W9-BNN-991

QuickBooks® 2009

Solutions Guide

for Business Owners and Accountants

Laura Madeira

800 East 96th Street,
Indianapolis, Indiana 46240

QuickBooks® Solutions Guide for Business Owners and Accountants

Copyright © 2009 by Que Publishing

All rights reserved. No part of this book shall be reproduced, stored in a retrieval system, or transmitted by any means, electronic, mechanical, photocopying, recording, or otherwise, without written permission from the publisher. No patent liability is assumed with respect to the use of the information contained herein. Although every precaution has been taken in the preparation of this book, the publisher and author assume no responsibility for errors or omissions. Nor is any liability assumed for damages resulting from the use of the information contained herein.

ISBN-13: 978-0-7897-3834-9
ISBN-10: 0-7897-3834-1

Library of Congress Cataloging-in-Publication data is on file.

Printed in the United States of America
First Printing: December 2009

Trademarks

All terms mentioned in this book that are known to be trademarks or service marks have been appropriately capitalized. Que Publishing cannot attest to the accuracy of this information. Use of a term in this book should not be regarded as affecting the validity of any trademark or service mark.

QuickBooks is a registered trademark of Intuit, Inc.

Warning and Disclaimer

Every effort has been made to make this book as complete and as accurate as possible, but no warranty or fitness is implied. The information provided is on an "as is" basis. The author and the publisher shall have neither liability nor responsibility to any person or entity with respect to any loss or damages arising from the information contained in this book or from the use of the CD or programs accompanying it.

Bulk Sales

Que Publishing offers excellent discounts on this book when ordered in quantity for bulk purchases or special sales. For more information, please contact

U.S. Corporate and Government Sales
1-800-382-3419
corpsales@pearsontechgroup.com

For sales outside the United State, please contact

International Sales
international@pearsoned.com

Associate Publisher
Greg Wiegand

Acquisitions Editor
Michelle Newcomb

Development Editor
Mark Cierzniak

Managing Editor
Patrick Kanouse

Project Editor
Deadline Driven Publishing

Copy Editor
Deadline Driven Publishing

Indexer
Ken Johnson

Proofreader
Kelly Maish

Technical Editor
Michelle Long

Publishing Coordinator
Cindy Teeters

Book Designer
Anne Jones

Compositor
Gina Rexrode

Contents at a Glance

Table of Contents

About the Author

Laura Madeira is the owner of American Computer Staffing, Inc., a software sales and consulting firm located in the greater Dallas, TX area. Her affiliations with Intuit includes being a member of the Intuit Trainer/Writer Network, Advanced Certified QuickBooks ProAdvisor, Certified QuickBooks Point of Sale ProAdvisor, and Enterprise Solutions Provider.

Laura has been teaching companies how to use Intuit's products beginning with Quicken in 1985 and then advancing to QuickBooks since its first version. Laura has instructed more than 10,000 individuals. She presents QuickBooks training to audiences that are comprised of accountants, consultants, and end users, representing Intuit as a select presenter for its yearly national multicity New Product Tour Launch seminars and QuickBooks Advanced Certification Training seminars. Laura continues to be a guest speaker for Intuit at national CPA trade shows.

Laura has been an advocate for the QuickBooks product line for more than 15 years and has been featured in several marketing articles on Intuit, QuickBooks, and in particular, the QuickBooks Certified ProAdvisor program.

In addition to the numerous speaking engagements, Laura also served on the first two Intuit Customer Advisory Councils from 2002–2005. This gave Laura an opportunity to meet Intuit executives and help influence changes in Intuit's relationship with accountants.

Laura also is a skilled technical writer and has provided Intuit with technical training and public presentation materials over the years. Her "QuickBooks at Year-End" document has been distributed by Intuit at several national events and is one of Intuit's most requested training and presentation documents.

Laura resides with her husband and two teenage sons outside Dallas, Texas. She graduated from Florida Atlantic University, May 2003, with her bachelor of science, majoring in accounting. Her hobbies include photography, art (watercolor), scrapbook making, and training two Cocker Spaniel dogs. Contact Laura at info@quick-training.com and www.quick-training.com.

About the Technical Editor

Michelle L. Long, CPA, MBA is an Advanced Certified QuickBooks ProAdvisor, author of the book *Successful QuickBooks Consulting*, and a member of the Trainer/Writer Network for Intuit. She has taught QuickBooks® seminars for the past eight years and college courses in accounting information systems, strategic management, entrepreneurial marketing, and FastTrac™ business planning.

Dedication

Dedicated to my husband Victor, sons Mark and Phillip, and my parents Ron and Joycelyn Demaree. —Laura

Acknowledgments

Thanks to all the audiences I have had over the years that have made me test and try out how to make QuickBooks work better. This book is a result of all those single requests for information.

Thanks to Michelle Long, technical editor, for sharing her extensive QuickBooks knowledge in technically reviewing the book's content. She worked long and hard hours providing me the needed technical oversight.

Thanks to several of my QuickBooks peers, including Joe Woodard, who was willing to try and test specific QuickBooks features with me.

Thanks to Alison Ball and Daniel Lowell with the Accountant Training and Relations team at Intuit for answering dozens of my emails and connecting me with the needed resources at Intuit. For the new content on the Client Data Review tool, a special thanks goes out to Victoria Dolginsky on the Intuit product development team for her late-night emails that answered many technical questions as I worked diligently to make this new content as accurate and complete as possible.

Thanks to my husband Victor for reviewing the book again himself and providing feedback.

Mostly thanks to my Dad and Mom. From a very young age, they taught me I could do anything I set my mind to. For that, I will be forever grateful.

I could not have done this without the technical help and guidance provided by Pearson. Michelle Newcomb, acquisitions editor, was forever patient with me as I struggled to meet the deadlines. Thanks to an incredible team of editors: Mark Cierzniak and Ginny Bess. I am now a much more skilled technical writer thanks to their expert editing and topic guidance.

—Laura

We Want to Hear from You!

As the reader of this book, *you* are our most important critic and commentator. We value your opinion and want to know what we're doing right, what we could do better, what areas you'd like to see us publish in, and any other words of wisdom you're willing to pass our way.

As an associate publisher for Que Publishing, I welcome your comments. You can email or write me directly to let me know what you did or didn't like about this book—as well as what we can do to make our books better.

Please note that I cannot help you with technical problems related to the topic of this book. We do have a User Services group, however, where I will forward specific technical questions related to the book.

When you write, please be sure to include this book's title and author as well as your name, email address, and phone number. I will carefully review your comments and share them with the author and editors who worked on the book.

Email: feedback@quepublishing.com

Mail: Greg Wiegand
           Associate Publisher
           Que Publishing
           800 East 96th Street
           Indianapolis, IN 46240 USA

Reader Services

Visit our website and register this book at informit.com/register for convenient access to any updates, downloads, or errata that might be available for this book.

Introduction

This is your QuickBooks solutions guide. This guide was written for both business owners and accountants. Much more than the typical "how to" of software books, this book makes reviewing QuickBooks data easy and trouble-free. For the business owner, it is like having a personal consultant working alongside you. For the accounting professional, this book makes working with clients' QuickBooks files easier than ever before.

This book provides easy-to-follow directions for properly setting up QuickBooks, reviewing your setup, checking your data for accuracy, and, when needed, making the proper corrections.

How This Book Is Organized

QuickBooks Solutions Guide for Business Owners and Accountants offers a wealth of information gathered from the author's years of working with business and accounting professionals who use the QuickBooks financial software product. To find just the right information, this book is organized into specific chapters, each focused on a particular task or account category of your QuickBooks data.

Chapter 1, "Creating a New QuickBooks Data File," Chapter 2, "Reviewing the QuickBooks Chart of Accounts," and Chapter 3 "Reviewing and Correcting Item List Errors," cover the following topics while using screen captures to enhance your understanding of each topic:

- Creating a data file
- Working with the chart of accounts
- Setting up items (an *item* is a QuickBooks tool that makes your accounting more accurate)

After you have the basics set up, Chapter 4, "Easily Review Your QuickBooks Data," and Chapter 5, "Power Reports for Troubleshooting Beginning Balance Differences," show you where to begin and prepare you to quickly and confidently review QuickBooks data. These chapters help you answer the following questions:

- Where do I start?
- What should I review?
- What "power reports" in QuickBooks can I use?

The remaining chapters conveniently address each specific account category. The following individual chapters provide details on setting up and reviewing QuickBooks and, when needed, methods for correcting QuickBooks data:

- Chapter 6, "Bank Account Balance or Reconciliation Errors"
- Chapter 7, "Reviewing and Correcting Accounts Receivable Errors"
- Chapter 8, "Reviewing and Correcting Errors with the Undeposited Funds Account"
- Chapter 9, "Handling Current Asset Accounts Correctly"
- Chapter 10, "Reviewing and Correcting Inventory Errors"
- Chapter 11, "Reviewing and Correcting Accounts Payable Errors"
- Chapter 12, "Reviewing and Correcting Sales Tax Errors"
- Chapter 13, "Reviewing and Correcting the Opening Balance Equity Account"
- Chapter 14, "Reviewing and Correcting Payroll Errors"

The book would not be complete without the discussion of two more important topics, making this book your own *QuickBooks Solutions Guide* tool:

- Chapter 15, "Sharing Data with Your Accountant or Your Client"
- Chapter 16, "Reporting Tips and Tricks," including a new reporting tool, Intuit Statement Writer 2009.

Finally, the book also looks at a revolutionary new detecting and correcting feature release with QuickBooks 2009:

- Chapter 17, "New for 2009! Detecting and Correcting with the Client Data Review Feature"

Conventions Used in This Book

The book is straightforward enough so that you can easily go to a specific chapter and find the needed information. It is worthwhile, however, to let you know how information is presented in this book.

Menu Commands

QuickBooks 2009 offers a variety of methods to accomplish a task. To simplify the instructions given, use the top menu bar in QuickBooks.

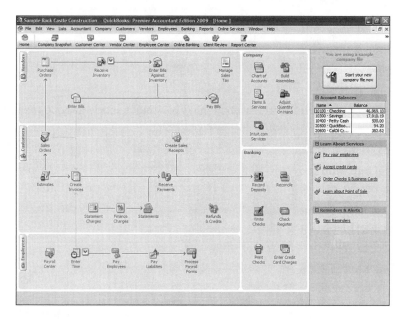

QuickBooks home page

For example, the instructions for preparing a report might look like the following:

1. Click **Reports, Vendors & Payables**.

This directive refers to clicking Reports on the menu bar, as shown in the previous figure, and then selecting Vendors & Payables as a submenu of Reports.

Additionally, for added clarity in the topic discussion, you can appreciate the frequent use of screen captures, which make following the instructions easy.

Web Pages and Manufacturer Information

A few web pages are listed in this book, mostly directing you to the **www.intuit.com** website. These addresses were current as this book was written; however, websites can change.

Special Elements

As you read through this book, you'll note several special elements, presented in what we call "margin notes." Different types of margin notes are used for different types of information, as you see here.

Digging Deeper

This is a tip that might prove useful for whatever you're in the process of doing.

Rescue Me!

This is a caution that something you might accidentally do might have undesirable results—so take care!

Chapter 1

Creating a New QuickBooks Data File

EasyStep Interview—Overview

Conver ting from Other Accounting Software to QuickBooks

Setting Up a QuickBooks Data File for Accrual or Cash Basis Reporting

EasyStep Interview—Overview

Over the years, I have helped hundreds of businesses troubleshoot problems with getting the proper financial and management information out of their QuickBooks data. I have found that improper setup of the data file was most often the primary cause, second only to judgment errors in posting transactions to the incorrect account.

The purpose of this book is to share with businesses and accounting professionals the many tools that QuickBooks provides for troubleshooting and correcting common data setup or entry errors. In QuickBooks, many preference settings and warnings will help prevent several of these common mistakes. Each chapter identifies these settings so you can make sure your data or your client's data is properly set up and maintained.

It is not my intention to offer any tax advice; I make comments throughout the text encouraging you to consult your accounting or tax professional before making any data corrections that might have a significant impact on a company's financials.

Recent editions of QuickBooks makes properly setting up the data file easy thanks to the question-and-answer format built in to the QuickBooks EasyStep Interview. These easy-to-follow prompts assist new QuickBooks users with properly setting up the data file by asking basic questions about their business.

To access the EasyStep Interview, open QuickBooks and select File, New Company. (See Figure 1.10, which is the startup screen of the EasyStep Interview.) You have the option to Start Interview, Skip Interview, or Convert Data from other financial software programs. For accounting professionals, the option to skip the interview is particularly useful if you are going to be providing your client predefined lists that you use commonly for all your clients.

When you choose the option to Skip Interview when creating a new data file, QuickBooks still requires the following:

> The company name and address details (see Figure 1.1)
>
> The company's financial structure (see Figure 1.3)
>
> The first month of your fiscal year (see Figure 1.5)
>
> An option to customize QuickBooks by selecting an industry-specific chart of accounts (similar to Figure 1.2)
>
> Requirement to name your data file and store it on your computer

After you store your data file, QuickBooks opens the new data file, and you will no longer have access to the EasyStep Interview. If you selected the Skip Interview option and you leave the EasyStep Interview before completing the

required steps in the previous bulleted list, QuickBooks will *not* save
your work.

If you choose the option to Start the Interview, QuickBooks provides a series of
question-and-answer type choices to help you properly set up your data file
and default certain features. If you have to leave the interview at any time
before finishing it, QuickBooks will remember where you left off in the process
when you return.

Have the following information on hand before setting up your QuickBooks
data file:

> Company name—This should be the company name or a name that
> best describes the business. By default, this is the filename given to the
> data file (.QBW extension) on your computer.

> Legal name—The legal name displays on certain reports and federal
> tax forms.

> Tax ID—Although this ID is not required to begin using QuickBooks,
> it is required if you want to sign up for one of the QuickBooks
> payroll services.

> Remaining information—This includes a phone number, e-mail
> address, Web site, and so on (see Figure 1.1), and can optionally
> be added to certain forms in QuickBooks, such as a customer
> invoice form.

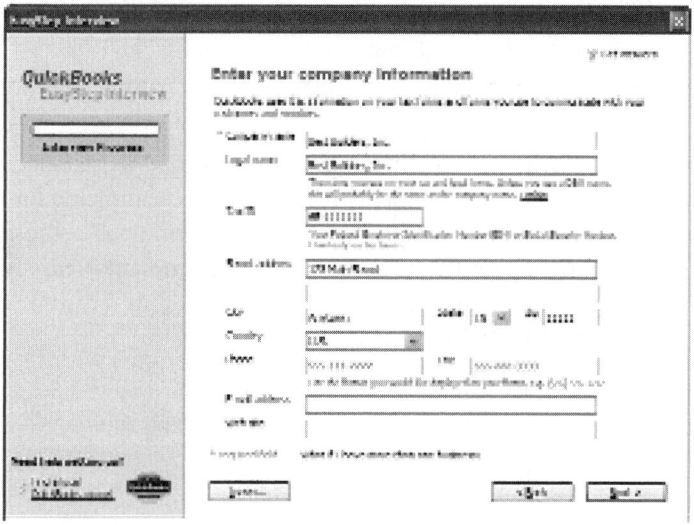

FIGURE 1.1

Entering company information in the EasyStep Interview.

Be prepared to answer the following questions that are asked as part of the EasyStep Interview process:

> Selecting your industry—QuickBooks recommends certain features that will be useful for the industry selected. QuickBooks also creates a Chart of Accounts list customized for the industry selected (see Figure 1.2). Additionally, some industry selections also create industry-specific items that are used to prepare customer and job estimates, sales orders, and invoices.

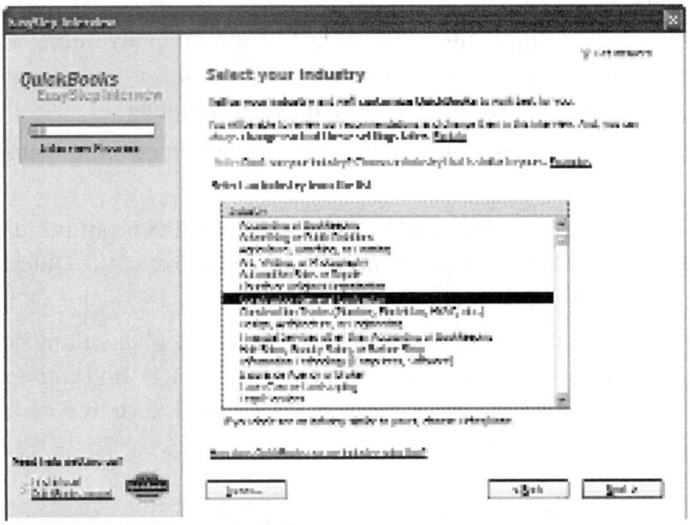

FIGURE 1.2

Customize QuickBooks for your specific industry.

> Identifying how your company is organized—This selection helps QuickBooks create the correct accounts, customizing for the legal type selected and assigning the proper tax form lines to those accounts (see Figures 1.3 and 1.4). These tax line assignments simplify the process of creating tax documents with tax preparation software, such as Intuit's TurboTax, ProSeries, or Lacerte.

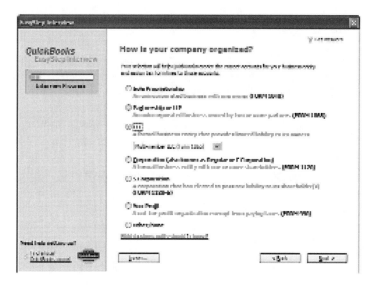

FIGURE 1.3

Selecting the legal organization of your company.

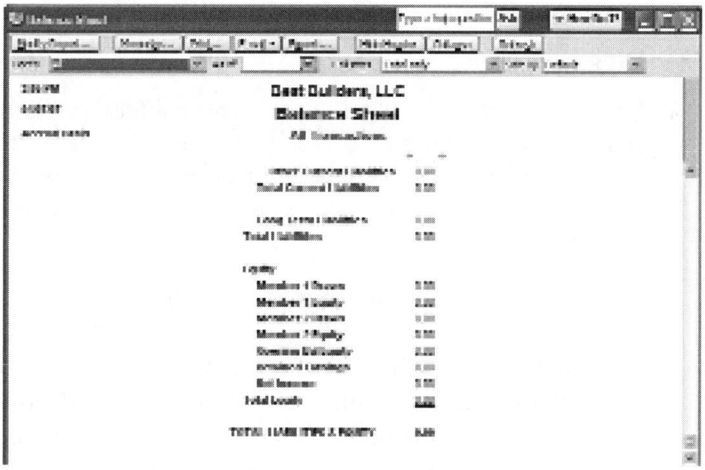

FIGURE 1.4

QuickBooks creates unique equity accounts when you select the company's legal organization.

Select the first month of your fiscal year—The answer to this EasyStep Interview question causes the reports that filter on fiscal year-to-date to know what month is the first month in the fiscal year (see Figure 1.5). For most companies, this is the first month of your income tax year.

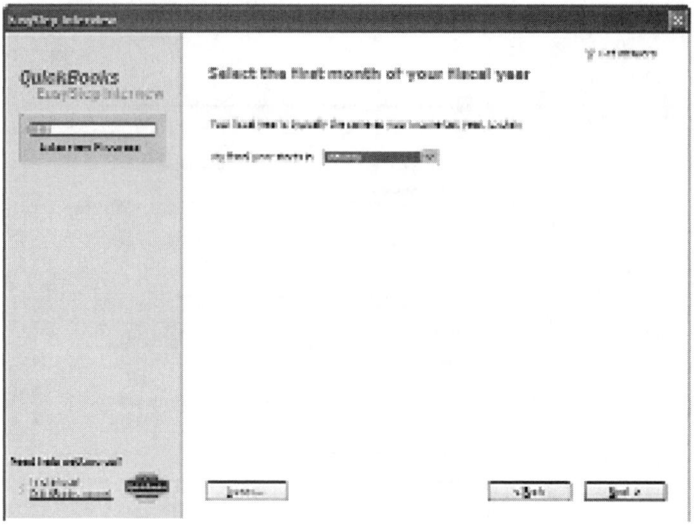

FIGURE 1.5

Selecting the first month of your year affects any fiscal year-to-date reports.

Digging Deeper

If the month selected as the first month of your fiscal year is incorrect, you can easily change it by choosing Company, Company Information. Changing this month does not affect individual transactions but does ensure that the reports that filter for fiscal year-to-date transactions are correct.

Setting an administrator password—Setting an administrator password is always a good practice (see Figure 1.6). If you do not set one during the EasyStep Interview, you can open a QuickBooks file with the default username of Admin and leave the password blank. Using a blank password is fine during the initial setup, but more security should be put in place after you enter sensitive information. You can also set up this password later.

At this point in the EasyStep Interview, QuickBooks asks where you want to store the company data file and what name you want to give it, if different than the default company name previously assigned.

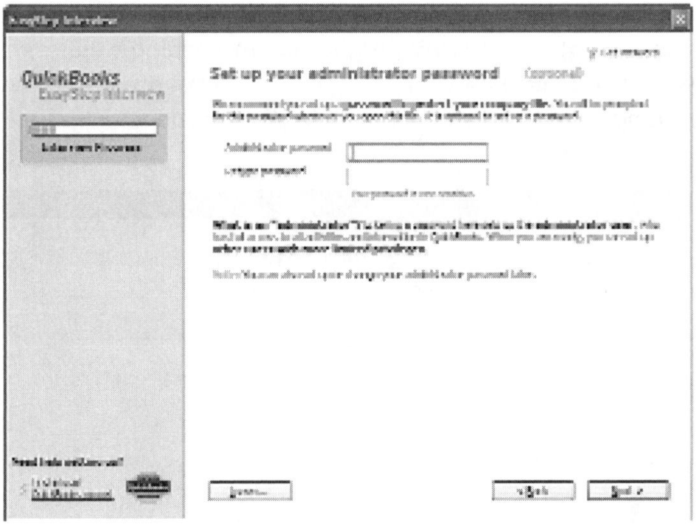

FIGURE 1.6

Create an Admin password and don't forget to write it down.

Digging Deeper

In QuickBooks 2009, the default directory for storing a QuickBooks data file is Shared Documents\Intuit\QuickBooks\Company Files. However, when a QuickBooks data file is initially created, you can select a specific file location different than the default.

If you need to leave the EasyStep Interview at any time, QuickBooks returns to the point you left off when you open the data file again.

The EasyStep Interview now prompts you for certain information based on what industry you selected. Your answers to the remaining questions will make certain features in QuickBooks the default. The purpose of this book is not to define each of these choices; most are self-explanatory. However, discussing the effect of several choices is useful.

Select a Start Date

One of the most important decisions you will make when beginning to work with QuickBooks is determining the start date (see Figure 1.7). You might want to discuss with your accountant what date to use. For most businesses, it is the day you begin entering data into QuickBooks. You select the start date during the EasyStep Interview, which defaults to the beginning of the current fiscal year; however, many companies begin using QuickBooks sometime during the year. The date you select is assigned to any opening balance entries entered when you create a list item on the chart of accounts or when you enter an opening balance for a new customer, job, or vendor.

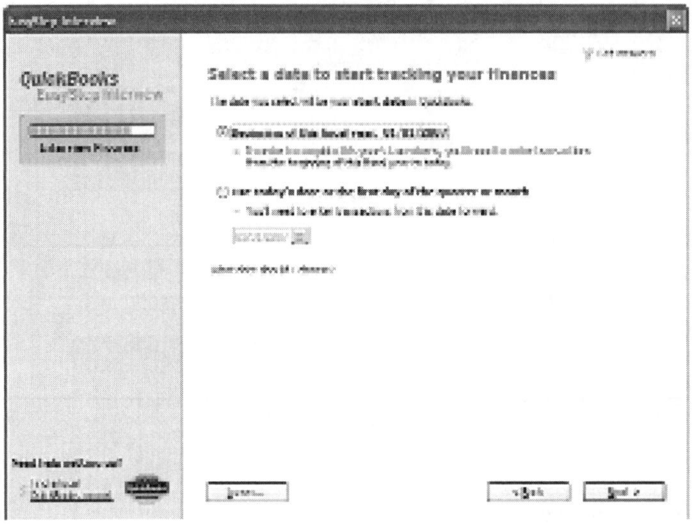

FIGURE 1.7
Selecting the date you will begin using QuickBooks.

The following are potential start dates:

> When you first begin your business activities (with no prior expenses or income). This date is the easiest one to work with because you have no historical balances or transactions to consider. You begin by paying vendors and invoicing customers. Everything else will fall into place.

> After you have established your business, but you decide to assign the start date as that of when your business began and enter historical transactions, thus recreating the business accounting from the beginning. This practice is common when a company is only a few months old. You follow the same advice as if your business were new. However, if the company is several months or years old, this method can be time-consuming and difficult to manage.

> At the beginning of a calendar year, such as January 1, 200x. This choice is common when the decision to begin using QuickBooks is at the end of a year or not long into the next year. Again, if the company has previously had business transactions, there will be beginning balances to enter. This information is discussed in detail in the section of

this chapter titled "Setting Up a QuickBooks Data File for Accrual or Cash Basis Reporting."

At the beginning of your fiscal year (for companies whose tax year does not coincide with the calendar year).

The first day of a month during the current calendar year or your fiscal year.

 ## Digging Deeper

For established companies that select a start date after the business has had activity, it is recommended that the start date be the beginning of a month. This practice makes reconciling balances to other software or to documents outside QuickBooks easier. If your bank statement or credit card statements ends within a month rather than at month end, request that the bank or lending institution change your statement ending date to the end of the month for future statements if possible.

Enter Bank Account Information

From your bank statement, tell QuickBooks the name of the bank account, the account number (optional), whether the account was opened before the QuickBooks start date, and the ending balance (see Figure 1.8).

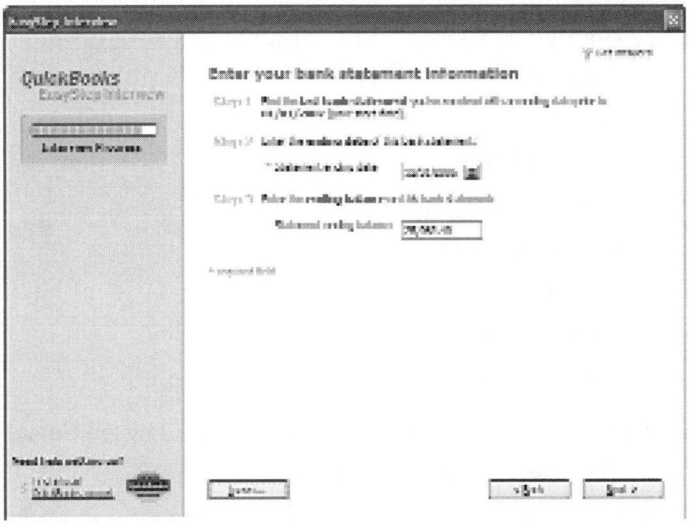

FIGURE 1.8

Enter the ending date and balance from your bank statement.

Digging Deeper

The bank account information you enter is necessary for you to properly reconcile your QuickBooks bank account. For the Statement ending date, use the last month's bank statement ending date before your selected start date. For the Statement ending balance, use the amount the bank shows on your printed bank statement *not including* any uncleared checks or deposits in transit (uncleared). You will enter these individually later.

Review Income and Expense Accounts

During the EasyStep Interview you might have selected a default chart of accounts for your new QuickBooks data file.

Even if you select None/Other when selecting a chart of accounts, specific accounts in QuickBooks is automatically created when related forms are opened for the first time:

> Accounts Receivable
>
> Inventory Asset
>
> Undeposited Funds
>
> Accounts Payable
>
> Payroll Liabilities
>
> Sales Tax Payable
>
> Opening Balance Equity
>
> Capital Stock
>
> Retained Earnings
>
> Shareholder Distributions
>
> Cost of Goods Sold
>
> Payroll Expenses
>
> Estimates (nonposting)
>
> Purchase Orders (nonposting)

To identify which charts of accounts were created by QuickBooks:

1. Click **Lists, Chart of Accounts**.
2. Click once to select a specific account you want to verify whether it is one of the default QuickBooks accounts.

3. After it's selected, click on **Account** and choose **Edit Account**.

4. If the Account type field is grayed out, this is a QuickBooks defaulted chart of accounts, and you should not create your own account for the same purpose. Instead, be sure to use this one.

These accounts are important to the QuickBooks functions. If a user deletes these accounts, QuickBooks recreates them when the related form is used. For example, if you delete the Accounts Receivable account and later open an invoice form, QuickBooks recreates the Accounts Receivable account.

Although QuickBooks defaults certain chart of accounts in the EasyStep Interview, you can conveniently remove any of the predetermined Income, Cost of Goods Sold, or Expense type accounts that you don't want in your file by removing the check mark next to the listed account name (see Figure 1.9) while in the EasyStep Interview.

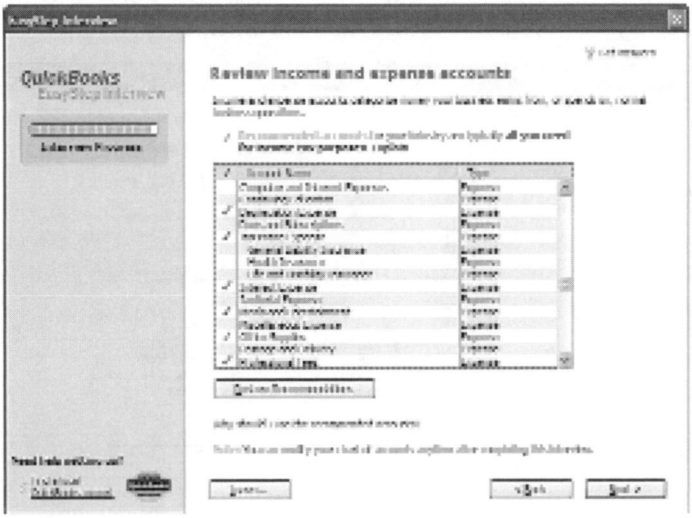

FIGURE 1.9

Select which default chart of account list items you want for your data file.

See Chapter 2, "Reviewing the QuickBooks Chart of Accounts," for methods to correct if you inadvertently create an account type that duplicates a QuickBooks created account.

Converting from Other Accounting Software to QuickBooks

QuickBooks has automated the process of converting files from other financial software into QuickBooks files, including the following:

Quicken

Peachtree by Sage

Small Business Accounting by Microsoft

Office Accounting

This section provides specific details about how QuickBooks handles these conversions and what you need to consider when making the choice to convert existing data from one of the listed financial software programs to a QuickBooks data file.

Converting from Quicken to QuickBooks

To begin the conversion, open QuickBooks, select File, New, and then select Convert Data directly from the EasyStep Interview opening screen (see Figure 1.10). The Conversion tool copies your Quicken data to a new QuickBooks file, leaving your original Quicken data file unchanged.

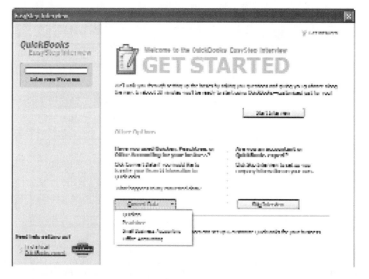

FIGURE 1.10

Converting files from other software packages right from the EasyStep Interview opening screen.

Table 1.1 shows you how the Quicken accounts are converted into QuickBooks accounts.

Table 1.1 Quicken Account Conversion	
This type of account in Quicken:	Becomes this type of account in QuickBooks:
Checking	Bank
Credit Card	Credit Card
Asset	Other Current Asset
Liability	Other Current Liability
Investment	Other Current Asset

Because QuickBooks does not offer the Investment tracking feature that is in Quicken, you can choose whether to include or exclude the value of your investments in the resulting QuickBooks balance sheet. If you choose to include them, QuickBooks converts the investment accounts into Other Current Asset chart of account type.

If you choose to exclude the investments, you are given the opportunity to delete the accounts before converting to QuickBooks. Any transfers that were recorded to or from the deleted accounts are recorded to your opening balance equity account. This is in keeping with the "debits equal credits" accounting that is going on behind the scenes in QuickBooks.

You are asked whether there is a Quicken Accounts Receivable account with customer payments. If you click Yes, the QuickBooks Conversion tool asks you to identify your Quicken Accounts Receivable account. QuickBooks then begins converting the Quicken transactions to QuickBooks Accounts Receivable transactions. This process can take several minutes.

During the conversion, you are informed of the following:

> QuickBooks creates an Opening Balance Equity account to compensate for deleted Quicken accounts.

> Memorized Invoices in Quicken might need to be reviewed.

> Duplicate check, invoice, or credit memo numbers are stored in a QBwin.log for review.

> Every payee name in Quicken must be on a QuickBooks list.

Because QuickBooks cannot determine which list an item belongs to, it places all items on the Other Name list (see Figure 1.11). In QuickBooks, users can then click Lists, Other Names List, Change Name Type for the one-time option to change the payee to a vendor, employee, or customer.

Rescue Me!

After you click OK to change the name type, you cannot undo the change. If you are not sure what list the payee belongs to, leave it as an Other Name.

Because Quicken allows for flexibility in how the accounting is documented—for example, allowing both business and personal funds to be comingled—my recommendation is for new QuickBooks users who are converting their Quicken data to hire a professional with accounting experience to make sure the resulting information is correct going forward.

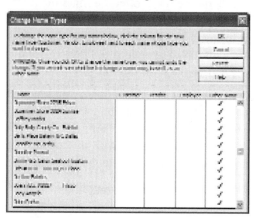

FIGURE 1.11
QuickBooks converts all Quicken payees to the Other Name list in QuickBooks.

Intuit offers a listing on the Internet of qualified QuickBooks Certified ProAdvisors in your area. In your QuickBooks data file, select Help, Find a Local Expert (you will need an Internet connection).

Converting from Peachtree, Small Business Accounting, or Office Accounting to QuickBooks

Just as in the Quicken conversion, QuickBooks can convert your Peachtree, Small Business Accounting, or Office Accounting data to QuickBooks data directly from the EasyStep Interview dialog. The conversion process leaves your original Peachtree, Small Business Accounting, or Office Accounting data untouched.

If you have not already downloaded the free Peachtree, Small Business Accounting, and Office Accounting QuickBooks Conversion tool, you are directed from the EasyStep Interview dialog to do so. The free downloadable tool converts Peachtree (any version 2001–2008), Microsoft Small Business Accounting (2006), and Office Accounting Express or Office Accounting Professional (2007) to QuickBooks Pro, Premier, or Enterprise Solutions. The tool can be used to convert multiple company files from any of the named software.

The Conversion tool works with Windows 98 Second Edition, 2000, XP, and Vista operating systems. You must have both the prior financial software installed and the QuickBooks software installed and registered for the conversion to work.

The download link as of the time of this writing for the free Conversion tool is http://quickbooks.intuit.com/product/about_quickbooks/peachtree_conversion.html. From this same site, you can also download a technical "white paper" that details the conversion specifics.

In the conversion process, you can select the specific Peachtree, Small Business Accounting, Office Professional, or Office Accounting Express file and the QuickBooks product version to which you will be converting it. Additionally, you can specify the conversion of Lists and transactions (including historical transactions) or Lists only.

You will also select a conversion date; any transactions dated after this date will not be converted.

Because of the differences between the two products, you are also given a choice to identify customers and vendors in QuickBooks with the name of the Peachtree, Small Business Accounting, Office Professional Accounting, or Office Accounting Express ID value. You must choose to use the name or the ID value in QuickBooks, so making this decision before performing the conversion is best.

The following Peachtree, Small Business Accounting, Office Professional, and Office Accounting Express files are converted.

Key lists include the following:

Chart of accounts

Customer/prospects

Jobs

Employees/sales reps

Vendors

Inventory item

Custom fields

Balance information

Open transactions include the following:

Open invoices

Open vendor bills

Customer transactions include the following:

Estimates

Sales orders

Invoices

Payment receipts

Deposits

Credit memos

Vendor transactions (new!) include the following:

Purchase orders

Bills

Bill payments

Checks

Bill credits

Converting from QuickBooks for Windows to QuickBooks Online Edition

With QuickBooks Online Edition, users can manage their business accounting information from anywhere—work, home, or on the road—at anytime. Monthly subscription fees are assessed for this product.

QuickBooks Online Edition allows a one-time conversion from QuickBooks Pro, or Premier for Windows. The process is simple and converts both lists and historical transactions.

To convert your QuickBooks for Windows software one-time, click File, Utilities and choose the option for Copy File for Online Edition.

Feature differences exist between the Online Edition and the Desktop versions; review the feature comparison chart at http://quickbooks.intuit.com/ product/ accounting_software/product_comparison.jhtml to see whether the Online Edition is right for you and your business or your client's business.

Converting from QuickBooks for Mac to QuickBooks for Windows

Users who are changing their operating system to Windows have the option to convert their QuickBooks for Mac data, lists, and transactions to a QuickBooks Pro for Windows data file. Only QuickBooks for Mac versions 6.0, 2005, 2006, 2007, and 2008 offer this capability. For version 6.0, click File, Create a File for QuickBooks for Windows.

In versions 2005–2007, click File, Back up to QuickBooks for Windows. In QuickBooks 2008–2009, click File, Utilities, and then select Copy Company File for QuickBooks Mac. Save this file to your desktop or computer hard drive. This is the file that will be converted, leaving your original file intact.

With each command, a .QBB backup file is created; this file is restored in QuickBooks for Windows. It is recommended that you restore the same-year version of a Mac file to a same-year version of the Windows program; that is, restore QuickBooks for Mac 2009 in a QuickBooks Windows 2009 file.

The conversion from QuickBooks for Mac to QuickBooks for Windows is a simple and worry-free process.

Converting from QuickBooks for Windows to QuickBooks for Mac

Users who are changing their operating system to a Mac have the option to convert their QuickBooks for Windows data, lists, and transactions to a QuickBooks Pro for Mac data file. Click File, Utilities, Copy Company File for QuickBooks Mac.

You can convert your QuickBooks for Windows file to work with QuickBooks for Mac 2009.

Before completing the conversion, make sure that you are *not* currently using any of these features not currently offered with the Mac edition:

> Payroll
>
> Merchant Services
>
> Integrated applications (third-party software)
>
> QuickBooks Online Bill Pay
>
> Multi-user
>
> Inventory Assemblies

The conversion process will keep your original data file in a Windows format, in the event that the Mac edition did not meet your needs.

Setting Up a QuickBooks Data File for Accrual or Cash Basis Reporting

Although the purpose of this book is not to give definitive accounting or tax advice on any of the topics covered, it is worth discussing the nature of accrual versus cash basis reporting because it pertains to creating a new data file.

Understanding the basics of these two types of reporting is important. When filing a tax return, businesses must specify cash or accrual as their accounting method. However, for management purposes, business owners can view one or both types of reports when making internal decisions. The capability to view reports in either accrual or cash basis is one of the features that sets the QuickBooks software apart from other accounting solutions.

The difference between the two methods is in the timing of when income and expenses are recognized in your financials. Table 1.2 shows how QuickBooks treats the different types of transactions in both reporting methods on the Profit & Loss statement.

Table 1.2 Accrual Versus Cash Accounting		
Transaction Type	**Profit & Loss Accrual Basis**	**Profit & Loss Cash Basis**
Customer Invoice	Revenue is recorded on the date of the invoice.	Revenue is recorded on the recorded on the date of the customer payment transaction.
Customer Credit Memo	Revenue is decreased on the date of the credit memo.	No impact.
Vendor Bill	Cost is recorded as of the date entered on the vendor bill transaction.	Cost is recorded on the date of the bill payment check.
Vendor Credit Memo	Cost is decreased on the date of the vendor credit memo.	No impact.
Check	Cost is recorded using the date entered on the check transaction.	Cost is recorded using the date entered on the check transaction.
Credit Card	Cost is recorded using the date entered on the credit card transaction.	Cost is recorded using the date entered on the credit card transaction.
General Journal	Cost or revenue is recorded using the date entered on the general journal transaction.	Cost or revenue is recorded using the date entered on the general journal transaction.
Inventory Adjustment	Date of inventory adjustment is the date the financials are affected.	Date of inventory adjustment is the date the financials are affected.

If you have just recently started a new business and QuickBooks is the first financial tracking software you have used, rest easy. QuickBooks makes it possible for you to do the daily tasks of paying vendors or employees and invoicing customers without any complicated startup procedures. Later, you can view reports in either Cash or Accrual basis.

However, if you are converting to QuickBooks from some other software application other than those currently supported with the QuickBooks conversion tool (see the section titled "Converting from Other Accounting Software to QuickBooks"), you will be manually entering open customer, vendor, and bank balances, in addition to additional balance sheet balances.

Earlier this chapter provided details on selecting a Start Date, the date that you first want QuickBooks to track your financial accounting. If the business had expenses or sold products and services before this start date, you most likely have open transactions. For example, if your start date is January 1, 20xx, then your beginning balances would be dated as of December 31, 20xx.

The following is a brief list of what you need to collect when creating a new QuickBooks data file. These lists should represent their respective value as of the day *before* your QuickBooks start date.

> Accounts Receivable—List by Customer of what customers owed you on the day before your start date, including any invoices where the payment was received but not deposited by the start date

> Accounts Payable—List by Vendor of those bills that you had not paid as of your start date

> Bank Ending Balance—Ending balance from your bank statement on the day before your start date

> Uncleared Checks and Deposits—List of all checks and deposits that have not yet cleared your bank account as of your start date

> Other Balances—List of all other assets, liabilities, and equity you have in the business

> Payroll—Year-to-date totals for each employee (if using payroll in QuickBooks)

To get your QuickBooks data ready for entering current transactions, you need to record these open balances. However, before doing so, you need to have a few things already set up in QuickBooks. You might refer to the following items as "Master Lists."

 **Digging Deeper**

Before you begin entering these startup balances, make sure you have the following created in your QuickBooks data file:

> **Chart of Accounts**—This list is usually created automatically for you in the EasyStep Interview process discussed earlier in this chapter.
>
> **Items List**—These are the services or products that you sell and the sales tax that you collect on these sales. See the section titled, "Using Item Types in QuickBooks," in Chapter 3 for a detailed discussion of setting up items. Be sure to take special consideration with Inventory items. This information is detailed in Chapter 10, "Reviewing and Correcting Inventory Errors."
>
> **Customer and Job Names**—To assign to open (unpaid) invoices.
>
> **Vendor Names**—To assign to open (unpaid) vendor bills.
>
> **Employee Names**—To assign to current year payroll transactions.
>
> **Payroll Items**—To assign for year-to-date payroll totals.

The following options are available when you're creating startup or opening transactions for a business that is beginning to use QuickBooks for an existing business, after using some other software or manual accounting method.

Cash or Accrual Basis Startup Transactions: Accounts Receivable

After you have completed the EasyStep Interview, you need to take some additional steps that are important to the successful setup of your new QuickBooks file.

To create a customer or job from the Customer Center, select New Customer & Jobs. You can enter an opening balance in the New Customer or New Job dialog (see Figure 1.12). However, I don't recommend entering the beginning balance here as I explain in this section.

Entering an amount in the Opening Balance field causes QuickBooks to do the following:

- **One invoice total**—A lump sum open invoice total is created for each customer.

- **Accrual Basis Reporting**—For this type of reporting, the Opening Balance field increases Accounts Receivable (debit) and increases Uncategorized Income (credit) assigned the date in the "as of" field on the New Customer or New Job dialog.

- **Cash Basis Reporting**—For this type of reporting, the field has no effect until the date of customer payment. When the customer payment is received, it increases (debit) the account you assign to customer payments (either the QuickBooks Undeposited Funds or the bank account) and increases Uncategorized Income (credit).

![New Customer dialog box showing the Opening Balance field circled, with Customer Name "Anthony's Pizza", as of 12/31/2006, and Address Info tab selected with company details.]

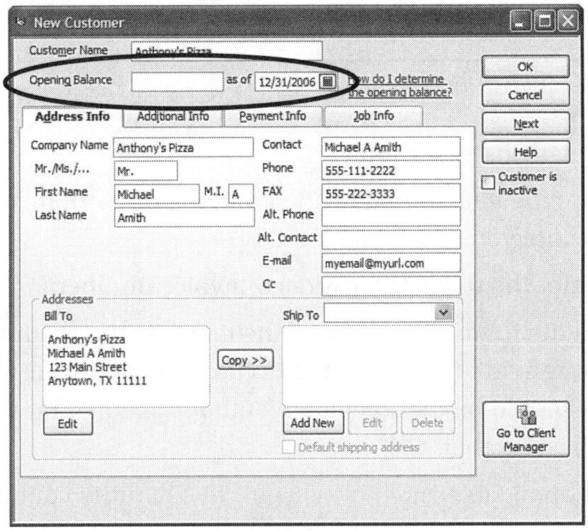

FIGURE 1.12

The Opening Balance field in a New Customer dialog.

You might well imagine that creating open customer invoices in the New Company or New Job dialogs is generally not recommended. Instead, follow these steps to create open customer invoices as of your start date:

1. Click **Customers**, **Create Invoices** (see Figure 1.13).

Digging Deeper

To access the invoice form, you can also use the shortcut key Ctrl+I or access it directly from the opening screen in QuickBooks, known as the Home page.

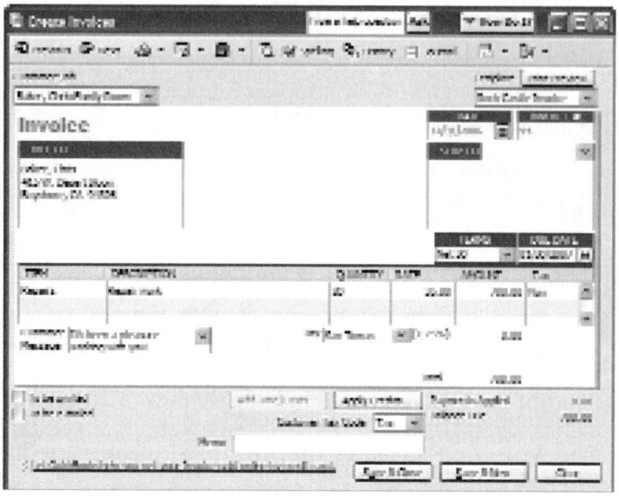

FIGURE 1.13

Creating an open customer invoice.

2. Enter **Customer:Job**.

3. Use the date drop-down to enter the original invoice date (it should be before your start date).

4. Enter the originally assigned invoice number.

5. In the Item column, enter the item(s)—the products or services that were sold—if you want to accurately track your revenue from this item. It should be the same item(s) that appeared on the original invoice to the customer.

6. If applicable, enter a value in the Quantity column.

7. If the rate did not default (because it was not included when the list item was created), enter a value in the Rate column.

8. The correct tax status on the line should default if the list item was set to the proper tax status. If some customers pay tax and others do not, you must first indicate the taxable status of an item by clicking **Lists**, **Item List**. Highlight the item in question and select the **Item** button and choose **Edit Item**. The Edit Item dialog opens, and you can mark the item with the appropriate tax code.

QuickBooks first determines whether an item is taxable, and then it checks whether the customer is a tax-paying customer before assessing tax on a customer balance.

9. Make sure the **To Be Printed** and **To Be E-mailed** check boxes in the lower left are not selected. Remember to select the appropriate box here when you create your first new invoice in QuickBooks. QuickBooks will remember the setting from the last saved or edited invoice.

10. Check your Balance due to make sure it agrees with the list item total from which you are working.

11. Click **Save & Close** if you are done, or click **Save & New** if you have more invoice transactions to record.

Partially Paid Open Customer Invoices on Cash Basis Reporting

To properly prepare reports on cash basis and to properly report on sales by item, you should perform additional steps for those open invoices that had partial balances paid as of your startup date. These steps are required if you want to accurately track sales by item:

1. Click **Lists, Chart of Accounts** and select the **Account** button, choosing the **New** option. The Add New Account dialog opens. Place a mark in the radial button next to **Bank** to select that account type.

2. Click **Continue**. The dialog opens where you can name the new bank account `Prior Year Payments Account`. This temporary deposit account is later closed to Opening Balance Equity, which is later closed to Retained Earnings. Click **Save & Close**.

3. Click **Lists, Item List** and click the **Item** button, choosing the **New** option. The New Item dialog opens. Assign the type as **Payment** and name it `Prior Year Payments`. Assign the Prior Year Payments account created in step 1 as the account to **Deposit To** (see Figure 1.14). Click **OK**.

4. To create the open invoice, click **Customers, Create Invoices**. Select the **Customer:Job** from the drop-down menu. Enter the original invoice date (it should be before your QuickBooks start date), and enter the invoice number that was originally presented to the customer for payment.

Continues...

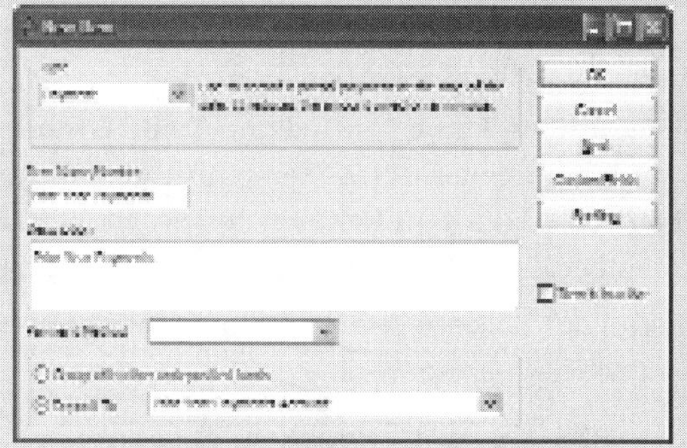

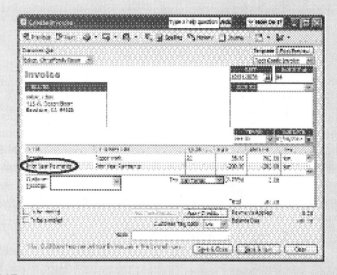

FIGURE 1.14

Create a payment item type to use on partially paid startup invoices.

5. On line 1 (or more if needed) of the customer invoice, enter your normal service or product item you sold to the customer. On the next available line, use the new Prior Year Payments item you created and enter the total of the customer's prior payments as a negative amount (see Figure 1.15). Click **Save & Close** if you are done or **Save & New** to create additional open customer invoices.

FIGURE 1.15

Creating an invoice that was partially paid before the start date.

6. Verify that the Balance Due amount on the invoice form accurately matches the open invoice total from your prior accounting list or report.

7. Compare your QuickBooks A/R Aging Summary report to your open invoices startup list total. If the balances agree, go to step 8. If they do not agree, review either the Summary or Detail A/R Aging report and identify which customer(s) balances are incorrect.

8. When your totals agree, click **Banking, Use Register** and select the **Prior Year Payments** bank account.

9. To close the fictitious bank account balance to the Open Balance Equity account, enter the following on the next available line of the register.

   For the date, enter the day before your startup date. Optionally for the number, use the term *Closing*. In the payment column, enter the same dollar amount as the register total displayed prior to this transaction. In the **Account** field, select the QuickBooks-created equity account named **Opening Balance Equity**.

10. Click **Record** to save the transaction.

   Your Prior Year Payments bank register should now have a zero balance. (See Chapter 13, "Reviewing and Correcting the Opening Balance Equity Account.")

Cash or Accrual Basis Startup Transactions: Accounts Payable

Accounts Payable startup refers to those vendor bills that were not paid as of your start date. Presumably, these are the vendor bills that we would be paying out in our first month of using QuickBooks.

Correctly setting up the starting Accounts Payable balance is just as important to your financials as the setup in Accounts Receivable.

1. Click **Vendor, Enter Bills** to open a new blank bill form (see Figure 1.16).

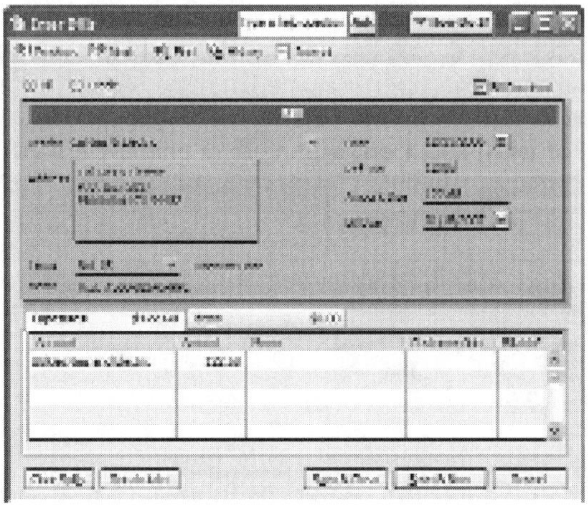

FIGURE 1.16

Enter a vendor bill that was unpaid at your start date.

2. Enter the bill **Date**. This date should be on or before your QuickBooks start date, and it is often the date on the vendor's bill you received.

3. Enter the vendor's bill number in the **Ref. No** field. This serves two important purposes: One is to optionally print the reference number on the bill payment stub that is sent to the vendor, and the other is that QuickBooks will warn you if a duplicate bill is later entered with the same Ref. No.

4. Enter a number in the **Amount Due** field, if you previously paid part of the bill; the amount should equal the balance remaining to be paid. (See the sidebar "Partially Paid Open Vendor Bills on Cash Basis Reporting.")

5. QuickBooks defaults the **Bill Due** date to the terms specified on the Additional Info tab in the Edit Vendor dialog; however, you can also override the Bill Due date on this screen, if necessary.

6. Click the **Expenses** tab and assign the appropriate expense account. If you are tracking costs by items, use the appropriate item on the **Item** tab. In accrual basis, the account or item selected is not as important because the expense was recorded on the vendor's bill date in your previous software or accounting method. For cash basis, it is most important because the cost is recorded to the expense account or item not when the bill is dated, but on the date of the bill payment check transaction, which should occur after the start date.

7. Click **Save & Close**.

8. Click **Report**, **Vendors & Paybles** and choose the **A/P Aging Summary or Detail** and compare the totals with your previous accounting software or manual records.

9. If the open bills you are entering are for inventory, make sure you read the details in Chapter 10.

Partially Paid Open Vendor Bills on Cash Basis Reporting

To properly prepare reports on cash basis, you should perform additional steps for those open vendor bills that have partial payments as of your startup date. These steps are required if you want to accurately track your costs by item.

Use the Prior Year Payments bank account that you created in the previous set of steps. This temporary payment account is later closed to Opening Balance Equity, which is later closed to Retained Earnings. (Refer to Chapter 13 on closing Opening Balance Equity to Retained Earnings.)

1. Click **Lists, Item List**. The Item List dialog opens. Click the **Item** button and choose **New**. Select the **Other Charge** item type. In the Item Name/Number, type **Prior Year Vendor Payments** (see Figure 1.17). Assign it to the **Prior Year Payments** bank account by selecting it from the Account drop-down menu. (This account was created in the previous set of steps. See the sidebar "Partially Paid Open Customer Invoices on Cash Basis Reporting.") Click **OK** to save.

FIGURE 1.17

Create an Other Charge type item to record prior year vendor payments.

2. Follow steps 1 through 6 in the preceding section titled "Cash or Accrual Basis Startup Transactions: Accounts Payable" with

Continues...

the exception that you want to record the full amount of the original bill. You can use the **Expenses** tab and assign the appropriate expense account, or if you are tracking costs by item, use the **Items** tab and assign the correct item.

3. On the Items tab, add the Other Charge type item called **Prior Year Vendor Payments**. Enter a negative amount equal to the total of all previous bill payments (see Figure 1.18).

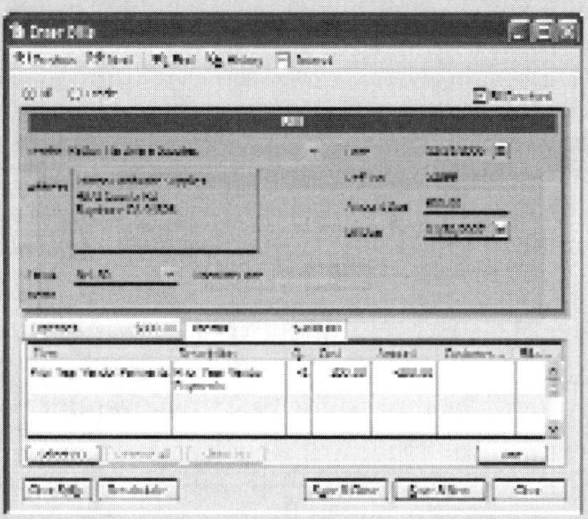

FIGURE 1.18

Create an open vendor bill including any prior year vendor payment line detail.

4. Verify that the Amount Due amount on the Enter bill form accurately matches the open vendor invoice total from your previous software (or accounting method) report.

5. Compare your QuickBooks A/P Aging Summary report to the open vendor bill startup list total from your previous software. If the balances agree with each other, go to the next step. If they do not agree, review either the Summary or Detail A/P Aging report and identify which vendor(s) balances are incorrect and make the needed changes.

6. When the totals of your prior accounting Payables agree with the new QuickBooks A/P summary report, click **Banking, Use Register** and select the **Prior Year Payments** fictitious bank account.

7. On the next available register line, enter the day before your startup date and the word `Closing` for the number. In the Deposit column, enter the total amount you see in the balance column of this register. In the Account field, select the QuickBooks-created equity account named **Opening Bal Equity**.

   Click **Record** to save your transaction. When completed, your fictitious Prior Year Payments account will have a zero balance. (Refer to Chapter 13 for more information.)

Digging Deeper

See Table 1.2 for details on how a Profit & Loss statement is affected in both accrual and cash basis for each QuickBooks transaction.

Digging Deeper

If your vendor bill, vendor credit, or check is for a Customer:Job for which you created an estimate and you want to track using the Job Profitability reports, you need to enter your cost detail on the Items tab. You can access the Items tab on any New or Edit vendor bill, vendor credit, or check form by selecting the Items tab, as shown in Figure 1.19.

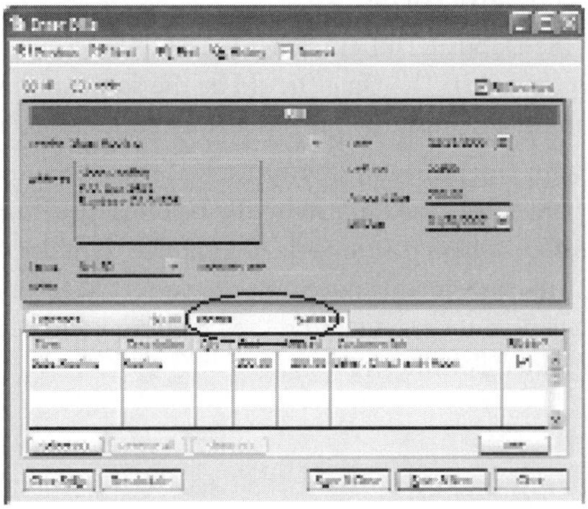

FIGURE 1.19

Create a vendor bill using items for proper Customer and Job profitability reporting.

Cash or Accrual Basis Startup Transactions: Bank Account Statement Balance

In addition to setting up the Accounts Payable and Receivable startup transactions, you also must record the balance the bank had on record as of the start date. Having accurate information is necessary when you are ready to reconcile the bank account in QuickBooks to the bank's records.

 Digging Deeper

If you completed the new bank information in the EasyStep Interview, you might have already entered your statement ending balance.

Click Banking, Use Register and select your bank account to open the register. If you have a balance in the register, check to see that it agrees with your bank balance as of the start date in QuickBooks. If the amount has a memo of Opening Balance, you can be sure it was probably created during the EasyStep Interview process.

If the amount is correct and agrees with your bank's statement ending balance, you are fine. If not, double-click the transaction and edit the amount. Otherwise, use the steps listed in this section for entering your opening bank balance.

To create your beginning bank balance:

1. Click **Banking, Make Deposits** to record your bank statement balance (if a positive balance).

2. In the **Deposit To** field, enter your bank account from your chart of accounts list. The Date should be the same as your bank statement ending date, usually the day before your QuickBooks start date.

3. Assign **Opening Bal Equity** to the **From Account** column (see Figure 1.20). The balance really belongs in Retained Earnings, but posting it here first gives you a chance to make sure the opening entries for your cash account are correct. (See Chapter 13 for a complete discussion on closing the Opening Balance Equity account to Retained Earnings.)

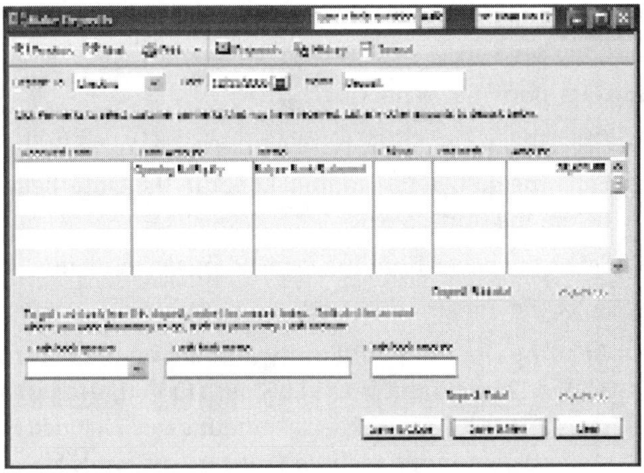

FIGURE 1.20

Entering the statement ending balance from the bank.

4. Enter an optional **Memo**.

5. Enter the **Amount**. The amount recorded here is the ending balance from the bank statement just before your QuickBooks start date. This amount *should not* include any uncleared checks or deposits that have not cleared the bank funds yet.

6. Click **Save & Close** to record the transaction.

If you have outstanding deposits that did not clear your bank funds, the way you enter them depends on the basis of accounting used:

Accrual basis users create the deposit(s) using the same steps as outlined for entering the beginning bank balance and date the transactions before the start date.

Cash basis users click Customers, Receive Payment and apply the deposit to an open invoice, which you created earlier in this chapter. Date this transaction *on* or *after* your start date

If your bank account had a negative balance as of your start day, you might also use a check form to record that amount.

Cash or Accrual Basis Startup Transactions: Checking Uncleared Bank Checks

You are almost done with the startup entries. The last thing to do is to record the checking account's uncleared checks and debits, as shown in Figure 1.21.

To complete the startup process for your banking transactions, follow these instructions to create your uncleared checks:

1. Click Banking, Write Checks.

2. Enter the actual check number that was issued in the **No.** field.

3. Enter the date of the original check in the **Date** field, which should be before the start date.

4. Select the payee from the Payee drop-down menu.

5. Enter the amount of the check.

6. Enter the **Opening Bal Equity** account on the Expenses tab (see Figure 1.21). (This account is used because in both accrual and cash basis reporting, the check expense amount was included in our prior software or accounting method Profit & Loss totals.)

7. Click **Save & Close** or **Save & New** until you are completed with this task.

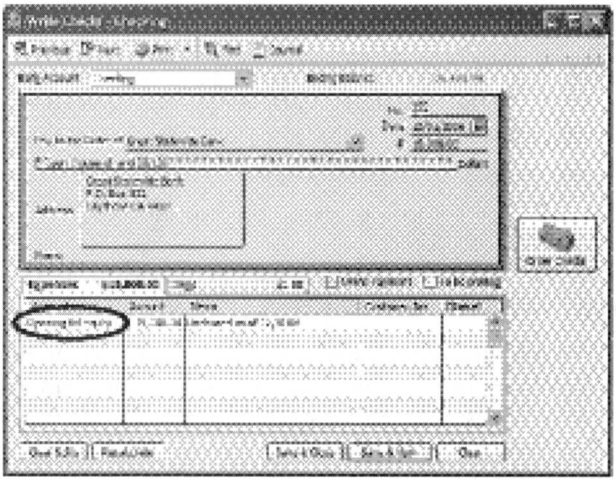

FIGURE 1.21

Entering a check that was not cashed by the bank as of the start date.

To verify the accuracy of the information, click Reports, Company & Financial, Balance Sheet Standard and set the date to be one day before your start date. Your bank account balance(s) should be equal to Bank Statement Ending Balance plus Outstanding (uncleared) Deposits less Outstanding (uncleared) Checks.

Chapter 2

Reviewing the QuickBooks Chart of Accounts

- Understanding the Chart of Accounts
- Importing a Chart of Accounts
- Preferences That Affect the Chart of Accounts
- Accounts That QuickBooks Creates Automatically
- Methods to Troubleshoot and Correct Chart of Account Issues

Understanding the Chart of Accounts

The chart of accounts is a list of asset, liability, income, and expense accounts to which you assign your daily transactions. This list is one of the most important lists you will use in QuickBooks; it helps you keep your financial information organized. If this list is created properly, you can capture information in a timely manner that will help you make good financial and management decisions for the business.

Understanding the chart of accounts isn't complicated; there are six standard accounting categories: assets, liabilities, equity, income, cost of goods sold, and expense.

Assets

Assets include items you have purchased in the past that will be used in the future to generate economic benefit. QuickBooks offers these categories in the order of how fluid the asset is, or in simple terms how quickly you can turn the asset into cash:

- Bank—You use this account type to track your cash in and out of the business. This account type (in addition to the credit card account type) is the only account type that you can select as the payment account in the Pay Bills or Write Checks dialog.

- Accounts Receivable—This account type requires a Customer or Customer and Job name with each entry. You use this account type when generating an invoice or credit memo form or when receiving a customer payment. You can create more than one Accounts Receivable type account if you want.

- Other Current Asset—This account type is general in nature and includes the QuickBooks Inventory Asset and the Undeposited Funds account. The Undeposited Funds account is used like a "desk drawer" in that it holds deposits to be totaled together on one deposit ticket.

- Fixed Asset—This account type shows purchases of goods or materials that will be used by the business long term in generating revenue. Accumulated Depreciation totals are also held in this account type as a negative fixed asset.

- Other Assets—User-defined other asset accounts are created in this section.

Liabilities

Liabilities are the debts the company has yet to pay. QuickBooks includes these subgroupings:

- Accounts Payable—This account type is reserved for the QuickBooks Accounts Payable account where vendor bills and bill payments reside.

- Credit Cards—Optionally, users can use this grouping to track the charges and payments made against a company credit card. One benefit is that you can reconcile this account like you do your bank account and download your credit card transactions directly into your data.

- Other Current Liability—This is debt that is expected to be paid within one year. This grouping includes the QuickBooks-created Payroll Liabilities and Sales Tax Payable, in addition to other user-defined liability accounts.

- Long-Term Liability—This is debt that will not be paid within one year.

Equity

The Equity account category holds the owner's (or owners') residual interest in the business after the liabilities are paid. Accounts for this section include Common Stock; Owner's Investments and Draws; Retained Earnings; and Open Bal Equity, an account created by QuickBooks that is discussed in more detail in Chapter 13, "Reviewing and Correcting the Opening Balance Equity Account."

Income

Money that is earned from the sale of your products or services is recorded as income. Your company might have one income account or several depending on the detail needed for your financial analysis. Other categories include Other Income, or income that is generated from the sale of a product or service not normal to your operations.

Cost of Goods Sold

The Cost of Goods Sold account is for costs that are *directly* related to producing a service or good for sale. There is a direct relationship between these costs and your revenue. If your company sells a product, your cost of goods sold (COGS) expenses would be the material, labor, and other costs incurred to make and sell the product. By contrast, your office expenses for rent or advertising are considered indirect and should not be posted to the Cost of Goods Sold account type.

Digging Deeper

When you are creating your Cost of Goods Sold accounts, consider using summary accounts, such as material, labor, and subcontract, and letting your Item List track more detail. For example, if you are a construction company and you have expenses for site work, concrete, framing, painting, and so on, rather than have a COGS account for each cost type, use the Item List. Select Lists, Item List to open the Item List dialog. Click Item, New and create an item for each cost type, assigning the Cost of Goods Sold account. Reports by item are available to break down the total of Cost of Goods Sold account into more detail.

Expense

An expense is recorded when an asset is used or there is an outflow of cash. The expense accounts created during the EasyStep Interview provides you with the basic classifications needed for properly tracking your expenses.

Although QuickBooks does not automatically create other groupings within the expenses category, a recommendation would be to group your expenses by fixed (or uncontrollable) and variable (or controllable). When you review your costs, these additional groupings make easy work of determining which costs you have more control over.

You can also categorize expenses as an Other Expense, which is an expense that is not normal to your operations.

Importing a Chart of Accounts

Are you familiar with Excel? Does your accountant have a preferred chart of accounts? Create the list in Excel with a few required fields. Then import the list into your QuickBooks data file. Before performing any import, it is recommended that you make a backup of your data file. The import is not reversible!

Importing from an Excel File Format

 Rescue Me!

When importing your chart of accounts from an Excel file format into a data file with an existing chart of accounts, you might encounter some import errors. However, the import tool provides a preview window that identifies whether any errors or duplications are expected with the import. If errors are detected in the import, QuickBooks gives you a dialog asking whether you want to save the error log file. A .csv log file is created that you can review for a line-by-line detail of the errors.

For accountants, the ability to import an existing chart of accounts from an Excel worksheet makes sharing a common chart of accounts with multiple clients easy.

Create a spreadsheet in Excel, shown in Figure 2.1, with the following fields:

- Type—This field is required. It refers to account categories and subcategories in QuickBooks. The spelling must be exactly like the QuickBooks account type.

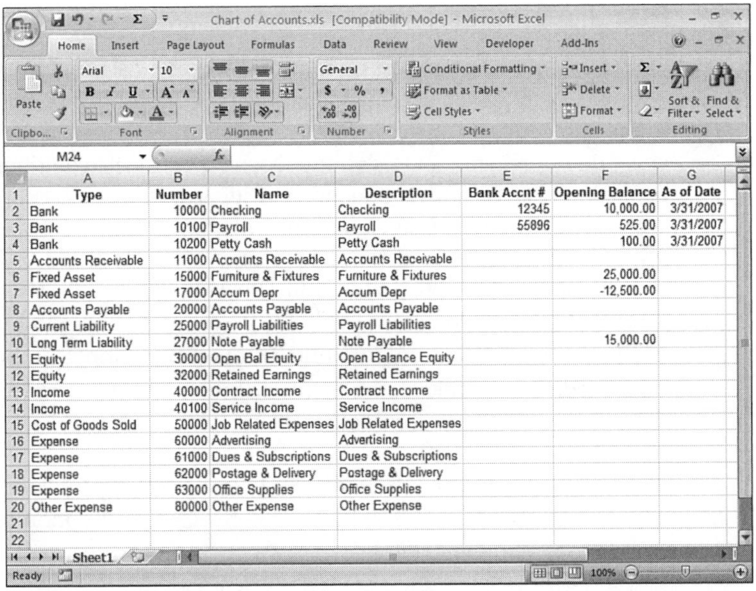

	A	B	C	D	E	F	G
1	Type	Number	Name	Description	Bank Accnt #	Opening Balance	As of Date
2	Bank	10000	Checking	Checking	12345	10,000.00	3/31/2007
3	Bank	10100	Payroll	Payroll	55896	525.00	3/31/2007
4	Bank	10200	Petty Cash	Petty Cash		100.00	3/31/2007
5	Accounts Receivable	11000	Accounts Receivable	Accounts Receivable			
6	Fixed Asset	15000	Furniture & Fixtures	Furniture & Fixtures		25,000.00	
7	Fixed Asset	17000	Accum Depr	Accum Depr		-12,500.00	
8	Accounts Payable	20000	Accounts Payable	Accounts Payable			
9	Current Liability	25000	Payroll Liabilities	Payroll Liabilities			
10	Long Term Liability	27000	Note Payable	Note Payable		15,000.00	
11	Equity	30000	Open Bal Equity	Open Balance Equity			
12	Equity	32000	Retained Earnings	Retained Earnings			
13	Income	40000	Contract Income	Contract Income			
14	Income	40100	Service Income	Service Income			
15	Cost of Goods Sold	50000	Job Related Expenses	Job Related Expenses			
16	Expense	60000	Advertising	Advertising			
17	Expense	61000	Dues & Subscriptions	Dues & Subscriptions			
18	Expense	62000	Postage & Delivery	Postage & Delivery			
19	Expense	63000	Office Supplies	Office Supplies			
20	Other Expense	80000	Other Expense	Other Expense			
21							
22							

FIGURE 2.1

An Excel worksheet created to import a chart of accounts into QuickBooks.

- Number—This field is optional and is the account number assigned in the Add New Account or Edit Account dialog. Using account numbers is optional in QuickBooks. See the section titled "Preferences That Affect the Chart of Accounts," later in this chapter, for information about account numbering preferences.
- Name—This field is required. You can set default preferences in QuickBooks for including name only, description only, or name and description on reports.

- Description—This field is optional. You can set default preferences in QuickBooks for including name only, description only, or name and description on reports. For more information about the appearance of the description on reports, see Chapter 16, "Reporting Tips and Tricks."

- Bank Account/Credit Card/Account Number—This field is optional and contains the account's number assigned by its holding institution.

- Opening Balance—This field is optional. If you enter a balance in this field, QuickBooks debits or credits the account, with the offset going to the Open Bal Equity account. If you do not enter any value, no transaction is created.

Rescue Me!

QuickBooks does not import from a spreadsheet a balance for Accounts Receivable or Accounts Payable type accounts due primarily to the one customer, one vendor per journal entry limitation. In general, I do not recommend using the Opening Balance column for beginning balances unless the import is supervised by an accounting professional who can review the resulting information for accuracy.

- As of Date—This field is optional. This is the date assigned to the transaction created when a value is placed in the opening balance column. If no date is entered and an opening balance amount was recorded, QuickBooks defaults the transaction date to today's computer system date.

Other fields you can include are reminder to order checks, track reimbursed income, income account for reimbursed expenses, and an option to mark the account as inactive in QuickBooks.

To import the list, you first must map the Excel column data to the appropriate QuickBooks data field.

From a new QuickBooks data file:

1. Click **File**, **Utilities**, and select **Import**, **Excel Files**. The Add Your Excel Data to QuickBooks dialog opens.

2. Select the **Advanced Import** button on the right, as shown in Figure 2.2.

3. In the **Import a File** dialog, browse to the file location where you stored the Excel document.

4. Select the Excel workbook sheet that you want to import.

5. Indicate whether there is a header row by clicking the check box.

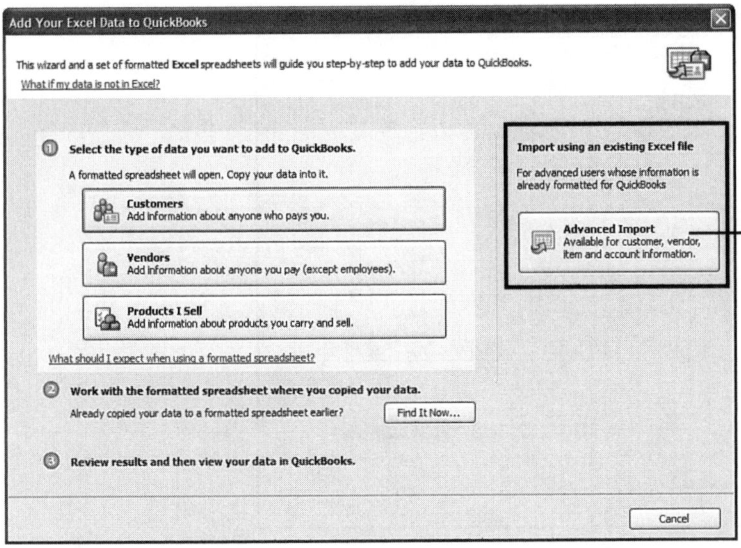

FIGURE 2.2

Released with QuickBooks 2008; the Add Your Excel Data to QuickBooks Wizard helps users import lists from Excel, including the Chart of Accounts.

6. Choose a mapping. If this is your first mapping, click < **Add New** >. If you are editing a previously saved mapping, select < **Edit** >, or if you have stored a previously created mapping, the name you gave it displays at the bottom of the drop-down list and you can select it here (see Figure 2.3). After selecting the mapping, a dialog opens, enabling you to change how the imported data will be assigned in QuickBooks.

7. After the mapping dialog is open (see previous step), you select the Import Type (Customers, Vendors, Items, or Accounts). QuickBooks lists on the left those fields in QuickBooks that you can populate with information from Excel. On the right side of the Mappings dialog, you see the column headers as you defined them in Excel. Select which column is assigned to which QuickBooks data field (see Figure 2.4).

8. Select the **Preview** item on the lower left of the Import a File dialog to review the data for any errors. Figure 2.5 shows the type name changed to Checking, and the import tool reported it as an invalid account type.

FIGURE 2.3

Choose a Mapping enables you to add a new mapping or edit a saved mapping.

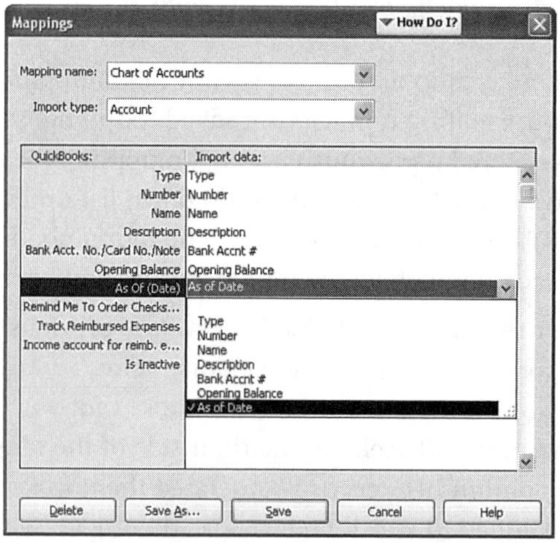

FIGURE 2.4

Setting the mapping rules for this saved mapping.

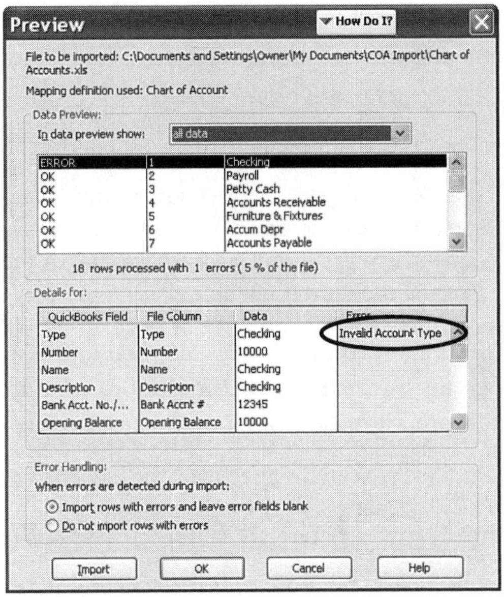

Preview   ▼ How Do I?   ☒

File to be imported: C:\Documents and Settings\Owner\My Documents\COA Import\Chart of Accounts.xls

Mapping definition used: Chart of Account

Data Preview:

In data preview show: all data   ▼

ERROR	1	Checking
OK	2	Payroll
OK	3	Petty Cash
OK	4	Accounts Receivable
OK	5	Furniture & Fixtures
OK	6	Accum Depr
OK	7	Accounts Payable

18 rows processed with 1 errors (5 % of the file)

Details for:

QuickBooks Field	File Column	Data	Error
Type	Type	Checking	Invalid Account Type
Number	Number	10000	
Name	Name	Checking	
Description	Description	Checking	
Bank Acct. No./...	Bank Acct #	12345	
Opening Balance	Opening Balance	10000	

Error Handling:

When errors are detected during import:

⦿ Import rows with errors and leave error fields blank
○ Do not import rows with errors

[Import]   [OK]   [Cancel]   [Help]

FIGURE 2.5

Preview the import before actually importing the data.

Rescue Me!

Clicking the Preview button enables you to see whether the information will import correctly.

Using the correct types is critical to the success of the import. QuickBooks recognizes these types:

- BANK
- AR (for Accounts Receivable)
- OCASSET (for Other Current Asset)
- FIXASSET (for Fixed Asset)
- OASSET (for Other Asset)
- AP (for Accounts Payable)
- CCARD (for Credit Card)
- OCLIAB (for Other Current Liability)
- LTLIAB (for Long Term Liability)
- EQUITY
- INC (for Income)
- COGS (for Cost of Goods Sold)

- EXP (for Expense)
- EXINC (for Other Income)
- EXEXP (for Other Expense)
- NONPOSTING (for Sales Orders, Estimates, and Purchase Orders)

If you do not include a type or you have an unrecognized type, QuickBooks provides an error log from the Preview window. Refer to Figure 2.5, where the term Checking was put in the account type instead of the proper term Bank.

Importing from Excel can be an easy method to use when you want to use a chart of accounts list from your accountant or want the flexibility of creating it in the Excel program. However, other options offer similar functionality, including the IIF format file.

Importing from an Intuit Interchange Format (IIF) File

The term *Intuit Interchange Format (IIF)* refers to data exchange functionality that has been around for some time. It is a method for exporting lists from one QuickBooks data file and importing these lists (not transactions) into a new QuickBooks data file. The process creates a comma-separated value format file with the extension of .iif. You can view and edit this file using Excel.

The most common use for this tool is to export lists from one QuickBooks data file to a new QuickBooks data file. The process is easy and relatively error free. Other uses for the tool include transaction imports. This book does not cover this topic; however, you can find more information about this utility by typing IIF in the search field at www.quickbooks.com\support\.

The IIF format is a preferred and easy method to use if you already have a QuickBooks data file with a chart of accounts (or other lists) that you want to duplicate.

The only disadvantage to working with an IIF format file is all the extra information that is in the worksheet, making it awkard to edit or add to the existing information.

Perform the following steps to export an IIF-formatted chart of accounts file from an existing QuickBooks file:

1. Click **File**, **Open** to open the QuickBooks file that has the chart of accounts (or other lists) that you want to export and duplicate in another file.

2. Click **File**, **Utilities**, select **Export**, **Lists to IIF Files**.

3. Select **Chart of Accounts** by clicking to place a check mark in the box, as shown in Figure 2.6.

FIGURE 2.6
The Export dialog shows choices of lists available for export.

 Digging Deeper

Creating individual IIF files for each of the master lists you want to export is preferred to creating one combined file. In other words, create one file for your Chart of Accounts separate from a file for Vendors or Customers. This way, if one list has trouble importing, it won't prevent the other lists from importing.

4. Click **OK**; you are prompted to save the file.

Figure 2.7 shows the exported QuickBooks chart of accounts in the IIF format in an Excel workbook. You can see that it is not as user friendly as the Excel import discussed previously.

	A	B	C	D	E	F	G	H	I	J	K	L
1	IHDR	PROD	VER	REL	IIFVER	DATE	TIME	ACCNTNT	ACCNTNT	SPLITTIME		
2	HDR	QuickBook	Version 17	Release R	1	4/7/2007	1.18E+09	N	0			
3	IACCNT	NAME	REFNUM	TIMESTAN	ACCNTTYI	OBAMOUI	DESC	ACCNUM	SCD	BANKNUN	EXTRA	HIDDEN
4	ACCNT	Checking	9	1.18E+09	BANK	10,000.00	Checking	10000	1535	12345		N
5	ACCNT	Payroll	10	1.18E+09	BANK	525	Payroll	10100	1535	55896		N
6	ACCNT	Petty Cash	11	1.18E+09	BANK	100	Petty Cash	10200	1535			N
7	ACCNT	Accounts I	12	1.18E+09	AR	0	Accounts I	11000	1537			N
8	ACCNT	Accum De	14	1.18E+09	FIXASSET	########	Accum De	17000	1555			N
9	ACCNT	Furniture &	13	1.18E+09	FIXASSET	25,000.00	Furniture &	15000	1555			N
10	ACCNT	Accounts I	15	1.18E+09	AP	0	Accounts I	20000	1573			N
11	ACCNT	Payroll Lia	4	1.18E+09	OCLIAB	0		24000	1577			N
12	ACCNT	Note Paya	16	1.18E+09	LTLIAB	########	Note Paya	27000	1581			N
13	ACCNT	Capital Stc	6	1.18E+09	EQUITY	0	Value of cc	30100	0			N
14	ACCNT	Opening B	5	1.18E+09	EQUITY	-8,125.00		30000	0		OPENBAL	N
15	ACCNT	Retained E	8	1.18E+09	EQUITY	0	Retained E	32000	0		RETEARN	N
16	ACCNT	Shareholde	7	1.18E+09	EQUITY	0	Distribution	31400	0			N
17	ACCNT	Contract Ir	17	1.18E+09	INC	0	Contract Ir	40000	0			N
18	ACCNT	Service Inc	18	1.18E+09	INC	0	Service Inc	40100	0			N
19	ACCNT	Job Relate	19	1.18E+09	COGS	0	Job Relate	50000	0			N
20	ACCNT	Advertising	20	1.18E+09	EXP	0	Advertising	6000	0			N
21	ACCNT	Dues & Su	21	1.18E+09	EXP	0	Dues & Su	6100	0			N
22	ACCNT	Office Sup	23	1.18E+09	EXP	0	Office Sup	6300	0			N
23	ACCNT	Payroll Ex	3	1.18E+09	EXP	0		66000	0			N
24	ACCNT	Postage &	22	1.18E+09	EXP	0	Postage &	6200	0			N
25	ACCNT	Other Expe	24	1.18E+09	EXEXP	0	Other Expe	8000	0			N

Chart of Account Template

Ready   NUM

FIGURE 2.7
A chart of accounts IIF format file.

Rescue Me!

The IIF file format is sensitive to changes in rows and columns. I recommend not changing the order or width of rows and columns when editing or adding data. Additionally, the file has several header rows that cannot be removed if the import tool is to work correctly when you import it with the IIF import menu option.

To import the saved IIF file into a new QuickBooks file, do the following:

1. Click **File**, **Open** to see the new QuickBooks file, preferably one that does not have a chart of accounts or other list types you are importing. (Importing into a file with an existing chart of accounts is possible. QuickBooks will reject the remaining portion of the import duplicate account number or name is detected.)

   If you have not already created your new file, click **File**, **New** and follow the prompts. (See Chapter 1, "Creating a New QuickBooks Data File," for more information on using the EasyStep Interview to create a new QuickBooks data file.)

2. Click **File**, **Utilities**, and select **Import, IIF Files**.

3. When the Import dialog opens, browse to the location of the stored IIF formatted file.

4. With your mouse pointer, select the file and click on **Open**.

5. QuickBooks then imports the IIF formatted file into the QuickBooks data file.

Now that you have your new data file with new lists from another file, you are ready to begin entering transactions. Just think of all the time you saved by not having to manually create each list item in the new file.

Preferences That Affect the Chart of Accounts

Using specific preferences, you can modify much of how the QuickBooks features work. Click Edit, Preferences and select the Accounting preference. Next, click the Company Preferences tab.

Here is a list of the preferences that affect the chart of accounts. They are all found in the Accounting preferences section.

- Use account numbers—Selecting this option turns on the data field that holds a numeric assignment for each chart of accounts. By default, this feature is *not* selected in a newly created QuickBooks file.

 Digging Deeper

For accounts that had an account number assigned, *not* selecting the Use Account Numbers option does not remove the account number; it simply makes the field not visible. For accountants, turn on the feature and assign your desired account numbers, and then turn the feature off when the file is returned to your client. When you review the file again, any accounts created since your last review will not have an account number, which makes locating them easy.

This is only one method you can use. For clients that have QuickBooks 2009, the new Client Data Review (CDR) feature, available for accountants with QuickBooks Premier Accountant 2009, will track any changes made to the chart of accounts including added, renamed, deleted, or merged to name a few. See Chapter 17, "Detecting and Correcting with the Client Data Review Feature."

- Show lowest subaccount only—If you have created a subaccount listing under a main (parent) listing, any drop-down menu will show only the lowest subaccount level, preventing users from posting to the main account.

 Digging Deeper

If you see a subaccount under a main account on a report called Other, it might be due to someone posting to the main (or parent) account rather than to the appropriate subaccount.

- Require accounts—By default, this feature is selected in a newly created QuickBooks file. If this feature is not selected, any transactions saved without an appropriate income or expense account will be posted to a QuickBooks automatically created uncategorized income or uncategorized expense account. This process follows the rule that there must always be a debit and credit side to each transaction. Fortunately, you do not have to know how to post a debit or credit because QuickBooks does this thinking for you with each transaction.

Accounts That QuickBooks Creates Automatically

Although you are given quite a bit of flexibility in creating the chart of accounts using a variety of methods, QuickBooks creates certain accounts that are hard-coded into the programming of the software, meaning you do not need to create them yourself.

A common mistake is to create these accounts, not recognizing that they were already created or will be created when the related form is chosen.

I usually tell my clients to accept the default chart of accounts because they can be modified at anytime. Even if you select None/Other during the EasyStep Interview when creating a chart of accounts, specific accounts in QuickBooks are automatically created. These accounts follow:

- Payroll Liabilities (Other Current Liability)
- Capital Stock (Equity)
- Opening Bal Equity (Equity)
- Retained Earnings (Equity)
- Shareholder Distributions (Equity)
- Payroll Expenses (Expense)

The specific default chart of accounts that QuickBooks creates varies depending on the type of entity you selected when creating your data file. For example, if you selected Sole Proprietor on the "How is your company organized" dialog as shown in Figure 1.3, QuickBooks will create an Owners Draw and Owners Equity, but no Capital Stock or Shareholder Distributions.

Additionally, if you selected None/Other during the EasyStep Interview when presented with a list of industry-specific chart of accounts, QuickBooks creates the following accounts only when the associated form or transaction is used or a related preference is selected:

- Inventory Asset (Asset)—Inventory item created
- Accounts Receivable (Asset)—Invoice form opened
- Sales Tax Payable (Liability)—Sales Tax preference enabled
- Accounts Payable (Liability)—Vendor bill form opened
- Purchase Orders (Non-Posting)—Purchase Order form opened
- Estimates (Non-Posting)—Estimate form opened

To determine whether an account was created by QuickBooks, edit the account in question; if the Account Type field is not active (grayed out), this account was automatically created by QuickBooks (see Figure 2.8).

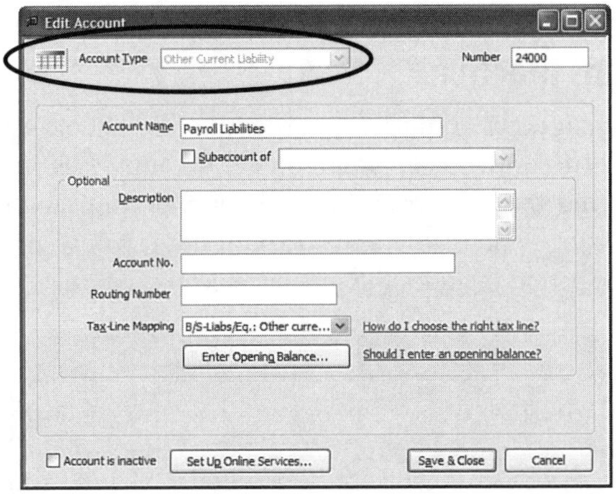

FIGURE 2.8

In the Edit Account dialog box, if Account Type is grayed out, this account was created by QuickBooks.

Methods to Troubleshoot and Correct Chart of Account Issues

When searching for reasons why your financial statements do not appear correct, the first place to look is often the chart of accounts. It is also important to carefully consider the impact of the change on your financials and make sure you choose the right method for correction.

There are many ways to resolve errors found on the chart of accounts. However, before attempting any of the suggested methods here, you should consider the following:

- The effect the change could have on prior-period financials
- The effect the change could have on previously recorded transactions
- The impact the changes would have on the records your accountant has kept for the company

A quick review of the chart of accounts should include the following:

- Duplicated accounts
- Unnecessary accounts (too much detail)
- Accounts placed in the wrong account type category
- Misplaced subaccounts

Removing Duplicated Accounts by Marking an Account Inactive

Marking an account inactive is usually the best choice when you have duplicate or extra list items on your chart of accounts (see Figure 2.9). Making an account inactive removes it from any drop-down list on any forms. However, for reporting periods where the account has a value, any reports generated for this time period includes the inactive account balance.

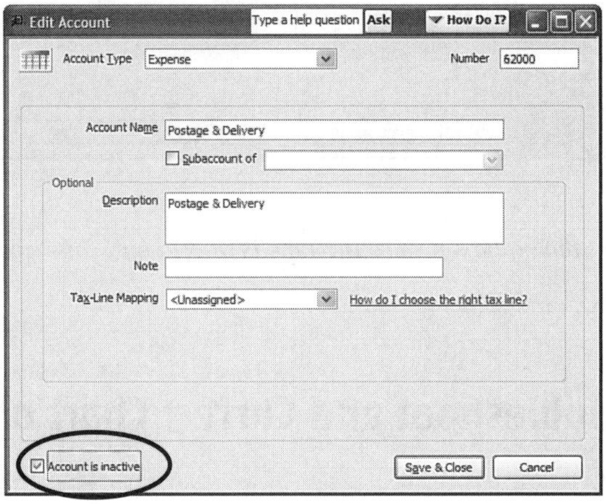

FIGURE 2.9
Select the Account is inactive check box to remove the list item from any drop-down menus.

Digging Deeper

In earlier versions of QuickBooks, you might have accounts that have an asterisk (*) in front of the name to indicate a duplicate account name. This situation usually only happens when you did not select to use one of the sample charts of accounts. QuickBooks has certain accounts that it creates automatically. For example, if you did not select a sample default chart of accounts and created your own Accounts Receivable account, later when you opened a customer invoice form, QuickBooks created the Accounts Receivable account but recognized that one existed with the same name. You should merge your created account (the one without the *) into the QuickBooks-created account. See the later section titled "Merging Duplicated Accounts" for instructions on how to merge two like accounts.

Digging Deeper

Need to mark several accounts as inactive? Simply select the Include inactive check box at the bottom of the Chart of Accounts list (after at least one account is inactive), as shown in Figure 2.10. You can mark any list item you want to become inactive by clicking in front of the list item name.

If you try to use an inactive account, QuickBooks will ask you if want to "Use it once" or "Make it active."

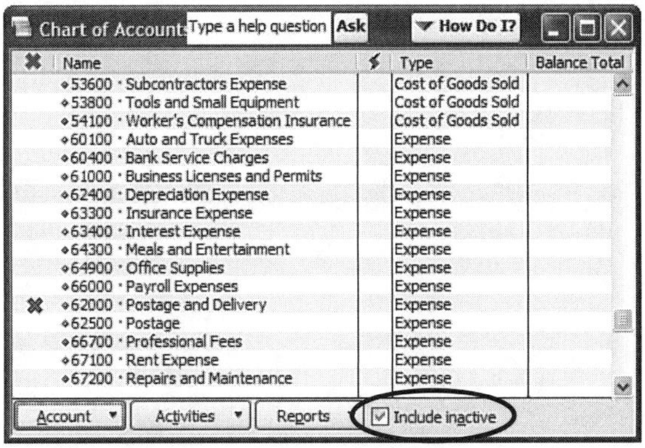

FIGURE 2.10

Easily mark accounts inactive from the Chart of Accounts dialog box.

Merging Duplicated Accounts

Another method to remove duplicated accounts is to merge the similar accounts. To perform a chart of accounts merge, both accounts must be in the same chart of accounts category; in other words, you cannot merge an Asset with a Liability type account.

Before merging accounts, be sure to perform a backup of your data, just in case the result is not what you expected. When the accounts are merged, all transactions previously assigned to the removed account now appear as if they were always assigned to the remaining account.

 Rescue Me!

This method potentially changes your financials and should be cautiously performed only after you have discussed the effect with the company's accountant and made a backup of the data file.

To merge two accounts, do the following:

1. Click **Lists**, **Chart of Accounts** and highlight the account you want to remove with the merge. With the account highlighted, press Ctrl+E on your keyboard to open the Edit Account dialog.

2. If you are using account numbering, replace the account number with the account number for the account you want to retain. (If you are not using account numbering, you can type the *exact* spelling of the name of the other account you are merging this one into.)

   QuickBooks cautions you that the name is already being used and asks whether you want to continue (see Figure 2.11). If you do not get this message, you didn't type the name or account number exactly the same. You will want to try again.

3. Click **Yes**.

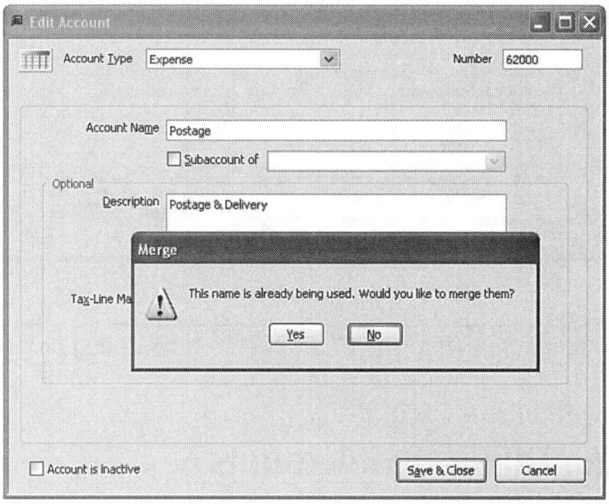

FIGURE 2.11

QuickBooks offers a word of caution when you are merging two Charts of Accounts lists.

Rescue Me!

Chart of accounts, customers, jobs, vendors, and other names lists can all be merged within their own type or category. Be careful—there is no undo function, making the action irreversible.

Wrong Account Type Assigned to a Chart of Accounts Listing

The mistake most often made when creating your own chart of accounts is assigning the wrong account type. QuickBooks provides additional subcategories under the six standard accounting types, as identified in the "Understanding the Chart of Accounts" section at the beginning of this chapter.

The Add New Chart of Account entry dialog, shown in Figure 2.12, reduces errors that occur when creating a new chart of accounts. When creating a new account, you select an account type, and QuickBooks provides a description of what a typical transaction would be for this type. In prior versions of the software, the default type was a Bank Account, and users would mistakenly create their accounts as if they were bank accounts.

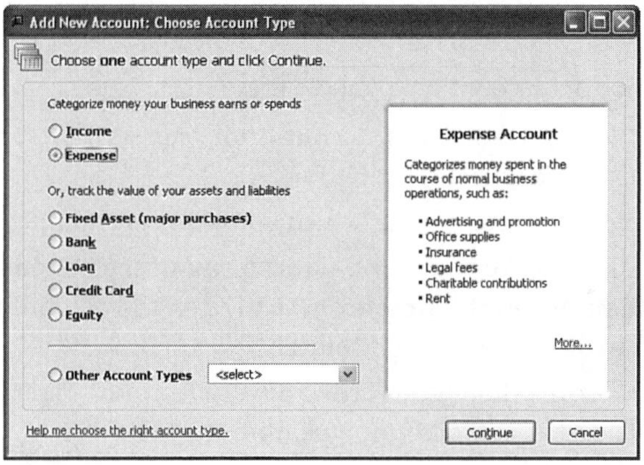

FIGURE 2.12

The Add New Account dialog.

Rescue Me!

Exercise caution before changing an account type. The change affects any prior-period financials. If this consequence is a limitation for your company, a simple solution would be to create a general journal to remove the amount from one account and assign it to another. This method preserves the integrity of prior-period financials. (See Chapter 5, "Power Reports for Troubleshooting Beginning Balance Differences," for more information on the Audit Trail report.) The Audit Trail report in QuickBooks does not track that a change was made to an account type.

Merging accounts can also be advantageous when you want to fix future transactions and prior-period transactions. For example, suppose you created a Current Asset account type instead of the correct Expense account type. Simply changing the account type via the Edit Account dialog box (see following steps) corrects all prior-period and future transactions to be assigned to the new account type.

However, you will not be able to change an account type, or merge a chart of an account if there are sub-accounts associated with that chart of account list item.

Rescue Me!

Any changes to account types and merging accounts are *not* captured by the "always on" audit trail. To track changes made to an account such as, modifying the name, changing the type, or merging accounts, see details on the new QuickBooks 2009 Client Data Review in Chapter 17.

To change an account type, follow these steps:

1. Click **Lists**, **Chart of Accounts** (or press Ctrl+A). The Chart of Accounts list dialog displays.

2. Select the account for which you want to change the type.

3. Click the **Account** drop-down menu at the bottom of the list. Select **Edit Account** (or press Ctrl+E to open the account for editing). The Edit Account dialog box displays.

4. Click the drop-down arrow next to **Account Type** (see Figure 2.13) and choose a new account type from the list.

5. Click **Save & Close**.

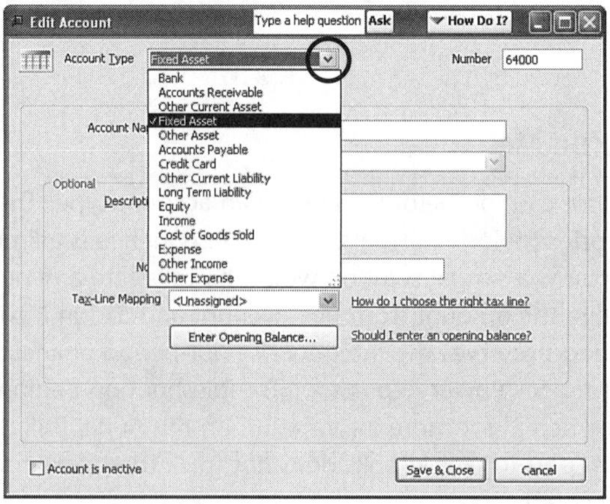

FIGURE 2.13

Changing an existing account's type.

Digging Deeper

Not all account types can be changed. Accounts Receivable, Accounts Payable, Credit Cards (with online access configured), and any of the default accounts created by QuickBooks cannot be changed to a different type. In addition, for any balance sheet account that the account type is changed to a non-Balance Sheet account type, QuickBooks warns that you can no longer enter transactions directly into the register.

Assigning or Removing a Subaccount Relationship

Often in accounting reports, you have specific accounts for which you want to see a more detailed breakdown of the costs. You can get this breakdown easily by creating the main account and associating subaccounts with the main account.

Figure 2.14 shows Utilities as a main account with an indented subaccount for each type of utility expense. To edit an existing account to be a subaccount of another main account:

1. Click **Lists**, **Chart of Accounts** (or press Ctrl+A). The Chart of Accounts list dialog displays.

2. Select the account for which you want to be a subaccount of another account.

3. Click the **Account** drop-down menu at the bottom of the list. Select **Edit Account** (or press Ctrl+E to open the account for editing). The Edit Account dialog box displays.

4. Place a check mark in the **Subaccount of** box and choose from the drop-down menu the account you want it to be associated with. (It must be of the same account type).

5. Click **Save & Close**.

Users can assign a subaccount that is only in the same general account type. For example, an Expense type cannot be a subaccount of a Current Asset type account (see Figure 2.15).

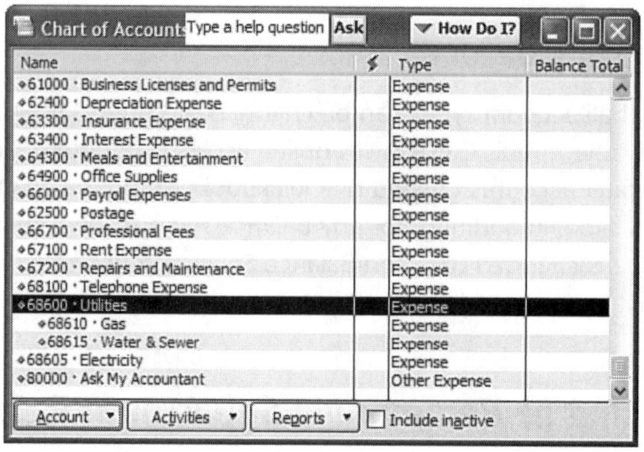

FIGURE 2.14

Chart of Accounts showing a subaccount relationship to main account.

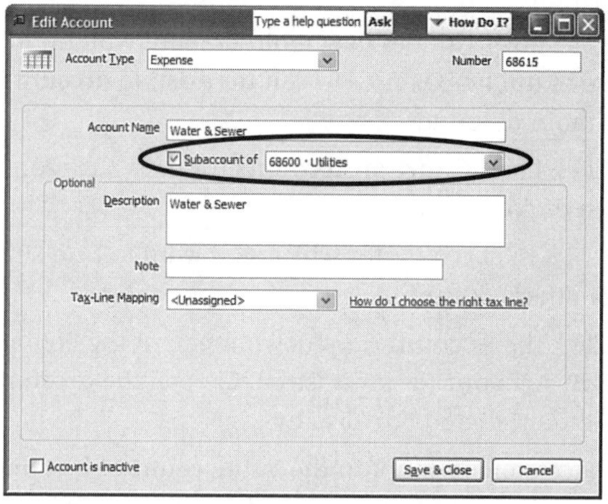

FIGURE 2.15

Edit Account dialog assigning a subaccount to main account.

Digging Deeper

If you need to change the subaccount to another General Ledger account type, first deselect the Subaccount of check box. Click Save & Close to save the change. Then edit the account and change the type. You cannot change subaccount types when they are associated with a main account. You also cannot change the account type when that account has subaccounts associated with it.

You can also change account relationships directly on the Chart of Accounts list:

1. To remove or add a subaccount directly from the list, place your mouse pointer over the diamond in front of the list item (see Figure 2.16). The cursor changes to indicate that you can drag the item.

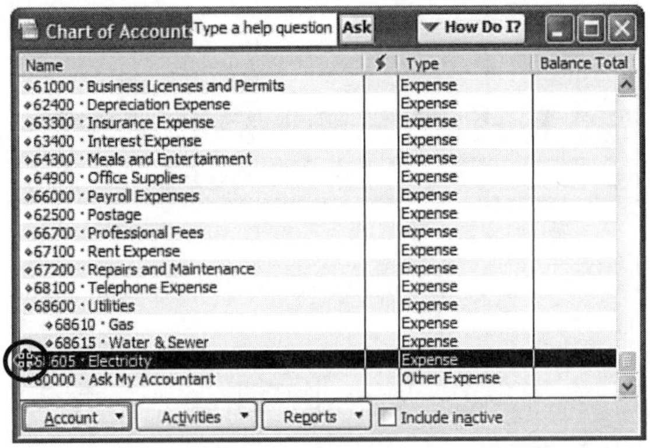

FIGURE 2.16

Select the diamond in front of the account name to change the placement.

2. Drag the diamond to the right and up using the dashed line that displays to help guide and properly place it under the main account (but it must be in same account category) to create a subaccount relationship (see Figure 2.17).

The Chart of Account list shows the corrected relationship (see Figure 2.18).

Financial reporting is more accurate when you take the time to review and correct your chart of accounts setup. Often, you can manage the information better when you group similar income or expense accounts using the subaccount feature.

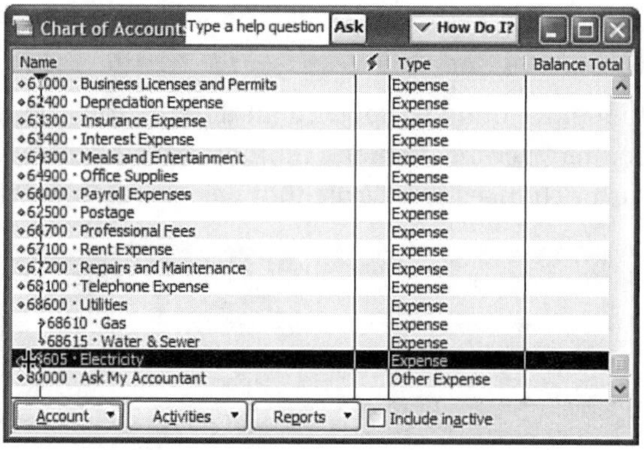

FIGURE 2.17

Dragging the diamond to the right and up creates the subaccount relationship.

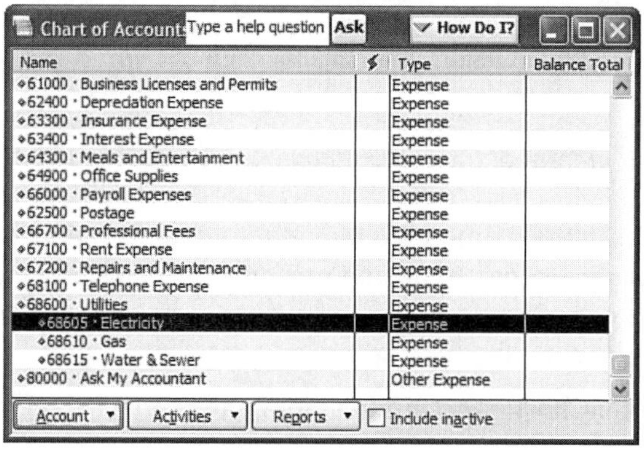

FIGURE 2.18

The chart of accounts view after the change is made.

Chapter 3

Reviewing and Correcting Item List Errors

- Understanding the Differences Among the Chart of Accounts, Items, Classes, and Customer Types

- Using Item Types

- Finding Item Errors in QuickBooks

- Fixing Item Errors in QuickBooks

- Creating Items as Subitems

Differences Between the Chart of Accounts, Items, Classes, and Customer Types

QuickBooks offers several methods for separating business results into meaningful segments. You have the chart of accounts list for organizing your transactions, the Items list for tracking the profitability of individual services and products you sell, classes for tracking different corporate profit centers, and the ability to view your profitability by user-defined customer types.

The QuickBooks accounting structure is generally easy to set up and define. What becomes problematic for some is how to efficiently use each of the available list types when you want to segment the business reporting activity in QuickBooks.

 Digging Deeper

A well-defined QuickBooks data file most likely includes the use of items, classes, and customer types, in addition to the chart of accounts.

Before reviewing and correcting item list errors, you need to understand the differences between items and the other lists available in QuickBooks.

Chart of Accounts

The chart of accounts list, in particular, the Profit & Loss accounts, should offer just enough detail for you to make financial decisions for your overall business, but not so much detail that you have too much information to analyze.

Keeping your Profit & Loss chart of accounts minimized enables you to easily analyze business finances. For example, a contractor might employ 30 or more different types of specialty trades when building a house, such as site work, concrete, plumbing, and so on. To create a Cost of Goods Sold account for each type of trade would be too much detail when reviewing financial reports for the overall business.

A better approach would be to create summary Cost of Goods Sold accounts that, for the contractor example, might be Cost of Goods Sold—Labor, Cost of Goods Sold—Material, Cost of Goods Sold—Equipment, and so on. Other industries that track many services or products would also benefit from including only summary accounts on the Profit & Loss statement.

Digging Deeper

Are you creating a new data file or using an existing file? Your accountant should review your chart of accounts and make sure that it meets certain accounting guidelines. Taking this extra step can save you lots of extra work at tax reporting time if you find you have not used the appropriate accounts.

Items

Items are what you sell or buy and are used on all customer forms and optionally on purchase forms. Items provide a quick means for data entry. However, a more important role for items is to handle the behind-the-scenes accounting while tracking item-specific costs and revenue detail.

Using the contractor example given previously, you could create an item for Site Work Labor, Concrete Labor, and Plumbing Labor and assign each item to your single Cost of Goods Sold—Labor chart of accounts. Using items enables you to capture cost detail by labor type rather than creating a Chart of Account for each type. Then when you view your Profit & Loss statement, you can easily see what your total Cost of Goods Sold is for all labor types.

A few of the reports that are dependent on the use of items include:

- Job Profitability Summary or Detail
- Job Estimates Versus Actuals Summary or Detail
- Item Profitability
- Time by Item

Classes

Another method for segmenting your QuickBooks financial information is by using classes. The use of classes is a preference setting and must first be enabled by logging in to the data file as the Admin or External Accountant user:

1. Click **Edit, Preferences**.
2. Select the **Accounting** preference on the left.
3. Click the **Company Preferences** tab.
4. Select the **Use Class Tracking** option, as shown in Figure 3.1.

Classes are typically used when a company has multiple revenue-generating business types or multiple profit centers. These class list items are then assigned to each transaction, as in Figure 3.2. Examples of classes might be a construction company that offers either new construction or remodel services, or a restaurant with multiple locations. In both examples, using classes that are assigned to each transaction line for both revenue and costs enables you to report profit and loss by class.

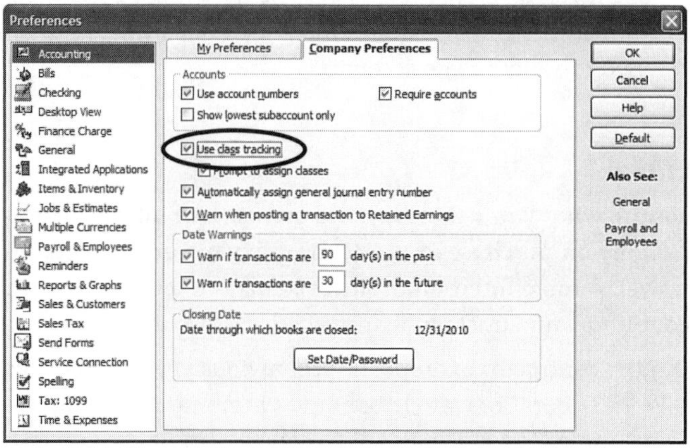

FIGURE 3.1

Enable the preference for class tracking.

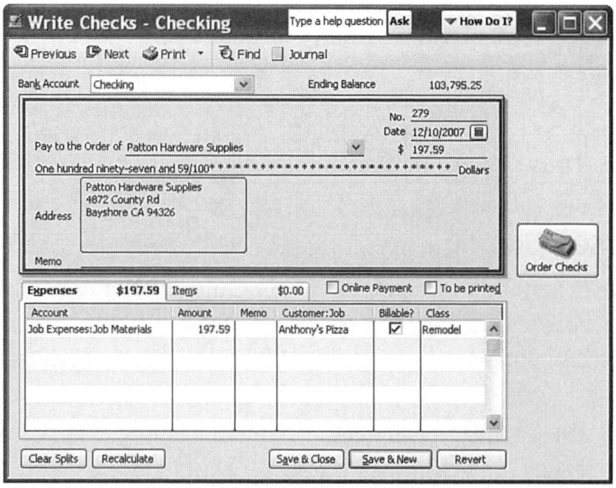

FIGURE 3.2

An example of a check with a class list item assigned on the transaction line.

Digging Deeper

When deciding to use classes, it is important that you have only one primary purpose for the class structure. If you try to track more than one "type" of class, the value in the reporting is diminished. For example, your company has both an east coast and west coast division. These represent the proper use of the QuickBooks class feature. However, using classes to also track the source of the business—for example, yellow pages, email marketing, and so on—would diminish the success of class reporting because you would be tracking two unrelated groupings. Instead, you can use classes for one purpose and customer types for another.

Customer Types

You can use customer types to categorize your customers in ways that are meaningful to your business. A retailer might use customer types to track retail versus wholesale; a medical office might track types of services; a service company might track what marketing event brought in the customer. You can filter certain reports by these customer types, giving you critical information for making business management decisions. These customer types can also be useful for marketing purposes when you want to direct a letter to a specific customer type.

To create or assign a customer type:

1. Click the **Customer Center** icon from the Home page.

2. Select a customer by double-clicking on the name.

3. Click the **Additional Info** tab and select a type from the drop-down menu or select **Add New** in Categorizing and Defaults, as shown in Figure 3.3.

Many of the customer reports can be filtered for customer type, making it another useful list for segmenting your data.

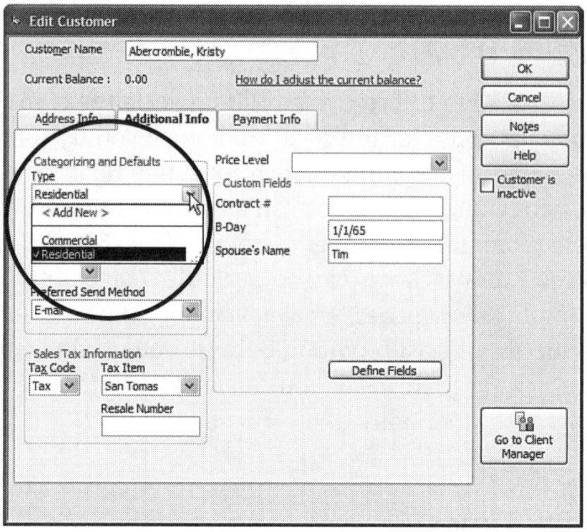

FIGURE 3.3

Assign a customer type in the Edit Customer dialog.

Using Item Types

QuickBooks has 11 item types to choose from (not including the Fixed Asset Item, Price Levels, or Billing Rates not discussed in this book, although some of the list items might not be listed in your data file if the related feature is not enabled. You can choose the type to assign to a list item; however, each type has certain unique characteristics. Here are some general guidelines about the proper use for item types:

- **Service**—You usually create this type for services you sell and, optionally, purchase.

- **Inventory Part**—This type appears only if Inventory and Purchase Orders are active on the Company tab of the Items and Inventory preferences (click Edit, Preferences, select Items and Inventory, and click the Company tab). Inventory is used to track products you make or buy, place in a warehouse location, and later sell to a customer. Inventory is increased with a received purchase order or bill and is decreased on a customer invoice.

Digging Deeper

If the item you purchase will never be included on a customer's invoice or sales receipt, then it should not be created as an Inventory Part, instead create it as a Non-inventory part.

- **Inventory Assembly**—This type is an assembling of multiple inventory components, as in a Bill of Materials. When an inventory assembly is built, the individual items (components of the assembly) are deducted from inventory and the quantity of the finished product is increased. The assembly functionality is only available in QuickBooks Premier or Enterprise.

- **Non-inventory Part**—This type is used for products you purchase but do not track as inventory. Correct use of this type would include products you purchase that are ordered for a specific customer and directly shipped to the customer, or for materials and supplies you purchase but do not sell to the customer.

- **Other Charge**—This is a multipurpose item type. Freight, handling, and other miscellaneous types of charges are examples of the proper use of the other charge item type. Using this type makes it possible to see your services separate from the other charge types of revenue and expense.

- **Subtotal**—This type is used to add subtotal line items on sales and purchase forms. This item is especially useful if you want to calculate a specific discount on a group of items on an invoice form.

- **Group**—This type is used to quickly assign a grouping of individual items on sales and purchase forms. Unlike assemblies, groups are not tracked as a separate finished unit. Groups can save you data entry time and enable you to print or not print the details on a customer's invoice.

- **Discount**—This type facilitates dollar or percent deductions off what your customers owe on a sales form. This item type cannot be used on purchase forms.

- **Payment**—This item type is not always necessary to set up. You create this item type if you record the payment directly on an invoice as a line item, such as is done with a Daily Sales Summary form (see the QuickBooks Help menu). On typical customer invoices, you should not record payments in this manner because there is no tracking of the customer's check or credit card number.

- **Sales Tax Item**—This type is available only if you enabled sales tax by selecting Yes to charging sales tax on the Company tab of the Sales Tax preferences (click Edit, Preferences and select Sales Tax). In most cases, QuickBooks automatically assigns this item to an invoice. In some states or industries where there are multiple sales tax rates for a given sale, you can also add this item to an invoice as a separate line item.

- **Sales Tax Group**—This type is used to group multiple tax district flat-rate sales tax items that are combined and charged as one sales tax rate.

Rescue Me!

Carefully determine the correct item type to use when creating items. After they're created, the following item types cannot be changed to any other item type: Service, Inventory Assembly, Subtotal, Discount, Payment, Sales Tax Item, and Sales Tax Group.

If you find you have set up the wrong item type, correcting it might require making an accounting adjustment. To avoid using the incorrect item on future transactions, mark the item as inactive by clicking Lists, Items. The Item List dialog opens. Select the Item button, choose Edit Item, and place a check mark in the Item is inactive check box. When this box is selected, as Figure 3.4 shows, the item is not included in any drop-down lists on forms, but is included in reports if used during the period being reported.

However, do not make an inventory type inactive if QuickBooks still shows available inventory quantity. This topic is discussed more fully in Chapter 10, "Reviewing and Correcting Inventory Errors."

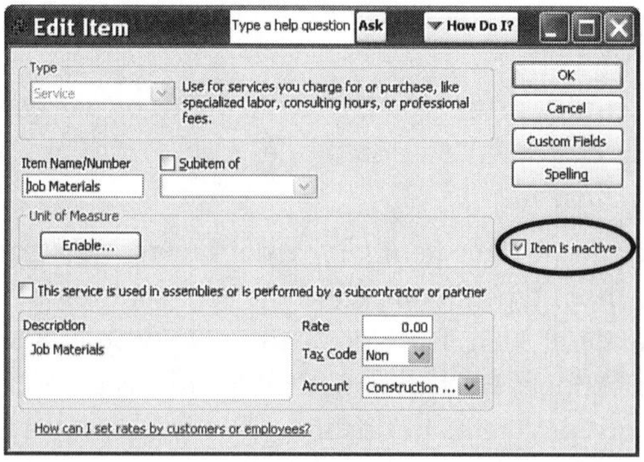

FIGURE 3.4

Marking a list item inactive only removes it from drop-down lists, not reports.

Finding Item Errors in QuickBooks

Want to quickly fix some of the most common errors in QuickBooks? Reviewing and correcting items in QuickBooks can be the best and easiest way to repair a company's data file. The most common reason or misstatement on a company's financials is often traced to incorrectly set up items. Often, it is easy to tell that the items were set up incorrectly. Some indicators of this might be understated revenue, negative costs, or just an overall lack of confidence in the financials. This is because items are "mapped" to the chart of accounts, if an item is improperly assigned to the wrong type of an account, this could create errors in accurate financial reporting.

To help you in those instances where incorrectly set up items might not be so apparent, the following sections offer a few methods for reviewing the item list.

Reviewing Accounts Assigned to Items

Adding and removing columns you view in the Item List dialog can help you notice any setup errors that exist. To customize the Item List Lookup dialog for items, do the following:

1. Click **Lists**, **Item List** and while highlighting any list item, right-click it and click **Customize Columns**, as shown in Figure 3.5.

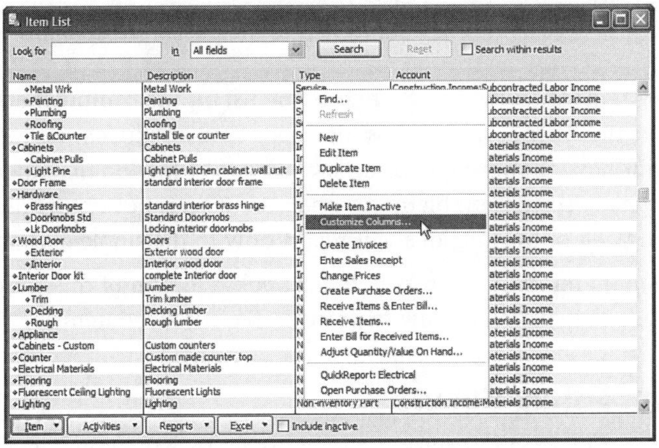

FIGURE 3.5

Customizing columns on the item list can help you see item errors easily.

2. In the dialog box that appears, add the COGS Account by highlighting it in the Available Columns pane, as you see in Figure 3.6, and clicking **Add** to include the account in the Chosen Columns pane on the right.

Add or remove from the Chosen Columns pane those fields that you want or don't want to see when viewing the Item List Lookup dialog.

3. Click the **Move Up** or **Move Down** buttons in the center of the dialog box to customize the order in which you want to view the columns (see Figure 3.6), and then click **OK**.

4. Optionally, to widen columns of displayed date on your computer screen, place your mouse on the right or left lines of any group in the grey bar header and drag to make the column wider or smaller.

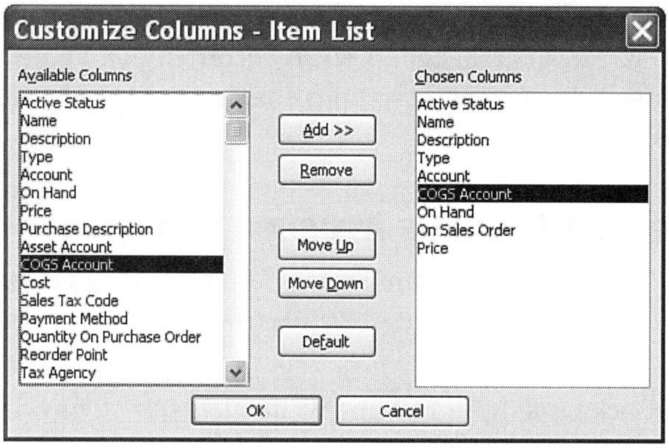

FIGURE 3.6
Choose the available columns you want to view in the Customize Columns - Item List.

Now, you can conveniently review the list on the computer screen for those items that do not have a Cost of Goods Sold or expense account assigned, or might have the wrong account assigned. Not having an expense account assigned becomes problematic when the item is both purchased and sold; both types of transactions will report only to the single account selected.

See the "Fixing Item Errors in QuickBooks" section of this chapter for a more detailed discussion of how to properly fix one-sided items.

Item Listing Report

Another method to review the item list setup is the Item Listing report (click Reports, Lists and select the Item Listing report). Click Modify on the report, and in the dialog box that appears, click the Display tab to select the columns to view. Useful columns include Item, Description, Type, Account, Asset Account (for inventory items only), COGS Account, and Sales Tax Code, as shown in Figure 3.7. Whenever the item is used on a purchase or sales transaction (such as an invoice, a sales receipt, a bill, a check, and so on), these columns show to which accounts QuickBooks records the transaction on the chart of accounts.

What exactly are you looking for on the list item report as shown in Figure 3.8? One thing you are looking for are items that you use on both purchase and sales forms but that have only the Account column details. Or you might also be looking for items with the incorrect account assigned. If you collect sales tax, be sure the correct sales tax code is selected. For a more detailed discussion of sales tax in QuickBooks, see Chapter 12, "Reviewing and Correcting Sales Tax Errors."

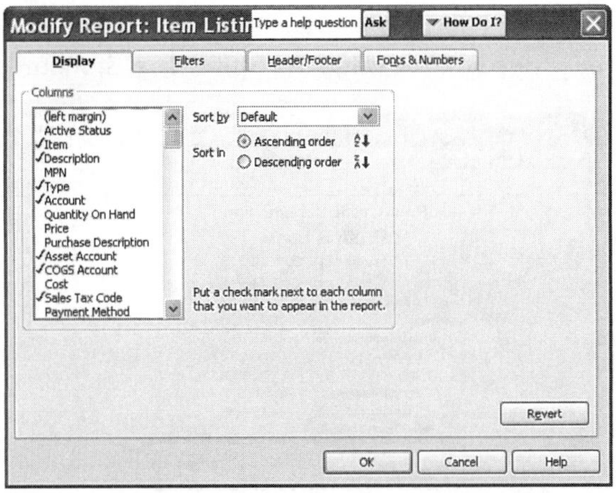

FIGURE 3.7

Modify a report to display specific detail.

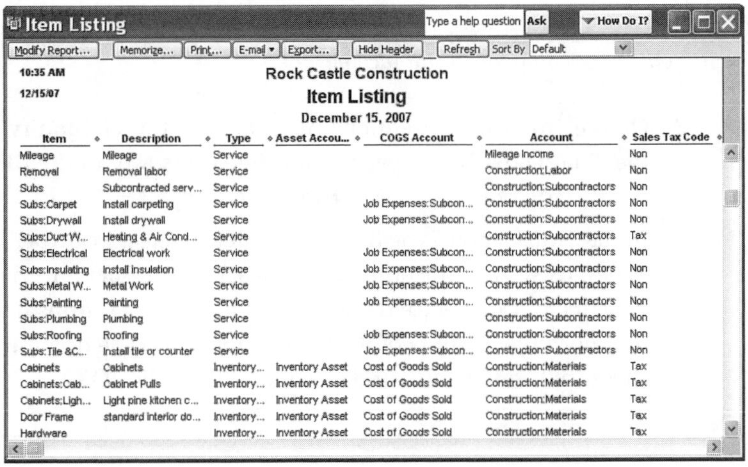

Item	Description	Type	Asset Accou...	COGS Account	Account	Sales Tax Code
Mileage	Mileage	Service			Mileage Income	Non
Removal	Removal labor	Service			Construction:Labor	Non
Subs	Subcontracted serv...	Service			Construction:Subcontractors	Non
Subs:Carpet	Install carpeting	Service		Job Expenses:Subcon...	Construction:Subcontractors	Non
Subs:Drywall	Install drywall	Service		Job Expenses:Subcon...	Construction:Subcontractors	Non
Subs:Duct W...	Heating & Air Cond...	Service			Construction:Subcontractors	Tax
Subs:Electrical	Electrical work	Service		Job Expenses:Subcon...	Construction:Subcontractors	Non
Subs:Insulating	Install insulation	Service		Job Expenses:Subcon...	Construction:Subcontractors	Non
Subs:Metal W...	Metal Work	Service		Job Expenses:Subcon...	Construction:Subcontractors	Non
Subs:Painting	Painting	Service		Job Expenses:Subcon...	Construction:Subcontractors	Non
Subs:Plumbing	Plumbing	Service			Construction:Subcontractors	Non
Subs:Roofing	Roofing	Service		Job Expenses:Subcon...	Construction:Subcontractors	Non
Subs:Tile &C...	Install tile or counter	Service		Job Expenses:Subcon...	Construction:Subcontractors	Non
Cabinets	Cabinets	Inventory...	Inventory Asset	Cost of Goods Sold	Construction:Materials	Tax
Cabinets:Cab...	Cabinet Pulls	Inventory...	Inventory Asset	Cost of Goods Sold	Construction:Materials	Tax
Cabinets:Ligh...	Light pine kitchen c...	Inventory...	Inventory Asset	Cost of Goods Sold	Construction:Materials	Tax
Door Frame	standard interior do...	Inventory...	Inventory Asset	Cost of Goods Sold	Construction:Materials	Tax
Hardware		Inventory...	Inventory Asset	Cost of Goods Sold	Construction:Materials	Tax

FIGURE 3.8

Modify the Item Listing report to review your item setup.

Profit & Loss Summary Report

If you suspect errors with your financials, drilling down (double-clicking with your mouse pointer) on the Total Income, Cost of Goods Sold, or Expense detail from a Profit & Loss Standard Report might provide clues to the mistakes. To generate this report, follow these steps:

1. Click **Reports, Company & Financial,** and select the **Profit & Loss Standard** report.

2. On the Profit & Loss Standard report, double-click the **Total Income** column total, as shown in Figure 3.9. A Transaction Detail by Account report appears, showing each line of detail that makes up the amount you viewed on the original Profit & Loss Standard report.

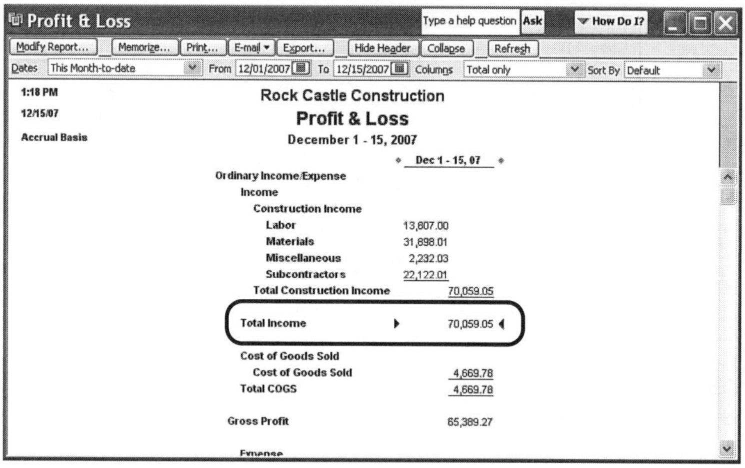

FIGURE 3.9

Review your Profit & Loss Standard Total Income.

3. On the Transaction Detail by Account report, click **Modify Report**. In the dialog box that appears, click the **Filters** tab. In the Choose Filter pane, scroll down to select **Transaction Type**.

4. In the Transaction Type drop-down menu, select **Multiple Transaction Types,** as shown in Figure 3.10. The Select Transaction Type dialog appears. Click to place a check mark next to each transaction type that normally would *not* be reported to an income account, such as a check, bill, credit card, and so on, and then click **OK**.

The resulting report now shows all purchase type transactions (or whatever transaction types you selected) that were recorded to income accounts. In the example shown in Figure 3.11, a vendor check transaction type appears in the totals for income. This is because on the vendor check an item was used that had only an income account assigned. After you determine that you have these types of errors in posting, you should review your item list for any one-sided items. This topic is discussed in the next section.

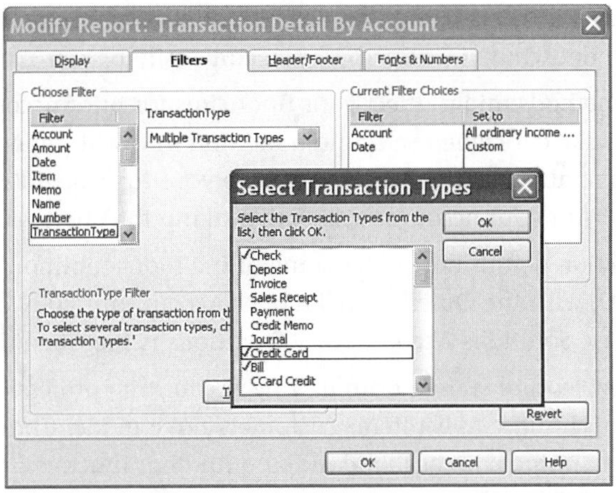

FIGURE 3.10
Modify the detail of Total Income from the Profit & Loss statement to help review whether items were set up correctly.

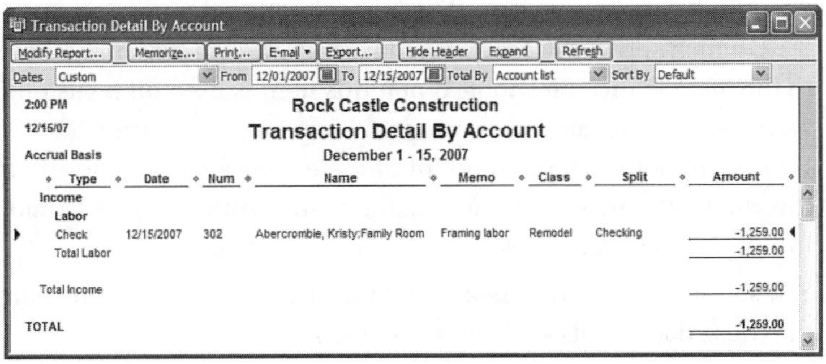

FIGURE 3.11
The Transaction Detail By Account report shows an expense type transaction reporting to a income account.

Fixing Item Errors in QuickBooks

This chapter has shown some effective ways to determine whether your items were incorrectly set up. In this section, you learn the methods of fixing these item setup errors in QuickBooks.

As with any data correction in QuickBooks, you should make a backup of the data before attempting these methods. The preferred backup method is a QuickBooks backup, or a file with the extension of .QBB. You can create a data backup by choosing File, Save Copy or Backup. If the result after fixing items is not what you expected, you can easily restore the backup file.

These methods might affect your financials for prior accounting periods. You should take care when selecting a method that will impact financial periods that have already been used to prepare your tax documents. Discuss these choices with your accountant before making the changes.

This section details how to fix some of the more common item mistakes. New for 2009, with the QuickBooks Premier Accountant 2009 and QuickBooks Enterprise Solutions Accountant 9.0 editions is the Client Data Review feature.

This new feature is used primarily by accounting professionals who want to view the changes to list items customers have made. Changes to accounts assigned, name changes, and making an item inactive are a few of the changes tracked. For more information on this, see Chapter 17, "New for 2009! Detecting and Correcting with the Client Data Review Feature."

Correcting One-Sided Items

A one-sided item is an item that has only one account assigned. See Figure 3.12, which shows the Framing item setup. Notice the only account assigned to this item is Income:Labor. When this item is used on a customer invoice, it increases the Income:Labor amount. However, if the same item is used on a vendor check or bill, the amount of the expense records directly to the Income:Labor income account as a negative number. This would cause both income and cost of goods sold to be understated.

You should never have one-sided items if you plan to use the item on both purchase documents and sales documents.

This section details how to fix some of the more common item mistakes. New for 2009, with the QuickBooks Premier Accountant 2009 and QuickBooks Enterprise Solutions Accountant 9.0 editions is the Client Data Review feature.

This new feature is used primarily by accounting professionals who want to view the changes to list items customers have made. Changes to accounts assigned, name changes, and making an item inactive are a few of the changes tracked.

For more detail information on this see Chapter 17.

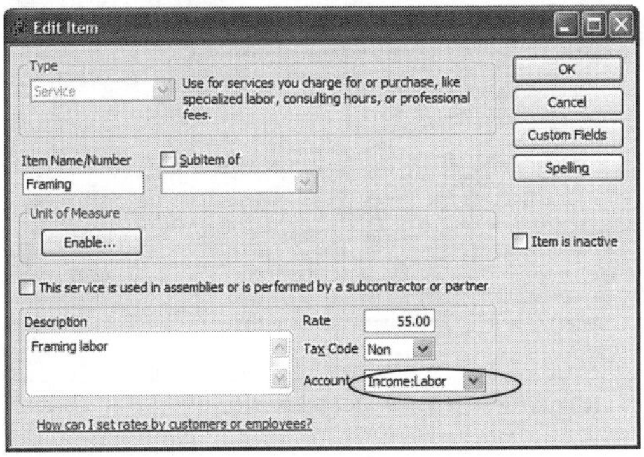

FIGURE 3.12

An example of a one-sided item in QuickBooks.

You might have several items on your list that can qualify to be one-sided because they are used only on sales forms and never on purchase forms, or always on purchase forms and never on sales forms. What can become problematic is that at some time, a user will mistakenly use the item on the other form.

I recommend you make all items two-sided (see Figure 3.13). You do so by selecting the check box labeled This service is used in assemblies or... (the rest of the label depends on what item type is selected) in the New or Edit Item dialog box. The results are new Purchase Information and Sales Information panes. Now, the "Account" has become an "Income Account" and you have a new Expense Account field to assign your proper expense account. This way, if you use the item on both a vendor bill or check and a customer sales form, your financials show the transaction in the proper account.

Rescue Me!

Before making these suggested changes, have you made a backup of your data? Some of the recommended changes are not reversible.

You might even consider printing reports before and after to compare and to verify that you achieved the desired end result with your change.

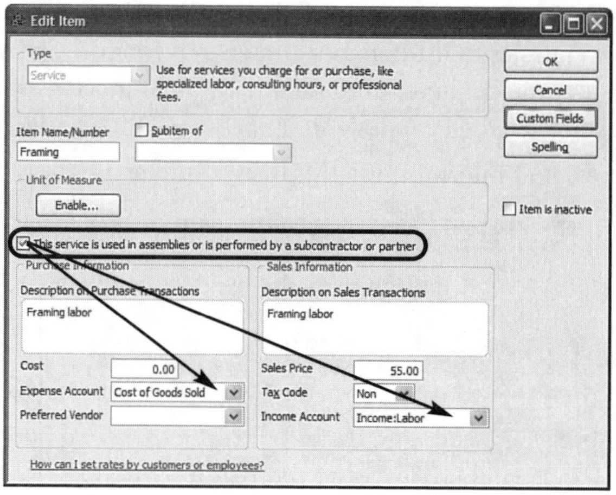

FIGURE 3.13

The one-sided item is now two-sided for accounting.

If you are editing an existing item to make it two-sided, QuickBooks now provides an Account Change warning, as shown in Figure 3.14. The decision made at this time is *critical* to your financials. Saying Yes to updating existing transactions causes all previous transactions to now report to the new account assigned. If you are attempting to fix historical transactions, this can be a timesaving feature because you do not have to change each individual transaction manually.

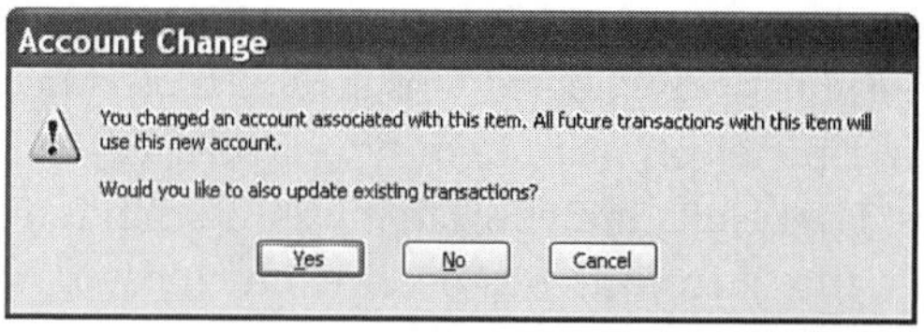

FIGURE 3.14

The QuickBooks warning that appears when you change the accounts in the Edit Item dialog.

Click No if you do not want to update prior period transactions. This option might be recommended if you have already prepared your tax data with QuickBooks financial information. The change then takes effect only for future transactions.

Carefully selecting the appropriate choice here determines whether the correction provides the result you were looking for. Beginning with QuickBooks version 2007, users are given a second chance to say No to affect prior period financials (see Figure 3.15). Reference is given in this warning to setting a closing date password. Although setting a closing date password is recommended, doing so does *not* prevent changes to prior period financials when you are modifying the accounts assigned to an item that has previously been used.

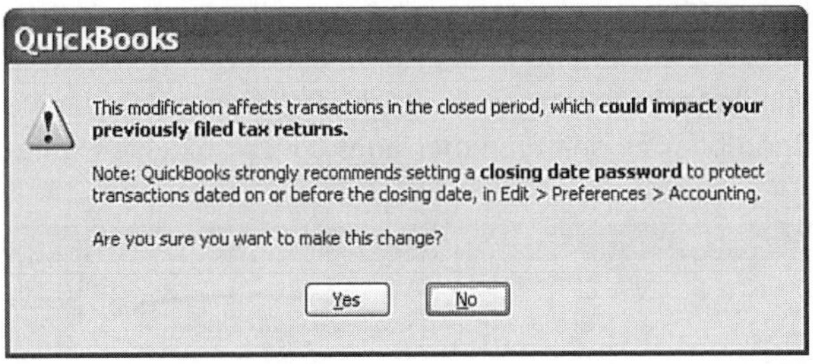

FIGURE 3.15

QuickBooks provides another warning when you change accounts on existing items.

Additional Warnings for One-Sided Items

You aren't completely on your own when it comes to locating one-sided item errors in item assignments. QuickBooks helps you recognize the potential error by displaying a warning message when you are using an item on a purchase form that is assigned in the New or Edit Item dialog to a revenue account only. Figure 3.16 shows the warning message you see when a check is being written to a vendor but the item used is assigned only to an income account. Be aware that this warning appears only if you have not checked the Do not display this message in the future check box.

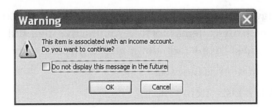

FIGURE 3.16

The warning message displayed when you use an item on a purchase form that is mapped to an Income Account only.

If you disregard the message, QuickBooks posts the expense to the revenue account selected in the Edit Item dialog. The effect of this is to understate revenue (an expense is a negative amount in the revenue account) and to understate your costs (because no cost was recorded to an expense account). Both of these messages distort your financial details, so be sure you don't disregard this important message.

Digging Deeper

Users often disregard these one-time messages and select the Do not display this warning in the future check box (refer to Figure 3.16). To enable these messages, click Edit, Preferences, General and select the Bring back all one time messages check box (see Figure 3.17).

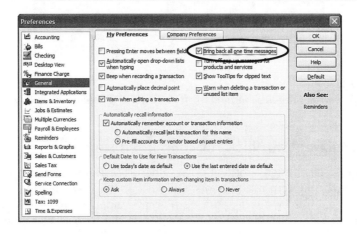

FIGURE 3.17

To be notified of transaction errors previously disregarded, select the Bring back all one time messages check box.

Making an Item Inactive

If you have found errors in your item list, a safe method of fixing them is to make the incorrect items inactive. An inactive item still appears in reports but is not included in any drop-down menus on sales or purchase forms.

To mark an item as inactive:

1. Click **Lists, Item List**.

2. Select the item you want to make inactive by clicking it once.

3. Click on the **Items** button and select **Edit Item**.

4. Place a check mark in the **Item is inactive** box.

Making an item inactive does not have any impact on the company's financials. If you want to correct your financials, you need to choose one of two options:

- Edit the account assignment on each item. This gives you the option to retroactively fix all previous transactions that used this item. (Use this cautiously because it changes prior period financials.) The effect of changing an account assignment on an item is the same as the one discussed in the section of this chapter titled "Correcting One-Sided Items."

■ Create a General Journal Entry transaction to reassign the numbers from one account to another. This method is typically done by your accountant.

Make a backup of your data before making these recommended changes and always discuss the method you choose with your accountant.

Need to Make Several Items Inactive?

Open the Item List by choosing Lists, Item List. Click to put a check mark in the Include Inactive box (in the lower center of the dialog). Click once to the left of any list item to make the item inactive, as shown in Figure 3.18.

If the check box is grayed out, you have not yet made any item inactive. After making the first item inactive, you can put a check mark in the box.

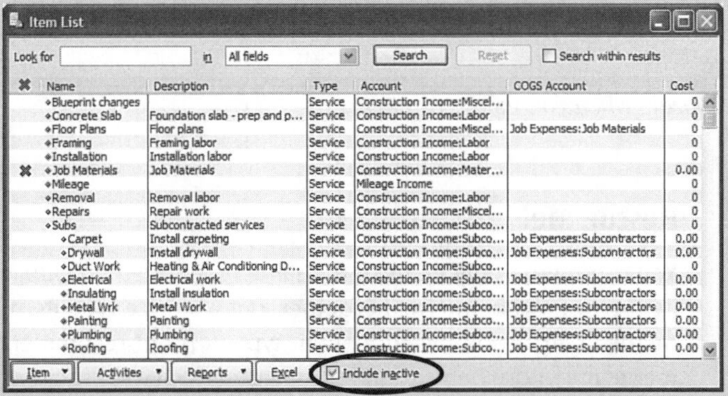

FIGURE 3.18

Marking Item List elements inactive causes the item not to show on drop-down lists.

Marking most items inactive is okay. The exception is inventory items. Only inventory items with a zero quantity on hand should be made inactive. See Chapter 10 for more details on handling inventory errors.

Merging Items

If you have duplicated items, one easy method for fixing the problem is to merge items of the same type. When merging two items, you first need to decide which item is going to be merged into the other item. The item merged will no longer exist on your item list.

To merge two items:

1. Click **Lists, Item List**.

2. Review the list for duplicate items; note the name of the item you want to remain.

3. Double-click the item you want to merge into another item. The Edit Item dialog appears.

4. Type in the **Item Name/Number** field the name exactly as you noted it in step 2. You can also use the Windows copy and paste command to avoid typing of lengthy names or long numbers.

5. Click **OK** to save your change. QuickBooks provides the warning message in Figure 3.19 that you are merging items.

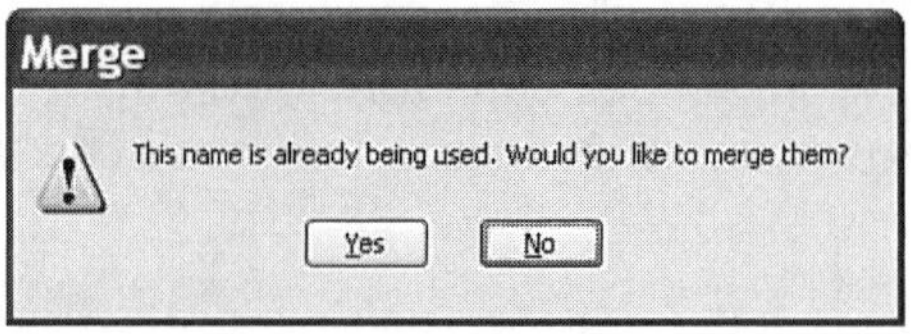

Merge

This name is already being used. Would you like to merge them?

Yes   No

FIGURE 3.19

A warning appears when you merge two items.

Rescue Me!

You can merge only items of the same type together. Duplicate service item types can be merged together, but a service type item cannot be merged with a non-inventory item type. It is not recommended to merge inventory items together; see Chapter 10 for more detail.

Carefully consider the consequences of merging before you do it (and be sure you have a backup of your QuickBooks file). All the historical transactions merge into the remaining list item.

Creating Items as Subitems

Creating an item as a subitem of another item is one way to easily filter reports for a group of similar items. Your accounting data is not affected by having or not having items as subitems.

To make an item a subitem of another item:

1. Click **Lists**, **Item List**.

2. Double-click the item you want to assign as a subitem. The Edit Item dialog opens.

3. Place a check mark in the **Subitem of** box, as shown in Figure 3.20.

4. From the drop-down menu, select the item you want to relate this subitem to.

You can create a subitem only within the same item type; for example, service items cannot be subitems of inventory items.

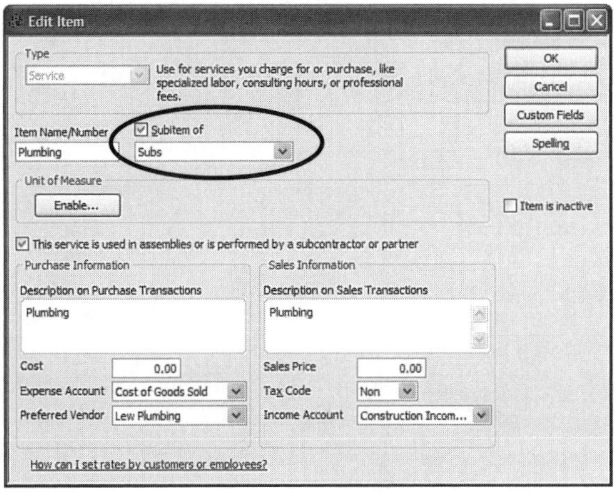

FIGURE 3.20

Mark an item as a subitem of another list item.

You can also rearrange the list by assigning a subitem to another item by using your mouse pointer on the Item List to move the item up or down and to the right or left. This functionality is the same as the example discussed in the section titled "Removing Duplicated Accounts by Marking an Account Inactive" in Chapter 2.

Digging Deeper

Did you know that if you want your customer to see the discount you are providing them on the invoice, you should not use Price Levels? Instead, create your invoice as usual and then include your discount item type on the invoice. This way your customer will see the benefit of the discount.

Chapter 4

Easily Review Your QuickBooks Data

- Client Data Review—*New for 2009!*
- Choosing a Reporting Basis
- Reviewing the Balance Sheet
- Additional Data Reviews

Client Data Review—*New for 2009!*

One of the most significant releases with QuickBooks 2009 is the Client Data Review (CDR) feature. Used primarily by accounting professionals, it is available in the QuickBooks Premier Accountant 2009 as well as the Accountant edition of QuickBooks Enterprise Solutions 9.0.

With the new Client Data Review feature comes more robust tracking of the changes your client makes to the data between your reviews. Additionally, if your client created an External Accountant user login for you, you will have access to these key benefits and features in non-accountant editions (see Chapter 17, "New for 2009! Detecting and correcting with the Client Data Review Feature" for more details):

- New troubleshooting tools and reports available only within the Client Data Review feature. These are identified in this chapter with the "tool" icon, such as the Troubleshooting Account Balances task that is a CDR-dependent feature.

- A trial balance that "remembers" the previously reviewed balances and compares to the same prior dated balances that QuickBooks calculates today.

- Stored, reviewed balances that your client cannot modify!

- Identifies what chart of accounts balances differ and the amount of the difference when compared to your prior period reviewed financials.

- View or modify the QuickBooks suggested adjusting journal entry created so that your reviewed balances agree with the current QuickBooks data for that prior period.

- Tracking changes to lists, additions, and name changes even tracking accounts or list items that were merged.

- Tracking changes to list items, accounts assigned or for payroll items tracking when a change to a rate is made.

- Working with the Open Windows dialog? Client Data Review will display in the Open Windows dialog enabling you to move efficiently between activities in QuickBooks.

- Conveniently work on Client Data Review in QuickBooks and modify or add transactions as normal with an immediate refresh of the data in your review.

- Functional in the Accountant's Copy file sharing format. (Some limitations specific to Accountant's Copy apply.) See Chapter 15, "Sharing Data with Your Accountant or Your Client" for more details.

There is not a better time to encourage your clients to upgrade to the newest version of QuickBooks. Only QuickBooks 2009 client files will offer this new innovative Client Data Review feature!

Choosing a Reporting Basis

Are you a business owner unsure of what critical information you should be reviewing in your data file and how often you should perform the review, or are you an accounting professional new to the QuickBooks software? This chapter provides you with the needed review and quick, easy-to-create reports with practical steps to manage your or your client's data. Each section references the chapter where you can find more detailed information.

If you are a business owner, you can use the quick methods in this chapter to better manage the results of your day-to-day transaction accuracy so that when you review reports, such as the Balance Sheet or Profit & Loss for your business, you can be confident the information is correct.

The frequency with which a business owner chooses to review his data often differs from the frequency with which an accountant reviews the same data. For a business owner, this review should be performed after the bank account is reconciled. Because so many transactions affect cash, reconciling the bank account often helps uncover data entry errors.

For the accounting professional, when your client learns how to review his data before your appointment, you can spend more time offering valuable business consulting with less time spent on transaction review.

Additionally, this book assumes that the business owner is not a graduated accountant. QuickBooks handles the "accounting" behind the scenes, making it easy to perform your day-to-day transactions. However, don't misunderstand me—you do need an accountant to review your data regularly and prepare financials for lending institutions, in addition to properly preparing your tax return.

This chapter provides a quick, step-by-step guide to navigating the many QuickBooks reports and alerts you to the ones that give you the valuable information you need.

When you review your QuickBooks reports, you have options for the accounting basis you want to report on. To set up the default reporting basis, click Edit, Preferences, select Reports & Graphs, and then click the Company preference tab (you must be logged in as the Admin or new External Accountant user). In the Preferences dialog that opens, select a Summary Report Basis of either Cash or Accrual:

- Cash Basis—Your Profit & Loss report shows expenses as of the date of the bill payment and income as of the date of your customer payment. No record of expense is recorded on the vendor bill date, and no income is recorded on the customer invoice date.

- Accrual Basis—Your Profit & Loss report shows expenses as of the date of the vendor bill and income as of the date of your customer invoice, whether or not these bills or invoices have been paid.

QuickBooks users can prepare reports in both types of basis. The need for selecting a specific basis is more a tax filing determination than a business management reporting decision. Certain Internal Revenue Service rulings govern what type of accounting is appropriate for certain businesses; this discussion is outside the scope of this book.

 Digging Deeper

My recommendation is that business owners view their business Profit & Loss report in accrual basis. This method more accurately matches their expenses with the related revenue in the same accounting period. The business's accountant can then review the data in either cash or accrual basis reports. For more information on sharing data with an accountant, see Chapter 15, "Sharing Data with Your Accountant or Your Client."

The reports discussed in the remaining sections of this chapter use accrual basis reporting. The reports I recommend reviewing are just a suggestion; your business (or client) might need to use all or just some of the review recommendations listed here. Where appropriate, I have also referenced the related chapter in this book where you can get more detailed information about the particular review topic.

Reviewing the Balance Sheet

Did you know that the report a business owner is least likely to look at is also one of the most important? To the business owner, the Balance Sheet report shows the balance of assets (what the business owns), liabilities (what the business owes others), and equity (what was put into the business or taken out of the business). Because these numbers are important, a business owner should first review this report.

Remember, this chapter presents the reports in accrual basis unless otherwise mentioned.

Begin by creating a Balance Sheet report of your data; this is the primary report we use for review:

1. Click **Reports, Company & Financial** and choose the **Balance Sheet Standard** report. The report dialog opens.

2. Leave the report with today's date. You are going to first review your report with today's date before using any other date. In the following instructions, if a different date is needed, it will be noted in the step-by-step details. Verify that the top left of the report shows Accrual Basis. If not, click the **Modify Report** button on the report, and select **Accrual Basis** from the **Report Basis** options.

3. Click **OK** to accept the change in basis.

Figure 4.1 shows a sample data Balance Sheet.

Account Types

Reviewing the account types assigned requires some basic knowledge of accounting. If as a business owner you are unsure, this review provides the perfect opportunity for your accountant to take a quick look at how your accounts are set up.

Review the names given to accounts. Do you see account names in the wrong place on the Balance Sheet? For example, does an Auto Loan account show up in the Current Asset portion of the Balance Sheet?

Follow these steps if you need to edit an account type:

1. Click **Lists, Chart of Accounts** to open the Chart of Accounts dialog.

2. Select the account in question with one click. Select the **Account** drop-down menu and select the **Edit** menu option. On the Edit Account dialog (see Figure 4.2), you can select the drop-down menu for **Account Type** to easily change the currently assigned account type (see Chapter 2, "Reviewing the QuickBooks Chart of Accounts").

Prior Year Balances

You should provide a copy of your Balance Sheet dated as of the last day of your tax year (or fiscal year) to your accountant and request that she verify that the balances agree with her accounting records used to prepare your tax return. This is one of the most important steps to take in your review because Balance Sheet numbers are cumulative over the years you are in business. You might need to provide the Balance Sheet report in both a cash and accrual basis. (See Chapter 5, "Power Reports for Troubleshooting Beginning Balance Differences," and Chapter 15 for a discussion about setting a closing date to protect prior year numbers.)

5:51 PM

12/15/07

Accrual Basis

Rock Castle Construction

Balance Sheet

As of December 15, 2007

	Dec 15, 07
ASSETS	
Current Assets	
Checking/Savings	
Checking	71,920.11
Savings	14,368.42
Total Checking/Savings	86,288.53
Accounts Receivable	
Accounts Receivable	81,798.70
Total Accounts Receivable	81,798.70
Other Current Assets	
Undeposited Funds	57,126.52
Inventory Asset	23,219.04
Employee Loans	62.00
Total Other Current Assets	80,407.56
Total Current Assets	248,494.79
Fixed Assets	
Buildings	325,000.00
Computers	28,501.00
Accumulated Depreciation	-121,887.78
Total Fixed Assets	231,613.22
TOTAL ASSETS	**480,108.01**
LIABILITIES & EQUITY	
Liabilities	
Current Liabilities	
Accounts Payable	
Accounts Payable	54,405.04
Total Accounts Payable	54,405.04
Credit Cards	
CalOil Card	5,127.62
Total Credit Cards	5,127.62
Other Current Liabilities	
Payroll Liabilities	9,258.55
Sales Tax Payable	5,502.94
Total Other Current Liabilities	14,761.49
Total Current Liabilities	74,294.15
Long Term Liabilities	
Bank of Anycity Loan	19,932.65
Total Long Term Liabilities	19,932.65
Total Liabilities	94,226.80
Equity	
Owner's Equity	
Owner's Contribution	25,000.00
Owner's Draw	-6,000.00
Total Owner's Equity	19,000.00
Retained Earnings	339,939.49
Net Income	26,941.72
Total Equity	385,881.21
TOTAL LIABILITIES & EQUITY	**480,108.01**

FIGURE 4.1

Review your Balance Sheet first, as in this example.

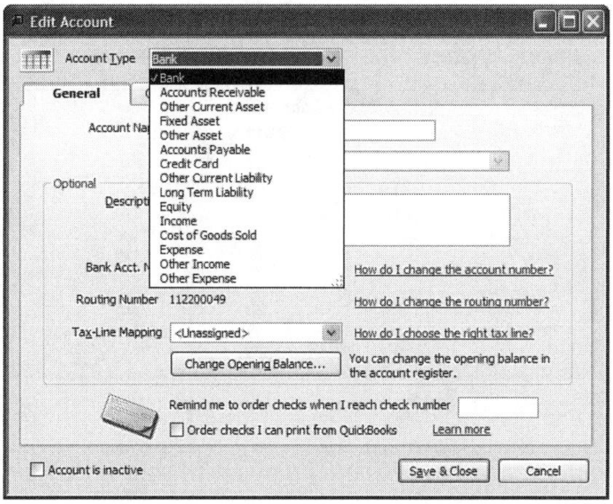

FIGURE 4.2

The Edit or New Account dialog is where you assign the account type for proper placement of financial reports.

Bank Account Balance(s)

Compare your reconciled bank account balances on the Balance Sheet report to the statement your bank sends you. Modify the date of the Balance Sheet to be the same as the last date of your bank statement balance. Your QuickBooks cash "book" balance should be equal to the bank's balance plus or minus any uncleared deposits or checks/withdrawals dated on or before the statement ending date (see Chapter 6, "Bank Account Balance or Reconciliation Errors").

Accounts Receivable

The Accounts Receivable balance on your Balance Sheet report should agree with the A/R Aging Summary report total, as shown in Figure 4.3. Accounts Receivable reports are available only in accrual basis (see Chapter 7, "Reviewing and Correcting Accounts Receivable Errors").

To create the A/R Aging Summary report, click Reports, Customers & Receivables and choose the A/R Aging Summary or A/R Aging Detail report. Click Collapse on the top of the report to minimize (remove from view) the line detail, making the report easier to view at a glance. The total should match the Accounts Receivable balance on the Balance Sheet report, as was shown in Figure 4.1.

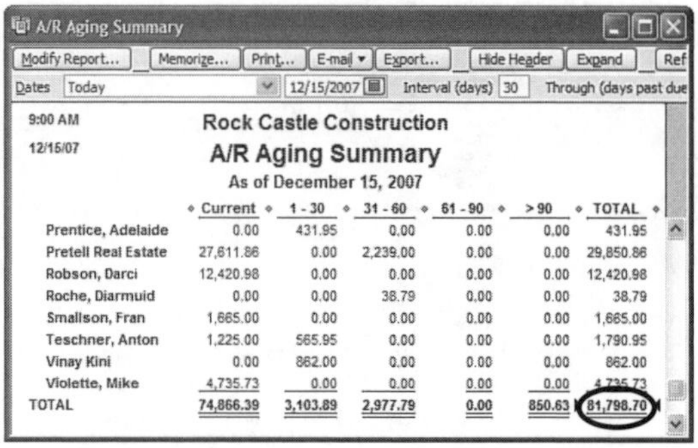

FIGURE 4.3
The A/R Aging Summary report total should agree with your Balance Sheet Accounts Receivable balance.

Undeposited Funds

The Undeposited Funds amount should agree with funds not yet deposited into your bank account, as shown in Figure 4.4 (use today's date on your Balance Sheet report). (See Chapter 8, "Reviewing and Correcting Errors with the Undeposited Funds Account.")

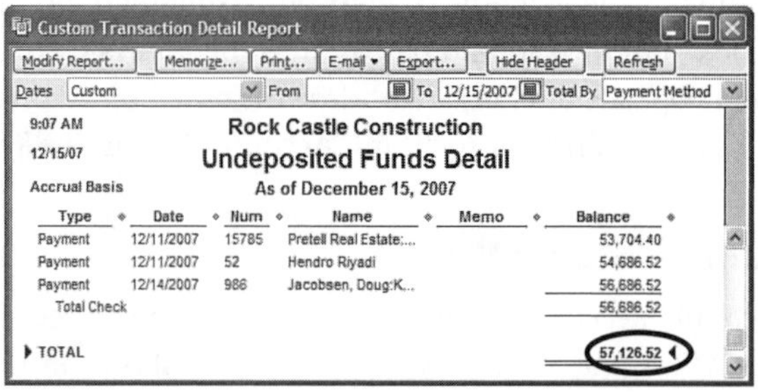

FIGURE 4.4
A custom report created to show the detail of undeposited funds.

Create the following custom report to review the Undeposited Funds detail sorted by payment method:

1. Click **Reports**, **Custom Transaction Detail**. The Modify Report dialog opens.

2. In the Report Date Range pane, select **All** (type an "a" without the quote marks and the date range defaults to All).

3. In the Columns pane, select those data fields that you want to view on the report and select **Payment Method** in the Total By drop-down menu.

4. Click the **Filters** tab; Account is already highlighted in the Choose Filter pane. Choose **Undeposited Funds** from the Account drop-down menu to the right.

5. Also in the Choose Filter pane, scroll down to select **Cleared**; on the right, choose Cleared **No**.

6. Optionally, click the **Header/Footer** tab and change the report title to **Undeposited Funds**. Click **OK** to view the report.

The amount of funds shown on this report should agree with the amount of funds you have not yet taken to the bank.

Inventory

The Inventory balance on the Balance Sheet report (refer to Figure 4.1) should agree with the Inventory Valuation Summary report total, as shown in Figure 4.5. The ending dates of both reports need to be the same.

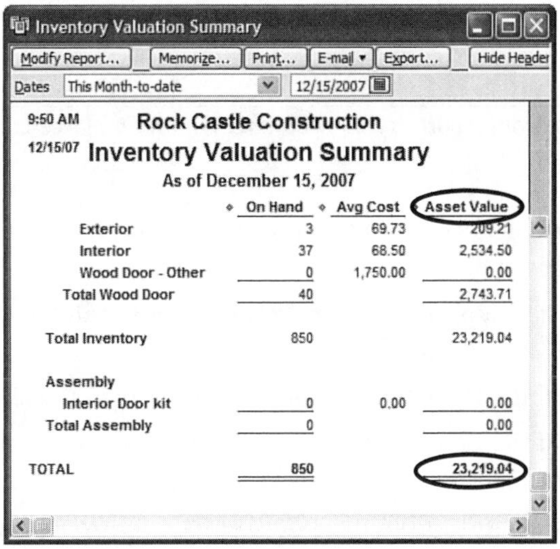

FIGURE 4.5

The total of the Asset Value column should agree with the Inventory balance on the Balance Sheet report.

To create the Inventory Valuation Summary report, click Reports, Inventory and choose the Inventory Valuation Summary report. The total in the Asset Value column should match the Inventory Asset balance of the Balance Sheet report (see Chapter 10, "Reviewing and Correcting Inventory Errors").

Other Current Assets

The Other Current Asset accounts can differ widely by company. If you have employee loans, make sure your records agree with employees' records. For any other accounts in the Other Current Assets category, look to documentation outside QuickBooks to verify the reported balances.

Need an easy report to sort the detail in these Other Current Asset accounts by a list name? In this example, I created a detail report of the Employee Loans account sorted and subtotaled by employee, as shown in Figure 4.6. You can create this same report for any of your accounts, sorting in a way that improves the detail for your review (see Chapter 9, "Handling Other Current Asset Accounts Correctly").

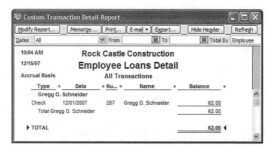

FIGURE 4.6

You can create a custom report to review balances in an Employee Loans account or any other asset account.

To create a detail report of your Other Current Asset accounts (in addition to other types of accounts):

1. Click **Reports**, **Custom Transaction Detail Report**. The Modify Report dialog appears.

2. On the Date Range pane drop-down menu, select **All**.

3. On the Columns pane, select what data you would like to see in the report.

4. Also on the Columns pane, select **Employee** from the Total By drop-down menu.

5. Click the **Filters** tab.

6. The Choose Filter pane already has selected the **Account** filter. On the right, from the Account drop-down menu, select the **Employee Loans** account (or select the specific account for which you want to see detail).

7. Optionally, click the **Header/Footer** tab and provide a unique report title. Click **OK** to create the modified report.

Verify the balances reported here with either the employees or outside source documents.

Fixed Assets

Fixed assets are those purchases that have a long-term life and for tax purposes cannot be expensed all at once but instead must be depreciated over the expected life of the asset.

Accountants can advise businesses on how to classify assets. If the numbers have changed from year to year, you might want to review what transactions were posted to make sure they are fixed asset purchases and not expenses that should appear on the Profit & Loss report.

If you have properly recorded a fixed asset purchase to this account category, provide your accountant with the purchase receipt and any supporting purchase documents for their depreciation schedule records.

If you see a change in the totals from one year to the next, you can review the individual transactions in the account register by clicking Banking, Use Register and selecting the account you want to review. Figure 4.7 shows the register for Fixed Assets—Computers. If a transaction was incorrectly posted here, you can edit the transaction by double-clicking the line detail and correcting the assigned account category.

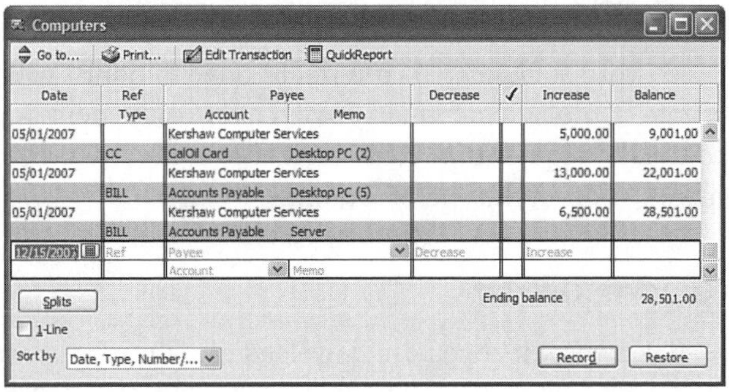

FIGURE 4.7

Use registers for certain accounts to see the transactions that affect the balances.

Accounts Payable

The Accounts Payable balance on the Balance Sheet report should agree with the A/P Aging Summary report total, as shown in Figure 4.8. Accounts Payable reports are available only in accrual basis (see Chapter 11, "Reviewing and Correcting Accounts Payable Errors").

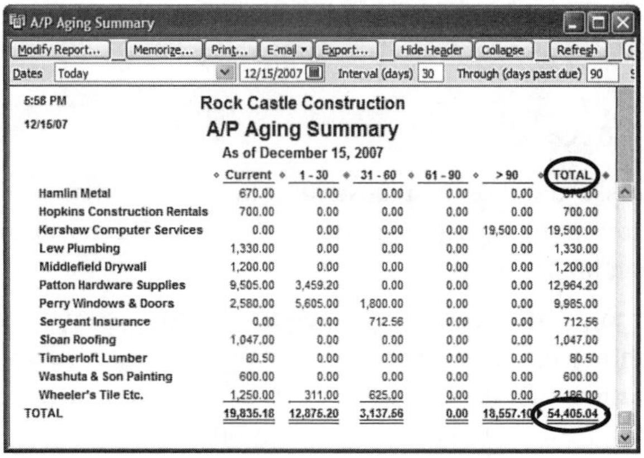

FIGURE 4.8

The A/P Aging Summary report total should agree with your Balance Sheet Accounts Payable balance.

To create the A/P Aging Summary or Detail report, click Reports, Vendors & Payables and select the A/P Aging Summary or Detail report. QuickBooks reports only Accounts Payable on an accrual basis (see Chapter 11).

Credit Cards

Your Credit Card account balance should reconcile with those balances from your credit card statement(s). You might have to adjust your Balance Sheet report date to match your credit card vendor's statement date. Now might be a good time to request that your credit card company provide you with a statement cut-off at the end of a month.

Digging Deeper

Did you know that you can download credit card transactions directly into your QuickBooks data? To find out more, click Banking, Online Banking, Participating Financial Institutions to see whether your credit card vendor participates.

Payroll Liabilities

The Payroll Liabilities balance on the Balance Sheet report should agree with your Payroll Liability Balances report total. Be careful with the dates here. If you have unpaid back payroll taxes, you might want to select a date range of All for this report. In Figure 4.9, I used This Calendar Year-to-Date as the date range (see Chapter 14, "Reviewing and Correcting Payroll Errors").

To create the Payroll Liability Balances report, click Reports, Employees & Payroll and select the Payroll Liability Balances report. Totals on this report should match your Balance Sheet report for the payroll liabilities account.

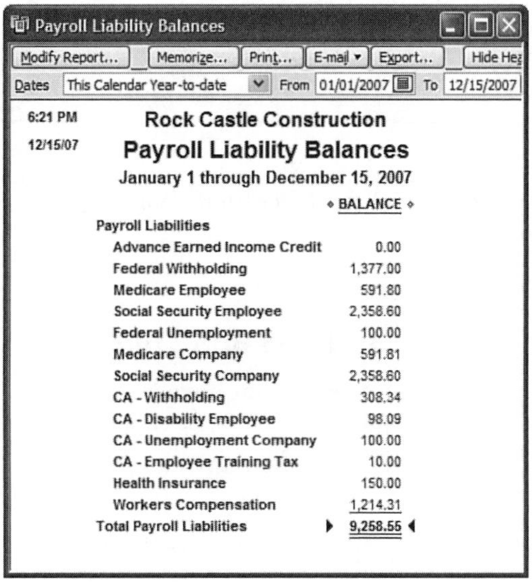

	BALANCE
Payroll Liabilities	
Advance Earned Income Credit	0.00
Federal Withholding	1,377.00
Medicare Employee	591.80
Social Security Employee	2,358.60
Federal Unemployment	100.00
Medicare Company	591.81
Social Security Company	2,358.60
CA - Withholding	308.34
CA - Disability Employee	98.09
CA - Unemployment Company	100.00
CA - Employee Training Tax	10.00
Health Insurance	150.00
Workers Compensation	1,214.31
Total Payroll Liabilities	9,258.55

FIGURE 4.9

The Payroll Liability Balances report total should agree with the same total on the Balance Sheet report.

Sales Tax Payable

The Sales Tax Payable balance on the Balance Sheet report should agree with the Sales Tax Liability report balance. You might need to change the Sales Tax Payable report date to match that of your Balance Sheet. Caution: If you have set up your Sales Tax Preference as Cash Basis, you cannot compare this balance to an Accural Basis Balance Sheet report (see Chapter 12, "Reviewing and Correcting Sales Tax Errors").

To create the Sales Tax Liability report, click Reports, Vendors & Payables and select Sales Tax Liability report.

Make sure the To date matches that of the Balance Sheet report date. The total, shown in Figure 4.10, should match the Sales Tax Payable total on your Balance Sheet report.

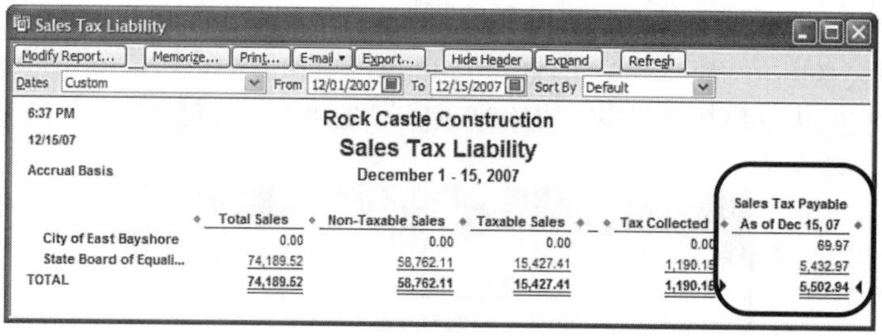

FIGURE 4.10
The Sales Tax Liability report total should match the Sales Tax Payable balance on your Balance Sheet report.

Other Current Liabilities and Long-Term Liabilities

Any other accounts that you might have in the Other Current Liabilities and Long-Term Liabilities account types should be compared with outside documents from your lending institutions.

Equity

Equity accounts differ for each company. These account balances should be reviewed by your accountant and might have tax adjustments made to them at year-end or tax time. Note: If you have an account called Open Bal Equity with a balance, this account should have a zero balance after the data file setup is completed (see Chapter 13, "Reviewing and Correcting the Opening Balance Equity Account").

The reports discussed in this chapter do not make up an exhaustive, end-all list for reviewing your Balance Sheet, but they are a great start to reviewing your own data or your client's data.

Additional Data Reviews

You can review some additional reports that add value to those discussed already. I discuss them in the remainder of this chapter, in no particular order.

Payroll Summary Total and Payroll Expense Total

It is important to compare your Payroll Summary report (if you are using QuickBooks to produce your employee's paychecks) to the payroll expenses listed on your Profit & Loss Standard report. If you are using some outside payroll service, you also want to compare its total payroll expenses to your Profit & Loss reported payroll expenses (see Chapter 14).

Follow these steps to create the Payroll Summary and Profit & Loss Standard reports:

1. Click **Reports, Employees & Payroll** and select the **Payroll Summary** report.

2. On the report dialog that opens, select the **Dates** drop-down menu and choose **This Calendar Year-to-Date** (because payroll is reported by the calendar year).

3. Click **Reports, Company & Financial** and select the **Profit & Loss Standard** report.

4. On the report dialog that opens, select the **Dates** drop-down menu and choose **This Fiscal Year-to-Date** if your business is a calendar year company, or select **Custom** and create the report for the same dates as the Payroll Summary report (because payroll is reported by the calendar year).

Compare your Payroll Expense account(s) totals on your Profit & Loss report to your Payroll Summary report totals. Identify those items, such as gross wages, and company paid payroll taxes on the Payroll Summary report that are costs to your business; this total should be what you have reported on your Profit & Loss report for payroll expenses.

Sales by Item Summary Compared to Total Income

Chapter 3, "Reviewing and Correcting Item List Errors," provides details on how the QuickBooks customer invoice requires the use of items. Therefore, another important review to perform is to generate a report showing Total Sales by Item and compare this total to the income that is recorded on your Profit & Loss report for the same report date range. Remember, you are reviewing these reports in accrual basis.

Follow these steps to create the Sales by Item Summary and Profit & Loss reports:

1. Click **Reports, Sales** and choose the **Sales by Item Summary** report.

2. On the Report dialog that opens, select the **Dates** drop-down menu and choose **This Fiscal Year-to-Date**. Compare the totals on this Sales by Item Summary report to the Profit & Loss report created in the next couple of steps.

3. Click **Reports, Company & Financial** and choose the **Profit & Loss Standard** report.

4. On the report dialog that opens, select the **Dates** drop-down menu and choose **This Fiscal Year-to-Date**.

The report totals from the Sales by Item Summary and Profit & Loss report total income should agree with each other. Note: If you report customer discounts as a negative income line item, you might need to add this total back in (see Chapter 3).

Net Income or (Loss) Agrees with Balance Sheet

QuickBooks automatically records Net Income or (Loss) to the Balance Sheet, but I still mention it because it is an important review to do, particularly at tax time.

1. Click **Reports**, **Company & Financial** and select the **Profit & Loss Standard** report.

2. On the Report dialog that opens, select the Date range of **This Fiscal Year-to-Date**.

Compare the Net Income (Loss) figure from the Profit & Loss report to the same figure in the equity section of the Balance Sheet report, making sure the reports are being prepared with the same accrual or cash basis. I've always seen these numbers match; however, if the numbers do not match, you want to verify data by clicking on File, Utilities and selecting Verify Data. If data integrity issues are reported, you can contact QuickBooks Technical Support for assistance at www.quickbooks.com/support.

Reconcile Discrepancies Account

More recent versions of QuickBooks now record any bank reconciliation discrepancies to an expense account automatically created by QuickBooks. (Earlier versions of QuickBooks used the Open Bal Equity account for these adjustments.) If an account named "Reconcile Discrepancies" appears at all on your Profit & Loss report, this account should have a zero balance. If it does not, you need to review why the bank account was reconciled with an adjustment (see Chapter 6). To remove a balance in this account, create a journal entry reassigning the expense to another account.

Cash Basis Balance Sheet Has Accounts Receivable or Payable

The problem of a cash basis Balance Sheet report having an accounts receivable or payable balance is perhaps more for the accounting professional than the business owner to review. The nature of accounts receivable and payable means that these accounts should have no balance when you're creating a Balance Sheet in a cash basis. There are, however, some reasons why this can happen:

- A/R or A/P transactions posting to other Balance Sheet accounts
- Inventory items on an invoice or credit memo
- Transfers between Balance Sheet accounts
- Unapplied A/R customer receipts or vendor A/P payments
- Payments applied to future-dated A/R or A/P invoices
- Preferences that contradict each other; for example, if you selected Cash Basis as your Summary Reports basis preference but Accrual Basis as your Sales Tax preference
- Data corruption; verify your data by clicking File, Utilities and selecting Verify Data

Create a transaction detail report to help you find these transactions:

1. Click **Reports, Company & Financial** and choose the **Balance Sheet Standard** report.

2. If your report is not currently prepared in cash basis (see top left of the report), click the **Modify Report** button on the report dialog. The Display tab is opened automatically.

3. Select **Cash** for the report basis.

4. Click **OK** to return to the report.

5. Double-click the **Accounts Receivable** or **Accounts Payable** amount in question. QuickBooks creates the Transaction by Account report.

6. Click the **Modify Report** button on the top of the report.

7. For the **Report Date Range**, remove the **From date** and leave the **To date**.

8. Click the **Advanced** button on the lower right and select the radial button in the Open Balance/Aging pane for **Report Date**.

9. Click the **Filters** tab.

10. From the Choose Filters pane, scroll down to select **Paid Status** and choose the **Open** option for Paid Status.

11. Click **OK** to create the modified Transaction by Account report.

This report now shows you the individual transactions that make up an unexpected balance in either Accounts Receivable or Payable on a Cash Basis Balance Sheet. Compare the transaction types listed on the report with the reasons they might appear as detailed earlier in this chapter. Knowing the transaction type will help you select the proper account(s) to correct.

Digging Deeper

Did you know that you can download a report template from the QuickBooks website that you can import into your data or your clients' data to provide this detail and other useful reports? See Chapter 16, "Reporting Tips and Tricks."

Go to www.quickbooksgroup.com. On the left, select QB Library. Then from the QB Library menu dialog, select Reports. QuickBooks provides a long list of reports available for you to download and import into your file or your clients' QuickBooks data files.

If you are a business owner, having completed this review of your data, you are now prepared with specific questions, and you can go to the specific chapter where you will find more detailed information. You have also gathered specific questions for your accountant and can request her advice on the methods you should use to make changes to your data.

If you are an accounting professional, you have easily identified areas of a client's file that might need more review. Refer to the appropriate chapter to find many useful step-by-step guidelines for troubleshooting and correcting any problems.

Chapter 5

Power Reports for Correcting Beginning Balance Differences

- How Can These Power Reports Help Me?
- Troubleshoot Account Balances—*New for QuickBooks 2009!*
- The Working Trial Balance Window
- Tracking Changes to Closed Accounting Periods
- Using the Audit Trail Report
- Using the Credit Card Audit Trail
- Using the Voided/Deleted Transactions Summary or Detail Report
- Creating the Retained Earnings QuickReport
- Using the Ctrl+Y Keyboard Shortcut
- Running the Transaction List by Date Report
- Documenting Changes Made to a Data File

How Can These Power Reports Help Me?

In Chapter 4, "Easily Review Your QuickBooks Data," a series of reports were provided that are useful for reviewing your business data file or, for accounting professionals, your client's data.

This chapter goes over some specific reports (I like to call them "power reports") that offer a quick way to get behind the numbers and identify just what might be causing issues, particularly with opening balance differences.

 Digging Deeper

What exactly do I mean by "opening balance differences"? This term often means that the numbers you gave your accountant for the prior year have changed, or that when you attempt to reconcile a new month's bank statement the beginning balance does not agree with the last month's ending balance.

These reports and activities include the following:

- Troubleshoot Account Balances—*New for QuickBooks 2009!*
- The Working Trial Balance window
- Closing Date Exception report
- Audit Trail report
- Voided/Deleted Transactions report
- Retained Earnings QuickReport
- Ctrl+Y keyboard shortcut (Journal Transaction report)
- Transaction List by Date report

The following are new for QuickBooks 2009, using QuickBooks Premier Accountant 2009 and QuickBooks Enterprise Solutions Accountant 9.0:

- Incorrectly Recorded "Sales Tax Payable" Payments
- Payroll Liabilities Pay by Regular Check

These additional reports can also be accessed in a QuickBooks Pro 2009 file and all other editions of QuickBooks Premier and Enterprise when logged into the file as the new External Accountant user type.

For more detailed information on these last two reports, see Chapter 17, "Detecting and Correcting with the Client Data Review Feature."

For the business owner or accounting professional, these reports can help pinpoint exactly what might have changed with the balances or what transactions were entered using an incorrect form since the last review of the data.

Digging Deeper

> Did you know that you can prevent changes to prior accounting periods by setting a closing date and optional password? To learn more about this feature, see Chapter 15, "Sharing Data with Your Accountant or Your Client." You also can troubleshoot other types of bank reconciliation issues using the information in Chapter 6, "Bank Account Balance or Reconciliation Errors."

The choices of reports QuickBooks offers you vary depending on the QuickBooks edition and version. Several of the reports discussed in this chapter were made available in the past few years, so if your file does not offer them, you might want to compare your version of QuickBooks to newer versions to see what other improvements besides the reports you are missing out on. To do so, go to www.quickbooks.intuit.com and select from the Products and Services link at the top, What's New for 2009.

The instructions given in this chapter are specific to QuickBooks Premier Accountant 2009; you might find some differences in the menus for QuickBooks Simple Start, Pro, Premiere-non accountant editions, and Enterprise.

Troubleshoot Account Balances—*New for QuickBooks 2009!*

The Troubleshoot Account Balances is not a report, but a menu activity in the new Client Data Review. Used by accounting professionals, the feature is designed to save time in identifying differences between prior period reviewed balances and the same balances as reported in today's QuickBooks file for that prior date.

This menu option is available in QuickBooks Premier Accountant 2009 and QuickBooks Enterprise Solutions Accountant 9.0.

Additionally, this tool can be accessed in a QuickBooks Pro 2009 file and all other editions of QuickBooks Premier when logged into the file as the new External Accountant user type.

For more detailed information on these last two reports, see Chapter 17.

The Working Trial Balance Window

One of the most useful tools for accounting professionals is the Working Trial Balance window. In this window, you have the same information accessible in reports, but offers so much more flexibility in creating new adjusting transactions and previewing the resulting effect on the client's financials from your changes.

This feature is available as a menu option in QuickBooks Premier Accountant Edition 2009 and the QuickBooks Enterprise Solutions Accountant 9.0.

To open the Working Trial Balance window (shown in Figure 5.1):

1. Click **Accountant**, **Working Trial Balance**.
2. From the **Selected Period** drop-down menu, identify the accounting period you want to review.
3. From the **Basis** drop-down menu, select **Accrual** or **Cash**.

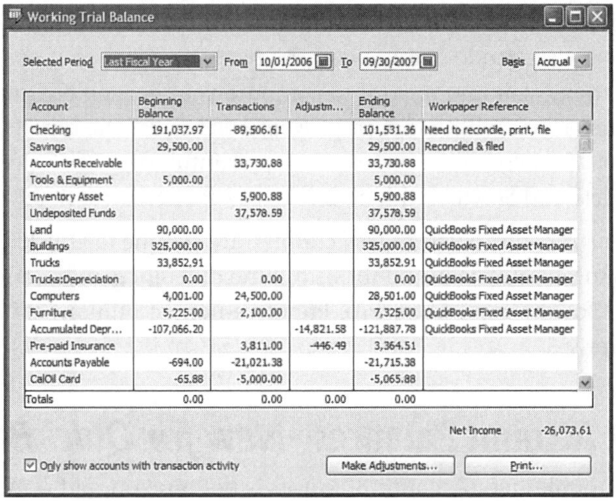

Account	Beginning Balance	Transactions	Adjustm...	Ending Balance	Workpaper Reference
Checking	191,037.97	-89,506.61		101,531.36	Need to reconcile, print, file
Savings	29,500.00			29,500.00	Reconciled & filed
Accounts Receivable		33,730.88		33,730.88	
Tools & Equipment	5,000.00			5,000.00	
Inventory Asset		5,900.88		5,900.88	
Undeposited Funds		37,578.59		37,578.59	
Land	90,000.00			90,000.00	QuickBooks Fixed Asset Manager
Buildings	325,000.00			325,000.00	QuickBooks Fixed Asset Manager
Trucks	33,852.91			33,852.91	QuickBooks Fixed Asset Manager
Trucks:Depreciation	0.00	0.00		0.00	QuickBooks Fixed Asset Manager
Computers	4,001.00	24,500.00		28,501.00	QuickBooks Fixed Asset Manager
Furniture	5,225.00	2,100.00		7,325.00	QuickBooks Fixed Asset Manager
Accumulated Depr...	-107,066.20		-14,821.58	-121,887.78	QuickBooks Fixed Asset Manager
Pre-paid Insurance		3,811.00	-446.49	3,364.51	
Accounts Payable	-694.00	-21,021.38		-21,715.38	
CalOil Card	-65.88	-5,000.00		-5,065.88	
Totals	0.00	0.00	0.00	0.00	

FIGURE 5.1

The Working Trial Balance window offers the features of reports with real-time convenience in editing or modifying transactions.

You now have easy access to the following:

- Beginning Balance—This represents the calculated balances as of the day before the From date selected in this window. In Figure 5.1, the beginning balance date would be 9/30/06.
- Transactions—These represent the transactions that are recorded to the specific account during the date range selected. Place your cursor over these numbers and double-click to see the detail behind the numbers.
- Adjustments—These represent journal entry transactions that are marked as Adjusting Entry (see Figure 5.2).
- Ending Balance—This represents the final balance after transactions and adjustments. In Figure 5.1, the ending balance is as of 9/30/07.

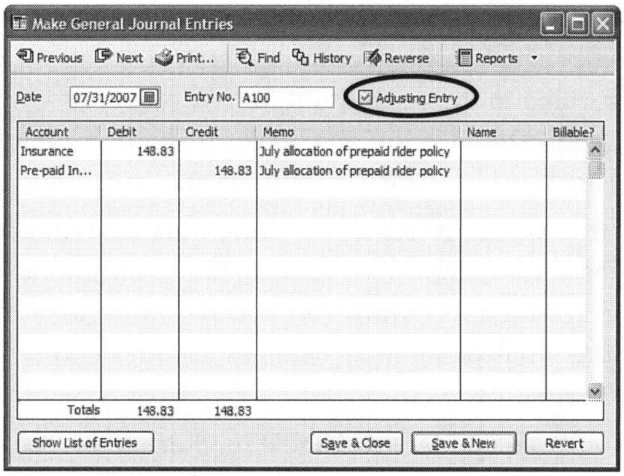

FIGURE 5.2

Create adjusting journal entries conveniently from the Working Trial Balance window.

- Workpaper Reference—Use this field to record any notes regarding the line detail.

- Make Adjustments—Click this button to open a Make General Journal Entries dialog with Adjusting Entry preselected, as shown in Figure 5.2.

Print the Working Trial Balance window by clicking Print. Other options include selecting to see only accounts with nonzero balances.

As you make changes to transactions, the QuickBooks Working Trial Balance window immediately reflects the net change to Income or (Loss) for the period being reviewed (see lower right of window).

If after your review of a data file you have found differences from the prior period ending balances, you can use any or all of the additional power reports that are detailed in this chapter to research and review what transactions were added, modified, voided, or deleted from the prior accounting period causing the difference. Use the details provided by the reports to recreate the transactions or make adjusting entries to balance the books to the prior period.

If you are working with a client's file in your Premier Accountant 2009 software, you will want to use the new Client Data Review feature for troubleshooting beginning balance differences (see Chapter 17).

Tracking Changes to Closed Accounting Periods

QuickBooks offers real flexibility for companies that want to protect prior period data and those that need or want to make changes to prior period accounting records. What exactly is a "closed" accounting period? A business can decide to close a month when tasks such as a bank reconciliation is done or a sales tax return is filed, or a business can close once a year when the data is provided to the accountant for tax preparation. Because QuickBooks does not require you to close the books, it is a decision of the business owner, perhaps based on the advice of your accounting professional (see Chapter 15).

The option of setting a closing date and password makes it easy to protect prior period transactions from unwanted modifications. With additional user-specific security settings, the business owner and accountant can also manage who has the privilege to make changes to transactions dated on or before a specific closing date.

The Closing Date option is available in QuickBooks Pro, Premier (all editions), and Enterprise (all editions). The Closing Date Exception report is available with the QuickBooks Premier Accountant and all versions of the QuickBooks Enterprise Solutions software.

The first step in controlling changes to closed accounting periods is to set a closing date (and optionally a closing date password that the user must provide when adding or modifying a transaction dated on or before the closing date).

The second step is to set user-specific security settings that give the selected user permission to change a transaction dated on or before the closing date.

With these controls in place, QuickBooks gathers information for the Closing Date Exception report.

Setting a Closing Date and Password

You must set a closing date and optionally a password if you want to track changes made to transactions dated on or before the closing date. When a closing date is not set, QuickBooks does not track the changes.

To set the closing date and optionally a password (different from the Admin password), follow these steps after first logging into the data file as the Admin or new External Accountant User:

1. Click **Company, Set Closing Date** to open the Accounting, Company Preferences dialog.

2. Click the **Set Date/Password** button. The Set Closing Date and Password dialog appears.

3. Enter a closing date and optional password. You might want to discuss this date with your accountant first.

4. Click **OK** to accept the closing date and optional password.

Setting a closing date was only step one. Next, you must set user-specific privileges for users who need access to adding or modifying a transaction dated on or before the closing date.

Setting User-Specific Security

To be certain that the closing date control is managed properly, review all users for their specific rights to change transactions before a closing date. To view the following menu, you need to log into the file as the Admin user:

1. Click **Company**, **Set Up Users and Passwords** and select the option to **Set Up Users**. The User List dialog opens.

2. To view a user's existing security privileges from the User List dialog, select the user with your cursor and click the **View User** button. You can view in summary form the security settings for that user, as shown in Figure 5.3.

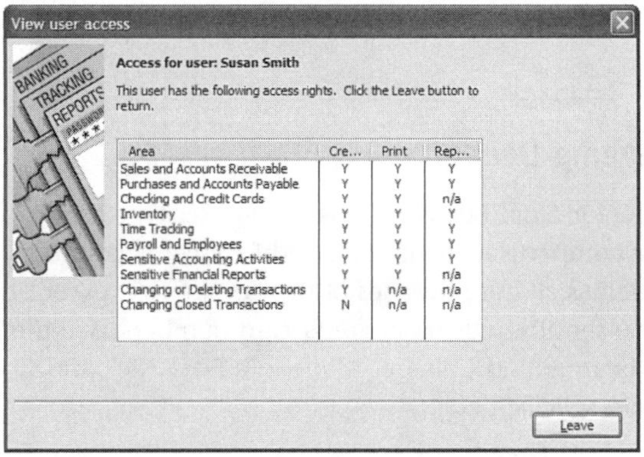

FIGURE 5.3

Review in summary form the user's security privileges.

3. Any user who should not have rights to changing closed period transactions should have an "N" placed in the last setting, Changing Closed Transactions (see Figure 5.3).

4. If after reviewing a user's existing security privileges you need to edit the setting referenced earlier, click **Leave** to close the View User Access dialog.

5. QuickBooks returns you to the User List dialog. Select the user name and click the **Edit User** button.

6. On the Change User Password and Access dialog, optionally modify the user name or password. Click **Next** to continue.

7. The User Access dialog for the specific user appears. Select **Selected Areas** and click **Next** to continue through each of the security selections until you reach the selection on Page 9, as shown in Figure 5.4.

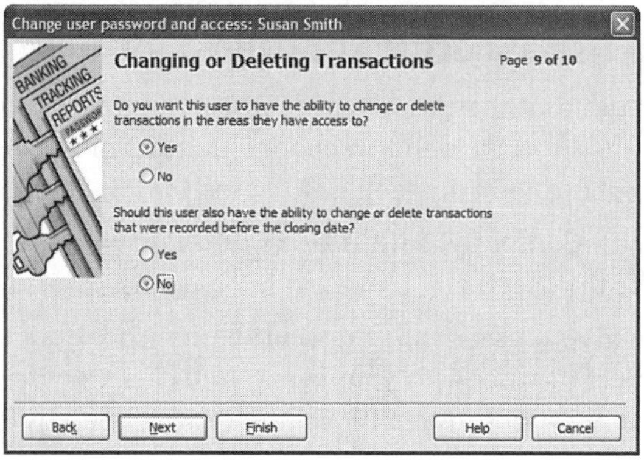

FIGURE 5.4

Be sure that each user is also set to No for changing closed period transactions.

Digging Deeper

New for QuickBooks 2009 is a new user type that can be assigned to the company accountant, called External Accountant. This new user type has all the privileges of the Admin user, except this user cannot view sensitive customer credit card numbers. See the last section titled "Documenting Changes Made to a Data File" and Chapter 17 for more specific details.

If after setting the user security levels in QuickBooks you want to have more levels of restriction, such as allowing users to access certain bank accounts but not others, you might want to consider the QuickBooks Enterprise product that offers more sophisticated security levels, as represented in Figure 5.5.

You set a closing date and optional closing date password and defined which users are allowed to add or modify transactions dated on or before the closing date; QuickBooks is now gathering information for the Closing Date Exception report.

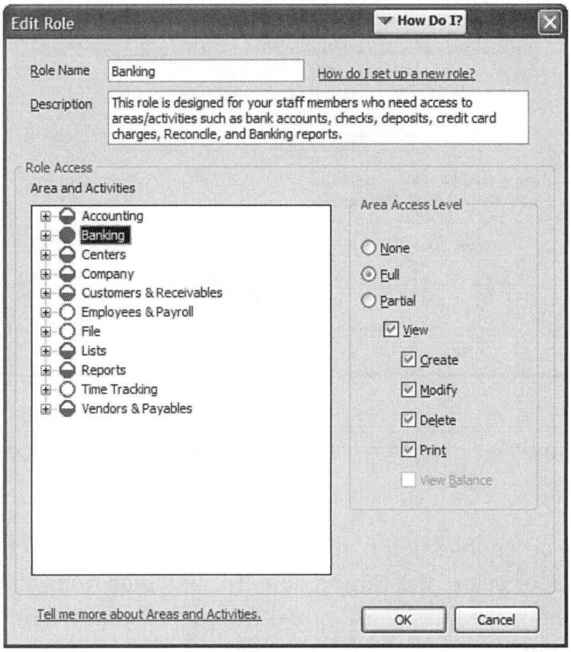

FIGURE 5.5

Expanded user security is available in the QuickBooks Enterprise Edition.

Creating the Closing Date Exception Report

To have QuickBooks track information for the Closing Date Exception report, you first had to set a closing date and optionally set specific users access to adding or modifying transactions on or before this date.

If you have compared your or your clients' data to prior year financials or tax returns and the ending balances for the "closed" period have changed (and you set a closing date for the file), you want to view the Closing Date Exception report to see exactly who made the change and what specific transactions were added or modified.

Rescue Me!

Exceptions, additions, and changes are *not* tracked during the time period that a closing date was not set.

To create the Closing Date Exception report, shown in Figure 5.6, click Reports, Accountant & Taxes and choose the Closing Date Exception Report.

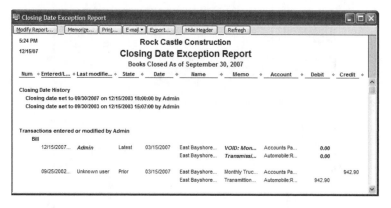

FIGURE 5.6

Review the Closing Date Exception report for changes made to transactions dated on or before a closing date.

This report enables you to identify changes that were made to transactions dated on or before the closing date. For modified transactions, the report details both the latest version of a transaction and the prior version (as of the closing date). With privileges to change closed period transactions, you can then recreate the original transaction or change the date of added transactions so that you can once again agree with the ending balance from the previously closed period.

Using the Audit Trail Report

The Audit Trail report provides details of additions and changes made to transactions, grouping the changes by user name. The detail on this report shows the prior and latest version of the transaction, if it was edited. You can filter the report to show a specific date range to narrow the amount of detail.

The Audit Trail report is available in QuickBooks Simple Start, Pro, Premier (all industry editions), and Enterprise (all industry editions). Further, since QuickBooks 2006, the Audit Trail feature is permanently enabled and the report cannot be "purged" of the detail.

To create the Audit Trail report shown in Figure 5.7, click Reports, Accountant & Taxes and select the Audit Trail report.

The report can be lengthy to review; however, if as a business owner or accountant you are trying to track down specific user activity with transactions, this can be a useful report to review because the changes are grouped by user name.

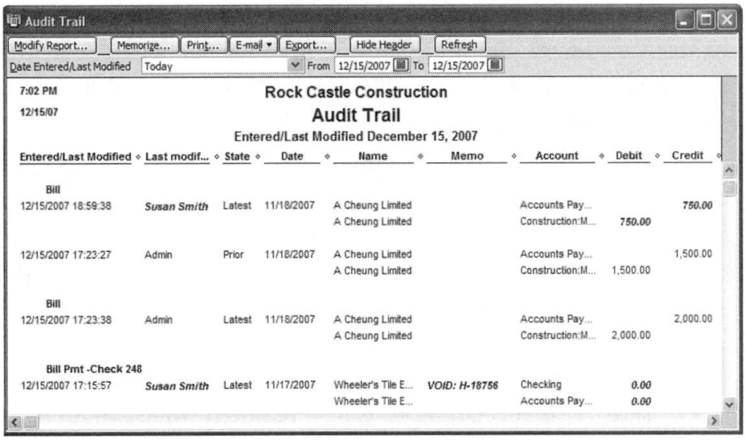

FIGURE 5.7

The QuickBooks Audit Trail report helps to identify what changes were made to transactions and by which user.

If you find undesired transaction changes, consider setting a closing date password and setting specific user security privileges, which were detailed in the sections titled "Setting a Closing Date and Password" and "Setting User-Specific Security."

Using the Credit Card Audit Trail

QuickBooks 2008 introduced added security surrounding the critical activity of maintaining a record of your customer's confidential credit card information. QuickBooks users can now stay in compliance with credit card industry security requirements by enabling security around who can view, add, or edit your customer's credit card numbers.

New for QuickBooks 2009 is a user type called External Accountant. When this type is assigned to your accountant, she cannot view these sensitive customer credit card numbers.

Additionally, when enabled, you can track which user viewed, edited, added, or removed a customer's credit card number with the new Credit Card Audit Trail report.

To use this new feature correctly, follow these three basic steps:

1. Enable the customer credit card protection feature.

2. Select which users are given security rights to view the credit card numbers and which users are not given this privilege.

3. View the new Credit Card Audit Trail report to track viewing, editing, adding, and deleting activity with your customer's credit cards.

The first step to viewing details on the Credit Card Audit Trail report is to enable Customer Credit Card Protection in QuickBooks. (Note: These instructions are provided for the QuickBooks Premier 2009; QuickBooks Enterprise Set Up Users dialog differ.)

1. Log in to the data file as the Admin user and click **Company**, **Customer Credit Card Protection** to open the Enable QuickBooks Customer Credit Card Protection dialog.

2. Click the **Enable** button to open the Customer Credit Card Protection Setup dialog, as shown in Figure 5.8. Type a complex password. The new complex password must be seven characters, including one number and one uppercase character. For example, coMp1ex is a complex password. This password is now required when the Admin user logs in.

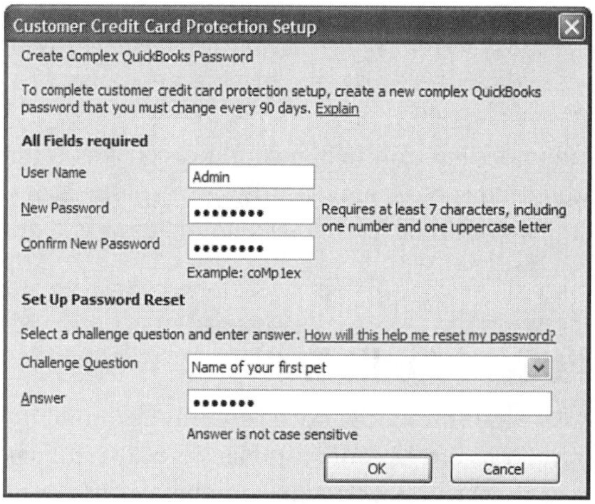

FIGURE 5.8

Protect the confidentiality of your customer's credit card numbers with added security setup.

3. You are also required to choose a challenge question from the drop-down menu and provide an answer to that question. This question will be used to reset your password if you forget it. Click **OK**.

4. A message dialog opens letting you know that you will be reminded in 90 days to change the password. Click **OK**.

5. QuickBooks notifies you that you have enabled Customer Credit Card Protection and details how to allow access by user to the credit card numbers (see step 6). Click **OK**. You are now returned to QuickBooks logged in as the Admin user.

6. To select which employees have access to view the full credit card numbers, add, or change customer credit card numbers, click **Company**, **Set Up Users and Passwords** and select the **Set Up Users** option.

7. The QuickBooks login dialog opens and requires you to enter the Admin password to gain access to user security settings. Click **OK** to open the User List dialog.

8. Select a user name and click the **Edit** button. Optionally, edit the user name or password, or click **Next** to accept these fields as they are.

9. The Access window for the specific user opens. Choose the **Selected Areas of QuickBooks** option. Click **Next**.

10. The Sales and Accounts Receivable access options are displayed. Choose either **Full Access** or **Selective Access**; either of these choices combined with a check mark in the **View complete credit card numbers** (as shown in Figure 5.9) enables the user to view and add, delete, or modify the credit card number. If no check mark is placed, the user sees only the last four digits of the customer's credit card when recording transactions that use this sensitive information.

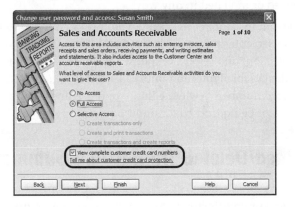

FIGURE 5.9

User-specific access to viewing complete customer credit card numbers.

11. Click **Finish** if this is the only setting you want to modify or click **Next** through additional security setting dialogs. Click **Finish** when completed. You are returned to the User List dialog. Click **Close** to close the User List dialog.

You have now properly enabled the customer credit card protection and granted or removed user access to these confidential credit card numbers.

With this feature enabled, your data file is now tracking critical user activity about your customer's credit card numbers. Track when the credit card security was enabled, and track when a user entered a credit card number, modified a credit card, or even viewed the credit card audit trail report (see Figure 5.10).

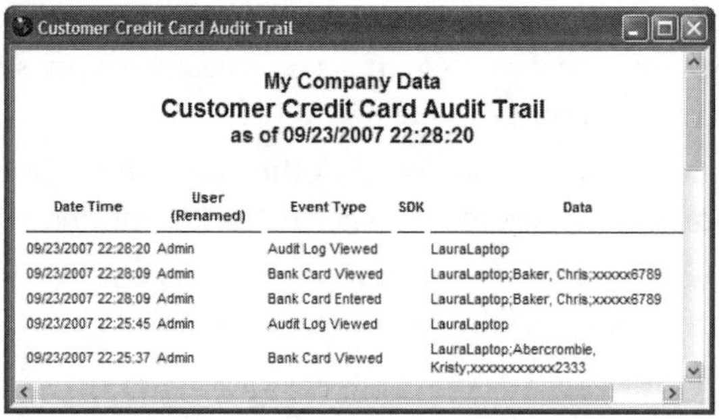

FIGURE 5.10

The new Customer Credit Card Audit Trail report cannot be modified, filtered, or purged.

This Customer Credit Card Audit Trail report is always tracking customer credit card activity as long as the feature remains enabled. The report cannot be filtered or modified in any way.

If you want to disable this setting, you must first log in to the data file as the Admin user, enter the complex password that was created when you enabled the protection, and select Company, Customer Credit Card Protection and select the Disable Protection button. Click Yes to accept that your customer's credit card number viewing, editing, and deleting activity by QuickBooks users is no longer being tracked for audit purposes.

Using the Voided/Deleted Transactions Summary or Detail Report

QuickBooks offers flexibility for handling changes to transactions. If you grant users rights to create transactions, they also have rights to void and delete transactions. Don't worry: You can view these voided transaction changes in the Voided/Deleted Transactions Summary (see Figure 5.11) or Voided/Deleted Transactions Detail reports.

To create the Voided/Deleted Transactions Summary report, click Reports, Accountant & Taxes and select the Voided/Deleted Transactions Summary or Detail report.

Use this report to view transactions before and after the change, and to identify which user made the change. After viewing this information, you might want to set additional user restrictions in security, as discussed in the section of this chapter titled "Setting User-Specific Security."

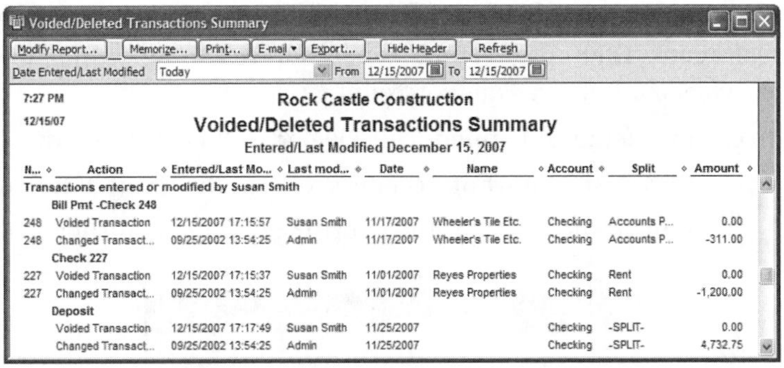

FIGURE 5.11

The QuickBooks Voided/Deleted Transactions Summary report quickly identifies which transactions were either voided or deleted, making troubleshooting much easier!

Creating the Retained Earnings QuickReport

Users familiar with QuickBooks know just how useful QuickReports can be. They can be created for many types of information, but one of the most useful, especially for accounting professionals, is the QuickReport that can be created for details in the Retained Earnings account.

To describe the QuickReport for the Retained Earnings account, you first must know that all Balance Sheet accounts have a QuickBooks register. Registers are available for nearly all Balance Sheet accounts. One method to access a register is to click Lists, Chart of Accounts and double-click any of the Balance Sheet accounts.

The registers make it easy to view a specific account's transactions without creating a report. You don't typically work in registers, but on occasion you might want to review the details found there.

The exception is the Retained Earnings account, a Balance Sheet account that does not have a register. The Retained Earnings account is where QuickBooks "closes" Net Income or (Loss) each year. Users do not have to manually do this entry; in fact, QuickBooks recalculates it each time you create a Balance Sheet report.

Typically, you never should be posting any transactions to this account, except when you close the Open Bal Equity account (another account that QuickBooks created automatically) into the Retained Earnings account. Typically, this is done only when you first begin using QuickBooks for a business with historical transactions.

For more information on these accounts, see Chapter 2, "Reviewing the QuickBooks Chart of Accounts," and Chapter 13, "Reviewing and Correcting the Opening Balance Equity Account."

To create a Retained Earnings QuickReport, follow these steps:

1. Click **Lists**, **Chart of Accounts** to open the Chart of Accounts list.

2. Double-click the **Retained Earnings** list item, as shown in Figure 5.12.

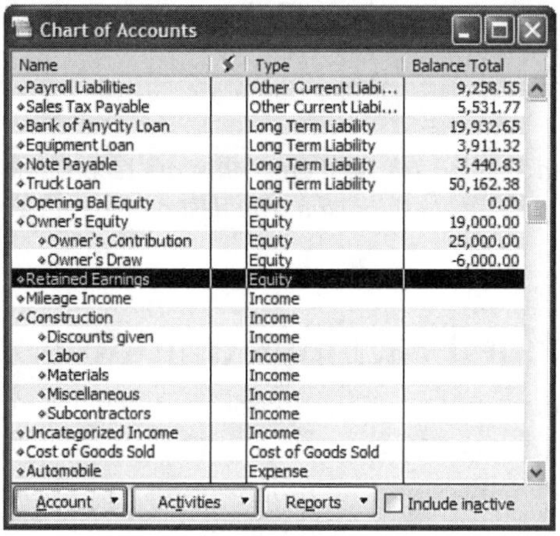

FIGURE 5.12

Create the Retained Earnings Account QuickReport by double-clicking the Retained Earnings account list item.

QuickBooks creates the Retained Earnings Account QuickReport, as shown in Figure 5.13.

The Closing Entry type entries shown in Figure 5.13 are those done automatically by QuickBooks; they are recalculated each time you generate the report.

Any other transaction types are user entered and, as with other reports in QuickBooks, you can double-click on a user-created transaction and "drill down" to the original transaction.

Rescue Me!

Did you know that you can set a preference to warn users if they try to record a transaction to the Retained Earnings account?

Click Edit, Preferences and select the Accounting preference on the left. Click the Company Preference tab (if you are logged in as the Admin or External Accountant user) and place a check mark in the Warn When Posting a Transaction to Retained Earnings check box. Users then receive the message shown in Figure 5.14.

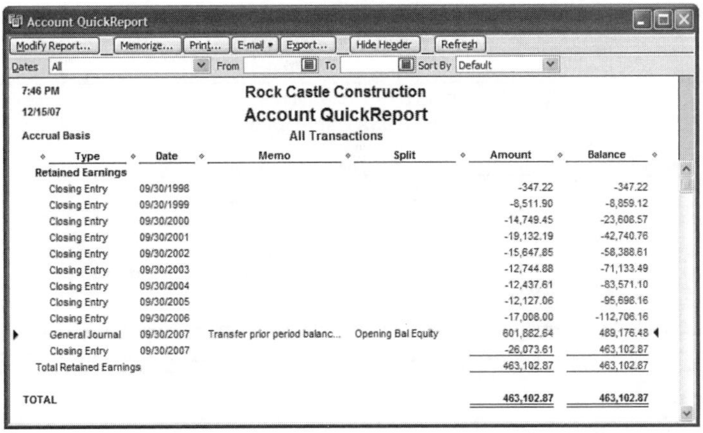

FIGURE 5.13

The Retained Earnings Account QuickReport helps you troubleshoot changes to prior period financials.

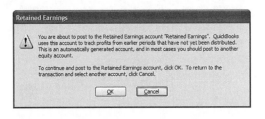

FIGURE 5.14

The warning enabled in preferences to alert users that they are posting to Retained Earnings.

Using the Ctrl+Y Keyboard Shortcut

The Ctrl+Y keyboard shortcut is one of the best-kept QuickBooks reporting secrets, yet it is especially useful for accounting professionals.

QuickBooks users do not have to be concerned with understanding debit and credit accounting. QuickBooks does all this behind the scenes. However, be assured that every transaction in QuickBooks creates a debit and credit transaction.

For accounting professionals, viewing the actual resulting debit and credit effect of a transaction can be useful. To do so, follow these steps:

1. Open any transaction. The example shown in Figure 5.15 is a vendor bill.

2. On your computer keyboard, press **Ctrl+Y**.

QuickBooks creates a Transaction Journal report on the specific transaction that was open, as shown in Figure 5.16.

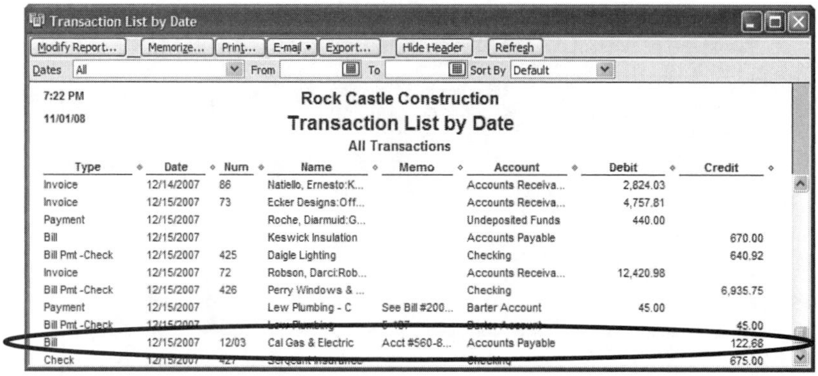

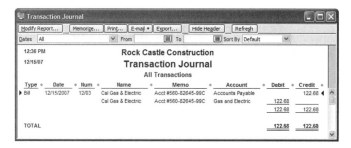

FIGURE 5.15

With a vendor bill or any other type of transaction open, press Ctrl+Y to create a Transaction Journal report for that transaction.

FIGURE 5.16

Conveniently view the debit and credit details of any transaction.

QuickBooks Premier Accountant opens the Transaction Journal report and shows the line totals in debit and credit format. Other editions of QuickBooks open the same report but do not show the totals in debit and credit format. If you want to see the report totals in debit and credit format, click Modify Report on the report and select the columns for debit and credit.

Running the Transaction List by Date Report

Although the title of Transaction List by Date report seems to not indicate as much "power" as the other reports discussed in this chapter, I use this report most often when reviewing a data file.

If you are new to QuickBooks, you will soon learn that the date you give your transactions is important. The year you assign to the transaction is the year that QuickBooks reports the transaction in your financials. If you record a transaction with a date error—for example, you wanted to create a 2009-dated transaction but in error typed 2090—this date would cause your financials not to show the effect until year 2090!

Follow these steps to create the Transaction List by Date report, shown in Figure 5.17:

1. Click **Reports, Accountant & Taxes** and select the **Transaction List by Date** report.

2. From the Dates drop-down menu, select **All** dates.

	Rock Castle Construction						
7:34 AM	**Transaction List by Date**						
12/15/07	All Transactions						
Type	Date	Num	Name	Memo	Account	Debit	Credit
Paycheck	12/15/2007		Elizabeth N. Mason		Checking		932.92
Paycheck	12/15/2007		Gregg O. Schneider		Checking		1,062.12
Paycheck	12/15/2007		Gregg O. Schneider		Checking		1,062.12
Transfer	12/16/2007			Funds Trans...	Savings		500.00
Build Assembly	12/17/2007				Inventory Asset	582.50	
Payment	12/18/2007		Hendro Riyadi		Undeposited Funds	1,816.25	
Bill Pmt -Check	12/19/2007		Wheeler's Tile Etc.	H-18756	Checking		625.00
Invoice	12/20/2007	88	Morgenthaler, Jenny		Accounts Receiva...	271.53	
Invoice	12/23/2007	87	Cuddihy, Matthew		Accounts Receiva...	129.30	
Invoice	12/30/2007	81	Abercrombie, Kris...		Accounts Receiva...	4,522.00	
Payment	12/31/2007		Abercrombie, Kris...		Checking	7,633.28	
Check	12/15/2030	1001	Sergeant Insurance		Checking		675.00

FIGURE 5.17

The QuickBooks Transaction List by Date report can be used to identify whether any incorrectly dated transactions exist.

You can use this report to see both the oldest dated transaction (when the file was started) and the furthest dated transaction (to identify whether date errors have been made). Then, as with all other QuickBooks reports, double-click a specific transaction to change the date if needed.

 Digging Deeper

Fortunately, QuickBooks preferences help avoid transaction dating errors by enabling you to set warning date ranges.

To open the date warning preference, follow these steps:

1. Log in to the QuickBooks data file as the Admin or new External Accountant user.

2. Click **Edit, Preferences**. In the Preferences dialog that appears, choose the **Accounting** preference on the left.

3. Click the **Company Preferences** tab.

4. Type in the user-defined date warning range you want to work with for past dated transactions and future dated transactions. QuickBooks sets the default warnings at 90 days in the past and 30 days in the future. An attempt to enter transactions dated before or after this date range prompts QuickBooks to give the user a warning message, as shown in Figure 5.18.

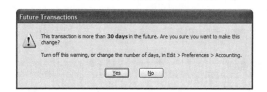

FIGURE 5.18
Set the Date Warning preference so that users will be warned when dating a transaction outside an acceptable date range.

 Digging Deeper

If you are using an older version of QuickBooks (before 2007), you might not have this important preference option.

Be cautious when making changes to the dates, especially if the year in question has already had a tax return prepared on the existing information.

Documenting Changes Made to a Data File

Setting up a QuickBooks user for each person that enters data provides a level of control over the sensitive data to be viewed by this user as well as giving access to specific areas in QuickBooks. Optionally, for additional control, a user-specific password can also be assigned.

New for QuickBooks 2009 is a new type of user called the External Accountant. When you create a new user (or edit an existing user) in QuickBooks, you can assign that user as an External Accountant. You are granting that user the same privileges as the default Admin user, except the new External Accountant user is not able to create or modify users or view sensitive customer credit card information.

If you are reviewing your client's data using the Accountant's Copy file type, this new External Accountant has to be created before your client creates the Accountant's Copy of his file.

With a unique user name assigned, you are able to report on the transaction changes that you have made to the file, separate and unique from those transactions your client records.

To create an External Accountant user, follow these steps:

1. Open the QuickBooks data file using the Admin user (the default user that QuickBooks creates with a new QuickBooks file), and enter the appropriate password if one was created.

2. From the **Company** menu, **Set Up Users and Passwords**, select the **Set Up Users** menu option.

3. Enter the Admin user password if one was originally assigned.

4. The User List dialog opens, listing the current users set up for this file.

5. Click the **Add User** button, to create a new user, or with your mouse pointer, select an existing user name and click the **Edit User** button.

6. The Set up or Change user password and access dialog is opened.

7. In the **User Name** field, type the name you want the user to be identified by in the file.

8. In the **Password** field, enter an *optional* password, and in the **Confirm Password** field, retype the password for accuracy.

9. Optionally, click the box to **Add** this user to my QuickBooks license. (See the explain link for more details.)

10. Click **Next**. If you receive a No Password Entered message, click **Yes** or **No** to create a password. If you select Yes, you will be taken back to step 8. Optionally, select the **Do not display** this message in the future.

11. Access for User:<user name> dialog opens.

12. Select the radial button for **External Accountant**.

13. Click **Next**.

14. QuickBooks provides a warning message, confirming that you want to give this new user access to all areas of QuickBooks except customer credit card numbers. Select **Yes** to assign the new External Accountant type privileges to this new or existing user.

15. The Access for User:<user name> dialog opens restating that the new External Accountant user has access to all areas of QuickBooks except sensitive customer credit card data. Click **Finish**, to complete the process.

All transactions added or modified are now recorded to this logged-in user. Creating an External Accountant user type for the accounting professional is important because you will create reports that are sorted by the user name assigned to the transaction.

Create an Audit Trail report as detailed earlier in this chapter. The default date range is set to Today. Scroll through the report until you see the transaction additions or modifications assigned to your user name; see the example in Figure 5.19.

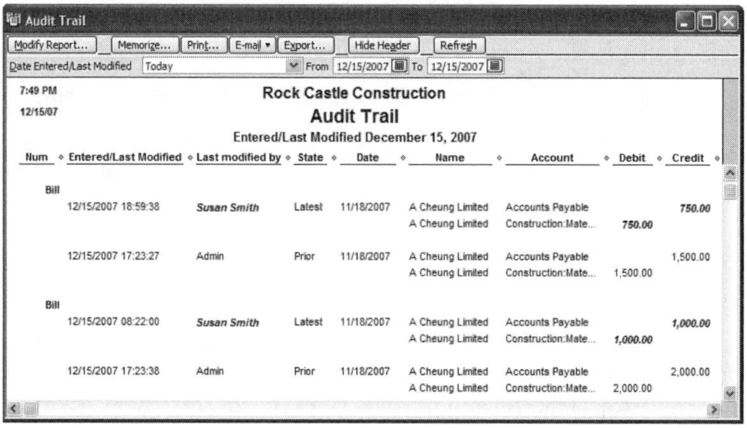

FIGURE 5.19

The Audit Trail report used to document changes you make to a data file.

The chapters so far in this QuickBooks Solutions Guide have prepared you with basic instructions for tools that you can use to make the review of your data efficient. You are now ready to dig into some more detailed reviews of specific accounts in QuickBooks!

Chapter 6

Bank Account Balance or Reconciliation Errors

- The Importance of Correct Bank Balances in Your QuickBooks Data

- Reconciling a Bank Account for the First Time

- Troubleshooting an Incorrectly Reconciled Bank Account

- Reconciling with an Adjustment

The Importance of Correct Bank Balances in Your QuickBooks Data

You might wonder why I would have to point out the importance of having the correct bank balances in your QuickBooks data, yet incorrect bank balances are often one of the most common problems I find when troubleshooting a client's QuickBooks data. One of the first questions I ask new clients is whether they have reconciled their bank account in QuickBooks. Most tell me that they have. I then review any bank transactions that are not marked as cleared and I will usually find older, dated transactions. (See the section "Reviewing Uncleared Bank Transactions" in this chapter.)

One of the most important reconciliations that you should do in QuickBooks is match your bank transactions recorded in QuickBooks with the same transactions reported by your bank on the monthly bank statement. Just reconciling your bank account balances fixes many errors on the Profit & Loss Statement.

Reconciling a Bank Account for the First Time

If your business is just starting, it is a good time to make sure that you include reconciling your bank account in QuickBooks with the statement you receive each month as part of your regular routine. However, what if you have been using QuickBooks for years or months and have never reconciled the bank account?

First determine how many months have gone by. Catching up with a few months of bank reconciliations takes much less effort than having to do several years or months of bank statement reconciliations. If you are going to go back to the beginning of the business and reconcile each month, you need to start with the first month of your bank activity and work your way month by month to the current month. Completing your bank reconciliation for each month is the most accurate and thorough process and provides a separate reconciliation report for each month.

However, it is often not practical to go back to the start of your business when you simply want to get the bank account reconciled in the current month.

Rescue Me!

As with any major task or adjustment you plan to make in your QuickBooks data, I recommend that you make a backup copy. You can easily create this backup by choosing File, Save Copy or Backup, and then following the instructions on the screen.

Complete the recommendations in the following sections before attempting to do a multiyear or multimonth bank reconciliation.

Verify That the Bank Account Has Not Been Reconciled

How can you tell whether your bank account has been reconciled? An easy method is to click Banking, Reconcile and check the "last reconciled on (date)" in the Begin Reconciliation dialog. A month/day/year indicates that the account has previously been reconciled (see Figure 6.1). If you have a Beginning Balance amount but no "last reconciled on (date)," no reconciliation has been completed. This beginning balance was most likely from entering your bank balance in the EasyStep Interview, which was detailed in the section "EasyStep Interview—Overview" in Chapter 1, "Creating a New QuickBooks Data File."

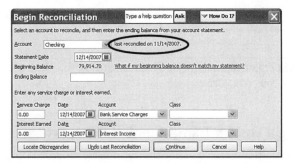

FIGURE 6.1

This bank account has been reconciled, as the "last reconciled on date" indicates.

Verifying That All Bank-Related Transactions Have Been Entered

Ensuring that all checks, bill payments, payroll checks, customer payments, and any other banking-related transactions have been entered in the QuickBooks data file is critical to the success in accurate reporting in your or your client's QuickBooks file. You don't want to complete a multiyear or multimonth bank reconciliation if handwritten checks or other bank transactions have not been recorded in the data.

Creating a Missing Checks Report

To help you determine whether any check transactions are missing, create a Missing Checks report:

1. Click Reports, **Banking**.
2. Select the **Missing Checks** report.
3. Select the bank account in the drop-down menu dialog that opens.

The resulting Missing Checks report shows all check or bill payment check type transactions sorted by number (see Figure 6.2). Look for any breaks in the detail with a *** *Missing* or *** *Duplicate* warning.

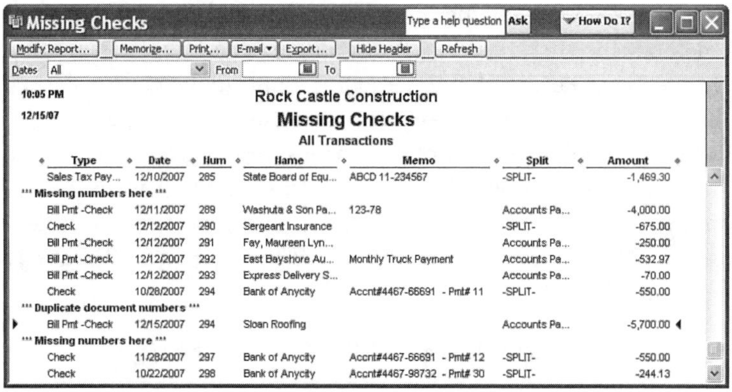

FIGURE 6.2

The Missing Checks report can help you determine whether you need to enter any missing transactions before you reconcile.

Creating a Custom Transaction Detail Report

Another method used to verify that you have recorded all your transactions requires a bit more effort on your part. Manually add the total of all deductions and additions from the statements your bank provides you and compare to the following report.

Create this report to help you manually verify that there are no missing transactions:

1. Click **Reports, Custom Transaction Detail**. The Modify Report dialog opens.

2. Remove the **From date** and enter the **To date** for the end of the month through which you are reconciling.

3. Click the **Filters** tab.

4. In the **Choose Filter** pane, with the **Account** filter highlighted, choose the bank account from the drop-down menu.

5. Select **OK**.

This report (see Figure 6.3) totals all debits (money into your bank account) and credits (money out of your bank account). To these totals, you have to add back in checks and deduct deposits that have not yet cleared the bank. If the resulting totals are exact or close to your manual totals, you can feel confident reconciling multiple years or months at one time.

Custom Transaction Detail Report

Item	Name	Memo	Split	Debit	Credit	Balance
9	Keenan, Bridget:Sun R...		-SPLIT-	102.85		102,670.55
289	Washuta & Son Painting	123-78	Accounts Payable		4,000.00	98,670.55
DED	Bad Check Charges		Bank Service Cha...		10.00	98,660.55
70	Teschner, Anton:Sun...	Check returned by ...	Accounts Receiva...		1,200.00	97,460.55
290	Sergeant Insurance		-SPLIT-		675.00	96,785.55
		Deposit	-SPLIT-	4,936.12		101,721.67
291	Fay, Maureen Lynn, C...		Accounts Payable		250.00	101,471.67
292	East Bayshore Auto M...	Monthly Truck Paym...	Accounts Payable		532.97	100,938.70
293	Express Delivery Serv...		Accounts Payable		70.00	100,868.70
		Deposit	-SPLIT-	4,700.00		105,568.70
				445,726.72	340,158.02	105,568.70

Rock Castle Construction
Custom Transaction Detail Report
As of December 14, 2007
Accrual Basis
10:25 PM
12/15/07

FIGURE 6.3

The modified Custom Transaction Detail Report shows the total of all money in and out of a bank account for the time period selected.

Identifying All Uncleared Transactions

Make a list of all the uncleared bank transactions as of the month and year you are reconciling through. See the following Digging Deeper for help with selecting this month. If you have been manually reconciling your bank account, simply find the paper statement for the selected month and look for the list of uncleared transactions.

For example, suppose it is April 2009 and you want to reconcile multiple years or months through December 31, 2008. Collect your bank statements for January through March of 2009. Identify any cleared transactions from these 2009 bank statements where the transaction date was on or before December 31, 2008, but did not clear your bank until year 2009.

 Digging Deeper

If you are choosing to complete a multiyear or multimonth bank reconciliation, consider reconciling through the last month of your previous fiscal year, which for most companies would be your statement ending December 31, 20xx. Choosing a month to reconcile through that is two to three months in the past will make identifying the transactions that had not cleared the bank as of the month you are reconciling much easier.

Completing the Multiple-Year or Month Bank Reconciliation

The steps for completing the multiple-year or month bank reconciliation follow:

1. Click **Banking, Reconcile**. The Begin Reconciliation dialog box appears (see Figure 6.4).

2. Select the correct **Account** from the drop-down menu, and type the Statement Date that you want to reconcile through. Enter the **Ending Balance** from the bank statement and click **Continue**. The Reconcile - Account displays. This example shows a reconciliation through December 31, 2006.

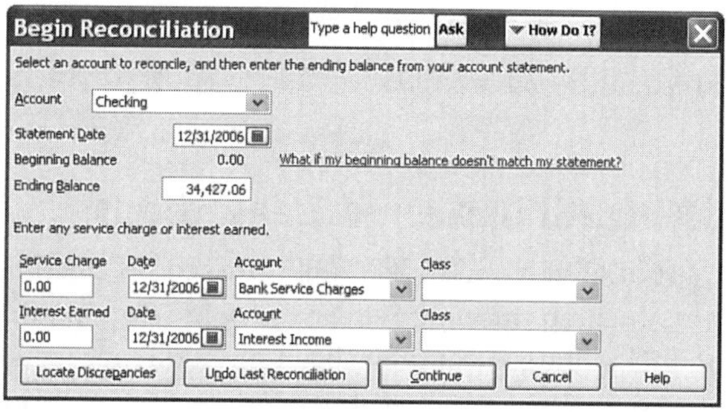

FIGURE 6.4

Beginning a bank account reconciliation for the first time.

3. Click the **Hide Transactions After the Statement's End Date** check box at the top right. Checking this box makes working with the remaining transactions easier.

4. Click the **Mark All** button. Now each transaction is marked as if it has cleared. Remove check marks from any transaction you previously identified as uncleared (see Figure 6.5). Your work is complete when the reconciliation shows a Difference of 0.00 at the lower right of the Reconcile - Account dialog.

| Reconcile - Checking | | Type a help question | Ask | ▼ How Do I? | | □ X |

For period: 12/31/2006   ☑ Hide transactions after the statement's end date

Checks and Payments

✓	Date	Ch...	Payee	Amount
✓	04/12/2006	105	East Bayshore Auto Mall	532.97
✓	04/17/2006	106	Kershaw Computer Servi...	714.00
✓	04/19/2006	108	Sergeant Insurance	712.56
✓	05/13/2006	109	East Bayshore Auto Mall	532.97
	12/18/2006	110	East Bayshore Auto Mall	532.97
✓	12/18/2006	111	East Bayshore Auto Mall	532.97
✓	12/25/2006	112	Sergeant Insurance	712.56
	12/28/2006	113	City of East Bayshore	225.00

Deposits and Other Credits

✓	Date	Chk #	Payee	Amount
✓	10/18/2006	2362	Easley, Paula:Garage	1,000.00
✓	11/04/2006	2356	Easley, Paula:Garage	1,519.39
✓	12/05/2006			5,079.48
✓	12/09/2006			1,867.89
✓	12/18/2006			3,516.05
✓	12/20/2006			1,867.89
✓	12/31/2006			25,625.86

[Mark All] [Unmark All] [Go To]   [Columns to Display...]

Beginning Balance		0.00		[Modify]	Service Charge	0.00
Items you have marked cleared					Interest Earned	0.00
7	Deposits and Other	40,476.56			Ending Balance	34,427.06
	Credits				Cleared Balance	34,427.06
10	Checks and Payments	6,049.50			Difference	0.00

[Reconcile Now]   [Leave]

Select Reconcile Now only
when the difference is 0.00.

FIGURE 6.5

Remove the check mark for those transactions that did not clear the bank.

5. Click **Reconcile Now**; QuickBooks creates a bank reconciliation report
you can print.

 Digging Deeper

What if the reconciled difference is not 0.00? First determine whether
the amount is significant. If the answer is yes, the best method for
finding errors is to review each item marked cleared in QuickBooks
with the transactions listed on your bank statements.

If the difference shown on the Reconcile - Account dialog is not significant, you can reconcile with an adjustment, as in Figure 6.6.
QuickBooks places this adjustment amount into an automatically created Expense account called "Reconciliation Discrepancies." (See the
section titled "Reconciling with an Adjustment," later in this chapter.)

New for QuickBooks 2009, when reconciling, you can sort the uncleared transactions by clicking once with your mouse pointer on the column header in the
Reconcile - <account name> dialog.

Not all bank account reconciliations are this easy to troubleshoot and correct.
Often, you need to dig deeper into the possible causes of reconciliation errors.
QuickBooks makes this task much easier by providing many different tools
and reports to help with this important process.

| Reconcile - Checking | | | | | | Type a help question | Ask | ▾ How Do I? | | | |

For period: 12/31/2006   ☑ Hide transactions after the statement's end date

Checks and Payments

✓	Date	Ch...	Payee	Amount
✓	01/11/2006	100	East Bayshore Auto Mall	532.97
✓	01/21/2006	101	Sergeant Insurance	712.56
✓	02/11/2006	103	East Bayshore Auto Mall	532.97
✓	03/11/2006	104	East Bayshore Auto Mall	532.97
✓	04/12/2006	105	East Bayshore Auto Mall	532.97
✓	04/17/2006	106	Kershaw Computer Servi...	714.00
✓	04/19/2006	108	Sergeant Insurance	712.56
✓	05/13/2006	109	East Bayshore Auto Mall	532.97

Deposits and Other Credits

✓	Date	Chk #	Payee	Amount
✓	10/18/2006	2362	Easley, Paula:Garage	1,000.00
✓	11/04/2006	2356	Easley, Paula:Garage	1,519.39
✓	12/05/2006			5,079.48
✓	12/09/2006			1,867.89
✓	12/18/2006			3,516.05
✓	12/20/2006			1,867.89
✓	12/31/2006			25,625.86

[Mark All] [Unmark All] [Go To]   [Columns to Display...]

Beginning Balance	0.00			
Items you have marked cleared		[Modify]	Service Charge	0.00
7 Deposits and Other	40,476.56		Interest Earned	0.00
Credits			Ending Balance	34,427.06
11 Checks and Payments	6,274.50		Cleared Balance	34,202.06
			Difference	**225.00**

[Reconcile Now] [Leave]

Clicking Reconcile Now will create an adjustment transaction.

FIGURE 6.6

Reconciling a bank account with a reconciliation difference.

Troubleshooting an Incorrectly Reconciled Bank Account

A simple way to determine whether your bank account is correctly reconciled is to compare your bank statement beginning balance to the QuickBooks Beginning Balance amount in the Begin Reconciliation dialog. Click Banking, Reconcile and select the appropriate Account. If you find that your QuickBooks data does not agree with your bank statement, you can use one, or a combination of several, of the methods listed in this chapter to figure out why.

Digging Deeper

What makes up the Beginning Balance, as shown in Figure 6.1? The beginning balance is the sum of all previously cleared checks, deposits, and other transactions. A check mark next to a transaction item in the bank account register indicates it has previously been cleared in the bank reconciliation in QuickBooks. An asterisk indicates the item is currently being reconciled, as shown in Figure 6.7. A lightning bolt (not shown) next to a transaction indicates that it has been downloaded and matched but has not yet been marked cleared.

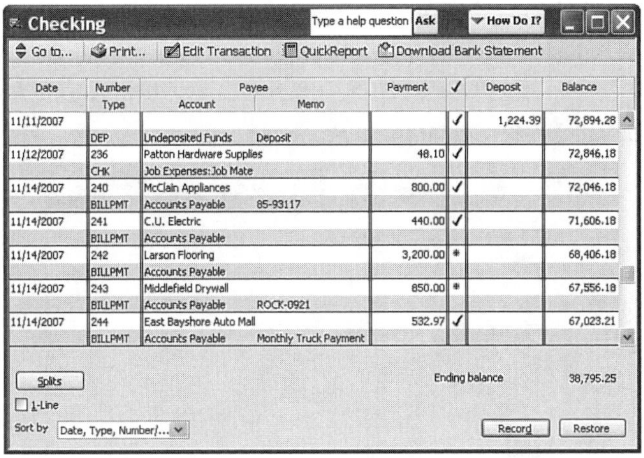

FIGURE 6.7

Transactions with a checkmark (✓) are previously cleared. Transactions with an asterisk (*) are currently in the process of being cleared.

Reviewing Uncleared Bank Transactions

If your bank account has previously been reconciled, reviewing your uncleared bank transactions is the best place to start when troubleshooting an incorrectly reconciled bank account.

Creating an Uncleared Transactions Detail Report

This report is one of the most useful to you as you research your bank reconciliation errors. You might want to memorize this report so that it can be reviewed again if needed.

You can create an uncleared bank transactions report by following these steps:

1. Click **Reports, Custom Transaction Detail**. The Display dialog opens. In the Report Date Range pane, select **All Dates**. If you have more than one bank account, choose **Total by Account list** to keep each bank account with separate totals. From the **Columns** pane, select the data you want to appear in the report.

2. Click the **Filters** tab. In the choose filter pane, with Account highlighted, select **All Bank Accounts**. Scroll down the Choose Filter list and select **Cleared**, and then click **No** next to the pane, as shown in Figure 6.8.

3. This report will be useful to you in the future, so go ahead and give it a specific name by clicking the **Header/Footer** tab and changing the Report Title as desired.

4. Click **OK** to create the report (see Figure 6.9).

5. Optionally, click **Memorize** to have QuickBooks store the report for future use. QuickBooks asks you to provide a name for the report.

6. Click **OK** to save the memorized report.

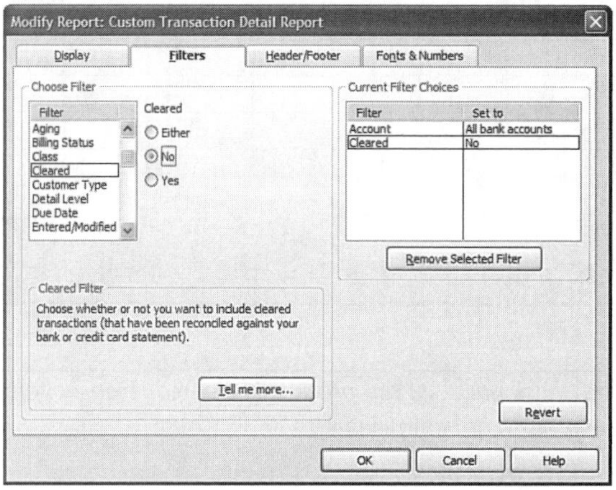

FIGURE 6.8

Filter the report to show only uncleared bank transactions.

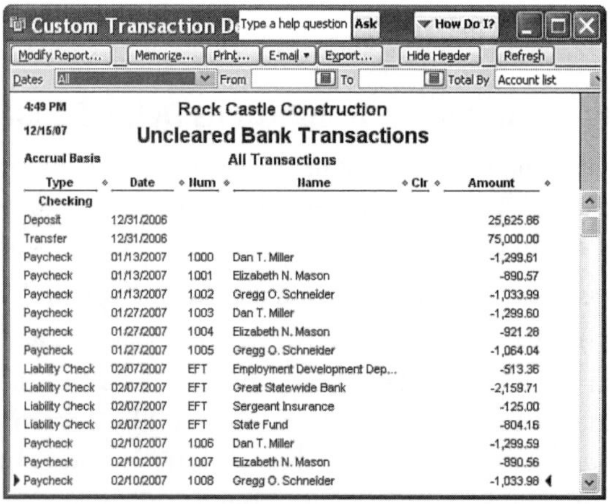

FIGURE 6.9

Create a customized report to easily view uncleared bank transactions.

Memorizing Reports

Memorizing customized reports for later use is easy. First make sure your Dates selection is appropriate. If your Dates selection is Custom, each time you create this report, it uses the custom dates. Selecting Dates, such as This Month-to-Date or any of the other choices, makes the memorized report more valuable in future months. Click Memorize in the report dialog. QuickBooks stores the report with the header name, or you can rename it. See Chapter 16, "Reporting Tips and Tricks," for detailed information on working with memorized report groups.

Another option is to add this report to your icon bar; with the report displayed, select View, Add <name of report> to Icon Bar.

Sorting Transactions

Another method for reviewing uncleared bank transactions is to open your bank register by choosing Banking, Use Register. On the lower left of the screen is a Sort By drop-down menu. Select the Cleared status. You can scroll through the register and view those transactions that are either cleared (check mark) in the process of being cleared (asterisk), or uncleared (no check mark or asterisk).

Often, a transaction that is cleared and should not have been cleared or a transaction that is uncleared and should have been cleared can be the cause of the opening balance not matching.

If you need to unclear a transaction or two, use your mouse pointer and double-click on the check mark next to the item in the bank register. QuickBooks replaces the check mark with an asterisk. You can also click once more to remove the asterisk if desired.

If you attempt to make a change to the cleared status of a transaction while in the bank register, QuickBooks warns you, as shown in Figure 6.10.

Using additional reporting tools in QuickBooks can help you find changes made to previously reconciled transactions. You will find that using a combination of the following reports when troubleshooting reconciliation errors is useful.

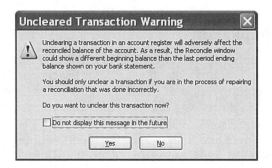

FIGURE 6.10

QuickBooks warns you when you remove the cleared status (check mark) from a transaction.

Reviewing Previous Bank Reconciliation Reports

If you determine that the file has been previously reconciled but no paper copy was kept, no need to worry. Click Reports, Banking, Previous Reconciliation. In the Select Previous Reconciliation Report dialog box, select the Statement Ending Date to view (see Figure 6.11). QuickBooks displays a list of all prior stored bank reconciliation reports. Choose from the following view options: Summary, Detail, or Both.

Additionally, you can view the reports in two ways:

- Stored PDF bank reconciliation—This stored report shows the bank reconciliation details as they were completed at the time the account was reconciled.

- Transactions cleared plus any changes—View this report to see how the bank reconciliation would look today, real-time.

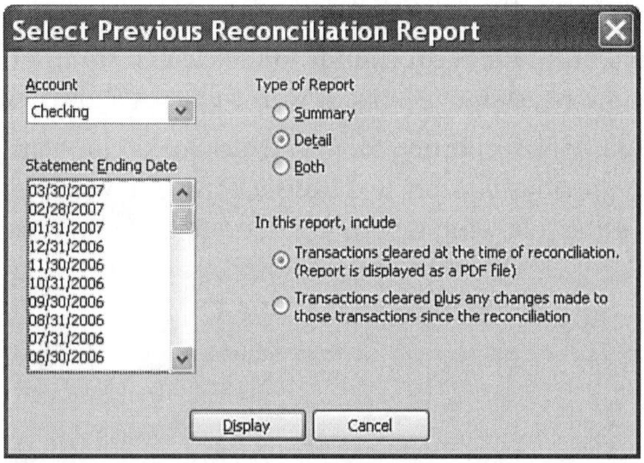

FIGURE 6.11

Select a previous bank reconciliation when troubleshooting errors.

Compare the stored PDF with the Transactions Cleared Plus Changes report. Any differences between the two should indicate what your discrepancies are. You might be able to find these discrepancies easily with the Reconciliation Discrepancy report, as discussed next.

Locating Bank Account Reconciliation Discrepancies

Click Reports, Banking, Reconciliation Discrepancy to open the specify account dialog. Choose the bank account from the drop-down menu and select OK to create the report. This report identifies any transaction that was modified after being cleared in the bank reconciliation process. For each transaction on this report, you see the modified date, reconciled amount, type of change (amount added or deleted), and the financial effect of the change (see Figure 6.12).

Date	Entered/Last Modified	Num	Name	Reconciled Amount	Type of Change	Effect of Change
12/31/2005	12/15/2007 14:40:15			10,571.57	Amount	49,428.43
11/01/2007	12/15/2007 17:15:37	227	Reyas Properties	-1,200.00	Amount	1,200.00
10/01/2007	12/15/2007 12:37:04		Dan T. Miller	-1,265.55	Deleted	1,265.55
10/15/2007	12/15/2007 12:37:25		Dan T. Miller	-1,272.75	Deleted	1,272.75
10/01/2007	12/15/2007 12:37:11		Elizabeth N. Mason	-954.29	Deleted	954.29
10/15/2007	12/15/2007 12:37:35		Elizabeth N. Mason	-905.13	Deleted	905.13
10/01/2007	12/15/2007 12:37:17		Gregg O. Schneider	-928.56	Deleted	928.56
10/15/2007	12/15/2007 12:37:42		Gregg O. Schneider	-819.09	Deleted	819.09
10/30/2007	12/15/2007 12:38:02	221	Dan T. Miller	-1,297.74	Deleted	1,297.74
10/15/2007	12/15/2007 12:37:54	211	Employment Devel...	-756.97	Deleted	756.97
10/15/2007	12/15/2007 17:11:59	212	Great Statewide B...	-6,465.58	Deleted	6,465.58

FIGURE 6.12
View details of previously cleared transactions that have been modified or deleted.

You can click Modify Report and add the user name that modified the transaction to help in identifying who made the change to the transaction.

After you have found the reconciliation discrepancy, you can view the Voided/Deleted Report (discussed in the next section) to help recreate the transaction(s).

Rescue Me!

Troubleshoot your bank reconciliation beginning balance differences with the Previous Reconciliation Discrepancy Report *before* completing the next month's reconciliation. Doing so is important because QuickBooks removes all detail from the discrepancy report when you complete a new reconciliation. This is due to QuickBooks determining that you have solved the issue or you would not have completed the next month's bank reconciliation.

This report does *not* track discrepancies caused by changing the bank account associated with a transaction.

Reviewing the Voided/Deleted Report

Another reporting tool to help locate problem transactions is the summary or detail Voided/Deleted Report. This report is available in newer versions of QuickBooks.

To create the Voided/Deleted Transactions Summary report, as in Figure 6.13:

1. Click **Reports, Accountant & Taxes**.

2. Select the **Voided/Deleted Transactions Summary or Detail** report.

If you are having trouble finding the problem, particularly when the beginning balance has changed, this report can help you find the transaction(s).

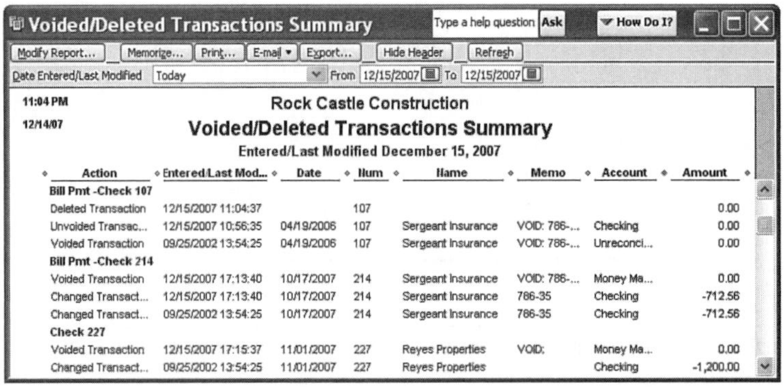

FIGURE 6.13

Use the Voided/Deleted Transactions Summary to locate transactions that are possibly causing your reconciliation errors.

Use this report for recreating the voided or deleted transactions as part of the process of fixing your bank reconciliations.

If there are more than a few transactions in error, restarting or undoing the previous bank reconciliation might be easier than researching each transaction marked as cleared.

Restarting a Previously Completed Bank Reconciliation

If your review shows a few minor issues with bank reconciliation accuracy, restarting your reconciliation might be the best action to take. To do so, click Banking, Reconciliation, Locate Discrepancies. The Locate Discrepancies dialog box appears. From this dialog box, click Restart Reconciliation.

Restarting your bank reconciliation retains your check marks on the cleared transactions, but enables you to put in a new statement date and ending balance. You can only restart the last month's banking reconciliation.

If you need to restart the reconciliation for more than one banking month, click Undo Last Reconciliation; you can repeat this undo for several months in a row all the way back to the first reconciliation if desired.

Undoing a Previous Bank Reconciliation

If you have determined that the integrity of the completed bank reconciliations is in question, you can easily undo each reconciliation, one month at a time. Click Banking, Reconciliation, and click Undo Previous Reconciliation. QuickBooks opens a dialog box, providing you with ample information about what to expect and recommending that you back up your company data file first (see Figure 6.14). As each month is undone, QuickBooks shows you the Previous Beginning Balance. You need only to undo bank reconciliations until you reach a statement where this amount agrees with the same month's bank statement beginning balance, so watch it closely.

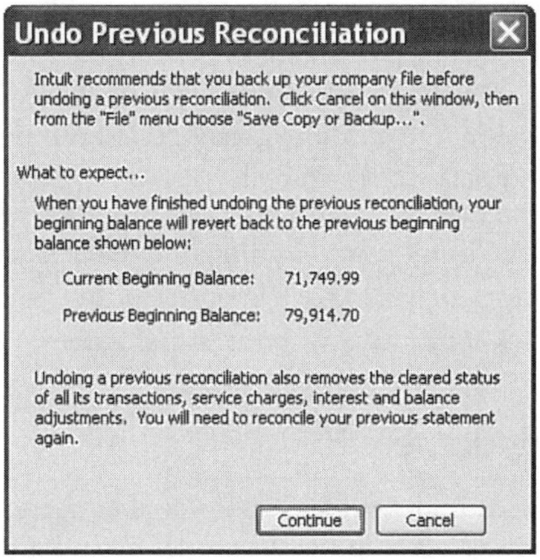

FIGURE 6.14

Details of what you can expect when you complete an Undo Previous Reconciliation process.

Click Continue after reviewing the message in Figure 6.14. You might undo the bank reconciliation one month at a time. You will know you are back to the first statement when the Undo Previous Reconciliation dialog shows the Previous Beginning Balance as 0.00. When you return to the Begin Reconciliation dialog, you no longer see a "last reconciled on date" or a "beginning balance" amount.

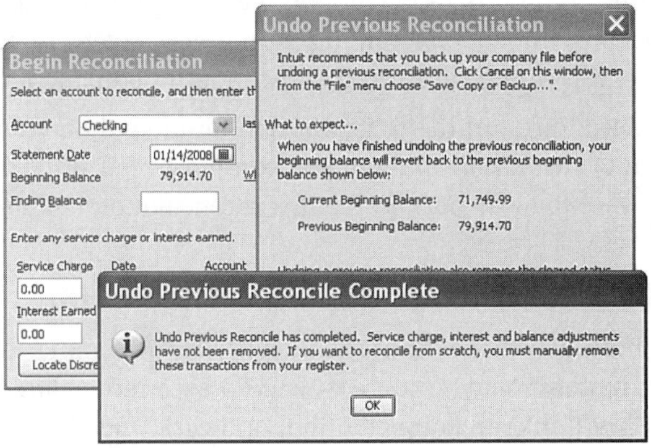

FIGURE 6.15

Message when the undo bank reconciliation is complete.

Digging Deeper

Use the Undo a Previous Bank Reconciliation feature when an incorrect statement date was entered on the bank reconciliation (refer to Figure 6.1 shown earlier). QuickBooks defaults the next bank statement date to 30 days from the last statement date. Before beginning the bank reconciliation in QuickBooks, verify that both the statement date and beginning balance are correct.

Now that all the bank reconciliations have been undone, you can begin reconciling the bank account each month. Match your reconciled activity each month in QuickBooks to your bank statement.

Digging Deeper

If your work is interrupted while you are reconciling a bank statement, you can click Leave in the Reconcile - Account dialog box; refer to Figure 6.6. Clicking Leave will keep the check marks you have assigned to transactions and let you finish your work at a later time.

Reconciling with an Adjustment

QuickBooks will create an adjustment to your bank account and financials if you choose to reconcile a bank account that does not have 0.00 in the Difference row of the Reconcile dialog box.

When you decide to reconcile with an adjustment for the difference amount (see Figure 6.16), you need to first consider the following:

- Have you made every attempt to find the difference using those techniques and reports you have read in this chapter?

- Is the difference as reported on the QuickBooks Reconcile dialog not a significant dollar amount?

If you can answer *yes* to these two items, let QuickBooks make an adjustment to your financials for the difference.

To reconcile with an adjustment created by QuickBooks, click Reconcile Now in the Reconcile - Account dialog or Enter Adjustment in Reconcile Adjustment dialog.

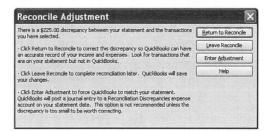

FIGURE 6.16

Letting QuickBooks enter an adjustment for the reconciliation difference.

QuickBooks details the amount of the adjustment and limits your choices to do the following:

- Return to Reconcile—Click this option if you want to look for the difference.

- Leave Reconcile—QuickBooks saves your changes, so you can return later and review your work.

- Enter Adjustment—This option forces QuickBooks' accounting to match your bank statement.

When you choose to Enter Adjustment, QuickBooks creates a journal entry and posts the difference to a Reconciliation Discrepancies expense account on your statement date, as shown in Figure 6.17. This is a new expense account automatically created by QuickBooks, first introduced in the 2006 version. Prior versions of QuickBooks find the adjustment posts to another QuickBooks-created account called Opening Bal Equity.

The Open Bal Equity account should not carry a balance after entering all startup balances. See Chapter 13, "Reviewing and Correcting the Opening Balance Equity Account," for more detail.

Profit & Loss Type a help question Ask ▼ How Do I? _ □ ✕	

Modify Report...	Memorize...	Print...	E-mail ▼	Export...	Hide Header	Colla

Dates Custom ▼ From 12/01/2006 🔳 To 12/31/2006 🔳 Column

10:07 PM
12/15/07
Accrual Basis

Rock Castle Construction
Profit & Loss
December 2006

	Dec 06
Expense	
Interest Expense	68.52
Job Expenses	
Subcontractors	1,000.00
Total Job Expenses	1,000.00
Reconciliation Discrepancies	-225.00
Tools and Machinery	810.00
Utilities	
Gas and Electric	122.68
Total Utilities	122.68
Total Expense	1,776.20
Net Ordinary Income	4,511.80

FIGURE 6.17

A journal entry reconciliation adjustment will be posted to a Reconciliation Discrepancies expense account on the Profit & Loss statement.

I never recommend reconciling with an adjustment. Sooner or later, you will have to identify what the adjustment was from and where it should be posted. However, making an adjustment for a small balance can often save time that would be better spent on activities that grow the business. Always put in place better processes so that these types of errors do not occur again.

 Digging Deeper

Any Balance Sheet type account can be reconciled, not just bank account types. Reconciling credit card accounts provides the same control over the accuracy of your financials. Did you know that any account that transactions flow in and out of can be reconciled? Do you have a car loan? Have you reconciled your car loan account to the lending institution's statement? Do you loan money to employees and then have them pay the loan back? These are all examples of accounts that would benefit from the same reconcile process used for bank accounts.

Chapter 7

Reviewing and Correcting Accounts Receivable Errors

- Accounts Receivable Forms and Workflow
- Preferences That Affect Accounts Receivable
- Reports to Review When Troubleshooting Accounts Receivable Errors
- Correcting Accounts Receivable Errors
- Unique Customer Transactions

It is not surprising to me and perhaps not to you either that the Accounts Receivable process is usually the most organized and "cared for" task in QuickBooks. Unlike reconciling a bank account, where no one needs to see the end result (so that task is often not completed), the process of producing a customer invoice is usually completed quickly because you have to provide a document to a customer to get paid.

What I have noticed over the years of consulting with clients is that many do not know the proper Accounts Receivable process. By following a recommended workflow, some of the more common errors can be avoided rather than having to be fixed at a later date.

Accounts Receivable Forms and Workflow

Within QuickBooks, you have some flexibility in how you handle your company's receivables workflow. Your company might use some or all of the forms listed in this chapter, depending mostly on the product or service that you sell. If you created your data file using the QuickBooks EasyStep Interview (see Chapter 1, "Creating a New QuickBooks Data File"), QuickBooks enabled all or some of the features discussed in this chapter depending on your answers to a few questions.

In the section titled "Preferences That Affect Accounts Receivable" in this chapter, I discuss the preferences that you can define after you determine what sales form or feature you need. Some of the forms and features are enabled automatically when QuickBooks first creates the data file.

Table 7.1 details the forms that are used in the Accounts Receivable module and their primary purpose.

Table 7.1 Accounts Receivable Forms	
Accounts Receivable Form Name	**Primary Purpose of Form**
Estimates	Create a job budget and proposal
Sales Orders	Record a committed sale
Invoices	Record the sale of services or products on account
Sales Receipt	Record the sale of services or products COD (Cash at the time of sale)

Accounts Receivable Form Name	Primary Purpose of Form
Receive Payment	Record customer payment of invoices
Online Payments	Download online customer payments (requires a monthly subscription)
Record Deposits	Recording the bank account deposit
Statement Charges	Assessing customers' recurring charges
Finance Charges	Assessed to customers with a past-due balance
Statements	Periodic statement provided to the customer of account activity
Refunds & Credits	Returns or credits given to customers

So whether you start with an estimate, sales order, or simply prepare an invoice for a customer, generally the proper workflow for recording a sale has at least these four steps:

1. Create an invoice, sales receipt, or statement charge.

2. Receive the customer payment.

3. Place the payment (automatically via a preference setting) into an Undeposited Funds account.

4. Complete the Make Deposits form.

Performing these related tasks in QuickBooks is easy from the Home page, as shown in Figure 7.1. Whether you are new to QuickBooks or are an experienced user, you will find the Home page useful in both getting around QuickBooks and in determining what the next transaction process should be. To modify the information on your Home page to match your company's specific workflow, click Edit, Preferences and select the Desktop View preference. Click the Company Preferences tab (must be logged into the data file as Admin or External Accountant user and in single user), and on the dialog shown in Figure 7.2 you can enable or disable features that will modify your Home page.

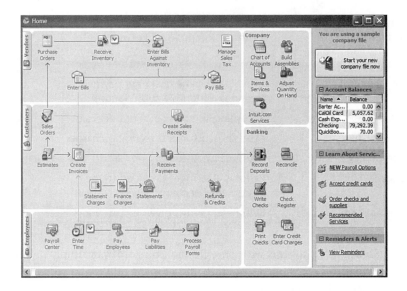

FIGURE 7.1

The QuickBooks Home page makes the Accounts Receivable workflow easy to follow.

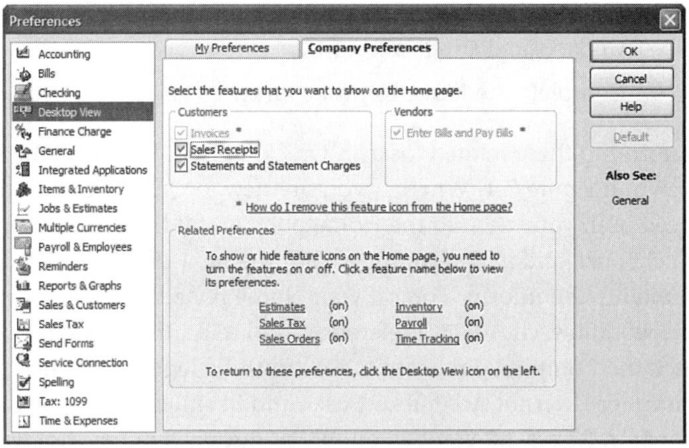

FIGURE 7.2

You can customize the Home page by enabling or disabling features within Preferences.

Preferences That Affect Accounts Receivable

You can simplify your Accounts Receivable tasks by setting certain QuickBooks preferences. Some of these preferences save you keystrokes, which can save data entry time.

Not every preference that affects Accounts Receivable impacts your financials directly. Some preferences simply enable specific features. To set preferences in QuickBooks, select Edit, Preferences and choose the type of preference on the left.

Preferences in QuickBooks come in two forms:

- My Preferences are settings that are unique to the user logging into the data file and are not shared by other users.

- Company Preferences are settings that are common for all users. When a preference is selected in the Company Preference window, the change or setting affects all users.

To set Company Preferences, open the file as the Admin or External Accountant user and switch to single-user mode (if you are using the data file in a multiuser environment).

Rescue Me!

The Admin user is the default user that is created when you create a new data file. Proper controls should be in place to allow only certain individuals to log into the data file as the Admin.

The sections that follow outline the preference settings that will improve your QuickBooks Accounts Receivable workflow.

Sales & Customers Preferences

These preference settings enable you to customize your QuickBooks, particularly around the tasks you have related to customers. You can also make it easy for your employees to do their daily tasks by customizing the Home page so that just the needed forms are available.

Company Preferences

To make changes to the Company Preferences for customer activities, you must first be logged in to the data file as the Admin or new External Accountant user and also be in single-user mode (choose File, Switch to Single User). Then, click Edit, Preferences and select the Sales & Customers preference.

Here are the specific preferences that are set for all users:

- **Sales Forms**—These settings enable you to set a default shipping method and FOB that will display on customer forms. Additionally, you can select to be warned when duplicate invoice numbers are detected.

- **Miscellaneous**—From the drop-down menu option, select the default invoice form you want to use when creating new customer invoices.

Digging Deeper

You can copy the QuickBooks-provided invoice forms and then modify them for your specific business needs, including adding your company's logo and rearranging the data fields on the invoice form.

To duplicate and then modify a form provided by QuickBooks, follow these steps:

1. Click **Lists, Templates**. A list of current templates displays.

2. Select with your mouse pointer the template you want to duplicate.

3. In the lower left of the displayed Templates dialog, click the **Templates** button. Choose the **Duplicate** menu option.

4. The Template Type dialog opens; place a mark in the radial button for the appropriate form type, choosing from Invoice, Credit Memo, Sales Receipt, Purchase Order, Statement, Estimate, or Sales Order.

5. After returning to the Templates dialog. Double-click to edit the newly created Copy of: <name of form>.

6. The Basic Customization dialog opens; you can assign attributes here, such as the font you use, place your logo on the form, and add additional business contact information to your invoice form.

7. Click the **Additional Customization** button to add or remove headers, columns, and footers, change the name of the columns, or perform other customizing choices.

8. Click the **Layout Designer** to modify column widths and select where the data will print and what the printed copy will look like.

You also can download ready-made custom invoice forms. Simply click Lists, Templates. On the Template List dialog, select the Templates button and choose Download Templates. Click OK to the optional message that you will need an Internet connection for the download. QuickBooks directs you to the QuickBooks Community Template Gallery for Forms, where you can download pre-made custom invoice forms as well as other types of forms.

- **Price Levels**—Click this box to enable the use of price levels. Create the price level by choosing Lists, Price Level and then associate this price level with a customer. Each time you sell a product or service to a customer with an assigned price level, QuickBooks defaults the sales price to match the price level. (This feature is available only in the QuickBooks Premier or Enterprise Solutions editions.) To assign a price level to a customer, from the Customer Center select a customer list item on the left. Click the Edit Customer button and choose the Additional Info tab. From the Price Level drop-down menu, select the proper price level to assign to this customer.

- **Sales Orders**—Similar to the Sales Forms preference settings, these settings enable the use of Sales Orders. For a description of the forms used in Accounts Receivable processes, see the section earlier in this chapter titled "Accounts Receivable Forms and Workflow." (This feature is only available in the QuickBooks Premier or Enterprise Solutions editions.)

- **Receive Payments**—These settings make it easier for you to assign customer payments to the customers' invoices.

  - **Automatically Apply Payments**—When you select this option and open the Receive Payment form, QuickBooks applies the recorded payment to an invoice of the same amount, or if no invoice amount matches exactly, the payment is applied to the oldest invoice.

  - **Automatically Calculate Payments**—When you select this option, you do not need to put a total in the Amount box on the Receive Payment dialog. QuickBooks calculates and prefills the amount as the sum total of each of the invoices marked as received.

  - **Use Undeposited Funds as a Default Deposit to Account**—When selected, this preference causes QuickBooks to place all customer payments into a current asset account that is automatically created by QuickBooks. Undeposited Funds are like a safe that holds your customer payments before they are taken to the bank for deposit.

 ## Digging Deeper

Do you have a balance in your Undeposited Funds Account? Be sure to read Chapter 8, "Reviewing and Correcting Errors with the Undeposited Funds Account," for more details on how to manage this account.

My Preferences

To make changes to the My Preferences for customer activities, click Edit, Preferences and select the Sales & Customers preference. Click the My Preference tab to select user-specific settings. These settings affect only the current logged-in user.

The following are the specific My Preferences:

- **Add Available Time/Costs to Invoices for the Selected Job**—You can choose whether to prompt users for time and costs to add, choose to not add any time and costs, or choose to have users prompted as to what they want to do when creating an invoice for a customer who has outstanding billable time and costs.

    Depending on the setting selected in My Preferences, you might see the message shown in Figure 7.3 displayed when you create an invoice for a customer who has outstanding billable time or costs.

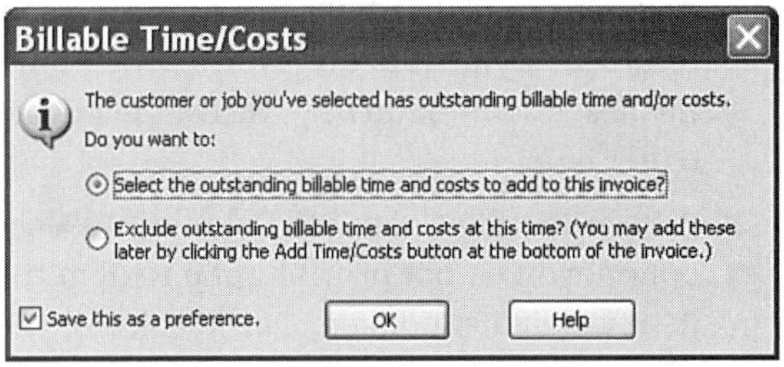

FIGURE 7.3
The user message displayed when creating an invoice for a customer with unbilled time or costs.

Checking Preferences

The Checking Preferences are for defining specific bank accounts for sales-related activities, such as depositing a customer's payment into a predefined bank account. Click Edit, Preferences and choose the Checking Preference from the left.

Company Preferences

There are not any Checking Company Preferences that would affect your workflow for Accounts Receivable.

My Preferences

The Open the Make Deposits form preference is optional; use it to specify the default bank account selected for making deposits. If you have multiple bank accounts that you make deposits to, you might not want to set a default on this tab.

Finance Charge Preference

Does your company charge late-paying customers a finance charge on open balances? If you do, you will want to set these preferences. Click Edit, Preferences and choose the Finance Charge Preference from the left.

Company Preferences

These preferences set your company's annual interest rate, minimum finance charge, grace period, and income account you want to credit. You must first be logged in as the Admin or External Accountant user and in single-user mode (choose File, Switch to Single-User). Then, to set the preferences, click Edit, Preferences and choose the Finance Charge preference from the left and then click on the Company Preferences tab.

The additional subsettings for each preference impact your financials and should be predetermined before you select the setting:

- **Assess Finance Charges on Overdue Finance Charges**—When selected, this option includes unpaid finance charge amounts previously invoiced in the new amount used to calculate additional late fees. Most clients do not take the time to invoice finance charges. However, my experience has shown that when you do, you become the "squeaky wheel" that does get paid.

- **Calculate Charges From**—The choices are Due Date or Invoice/Billed Date. For example, if you create an invoice for a customer for $1,000.00 that is due in 30 days, and you select the Calculate Charges From Due Date option, the amount is not considered overdue until 30 days from the invoice date when calculating the amount due.

- **Mark Finance Charge Invoices "To Be Printed"**—If this option is not selected, you can simply send a statement to the customer at the end of your billing cycle to communicate the amounts that are currently owed instead of sending an invoice for the finance charges assessed.

My Preferences

There are no My Preferences for Finance Charge settings.

Jobs & Estimates

The preference settings found in this section enable certain accounts receivable form types in QuickBooks. Click Edit, Preferences and select the Jobs & Estimates Preference from the left.

Company Preferences

These choices have to do with enabling specific estimating and invoicing features in QuickBooks as well as defining custom job status descriptions.

My Preferences

There are no My Preferences for Jobs & Estimates.

Reminders

The Reminders Preferences can be useful if you want QuickBooks to prompt you on certain accounts receivable lists or tasks. To set this preference, click Edit, Preferences and choose the Reminders Preference from the left.

Company Preferences

The Company Preferences for Reminders, as shown in Figure 7.4, sets the defaults for how QuickBooks shows reminders. Summary, List, or Don't Remind Me are the options. If you want to see the reminders, be sure to select the My Preferences setting also.

My Preferences

Users can specify whether they want to see the reminders when they open the QuickBooks data file. After the program is open, any user can click Company, Reminders at any time to review the reminder list entries.

Reports & Graphs

Choose Edit, Preferences and select the Reports & Graphs Preference from the left. The primary preference for this setting is found on the Company Preference tab, so you will need to be sure to log in to the data file as the Admin or External Accountant user and in Single-User Mode (choose File, Switch to Single-User Mode) if you have multiple users that access the same data file.

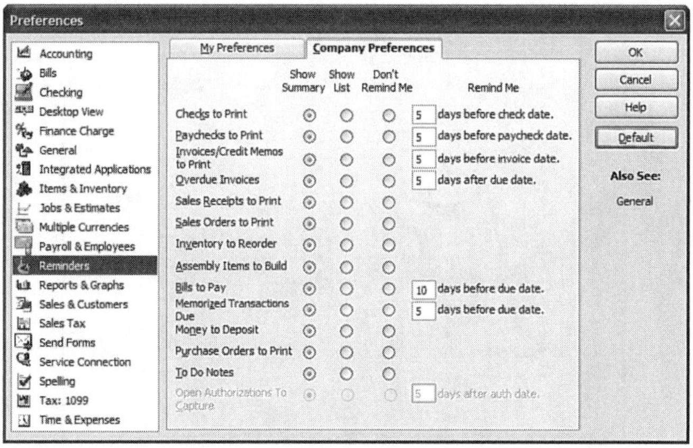

FIGURE 7.4

Set the default Company Preferences for how QuickBooks displays reminders for all users.

Company Preferences

Review each of the listed preferences; they will often impact how certain accounts receivable reports will calculate.

- **Summary Report Basis**—This preference is worth discussing because despite what you select on this pane, Accounts Receivable reports will always be in Accrual basis.

- **Aging Reports**—This option sets the default for calculating overdue invoices. You can choose to age from due date or from transaction date. Typically, aging from transaction date causes invoices to show as overdue earlier than if you aged from due date.

- **Format**—This option enables you to override the default header, footer, and font for the report. You should not override the Report Title, Subtitle, or Date Prepared because QuickBooks will accurately fill in this information for you each time you prepare the report.

- **Reports - Show Accounts By**—This setting offers you the following options for displaying reports:
  - **Name only**—Reports display only the name and account number (if the preference to enable account numbers is selected).
  - **Description only**—Reports display the description typed in the New or Edit Account dialog (see Figure 7.5). No account numbers are displayed on the reports.

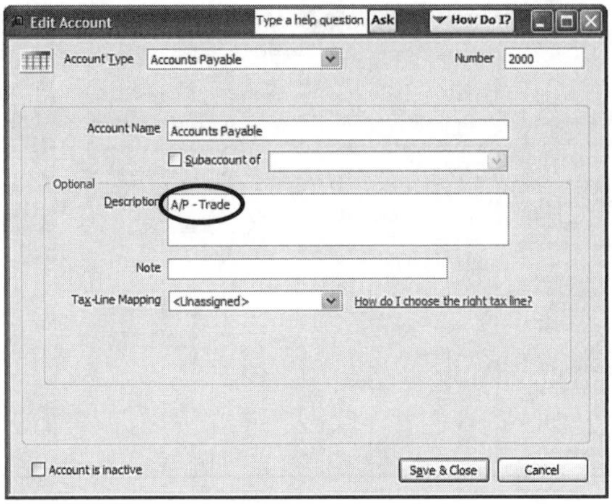

FIGURE 7.5

The Edit Account window with an optional description that will display on reports.

■ **Name and Description**—Reports display the account number (if enabled in preferences), the name, and in parentheses, the description as typed in the New or Edit Account dialog (see Figure 7.6).

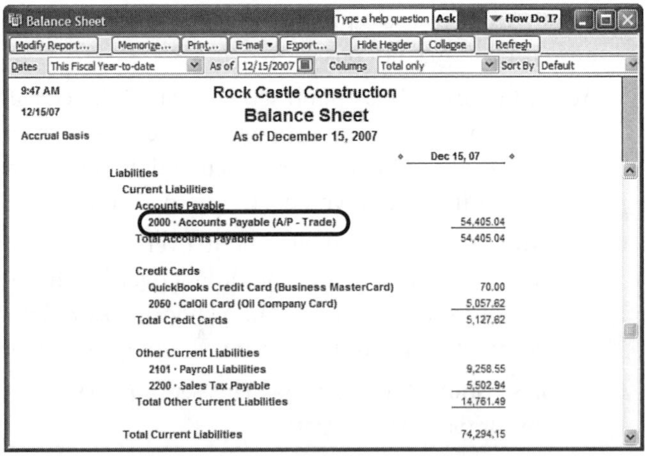

FIGURE 7.6

The report shows additional detail when you select the Name and Description reporting preference.

My Preferences

The My Preferences selections include:

- **Modify Report**—Selecting this automatically opens the Modify Report dialog with each created report.

- **Reports & Graphs**—Refresh options for reports and graphs when data changes. They prompt the user to refresh or not to refresh.

Sales Tax Preference

The Sales Tax Preference shown in Figure 7.7 is important if your business is required to collect sales tax on sales made to your customers. Be sure you have researched with the state tax authority for each state's proper guidelines are on collecting and remitting your sales tax in a timely manner.

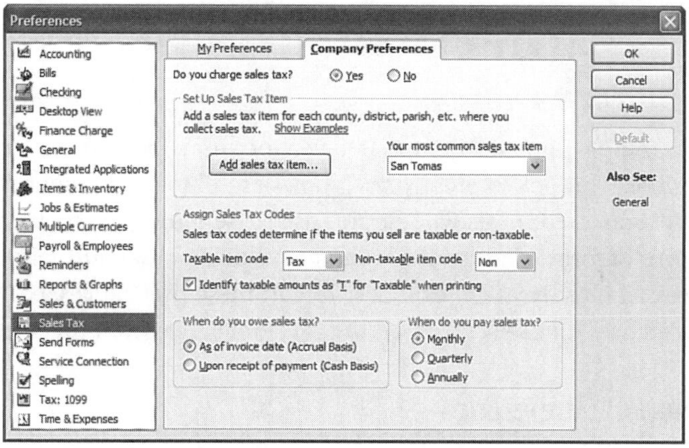

FIGURE 7.7

Company Preferences to set the Sales Tax defaults in QuickBooks.

Company Preferences

If your company charges and collects sales tax, then you need to enable the sales tax tracking by selecting Yes for the Do you charge sales tax? option.

- **Set Up Sales Tax Item**—When you click the Add Sales Tax Item button, QuickBooks takes you to the Add Sales Tax Item window where you create your sales tax items. You must also select your most common sales tax item.

- **Assign Sales Tax Codes**—This is the description you give to the code that is assigned to items you sell. Additionally, you can select to have a "T" print on your customer invoices for items that are taxable. This option is useful if on one invoice, you sell both taxable and non-taxable items.

- **When Do You Owe Sales Tax?**—If you are not sure what each state department of revenue requires, review their websites or simply make a call to get the correct information.

- **When Do You Pay Sales Tax?**—This setting simply tells QuickBooks what date range to select automatically when paying your sales tax. For example, if you select Monthly, QuickBooks will compute the amount owed for the previous month in the Pay Sales Tax Liability dialog.

My Preferences

There are no My Preferences for Sales Tax.

Send Forms

Beginning with QuickBooks 2008 version, users have the option to use Outlook, Outlook Express, or Windows Email to send emails from within QuickBooks. For users who do not use these mail types, you can still send emails of forms and reports using the QuickBooks email server, which is accessed directly in QuickBooks. To edit these preferences, click Edit, Preferences and select the Send Forms Preference from the left pane.

Company Preference

This preference enables you to set email defaults including a default message when sending supported forms or reports.

My Preference

Users can use Outlook, Outlook Express, Windows Email, or the QuickBooks email server as the preferred method for sending reports and forms from within QuickBooks. The benefit of using an email provider outside of QuickBooks is that a record of the sent email is stored in your Sent folder.

Spelling

Click Edit, Preferences and choose the Spelling Preference from the left pane to manage how QuickBooks can assist you with spelling on Accounts Receivable forms.

Company Preference

There is no Company Preference for the Spelling Preference.

My Preference

Users can set QuickBooks to check spelling before printing, sending, or saving supported forms.

Time and Expenses

The Time and Expenses Preference was greatly improved with the release of QuickBooks 2008. Time and Expenses is a specific method of invoicing common to the professional services industry, where customers' sales are invoiced based on hours or costs of the project plus an agreed-to markup or overhead fee.

The Time and Expenses Preference is available in QuickBooks Pro, Premier (all editions) and QuickBooks Enterprise (all editions). However, when creating a new data file, only the QuickBooks Premier Professional Services edition will default with the feature enabled. For all other editions, you need to enable the feature by following these steps:

1. Log in to the data file as the Admin or External Accountant user in single-user mode.

2. Click Edit, Preferences and select the Time and Expenses Preference from the left.

3. Click the Company Preferences tab. (More detail on the specifics of these settings is provided in the following section.)

Company Preferences

If your company needs to provide customers with an invoice showing your individual costs plus an added markup, you will want to enable this preference.

- **Time tracking**—Select Yes if you want to enable the timesheet function in QuickBooks where you can record employee or vendor hours to specific tasks and jobs. Additionally, in this preference you also indicate which day is the first day of your work week.

- **Invoicing options**—Create Invoices from a List of Time and Expenses enables the newly redesigned feature. When users enable this preference, there is a new menu option. You will find this menu option by clicking Customers, Invoice for Time and Expenses. This redesigned feature released with QuickBooks 2008 offers a single-screen view of each customer with billable time and expenses and the capability to create an invoice for the time with one click (see Figure 7.8).

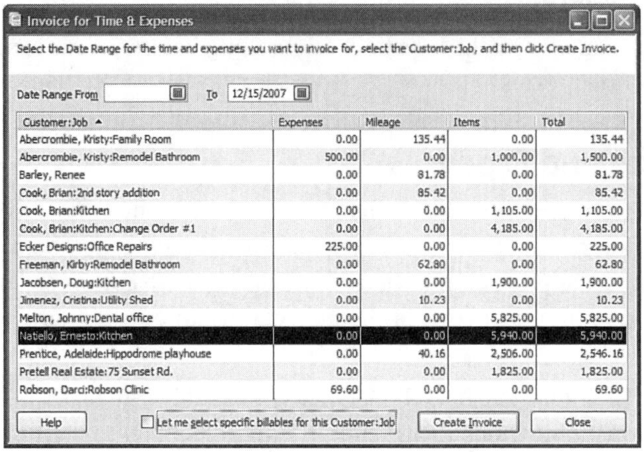

FIGURE 7.8

The new preference enables an easy-to-use invoicing list of customers with time and expenses.

Additionally, you can select to track reimbursed expenses as income. When enabled, QuickBooks provides an additional field on the Add New or Edit Account dialog indicating the income account to be used when invoicing for costs associated with this expense account (see Figure 7.9).

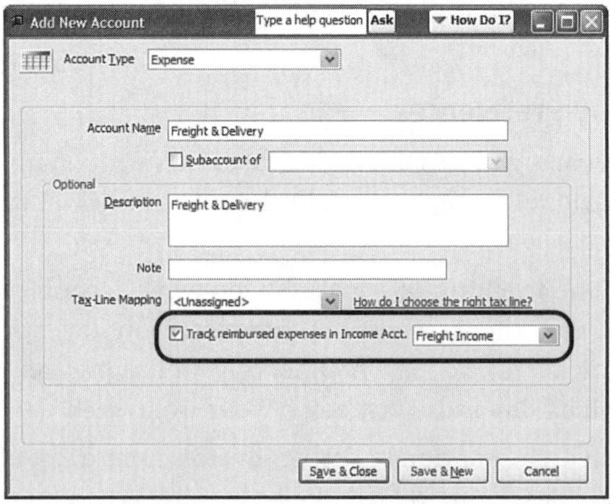

FIGURE 7.9

Selecting Track reimbursed expenses in Income Acct. adds the option to assign an income account for the reimbursed expenses on the Add New or Edit Account window.

My Preferences

There is no My Preference for the Time and Expenses Preference.

Reports to Review When Troubleshooting Accounts Receivable Errors

Sometimes the most difficult task when troubleshooting data errors is not knowing exactly what you are looking for. This section details some of the more common reports used to identify whether or not your Accounts Receivable information is correct.

Reconcile Balance Sheet Accounts Receivable Amount to A/R Aging Summary Total

With QuickBooks, you don't have to worry that the Balance Sheet report and Accounts Receivable Aging Summary report match because any transaction posting to the Accounts Receivable account must have a customer assigned. You want to make sure that you always create your Balance Sheet with the Accrual Basis (click Modify Report and select Accrual from the Display dialog that opens) because the A/R Aging Summary report provides details only on an Accrual Basis.

1. Select **Reports, Company & Financial, Balance Sheet Standard**. The selected report is displayed. For the date, select the As of Date you want to compare to. To accurately compare your Balance Sheet report with the A/R Aging Summary report, you must create your Balance Sheet in accrual basis. If your reporting preference default is for cash basis, you can change it temporarily to accrual basis—in the active report window, just click the Modify Report button at the top of the report and select Accrual as the reporting basis.

2. In the Balance Sheet report that displays, note the balance in your Accounts Receivable account(s) (see Figure 7.10).

3. Select **Reports, Customers & Receivables, A/R Aging Summary**, making sure the field shows the same date as the date selected in step 1. Figure 7.11 has been "collapsed" to make viewing the information easier. To expand to see more detail, click on the **Expand** button at the top of the report.

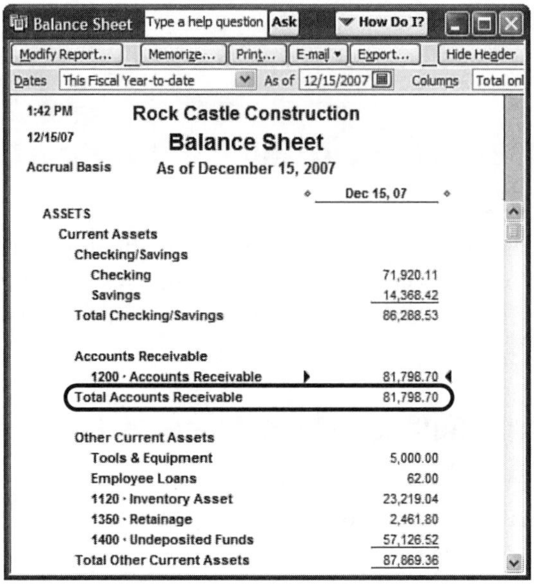

1:42 PM
12/15/07
Accrual Basis

Rock Castle Construction
Balance Sheet
As of December 15, 2007

	Dec 15, 07
ASSETS	
Current Assets	
Checking/Savings	
Checking	71,920.11
Savings	14,368.42
Total Checking/Savings	86,288.53
Accounts Receivable	
1200 · Accounts Receivable	81,798.70
Total Accounts Receivable	81,798.70
Other Current Assets	
Tools & Equipment	5,000.00
Employee Loans	62.00
1120 · Inventory Asset	23,219.04
1350 · Retainage	2,461.80
1400 · Undeposited Funds	57,126.52
Total Other Current Assets	87,869.36

FIGURE 7.10

Use your Balance Sheet report (accrual basis) to reconcile your Accounts Receivable report.

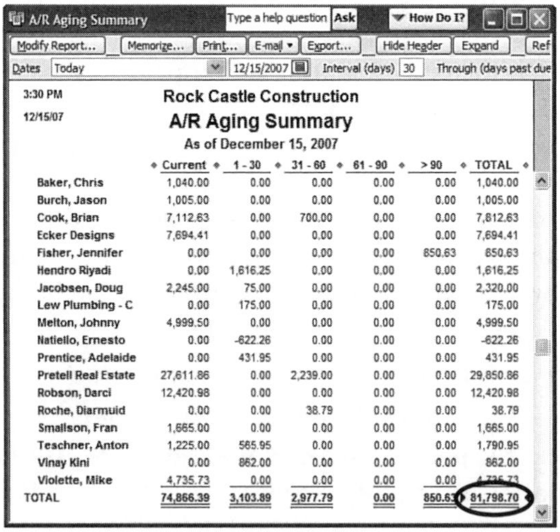

3:30 PM
12/15/07

Rock Castle Construction
A/R Aging Summary
As of December 15, 2007

	Current	1 - 30	31 - 60	61 - 90	> 90	TOTAL
Baker, Chris	1,040.00	0.00	0.00	0.00	0.00	1,040.00
Burch, Jason	1,005.00	0.00	0.00	0.00	0.00	1,005.00
Cook, Brian	7,112.63	0.00	700.00	0.00	0.00	7,812.63
Ecker Designs	7,694.41	0.00	0.00	0.00	0.00	7,694.41
Fisher, Jennifer	0.00	0.00	0.00	0.00	850.63	850.63
Hendro Riyadi	0.00	1,616.25	0.00	0.00	0.00	1,616.25
Jacobsen, Doug	2,245.00	75.00	0.00	0.00	0.00	2,320.00
Lew Plumbing - C	0.00	175.00	0.00	0.00	0.00	175.00
Melton, Johnny	4,999.50	0.00	0.00	0.00	0.00	4,999.50
Natiello, Ernesto	0.00	-622.26	0.00	0.00	0.00	-622.26
Prentice, Adelaide	0.00	431.95	0.00	0.00	0.00	431.95
Pretell Real Estate	27,611.86	0.00	2,239.00	0.00	0.00	29,850.86
Robson, Darci	12,420.98	0.00	0.00	0.00	0.00	12,420.98
Roche, Diarmuid	0.00	0.00	38.79	0.00	0.00	38.79
Smallson, Fran	1,665.00	0.00	0.00	0.00	0.00	1,665.00
Teschner, Anton	1,225.00	565.95	0.00	0.00	0.00	1,790.95
Vinay Kini	0.00	862.00	0.00	0.00	0.00	862.00
Violette, Mike	4,735.73	0.00	0.00	0.00	0.00	4,735.73
TOTAL	74,866.39	3,103.89	2,977.79	0.00	850.63	81,798.70

FIGURE 7.11

A/R Aging Summary report collapsed for reviewing report totals.

Your balance from the Balance Sheet report should match the total on the A/R Aging Summary. If it does not, the cause might be a "broken" transaction(s) link. You can detect these types of issues by choosing File, Utilities, Verify Data. If your Verify Data report comes back with a loss of data integrity, you should contact QuickBooks technical support to resolve it.

Review Open Invoices Report

Unlike the A/R Aging Summary report, the Open Invoices report is useful because it shows individual lines for each open item grouped by customer and job. This report is a "dynamic" report, meaning it will show open invoices only as of today's date and not some fixed time in the past without modifying as suggested in the following steps.

To create an Open Invoices report modified, so that you can compare it to your Balance Sheet report for some specific date in the past, follow these steps:

1. Click **Reports, Customers & Receivables, Open Invoices**. This report includes all payments made by your customer as of today's computer system date. If you are creating this report for some date in the past, it is important that you click **Modify Report**, select the **Display** tab, and click **Advanced**. In the **Open Balance/Aging** pane of the Advanced Options dialog, select the **Report Date** option (see Figure 7.12). This modification to the report enables you to see each invoice balance detail as of the report date. If you do not modify this report, QuickBooks displays the date on the report, but also reduces the balances owed for payments made after the report date.

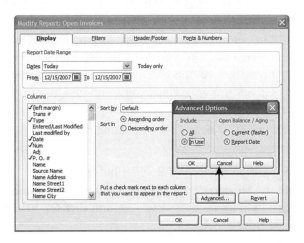

FIGURE 7.12

Open Invoices report, when modified, can be compared to the totals on your Balance Sheet report for some time in the past.

2. Compare your total from the Open Invoices report with the Balance Sheet Standard (Accrual Basis) Accounts Receivable total and make sure that it agrees (see Figure 7.13 and refer to Figure 7.10). If it does not agree, refer to the Verify Data utility discussed at the end of step 3 in the previous section.

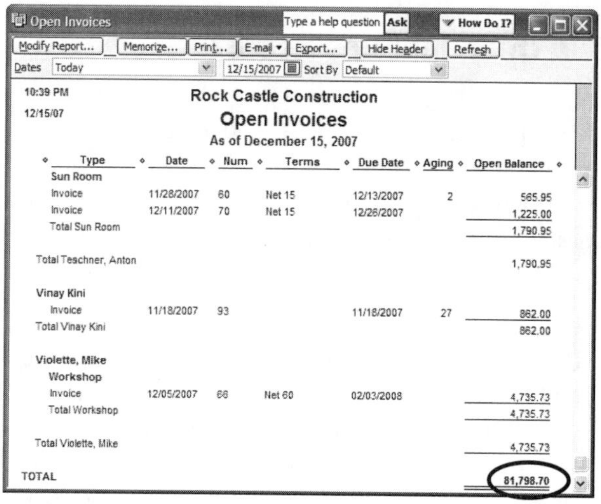

Type	Date	Num	Terms	Due Date	Aging	Open Balance
Sun Room						
Invoice	11/28/2007	60	Net 15	12/13/2007	2	565.95
Invoice	12/11/2007	70	Net 15	12/26/2007		1,225.00
Total Sun Room						1,790.95
Total Teschner, Anton						1,790.95
Vinay Kini						
Invoice	11/18/2007	93		11/18/2007	27	862.00
Total Vinay Kini						862.00
Violette, Mike						
Workshop						
Invoice	12/05/2007	66	Net 60	02/03/2008		4,735.73
Total Workshop						4,735.73
Total Violette, Mike						4,735.73
TOTAL						81,798.70

FIGURE 7.13

I prefer this report because it easily shows unpaid balances as well as any unapplied customer credits.

Generate a Missing Customer Invoices Report

Most companies have some control over the process of creating customer invoices. One control, especially if invoices are created manually in the field and later entered into QuickBooks, is to maintain a numeric invoicing pattern. Usually each invoice is one number larger than the prior invoice. This method of invoice recordkeeping can be an important process to have if your company is ever audited and you are required to provide a list of all invoices.

To see whether your data has any missing numbers in the invoicing sequence, follow these steps:

1. Click **Reports, Banking, Missing Checks.**
2. In the Missing Checks dialog, select **Accounts Receivable** from the Specify Account drop-down list, and click **OK** to generate the report (see Figure 7.14).

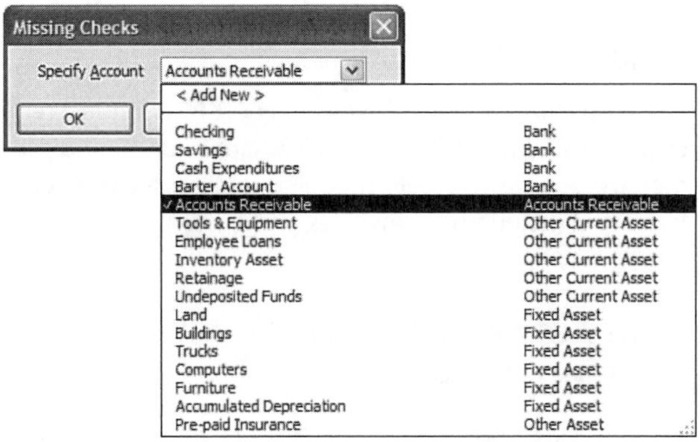

FIGURE 7.14

In the Missing Checks dialog, select the Accounts Receivable account.

3. I also recommend that you rename the report by choosing **Modify Report**, clicking the **Header/Footer** tab, and typing a new title for the Report Title field, such as **Missing Invoices**.

The newly created Missing Invoices report makes the process of identifying missing or duplicated invoice numbers easy (see Figure 7.15). Use this information to determine whether you need better company practices to avoid this situation. By default, this report shows only invoices that are greater than or equal to the value of -0-.

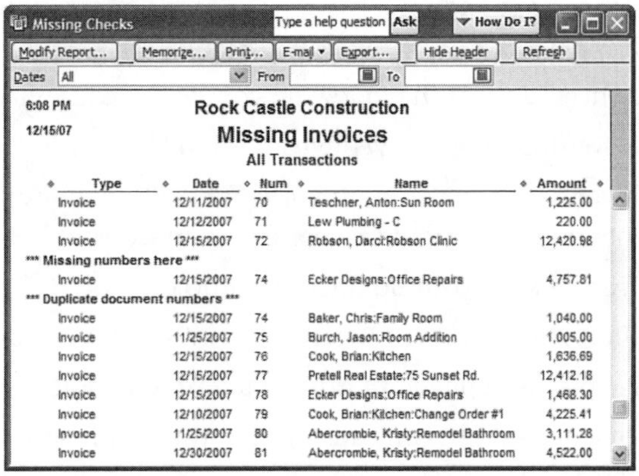

FIGURE 7.15

This modified report shows a list of all missing or duplicated invoice numbers.

Digging Deeper

The customized Missing Invoices report filter omits credit memos and customer payments. If you use the same numbering scheme for credit memos, you need to set an additional filter for multiple transaction types and include both invoices and customer payments.

When an Accounts Receivable Balance Appears on a Cash Basis Balance Sheet

The nature of Cash Basis reporting implies that you would not see an Accounts Receivable balance on your Balance Sheet. Table 7.2 describes how accounts receivable transactions are handled for both Accrual and Cash Basis reporting.

Table 7.2 Accounts Receivable on Accrual and Cash Basis Balance Sheet

Form Name	Accrual Basis	Cash Basis
Invoice	Revenue recognized on date of invoice	Revenue recognized on date of customer payment
Sales Receipt	Revenue recognized on date of sales receipt	Revenue recognized on date of sales receipt
Credit Memo	Revenue reduced on date of credit memo	No effect

So, why exactly do I see an Accounts Receivable balance on a Cash Basis Balance Sheet? Any of the following can be the cause:

- A/R transactions have items posting to other Balance Sheet accounts.
- Inventory items on an invoice or credit memo (typically, inventory management should be done only in Accrual Basis reporting).
- Transfers between Balance Sheet accounts.
- Unapplied Accounts Receivable customer receipts.
- Payments applied to future-dated Accounts Receivable invoices.
- Preferences that contradict each other. (This situation can happen if you select Cash Basis on your Summary Reports, but Accrual Basis as your Sales Tax preference.)
- Data corruption (click File, Utilities, Verify Data to check for data corruption).

When You Have Accounts Receivable Balances on a Cash Basis Balance Sheet

What can you do if you do have an Accounts Receivable balance on your Cash Basis Balance Sheet? First, modify the following report, as shown in Figure 7.16, to help you locate the transactions making up this balance:

1. Click on **Reports, Company & Financial**.

2. Select **Balance Sheet Standard**.

3. Click the **Modify Report** button.

4. The Display tab opens. Select **Cash** for the report basis.

5. Click **OK**.

6. With your mouse pointer, double-click the **Accounts Receivable** amount in question.

7. The Transaction by Account report is created.

8. Click the **Modify Report** button. The Display dialog opens.

9. For the **Report Date Range**, remove the **"From"** date and leave the **"To"** date.

10. Select the **Advanced** button, and from the **Open Balance / Aging** pane, select **Report Date**.

11. Click the **Filters** tab.

12. In the **Choose Filters** pane, scroll down to select **Paid Status**.

13. Select the Open for Paid Status radial button.

14. Click **OK**.

Look for transactions that fall into any of the categories described previously. Figure 7.17 shows that an item was used on Invoice No. 69 that debited another Balance Sheet account named Retainage. Any item used on a customer invoice that is mapped to another Balance Sheet account will display on a Cash Basis Balance Sheet report. (See Chapter 3, "Reviewing and Correcting Item List Errors," for a discussion of setting up items.)

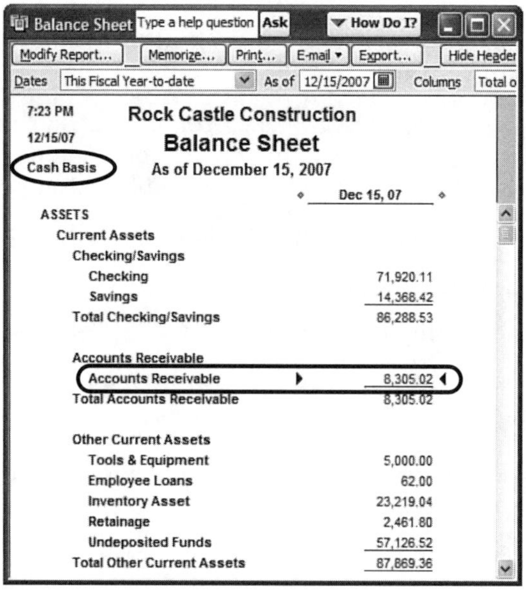

FIGURE 7.16

The Cash Basis Balance Sheet shows an Accounts Receivable balance.

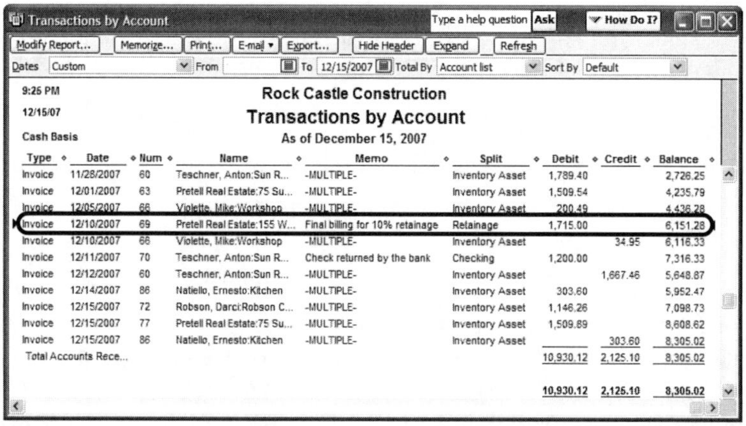

FIGURE 7.17

This modified report identifies the individual transactions that are included in the Accounts Receivable amount showing on a Cash Basis Balance Sheet.

So far, I have identified preferences that affect Accounts Receivable and reports to identify common errors. The next section discusses how you can easily fix these errors.

Correcting Accounts Receivable Errors

After you have identified the errors in Accounts Receivable, you need to determine the best method to correct the errors. When deciding which method is best, you should ask yourself the following:

- **Are the errors in an accounting year that I have already filed a tax return for?** If yes, then adjusting these transactions by dating the modifying entry in the current tax year and not modifying the original transaction is best. Some methods listed in this section will not enable you to select a date different from the original transaction date.

- **Are the errors significant in the dollar amount, collectively or individually?** If yes, you should obtain the advice of your accountant before making any adjustments so changes that will impact your tax status are carefully considered.

- **Am I going to fix detail or summary information?** In other words, are you going to fix individual invoices or correct a group of customer invoices with one adjusting transaction?

- **Am I modifying an invoice with sales tax recorded on the invoice?** If yes, refer to Chapter 12, "Reviewing and Correcting Sales Tax Errors," for a detailed discussion on adjusting invoices with sales tax. These corrections should be made with transactions dated in the current accounting month.

Removing an Open Balance from a Customer Invoice

There are several reasons you might have open balances on your Accounts Receivable invoices. There are also several methods to correct overstated or understated balances, each with its own impact on your company's financials.

If you are an accounting professional, you will want to review the detail in Chapter 17, "New for 2009! Detecting and Correcting with the Client Data Review Feature," in the "Fix Unapplied Customer Payments and Credits" section. This is a new time-saving feature available with the QuickBooks Premier Accountant 2009 and QuickBooks Solutions Enterprise Accountant 9.0. Accounting professionals might also access this feature by logging into a client's Pro or non-Accountant Premier data file using the new External Accountant user type, as detailed in Chapter 17.

Included in the Client Data Review (CDR) used primarily by accountants, this new feature streamlines applying open customer payments and credits to open customer invoices.

Writing Off a Customer Balance by Modifying the Original Customer Receive Payment Form

The method of modifying the original customer payment form to write off a customer balance records the change as of the date of the receive payment transaction and allows only a write-off amount equal to the underpayment amount.

If the amount due is an insignificant amount, you might not want to take the time to collect it. The easiest method of dealing with it would be to write off the remaining amount on the date the receive payment is recorded. If you do not write off the remaining amount, QuickBooks will warn you of the underpayment. You can also use this method after the payment is recorded by returning to the receive payment document.

Click Customer Center from the Home page and select the appropriate customer, from the show drop-down, select Payments and Credits or just Received Payments and any other date criteria you want to use, as shown in Figure 7.18.

FIGURE 7.18

You can easily find customer payments from the Customer Center.

Double-click the selected customer payment to open it. In the example shown in Figure 17.19, the customer paid $1.00 less than the amount due. Easily write off this amount by selecting Write Off the Extra Amount on the lower left of the Receive Payments dialog. QuickBooks then asks you to identify the account to assign the write-off amount to.

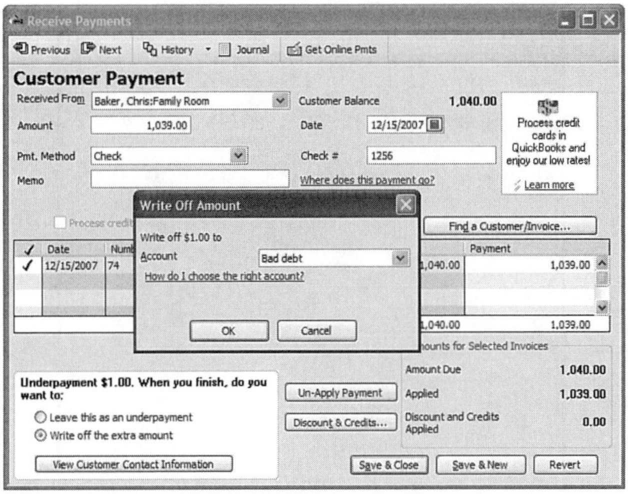

FIGURE 7.19
When you select to write off an amount due, QuickBooks requires that you assign the amount to an account.

Recording a Discount to Remove a Customer Balance

Another way to remove an open customer balance is to record a discount. This method records the change as of the date of the receive payment transaction. A discount can be recorded initially when the customer's short payment is recorded, or on a later date by creating a new receive payment document without placing any dollars in the Amount field and choosing the Discounts & Credits option. However, the discount amount cannot be in excess of the amount due.

Typically, the difference between a write off and discount is the placement on the Profit & Loss statement. A write off is usually used when the debt has gone bad and cannot be collected. In contrast, the discount is used when you decide not to collect the debt or you are reducing the sale price.

To record a discount, from the Receive Payment window, simply click the Discount & Credits button in the lower center. Similarly to the Write Off Amount window, you will be asked to identify an account to post the amount to (see Figure 7.20).

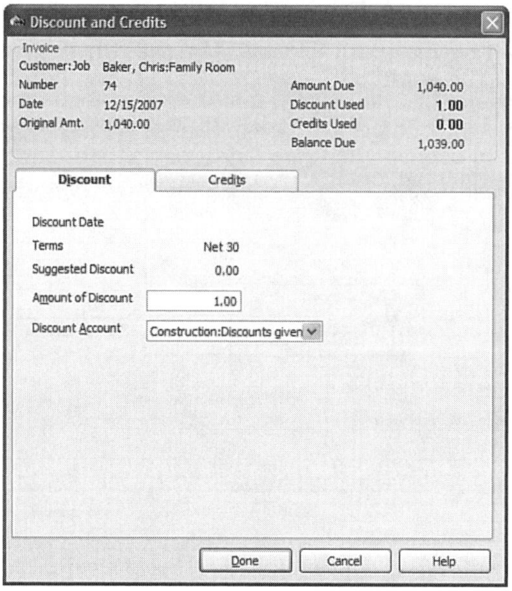

FIGURE 7.20

From the Discount and Credits window, select the account to post the discounted amount to.

Caution When Adjusting Receive Payment Transactions

Before adjusting your Accounts Receivable, you should review the Open Invoices report by choosing Reports, Customers & Receivables, Open Invoices Report as of today's date. If the amount due is not showing open now, but the report created for a prior date did, you might need to review the date recorded in the Receive Payment window.

You can verify the accuracy of your recorded payment date by clicking History on the top center of any open invoice form, as shown in Figure 7.21. From the Transaction History - Invoice window, you can highlight the payment in question and click Go To.

However, if the payment has been included in a deposit, you will not be able to modify it unless you first remove it from the deposit form. Simply use the same process of selecting History from the Receive Payment window, highlighting the deposit, and clicking Go To (see Figure 7.22). If the payment has been included on a Make Deposit form, you can follow the instructions in the section titled "Payment Applied to the Wrong Customer or Job" to remove the receive payment from the recorded deposit.

FIGURE 7.21

Select History from the top of any invoice form to see a list of the payments or credits applied to the invoice.

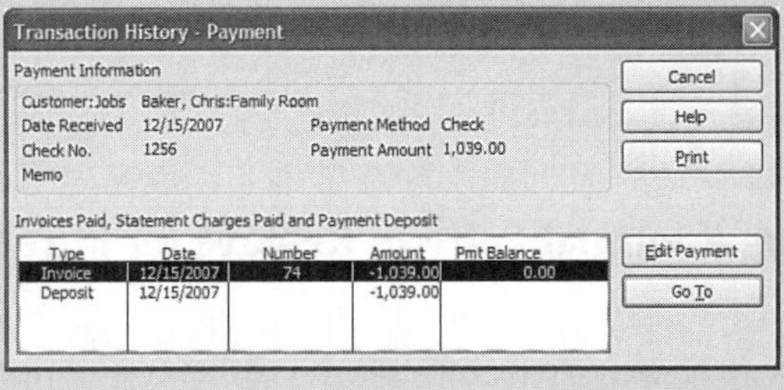

FIGURE 7.22

If you need to modify a payment already deposited, you can easily get to the deposit by clicking History from the Receive Payment window.

Recording a Credit Memo to Remove a Balance Due

The most accurate method for removing a balance due is to record a credit memo, because it creates a good audit trail. Additionally, you can date the credit in a period you want to reduce the appropriate income account and, if applicable, sales tax due.

1. From the **Customer** menu, select **Create Credit Memos/Refunds**.

2. In the dialog that displays and using the same item(s) on the original invoice, create a credit memo that totals the amount being credited.

3. After the memo is created, select the **Use Credit To** icon on the top right, as shown in Figure 7.23, to apply the credit to an invoice. QuickBooks then saves the credit memo and provides a list of all open invoices available to apply the credit to.

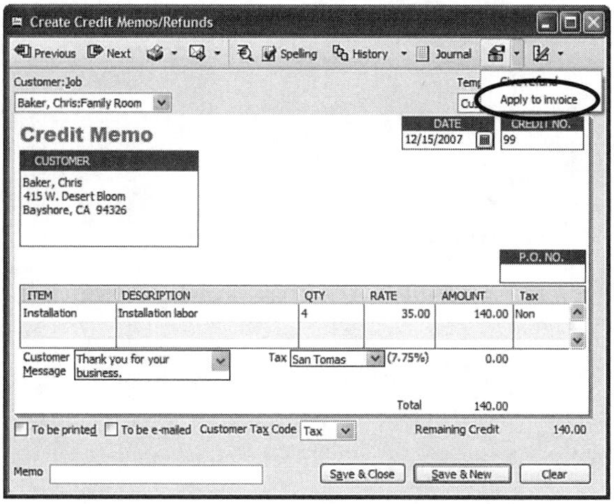

FIGURE 7.23

Apply a credit memo to a customer's invoice directly from the Create Credit Memos/Refunds dialog.

Recording a Journal Entry to Remove (or Increase) a Customer Balance

Another way to remove or increase a customer balance is to record a journal entry. This type of transaction is commonly used at tax time by the company's accountant when making adjustments to Accounts Receivable.

If you are going to record a Journal Entry adjustment, you need to keep in mind the following:

- Only one customer is allowed per Journal Entry.
- If the General Journal Entry has other noncustomer-related adjustments, the first line of the journal entry should remain blank.
- The date of the General Journal Entry is the date the transaction will impact your financials both for Accrual or Cash Basis.
- You can enter and apply one lump sum to multiple open customer invoices.

Rescue Me!

Did you know that if you use a customer on the first line of a journal entry, every other adjustment made—even noncustomer adjustments—will display on the Profit & Loss by Job report? This situation is due to the first line of any journal entry being a source line and causing a relationship with transactions below the first line.

To avoid this problem, always leave the first account line of a journal entry blank, as shown in Figure 7.24. Including a memo on the first line is perfectly acceptable.

1. Click **Company, Make General Journal Entries**, and in the form that displays, record a debit (to increase Accounts Receivable) or credit (to reduce Accounts Receivable), as shown in Figure 7.24. Be sure to assign the customer name to each line (except the first line, see the previous Rescue Me) so that a Profit & Loss by Job report accurately shows the adjustment.

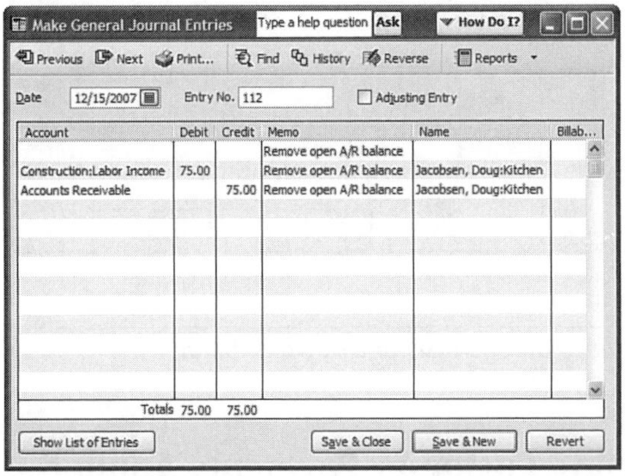

FIGURE 7.24

General Journal Entry created to remove an Accounts Receivable balance.

2. You now need to assign the General Journal Entry to the appropriate customer invoice. From the **Customer** menu, select **Customer Center**. Select the correct customer from the list on the left, and in the Show drop-down menu, select **Invoices**. Double-click the appropriate invoice list item.

3. The Create Invoices dialog opens; select **Apply Credits**. QuickBooks then provides a list of available credits to choose from (see Figure 7.25).

4. On the **Apply Credits** dialog that opens, select the appropriate credits by placing a check mark next to the credit. Click **Done** to assign the credit(s) to the customer invoice form.

5. Click **Save & Close**.

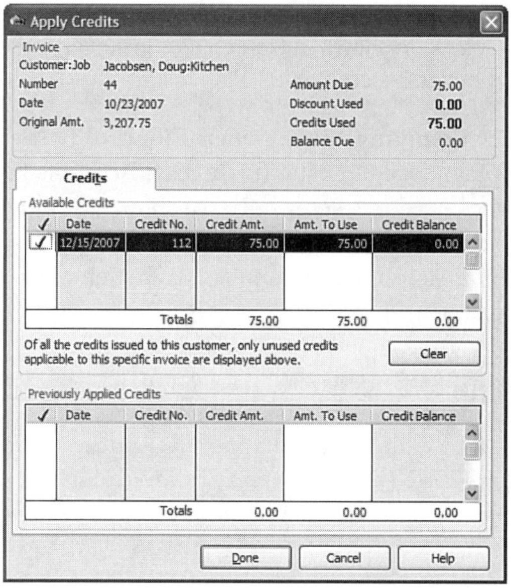

FIGURE 7.25

Apply an open credit to an open customer invoice balance.

Correcting Customer Payments Applied to the Incorrect Invoice, Customer, or Job

Applying the customer's payments exactly as the customer intended is important. If you apply the customer's payment to an invoice of your own choosing, communicating any discrepancies with open invoice balances can be more confusing than necessary.

However, many times your customer does not provide you with the correct invoice number and you apply it to an incorrect invoice. QuickBooks makes changing how you applied the payment to an invoice easy.

Payment Applied to the Wrong Invoice Number

If, after you review your customer's records with yours, you find you have applied the payment to the wrong invoice, follow these steps to unapply the payment and then reapply to the correct invoice:

1. From the **Customer** menu, click the **Customer Center**.

2. On the list on the left, select the appropriate customer.

3. In the pane to the right of the customer list, select the **Show** drop-down menu list, select **Received Payments**.

4. Optionally, choose specific payment methods or select a specific date range from the appropriate drop-down menus.

5. QuickBooks will list all Received Payment transactions for this customer.

6. Double-click the payment that was misapplied.

7. The Receive Payments dialog opens, as shown in Figure 7.26. Remove the check mark from one invoice and place it next to the correct invoice. Be careful that the total amount of the payment total does not change. Click **Save & Close**.

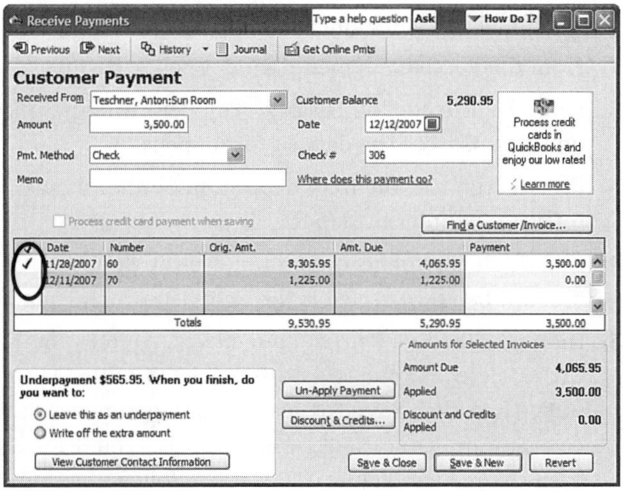

FIGURE 7.26
To change the invoice a customer payment is assigned to, remove the check mark in front of the invoice number.

Payment Applied to the Wrong Customer or Job

From the Customer Center, find the appropriate customer, filter for Received Payments, and locate the payment in question. See the previous section for specific steps to locating the payment.

Determine whether the payment has already been included on a deposit form by clicking History in the Receive Payments screen. If you attempt to change the customer name on the payment screen, QuickBooks warns you that the payment first needs to be deleted from the deposit (see Figure 7.27).

FIGURE 7.27

The warning that displays if you attempt to change a customer name on a customer payment already included in a deposit amount.

If the payment has been included on a deposit form, follow these steps to correct the customer or job assigned:

1. From the Receive Payments window, click **History**.

2. From the Transaction History - Payment window, select the **Deposit** and click **Go To**. The deposit form opens.

3. Record on paper the total deposit amount and date. You will need this information later in step 8.

4. If multiple payments are on the deposit, go to step 5. If the payment amount being corrected is the only deposit line item, then go to step 9.

5. Highlight the line item to be removed, as in Figure 7.28, and press **Ctrl+Delete** on your keyboard. Click **OK** to the delete warning message. Then click **Save & Close**. This step removes the line item from the deposit form. QuickBooks will also warn you if the item has previously been cleared (see Figure 7.29). If you follow the steps carefully, you will restore your deposit back to the correct amount and you will not have any reconciliation differences.

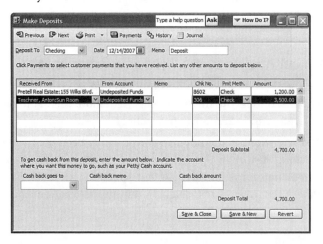

FIGURE 7.28

Select the line item and on your keyboard use the Ctrl+Delete key to easily remove entire line.

FIGURE 7.29

QuickBooks provides a warning message when you attempt to delete the customer payment from a deposit form.

6. Locate the customer payment that was in error and change the Customer or Job assigned.

7. Return to the bank register and locate the deposit form. Double-click the deposit. With the deposit form open, select **Payments** at the top and place a check mark next to the payment with the corrected Customer or Job (see Figure 7.30). Click **OK** to add the payment to the deposit form.

8. Verify that the total of the deposit agrees with the original amount you recorded on paper. When this transaction is saved with the same original amount, your bank reconciliation will not show a discrepancy. The process is now complete (see Figure 7.31).

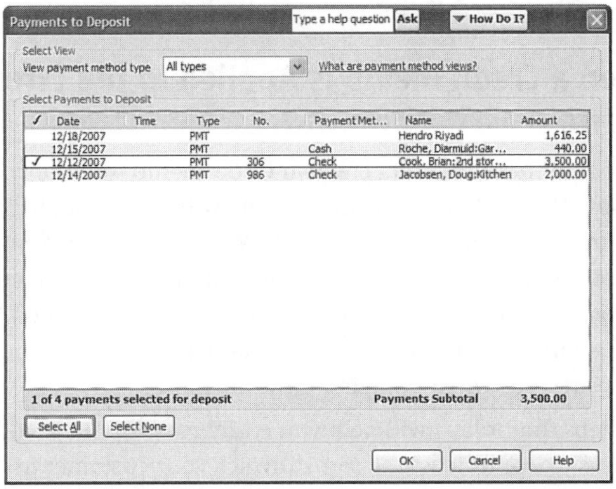

FIGURE 7.30

Click Payments at the top of the deposit form to add the corrected receive payment.

9. If the payment you are correcting is the only deposit line item, then first create a **Receive Payment** by clicking on **Customers, Receive Payments** and record the information for the correct customer or job.

Then, follow steps 7 and 8 to assign your newly created payment to the existing deposit. Next, delete the incorrect line item and save the deposit.

10. From the **Customer Center**, locate the incorrect payment and void or delete it.

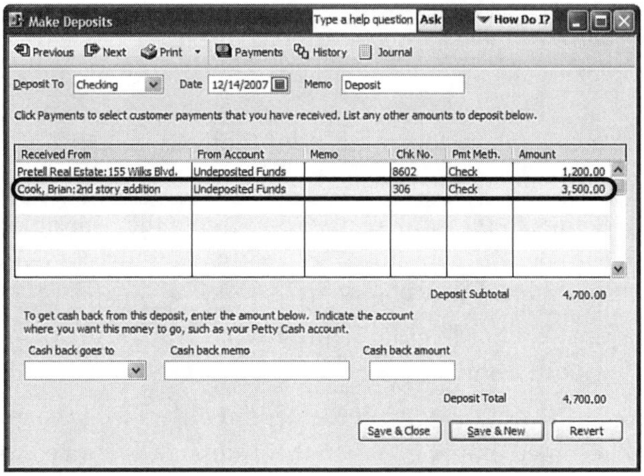

FIGURE 7.31

Deposit now shows corrected Customer and Job.

When a Credit Memo Is Applied to the Wrong Customer Invoice

It often happens that you create a credit memo and apply it to a specific invoice. Then, when you communicate with the customer, you find out he or she applied it to a different invoice. When you are making those credit and collections calls, the discrepancy can end up costing you critical time in getting paid on invoices that you show as open. If in the end the total due from the customer remains the same, I usually find it easier to agree with the customer's records when applying credit memos.

The steps that follow will help you easily reassign the credit memo to the correct invoice, or at least the same invoice your customer assigned it to. Without agreeing with the customer, your collections process would be delayed as both parties sort out what remains unpaid.

1. From the **Customer Center**, locate the customer that had the credit memo applied incorrectly. If you are not sure, simply click the Customer Center's **Transactions** tab and select **Credit Memos** from the list of available transactions. You can filter for **Open** or **All Credit Memos**

as well as transaction dates to narrow your search, as shown in Figure 7.32.

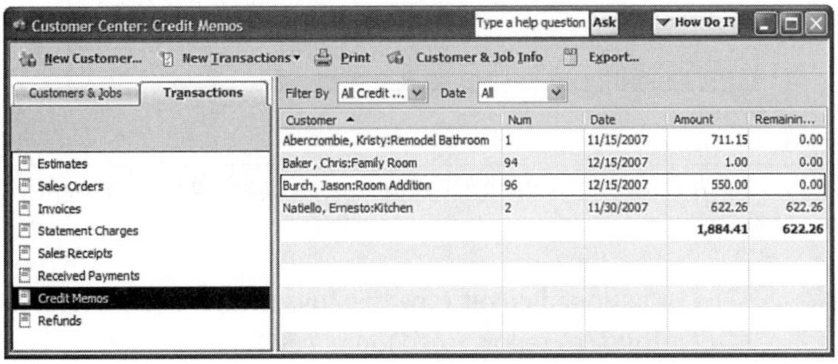

FIGURE 7.32

Using the Transactions tab of the Customer Center can make it easy to see all transactions of one type.

Digging Deeper

Did you know that you can click on the headers in any of the columns, as shown in Figure 7.32, and QuickBooks will sort the data by that column?

2. To reassign the incorrectly assigned credit memo to another invoice, open the credit memo and change the Customer or Job name. Click **Save & Close** to save the reassigned credit memo.

3. QuickBooks warns that switching between customers can have negative effects for sales tax. Click **OK** if you want to change it, as in Figure 7.33.

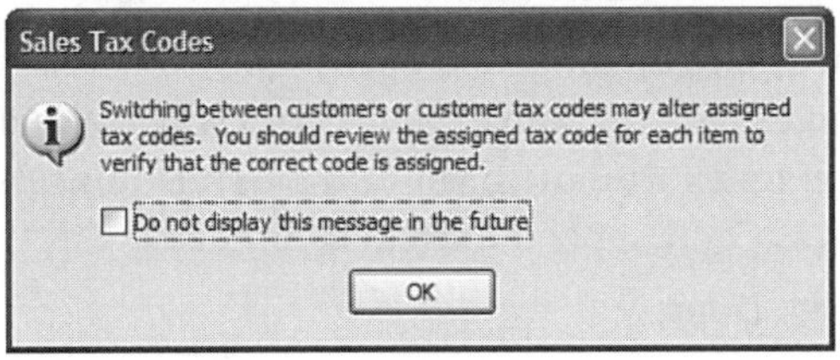

FIGURE 7.33

QuickBooks warns the user about changing credit memos between customers or tax codes.

QuickBooks warns you, as shown in Figure 7.34, that the transaction is connected to other transactions. Click **Yes** if you want to make the change.

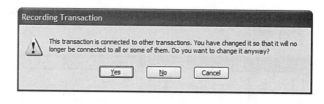

FIGURE 7.34

QuickBooks warns that the credit memo was previously applied and saving these changes will affect those transactions.

The unassigned credit now displays in the Customer Center and on the Open Invoices report (see Figure 7.35).

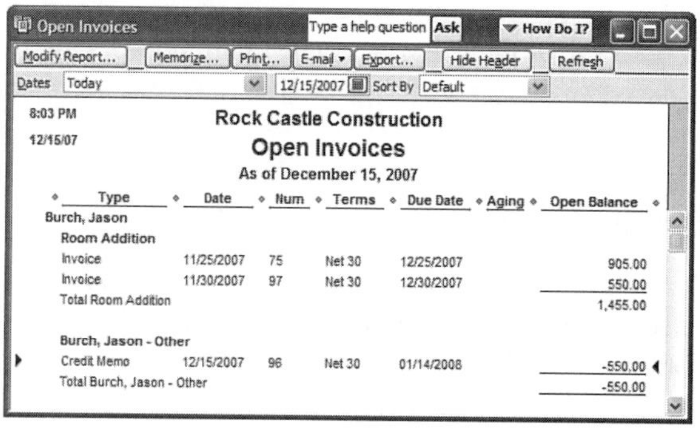

FIGURE 7.35

The open credit is now available to assign to the correct invoice.

4. Use the instructions from step 1 to locate the unapplied credit memo. Double-click the unapplied credit and click the **Use credit to** icon at the top right of the Create Credit Memos/Refunds dialog and select **Apply to Invoice**, as shown in Figure 7.36.

5. The Apply Credit dialog opens. Place a check mark next to the appropriate credit amounts. QuickBooks will, by default, select the invoice with an exact match; you can override this selection by unchecking the default and apply the credit as needed.

6. Select **Done**.

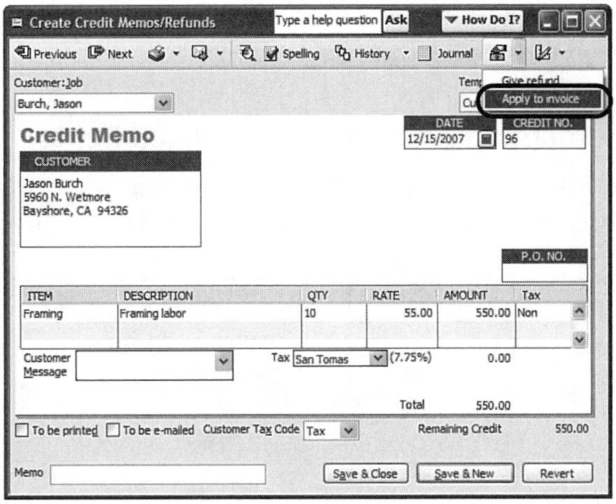

FIGURE 7.36
From the Create Credit Memos/Refunds dialog, select Apply to invoice from the icon.

When Deposits Were Made Without Using the Receive Payment Form

In the section of this chapter titled "Accounts Receivable Forms and Workflow," four steps were identified as basic to Accounts Receivable management:

1. Create an invoice, sales receipt, or statement charge.

2. Receive the customer payment.

3. Place the payment (automatically by preference setting) into the Undeposited Funds account.

4. Complete the Make Deposits form.

This section details how to correct your QuickBooks data when the receive payments step was skipped in recording deposits to the bank account.

How can you know when this situation happens? You need to do a little troubleshooting first to identify the problem:

- Do you have open invoices for customers who you know have paid you?

- Is your bank account balance reconciled and correct?

- Does Income appear to be too high?

If you answered yes to these questions, you need to determine just how the deposits in the bank account register were recorded.

Troubleshooting with the Deposit Detail Report

In QuickBooks, click Reports, Banking, and then select Deposit Detail. This report lists your deposits in date order, as shown in Figure 7.37.

FIGURE 7.37

The Deposit Detail report; look for deposits that are recorded directly to your income accounts.

You are reviewing this report to see whether a pattern exists. For example, in Figure 7.37, you can see a deposit correctly done for $4,936.12, which is comprised of two checks from customer Nguyen. In this situation, the Receive Payments form was applied to open invoices, and the payments were "sent" to the Undeposited Funds account (see the section "Preferences That Affect Accounts Receivable"). Next, a Make Deposit form was completed and totaled to agree with the actual deposit.

This process differs from the deposit for the Jacobsen customer. Instead of applying this deposit to the customer's open invoice, a Make Deposit form was used and the amount was recorded directly to the Construction Income account. (See Type column.)

Technically, in Cash Basis reporting, your reports would be correct. You could just void the open invoices. However, on Accrual Basis reports, your income and accounts receivable have been overstated because both the original invoice and the customer deposit increase income.

Fix Unapplied Customer Payments and Credits

New for QuickBooks 2009 is the Client Data Review (CDR), which includes a tool called Fix Unapplied Customer Payments and Credits.

This tool is available in QuickBooks Premier Accountant 2009 and QuickBooks Enterprise Solutions Accountant 9.0. Additionally, it can be used with QuickBooks Pro 2009 and all editions of QuickBooks Premier 2009 when logged into the file with the new External Accountant user type.

Used primarily by accounting professionals, this feature is designed to provide a single window where multiple customer's payment forms could be applied to the related Make Deposit Form created in error as the next section details.

For more detailed information about how accounting professionals can use this new feature, see Chapter 17.

Assigning the Make Deposits Form to the Customer Invoice

For the business owner, assigning the Make Deposits form to the Customer Invoice is a two-step process. If you have the time to correct individual transactions, this method retains your bank reconciliation and identifies the payment with the customer's open invoice. Be prepared for a bit of tedious work. You need to have a good record of which deposit was paying for which customer invoice. Remember, these steps are to correct only transactions that have been recorded incorrectly.

1. Click **Banking, Use Register**.

2. The Use Register dialog opens. Select the bank account to which the deposit was made.

3. Locate the deposit in the checkbook register and double-click it to open the Make Deposits form. Change the account assigned in the From Account column from Income to **Accounts Receivable**. The effect of this step is to "credit" Accounts Receivable (see Figure 7.38). Click **Save & Close**.

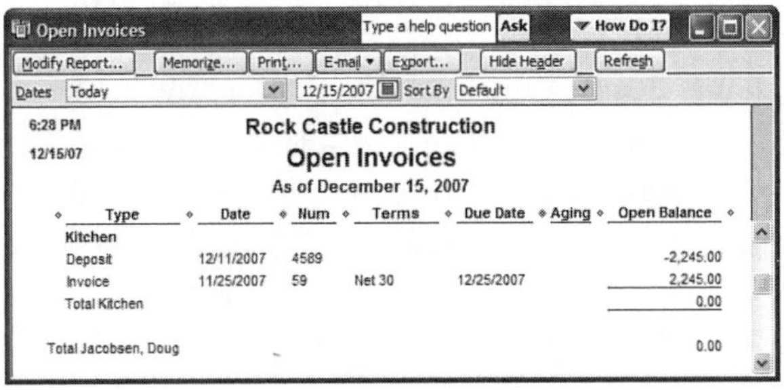

FIGURE 7.38

The Open Invoices report now shows the open credit, which comes from the deposit form.

4. Click **Reports, Customers & Receivables**, select **Open Invoices**, and double-click on the invoice form. (I like using this report simply because I can see both the credit and open invoice.)

5. Click the **Apply Credits** button and select the credit that pertains to this invoice.

6. Click **Done** to close the Apply Credits dialog. Click **Save & Close**.

You have now corrected the deposit and assigned the amount to the open customer invoice, all without changing your bank reconciliation status of the item. This process works well, but can certainly be tedious if you have many transactions with this type of error.

Grouping Deposited Items

Unless you take each and every check or cash payment made for your product or service to the bank on a separate bank deposit ticket, your customer payments should be grouped together with the total matching your bank deposit slip.

If you group your customer payments together on the same Make Deposits form and match the total deposited to your bank deposit ticket, your bank reconciliation will be much easier to complete each month.

You should not attempt this method if you have reconciled your bank account in QuickBooks. Also, if you are correcting years of unreconciled transactions, you need to review Chapter 6, "Bank Account Balance or Reconciliation Errors," for methods to reconcile multiple months or years at one time.

Additionally, the previous section in this chapter titled "Preferences That Affect Accounts Receivable" details how you can avoid these errors for future transactions.

The easiest place to see the problem is in your bank account register. Click Banking, Use Register and select the appropriate bank account.

As shown in Figure 7.39, assume the deposit total per the bank statement was $5,464.78, but in the checkbook register, you recorded two individual deposits.

This situation was caused by choosing Checking as the Deposit To account when receiving the customer's payment (see Figure 7.40). The preferred method would have been to select Undeposited Funds and group them together on one Make Deposit form.

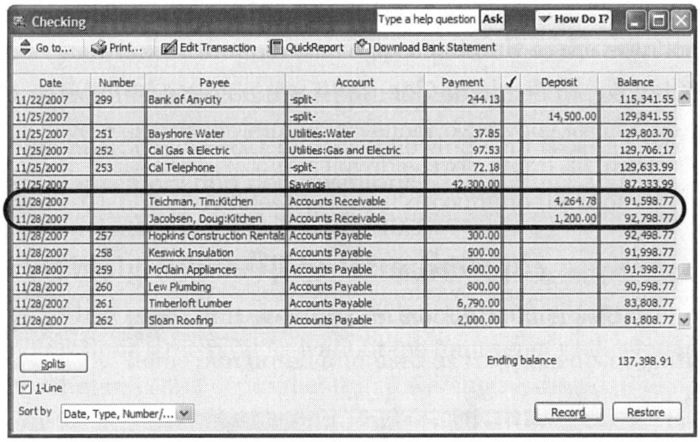

FIGURE 7.39

Customer payments that were deposited directly into the checking account without being grouped together on a Make Deposits form.

FIGURE 7.40

Deposits were individually added to the bank account register because the account selected in the Deposit To field was the Checking account and not the Undeposited Funds account.

To correct this error, edit the Receive Payments form by selecting the Deposit To drop-down menu and choosing Undeposited Funds (see Figure 7.41).

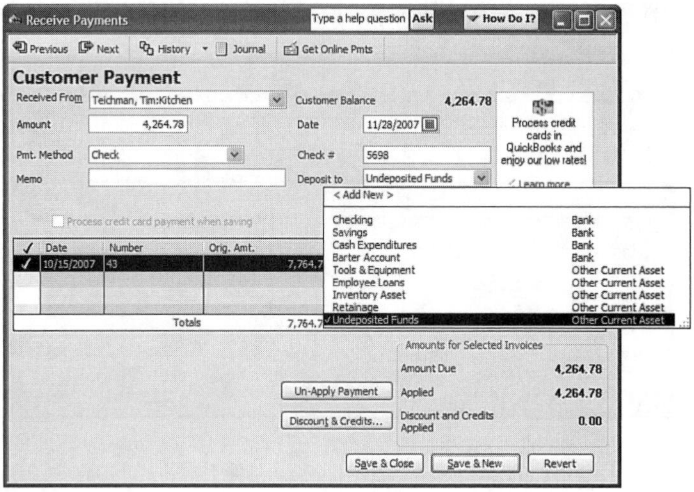

FIGURE 7.41

Selecting the Undeposited Funds account as the Deposit To account will enable you to group deposited items together.

To complete the process, from the QuickBooks main menu, click Banking, Make Deposits. QuickBooks displays a list of all the payments received, but not yet included on a deposit form (included in the Undeposited Funds balance sheet account balance). Click to place a check mark next to the grouped payments, verify that the total deposit agrees with your bank deposit, and then click OK (see Figure 7.42).

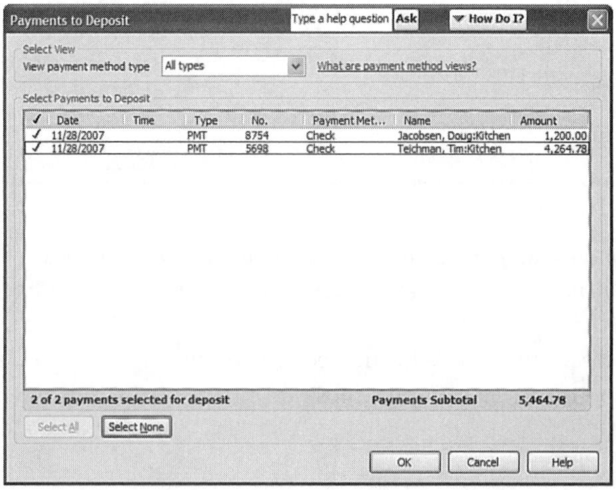

FIGURE 7.42

To correct, select the customer payments that were included in the total bank deposit.

The Make Deposit form now agrees with the actual bank deposit recorded by the bank.

Eliminating the Print Queue for Customer Invoices Marked to Print

At the bottom left of each customer invoice form is the option to select the invoice to be printed. QuickBooks remembers the setting from the last stored invoice form, which can sometimes hinder your own company process.

If you find that you have many invoices selected to print and you don't intend to print them, try this easy solution:

1. Place one or two sheets of paper in your printer. Click **File, Print Forms, Invoices**. The Select Invoices to Print dialog box displays the invoices that are marked to be printed (see Figure 7.43).

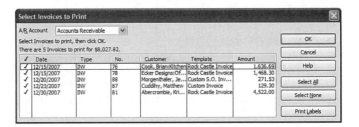

FIGURE 7.43

Click File, Print Forms, Invoices to see a list of customer invoices marked to print.

2. The check mark next to the invoice tells QuickBooks you want to print the invoice on paper. Click **OK** to send the forms to the printer.

3. After a couple of invoices print, a message displays similar to the one in Figure 7.44 showing a list of the forms that did not print. Because you don't want to print them, click **OK** and each form will be marked in QuickBooks as if it were printed.

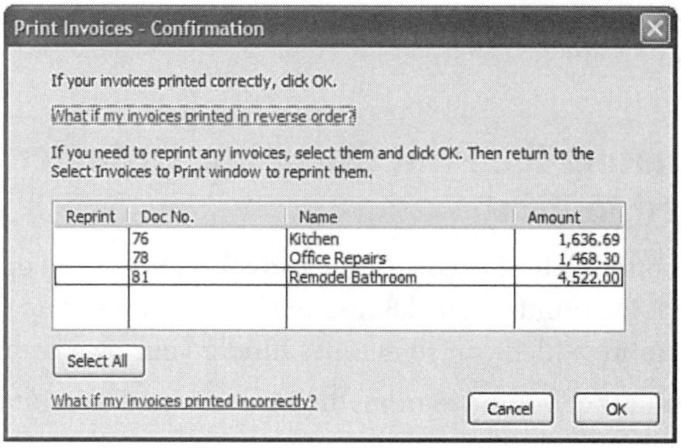

FIGURE 7.44

Clicking OK without marking the unprinted invoices to print tricks QuickBooks into thinking each invoice was printed.

Unique Customer Transactions

This chapter has provided a brief summary of the workflow for accounts receivable, provided ways you can review and troubleshoot your data, and provided instructions on how to fix many of the common Accounts Receivable errors.

This section of the chapter shares some ways to handle unique transactions— transactions you might come across but just are not sure how to enter.

Recording Your Accountant's Year-End Adjusting Journal Entry to Accounts Receivable

Often, adjustments at tax time might include adjustments to your Accounts Receivable account. This transaction is usually in the form of a General Journal Entry. What can make the entry more difficult for you is when no customer(s) are identified with the adjustment.

Preferably, you can request a breakdown by customer of the adjustments made to the Accounts Receivable account. If that is not immediately available, and you simply need to enter the adjustment, you might want to consider using the following method:

1. From the **Customer Center**, create a fictitious customer name— something like, **Accountant YE Adj**.

2. Use this customer to apply the line item to in the **Make Journal Entry** form. Remember that this is only a temporary fix and the balance will display on your Open Invoices report.

Later, when you are able to collect the actual customer(s) who make up the adjustment, you can enter a reversing entry to the fictitious customer and new entries to the correct customers.

When a Customer Is Also a Vendor

Often, I am asked how to handle a transaction when you are selling your company's product or service, but instead of getting paid, you are trading it for the products or services of your customer.

 Digging Deeper

Before attempting these steps, be sure that you have created a customer for your "vendor." You can easily add new customers by selecting the Customer Center from the QuickBooks Home page.

However, QuickBooks does not let you use the same name on the customer list as the vendor list. A little trick can help with this. When naming the new "fictitious" customer, enter a "- C" after the name as you see in Figure 7.45. This naming convention will not display on invoices, but when selecting this name from lists, it will easily bring to your attention that you are using the "customer" list item.

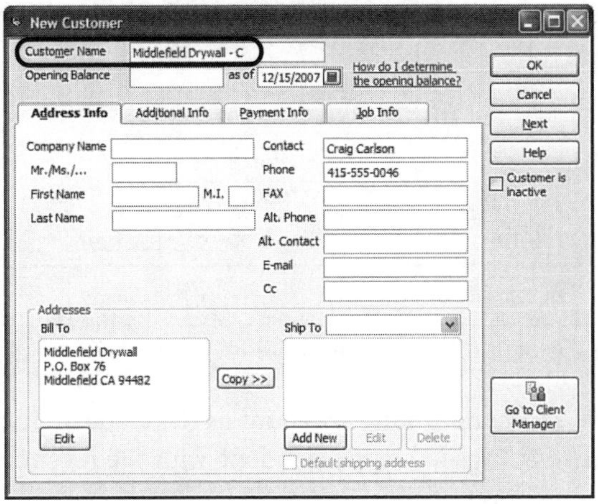

FIGURE 7.45

QuickBooks does not allow duplicate names, so add a "- C" after the name for this fictitious customer that is also your vendor.

Follow these easy steps to keep track of both the revenue and costs:

1. Click **Lists, Chart of Accounts** to open the Chart of Accounts dialog.

2. Click the **Account** button. Select **New** and create an account named **Barter Account** as a bank account type following the instructions on the screen. Click **Save & Close**.

3. Click **Customers, Create Invoices**. Select the new customer you created (your vendor now added to the customer list). Enter the information as if you were selling your products or services to this customer. Click **Save & Close**.

4. Click **Customers, Receive Payments**. Select the new customer you created and record the amount of the payment, placing a check mark next to the appropriate "fictitious" invoice, as shown in Figure 7.46.

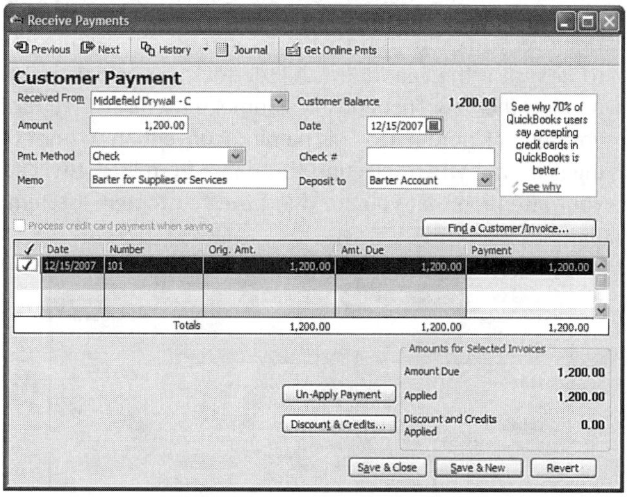

FIGURE 7.46

Record a fictitious payment from the new customer (your vendor).

5. Select the new Barter Account as the **Deposit To** account and click **Save & Close** and you are done with the revenue part of the transaction.

   However, if your default preference is set to have all customer payments, go to Undeposited Funds and continue on to steps 6 and 7.

6. Click **Banking, Make Deposits** to open the Payments to Deposit dialog. Place a check mark next to the appropriate Receive Payment form(s), and click **OK** to advance to the **Make Deposits** form.

7. On the **Make Deposits** form, choose the Barter Account as the **Deposit To** account and select the date you want this transaction recorded. Click **Save & Close** when done.

You have recorded the "potential" revenue side as well as the "fictitious" payment of the invoice of the barter agreement. Now you need to record the expense side of the transaction.

I recommend that the transactions going in and out of the barter account are equal in value; if not, you will need to make an adjustment in the register (Click on Banking, User Register selecting the Barter Account and increasing or decreasing the amount to an income or expense account as determined by the amount left in the account).

To record the expense with a check form, follow these steps:

1. Create a vendor list item for your customer that is also a vendor. I typically append the name with a – V so that when I select the name, I will know that I am using the Vendor list item and not the Customer list item.

2. To create a check form, click on **Banking, Write Checks**.

3. Select the **Barter Account** as the checking account.

4. For the check number, use any number or alpha characters you want.

5. For the payee, use the newly created **vendor list item** (a vendor record for your customer).

6. Record to the normal expense account and amount as if you were purchasing the goods or services.

7. Click **Save & Close**.

To record the expense with a vendor bill form, follow these steps:

1. Click **Vendors, Enter Bills**.

2. Select the **Vendor**, enter a date, vendor reference number, and amount.

3. Assign the expense to the appropriate expense account. When done, click **Save & Close**.

4. To pay the bill, click **Vendors, Pay Bills**.

5. Place a check mark next to the appropriate bill that has actually been paid by providing the vendor with your product or services.

6. In the Payment Method pane, select the choice to **assign check number** because we don't expect to print a check to give to the vendor.

7. In the Payment Account pane, select the newly created **Barter Account** as the payment account, as shown in Figure 7.47.

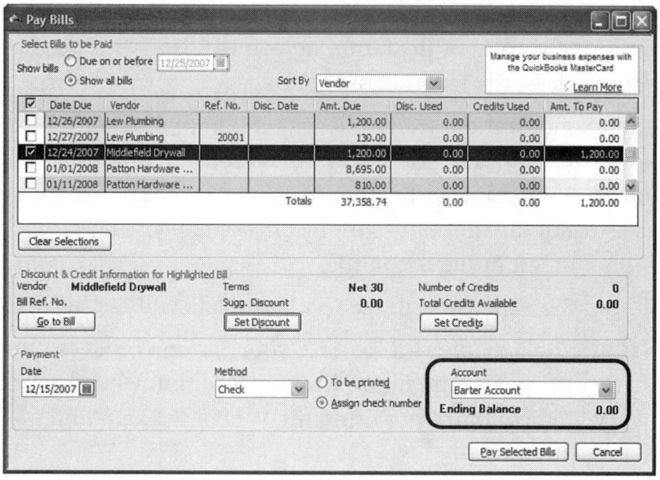

FIGURE 7.47
Record the fictitious bill payment to the Barter Account.

8. Click **Pay Selected Bills** and the Assign Check Numbers dialog displays. Assign a fictitious check number of your choosing. You can even put the term "Barter" in for the check number. Click **OK** and QuickBooks provides a payment summary window; select **Done**.

When this process is finished, your Barter Account should have a zero balance as indicated earlier in this section. You might even want to perform a bank reconciliation of the Barter Account to clear both equal sides of the transaction.

Recording Customer's Bounced Check

If you have ever had a customer's payment check bounce, you know how important correct accounting is. When a check is bounced, often your bank account automatically debits your bank balance and might also charge an extra service fee.

So just how do you record these transactions and also increase the balance your customer now owes you? Follow these steps:

1. To create a bounced check item, click **Lists, Item List**. Click on the **Item** button and select **New**.

2. The New Item dialog box displays. Select an **Other Charge item type**. In both the **Number/Name** field and **Description** field, type Bounced Check.

3. Leave the Amount field blank; assign **Non** as the Tax Code. For the **Account**, select the bank account that was deducted for the returned check (see Figure 7.48).

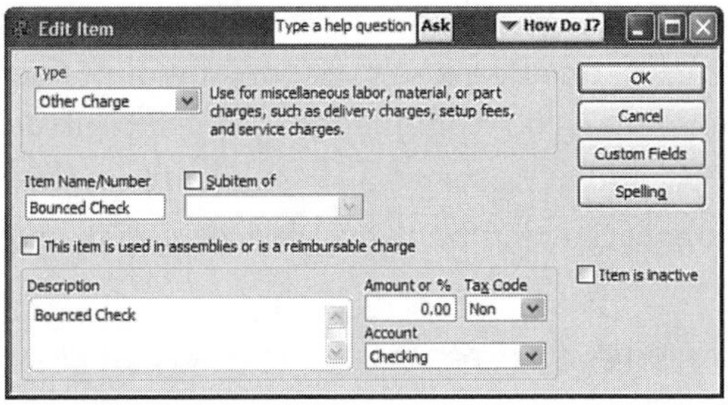

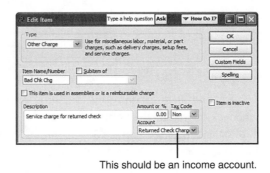

FIGURE 7.48

This item will be used to record the deduction to your bank account for the bounced check amount.

4. Using the preceding steps, create an additional Other Charge item type to be used to invoice the customer for the bank fee you incurred. Name the item Bad Chk Chg.

5. Leave the Amount blank, set the Tax Code as **Non**, and for the Account, select an income account, such as **Returned Check Charges**, as shown in Figure 7.49.

This should be an income account.

FIGURE 7.49

This other charge item will be used to invoice the customer for the fee you were charged by the bank.

6. Click **Customers**, **Create Invoices**, and in the dialog that displays, select the customer with the bounced check. On the first line of the invoice, use the Bounced Check item and assign the amount of the bounced check. On the second line of the invoice, use the Bad Chk Chg item and assign the amount of the fee your bank charged you. (See Figure 7.50.) Click **Save & Close**.

The impact is to increase Accounts Receivable (debit), increase Income for the bank fee (credit), and decrease your bank account (credit). The reduction in the bank account is to record the fact that the bank deducted the amount from your account.

When you reconcile your bank account, be sure to enter the service fee charged.

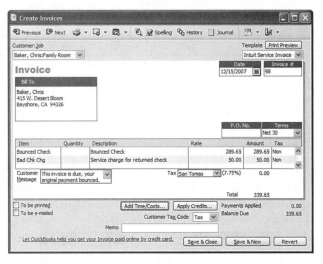

FIGURE 7.50

Create an invoice to collect the bounced funds and fee from the customer.

Although this method provides a process to charge your customer again for the returned check as well as the bank fee, it does have one "symptom" you might want to consider. When you create a Balance Sheet on a cash basis, you might see this amount in Accounts Receivable. More information on this topic is provided in Chapter 4, "Easily Review Your QuickBooks Data."

Chapter 8

Reviewing and Correcting Errors with the Undeposited Funds Account

- The Purpose of the Undeposited Funds Account
- Preference Settings that Affect Undeposited Funds
- Reviewing the Balance in the Undeposited Funds Account
- Fixing Errors with the Undeposited Funds Account

The Purpose of the Undeposited Funds Account

The Undeposited Funds account is part of the suggested workflow for Accounts Receivable. Recall from the discussion in Chapter 7, "Reviewing and Correcting Accounts Receivable Errors," that there are typically four common steps to processing Accounts Receivable transactions:

1. Create an invoice, sales receipt, or statement charge.

2. Receive customer payments.

3. Optionally, place payments into the Undeposited Funds account (preference setting will automate this).

4. Complete the Make Deposits form, grouping the multiple customer payments onto a single Make Deposits form in QuickBooks.

This Undeposited Funds account is needed to hold payments received but not yet deposited. When you receive payment checks from your customers, you put them in your safe and then later take them to the bank; your Undeposited Funds account serves a similar purpose to your safe.

The Undeposited Funds account also plays an important role in making the bank reconciliation process easier and potentially more accurate. For example, if you normally list multiple customer payments on one deposit ticket taken to the bank, you need to match this deposit ticket total to the amount recorded in QuickBooks. By setting the preference to have QuickBooks automatically forward all your customer payments into a temporary Undeposited Funds account, you can then conveniently "group" these individual payments in QuickBooks using the Make Deposit form, so that your bank register deposit total matches the records on your bank statement.

Preference Settings that Affect Undeposited Funds

For several years, QuickBooks users have had the choice about whether to use the Undeposited Funds account for all accounts receivable payment transactions. When you create a new QuickBooks data file, the preference to automatically use the Undeposited Funds account for customer payments is already set. To view the preference for your own data, select Edit, Preferences, and click Sales & Customers. Click the Company Preferences tab, as shown in Figure 8.1. You must be logged in to the file as Admin or External Accountant user type to view the Company Preferences tab.

If the preference shown in Figure 8.1 is not selected, use the Undeposited Funds account on a customer's receive payment transaction when you have a multi-customer deposit. Figure 8.2 shows a deposit slip taken to the bank. Notice that there are three separate checks on the deposit ticket totaling $21,270.29. When you receive your monthly bank statement, your bank will list one deposited line item for the total of the deposit slip and not the three individual deposited checks.

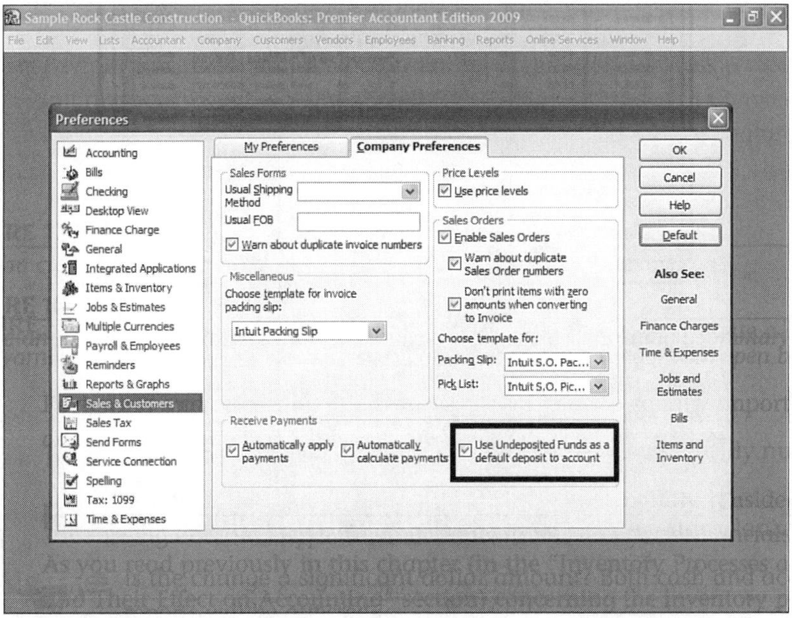

FIGURE 8.1

Set a preference to use the Undeposited Funds account as a default deposit account.

If you did not have the Undeposited Funds preference set, as shown previously in Figure 8.1, you might have selected to deposit the checks received directly to the Checking account, as shown in Figure 8.3.

When performing the bank reconciliation, the Deposits and Other Credits pane on the Reconcile–Checking dialog would show three individual line deposits, as shown in Figure 8.4. How likely is it that you will not clear the right number of deposited items? Multiply this effect by several deposits in a month and you can see the bank reconciliation process would certainly be more difficult.

However, if the Reconcile–Checking pane showed only the total deposit amount, it would be easier to identify it as the cleared bank account deposit.

By choosing to use the Undeposited Funds as the default Deposit to account preference, your bank reconciliation process will be less time-consuming and your bank register will reflect the correct total deposit.

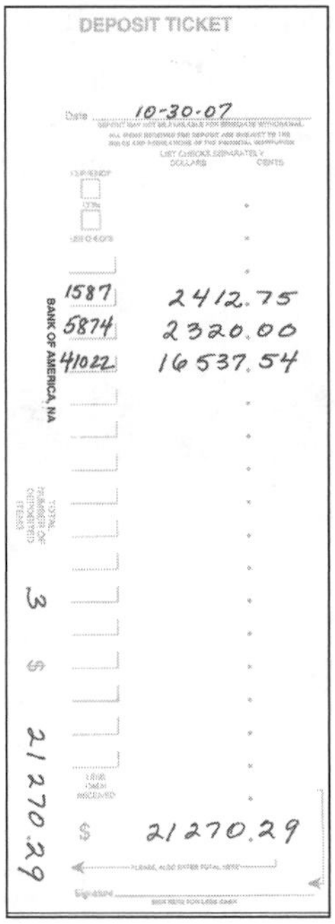

FIGURE 8.2

Your bank will show on the bank statement one line total for this multiple-check deposit ticket.

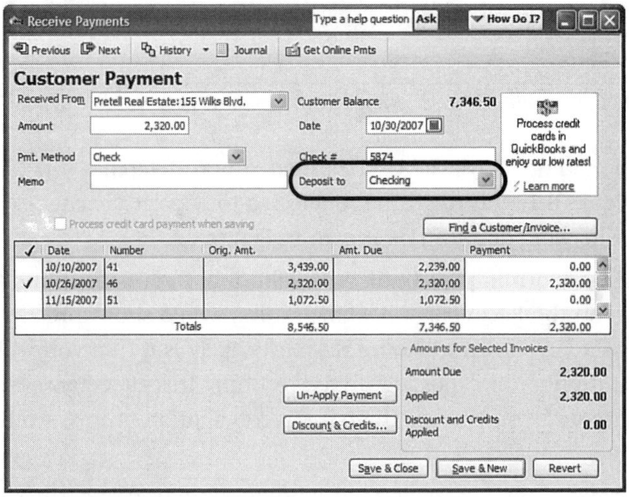

FIGURE 8.3

Depositing an individual payment directly to the Checking account.

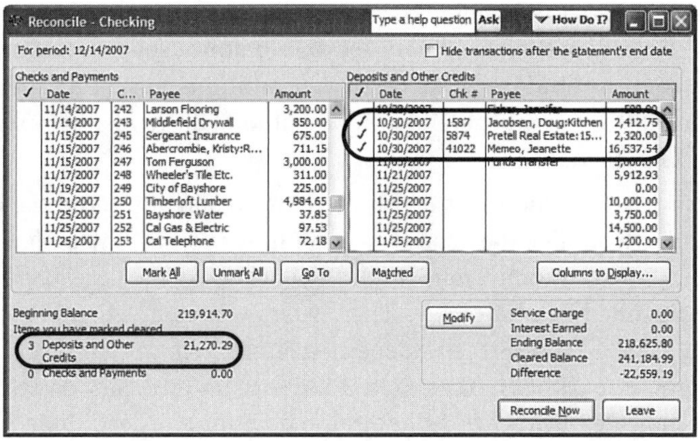

FIGURE 8.4

Reconciling is more difficult for deposits that were individually deposited to the Checking account.

Reviewing the Balance in the Undeposited Funds Account

Before you can begin to agree or disagree with your Undeposited Funds account balance, it is best to review your QuickBooks data, concentrating on certain reports that will help you simplify the review process.

This section provides instructions on creating specific reports that you can use for this task. Later in this chapter, the section "Fixing Errors with Undeposited Funds Account" shows easy-to-follow steps if you need to correct your Undeposited Funds account balance after completing your review.

Rescue Me!

Before you troubleshoot your undeposited funds detail, reconcile your bank account. Identify what transactions have cleared your bank and which transactions have been recorded in QuickBooks but did not clear your bank in a timely manner.

More information about the bank reconciliation task can be found in Chapter 6, "Bank Account Balance or Reconciliation Errors."

Creating an Undeposited Funds Detail Report

The first report I create for a client is a custom report titled "Undeposited Funds Detail." This is not a ready-made report in QuickBooks, but it is easy to create, as you will see.

This report is fundamental because you cannot troubleshoot a total balance for the undeposited funds you see on a balance sheet report not knowing the detail behind the numbers. If you print the register for the account, you will see too much detail, making it difficult to identify exactly what is not deposited.

How do transactions get to this account? When you select the Undeposited Funds account as the deposit-to account (or you set the preference to have QuickBooks automatically do this), QuickBooks increases the balance in the Undeposited Funds account. Then, when you complete a Make Deposit form, QuickBooks reduces the Undeposited Funds account balance, and behind the scenes, it marks both the original increase and the new decrease as cleared (as indicated by a check mark in the account register). Table 8.1 shows the relationship of these forms to your accounting.

Table 8.1   Transaction Effect on Undeposited Funds Account

Transaction Type	Accounts Receivable	Undeposited Funds	Bank Account
Customer Receive Payment form with Undeposited Funds account selected as the "Deposit to" account	Decreases (credit)	Increases (debit)	No effect
Make Deposit form	No effect	Decreases (credit)	Increases (debit)

Before we dig too deep, let's see if you agree with the detail of the Undeposited Funds balance in your QuickBooks data. You also might want to memorize this report for the convenience of reviewing the detail often, avoiding any data entry errors this chapter might help you uncover (see Chapter 16, "Reporting Tips and Tricks").

To create this *Undeposited Funds Detail* report, follow these easy steps:

1. Select **Reports, Custom Transaction Detail**. The Modify Report dialog automatically opens.

2. Display the date range as **All**. (Tip: Simply type an "a" without the quote marks to make the date range default to All.)

3. For **Total by**, select **Payment Method** from the bottom of the list.

4. For **Columns**, select those that you want to view on the report.

5. Click the **Filters** tab. On the Choose Filters pane, select **Accounts**, and choose the **Undeposited Funds Account** from the drop-down menu.

6. Also from the **Filters** tab, select **Cleared** and click the **No** button.

7. Click the **Header/Footer** tab. Change the report title to Undeposited Funds Detail. Click **OK**.

Rescue Me!

The modified custom report you named Undeposited Funds Detail will always show the present state of the transaction, which means that when a payment is received and is included on a Make Deposits form, the report for a prior date will no longer show that item as undeposited. Behind the scenes, QuickBooks is marking the transaction as "cleared" as of the transaction date; therefore, you cannot get a historical snapshot with this report.

Creating a General Ledger Report of the Undeposited Funds Account

You can review a General Ledger report of the Undeposited Funds account balance that will agree with the ending balance on your Balance Sheet report, but without quite a bit of manual work, you cannot identify each individual transaction that makes up the Undeposited Funds account for a specific prior period. Why? Because each time you deposit a Receive Payments form, QuickBooks marks the original dated line item as cleared. This is why we first create a custom report to see if the current (today's date) detail is correct.

If you normally review your balances monthly, you need to print out the Undeposited Funds Detail report that you created earlier in this chapter, on the last day of your accounting month. Save this report in your paper file for future reference because you cannot go back to a historical date and get the same information. This was discussed in the previous section titled "Creating an Undeposited Funds Detail Report."

Additionally, if you take credit cards as payments from your customers, I recommend that you not complete the "Make Deposits" task until you view a bank statement showing the funds deposited into your bank account. This usually does not mean waiting a month for the statement to arrive, because most financial institutions now offer online account access to your account statements.

For those clients, particularly retail businesses, where there is often a large volume of customer receipts in any day, I recommend reviewing the modified report as part of the month, quarter, or year-end process. Notice whether any old dated transactions are on the list. If you find none, you can assume that the Balance Sheet balance in Undeposited Funds as of the prior period date is probably correct.

To generate a General Ledger report, follow these steps:

1. Select **Reports, Accountant & Taxes,** and select the **General Ledger** report.

2. Select **Modify** from the report screen.

3. On the Modify dialog that opens, enter an appropriate **Report Date Range**.

4. From the **Columns** pane, select those you want to see. (You might want to include Clr for seeing the cleared status of transactions.)

5. Click the **Filters** tab, choose to filter for **Account,** and select the **Undeposited Funds** account from the drop-down menu.

You can use this General Ledger report to see details for the Undeposited Funds account and to verify if the running balance in this report agrees with your Balance Sheet report. However, you still cannot use this report to identify exactly which receive payments transaction was not deposited as of the report date because QuickBooks does not capture the information with an "as of" date.

Reviewing the Open Invoices Report

After reviewing the custom-made Undeposited Funds Detail report, if you find some items on the report that have already been taken to your bank, you might need all or some of the following reports to identify why QuickBooks would show the amount as undeposited.

One of the important places to begin troubleshooting the balance in the Undeposited Funds account is to first review the Open Invoices report (click Reports, Customers & Receivables, and choose the Open Invoices report). See Figure 8.5.

Don't just void or delete the incorrect transactions that should not be on the Undeposited Funds Detail report you created. First, review the Open Invoices report to identify what the appropriate correction should be. Corrections to transactions that affect the Undeposited Funds account are detailed in the "Fixing Errors with Undeposited Funds Account" section.

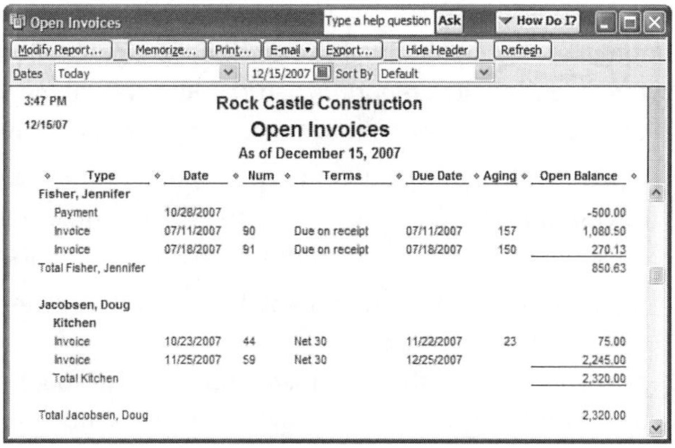

Open Invoices
Type a help question Ask
How Do I?
Modify Report... Memorize... Print... E-mail Export... Hide Header Refresh
Dates Today 12/15/2007 Sort By Default
3:47 PM
12/15/07
Rock Castle Construction
Open Invoices
As of December 15, 2007
Type Date Num Terms Due Date Aging Open Balance
Fisher, Jennifer
Payment 10/28/2007 -500.00
Invoice 07/11/2007 90 Due on receipt 07/11/2007 157 1,080.50
Invoice 07/18/2007 91 Due on receipt 07/18/2007 150 270.13
Total Fisher, Jennifer 850.63
Jacobsen, Doug
Kitchen
Invoice 10/23/2007 44 Net 30 11/22/2007 23 75.00
Invoice 11/25/2007 59 Net 30 12/25/2007 2,245.00
Total Kitchen 2,320.00
Total Jacobsen, Doug 2,320.00

FIGURE 8.5

Review the Open Invoices report before making corrections to the Undeposited Funds account.

Look for any or all of the following on your Open Invoices report:

- Negative balance items—These balances represent customer payments or credits recorded but not applied to a customer invoice. You might see payment, credit memo, checks, and even journal entry type transactions. Review Chapter 7 for more detailed instructions on how to correct each different transaction type.

  In Figure 8.5, customer Jennifer Fisher has a payment type transaction of –$500.00, which is "unapplied" to any open invoice.

  Ask yourself the following as you look at this transaction:

  - Is this same $500.00 showing up on my Undeposited Funds Detail report we created?
  - Is the invoice being paid by this check not showing on the Open Invoices report?

  If you answered yes to these questions, you might have entered a duplicate customer payment. Follow the instructions given in the next section to remove this payment from your Undeposited Funds account balance.

Digging Deeper

If you are an accounting professional and reviewing your client's data file for these and other types of data entry errors, be sure to read Chapter 17, "New for 2009! Detecting and Correcting with the Client Data Review Feature" for details on how to streamline your correcting tasks.

If you answered no, you simply might need to associate the payment to the correct open invoice by clicking the payment transaction from the Open Invoices report. When the Receive Payments form opens, place a check mark next to the invoice being paid with the payment.

■ Open invoices that you know your customer has paid—These open balances might be the result of making the customer funds bank deposit on some other form instead of the receive payments form.

If you see open invoices that you know your customer has paid, and if your bank account balance has the correct deposits, you must determine how you recorded the original deposits in QuickBooks. To help with this task, you will want to review the checkbook register and the Deposit Detail report, as discussed in the following two sections of this chapter.

Viewing Deposits in the Bank Register

An easy way to determine how deposits were made to the bank account is to view the deposits directly in your bank register. To open a bank register, choose Banking, Use Register and select the appropriate bank account.

The deposits that were recorded directly to the bank account from the Receive Payments window will have Accounts Receivable visible in the Account field, as shown in Figure 8.6. The three deposits dated 10/31/07 were each individually recorded directly to the Checking account.

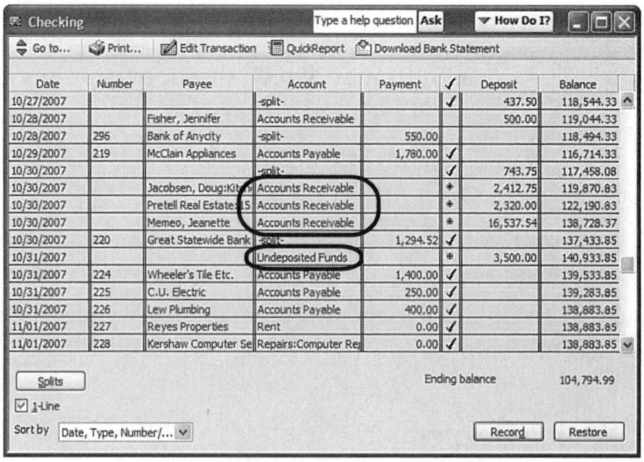

FIGURE 8.6
Review the source of your deposits in your bank account register.

In the checkbook register view, the account shown represents the account from which the transaction originated. You might see your income account as the "account" or you will see "-Split-," which indicates that there are several lines of detail for this single transaction. To view the "-Split-" detail, just double-click on the transaction itself to open the originating QuickBooks form.

By contrast, look at the deposit dated 10/31/07 for $3,500.00. The account shown is Undeposited Funds, which is the account where the information originated.

To summarize, look for a "pattern" of how deposits were made to your QuickBooks data. The examples here show two types of deposits: ones that were recorded directly to the checking account and others that first went through the Undeposited Funds account. You might have others in your data where the account shown is your income account. This type of transaction is discussed in the next section, "Viewing the Deposit Detail Report."

You will also be looking to see which transactions have been cleared in the bank reconciliation and which deposits remain uncleared. Chapter 6 covers the bank reconciliation topic, and in fact, it would be best if the reconciliation task were completed before you begin fixing your deposit details. Why? If you see an uncleared deposit, it would help you identify your potential errors in the Undeposited Funds account.

Viewing the Deposit Detail Report

This report easily identifies customer receive payment transactions that were directly deposited to the bank account without first going through the Undeposited Funds account.

1. Click **Reports, Banking,** and choose the **Deposit Detail** report.

2. Click the **Modify Report** button at the top of the report.

3. Click the **Filters** tab. In the Choose Filter pane, the Account filter is already selected. From the drop-down menu select your bank account or use the default **all bank accounts**.

4. On the same Filters pane, select **Transaction Type** and choose **Payment** from the drop-down menu. As shown in Figure 8.7, the other filters are already defaulted with this report for you. Click **OK**.

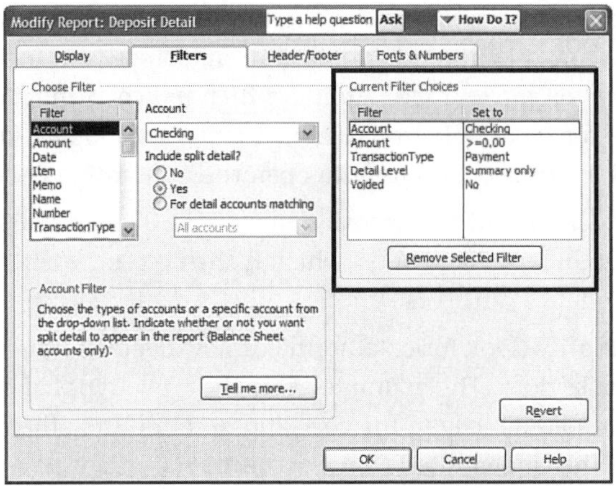

FIGURE 8.7

Modify the Deposit Detail report to show Receive Payment forms that were recorded directly to the bank account register.

Creating a Payment Transaction List Detail Report

Do you find the Deposit Detail report too lengthy and difficult to read? You can create a report that shows the detail in a list form and provides a total of the column detail.

Select Reports, Custom Transaction Detail Report. The report automatically opens with the Modify Report tab selected. Select the Report Date Range you want to view, as well as the columns you want to see on the report. From the Filters tab, select the account and filter for your specific bank account. Set an additional filter for a transaction type of payment.

Now you can easily view in a list format all payments that were recorded directly to the Checking account (see Figure 8.8).

FIGURE 8.8

Modify the Custom Transaction Detail report to show in a list format the payments that were deposited directly to the bank account register.

Fixing Errors with the Undeposited Funds Account

Did you make it through the review of each of the referenced reports in the earlier section of this chapter? You don't want to jump into fixing transactions that affect accounts receivable without due diligence in researching what the correct balance should be. Without the review and troubleshooting time, you might hastily delete, void, or modify a transaction only to compound the problem.

This section details specific steps for correcting the errors you might find. It was important to first discover why the error was made and then fix it so you can avoid the same error on future transactions.

Clear Up Undeposited Funds Account—*New for QuickBooks 2009!*

New for QuickBooks 2009 is the Client Data Review, which has a tool to clear up the Undeposited Funds Account.

This tool is available in QuickBooks Premier Accountant 2009 and QuickBooks Enterprise Solutions Accountant 9.0. Additionally, it can be used with QuickBooks Pro 2009 and all editions of QuickBooks Premier 2009 and Enterprise Solutions 9.0 when logged into the file with the new External Accountant user type.

Used by accounting professionals, this tool is designed to provide a single window where multiple customer payment forms recorded to the Undeposited Funds Account can be applied to the related Make Deposit form when the client created a second transaction to record the deposit.

For more detailed information about how accounting professionals can use this new feature, see Chapter 17.

Removing Old Dated Payments in the Undeposited Funds Account

Did your review of the data uncover old dated payment transactions still in the Undeposited Funds account? If yes, you can use the method described in this section to correctly remove these payments without editing or modifying each transaction.

This method makes the following assumptions:

- Your bank account is reconciled before making these changes.
- You have reviewed and corrected your Accounts Receivable Aging reports, as discussed in Chapter 7.

- You have identified which payment amounts are still showing in the Undeposited Funds account, and these are the same amounts that have already been deposited to your bank register by some other method.

- You have identified the specific chart of accounts (income accounts, presumably) to which the deposits were incorrectly recorded.

This method enables you to remove the unwanted balance in your Undeposited Funds account with just a few keystrokes:

1. If the funds that remain in your Undeposited Funds account are from more than one year ago, you first must identify the total amount that was incorrectly deposited for each year. See the sidebar titled "Creating a Payment Transaction List Detail Report" in the previous section. Filter the report for the specific date range.

2. Now "remove" these identified Undeposited Funds items by clicking **Banking**, **Make Deposits**. (see Figure 8.9).

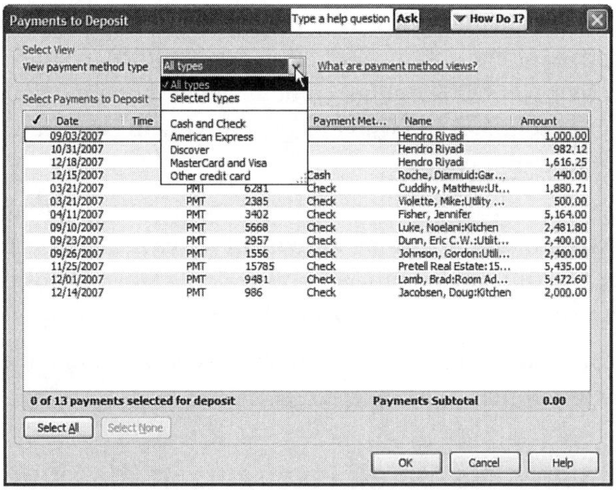

FIGURE 8.9

To easily select the correct payments to deposit, leave the View Payment Method Type as All Types.

3. Select all the payments for deposit with dates in the date range you are correcting by clicking to place a check mark next to the payment item, as shown in Figure 8.10, and then click **OK**.

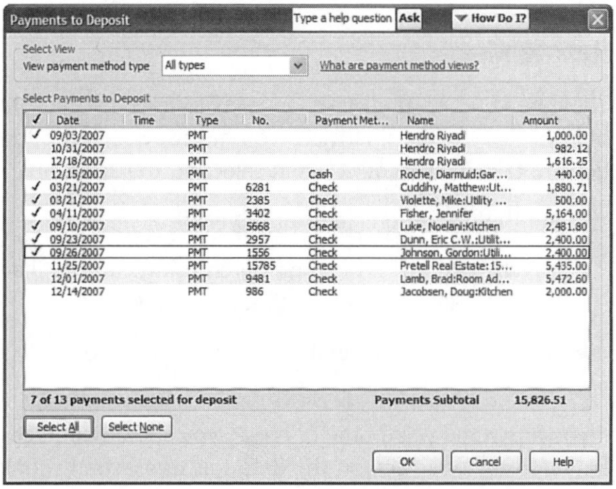

FIGURE 8.10
Select for deposit the payments that need to be removed from the Undeposited Funds account.

4. The Make Deposits dialog opens with each of the previously selected payments included on a new **Make Deposits** form. On the next available line, enter the account to which the incorrect deposits were originally recorded. In this example, you discovered that the Construction Income account was overstated by the incorrect deposits. The effect of this new transaction is to decrease (debit) the Construction Income account and decrease (credit) the Undeposited Funds account without any effect on the checking account, as shown in Figure 8.11.

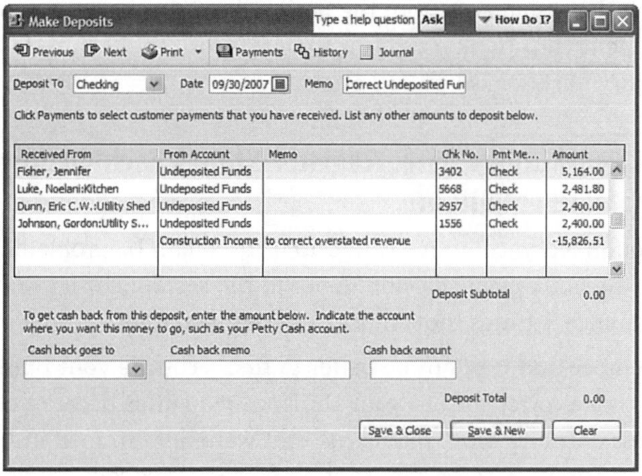

FIGURE 8.11
Enter a line with a negative amount recorded to the account that was previously overstated.

Rescue Me!

The date you give the Make Deposits form is the date the impact will be recorded in your financials. You have several important considerations to take into account when selecting the appropriate date:

- Are the corrections for a prior year?

- Has the tax return been prepared using current financial information from QuickBooks for that prior period?

- Has another adjustment to the books been done to correct the issue?

If you answered yes to any of these, you should contact your accountant and ask her advice on the date this transaction should have.

5. Make sure to reconcile this net -0- deposit in your next bank reconciliation.

You should now be able to review the Undeposited Funds Detail report and agree that the items listed on this report as of today's date are those that you have not yet physically taken to your bank to be deposited or that the credit card vendors have not yet credited to your bank.

Reconciling Your Bank Register with the Bank Statement's Deposits

You might run into a situation where deposits in your bank register do not match the statements from the bank. There can be several reasons why the statement your bank gives you shows deposit totals that do not match those in your QuickBooks bank register.

Your QuickBooks Bank Register Shows Each Customer Payment as a Separate Line Item

Although technically this is not an error, it can be problematic when you perform the bank reconciliation. Refer to the section earlier in this chapter titled "Preference Settings that Affect Undeposited Funds."

Remember that it might be better to first reconcile your bank account and then make corrections to your Undeposited Funds account detail. Also, the process of fixing those payments that were not grouped in the past can be time-consuming, so be sure that doing so makes sense. If your bank account has been reconciled, I would not recommend making this type of correction.

Follow these steps to group customer payments that were previously recorded and deposited directly to the checkbook register:

1. Click **Edit**, **Preferences**, and then select **Sales & Customers**. Click the **Company Preferences** tab. Verify that there is *no* check mark in the Use Undeposited Funds as a Default Deposit To Account. Removing this check mark in the Sales & Customers, My Company preference dialog enables the Receive Payments window to show a drop-down Deposit To account selection that otherwise is not available.

2. Access the checkbook register by clicking **Banking**, **Use Register** and select your specific bank account.

3. Select the specific customer payment to be modified by double-clicking the transaction in the open register.

4. The Receive Payments dialog opens. Select **Undeposited Funds** from the **Deposit To** drop-down list (see Figure 8.13).

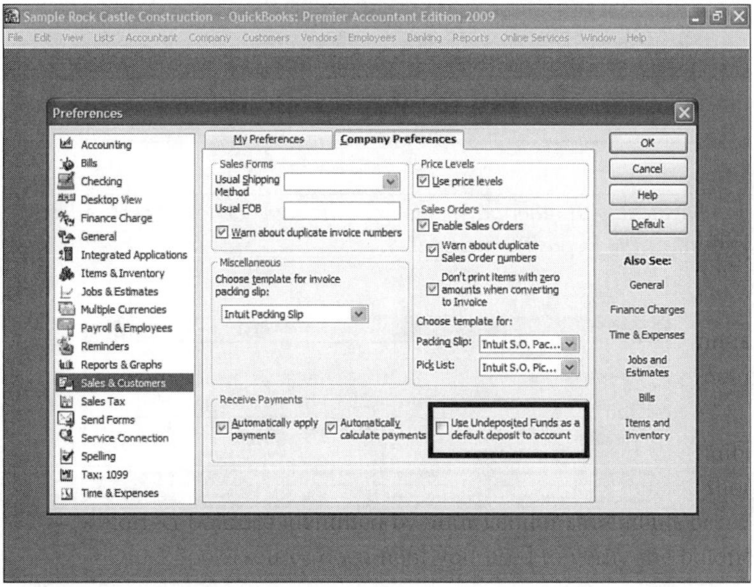

FIGURE 8.12

For this type of correction, be sure to remove the check mark from the Use Undeposited Funds as a Default Deposit to Account box.

5. To group the payments together, select **Banking**, **Make Deposits**. In the Payments to Deposit dialog box, select the payments that belong together. Figure 8.14 shows that the two customer payments recorded with an 11/25/07 date belonged together on the same bank deposit ticket.

6. Click **OK** when the total of the Make Deposits agrees with your bank statement deposit. If the total does not agree with your bank statement, review your manually created bank deposit ticket to see what line information differs from your QuickBooks deposit form detail. Be sure to cancel out of the dialog to correct transactions if needed.

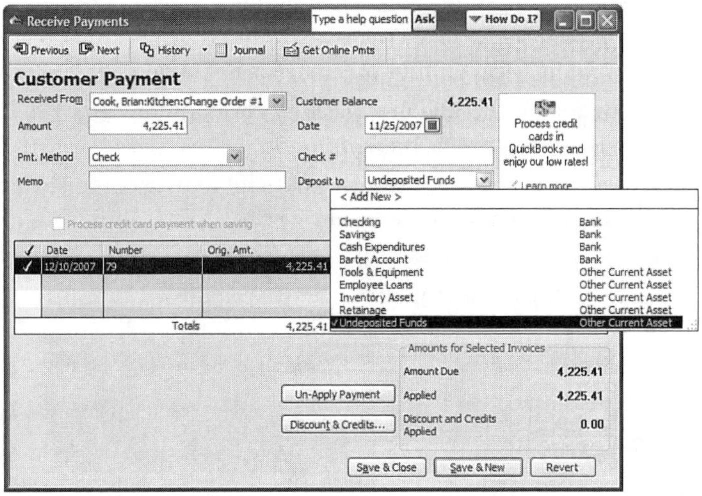

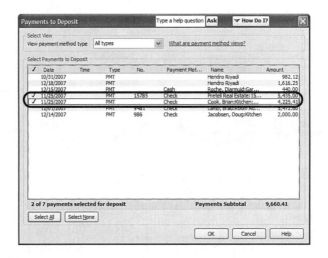

FIGURE 8.13
To group a payment with other payments from the same deposit ticket, select the Undeposited Funds account as the Deposit to account.

FIGURE 8.14
Select the individual payments that belong on the same deposit transaction.

The Make Deposits form (see Figure 8.15) will now record to your bank account one deposit instead of two individual line deposits. This makes your bank reconciliation process easier to complete by showing in the Deposits & Credits pane of the Reconcile dialog window one transaction for the total instead of multiple individual transactions.

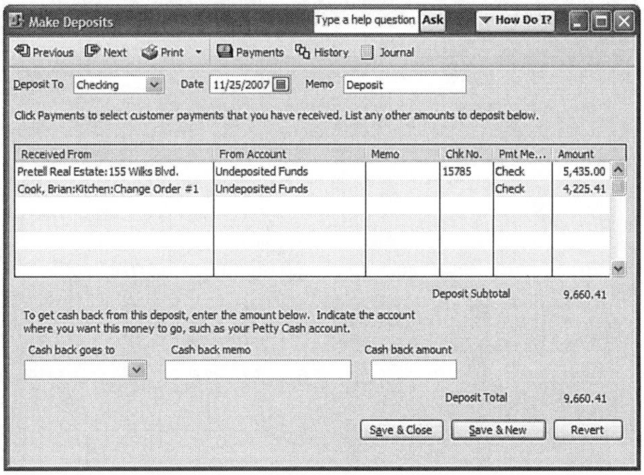

FIGURE 8.15
Individual customer payments are grouped onto one Make Deposits form to agree with the bank's actual deposit ticket.

Recording Credit Card Deposits Less a Discount Fee

If you collect credit card payments from your customers, having a defined receive payment and make deposit process that you can consistently follow is important. Because you don't physically hold the payment from your customer as you do with cash or check payments, tracking these credit card payments accurately and reconciling with the bank's monthly statement helps you avoid some common mistakes.

Does your merchant vendor charge a discount fee by reducing the total amount that is deposited to your bank account? If so, during your review of the data, you might have found that the credit card deposits were made to your bank register for the gross amount and did not deduct the credit card fee.

To correct this error, you can take either of two courses of action if you used a Make Deposit form to record these increases in your bank account:

- Edit each Make Deposits form and make the correction (this is the most time-consuming).

To edit a recorded Make Deposits form, open the form from the checkbook register and add an additional line to the deposit, assigning the Credit Card Service Fees expense account with a negative amount equal to the credit card fee withheld (see Figure 8.16). Your net deposit should now agree with the bank's deposit records.

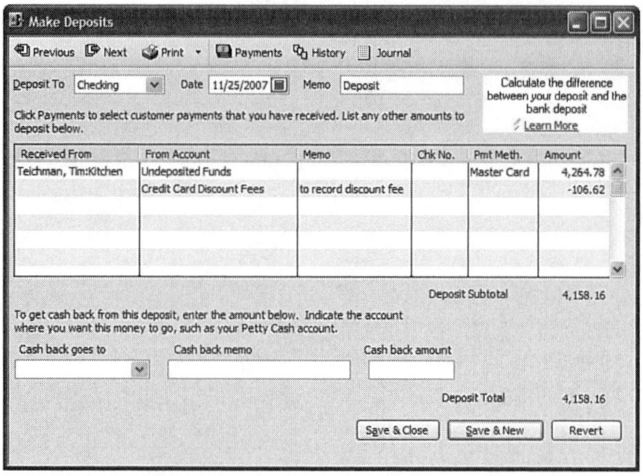

FIGURE 8.16
Recording the credit card discount fee deducted from the actual money received.

- Create a journal entry with a debit to Credit Card Services Fees expense and a credit to the Banking account. Click **Company**, **Make General Journal Entries**. Select a date for the entry and assign an Entry No. of your choosing. Leave the first line blank; on the second line in the account column, enter the Credit Card Service Fees expense account and the amount of the merchant fee in the debit column. You can also enter an optional memo. On the third line in the account column, enter the bank account that was charged the fee and enter the merchant fee amount in the credit column, again with an optional memo. Click **Save & Close** when done.

Chapter 9

Handling Current Asset Accounts Correctly

- Defining an Other Current Asset
- Reviewing and Troubleshooting the Other Current Asset Accounts
- Troubleshooting and Creating Unique Other Current Asset Account Transactions

Defining an Other Current Asset

The Other Current Asset section on the Balance Sheet includes the value of noncash assets that are typically due to the company within one year (see Figure 9.1). This section is appropriate for recording prepaid expenses and cash advances to employees. This section differs in purpose from the Fixed Assets, which tracks the cost and depreciation of the land, equipment, and buildings your business owns (not rents) in the production of the service or product you sell.

FIGURE 9.1

Sample Chart of Accounts list showing placement of the Other Current Asset accounts.

Additionally, QuickBooks offers another asset section, Other Asset, which is typically used for those other assets that are not convertible to cash within one year.

Reviewing and Troubleshooting the Other Current Asset Accounts

All too often, I see companies ignore the balances in the other current asset section. I think it is primarily due to the attention companies normally pay to their Profit & Loss statements and the lack of the same attention given to the Balance Sheet statement. However, often the balances in these accounts have a direct relationship to the company's current period Profit & Loss statement. This is because other current asset accounts typically are for prepaid expenses, or expenses that are paid to the vendor in anticipation of the expense.

The next few sections detail ways in which you can accurately review these accounts and methods to correct the balances when you need to.

Matching Other Current Asset Balances to an Outside Document

Just as you have taken care to review your Bank Account and Accounts Receivable balances, you should also review the balances in your Other Current Asset accounts. These balances indirectly affect the Profit & Loss statement for your company. They represent expenses that have been paid but not recorded as a current expense to your company, or they might represent money that is owed to your company.

When possible, obtain a document outside QuickBooks to substantiate any balances you have in your Other Current asset accounts. If you have been using these types of accounts for recording your prepayments, it is important that you match their balances with the records of the vendor you have prepaid.

For example, if you have recorded a prepayment of your business insurance, you need to compare this balance to your insurance vendor's records.

 Digging Deeper

In the section of this chapter titled "Troubleshooting and Creating Unique Other Current Asset Account Transactions," you learn some preferred methods to properly record these special transactions.

Creating a Custom Transaction Detail Report

One of the most common reports to use for reviewing the detail in your Other Current Asset accounts is the Custom Transaction Detail report available via the Reports menu. You simply modify and filter the report to view the details for the specific account or accounts.

The following steps show you how to get the Custom Transaction Detail report for an Employee Loans account. If your business loans money to your employees, review this report often and verify it with the employee's own records.

To create the report, do the following:

1. Click **Reports, Custom Transaction Detail**.
2. The Modify Report dialog opens. In the Report Date Range pane, select the appropriate date range you want to review.

3. From the Columns pane, select the columns you want to see in the resulting report.

4. To see the detail sorted and subtotaled by Employee, select **Employee** from the **Total by** drop-down (see Figure 9.2).

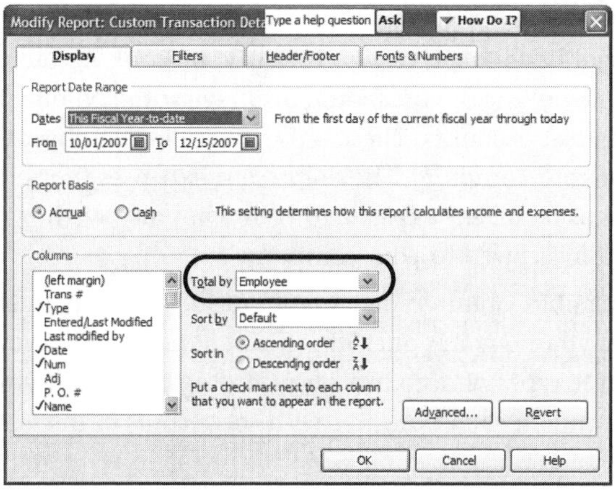

FIGURE 9.2

Total the report by Employee to see which employee balances make up the Employee Loans account total.

5. Click the **Filters** tab. In the Filter pane, the Accounts filter is selected. From the Account drop-down menu, select **Employee Loans**. You also might want to go to the **Header/Footer** tab and give the report a unique title.

Figure 9.3 shows the finished report.

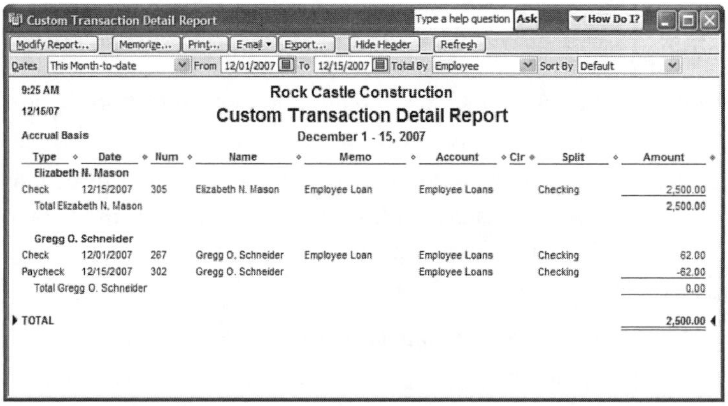

FIGURE 9.3

The report totaled by Employee organizes the information so you can easily verify balances by employee.

You can filter this report for other accounts and change the Total by option to organize the information according to your specific needs.

Reconciling Other Current Asset Accounts

Over time, the Custom Transaction Detail report might become lengthy with a lot of line item detail information that you no longer need to review.

In the earlier example of reviewing the balances in the Employee Loans account, you did not need to see the balance for employee Gregg Schneider because his loan was completely paid off.

The following steps show a method of removing this detail by reconciling the Other Current Asset account and then creating the Custom Transaction Detail report filtered for uncleared transactions:

1. Click **Banking**, **Reconcile**.

2. The Begin Reconciliation dialog opens. From the Account drop-down menu, select **Employee Loans** (see Figure 9.4) and click **Continue**. In this example, you reconcile the account only when an employee has fully paid off the loan.

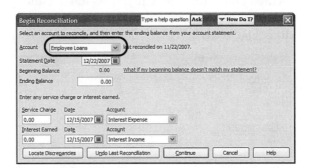

FIGURE 9.4

Reconcile the Employee Loans account so that you can filter the report for uncleared transactions.

3. Place a check mark next to the original loan payment (check) for each item that represents the complete repayment of the loan (deposit) (see Figure 9.5).

4. Click the **Reconcile Now** button when the cleared balance is -0-. Remember, you reconcile the items only when the total amounts going in and out of the account are equal over time.

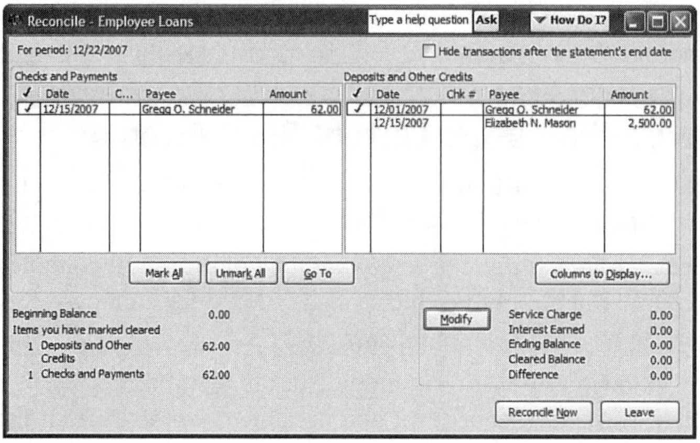

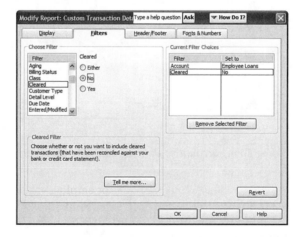

FIGURE 9.5

In the Reconcile dialog, you will mark both the payment of the loan and the employee's repayment cleared.

5. When you create the Custom Transaction Detail report, click the **Modify** button at the top of the report. In the Choose Filter pane, select **Cleared** and place a mark in the **No** radial button (see Figure 9.6). The report now shows only those transactions that make up the current balance.

FIGURE 9.6

Filter the Custom Transaction Detail report for Uncleared Items.

The important thing to remember about this method is that you are only marking as cleared those list groups (that is, employees, customers, and so on) that are prepaid, or additional receivable is totally paid off. The resulting report shows only those transactions that are not cleared, making the report much shorter and easier to review (see Figure 9.7).

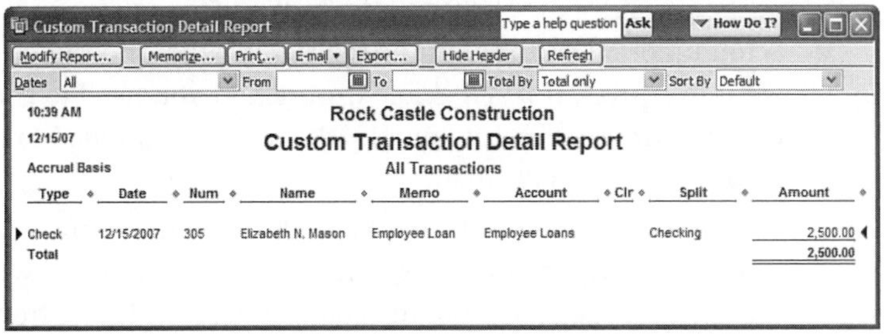

FIGURE 9.7

Employee Loans Detail report after filtering out all Uncleared transactions.

Troubleshooting and Creating Unique Other Current Asset Account Transactions

Often the Other Current Asset accounts are not reviewed periodically for accuracy. Typically, this is because you might not have set up some process and procedures to review these numbers. This section is intended to help you correct any errors found in the Other Current Asset accounts in your QuickBooks data and to identify some ways to handle unique transaction types in these accounts.

Correcting Balance Errors in Your Other Current Asset Accounts

After you review your vendor statements for prepaid balances or after you review the balances QuickBooks shows for employee loans, if you find errors, you can correct them via a simple process. Unlike some of the other account types you have learned about so far in this book, the Other Current Asset type account has no restrictions.

The first step in correcting your data is to identify to which chart of account the original transaction was recorded so that you can reverse all or part of the transaction properly. Use these steps to identify and fix any errors:

1. Click **Banking**, **Use Register** and in the resulting drop-down account menu, select the **Other Current Asset** account you are correcting. This opens the selected account in a register view.

2. Scroll up or down through the register view to find the transaction you want to correct. If it is a single transaction you need to correct, double-click the transaction and modify the account assigned to the correct chart of accounts list item.

   Far more often, you will need to modify a total balance that is the result of several transactions, and the previous method would just be too tedious. Take a note of the chart of account in the transaction you want to modify.

3. To make a correction to the total balance without modifying each individual transaction, you can use a Journal Entries form. Click **Company**, **Make General Journal Entries**.

4. In the Make General Journal Entries dialog, enter the date you want to affect the balances, and enter an optional **Entry No**.

5. Leave the first line of the Make General Journal Entries blank. (See the Rescue Me discussed in Chapter 7, "Reviewing and Correcting Accounts Receivable Errors," page 170–171).

6. On the second line of the Make General Journal Entries, enter the **Other Current Asset** account balance you want to modify. Enter the dollar amount of the adjustment you determined from your review (see the previous section in this chapter).

   - Debit Column—Enter the amount here to *increase* this account balance.

   - Credit Column—Enter the amount here to *decrease* this account balance.

7. If the account is tracking employee, vendor, or customer names, be sure to include the appropriate list name in the **Name** column on the second line of the Make General Journal Entries. This is important if you want your resulting reports to sort or subtotal by the list name.

8. On line three of the Make General Journal Entries, enter the chart of account list item (often an expense account) that you want to adjust. This is the same account you identified in step 2 previously. Enter the same amount as line 2, only enter it in the opposite column from the one selected in step 6.

9. Click **Save & Close** when you see that the debits column is equal to the credits column. If they are not equal, QuickBooks will not allow you to save the transaction.

10. To check your work, create the Custom Transaction Detail report as detailed in the previous section. The resulting balance should be the correct balance identified by your vendor statements or an outside QuickBooks source document you used to verify the balance.

Rescue Me!

Take care with the date you choose for the transaction; your correction impacts your financials on the date you assign to the transaction. The impact is the same for both cash- or accrual-based reports.

If you are correcting a prior year, make sure your adjustment agrees with the filed tax return totals for that account or check with your accountant before making the change.

Deducting Employee Loan Payments from the Employee's Payroll Checks

Tracking employee loans and repayments is just as critical as other types of other current asset account tracking. When you have employee loans for which you are tracking the repayment, make sure you periodically check your records with the employee's record to verify the balances you have recorded.

Perhaps you loaned your employee money and the employee agreed to pay back the loan in equal amounts over several paychecks.

Rescue Me!

The method described in this section for deducting employee loan repayments from the employee's payroll check assumes that you create your payroll checks in QuickBooks using one of Intuit's Payroll Solutions, available at www.payroll.com.

Use these steps to create an employee loan repayment deduction payroll item:

1. To view your current list of payroll deduction type items, click **Lists**, **Payroll Items List**.

2. The payroll item list dialog opens. Review the contents of the list to make sure you do not already have an employee loan deduction type payroll item.

3. To create a new employee loan deduction item, click on the **Payroll Item** button at the bottom of the list. Select **New**.

4. Click the **Custom Setup** button, and click **Next**.

5. In the dialog that displays, click the **Deduction** payroll item type and then click **Next**.

6. Name the deduction item Employee Loans Repay, as shown in Figure 9.8, and click **Next**.

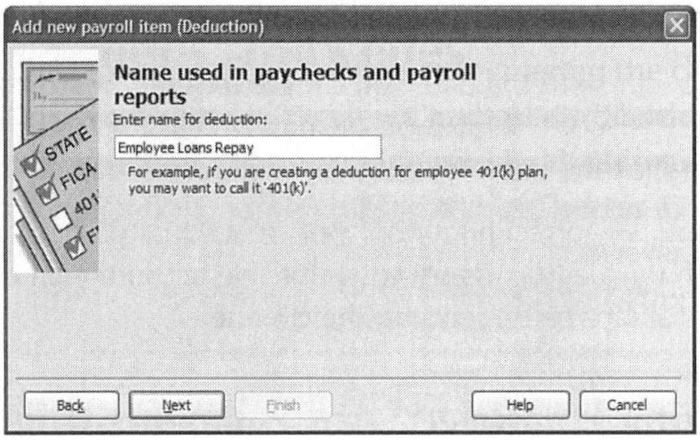

FIGURE 9.8

Name the payroll deduction type.

7. You can leave blank the name of the agency and the number for the agency because you are not remitting this payment back to some other collection source.

8. For the Liability Account assign the Employee Loans Other Current Asset type account (see Figure 9.9) and click **Next**.

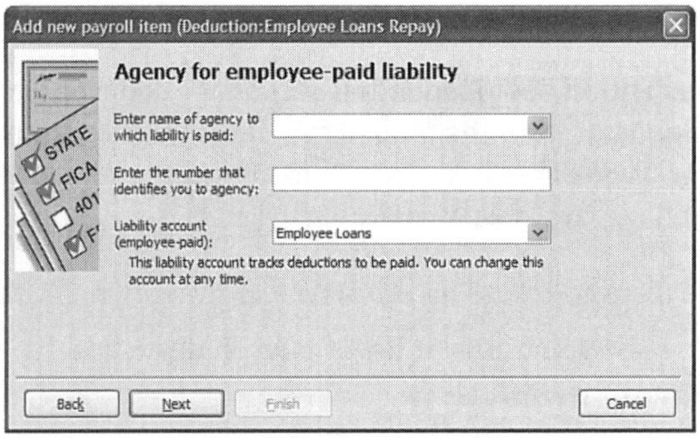

FIGURE 9.9

Assign the Other Current Asset account Employee Loans.

9. Leave the default Tax Tracking Type as **None** and click **Next**.

10. On the Taxes dialog, accept the default of none of the list items selected.

11. In the Calculate Based on Quantity dialog leave, the default of **Neither** selected and click **Next**.

12. On the Gross vs. Net dialog, leave the default of Gross Pay selected and click **Next**.

13. On the Default Rate and Limit dialog, leave the default of 0.00 as well as the default check mark selected for this is an Annual Limit box, and click **Finish**.

Now you need to assign the deduction to the employee's record, as described in the following steps:

1. From the Employee Center (accessible from the icon bar), select the employee to edit by double clicking the employee name.

2. In the Edit Employee window, choose **Payroll and Compensation Info** from the **Change Tabs** list.

3. Assign the **Employee Loans Repay** item in the Additions, Deductions, Employee Contributions pane. Enter the amount to be deducted each pay period in the **Amount** column (see Figure 9.10). You should put an amount in the **Limit** column. QuickBooks will stop the deduction when the limit is reached.

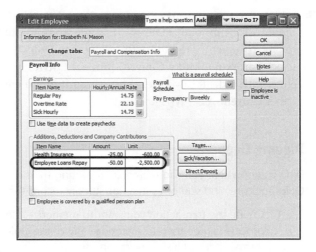

FIGURE 9.10

Assign the Loan Repay deduction payroll item type via the New or Edit Employee window.

Recording Prepaid Expenses in QuickBooks

Often you will have expenses that must be paid in advance of the benefit of the service or product being purchased. An example is a business's General Liability insurance. Typically you pay many months in advance for this type of insurance. To record this annual or semi-annual expense all in one month would make that month unfairly take on the total expense.

A preferred method is to record the expense in equal monthly increments. The following steps show you how to record the original prepaid expense and record the expense to the individual months.

To accomplish this task, you will pay the insurance vendor and assign the expense to an Other Current Asset account, and then create a recurring entry that QuickBooks uses to remind you to enter the expense; or QuickBooks will automatically enter the expense each month, depending on how you set up the reminder. This example shows how you would prepay a General Liability insurance bill of $12,000 for 12 months of coverage.

1. Create the vendor bill (or check form) to your insurance provider (or whatever type of prepaid expense you are recording). Instead of assigning the usual expense account on the form, assign the prepaid Other Current Asset type account. In this example, the account is Pre-paid General Lab Insurance.

2. Pay the bill to the vendor as normal.

3. Set up a recurring transaction to charge 1/12 of the total to each month. If the amount remains the same from month to month, set up the recurring entry to automatically post to QuickBooks. To do so, select **Company**, **Make General Journal Entries**. Create a journal entry with a debit to your expense account and a credit to the prepaid Other Current Asset type account.

 Digging Deeper

Did you know that you can memorize repeating transactions and let QuickBooks remind you or even automatically record them?

1. Create the transaction you want to memorize. However, this process can be used to memorize any of the QuickBooks forms, checks, bills, invoices, and so on.

2. Press Ctrl+M on your keyboard or from the Edit menu select Memorize to open the Memorize Transaction dialog box.

3. Choose to have QuickBooks remind you on a specific frequency, or choose to have QuickBooks automatically enter the transaction (see Figure 9.11).

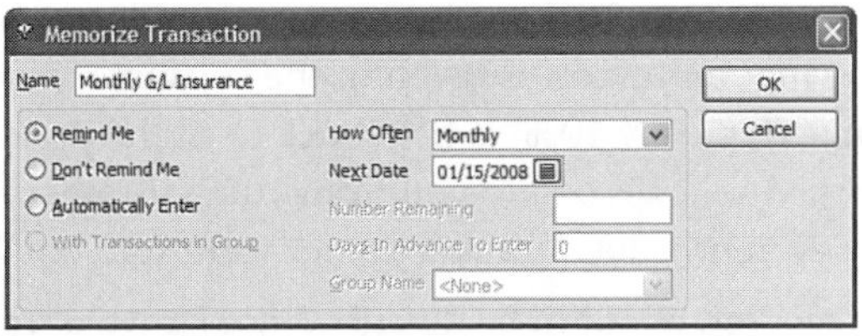

FIGURE 9.11

To automate data entry, memorize the transaction.

QuickBooks will list memorized transactions on the Memorized Transaction List, which is available by selecting Ctrl+T on your keyboard. You can also access this menu by selecting Lists, Memorized Transaction List.

You also might want to check your reminders (select Edit, Preferences, Reminders) to be sure you include a reminder for showing your memorized transactions.

When Another Software Program Is Used to Track Accounts Receivable or Inventory

You can use the Other Current Asset type account to record net changes to account balances (such as Accounts Receivable) for which you do not need to track details in QuickBooks. This is useful when other software is used to track the detail owed by a customer. Examples of this type of use might be a medical office that has billing software that tracks the patient's receivables, and QuickBooks needs to record only the net change to Accounts Receivable.

Using an Other Current Asset type account makes tracking the net change to your Accounts Receivable easy because no customer name is required to record an entry to this type of account.

The same is true for using this type of account in place of the Inventory account type for a business that has another software program to track the inventory details.

Tracking Customer Retainage in QuickBooks

Another common use for the Other Current Asset range of accounts is to track amounts that are invoiced to a customer, but are not due immediately and do not age. This practice is common in the construction industry and is referred to as *retainage*.

Basically, when an invoice is given to the customer, a percentage of the amount due (typically 10%) is held back until the project is completed. So, although the money is due to you from your customer, the 10% retainage portion is not currently due and you do not want it to age in your receivables.

Using the method about to be described does have a tradeoff. If you are a cash basis taxpayer, you would not expect to see a balance in your Accounts Receivable account when the Balance Sheet report is prepared on a cash basis. However, when you use this method, you will most likely see an Accounts Receivable balance on a cash basis Balance Sheet report. One of the causes of this is that QuickBooks reports an Accounts Receivable balance on a cash basis Balance Sheet report when items are used that map to other Balance Sheet accounts. You can find more detail about this in Chapter 4, "Easily Review Your QuickBooks Data."

To properly use the Other Current Asset type account for tracking customer retainage, you need to create the necessary chart of accounts and items following these steps:

1. Click **Lists, Chart of Accounts**.

2. Click the **Account** button at the bottom of the screen and select **New**.

3. In the Add New Account dialog that opens, select **Other Account Types**. From the Other Account Types drop-down list, select the Other Current Asset type account and click **Continue**.

4. The Add New Account dialog opens. Type an account name of Retainage and optionally, provide a description and tax line mapping. Click **Save & Close**.

5. Click **Lists, Item Lists**.

6. Click the **Item** button on the bottom of the list and select **New**.

7. From the New Item type drop-down menu, select **Other Charge**.

8. In the Item Name/Number field, enter a name such as Retainage Withheld. Enter an optional description and select the **Retainage** account from the Account drop-down menu, as shown in Figure 9.12. If your retainage is always 10%, you can put a –10% in the amount; if the amount varies, you can leave it blank. Optionally, you can create multiple retainage items for different percentages.

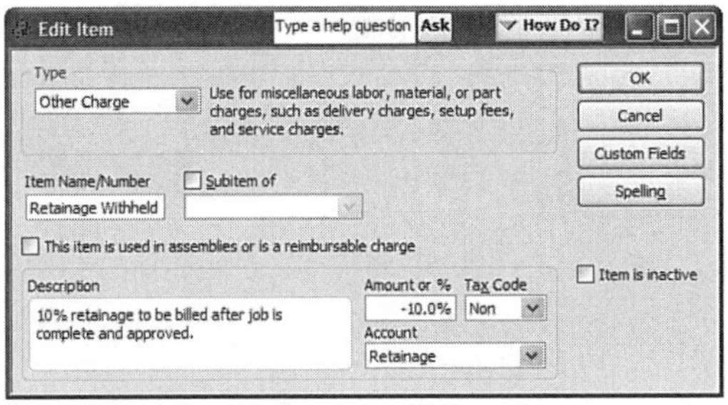

FIGURE 9.12

Creating the retainage withheld item to be used on customer invoices.

9. Follow steps 5 and 6 again to create another Other Charge list item and name it Retainage Billed (see Figure 9.13). Assign the Retainage account you just created. No default amount needs to be entered here.

10. Prepare your invoice to the customer for the full amount (in this example, $10,000.00) and on the next available line, enter the Retainage Withheld item (see Figure 9.14). Table 9.1 shows the financial effect. If you have more than one line on the invoice form, you might want to first place a Subtotal item, and then list your retainage withheld item.

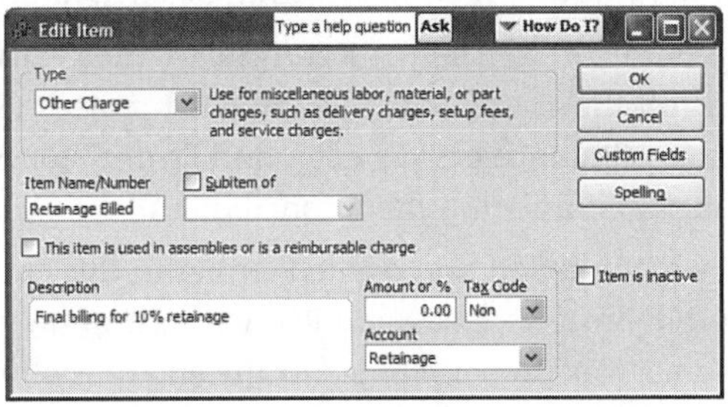

FIGURE 9.13

Create the final billing retainage item.

Table 9.1 Retainage Withheld Invoice Example		
Name	**Debit**	**Credit**
Accounts Receivable	$9,000.00	
Retainage Receivable	$1,000.00	
Construction Income (the income account that is assigned to the invoice item)		$10,000.00

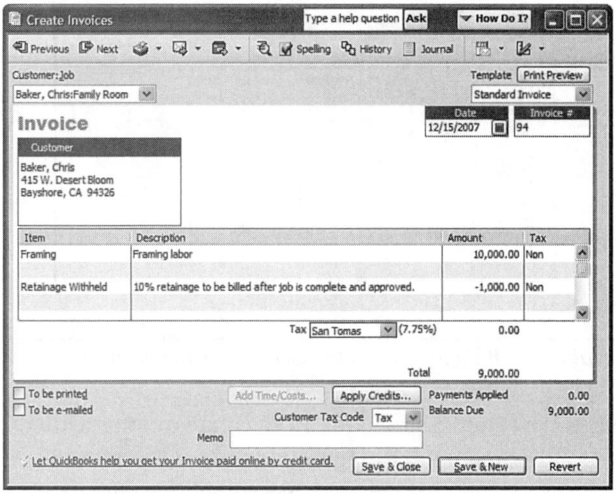

FIGURE 9.14
Creating a customer invoice with retainage withheld.

11. When the project is completed and you are ready to collect payment on the retainage amount withheld, create your final invoice and use the **Retainage Billed** item with a positive amount.

12. Optionally, reconcile the **Retainage Other Current Asset** account and clear all the entries for the completed project. (See Chapter 6, "Bank Account Balance or Reconciliation Errors," for more information on properly completing the reconciliation.)

13. Review the report you created earlier in this chapter (in the "Creating a Custom Transaction Detail Report" section) to verify the correct amount was properly billed at the end of the project.

These are just some of the many ways you can use the Other Current Asset account to improve your financial recordkeeping. Feel free to use this type of process for other accounting needs such as tracking vendor prepaids or even tracking receivables between multiple legal entities that you might own.

Chapter 10

Reviewing and Correcting Inventory Errors

- Overview of the Accounting for Inventory
- Preferences That Affect Inventory
- Inventory Processes and Forms and Their Effect on Accounting
- Reviewing and Troubleshooting Inventory Balances
- Correcting Inventory Errors
- How QuickBooks Handles Negative Inventory

Overview of the Accounting for Inventory

Inventory can be described as a company's merchandise, raw materials, and finished and unfinished products that have not yet been sold.

QuickBooks can track the products you purchase, stock, and then later sell to customers. QuickBooks can also track the products that you assemble (component) and use to create a product for sale (finished good).

QuickBooks has a perpetual inventory system, meaning that each time you record a purchase document, inventory is increased, and when you record a sales document, inventory is decreased. (See the "Inventory Processes and Forms and Their Effect on Accounting" section later in this chapter.)

Also, QuickBooks records the cost for inventory using the Average Cost method as apposed to LIFO (Last In First Out) or FIFO (First In First Out). This means that the cost recorded at any time is equal to the number of inventory units divided by the total cost of the units. QuickBooks automates this process for you. As long as you record your documents correctly and date them appropriately, QuickBooks will assign the correct average cost.

Ask yourself these important questions before beginning to create and track inventory items:

- Will you be selling what you buy, and do you not know the customer at the time of purchase? An example might be a furniture store that purchases furniture for resale to customers, or a retail store that purchases medical supplies that are sold to customers. These qualify as the proper use of inventory items.

- Are you manufacturing what you sell? In other words, you buy components (raw materials) and later assemble the components into a finished product that is sold to a customer. An example might be a bike store that purchases wheels, steering columns, chains, and so on and then assembles the components into a completed bike for sale to the customer. This qualifies as the proper use of inventory items.

- Are you purchasing materials that you use, but do not sell? For example, a car repair business might purchase buffing pads and paint supplies. These items are stored in inventory, but are not sold directly to a customer. This example is a more appropriate use of non-inventory items.

- Is the dollar value of your inventory not significant? Often, companies carry a small amount of inventory, but the majority of their sales are drop-shipped directly to the customer from the vendor that the product is purchased from. For example, a construction company can order appliances for a new home but does not generally stock them. Instead, they have the appliances shipped directly to the new home from the vendor. This example is a more appropriate use of a non-inventory item.

In summary, QuickBooks has the following item types for use in the management of inventory and non-inventory:

- Inventory items (see Figure 10.1)
    - Items both purchased and sold
    - Items that are stored in stock and later sold
    - Items purchased and used as components of a finished product

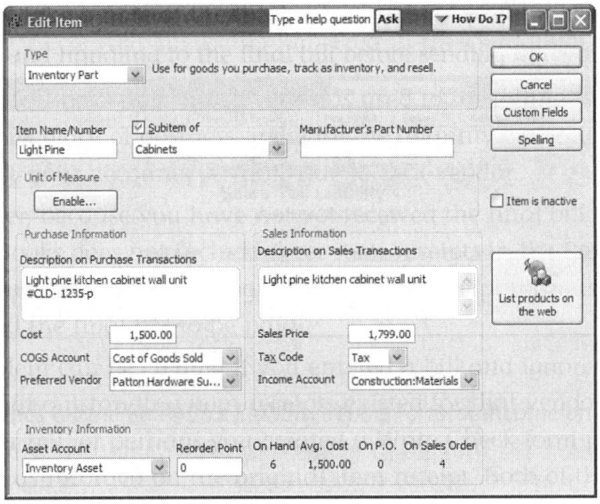

FIGURE 10.1

An inventory part.

- Non-inventory items (see Figure 10.2)
    - Purchased but not sold
    - Sold but not purchased
    - Purchased and resold, but not tracked as stock

Inventory items require assigning an expense account (usually a Cost of Goods Sold type), an income account, and an asset account.

Non-inventory items only require one account by default. This is okay if you don't both purchase and sell the item. It is recommended that when creating a non-inventory item type, you place a check mark in the "This item is used in assemblies or is purchased for a specific customer:job" box, as shown in Figure 10.2. This enables you to assign both an expense and income account in the event you do both purchase and sell the item.

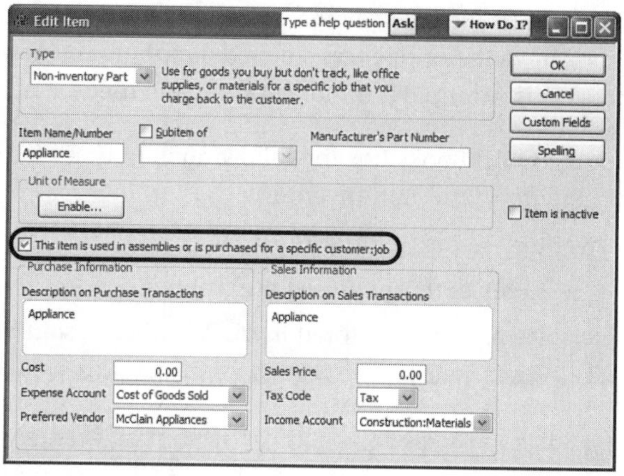

FIGURE 10.2

Non-inventory part with this item is used in assemblies or is purchased for a specific customer:job selected.

Digging Deeper

Optionally, you can record a default cost (recommended), default sales price, and default preferred vendor for both types.

Before you begin tracking inventory, you should know the commitment you are making to additional accounting responsibilities. When choosing to track inventory in the normal course of your business, you need to use purchase forms to increase inventory, and sales forms to decrease inventory. You also need to commit to periodic inventory counts because your inventory can often get out of sync with your accounting information.

Preferences That Affect Inventory

To begin using QuickBooks to track inventory, you must first turn on the feature found in the Items and Inventory preference in QuickBooks. By default, when creating a new company data file, inventory management is not enabled. To turn on the inventory feature, follow these steps:

1. Log in to the data file as the Admin or External Accountant user.

2. Select **Edit, Preferences** and choose the **Items and Inventory** preference.

3. Click the **Company Preferences** tab and place a check mark in **Inventory and purchase orders are active**.

4. Click **OK** to save the preference.

These preferences do not affect the accounting for inventory, but rather enable specific features within inventory management (see Figure 10.3).

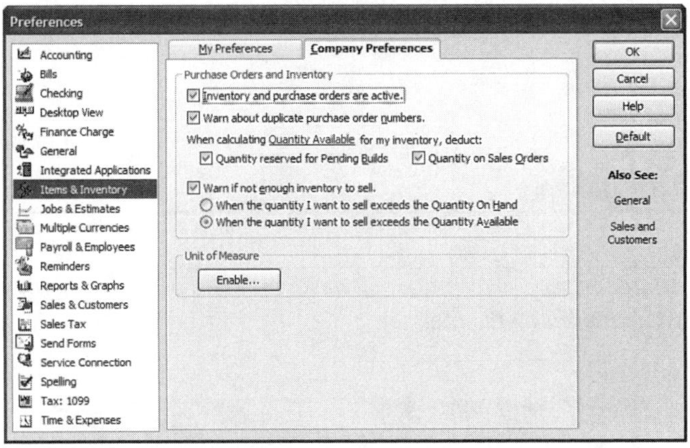

FIGURE 10.3

Preferences that enable QuickBooks inventory.

Your QuickBooks Home page now shows the inventory workflow. To view the Home page (if it does not automatically open), select Edit, Preferences, and choose the Desktop View preference. Click the My Preferences tab and place a check mark in the Show home page when opening a company file box.

One additional preference that can affect your setup of inventory is found in the Time and Expenses, Company Preferences tab (accessed like you did previously for the Item and Inventory preference). When a percentage is entered in the Invoicing options pane for the Default Markup Percentage setting, QuickBooks automatically makes the default Sales Price to be the cost multiplied by the markup on a new item when the cost is first recorded (see Figure 10.4).

For example, when you create a new inventory list item and enter a cost of $3.00, QuickBooks will default the sales price of $3.30, or $3.00 + 10% markup, as shown in Figure 10.5.

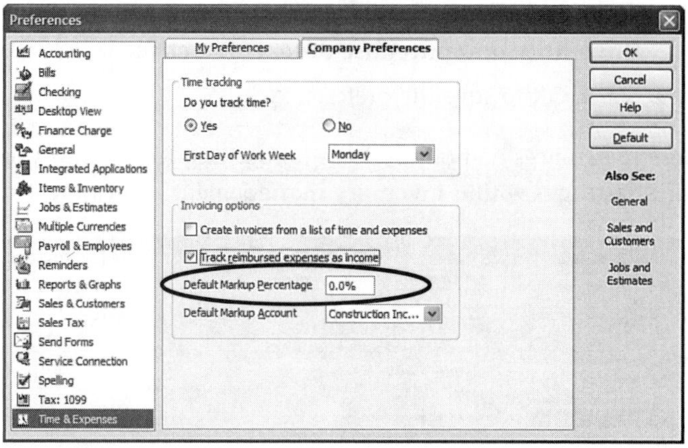

FIGURE 10.4

Including a default markup percentage will make the sales price of a newly created inventory item to be cost multiplied by the markup.

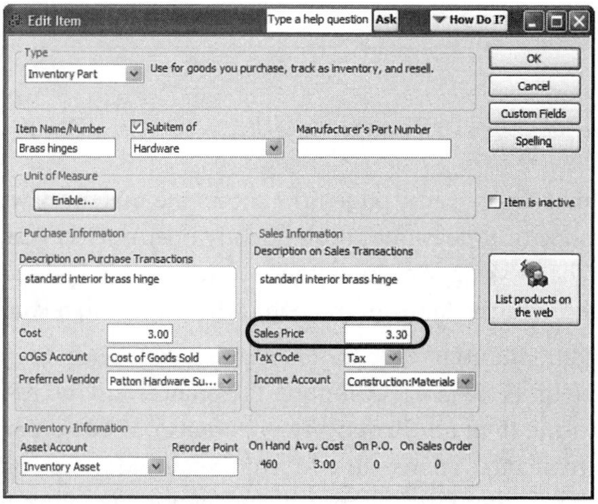

FIGURE 10.5

QuickBooks automatically calculates the sales price when you set the preference for default markup in Time and Expenses Preference.

Another feature that was introduced with QuickBooks 2007 is the Unit of Measure. With this feature, you can define the following for inventory items or non-inventory items in QuickBooks:

- **Single Unit of Measure.** Choose this if you buy, stock, and sell each item by the same unit of measure. If you buy by the pound, sell by the pound, and track your inventory by the pound, this option is the best choice.

- **Multiple Unit of Measure.** If you buy in one measurement, for example, you purchase cases (such as a case of canned soda) and sell to the customer in single units (a can of soda), but track inventory in skids (multiple cases of soda), the Multiple Unit of Measure option is the best choice.

When you select Multiple Unit of Measure and assign it to an inventory or non-inventory item, you can also define your default units of measure for purchase, sales, and shipping forms, as shown in Figure 10.6.

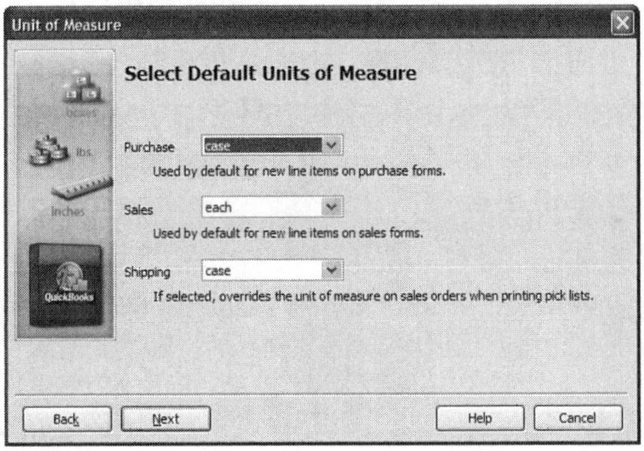

FIGURE 10.6

When Multiple Unit of Measure is enabled, you can define your default units for specific purchase and sales forms.

Unit of Measure settings indirectly affect your accounting by defaulting the unit and the associated cost and sales price. Using this feature can improve your buying and selling accuracy on your documents.

Inventory Processes and Forms and Their Effect on Accounting

Understanding the proper inventory process and the associated forms can help you use the inventory feature properly. If you are new to inventory management, QuickBooks makes getting started with it easy, via the workflow outlined on the Home page, as shown in Figure 10.7.

Use a purchase order if you want to compare the bill that the vendor sends with the original agreed-to quantity and cost. With purchase orders, you can also keep track of what items have been ordered and have not yet been delivered.

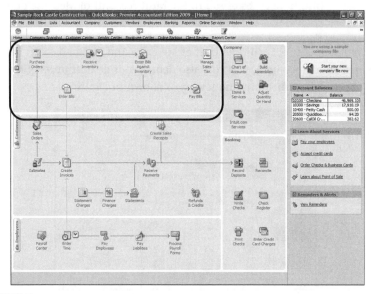

FIGURE 10.7

Use the Inventory workflow from the QuickBooks Home page.

You can receive inventory in one of two ways. With one method, you receive inventory with the vendor's final bill. If you record full receipt of the quantity, QuickBooks will then mark the purchase order as closed. You can also choose to receive inventory without a bill. QuickBooks will create an Item Receipt document that can be viewed in the accounts payable reports and ages with other vendor bills, but cannot yet be paid in the Pay Bills window.

Rest assured that as you create the vendor's final bill, QuickBooks will recognize if you have outstanding purchase orders or item receipts that you want to associate with the vendor's bill.

Table 10.1 shows a listing of all forms that you should use when working with Inventory items and their related effects on the company's accounting.

Table 10.1   Inventory Items

Form Name	Purpose of Form	Effect on Accounting
Purchase Order	Record order placed with vendor	No effect
Item Receipt without Bill	Record receipt of inventory items	Increase inventory, increase accounts payable (bill *cannot* be selected in the Pay Bills window)
Item Receipt with Bill	Record receipt of inventory items	Increase inventory, increase accounts payable (bill can be selected in the Pay Bills window)
Bill	Record bill (optionally assign purchase order or item receipt)	Increase inventory, increase accounts payable
Check	Items tab used (optionally assign purchase order or item receipt)	Increase inventory, decrease cash
Estimates	Record quote for sales of items to a customer	No effect
Sales Order	Manage sales of inventory by committing it for sale (used to manage back orders of inventory)	No effect, except to show the items in inventory as committed
Invoice	Record sale of inventory to customer	Decrease inventory, increase Cost of Goods Sold, increase Income
Sales Receipt	Record sale of inventory to customer	Decrease inventory, increase Cost of Goods Sold, increase Income
Inventory Adjustment – Quantity	Record a change to the quantity of stock on hand	Decrease or increase inventory and decrease or increase Inventory Adjustment account (Cost of Goods Sold type or Expense type)
Inventory Adjustment – Value	Record a change to the value of the stock on hand	Decrease or increase inventory and decrease or increase Inventory Adjustment account (Cost of Goods Sold type or Expense type)

Reviewing and Troubleshooting Inventory Balances

For companies that do track inventory, I find Inventory balances are one of the last numbers in QuickBooks that truly gets a good look. You review your accounts receivable because you have customers that need to pay you. You keep up with your accounts payable because you have vendors that won't supply you without first getting paid. Why exactly is it that Inventory "reconciling" is often at the bottom of the list, yet it can have the greatest impact on your company's financials?

Experience has taught me that most companies simply do not know how in QuickBooks to properly review and audit their inventory balances. This section outlines specific reports and methods you can use in QuickBooks to make sure your Inventory balances are correct.

If you are using Inventory in your QuickBooks data, it is preferred that you view your financial reports in accrual basis. Most companies that have inventory report their tax financials in accrual basis. However, a more important reason is that on accrual basis reporting, QuickBooks will match the cost with the related sale. The exception is when using non-inventory items. These items, when purchased, do not increase an Inventory asset account. Instead, they are recorded directly to the Cost of Goods Sold account, or the Expense account that was assigned when the item was created.

Perform a Physical Inventory Count

All too often, here is where I find a complacent attitude about inventory management. I agree this is a time-consuming task. However, if effort is put to this task, your overall financials will be more accurate.

Select Reports, Inventory, and then select the Physical Inventory report to make recording the count easier. The report cannot be modified or filtered, so you should run the report at the same time you plan to do your physical count (see Figure 10.8). If you want to keep a record of the original worksheet, you can export it to Excel or email it as a PDF attachment.

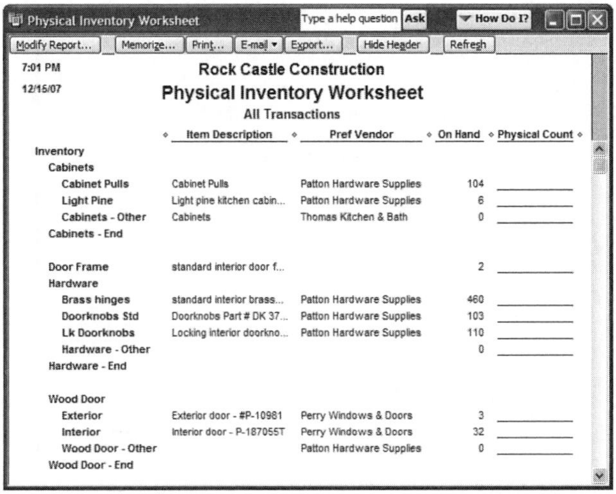

FIGURE 10.8

Create a physical inventory worksheet to record the actual inventory counts.

After completing a physical inventory count, you can then confidently create an inventory adjustment so that the accounting records will match your actual physical inventory.

Reconciling the Inventory Valuation Summary Report with the Balance Sheet Inventory Balance

Another equally important task in inventory management is to compare your Inventory Valuation Summary report to your Balance Sheet Inventory Asset balance (accrual basis).

1. Select **Reports, Inventory, Inventory Valuation Summary**, and select the specific date that you are reconciling your Balance Sheet Inventory balance to.

2. Compare your Balance Sheet Inventory balance to the total Asset Value on the Inventory Valuation Summary report (see Figures 10.9 and 10.10).

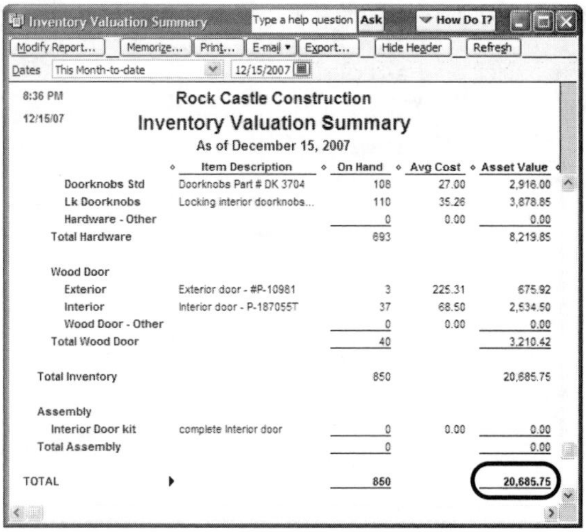

FIGURE 10.9

Compare your total Asset Value with your Balance Sheet Inventory balance.

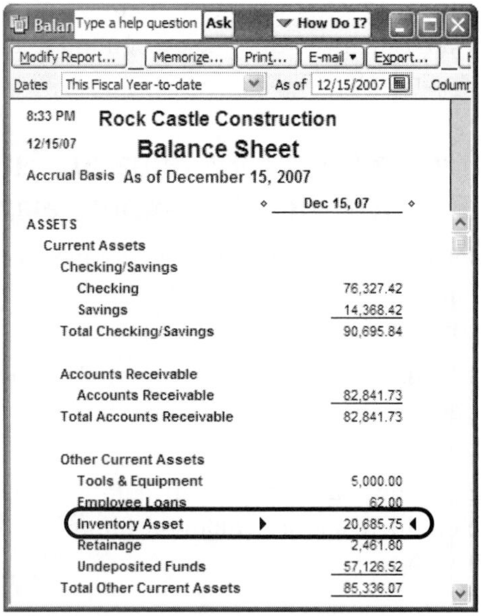

FIGURE 10.10

Compare your Balance Sheet Inventory balance to the total Asset Value on the Inventory Valuation Summary.

What if the two balances do not match? The most common cause for the two reports not to match is entering a transaction that affects the Inventory Asset account, but it does not affect inventory items. The Inventory Summary report only shows the results of transactions that use inventory items. If a General Journal has been used to adjust the Balance Sheet balance, those transactions will not affect the Inventory Valuation Summary report.

Rescue Me!

When working with inventory adjustments, never use a General Journal form. The specific reason is because a General Journal form does not use Items, and any adjustments using this form affect only the Balance Sheet balance, not the Inventory Valuation Summary report.

Instead, perform the appropriate type of adjustment by selecting Vendors, Inventory Activities, and selecting Adjust Quantity/Value on Hand, as discussed in the "Correcting Inventory Errors" section of this chapter.

To find General Journal entries that might be causing the out-of-balance amount, double-click the Balance Sheet Inventory balance. QuickBooks creates the Transactions by Account report. To locate the General Journal entries, on the top, right of the report, select Type from the Sort By list, as shown in Figure 10.11. QuickBooks now organizes the data by transaction type. Look for General Journal type transactions.

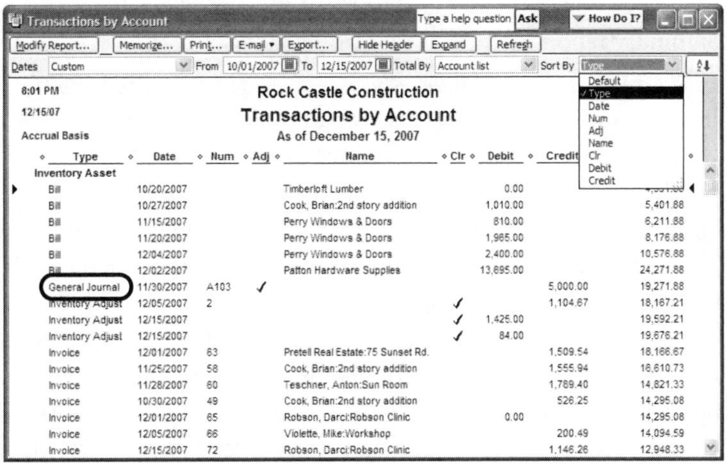

FIGURE 10.11

Sort by Type on the Transactions by Account report to locate General Journal transactions.

You should not delete or void these transactions, especially if they were used in accounting periods that have already had tax returns prepared using the current financial information. Continue with the remaining methods in the sections that follow, before making any corrections.

Reviewing the Recorded Average Cost Valuation

As mentioned earlier in this chapter, QuickBooks uses the Average Cost method for valuing inventory.

As an example, you are selling an item called Widget A.

	Quantity	Cost per		
Date	Purchased	Unit	Total Cost	Average Cost
12/15/07	100	$10.00	$1,000.00	$10.00
12/25/07	50	$8.50	$425.00	$9.50
TOTAL	150		$1,425.00	(1425/150)

Table 10.2   Calculating Average Cost

Sales documents that are dated on or between 12/15/07 and 12/24/07 selling this item will record Cost of Goods sold at $10.00 per unit.

Sales documents that are dated on or after 12/25/07 will record Cost of Goods sold at $9.50 per unit.

Average costing is a perfect fit for a business that sells a product that does not fluctuate significantly in cost from one period to the next. However, this is not always the case, so it becomes important that you verify the relative accuracy of the average cost that QuickBooks has recorded on the Inventory Valuation Summary report.

In Figure 10.9 shown previously, the average cost for the Interior Wood Door is listed as $68.50. Compare this amount to a recent vendor bill. If the amount is significantly different, you will need to research the purchase details for the item.

To easily create an Inventory Valuation Detail report for an item while viewing an Inventory Valuation Summary report, simply double-click the Avg Cost column for the item in question.

In Figure 10.12, the Inventory Valuation Detail is shown for the Interior Wood Door. Reviewing the individual lines in the Average Cost column can help you determine whether an issue exists with the average cost. If the average cost changes dramatically, you might want to review the specific bill or check form used to purchase the product.

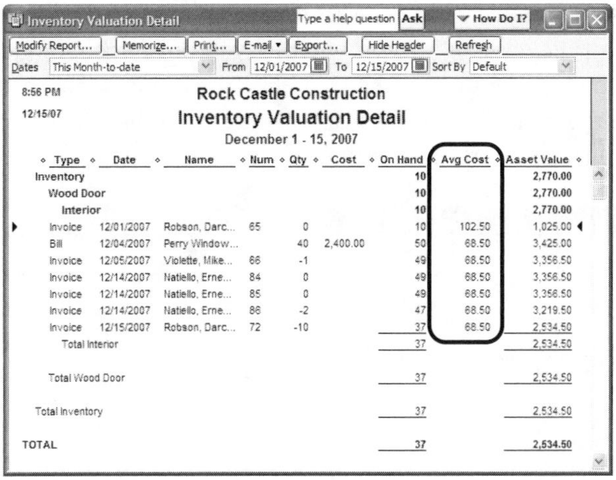

FIGURE 10.12

Create an Inventory Valuation Detail report from the Inventory Valuation Summary report.

Reviewing and correcting the average cost of items is equally important to adjusting the quantity on hand.

Reviewing Aged Open Item Receipts

As you read previously in this chapter (in the "Inventory Processes and Forms and Their Effect on Accounting" section) concerning the inventory process, one of the optional methods of receiving inventory is without the vendor's bill.

The effect of receiving inventory without a bill is to increase your inventory asset (debit) and increase your accounts payable (credit). The unique feature of this method is that QuickBooks creates an item receipt form that *will not* show in the Pay Bills window. QuickBooks recognizes that because you did not receive the bill, it is not likely that you should be paying it without the final bill details.

Often, goods will arrive at your business without a bill. A couple of reasons exist for a vendor to ship the goods to your place of business without a final bill:

- Shipping charges need to be added to the bill. Often, the vendor will not know the shipping charges when the goods are initially shipped.
- Vendors do not want to disclose the value of the inventory, so that those who handle the inventory during shipping will not know the value of the goods being shipped.

What you might not know is that item receipts age just like an outstanding accounts payable bill. To see whether you have open, outdated item receipts, go to the Vendor Center and click the Transactions tab (see Figure 10.13). Select the Item Receipts transaction type. Filter by All Dates and double-click on the Date column to sort the transactions by date.

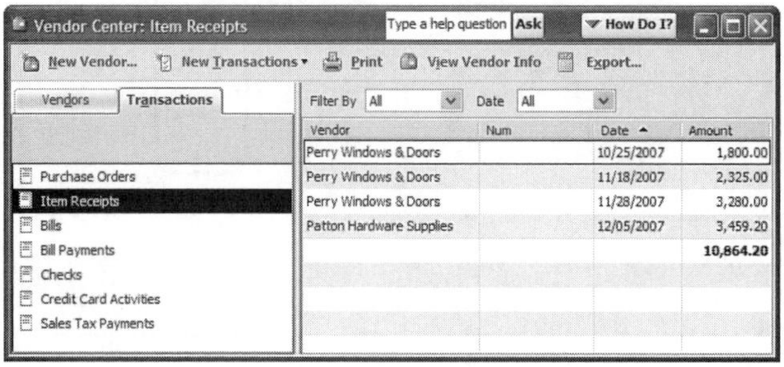

FIGURE 10.13

Use the Transactions tab of the Vendor Center to see all open item receipts.

You might discover that you have created item receipts and instead of associating a bill with the item receipt, you created checks to the vendors. To see whether this might be the case, select the Checks transaction type. If you do find that this happened, then the user had to have first bypassed the warning shown in Figure 10.14 when creating the check for the vendor.

FIGURE 10.14

Warning provided when creating a check to a vendor with an open item receipt.

Digging Deeper

The warning shown in Figure 10.14 also offers the option to not display the warning again. If you think this option was selected and you are no longer being warned, you can turn the warning (as well as others) back on. Select Edit, Preferences, and click the My Preferences tab. Click General, and click the Bring back all one time messages check box, as shown in Figure 10.15.

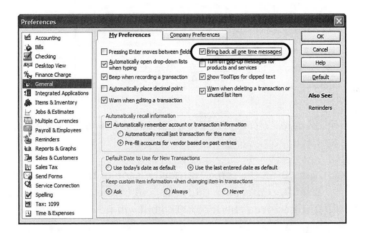

FIGURE 10.15

By selecting the Bring back all one time messages, warnings that have been previously bypassed will again be shown when a user attempts to do something for which QuickBooks supplies a warning.

To associate a check with an item receipt, follow these steps. Make sure that the dates of the transactions being modified are not in an accounting year that has already had a tax return prepared using those prior period balances.

1. After locating the check on the Vendor Center, Transactions tab as described earlier, double-click the check to open up the Write Check form. Modify the Account to **Accounts Payable**, as shown in Figure 10.16. Next, assign the Vendor name in the **Customer:Job** column. The effect of this is to decrease (debit) Accounts Payable and decrease (credit) Cash.

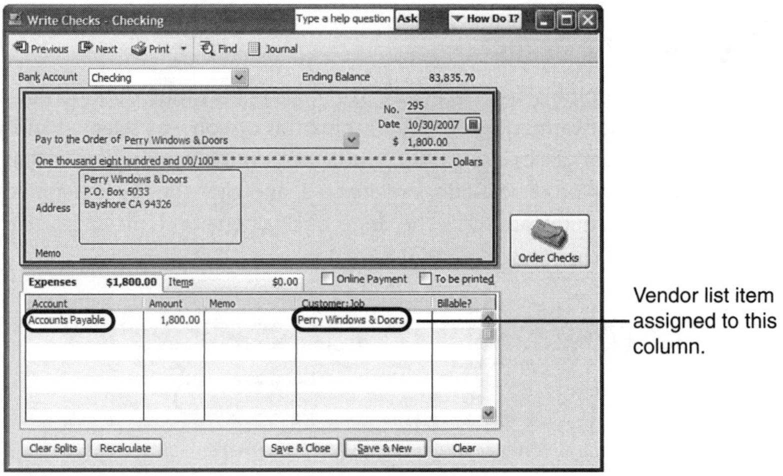

Vendor list item assigned to this column.

FIGURE 10.16

Changing the account to Accounts Payable and adding the vendor name on the same line creates a vendor credit.

2. Next, from the same Transactions tab of the Vendor Center, select the **Item Receipts** form that was paid by the Write Check form, click the **Bill Received** check box. The bill will now be included in the Pay Bills window (see Figure 10.17).

3. Select **Vendor, Pay Bills** to open the Pay Bills dialog box. Select the bill (now visible because it is no longer an item receipt). After the bill is selected, QuickBooks recognizes that there is a credit available to be assigned in the Set Credits information of the Pay Bills dialog (see Figure 10.18).

4. Click the **Set Credits** button to assign the modified check transaction from step 3 to the open vendor bill (see Figure 10.19).

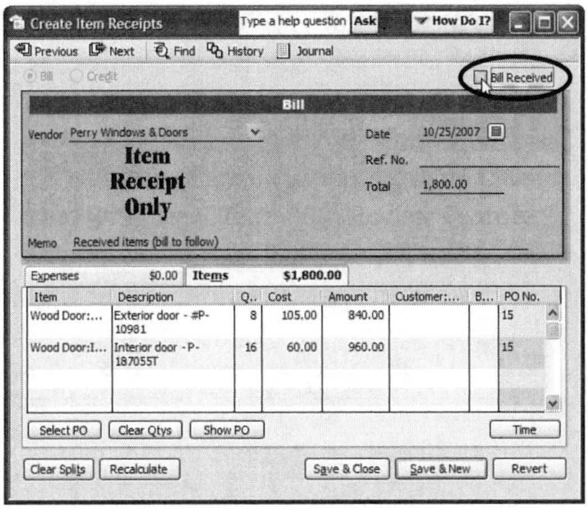

FIGURE 10.17
Checking the Bill Received check box changes the status from Item Receipt to Bill, enabling you to assign the credit to the bill.

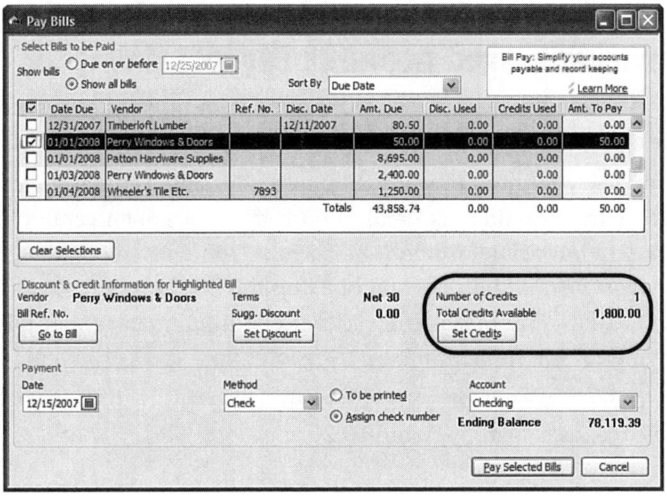

FIGURE 10.18
When a vendor has credits available, they appear in the Set Credits information in the Pay Bills dialog.

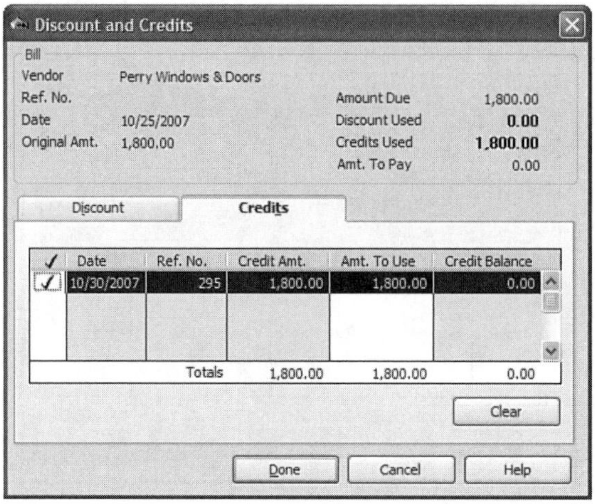

FIGURE 10.19

QuickBooks automatically matches a credit with a bill of the same amount, or you can select the credit and modify the amount assigned.

Reviewing Aged Accounts Payable

At the same time you review your open item receipts, you should also review your accounts payable open invoices that are aged more than 60 days.

To review your accounts payable, select Reports, Vendors & Payables and choose the Unpaid Bills Detail report. If you see open vendor bills you are sure you have paid, it might be because you created a Write Check form to pay your vendor bills instead of using the Bill Payment form (accessed from the Vendors, Pay Bills menu). Having both an open vendor bill and check paying for the same purchase overstates your costs or inventory.

QuickBooks tries to prevent you from doing this by providing a warning message, as shown in Figure 10.20.

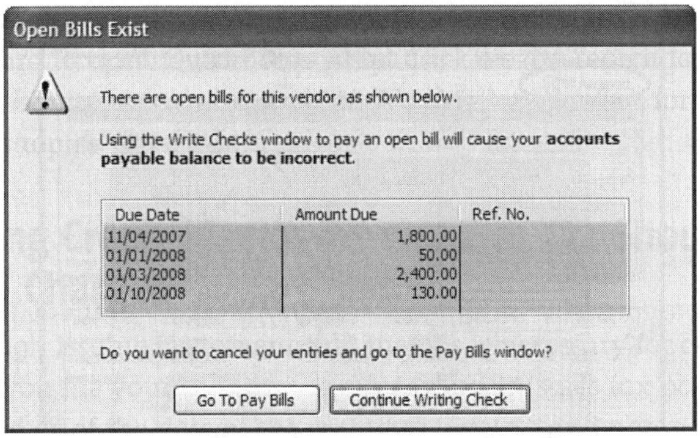

FIGURE 10.20

If you pay a vendor with open bills using a check form, QuickBooks will redirect you to the Pay Bills dialog.

To assign a Write Check form previously issued to a vendor in payment for a currently open vendor bill, follow these steps:

1. Select the **Vendor Center** from the icon bar. Highlight the vendor in question.

2. In the pane to the right of the vendor's name, select the **Show** drop-down menu and select **Checks**.

3. Optionally, filter for a specific bank account and date range or select All to not filter on these fields.

4. Locate the check in question. Double-click the check to open the Write Checks form. Edit the account column to be the **Accounts Payable** chart of accounts list item.

5. In the Customer:Job column, enter the **Vendor Name** from the vendor list. The result is to decrease (debit) your Accounts Payable for this vendor and decrease (credit) cash for the bank account selected on the Write Check form. Click **Save & Close**.

6. To associate this vendor "credit" with the open bill, click **Vendors**, Pay Bills. The Pay Bills dialog opens. Find the open vendor bill and place a check mark next to the bill.

7. Click the **Set Credit** button that is enabled. The Set Credits dialog enables you to assign the "check" credit to the bill. Select **Done** to assign the credit. More detailed information on Accounts Payable processes can be found in Chapter 11, "Reviewing and Correcting Accounts Payable Errors."

You have now successfully assigned the Write Check form to the Open Vendor Bill that should have been paid by a Bill Payment check. This correction has now removed the expected overstatement in your costs and removed the bill from being included in your open Accounts Payable balances.

Correcting Inventory Errors

Any company that manages inventory needs to manage inventory errors. Business owners will list any of the following reasons for having to correct his or her accounting inventory errors:

- Errors in the physical counted results
- Damaged goods
- Theft of inventory
- Open vendor item receipts or bills that are not due to the vendor
- Incorrect valuation given to the inventory at the startup of a data file

This section discusses the methods for correcting inventory errors you might find in your QuickBooks data. If you have a good inventory count commitment and manage the resulting information from the QuickBooks Inventory Valuation Summary report, you should see little to no data entry errors and instead probably will be adjusting inventory only for damage or theft.

Creating an Inventory Quantity Adjustment

If you discovered quantity differences between your accounting records and your physical inventory account, you should record an inventory quantity adjustment to correct your accounting records.

Before creating the accounting adjustment, make sure you have created an account in the Chart of Accounts to hold the value of the inventory adjustment. The account type can be either a Cost of Goods Sold type or an Expense type. For the business owner, consult your accountant when making this decision.

To create an inventory quantity adjustment, follow these steps:

1. Select **Vendors, Inventory Activities** and choose **Adjust Quantity/Value on Hand,** as shown in Figure 10.21.

2. Enter an **Adjustment Date** and optional Ref. No. Optionally, assign a Customer:Job and select your Inventory Adjustment chart of accounts (this can be either a Cost of Goods Sold or Expense type chart of account list item).

3. In the **New Qty** column, enter your count from the completed physical inventory or optionally enter the change in the **Qty Difference** column.

4. QuickBooks will provide the Total Value of the Adjustment at the bottom of the dialog for your review as you make the needed changes. Select **Save & Close** when completed.

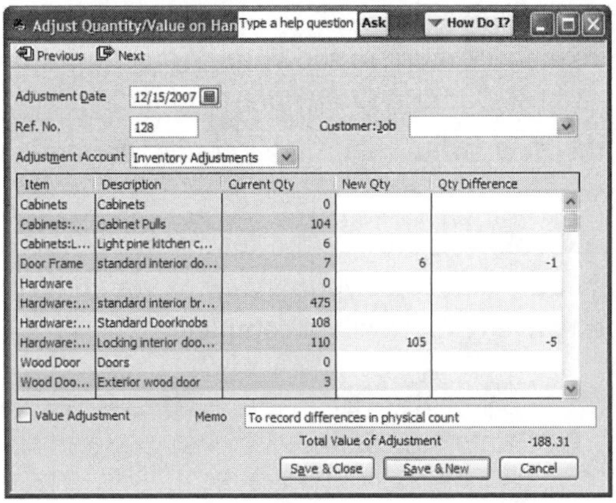

FIGURE 10.21

Record an adjustment for inventory quantity differences after performing a physical inventory count.

The accounting effect of the transaction in Figure 10.21 is to reduce the quantity on hand for each of the items shown, reduce (credits) the Inventory asset balance by $188.31, and increase (debits) the Inventory Adjustments account (either a Cost of Goods Sold type or Expense type).

Creating an Inventory Value Adjustment

Timing is important when doing a valuation adjustment. Value adjustments, if appropriate, should be carefully considered for their impact on the company's resulting financials.

Rescue Me!

This type of adjustment is generally not done as often as quantity adjustments. The purpose of this book is not to explore or offer tax advice, but certain guidelines exist for when an inventory valuation adjustment is appropriate. Ask your tax accountant to provide them for you.

To create an inventory value adjustment, follow these steps:

1. Select **Vendors, Inventory Activities** and choose the **Adjust Quantity/Value on Hand**, as shown in Figure 10.22.

2. Enter an **Adjustment Date** and optional Ref. No. Optionally, assign a Customer:Job and select your Inventory Adjustment chart of accounts (this can be either a Cost of Goods Sold or Expense type chart of account list item).

3. Place a check mark in the **Value Adjustment** box in the lower-left of the Adjust Quantity/Value on hand dialog.

4. In the **New Value** column, enter your current total dollar value for the inventory.

5. QuickBooks will provide the Total Value of the Adjustment at the bottom of the dialog for your review as you make the needed changes. Select **Save & Close** when completed.

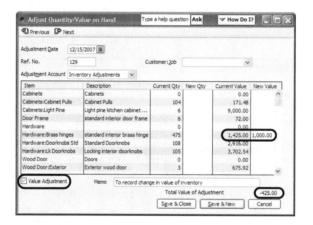

FIGURE 10.22

Record an inventory value adjustment.

The accounting result of this inventory value adjustment as shown in Figure 10.22 is no net change to inventory quantities, a decrease (credit) to your Inventory Asset account and an increase (debit) to your Inventory Adjustments account (either a Cost of Goods Sold type or Expense type). A new average cost will be computed based on the (`Original Asset Value + or - the Value Difference`) / `Quantity on Hand` as recorded on the inventory value adjustment.

The new average cost will be recorded when a sales document uses this item, *on or after* the date of the inventory adjustment.

Rescue Me!

Did you know how important the date is when assigning the inventory adjustment? If you back date your inventory adjustment, QuickBooks will recalculate your Cost of Goods Sold from that date forward using the new average cost as of the date of the sales form. Care should be taken not to date an inventory adjustment in a prior year where tax returns have already been filed.

Digging Deeper

There are two ways to control dating transactions. To access them, log in as the Admin or new External Accountant user in single-user mode. Click Company, Set Closing Date to open Company Preferences for Accounting (see Figure 10.23). Setting Date Warnings enables a user to be warned when a transaction is either dated so many days in the past or in the future. Set Date/Password is another option to "close" QuickBooks to adding, voiding, or deleting transactions prior to a selected closing date. Setting a closing date and related features is discussed more fully in Chapter 15, "Sharing Data with Your Accountant or Your Client."

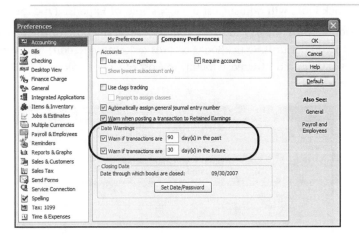

FIGURE 10.23

Choices for controlling past- or future-dated transactions.

How QuickBooks Handles Negative Inventory

QuickBooks enables selling of inventory, even if you do not have enough quantity available for sale. This situation is referred to as selling negative inventory. What it means is that you can include an inventory item on a customer invoice before you have recorded the receipt or purchase of the item into your inventory.

Although this method can be useful for getting the invoice to the customer, it can create issues with your company's financials. The following sections detail how QuickBooks handles the costing of the inventory behind the scenes when you sell negative inventory and provides information on how to avoid or minimize the negative effect it can have on your company's financials.

When Inventory Has an Average Cost from Prior Purchase Transactions

If you review the Inventory Valuation Detail report (click Reports, Inventory, Inventory Valuation Detail) for the item(s) that have negative values, and there are previously recorded average cost amounts, QuickBooks will assign the most recent average cost dated on or before the invoice date that created negative inventory. When the purchase document is later recorded, QuickBooks will adjust Cost of Goods Sold or Expense type for any difference.

Figure 10.24 shows that the average cost on the date of the invoice was $150.00 per unit. QuickBooks records a decrease (credit) to inventory of $300.00 and an increase (debit) to Cost of Goods Sold of $300.00 for the two units sold.

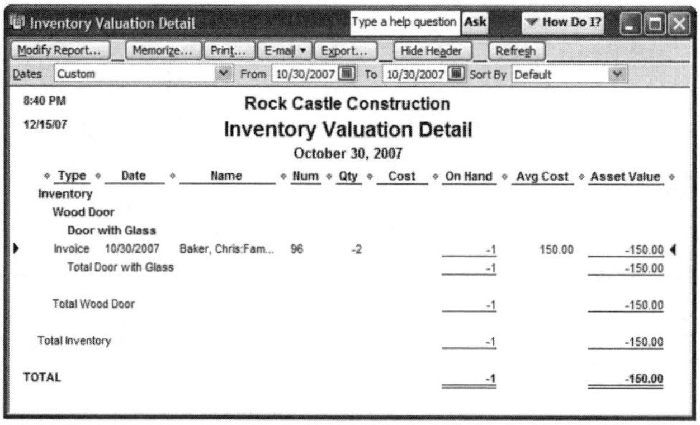

FIGURE 10.24
QuickBooks records the Cost of Goods Sold for negative inventory items at the last known average cost.

To show how important the date of the purchase document is, the following example shows how to create a bill replenishing inventory dated 11/15/07, or 15 days after the invoice form creating negative inventory, for 3 units at a cost of $200.00 per unit.

The new inventory asset value is calculated as

($150.00)	Inventory asset value as of 10/30/07
<u>$600.00</u>	11/15/07 purchase of 3 units @ $200.00 / unit
$450.00	Asset value before QuickBooks' automatic adjustment to COGS

Actual inventory value is 2 remaining units at $200 each or $400.00 total

<u>$(50.00)</u>	11/15/07 vendor bill document created. QuickBooks automatically decreases (credits) Inventory asset and increases (debits) COGS with no association of the increased per unit cost to the customer.
$400.00	Resulting Inventory Asset value on 11/15/07 as shown in Figure 10.25.

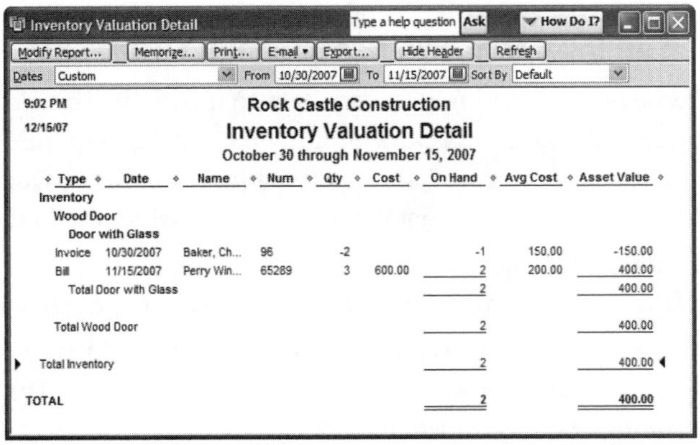

FIGURE 10.25

The Inventory Valuation Detail shows the actual inventory value after recording the purchase document.

Digging Deeper

What is important to note here is that QuickBooks does not retroactively record the additional cost back to the customer's negative inventory invoice date. In fact, QuickBooks records the adjustment as of the date of the purchase document and will not associate the adjustment with the original customer at all, overstating gross profit on a Profit & Loss by Job report.

The date of the replenishing purchase document becomes increasingly important to manage when you let inventory go negative at the end of a fiscal or tax year in your data.

When Inventory Does Not Have a Prior Average Cost

There might be times when you stock a new item and you add it to a customer invoice before recording any purchase activity for the item. If this happens, you should be sure to at least record a default cost on the Edit Item window.

When an Inventory Item Has a Default Cost

If you have assigned an inventory item to a customer invoice that you have not yet purchased (that is, the quantity on hand is zero) and if you *did* define a default cost when you first created the inventory item, QuickBooks will use this default cost as the suggested per-unit cost when the invoice is recorded.

Let's suppose you stock a new inventory item for a Door with Glass. When creating the item, you record a default cost of $150.00, as shown in Figure 10.26.

Before any purchase is recorded for this item, it is sold on a customer invoice. When you create an invoice where there is no inventory, QuickBooks provides a warning, as shown in Figure 10.27.

QuickBooks has to estimate the cost of the item and in this example uses the cost assigned to the item in the Edit Item dialog. When you save this invoice, QuickBooks will increase (debit) Accounts Receivable, increase (credit) Income, decrease (credit) Inventory Asset, and increase (debit) Cost of Goods Sold, and in this example, will increase (credit) Sales Tax Payable. The transaction journal report details the accounting automatically recorded by QuickBooks (see Figure 10.28).

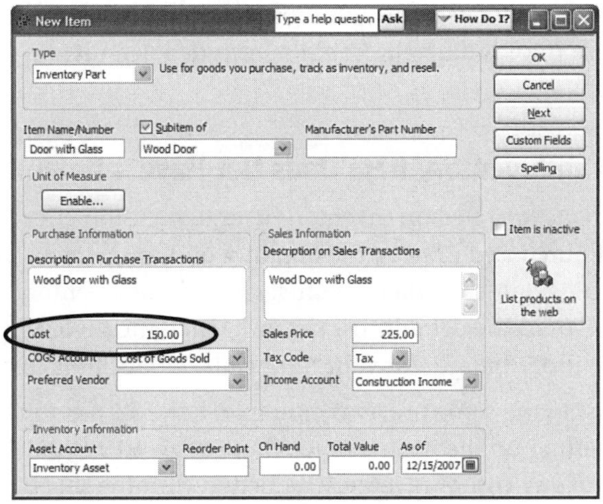

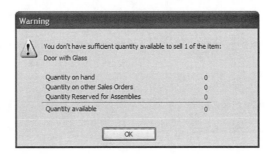

FIGURE 10.26

New stock item created in QuickBooks with a default cost of $150.00.

FIGURE 10.27

The warning provided when you try to sell more inventory than is available for sale.

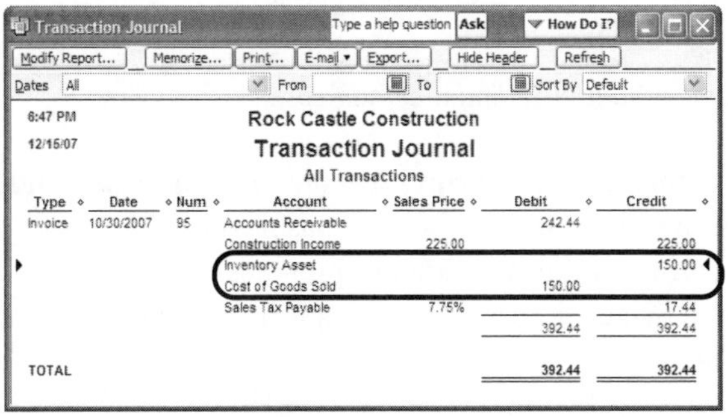

FIGURE 10.28

QuickBooks uses the cost assigned in the Edit Item window when you sell inventory that you have not recorded any purchase documents for.

This impact to your financials (positive or negative) can be significant if the purchase price is different from the recorded default cost on the Add New or Edit Item dialog.

When an Inventory Item Does Not Have a Default Cost

If you have assigned an inventory item to a customer invoice that you have not yet purchased (that is, the quantity on hand is zero) and if you *did not* define a default cost when you first created the inventory item, QuickBooks will use -0- as the default cost per unit when the invoice is recorded, showing a 100% profit margin for your financials and for that customer!

Now, using the same previous example, only *not* recording a default cost when setting up the item, as shown in Figure 10.29, QuickBooks will not calculate any cost or inventory reduction with the sale of the inventory (see Figure 10.30).

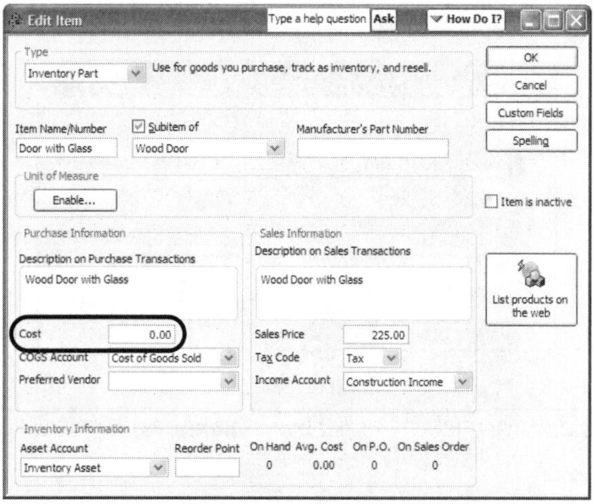

FIGURE 10.29

Setting up an item without including a default cost.

Imagine the impact this can have on your financials and the profitability reports you might review for your business or clients. Simply heeding the many warnings that QuickBooks provides about the impact of selling negative inventory can prevent this from happening in your or your client's data file.

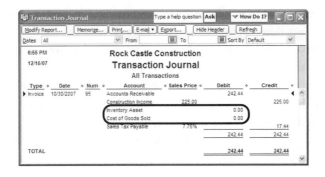

FIGURE 10.30

No inventory decrease or cost is recorded when selling an item you do not have in inventory, have not purchased, and did not record a default cost for.

When a Replenishing Purchase Document Is Created

What exactly happens when you do record the purchase documents? The date recorded on the purchase document is important in how QuickBooks will handle this transaction.

If we use the example from Figure 10.25 that 1 unit was sold on 10/30/07 and 1 unit was purchased on 11/15/07, QuickBooks records the revenue in the month of October and the cost in the month of November. From month to month, it might not be noticeable, but if the transactions cross years, revenue would be overstated in one year and costs in another. Additionally, the revenue is tracked by the customer assigned to the invoice, but the cost *is not* tracked by the customer because the cost is recorded on the date of the purchase document.

To limit the negative impact, simply date your replenishing purchase documents *before* the date of the customer invoice that caused the negative inventory. QuickBooks will recalculate the average cost of all sales documents dated after this "replenishing" purchase document. And of course, it is simply best not to sell negative inventory altogether.

How To Avoid Incorrect Inventory Valuation

Troubleshooting negative inventory can be an eye opener as to how important proper inventory management is. To help with this task, rely on the Inventory Valuation Detail report, shown previously in Figure 10.12.

You can avoid these issues if the purchase documents or inventory adjustments are dated on or prior to the date of the sales documents creating the negative inventory. Backdating inventory adjustment documents can be a powerful solution for correcting months of misstated financials, so use it where appropriate after discussing it with your accountant.

Have in place inventory management processes that will avoid recording negative inventory. If you do have negative inventory, be sure to correct it at the end of your tax year or your tax return information will potentially be incorrect.

Additionally, you might want to read Chapter 11.

 Digging Deeper

Do you want to "commit" inventory to a customer ahead of purchasing the inventory? Consider using the QuickBooks sales order form available with QuickBooks Premier or QuickBooks Enterprise, all editions.

With a sales order, you can set aside the inventory for sale to a customer, provide the customer a sales order for prepayment, and then later create the customer invoice directly from the sales order form.

Sales orders are considered a nonposting document, meaning that when they are created they do not affect inventory, revenue, or costs until the sales order is converted to an invoice.

Using this form often can be the best solution if you must provide a sales document to a customer before he or she receives the merchandise.

Chapter 11

Reviewing and Correcting Accounts Payable Errors

- Accounts Payable Forms and Workflow

- Preferences That Affect Accounts Payable

- Reports to Review When Troubleshooting Accounts Payable Errors

- Correcting Accounts Payable Errors

- Unique Accounts Payable Transactions

Accounts Payable Forms and Workflow

Similar to the flexibility found in the QuickBooks accounts receivable tasks in Chapter 7, "Reviewing and Correcting Accounts Receivable Errors," you also have choices in how to manage your company's purchasing workflow. Your company can choose to use the purchase order form for controlling and monitoring costs, or you can simply create a bill and later pay the bill.

If you created your data file using the QuickBooks EasyStep Interview, QuickBooks enabled all or some of the features discussed in this chapter, depending on your answers to a few questions.

If you did not use the EasyStep Interview, QuickBooks will create specific accounts or turn on features after you open a vendor form or enable the related preference. (See Chapter 2, "Reviewing the QuickBooks Chart of Accounts," in the section titled, "Accounts That QuickBooks Creates Automatically.")

Accounts Payable Forms

If you are considering using the accounts payable process for the first time, be sure to review Chapter 3, "Reviewing and Correcting Item List Errors," which discusses the use of items in QuickBooks and how to set them up properly.

If you choose to use the purchase order form, you will need to create items. Items are simply a list of the products or services that you buy (and can also be those that you sell). The primary purpose of items is to perform the accounting behind the scenes and to automate the data entry process by defaulting descriptions, costs, and sales price on both purchase and sales forms.

What If You Buy and Sell the Same Item?

Did you know that if you create an item in QuickBooks and assign only one account, all your expenses and revenue associated with that item will record to that single account? The Add New Item or Edit Item dialog for the item types of Service, Non-inventory part, and Other Charge are the only items that by default show only one account assignment, the primary cause of the issue being discussed in this sidebar.

An easy but all-too-often-overlooked solution is to assign both an expense and an income account in the Add New Item or Edit Item dialog (select Lists, Item List, click the Item button, and click New Item or Edit Item). Figure 11.1 shows where you can place a check mark in the This service... or This item is used... box (depending on what type of item you are creating) when creating a new item or editing an existing item. Chapter 3 offers more detail on creating items.

When you create an item, these settings are optional except for the inventory item list type, which should have a value entered in the default cost field:

- Purchase and sales description

- Default cost and sales price

- Preferred vendor

These settings are required:

- A name for the item

- At least one account (usually an expense account if you sell the item or an income account if you buy the item)

- An inventory asset account (if creating an inventory item type)

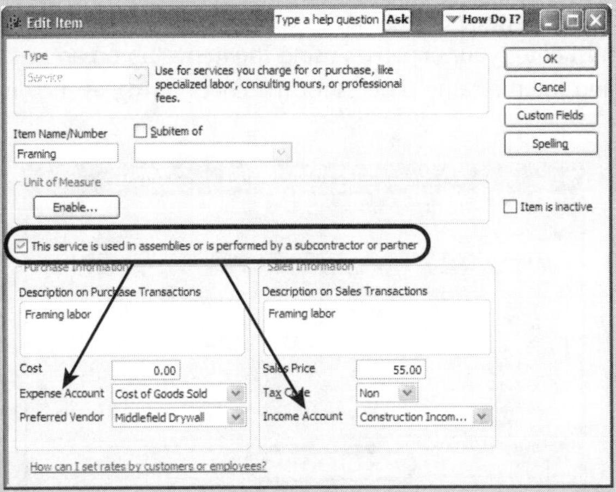

FIGURE 11.1

Place a check in the This service... box so that you can use the same item on both a purchase document and sales document.

Choosing to set up items correctly can be one of the most important decisions you will make in using accounts payable properly.

Should you use items even if you do not plan on using the QuickBooks purchase order or item receipt documents? I recommend that you do, especially if you follow the instructions in the preceding sidebar. A powerful feature of items is that each time the item is purchased or sold, QuickBooks records the amount to the specific account(s) originally defined in the Add New or Edit Item dialog, reducing or entirely eliminating potential errors created from recording the transaction to the wrong account when using the Expense tab of a purchase document.

Digging Deeper

How can items help me track my customer's profitability? Many of the QuickBooks reports that provide customer and job profitability information are based on transactions recorded using items and will not provide the same information provided by using only the Expenses tab on a transaction.

For example, a home builder creates a budget for the project (using an estimate form) and wants to track actual versus budgeted expense. To take advantage of the many customer and job profitability reports, you must enter your expenses using the Items tab on an accounts payable bill (and use the same process for the check form), as shown in Figure 11.2.

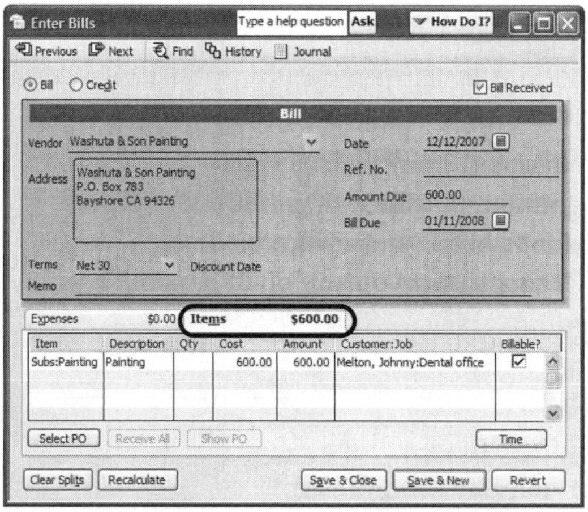

FIGURE 11.2

Use the Items tab to record expenses that you want to track in customer or job profitability reports.

Table 11.1 lists the transaction forms available in accounts payable and the purpose each form serves. You will also want to review Table 11.2 (later in this chapter), which outlines the accounting that goes on behind the scenes with the forms.

Table 11.1 Accounts Payable Forms	
Accounts Payable Form Name	**Primary Purpose of Form**
Purchase Order	Document issued by a buyer to a seller indicating the products or services, quantity, and rates that the buyer will pay.
Item Receipt (Receiving inventory or non-inventory without the vendor bill)	QuickBooks-specific document recording receipt of inventory or non-inventory items without receiving a vendor bill.
Bill	Records an expense or outflow of money through a liability account.
Vendor Credit Memo	Records a decrease of what is owed to the vendor.
Bill Payment Check	Pays the vendor bill and decreases cash balances.

Accounts Payable Workflow

I hope you are convinced by now about the importance of using the accounts payable process instead of simply writing a check for your business expenses. The QuickBooks Home page and Vendor Center, as shown in Figures 11.3 and 11.4, respectively, make managing all your purchasing activities easy.

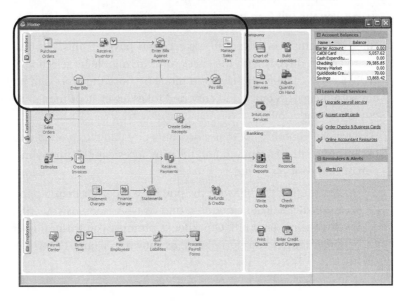

FIGURE 11.3

Use the QuickBooks Home page to manage your purchasing processes.

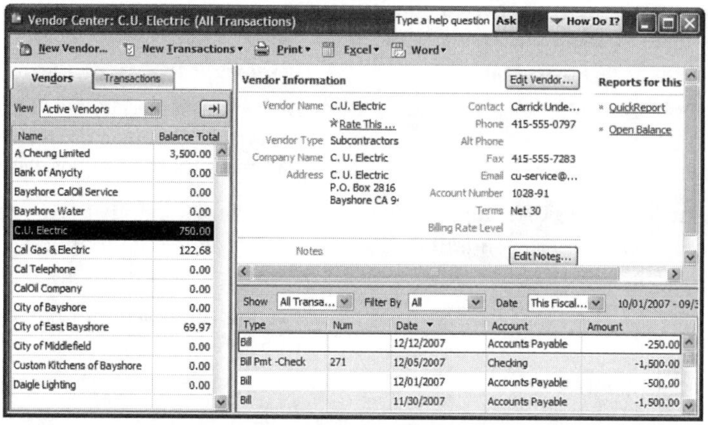

FIGURE 11.4

Use the Vendor Center to manage the vendor list information.

You can easily perform typical vendor-related activities from the QuickBooks Home page, as shown in Figure 11.3:

1. Create a vendor (you do this just one time).

2. Create a purchase order to the vendor (optional).

3. Receive items without a bill (optional).

4. Create a bill to the vendor.

5. Pay the bill (can be a date different from when the bill is dated).

Some companies choose not to use accounts payable bills, but instead pay their vendors directly with the check form (available by selecting Banking, Write Checks). Often, this choice is made because the process of paying a vendor with a check is quick and easy and takes fewer steps than creating and paying a vendor bill.

However, by choosing *not* to use accounts payable bills, you ignore several important controls for managing the purchases your company makes. These purchasing controls include:

■ Associating the bill with the purchase order (or item receipt) to automatically calculate quantity and cost—As soon as you enter the vendor's name on a bill, QuickBooks prompts you with an open purchase order (or item receipt) dialog, as shown in Figure 11.5.

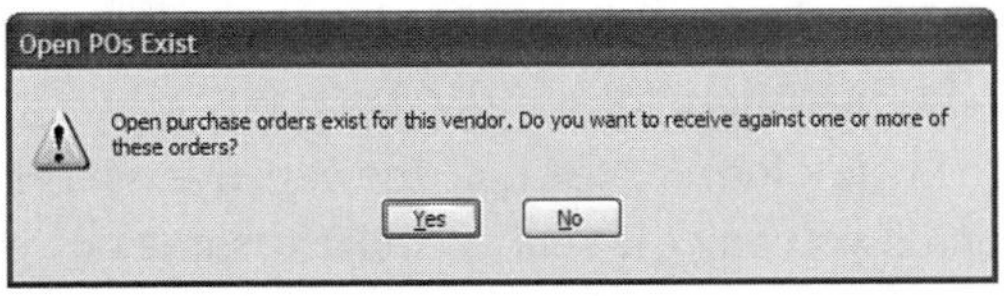

FIGURE 11.5

Warning provided when you enter a bill for a vendor that has an open purchase order.

For example, you agree to purchase from the vendor a service or product for a specific amount. Later when you receive and enter the bill, QuickBooks prefills the bill with the quantity and cost as recorded on the purchase order document. You can then compare the billed quantity and cost to the ordered quantity and cost. (To learn more about the use of items in QuickBooks, refer to Chapter 3.)

- Receiving a warning when entering a vendor invoice number twice—It can happen: A vendor sends you a bill more than once and you pay it more than once. However, if you choose to use a bill form (versus the Write Check form) and you enter the vendor's invoice number in the Ref No. field of the Enter Bills dialog, QuickBooks warns you if the invoice number was used on a previous bill, as shown in Figure 11.6.

This warning is enabled in the Bills preference; see the "Preferences That Affect Accounts Payable" section later in this chapter.

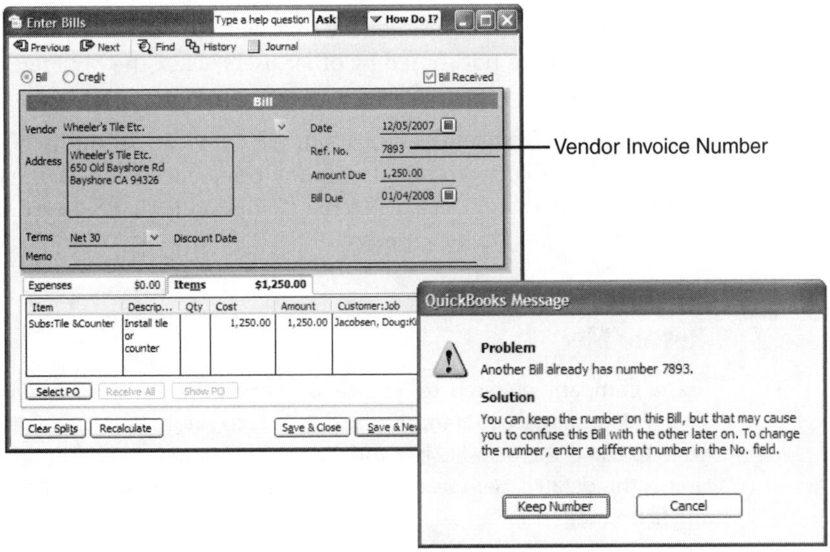

FIGURE 11.6

QuickBooks provides a warning message when you enter a bill with the same reference (vendor invoice) number.

- Not recognizing costs in the month they were incurred—When you opt to use a Write Check form instead of a bill form, QuickBooks uses the date of the check form as the date the expense is recorded (recognized). How often do you pay the vendor's bill the same day or month that you receive it? You might be overstating or understating the expenses incurred in a specific month if you use the check form instead of the bill form.

The purchasing controls and warnings provided in QuickBooks make using the accounts payable process a smart choice for your company. Additionally, your company will benefit from having financials that can be viewed in both cash and accrual basis. To learn more about the differences between these two types of financial reporting preferences, see the section titled "Choosing a Reporting Basis" in Chapter 4, "Easily Review Your QuickBooks Data."

Preferences That Affect Accounts Payable

Did you know that you can simplify your processes in accounts payable by setting certain QuickBooks preferences? These preferences can save you keystrokes, which in turn can save data entry time.

Not every preference that affects accounts payable impacts your financials directly; some preferences simply enable specific features. To set preferences in QuickBooks, click Edit, Preferences and select the type of preference on the left.

Preferences in QuickBooks come in two forms:

- My Preferences—Settings that are unique to the user logging in to the data file and are not shared by other users. Click the My Preferences tab to modify the logged-in user-specific settings.

- Company Preferences—Settings that are common for all users. When a preference is selected on the Company preference window, the change or setting affects all users. Click the Company Preferences tab to modify settings globally for all users.

Rescue Me!

To set company preferences, you need to open the file as the Admin or new External Accountant user and switch to single-user mode (if you are using the data file in a multiuser environment). The Admin user is the default user created when you begin using QuickBooks for the first time.

Proper data entry security includes limiting which employees have access to logging in as the Admin and setting company preferences that are global for all users.

The following sections detail the preferences that can affect your use of the accounts payable forms.

Accounting

The Accounting preferences are important to review when you first create your data file. These choices affect much of how your accounting information is recorded in accounts payable.

Company Preferences

Company preferences are shared globally by all users. The Accounting preferences include:

- Accounts—These settings are important for proper management of recording revenue and expenses. The following are the preference settings for Accounts:
  - Use account numbers—Requires the use of an account number in addition to account name when creating a new chart of account list item. Users can type either the number or the name to place that account on a transaction line.
  - Show lowest subaccount only—You can only choose this option if account numbering is enabled and all the chart of account items have a number assigned. This setting only changes how the account name is displayed. If you see an "other" named account on your financials, users probably recorded a transaction to the parent account and not to one of the available subaccounts.
  - Require accounts—If not selected and a transaction is recorded without an account assigned, QuickBooks will assign it to an automatically created uncategorized income or uncategorized expense account, depending on the transaction form used. Note: When creating a new data file, this default is automatically selected.
- Use Class Tracking—See the QuickBooks Help menu for more information on how you can use class tracking to track multiple profit centers on your income statement.
- Automatically Assign General Journal Entry Number—This preference sequentially numbers any general journal entries automatically. Each entry number can be modified at the time of input.
- Warn When Posting a Transaction to Retained Earnings—You can post to the Retained Earnings account but you should not because QuickBooks uses this account at year end to close out the year's Profit

or Loss totals. Note: When creating a new data file, this default is automatically selected.

- Date Warnings—When you create a new data file, the default date range set is from 90 days in the past to 30 days in the future, calculated from your current computer system date. Users can modify these date ranges, and QuickBooks will warn users when they enter or modify a transaction outside these dates.

- Closing Date—The Admin or External Accountant user login can set a date in the past for which transactions cannot be modified added or deleted prior to, that date without entering the closing date password (if one was created). (Review Chapter 15, "Sharing Data with Your Accountant or Your Client," for more details on setting a closing date and controlling which employees have access to transactions in closed periods.)

My Preferences

There are no My Preferences that would affect your workflow for accounts payable.

Bills

Review your Bills preferences to determine whether the defaults set by QuickBooks are appropriate for your company's needs.

Company Preferences

Company preferences are shared globally by all users. The following are the Bills preferences:

- Entering Bills—This is the global default for terms of all vendors for aging the due date of the vendor's bill. You can change this global default on each vendor's list information or on a specific transaction. By default, QuickBooks sets the default due date for bills (where a vendor record does not have payment terms set) to 10 days. Users can modify this for their company's specific bill-paying terms.

- Warn About Duplicate Bill Numbers from the Same Vendor—Being warned of this situation is one of the important reasons for using accounts payable.

- Paying Bills—The Automatically Use Discounts and Credits option enables QuickBooks to apply the discount to your vendor bill payments automatically if your vendor is set up with discount terms and the bill is being paid within the discount date defined.

My Preferences

There are no My Preferences that would affect your workflow for accounts payable.

Checking

The Checking preferences improve the accuracy of your day-to-day data entry. Be sure to review them carefully when setting up a new data file.

Company Preferences

Company preferences are shared globally by all users. The following are the Checking preferences:

- Print Account Names on Voucher—This option has no effect for vendor bills. The default is to print the General Ledger account on Write Check forms only (not bill payment checks).

- Change Check Date When Check Is Printed—If you prepare your bill payment checks several days in advance of printing them, this setting will change the check date to the current system date when you print the checks.

- Start with Payee Field on Check—When selected, your cursor will be on the payee field of the check (and skips the check number and check date fields).

- Warn About Duplicate Check Numbers—QuickBooks will warn the user if reusing a check number that the system has already recorded.

- Auto-fill Payee Account Number in Check Memo—You can assign the account number with which your vendor has identified you and have this number print on the Memo field of the bill payment check.

  To assign the vendor account number to the vendor record, follow these steps:

  1. Click **Vendors** from the QuickBooks Home page.
  2. Click to select the vendor to which you want to assign the account number.
  3. Click the **Edit Vendor** button.
  4. Click the **Additional Info** tab.
  5. Type the account number the vendor has assigned to your account (see Figure 11.7). Click **OK**.

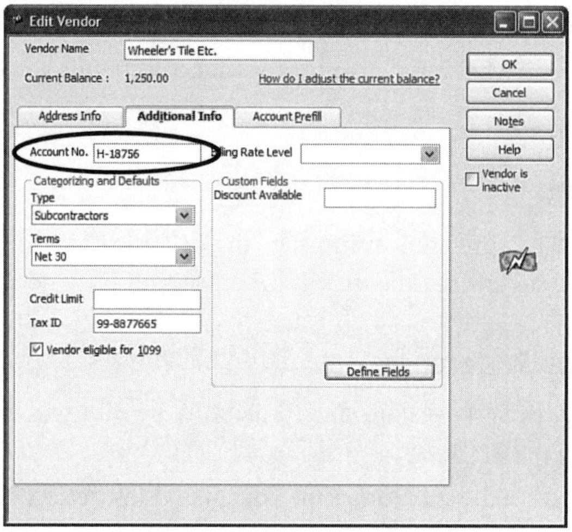

FIGURE 11.7

Add the account number your vendor has assigned to your business and QuickBooks will optionally print it on the memo line of a check or bill payment check.

- Select Default Accounts to Use—You can assign the default bank accounts QuickBooks uses when creating paychecks or payroll liability checks.

My Preferences

My Preferences are unique to the user name logged in to the data file. These settings are not shared globally.

- Select Default Accounts to Use—Assign what account you write your bill payment checks from. This setting can be unique for each user that manages different bank accounts.

General

Every company using QuickBooks needs to review the settings in General Preferences. Although I have named only a couple here, many are worth selecting and customizing for your company's specific needs.

Company Preferences

There are no Company preferences that would affect your workflow for accounts payable.

My Preferences

My Preferences are unique to the user name currently logged in to the data file. These settings are not shared globally.

- Automatically Recall Information—Select this option to recall both the previously assigned account and the amount or just the account when creating a new vendor transaction.

- Default Date to Use for New Transactions—Exercise caution to ensure that the appropriate choice is selected. If you are entering transactions from the past, you might want to choose the last entered date. Otherwise, I recommend setting the default to use today's date.

Reminders

When setting the Company preferences for reminders, do not forget to also set the My Preferences for this section.

New for QuickBooks 2009 is the Company Snapshot, a digital dashboard that includes a view of your reminders. Defining this preference properly here displays for all users on the Company Snapshot, reminding them of important tasks or documents.

Company Preferences

On the Reminders preference page, you can tell QuickBooks reminders to show a list or summary of all checks to print, bills to pay, or purchase orders to print.

My Preferences

If you want reminders to show when you open the QuickBooks data file, select the My Preferences tab of the Reminders preference and choose to Show Reminders List when opening a Company file.

Reports and Graphs

The person responsible for how QuickBooks reports your Accounts Receivable Aging and Accounts Payable Aging will want to review these preferences choices.

Company Preferences

Company preferences are shared globally by all users. The Reports and Graphs preferences include:

- Summary Reports Basis—This feature is important because it tells QuickBooks what basis you want to view your Balance Sheet and Profit & Loss report in by default. You can always override the default when you prepare the report.

- Aging Reports—You can choose to age your reports from the due date or from the transaction date.

The remaining preferences affect how your reports look, but they have no effect on accounting transactions.

My Preferences

There are no My preferences that would affect your workflow or accounting for accounts payable.

Tax:1099

Setting up your vendors for proper 1099 status is important. However, be assured that if after reviewing this information you determine the original setup was incorrect, any changes made to this preference will correct prior- and future-dated reports and forms.

The Internal Revenue Service requires that a business provide a 1099—Misc. Income form at the end of the tax year to any person paid $600 or more for services in one year. Most incorporated businesses are not required to get a 1099—Misc. Income form. You should contact your accountant for more specific information.

Company Preferences

You can select the Do You File option to let QuickBooks know that you will be providing 1099 forms to your vendors at the end of the year.

The dialog shown in Figure 11.8 lists several 1099 categories. However, QuickBooks will track the information, but prints only the 1099—Misc. Income form (or the Box 7 data).

To finish setting up this option, you must assign a QuickBooks account on the specific 1099 category and box detail line. Highlight the appropriate 1099 tax line you want to assign, and from the drop-down menu, select the account you want to assign. You can also assign multiple accounts (as shown in Figure 11.8).

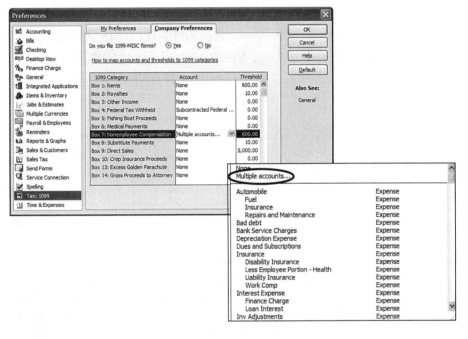

FIGURE 11.8

Setting the Tax:1099 preference to map multiple accounts.

See the section titled, "Reviewing and Printing Year-End Vendor Tax Forms" later in this chapter for more information on how to properly set up vendors and prepare 1099 documents at the end of the year.

My Preferences

There are no My preferences that would affect your workflow for accounts payable.

Reports to Review When Troubleshooting Accounts Payable Errors

Accounts payable mistakes often can be one of the primary reasons for misstated company financials. Knowing which reports are best to review will make you much more efficient at keeping your accounts payable "clean," meaning the data is correct and up to date. Often, the most difficult task when troubleshooting data errors is not knowing exactly what you should be looking for. This problem is addressed in the next section, which explains some of the more common reports used to identify whether your accounts payable information is correct.

Reconcile Balance Sheet Report Accounts Payable Balance to A/P Aging Summary Report Total

An important check to do with your file is to compare your Balance Sheet report balance for accounts payable with the A/P Aging Summary report total.

With QuickBooks, you don't have to worry that the Balance Sheet accounts payable balance will not match the A/P Aging Summary report total because any transaction posting to the accounts payable account must have a vendor assigned. When providing year-end documentation to your accountant, be sure to include the A/P Aging Summary or Detail report and compare the total amount from these reports to the Balance Sheet balance for accounts payable.

To compare the Balance Sheet Standard report balance for accounts payable with the A/P Aging Summary report total, do the following:

1. Click **Reports, Company & Financial**, and select **Balance Sheet Standard**. On the report dialog that opens, select the **As of Date** you want to compare to. To accurately compare Balance Sheet report accounts payable balance and the A/P Aging Summary report total, you *must* create your Balance Sheet in Accrual Basis. If your reporting preference default was for Cash Basis, you can change the reporting basis temporarily by clicking the **Modify Report** button on the active report window and selecting **Accrual** as the report basis. Click **OK** to return to the report dialog.

2. Note the balance of your accounts payable account(s) on your Balance Sheet report (see Figure 11.9).

3. Click **Reports, Vendors & Payables** and select **A/P Aging Summary**, as shown in Figure 11.10, making sure the date is the same as the date you selected in step 1.

Your accounts payable balance on the Balance Sheet Standard report should match the total on the A/P Aging Summary report. If it does not, the reason might be a data integrity issue. I don't recall seeing this myself with any client. If you find the two balances do not match first, make sure your Balance Sheet Standard report is created in the accrual basis. Then perform a verify data by clicking File, Utilities, and selecting Verify Data. If you receive a data integrity message, you should contact QuickBooks Technical Support for assistance.

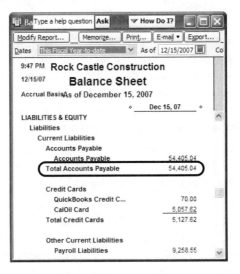

FIGURE 11.9

Use your Balance Sheet (Accrual Basis) to reconcile your accounts payable reports to.

	Current	1 - 30	31 - 60	61 - 90	> 90	TOTAL
A Cheung Limited	0.00	3,500.00	0.00	0.00	0.00	3,500.00
C.U. Electric	750.00	0.00	0.00	0.00	0.00	750.00
Cal Gas & Electric	122.68	0.00	0.00	0.00	0.00	122.68
East Bayshore Auto Mall	0.00	0.00	0.00	0.00	-942.90	-942.90
Hamlin Metal	670.00	0.00	0.00	0.00	0.00	670.00
Hopkins Construction Rentals	700.00	0.00	0.00	0.00	0.00	700.00
Kershaw Computer Services	0.00	0.00	0.00	0.00	19,500.00	19,500.00
Lew Plumbing	1,330.00	0.00	0.00	0.00	0.00	1,330.00
Middlefield Drywall	1,200.00	0.00	0.00	0.00	0.00	1,200.00
Patton Hardware Supplies	9,505.00	3,459.20	0.00	0.00	0.00	12,964.20
Perry Windows & Doors	2,580.00	5,605.00	1,800.00	0.00	0.00	9,985.00
Sergeant Insurance	0.00	0.00	712.56	0.00	0.00	712.56
Sloan Roofing	1,047.00	0.00	0.00	0.00	0.00	1,047.00
Timberloft Lumber	80.50	0.00	0.00	0.00	0.00	80.50
Washuta & Son Painting	600.00	0.00	0.00	0.00	0.00	600.00
Wheeler's Tile Etc.	1,250.00	311.00	625.00	0.00	0.00	2,186.00
TOTAL	19,835.18	12,875.20	3,137.56	0.00	18,557.10	54,405.04

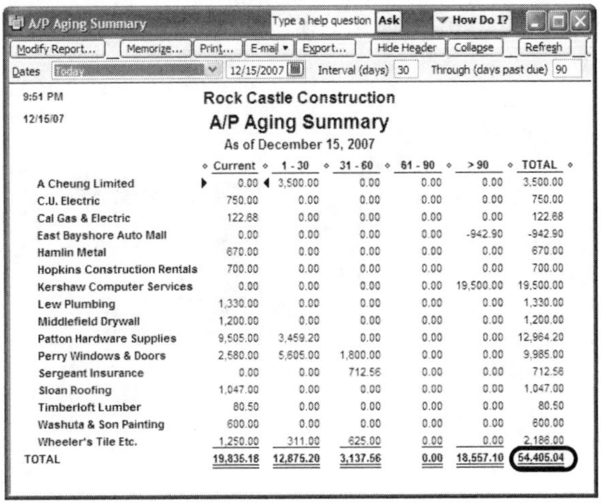

FIGURE 11.10

You can use the A/P Aging Summary report to compare to the Balance Sheet accounts payable total.

Review the Unpaid Bills Detail Report

Unlike the A/P Aging Summary report, the Unpaid Bills Detail report is useful because it groups by vendor the individual lines for each open vendor transaction.

By default this report is perpetual, which means that even if you create it using a date in the past, QuickBooks will show only those open vendor bills, or unapplied credit memos, as of *today's* computer system date. The following steps show you how to override this default, and then properly reconcile the Unpaid Bills Detail report to your Balance Sheet and your A/P Aging Summary report for a date prior to today's date:

1. Click **Reports, Vendors** and select the **Unpaid Bills Detail** report. As mentioned previously, this report includes all payments made to your vendor as of today's computer system date.

2. If you are creating this report for a date other than today, it is important that you click the **Modify Report** button on the active report window. On the **Display** tab that opens, click the **Advanced** button. The Advanced Options dialog box opens. Under **Open Balance/Aging Report Date**, select the **Report Date** option, as shown in Figure 11.11, and click **OK** to close the Advanced Options dialog. Click **OK** to return to the report.

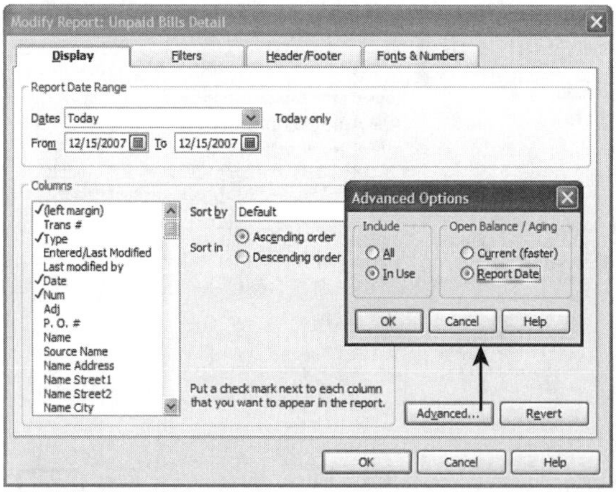

FIGURE 11.11

Modify the Unpaid Bills Detail report so that it will agree with the Balance Sheet for a date in the past.

Modifying the report enables you to see each open vendor bill or unapplied credit detail as of some date in the past. This report becomes very useful for reconciling your accounts payable unpaid bills or open credit detail to your

Balance Sheet accounts payable total. Be sure to send a copy of this modified report to your accountant after verifying that it agrees with the Balance Sheet.

If an amount is listed on this report, it is presumed that you owe the money, or in the event of a credit, that your vendor owes you. See the section in this chapter titled "Correcting Accounts Payable Errors" for a discussion of how you can remove old, aged payables from your accounting that you do not owe.

Reviewing Aged Open Item Receipts

Often, when goods are purchased for both inventory and non-inventory, your vendor will ship the product without the final vendor bill. One reason for doing this is that receiving departments in a warehouse should not know the value of the goods being delivered. Another reason might be that the vendor needs to add freight and handling to the final bill before sending it to your company.

The QuickBooks Item Receipt form is used to record the receipt of the stock into your place of business, increase the quantity on hand for this item, and increase your accounts payable due to that vendor.

However, because you have not yet received the final bill from the vendor, QuickBooks does not include these item receipts in the Pay Bills window. This is because QuickBooks recognizes an Item Receipt form as not yet having received the final bill to be paid.

A problem can be created if you entered a bill and ignored the warning message that outstanding item receipts existed for that vendor and created another bill, or perhaps you created a Write Check form paying for the same charge as recorded on the original item receipt. Both of these types of mistakes would overstate your expenses or inventory value.

First, to see if this issue is a problem for your data file, create the Unpaid Bills Detail report by clicking Reports, Vendors, and selecting the Unpaid Bills Detail report. On the report, do you have line items with a transaction type of Item Receipt (see Figure 11.12)? If you do, these are from receiving inventory or non-inventory items *without* receiving the vendor bill in QuickBooks.

Rescue Me!

How exactly does QuickBooks manage the use of Item Receipt documents?

- They age like other open payables on the A/P Aging Summary report.

- The Unpaid Bills Detail report does not show any days in the aged column, yet they are aging.

- QuickBooks does not let you pay an item receipt in the Pay Bills dialog.

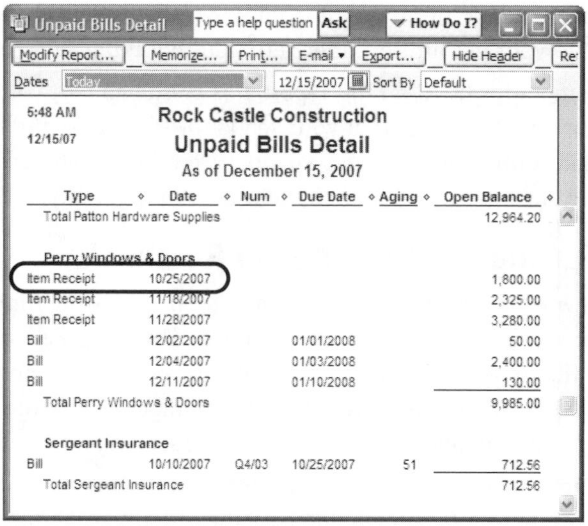

FIGURE 11.12
Unpaid Bills Detail report showing aged Item Receipts.

If after reviewing your Unpaid Bills Detail report, you find outdated Item Receipts that you do not owe the vendor, determine whether they have been paid by requesting an open payables statement from your vendor. To see if the bill was paid with a Write Check form instead of the proper Bill Payment check form, follow these steps:

1. Click the **Vendors** button from the Home page, as shown in Figure 11.3 at the beginning of this chapter.

2. Select the **Vendor** name on the left. You can also type the first letter of the name and QuickBooks will jump to the first list entry with that letter.

3. Click the **Show** drop-down list to select the **Checks** transaction type, as shown in Figure 11.13.

You can print the transaction list via the Print tab at the top of the Vendor Center dialog.

In the example shown previously in Figure 11.12, Perry Windows has an open item receipt dated 10/25/07. To easily see whether a check form was used to pay this vendor, follow the steps listed previously to see any checks (not bill payment checks) that were written to the vendor.

The "Correcting Accounts Payable Errors" section discusses options you have for fixing this type of error.

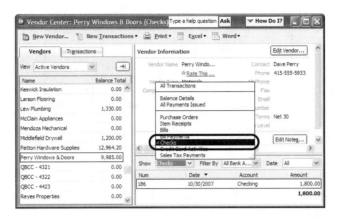

FIGURE 11.13

Reviewing checks written to a vendor (not bill payment checks) from the Vendor Center.

Reviewing Item Setup

As discussed in this chapter in the earlier sidebar titled, "What If You Buy and Sell the Same Item?," items play an important part in the accounts payable process if you use purchase orders, item receipts, or enter bills and checks using the Items tab.

Previously in Figure 11.1, you can see a service type item with a check mark placed in the box titled, "This Service Is Used...." Having this check mark is important if you buy and sell the same item. If this option is not selected and you use the same item on a purchase and a sales document, QuickBooks will record both the revenue and the expense to the single account selected on the New or Edit item dialog.

It is perfectly acceptable to create an item with only one account if you know you will never both buy and sell the same item. However, I usually recommend that each item be set up as two-sided, or needing both an expense and an income account.

Properly setting up items is discussed in more detail in Chapter 3. This section focuses on how you can determine whether your items are the cause of errors on your financials for a company data file with transactions. If your data file does not have transactions in it yet, you will not be using this report to check your item setup.

Presume that an item was created with only an income account assigned. The item was used on a vendor bill and the user decided to ignore the warning shown in Figure 11.14.

FIGURE 11.14

The warning you receive when using an item on a vendor purchase document that has only an income account assigned.

To see whether this type of error affects your or your client's data, create the following report:

1. Click **Reports, Company & Financial** and select **Profit & Loss Standard**.

2. Double-click the **Total Construction Income** amount, as shown in Figure 11.15. QuickBooks creates a Transaction Detail by Account report displayed in Figure 11.16.

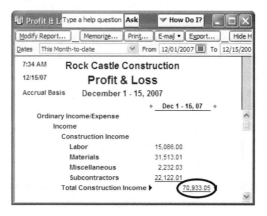

FIGURE 11.15

Double-click the Total Construction Income amount to create a Transaction Detail by Account report.

3. On the top right of the resulting Transaction Detail by Account report, select **Type** from the **Sort By** drop-down menu. QuickBooks groups all transactions by type within each income account or subaccount. Notice in Figure 11.16 that the Construction Income subaccount, Materials,

has a vendor bill transaction posting to an income account. Refer to the "Fixing Item Errors in QuickBooks" section in Chapter 3 for methods to fix these types of errors.

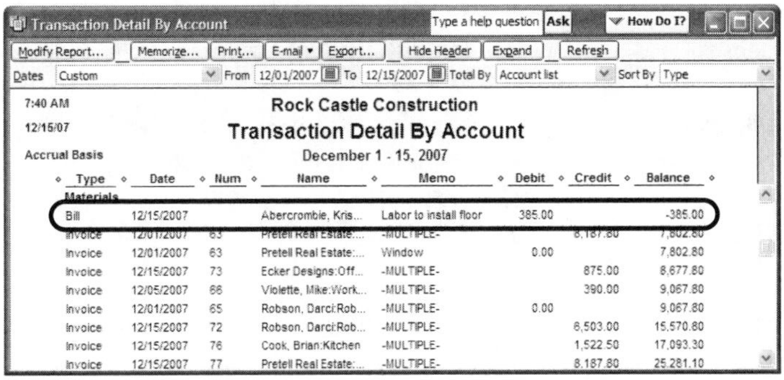

FIGURE 11.16

Sorting your Transaction Detail by Account report by transaction type helps identify improperly set up items.

When an Accounts Payable Balance Appears on a Cash Basis Balance Sheet

The nature of accounts payable suggests that when you are reviewing your financials in cash basis, you would not see an accounts payable balance. See Table 11.2 for a listing of the forms you can use in accounts payable and the effect the form has on both accrual and cash basis reporting.

Table 11.2 Accounts Payable on Accrual and Cash Basis Balance Sheet		
Form Name	**Accrual Basis**	**Cash Basis**
Purchase Order	No effect	No effect
Item Receipt Receive inventory *without* the bill	Date of Item Receipt—increase (debit) inventory; increase (credit) accounts payable. Note: Bill *cannot* be paid in Pay Bills dialog.	No effect
Item Receipt Receive non-inventory *with* the bill	Date of Item Receipt—increase (debit) inventory; increase (credit) accounts payable. Note: Bill *can* be paid in Pay Bills dialog.	No effect

Continues

Table 11.2 Continued

Form Name	Accrual Basis	Cash Basis
Vendor Bill For non-inventory or general expenses	Date of Bill—increase (debit) cost of goods sold (or expense account); increase (credit) accounts payable.	No effect until date of bill payment check
Vendor Credit Memo	Date of Credit Memo—decrease (debit) accounts payable; decrease (credit) inventory, cost of goods sold (or expense account).	No effect

Why exactly do you have an Accounts Payable balance on a cash basis balance sheet? Any of the following can be the cause:

- A/P transactions have expenses or items posting to other balance sheet accounts.
- Inventory items on an invoice or credit memo (typically, inventory management should be done only in accrual basis reporting).
- Transfers between balance sheet accounts.
- Unapplied accounts payable vendor payments.
- Payments applied to future-dated vendor bills.
- Preferences that contradict each other. (This can happen if you select cash basis on your summary reports and accrual basis as your sales tax preference.)
- Data corruption. To confirm this problem, select File, Utilities, Verify Data.

When You Have Accounts Payable Balances on a Cash Basis Balance Sheet

Some of the reasons why you might have an accounts payable balance on your cash basis balance sheet as shown in Figure 11.17 were listed previously. What can you do if you do have an accounts payable balance on your cash basis balance sheet? First, modify the following report to help you locate the transactions making up this balance:

1. Click on **Reports, Company & Financial**.

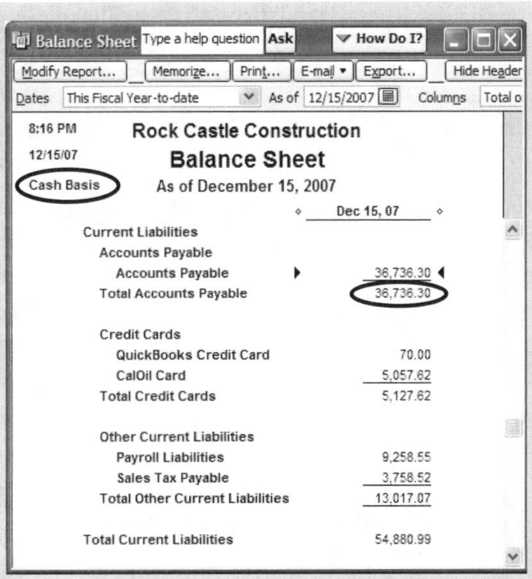

FIGURE 11.17
Cash basis balance sheet with accounts payable balance.

2. Select **Balance Sheet Standard**.

3. Click on the **Modify Report** button, the display tab opens.

4. Select Cash for the report basis.

5. Click **OK**.

6. With your mouse pointer, double-click the Accounts Payable amount in question.

7. The Transaction by Account report is created.

8. Click on the **Modify Report** button. The Display dialog opens.

9. For the Report Date Range, remove the "From" date and leave the "To" date.

10. Select the **Advanced** button and from the **Open Balance/Aging** pane, select Report Date as shown in Figure 11.18.

11. Click the **Filters** tab.

12. In the **Choose Filters** pane, scroll down to select **Paid Status**.

13. Select the radial button **Open** for Paid Status.

Continues...

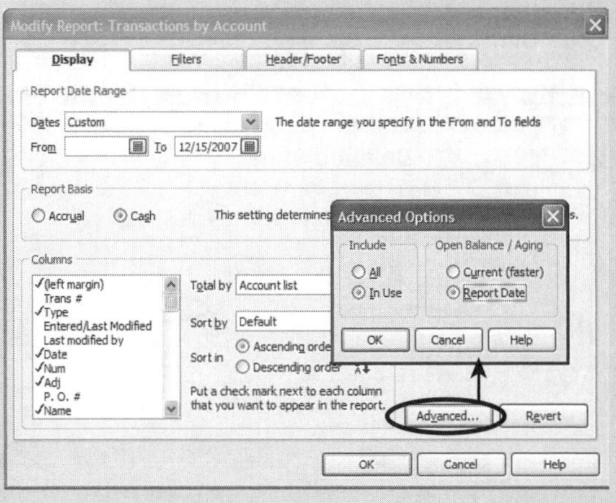

FIGURE 11.18

Clicking the Advanced button on the Modify Report window to filter a report for transaction status as of a specific date in the past.

14. Click **OK** to return to the report and look for transactions that fall into any of the categories described earlier. The Transaction Detail report shown in Figure 11.19 shows several inventory transactions, one of the causes of accounts payable showing on a cash basis balance sheet.

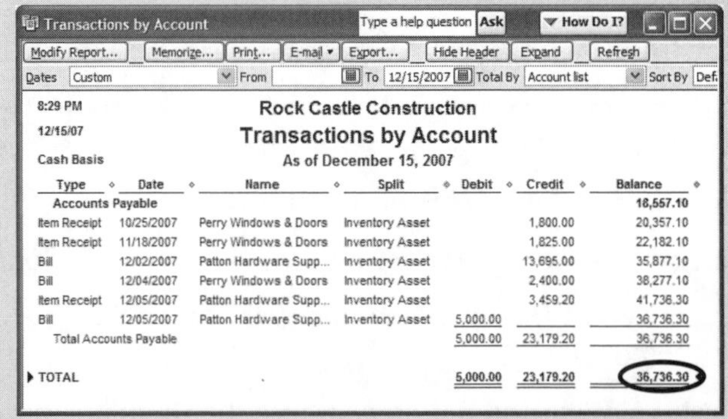

FIGURE 11.19

The modified report identifies the individual transactions that are included in the accounts payable balance showing on a cash basis balance sheet.

Reviewing and Printing Year-End Vendor Tax Forms

If your company pays individuals and certain types of business (refer to your accountant for advice) $600.00 or more in one tax year, you are required by the Internal Revenue Service to provide that person or certain types of businesses with a 1099—Misc. Income form at year end. The 1096 document is a summary document the IRS requires along with the detailed 1099—Misc. Income forms. QuickBooks will print the both 1096 summary and individual 1099 forms, but only using prepared tax forms available through Intuit or most office supply stores.

Earlier in this chapter, details were provided for setting up the Company preference for how QuickBooks will handle the accounting for your 1099 forms. You can also use the 1099/1096 Wizard to set up QuickBooks and your vendors for 1099 filing.

To prepare to process your 1099 forms, follow these steps:

1. Click **Vendors, Print 1099s/1096**; the wizard opens, as shown in Figure 11.20.

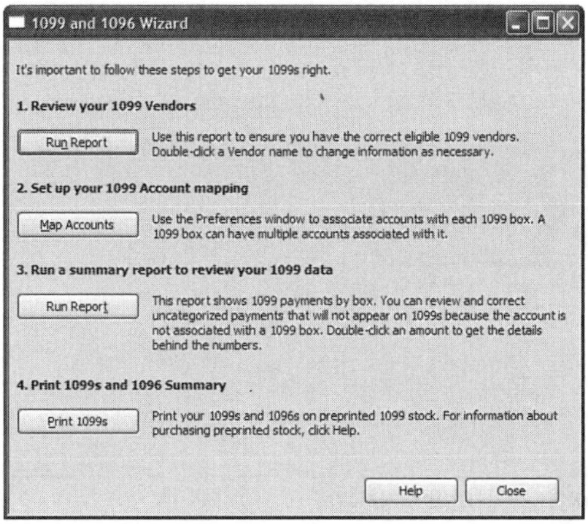

FIGURE 11.20

The 1099 and 1096 Wizard provides a step-by-step process to make sure your documents have the correct information.

2. From the wizard dialog, you can review your 1099 vendors by clicking the **Run Report** button to create a Vendor 1099 Review report, as shown in Figure 11.21. Use this report to check that you have the needed information for each of your vendors. With your cursor on any vendor name on this report, double-click to access the Edit Vendor dialog. Select the **Additional Info** tab, as shown in Figure 11.22, to add or modify the information you see on the report.

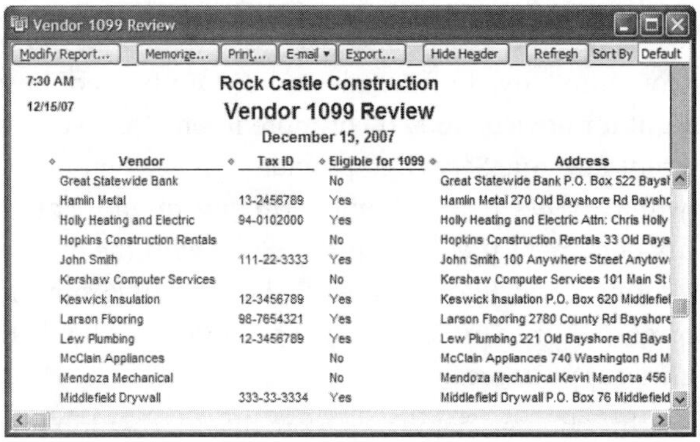

FIGURE 11.21

Review the Vendor 1099 Review report before printing your 1099—Misc. Income forms at year end.

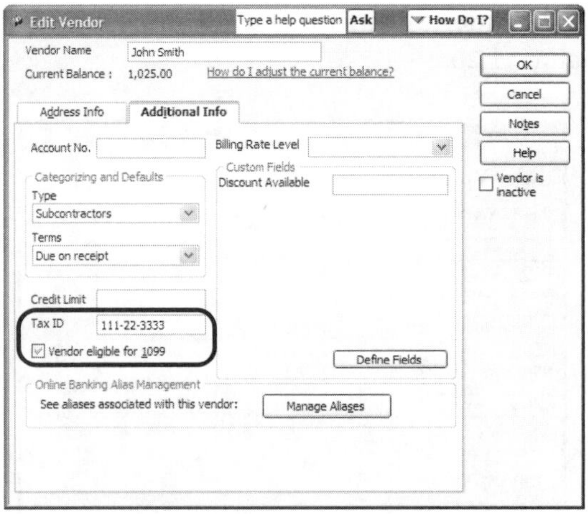

FIGURE 11.22

Recording the vendor's tax ID number and eligibility for receiving a 1099 form at year end.

3. Set up your 1099 chart of account mapping by clicking the **Map Accounts** button and editing or adding Company preferences settings for Tax: 1099. (Refer to Figure 11.8 and the "Preferences That Affect Accounts Payable" section.) The significance of this mapping is that if a vendor is paid for multiple types of expenses, you can properly instruct QuickBooks to prepare the 1099 amount only for expenses subject to 1099 reporting (see Figure 11.23).

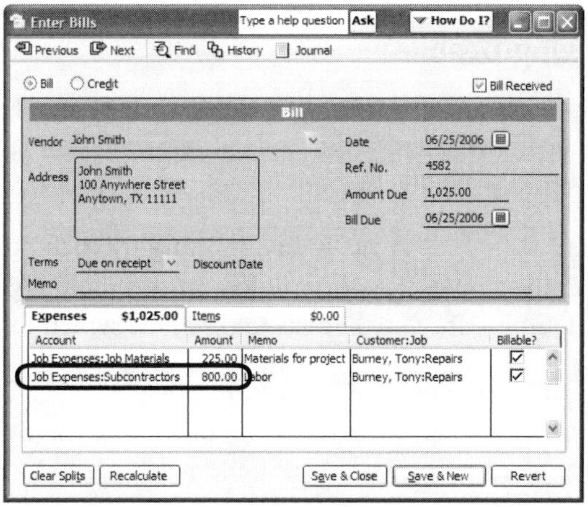

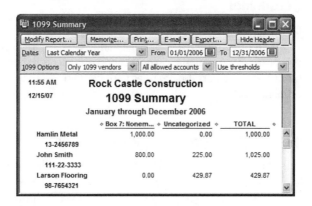

FIGURE 11.23

Only the amount recorded to the Subcontractors account will be reported on the vendor's 1099—Misc. form.

4. Click the **Run Report** button to create a 1099 Summary report so you can review your 1099 data. This report is automatically filtered for the last calendar year: all vendors marked eligible for 1099 (refer to Figure 11.22) and all allowed accounts (references those accounts that you assigned in step 3 for account mapping). Double-click any line listing to see the individual transactions. Uncategorized indicates that a payment was made to a 1099 eligible vendor but not recorded to one of the mapped 1099 accounts (see Figure 11.24).

FIGURE 11.24

The vendor 1099 Summary report can help you identify payment totals made to your vendors who are eligible for 1099s.

Digging Deeper

QuickBooks reports 1099 earnings on cash basis only, or amounts for bills that have been paid in the tax year that the 1099–Misc. Income forms are being created.

5. Print your 1099s and 1096 Summary by clicking the **Print 1099s** button to open the Print dialog. In this dialog, you will specify a date range for QuickBooks to calculate which forms to print.

Properly setting up your 1099 tax form preferences in QuickBooks will ensure compliance with federal tax reporting guidelines. If you have specific questions about what type of vendor should receive this document, refer to the www.irs.gov website or contact your company's accountant.

Correcting Accounts Payable Errors

The previous topics in this chapter have provided recommended workflow and preference settings that will help you avoid making mistakes with your accounts payable transactions. This section provides specific details about methods you can use to correct existing accounts payable errors.

The purpose of this book is not to give your business specific accounting or tax advice, but rather to introduce you to ways you might consider fixing specific mistakes you have found.

Rescue Me!

Before making any of the suggested changes, be sure you have made a backup of your data in case the change does not give you the desired result. Additionally, contacting your accountant and obtaining his or her advice on the changes you are going to make would be prudent.

When a Vendor Was Paid with a Check

Earlier in this chapter, in the "Review the Unpaid Bills Detail Report," section, you were provided a way to reconcile your A/P Aging Summary report total to your Balance Sheet accounts payable total (refer to Figure 11.10). As important as this task is, it is also necessary for you to review those items listed as unpaid to your vendor. If you notice an open bill that you know you do not owe the vendor, it might be because you paid the vendor with a Write Check form instead of the proper Bill Payment form.

You should experience fewer of these types of mistakes because QuickBooks directs you to the Pay Bills dialog, as shown in Figure 11.25, when you attempt to write a check to a vendor with open bills.

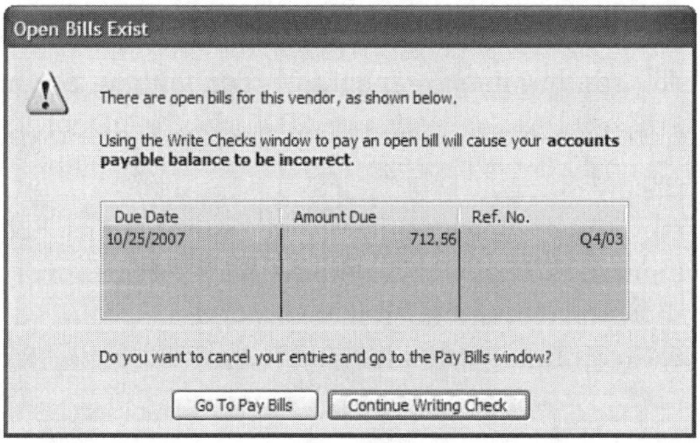

FIGURE 11.25

The warning provided if you attempt to create a check to pay a vendor with open bills.

Modifying the Vendor Check

If you choose to modify the original vendor check, carefully consider the accounting effect this type of correction will have on your financials:

- Is the change a significant dollar amount? Both cash and accrual basis reports will be affected.

- Consider the date of the check and the date of the bill—are they in different tax years?

- Is the correction going to affect a year where the data has already been used to prepare a tax return?

If you answered yes to any of these questions, be sure to discuss with your accountant the impact this change could have on your financials.

Use the following steps to modify this check, making the check become a vendor credit. In other words, it will decrease (debit) accounts payable and maintain the original decrease (credit) to your cash account:

1. Locate the vendor check. One easy way is to click the **Vendors** button on the Home page to open the Vendor Center. With your cursor, select the vendor from the list on the left and choose **Checks** from the **Show** drop-down menu, as shown previously in Figure 11.13.

2. Double-click the check to open the **Write Checks - Checking** dialog box for the selected transaction.

3. On the **Expenses** tab, in the account column, replace the currently listed account with the accounts payable account. This creates a decrease (debit) to the accounts payable account.

4. Select the vendor name from the drop-down menu in the Customer:Job column. This assigns the accounts payable decrease to a specific vendor. You cannot save the transaction without assigning a vendor name.

5. Click **Save & Close**, and then click **Yes** to record your changes.

6. Click **Vendors, Pay Bills** and use the arrow key on your keyboard to move up and down through the list of vendors. Before placing a checkmark in the box next to the vendor's specific invoice, QuickBooks will show the total number of credits and their total value in the Discount & Credit Information for Highlighted Bill pane. (See Figure 11.26.)

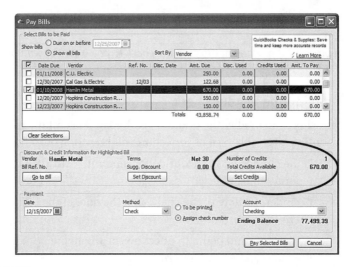

FIGURE 11.26

When a vendor has available credits, QuickBooks will display the total of the credits in the Pay Bills dialog.

7. When you have located the correct bill, place a check mark in the box to the left of the Date Due column. When an invoice is selected, QuickBooks will automatically apply the available credits to the selected vendor invoice (if the preference was set). If not and you want to modify the amount or which credits are selected, click the **Set Credits** button. The Discount and Credits dialog appears as shown later in the chapter in Figure 11.28. Users can modify which credit is selected by changing the check mark from one credit to another or by manually overriding the amount of the credit.

8. Click the **Done** button when the credit is assigned.

9. QuickBooks shows in the Pay Bills window that the bill is being paid by a credit (if the entire bill is being paid by the credit, QuickBooks will not create a check). Click **Pay Selected Bills** when you are finished.

10. QuickBooks offers you Pay More Bills or Done choices. Click **Done** if you do not have any other transactions to correct using this method.

Creating and Applying a Vendor Credit

Often, the safest way to not inadvertently affect the prior year financials is to create another correcting transaction in the current year, especially if you have already used your prior year's data to prepare and file a tax return.

The vendor credit enables you to correct prior year Accounts Payable errors, but gives you the opportunity to date the credit in the current tax year. (Refer to Table 11.2 for a listing of accounts payable forms and their effects on your accounting.) To create a vendor credit, follow these steps:

1. Click **Vendors**, **Enter Bills** and, as shown in Figure 11.27, select **Credit** at the top of the form. Select the appropriate vendor, date, vendor reference number (optional), and amount, and on the **Expenses** tab, select the appropriate account or use the Items tab and use the same item that was on the original bill.

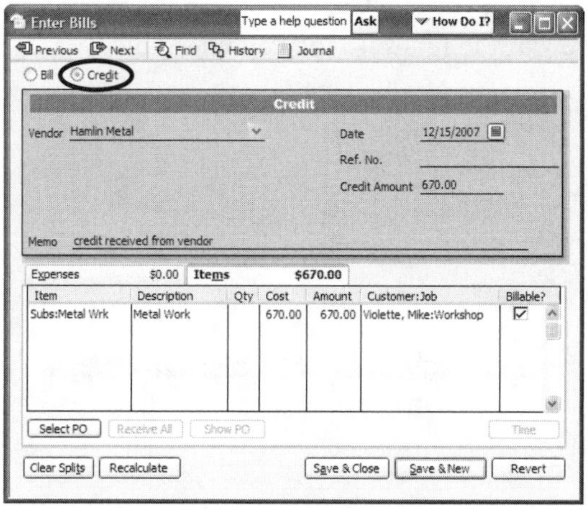

FIGURE 11.27

Select Credit on the Enter Bills dialog to create an Accounts Payable credit memo.

2. Click **Save & Close**. QuickBooks records this transaction as a credit memo or decrease (debit) to accounts payable and a decrease (credit) to the account on the Account column of the Expenses tab or, if you're using the Items tab, the expense account assigned to that item. You are not yet done; this vendor credit now needs to be assigned to the unpaid vendor bill.

3. Click **Vendors, Pay Bills** and move up and down through the list of vendors. Before placing a check mark in the box next to the vendor's specific invoice, QuickBooks will show the total number of credits and their total value in the Discount & Credit Information for Highlighted Bill pane (see Figure 11.26).

4. When you have located the correct bill, place a check mark in the box to the left of the Date Due column. When an invoice is selected, QuickBooks automatically applies the available credits to the selected vendor invoice (if that preference was selected). If you want to modify the amount or which credits are selected, click the **Set Credits** button. The Discount and Credits dialog displays as shown in Figure 11.28. Users can modify which credit is selected by changing the check mark from one credit to another or by manually overriding the amount of the credit.

5. Click **Done** to close the Discount and Credits dialog. Click **Pay Selected Bills** to exit the Pay Bills dialog. If you are only associating a credit memo with a vendor bill, no additional check transaction will be created.

6. Click **Done** in the Payment Summary dialog or click **Pay More Bills** if you want to return to the Pay Bills dialog.

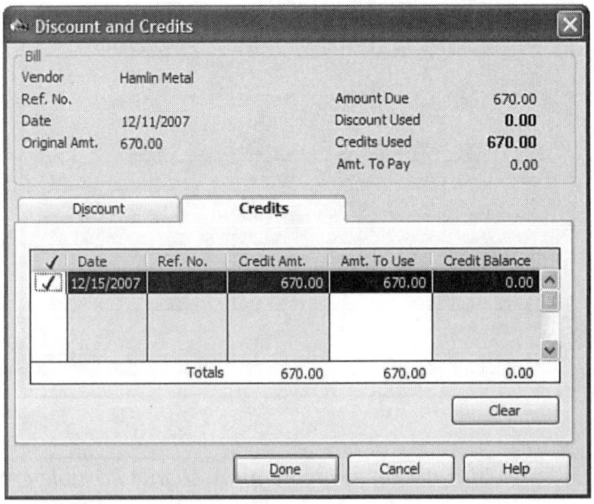

FIGURE 11.28

Assign the credit amount to an open vendor invoice.

As noted, new for QuickBooks Premier Accountant 2009 and the QuickBooks Enterprise Solutions Accountant 9.0 is the Client Data Review feature. From one convenient window, you can assign the vendor unapplied credit memo to the open accounts payable bill, replacing the previous steps numbered 3–6. To learn more about these features, see Chapter 17, "New for 2009!, Detecting and Correcting with the Client Data Review Feature."

Misapplied Vendor Credit

Have you ever been given a credit from a vendor, only to find out later that your vendor applied the credit to a different open bill than you did in your data?

Follow these easy steps to reassign a vendor credit from one accounts payable bill to another bill:

1. Click the **Vendors** button on the Home page to open the Vendor Center.

2. Select the vendor with the misapplied credit.

3. From the **Show** drop-down menu, select **Bills** (this will also show vendor credits).

4. From the transactions listed, select the misapplied credit memo by double-clicking it. The Credit dialog opens for that transaction.

5. On the vendor line of the credit, select a different vendor. (Remember to whom you assign it.)

6. Click **Save & Close**. QuickBooks removes the credit transaction from the vendor bill it was previously associated with.

7. QuickBooks also warns that the transaction you are editing will no longer be connected. Click **Yes** to continue (see Figure 11.29).

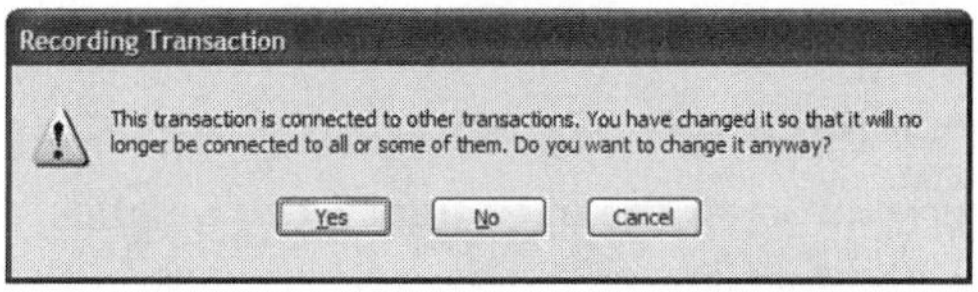

FIGURE 11.29

Warning when you unapply a previously applied vendor credit.

8. From the same Vendor Center, select the other vendor to which you assigned the credit. From the **Show** drop-down menu, select **Bills** and double-click the credit that you just assigned in step 5. The credit dialog displays.

9. On the vendor line, select the original vendor.

10. Click **Save & Close** and **Yes** to making the change.

QuickBooks now shows the credit as unapplied to your original vendor, and you can follow the steps outlined previously for applying the credit to the correct open vendor bill.

Removing Aged Open Item Receipts or Vendor Bills

One of the more important tasks you can do to maintain a correct data file is to remove old, aged item receipts or payables that you do not owe.

Rescue Me!

Before making any of the suggested changes, be sure you have made a backup of your data in case the change does not give you the desired result. Additionally, contacting your accountant and obtaining his or her advice on the changes you are going to make would be prudent.

You have three options when you want to remove these aged (old) transactions:

- Create a credit memo and apply it as discussed earlier in this chapter.
- Void the item receipt or bill.
- Delete the item receipt or bill.

To create and apply a credit memo to a vendor bill, follow the same steps as listed in the earlier section, "Creating and Applying a Vendor Credit."

You must give special consideration to applying a credit memo to an open item receipt. First, convert the item receipt to a bill:

1. Locate the open item receipt using any of the methods suggested in this chapter.

2. When you select the open item receipt, QuickBooks opens the Create Item Receipts dialog. Place a check mark in the **Bill Received** box at the top right, as shown in Figure 11.30.

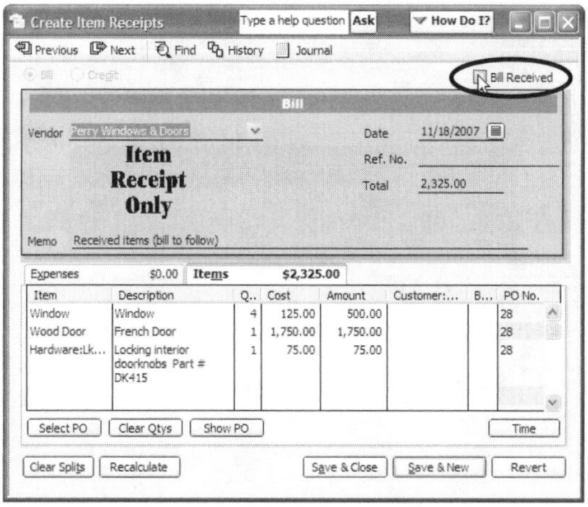

FIGURE 11.30

Converting an open item receipt to a bill is necessary before applying a vendor credit memo.

You can now apply your credit memo to the item receipt form, which has been converted to a bill.

When considering whether to void or delete, I always prefer the void option because it leaves a record of the original transaction.

Before Voiding or Deleting

Before voiding or deleting, you need to verify that the aged open item receipts or bills do not have any other transactions associated with them. To verify this, follow these steps:

1. Open the item receipt or bill using any one of the many methods discussed in this chapter.

2. From the Enter Bills or Create Item Receipts dialog, click the **History** link at the top. QuickBooks opens the Transaction History - Bill or Item Receipts dialog, as shown in Figure 11.31. If no history exists, you will get a warning message indicating the same.

If you had voided or deleted the example shown in Figure 11.31, you would have created an unapplied vendor payment. In effect, you would have traded one correction for another problem. So be careful when making corrections to your accounts payable transactions.

Continues...

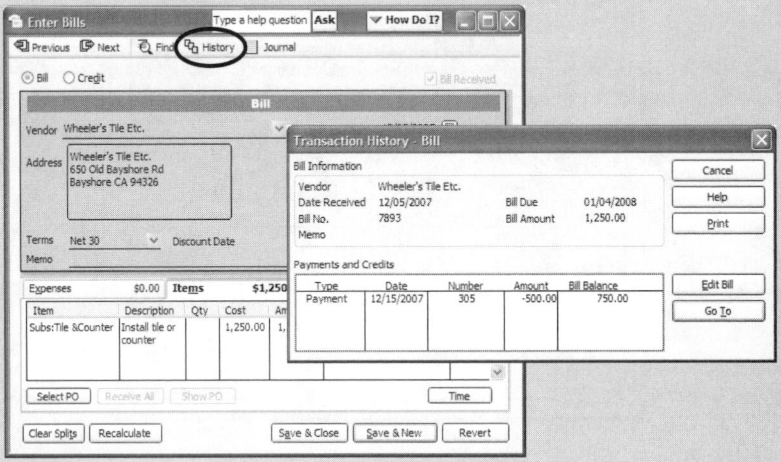

FIGURE 11.31

Before voiding, deleting, or modifying a bill, click the History link at the top of the form to see whether any transactions are associated with this bill.

General Journal Adjustments to Accounts Payable

All too often, I find that accounting professionals are quick to make adjustments to accounts payable using the Make General Journal Entries form, also referred to as a journal entry. The following are some of the issues surrounding the use of a general journal entries form:

- Only a single vendor or a customer name can be in the general journal entries form, not both a vendor and customer in the same form, minimizing the use of the form for large volume corrections.

- General journal entries do not include the option to assign an item, including service, non-inventory, inventory, and so on. The adjustment would affect the Profit & Loss reports, but not specific QuickBooks reports that use item information, such as the job profitability reports or inventory valuation reports.

- You will still need to go to the Pay Bills dialog to assign the general journal to the other related vendor transactions.

Caution When Using General Journal Entries

Often, the use of the general journal entries does not provide the desired results in your reporting. Did you know that the first line of any general journal entry form is considered a "source" line? Specifically, this means that if the first line of a multiple-line general journal entry form includes a vendor, customer, or any list item name in the Name column, as shown in Figure 11.32, that name element will display in reports on the lines below the first line, even if there is no relationship (see Figure 11.33).

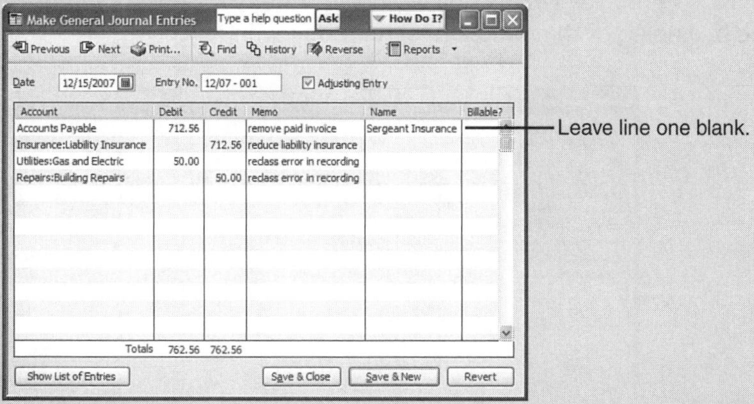

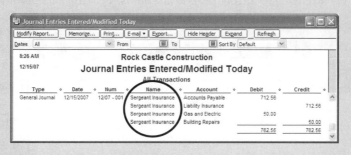

FIGURE 11.32

When the first line of a multiple-line general journal form includes a list name in the Name column, QuickBooks associates the name entry with all lines of the form.

FIGURE 11.33

QuickBooks associated the vendor's name with all lines of the journal entry because the vendor list name was on the first line of the general journal.

Continues...

This type of error is more apparent when a Customer:Job Name is included on the first line of a multiple-line general journal entry form. When preparing a Profit & Loss by Job report, QuickBooks would include all lines of the general journal entry as belonging to that job!

A quick fix is simply to add a blank line at the beginning of each general journal entry. Another recommendation is to create a fictitious bank account and call it Adjusting Entries. If you assign the first line of the entry to this account, QuickBooks provides a "register" for you to easily locate these types of transactions and at the same time avoid the issue addressed in this section. See Figures 11.34 and 11.35 to see how adding the line at the beginning of the form solves the problem in reporting.

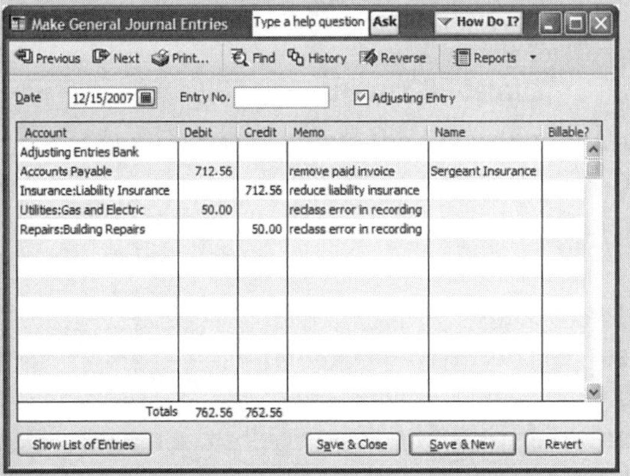

FIGURE 11.34
Including the fictitious bank account on the first line of a general journal entries form prevents the source line (line 1) from being associated with each additional unrelated line.

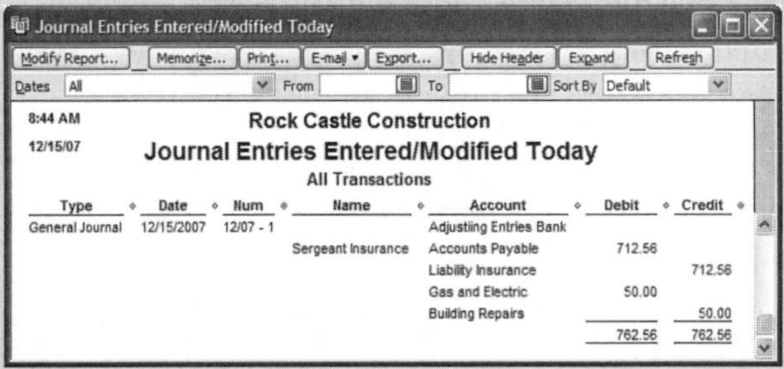

FIGURE 11.35
QuickBooks no longer associates the vendor's name with the unrelated general journal lines.

Often, just these simple tips can help make your QuickBooks data much more accurate!

If you have journal entries recorded to your accounts payable, your unpaid bills report might look something like Figure 11.36.

FIGURE 11.36

Your Unpaid Bills Detail report might show the general journal entry as unapplied.

To remove these types of transactions, simply follow steps 3 through 6 as out-lined earlier in this chapter in the "Creating and Applying a Vendor Credit" section.

Unique Accounts Payable Transactions

So far in this chapter, you have learned about the accounts payable forms and workflow, preferences that you can set to improve your data entry, reports to review when troubleshooting errors, and methods of correcting accounts payable errors. This section offers specific solutions to some of those unique transactions you might need to record.

When Your Vendor Is Also Your Customer

Having a vendor who is also a customer is commonly referred to as *bartering*. This is when your vendor also purchases your goods or services and you are going to "swap" and not pay each other for the items purchased from each other.

If you want to track the exchange of goods, you can follow these steps:

1. Click **Lists**, **Chart of Accounts** and click the **Account** drop-down menu. Select **New** to create a new bank account type named **Bartering**. This bank account will always have a net zero balance if the transactions are recorded properly.

2. Click **Save & Close**.

3. Click **Vendor**, **Enter Bills** to record your vendor bill as if you were going to make the purchase from the vendor.

4. Click **Vendor, Pay Bills**. The Pay Bills dialog opens. Select the vendor's bill you will barter with.

5. In the Pay Bills dialog (click **Vendors, Pay Bills**), select the **Bartering Account** as the payment account (as displayed in Figure 11.37). You can then choose to assign a fictitious check number.

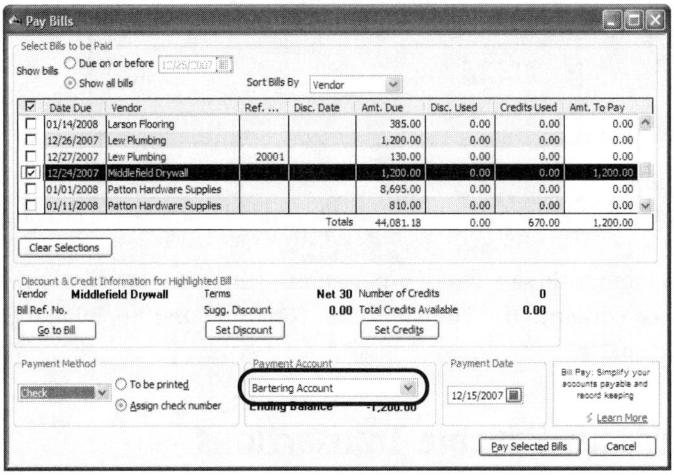

FIGURE 11.37

When you are bartering goods with your vendor, choose the fictitious bank account when recording the "payment" of the vendor bill.

6. Click the **Customers** button on the Home page to open the Customers Center.

7. If you need to create the vendor as a customer, click the **Customer** button on the Home page. Select **New Customer & Job, New Customer or Add Job**, and complete the contact information for the new customer; otherwise, double-click the customer or job you will be bartering with to select it. Note: QuickBooks will not allow the same name to reside on multiple lists. To get around this limitation, when creating the customer name for your vendor, follow this convention: Johns Plumbing – C. I have simply added a – C after the "vendor name" on my customer list. This is helpful when picking the name from a list and you need to select the customer list item.

8. From the Customers Center, click the **New Transactions** drop-down menu and select **Invoices**. Prepare the invoice to the new customer (also your vendor) using the same items on the invoice as if you were selling them to a customer. Click **Save & Close**.

9. From the Customers Center, click the **New Transactions** drop-down menu and select **Receive Payments**. Record the fictitious payment from the customer (your vendor). Click **Save & Close**.

10. Depending on how your preferences are set up for customer payments (see Chapter 7 and refer to the "Preferences That Affect Accounts Receivable" section), deposit the fictitious customer payment into the same Bartering bank account created earlier.

11. If the value of what you purchased is equal to the value of what you sold, your Bartering bank account will have a net zero ending balance. If not, you will need to enter an adjusting entry to remove the balance or adjust your purchase or sales form total. If needed, you can easily create an adjusting entry by clicking **Banking**, **Use Register** and selecting your Bartering bank account from the **Use Register** drop-down menu. On the next available line in the account register, record a payment or deposit as needed to clear the account. You will want to ask your accountant what account is appropriate for the adjustment.

Recording Vendor Prepayments

If your business is required to prepay your vendor for purchases, you can choose from a couple of methods:

■ Assigning expenses to the Other Current Asset type account typically named Prepaid Expenses. (See Chapter 9, "Handling Other Current Asset Accounts Correctly," specifically the section titled "Recording Prepaid Expenses in QuickBooks.")

■ Recording a decreasing (debit) transaction to accounts payable.

To record a debit balance to the vendor's accounts payable account, follow these steps:

1. Click **Banking**, **Write Checks**.

2. In the **Pay to the Order of** field, select the vendor's name.

3. Enter the amount of the prepayment.

4. On the **Expenses** tab, in the account detail area, select the accounts payable account (see Figure 11.38).

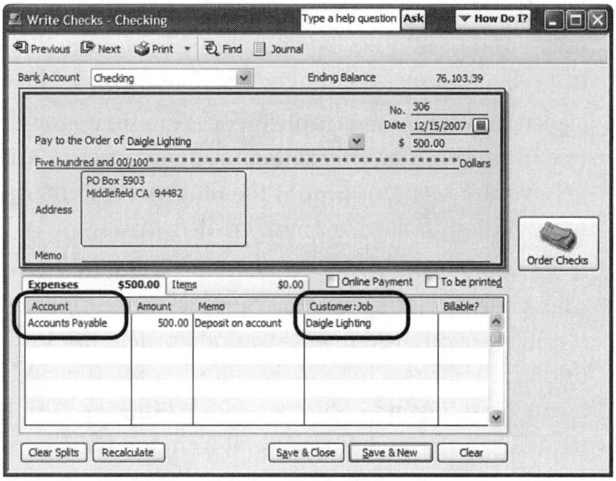

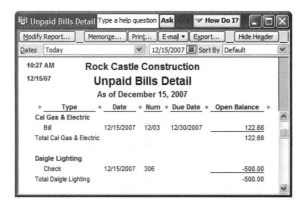

FIGURE 11.38

Assign the accounts payable account and the vendor name to a check form when recording a vendor prepayment.

5. In the **Customer:Job** column, enter the vendor's name (must be a vendor type for this method to work).

6. Click **Save & Close**.

QuickBooks now records a vendor credit (debit to accounts payable) as in Figure 11.39.

FIGURE 11.39

QuickBooks records the vendor prepayment as a negative entry to accounts payable (or a debit to accounts payable).

At a later date, you would record a bill for the full purchase price and assign this credit as discussed in this chapter.

Entering Mid-Year 1099 Balances

If you start your QuickBooks data file mid-year (or at some other time than the first of a new calendar year), you might have amounts paid previously to vendors who are eligible to receive the 1099—Misc. Income form. (See the section in this chapter titled, "Reviewing and Printing Year-End Vendor Tax Forms.")

To properly record the amounts paid to vendors in your prior accounting software and to make sure that QuickBooks reports all amounts paid to the vendor on the 1099—Misc. Income form, follow these steps:

1. Click **Company**, **Make General Journal Entries**. In the dialog that displays, leave the first line blank, or as discussed in the "Caution When Using General Journal Entries" sidebar on page 299, use the Adjusting Entries fictitious bank account on the first line with no dollar amount assigned.

2. On the following lines (one line per vendor), in the **Account** column, enter the cost of goods sold account or expense account assigned in the preferences for Tax: 1099. (See the section in this chapter titled "Preferences That Affect Accounts Payable.")

3. For each Debit line amount, be sure to select the vendor's list name (this must be a vendor type) in the **Name** column.

4. On the last line, enter one line total assigning the same account as the other lines so that the Debit column is equal to the Credit column (see Figure 11.40).

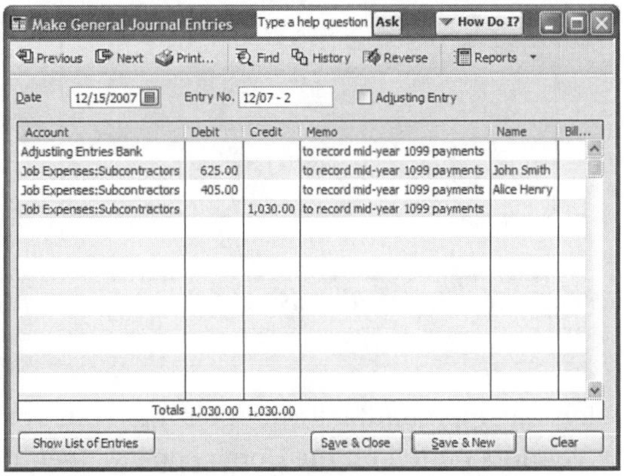

FIGURE 11.40

When starting a QuickBooks file mid-year, create a general journal entries form to record year-to-date vendor 1099—Misc. Income tax payments.

Your overall financials will not change because the same account was used for both the debit and credit side of the transaction. Including the vendor name on the debit side of the transaction lines causes QuickBooks to include the amount in the reported 1099—Misc. Income amount.

Taking Discounts on Vendor Bills

Your company might be able to save money by paying your vendors within their allowed discount terms. Discounts are offered by some vendors to encourage quick payment of their invoices.

The steps to automate taking a vendor discount are as follows:

1. Set the Bills preference to automatically calculate the discount. (See the section in this chapter titled "Preferences That Affect Accounts Payable.")

2. Make sure your vendor's discount terms are included in the global terms list by clicking **Lists**, **Customer & Vendor Profile Lists** and selecting **Terms List**. The terms list dialog opens as shown in Figure 11.41. If your specific terms are not included, click the **Terms** drop-down menu to create a new term or highlight with your cursor and select **Edit Terms**. Click **OK** and when completed, click on the red X to close the terms list.

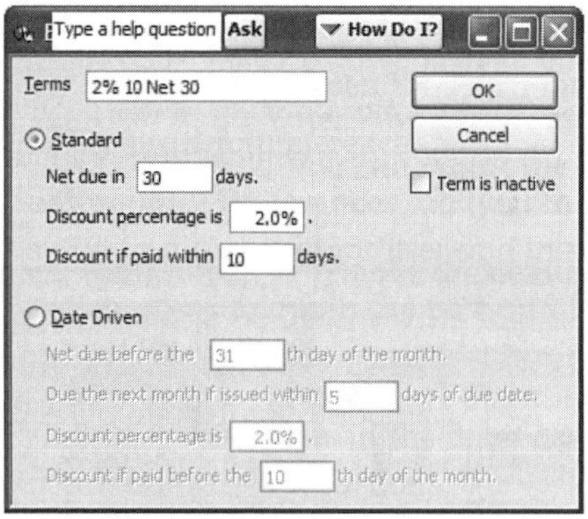

FIGURE 11.41

Set up terms in QuickBooks to calculate the discounts available when vendors' invoices are paid quickly.

3. Assign the appropriate discount term to your vendor record by clicking the **Vendors** button on the Home page to open the Vendors Center and selecting **New Vendor**, or by double-clicking an existing vendor to open the respective New or Edit Vendor dialog box. Click the **Edit**

Vendor button for an existing vendor, and then click the **Additional Info** tab for either a new or existing vendor. Assign the terms from the drop-down menu in the **Categorizing and Defaults** pane. Click **OK** to store the information.

4. When a discount term is entered on the vendor record and you enter a vendor bill, QuickBooks automatically applies the discount terms to the transaction.

5. Click **Vendors, Pay Bills** and select the vendor you will be paying. If you are paying the vendor within the discount terms date, QuickBooks will automatically calculate the discount amount as shown in Figure 11.42 and reduce the amount that is due on the bill.

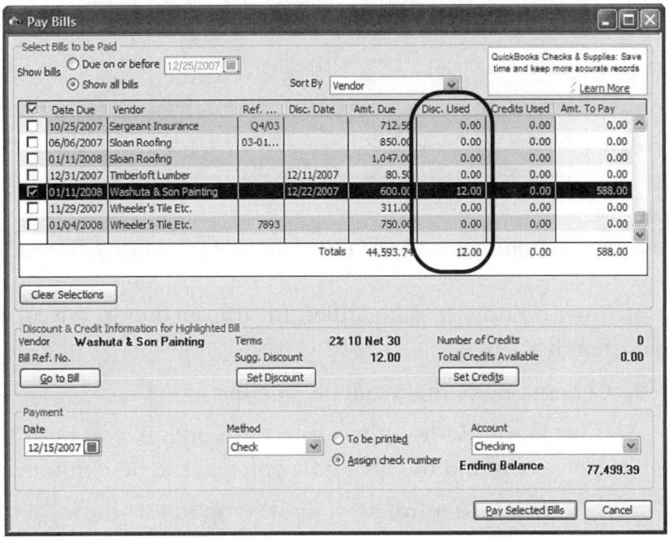

FIGURE 11.42

QuickBooks automatically applies the discount amount if preferences and transactions are entered correctly.

Click the Set Discount button if you want to override the amount calculated or the account assigned. If you are going to use this method, record your bills at the "gross" amount, or total amount before any discount. Then, over time you can watch the amount you have saved grow!

Memorizing Recurring Transactions

QuickBooks can also make it easy to not forget a recurring accounts payable bill. Memorized bills work best if the amount being paid is the same from month to month (or whatever frequency you set). An example might be your rent payment.

Here are the steps to memorize a recurring accounts payable transaction:

1. Create a vendor bill as normal, assigning the amount and expense account with which you want it to be associated.

2. With the Enter Bills dialog open, press **Ctrl+M** to open the Schedule Memorized Transaction dialog (see Figure 11.43).

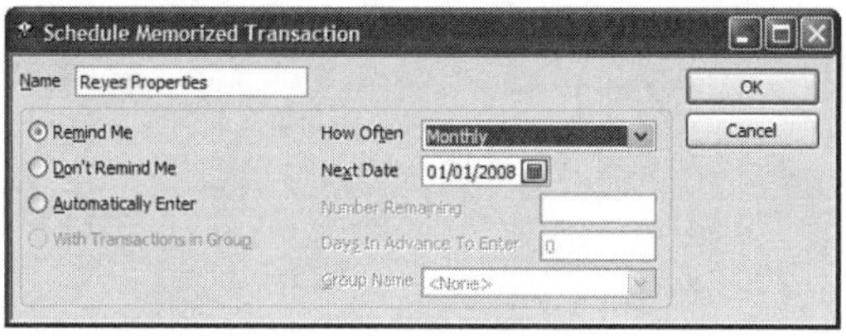

FIGURE 11.43

Press Ctrl+M from any transaction to open the Schedule Memorized Transaction dialog.

3. Enter a name that identifies this transaction in the memorized transaction list.

4. Choose one of the available options:

   ■ **Remind Me**—If you select this option, you need to choose how often and the next date you want to be reminded.

   ■ **Don't Remind Me**—Use this option if you want to stop permanently, or even temporarily, your reminders for this transaction.

   ■ **Automatically Enter**—Use this option if you want QuickBooks to create the entry without asking.

   ■ **With Transactions in Group**—You can assign multiple transactions to a group and then process them with one keystroke. First, create a group by clicking **Lists, Memorized Transaction List**. Click the **Memorized Transaction** drop-down menu, and select **New Group**. Give the group a name and choose options for the group from the same Remind Me, Don't Remind Me, or Automatically Enter options.

5. Click **OK** to close the Schedule Memorized Transaction dialog.

6. Click **Save & Close** on your bill only if you want to create the vendor bill now and add it to your memorized transaction list. If not, select **Clear** to remove the bill details, knowing that QuickBooks will prompt you to enter it on the frequency and date you selected.

To manually enter the transactions (if they're not set to automatically enter), click Lists, Memorized Transaction List, or press Ctrl+T to quickly call up the list. Select the group or individual transactions you want to post by double-clicking the group or the individual item from the memorized transaction list.

If you clicked on a memorized group, QuickBooks will create each of the transactions in the group, asking you to assign a transaction date globally to all the transactions in the group. If you created individual transactions, QuickBooks will enable you to modify the information on the individual transaction if necessary before saving the memorized transaction.

Use the memorized tool to save time and to remind you to pay those important bills.

Depositing a Vendor Refund

Use this method to add a vendor refund check to your bank deposit:

1. Create your deposit (normally done with customer invoice payments) as usual. (For more detailed information, see Chapter 7.)

2. On the next available deposit line, choose one of two options:

    ■ If you do not have an open vendor credit in your Accounts Payable, enter the vendor name in the **Received From** column, and select the expense account you want to reduce in the **From Account** column.

    ■ If you do have an open vendor credit that you want to associate this refund with, enter the vendor name in the **Received From** column, and select the **Accounts Payable** account in the **From Account** column. Then apply the deposit to the open credit, as discussed in this chapter in the "Creating and Applying a Vendor Credit Memo" section.

3. Enter an optional memo.

4. Enter the amount.

5. Click **Save & Close** when the total of the deposit agrees with the bank deposit total.

Paying and Recording a Credit Card Bill

You have flexibility in how you choose to record and pay your credit card bills. The decision is based on your own circumstances because no one way is the right way.

Options for recording credit card expenses include the following:

- Enter a bill to the credit card vendor, summarizing the total charges on one bill and entering a separate line for each expense account amount.

- Enter individual credit card charges. Click **Banking, Enter Credit Card Charges**. You first need to create a credit card type account as discussed in Chapter 2.

- Use the QuickBooks Online Banking feature and automatically download your credit card charges and payments directly into your QuickBooks data file. (Not all credit card providers offer this functionality. To see whether your card offers this option, click **Banking, Online Banking**, and select **Participating Financial Institutions**.)

Options for paying your credit card bill include the following:

- If you selected to enter a bill to your credit card vendor, simply pay the bill as you do other bills, paying it partially or in full.

- If you selected one of the other two options, you need to create a vendor bill, and in the Account column of that bill, assign the Credit Card type account you previously recorded the transactions to. The vendor bill simply decreases the balance owed on the credit card liability account.

The cash basis balance sheet often shows this amount if it is not paid by the date you prepare your financials. For more information about how QuickBooks handles certain accounts on a cash basis, see the "When You Have Accounts Payable Balances on a Cash Basis Balance Sheet" sidebar earlier in this chapter.

Assigning Default Expense Accounts to Vendors

Have you ever found that QuickBooks users will assign a different expense account each time they create a check or bill to pay for costs of the business? This can make reviewing your specific expenses for the business less accurate.

For several years, QuickBooks had the Automatically Recall option (click Edit, Preferences and select the General, My Preferences tab). The problem with recall was that when you created a new transaction for the vendor, it not only recalled the expense account, but it also recorded the previous amount. Later, QuickBooks had a Pre-fill Accounts choice that would prefill the expense account(s), but not the amount.

With the release of QuickBooks 2008, users can now assign up to three different default chart of accounts to each vendor record. Follow these steps to add these accounts:

1. From the Home page, click **Vendors** to open the Vendor Center.

2. Select the vendor to which you want to assign accounts, and click **Edit** to open the Edit Vendor dialog.

3. Click the **Account Prefill** tab. In the fields provided, select the desired accounts from the drop-down list, as shown in Figure 11.44.

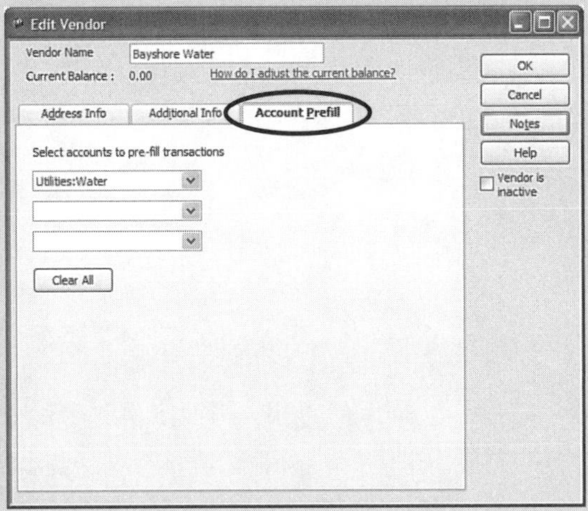

FIGURE 11.44
QuickBooks 2008 added the capability to assign multiple expense accounts to the vendor record.

The selected accounts will override any preference setting for Recall or Prefill and will instead insert these accounts automatically on a Write Check or Bill form. This is just another method that you will find helps you keep your accounting accurate.

Chapter 12

Reviewing and Correcting Sales Tax Errors

- Preferences That Affect Sales Tax
- Sales Tax Items, Groups, and Codes
- Assigning Sales Tax Codes to Products or Services
- Assigning Sales Tax Codes and Items to Customers
- Reports to Review When Troubleshooting Sales Tax Errors
- Properly Paying Sales Tax
- Correcting Sales Tax Errors
- Unique Sales Tax Transactions

Your business might sell a product or service for which the states you sale in require you to charge and collect sales tax at the time of sale. If your business does collect sales taxes, you are simply acting as an agent for these states by collecting this fee and later remitting it to the respective state. Each state, county, or city might have its own sales tax rates and lists of products or services that are taxable or exempt from being taxed.

You should contact your accountant or the city/state sales tax government office to make sure your business complies with the sales tax requirements for that jurisdiction. The mistakes caused by not setting up your QuickBooks sales tax correctly, or not following the state's sales tax guidelines, can be expensive to correct, especially if you find your business is subject to a sales tax audit by the taxing authority.

To determine whether sales tax is to be charged to a customer, QuickBooks uses the following criteria for each transaction:

- Is the sales tax preference enabled? If not, QuickBooks will not track or compute sales tax.

- Is the item being sold as a taxable item? If not, QuickBooks will not compute sales tax for that specific item.

- Is the customer taxable? If not, QuickBooks will not compute sales tax for any items for that customer, even taxable items.

To ensure QuickBooks correctly charges and tracks your sales tax, take the following required steps:

1. Set your sales tax preferences (by selecting **Edit**, **Preferences**).
2. Create your sales tax items or groups defining the rate and taxing authority to be paid.
3. Assign a Taxable or Non-taxable code to your products or services.
4. Assign the appropriate sales tax code and sales tax item to your customer.

Each of these steps is discussed in this chapter, as are techniques for troubleshooting and fixing errors in your sales tax setup.

Preferences That Affect Sales Tax

Only one preference in QuickBooks directly affects sales tax collection and reporting. To locate that preference setting, you must log in as the Admin or External Accountant user in single-user mode:

1. Click **Edit**, **Preferences**.

2. Select the preference for **Sales Tax** in the left pane.

3. Click the **Company Preferences** tab (see Figure 12.1).

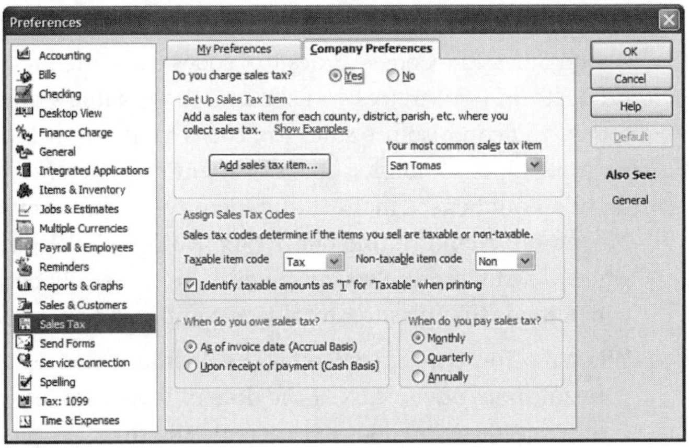

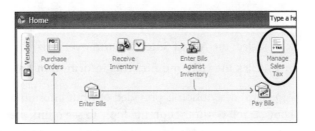

FIGURE 12.1

Set Sales Tax preferences.

Alternatively, you can access the Sales Tax preferences from the Home page by selecting Manage Sales Tax, as shown in Figure 12.2. (Sales Tax must first be enabled in Edit, Preferences, Sales Tax, Company Preferences.)

FIGURE 12.2

If Sales Tax is enabled, you can optionally get to the Sales Tax preferences from the Home page's Manage Sales Tax icon.

You must define each of the preference settings for your specific business needs:

- Do You Charge Sales Tax?—Click Yes if your company tracks sales tax. When a new QuickBooks data file is created without using the EasyStep Interview, QuickBooks defaults this setting to "No." (See the section titled "EasyStep Interview—Overview" in Chapter 1, "Creating a New QuickBooks Data File.") You can return later to this preference dialog and turn on the preference.

- Set Up Sales Tax Item—Sales Tax type items in QuickBooks record the default tax rate to charge your customers and record the taxing authority to which the sales tax collection is remitted. For more detailed information, see the "Sales Tax Items, Groups, and Codes" section later in this chapter.

- Assign Sales Tax Codes—Sales tax codes track the taxable status of the products and/or services you sell and the taxable status of the customer. You can also use sales tax codes to get reporting breakdowns on multiple types of non-taxable sales. In this preference, be sure to place an additional check mark in the Identify Taxable Amounts as "T" for "Taxable" When Printing check box. Doing so is recommended so that when a customer receives an invoice, he can easily determine exactly which items the sales tax total was computed on.

- When Do You Owe Sales Tax?—The Accrual Basis selection increases your sales tax payable as of the date of the customer's invoice. The Cash Basis selection does not increase the sales tax payable until the date of the customer payment. This setting is governed by the state or local government jurisdiction in which you are selling. If you are not sure what the state's guidelines are, you can find Internet links to each state's sales and use tax website from within the QuickBooks Help menu (see Figure 12.3):

  1. To open the QuickBooks Help menu, press the **F1** key on your keyboard.

  2. On the **Search** tab, type the keyword **Sales Tax**.

  3. Select the **About Sales Tax (an overview)** link.

  4. Click the **Help me find this information** link.

  A general description is provided of what information you need to know. Scroll down though the topic to see a link specific to the state's government sales tax Internet site (an Internet connection is required).

- When Do You Pay Sales Tax?—Select the appropriate payment frequency for your business as determined by the state tax authority. This setting causes QuickBooks to use this date range when it's preparing the sales tax liability reports and creating your sales tax payment.

If you are setting up sales tax for the first time in a QuickBooks file with existing items and customers, QuickBooks prompts you with the message in Figure 12.4 to automatically set each customer and each item as taxable.

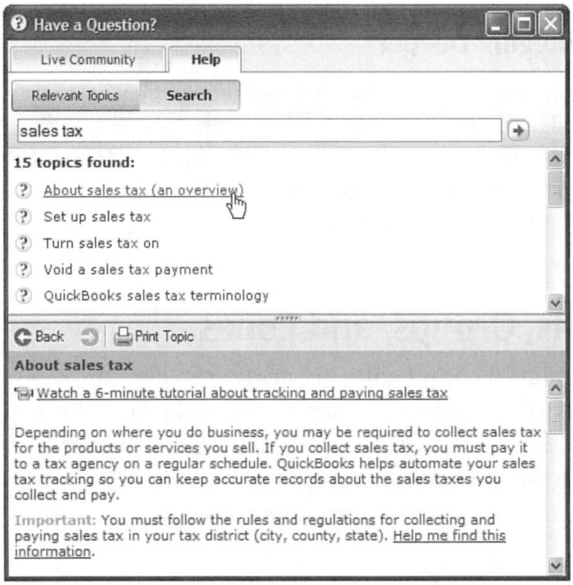

FIGURE 12.3

Use the QuickBooks Help menu to research your state's or city's sales tax guidelines.

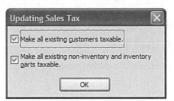

FIGURE 12.4

When you set up sales tax in an existing file, you can have QuickBooks automatically mark each customer or referenced item as taxable.

Place a check mark in the Make all existing customers taxable check box if you want QuickBooks to assign your most common sales tax item as defined in the preferences.

Place a check mark in the Make all existing non-inventory and inventory parts taxable check box if most of these items are taxable. QuickBooks does not automatically assign the taxable item code to other item types on your item list.

Digging Deeper

Because each state has different requirements and rates for reporting sales tax, taking the time to research them and then setting up QuickBooks correctly can save your business the costly penalties incurred if you are subjected to a sales and use tax audit and found not to be in compliance.

Sales Tax Items, Groups, and Codes

As mentioned earlier, sales tax items and sales tax codes are required when setting up your sales tax tracking in QuickBooks. If you created your data file using the EasyStep Interview as discussed in Chapter 1, you probably have already set up your sales tax items and codes. However, I still recommend that you review this topic to make sure your initial sales tax setup is correct.

Creating and Using Sales Tax Items

Sales tax items are used to identify specific rates charged to your customers and the tax authority vendor to which you remit the sales tax. You might have one sales tax item, or several, on your item list.

To create a sales tax item, follow these steps:

1. Click **Lists, Item List**.

2. From the **Item** drop-down menu, select **New** to open the New Item dialog.

3. Choose **Sales Tax Item** in the **Type** drop-down, as shown in Figure 12.5.

FIGURE 12.5

Choose a Sales Tax Item type from the Type list.

4. Enter a sales tax name for the sales tax item; the name should identify the state, district, or city the tax is collected for (see Figure 12.6).

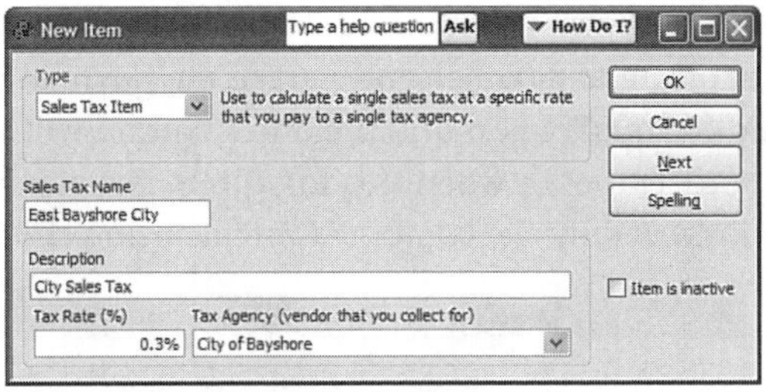

FIGURE 12.6

New Item setup for a Sales Tax Item type.

5. In the **Tax Rate (%)** box, enter the rate the tax entity charges.

6. From the **Tax Agency (vendor that you collect for)** drop-down list, select the vendor to which you remit your sales tax payments. If your vendor is not currently set up in QuickBooks, select **Add New** at the top of the list and follow the dialogs to create your vendor.

7. Click **OK** to save the sales tax item.

With sales tax items created, you can group them into sales tax groups if the state requires collection and reporting on multiple tax entities.

Creating and Using Sales Tax Group Items

Sales tax groups are optional in QuickBooks. In many states, you are required to report the collection of sales tax for a combination of city, county, and state but you want to show the customer only one tax rate. In QuickBooks, you can accomplish this by first creating your individual city, county, and state sales tax items, and then assigning them to a Sales Tax Group item type. The Sales Tax Group item is then assigned to the customer.

To create a Sales Tax Group item, follow these steps:

1. Click **Lists, Item List**.

2. From the **Item** drop-down menu, select **New** to open the New Item dialog.

3. Select **Sales Tax Group** item from the type drop-down menu.

4. Enter a Group Name or Number that identifies the group.

5. In the **Description** box, enter the description you want printed on the customer's invoice.

6. In the **Tax Item** column, from the drop-down menu, select the appropriate city, county, or state sales tax items previously created (see Figure 12.7).

7. Click **OK** to save the new Sales Tax Group item.

In the example shown in Figure 12.7, you are going to collect and pay the sales tax at a rate of 8.05 percent. Part of the payment will be made to the State Board of Equalization and the other portion will be paid to the City of East Bayshore. However, when this tax group is assigned to a customer, the invoice will show only the combined rate as being charged.

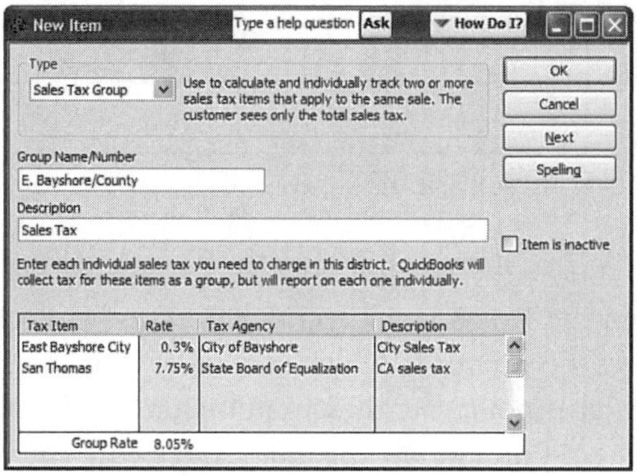

FIGURE 12.7

Use sales tax groups to track multiple taxes, but show only one tax rate on a customer's invoice.

Creating and Using Sales Tax Codes

The primary purpose of sales tax codes in QuickBooks is to identify a product or service as taxable or non-taxable and identify a customer as taxable or non-taxable. If you track sales tax, you have at least one tax code for taxable but might have multiple non-taxable tax codes.

Another use of sales tax codes is for when the state has reporting requirements on the types of non-taxable sales you make. Creating a unique non-taxable sales code for each of these non-taxable sales types enables you to report the total sales on each non-taxable sales tax type.

Examples of non-taxable tax codes might include some or all of the following:

- Non-taxable reseller
- Out-of-state sale
- Sale to a nonprofit organization
- Government entity

To see a list of suggested non-taxable tax codes, press the F1 key on your keyboard to open QuickBooks Help. Type `sales tax code` and select the non-taxable sales tax codes examples topic. QuickBooks will provide a list of commonly used sales tax codes. See Figure 12.8 for a sample sales tax code list.

When creating a customer invoice and before charging sales tax to the customer, QuickBooks determines whether the item being sold is taxable and whether the customer is assigned a taxable or non-taxable sales tax code before computing any sales tax charge on an invoice.

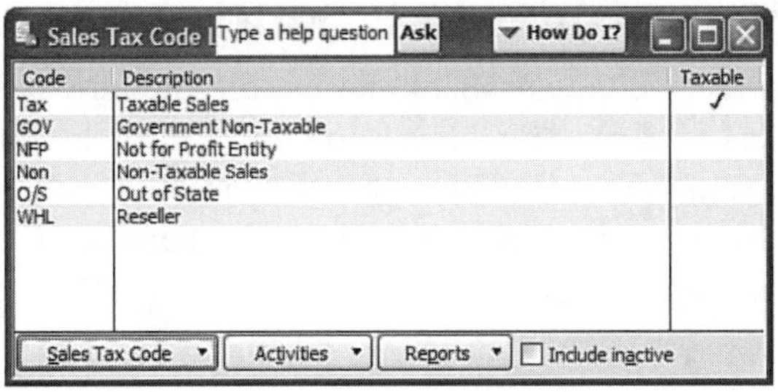

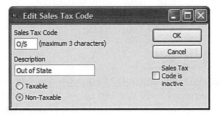

Code	Description	Taxable
Tax	Taxable Sales	✓
GOV	Government Non-Taxable	
NFP	Not for Profit Entity	
Non	Non-Taxable Sales	
O/S	Out of State	
WHL	Reseller	

FIGURE 12.8

Sales tax code list.

To create a sales tax code list or edit the existing sales tax codes, follow these steps:

1. Make sure you have enabled the sales tax preference as discussed in the section of this chapter titled "Preferences That Affect Sales Tax."

2. Click **Lists, Sales Tax Code List**.

3. From the **Sales Tax Code** drop-down menu, click **New** or select a sales tax code from the list and from the same drop-down menu, select **Edit Sales Tax Code**. (Note that a new QuickBooks data file automatically defaults with one taxable tax code and one non-taxable tax code.)

4. In the New or Edit Sales Tax dialog, enter a three-character code in the **Sales Tax Code** field. Make the three-digit code something meaningful. You will see this code on a New or Edit Item dialog, New or Edit Customer dialog, and optionally on the lines of the customer's invoice (see Figure 12.9).

FIGURE 12.9

Create a new sales tax code assigned to your customers with out-of-state sales.

To complete the process, assign the appropriate code to your customer record. More detail on this is discussed in the section in this chapter titled "Assigning Sales Tax Codes and Items to Customers."

Assigning Sales Tax Codes to Products or Services

Items are created in QuickBooks for use on sales and purchase forms. The primary purpose of creating items is to handle the behind-the-scenes accounting and to assign the taxable status for an item on a customer invoice. For general information about properly setting up items, see Chapter 3, "Reviewing and Correcting Item List Errors."

The following items in QuickBooks enable you to assign a taxable code, as shown in Figure 12.10:

- Service Item
- Inventory Part
- Inventory Assembly
- Non-inventory Part
- Other Charge
- Discount

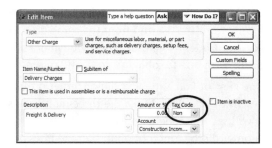

FIGURE 12.10

Other Charge item type marked as "Non" for non-taxable.

 Digging Deeper

Items are typically assigned only a generic tax or non-taxable sales tax code. You might have created other sales tax codes for resellers or out-of-state sales; these more specific tax codes would be on the same list, but they would be assigned to customers and not the items.

If you expect to charge sales tax on an item, it should be marked as taxable even if it is sold to a non-taxable customer. As discussed in the beginning of this chapter, QuickBooks checks whether an item is taxable and then verifies that the customer is taxable before it charges sales tax.

If the item is always non-taxable, even if it is sold to a taxable customer (for example, labor), it should be assigned a non-taxable sales tax code so that it will never have sales tax calculated on the sale of that item.

Some states require the sale of labor services to be taxed if they are invoiced with products and not taxed if they are invoiced separately. Although this might not be the requirement for the state jurisdictions you sell in, to handle this situation, create two Labor Service type items—one named Taxable Labor and assigned a taxable tax code, and another named Non-Taxable Labor and assigned a non-taxable tax code. Then, depending on how you invoice your customer, you select one or the other labor item.

Assigning Sales Tax Codes and Items to Customers

Enabling the sales tax preference and creating sales tax items, groups, and codes are part of the sales tax setup. You also need to assign a tax code and a tax item to each customer.

To assign or edit a customer's tax code (as well as tax item), as shown in Figure 12.11, do the following:

1. Click **Customers** from the Home page to open the Customer Center.

2. Select the customer for whom you want to assign or edit a tax code.

3. Click the **Edit Customer** button on the Customer Center dialog. (Or if creating a new customer, continue to the following step.)

4. In the Add New or Edit Customer dialog that displays, click the **Additional Info** tab.

5. Enter the appropriate Tax Code and Tax Item from the drop-down lists in the Sales Tax Information pane of the dialog.

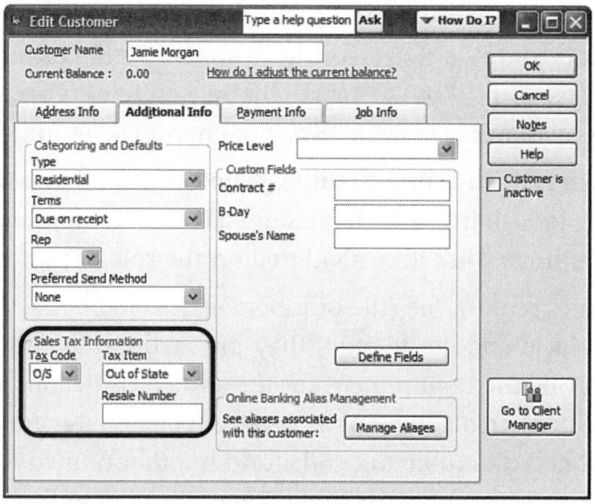

FIGURE 12.11

Assign the proper sales tax code and sales tax item to your customer.

 Digging Deeper

You can assign only one tax code and one tax item to each customer. You cannot assign a tax code or tax item to a job. If you have a customer with multiple locations and you are required to charge different tax rates for each location, you need to create a unique customer for each location.

The sales tax code defines the customer as taxable or not. The sales tax item defines the rate to be charged to the customer.

Because QuickBooks enables you to save a customer record without one or both of these settings, be sure to review your customer sales tax list (discussed in the "Reviewing Customer Lists for Tax Code and Tax Item Assigned" section in this chapter) often to make sure your sales tax is properly assigned to each of your customers.

Reports to Review When Troubleshooting Sales Tax Errors

This section's title can be a bit misleading because the reports I'm referring to are reports that I recommend you review each time you get ready to pay your sales and use tax to the taxing authority. Properly "reconciling" these reports to each other helps minimize any chance that your QuickBooks data will not support what you filed on your sales tax return.

Reviewing Customer Lists for Tax Code and Tax Item Assigned

Check your customer's taxable status often. This task is quite easy to do and helps prevent the costly mistakes caused by not charging sales tax or charging the incorrect rate.

1. Click **Reports**, **Lists** and select the **Customer Phone List** report.
2. Click the **Modify Report** button on the top left of the report.
3. In the Display dialog that opens, in the Columns pane, click to place a check mark next to items you want to review for the list, including **Sales Tax Code** and **Tax Item**, and include the **Resale Num** if you track this number for your wholesale customers.
4. Optionally, select **Sort by** at the top right, and from the drop-down list, select **Sales Tax Code**.
5. Optionally, click the **Header/Footer** tab to change the report title.

From this list shown in Figure 12.12 you can conveniently double-click any line item detail to open the Edit Customer dialog and make any needed changes.

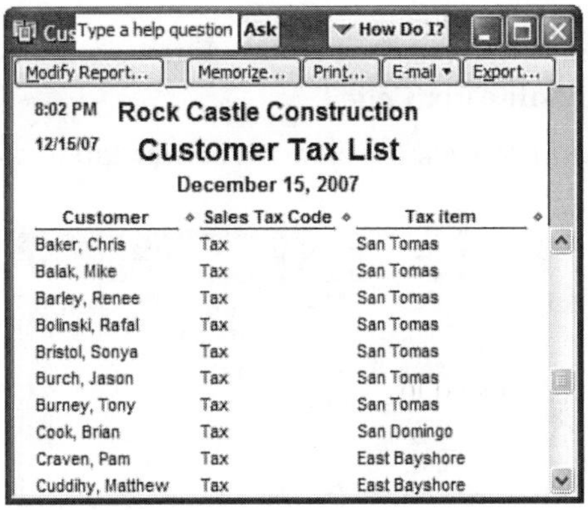
Type a help question
Ask
How Do I?
Modify Report...
Memorize...
Print...
E-mail
Export...
8:02 PM
Rock Castle Construction
12/15/07
Customer Tax List
December 15, 2007
Customer
Sales Tax Code
Tax item
Baker, Chris	Tax	San Tomas
Balak, Mike	Tax	San Tomas
Barley, Renee	Tax	San Tomas
Bolinski, Rafal	Tax	San Tomas
Bristol, Sonya	Tax	San Tomas
Burch, Jason	Tax	San Tomas
Burney, Tony	Tax	San Tomas
Cook, Brian	Tax	San Domingo
Craven, Pam	Tax	East Bayshore
Cuddihy, Matthew	Tax	East Bayshore

FIGURE 12.12

Prepare this report often to review the sales tax codes and items assigned to your customers and to verify the accuracy of your setup.

Digging Deeper

When you make a change to a customer's assigned tax code or tax item or to the tax code assigned to a product or service you sell on your item list, QuickBooks will *not* correct or modify prior saved transactions. Only new transactions will show the change in the sales tax status or rate.

Reviewing the Item List for Tax Code Assigned

Another review that I recommend you do periodically is to look at the list of services and products that you sell and determine whether the proper tax code has been assigned (see Figure 12.13).

1. Click **Reports**, **Lists** and select the **Item Price List** report, which you will modify.

2. Click the **Modify Report** button at the top left of the report.

3. In the Display dialog that displays, remove check marks from those data fields you do not want displayed on this report. Place a check mark next to date fields you want to review for the list, including Sales Tax Code.

4. Optionally, select **Sort by** at the top right, and from the drop-down list, select **Sales Tax Code**.

5. Optionally, click the **Header/Footer** tab to change the report title.

FIGURE 12.13

Prepare a report of your items and the sales tax codes assigned to them to verify the accuracy of your setup.

Reconciling Total Sales to Total Income

The term *reconciling* (also known as proofing) refers to the need to compare two related numbers from two different reports. The importance of this task cannot be overstated. If your company is selected to have a sales tax audit, one of the first numbers the auditor will want to determine is the total sales you reported on your tax returns for the time period being audited.

To compare your total sales on the Sales Tax Liability report to your total income on the Profit & Loss Report, follow these steps:

1. Click **Reports, Vendors & Payables** and select the **Sales Tax Liability** report.

2. Make a note of the total sales on this report, as shown in Figure 12.14.

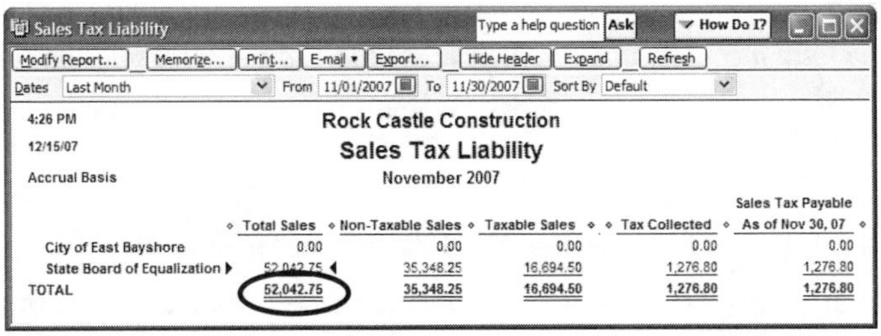

FIGURE 12.14
Compare total sales on the Sales Tax Liability report to total income on the Profit & Loss report.

3. Click **Reports, Company & Financial**, and select the **Profit & Loss Standard** report.

4. Compare total income (see Figure 12.15) to the total sales from the Sales Tax Liability report. Note: You might have to deduct any non-sales income on your Profit & Loss Total Income amounts.

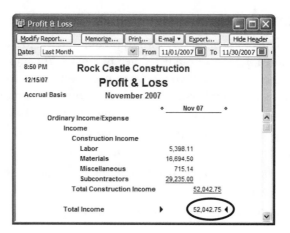

FIGURE 12.15

Compare the total income on the Profit & Loss report to the total sales on the Sales Tax Liability report.

When Total Sales Does Not Match Total Income

What can cause your total sales on your Sales Tax Liability report not to match your total income on your Profit & Loss report? Some of the reasons might be the following:

- **Different accounting basis between reports**—Your Sales Tax Liability report basis is in conflict with your Profit & Loss reporting basis. The basis of the report is by default printed on the top left of the report. Both reports must be either Accrual Basis or both must be Cash Basis before comparing. (See the section titled "Preferences That Affect Sales Tax.")

- **Non-sales form transactions recorded to income accounts**—A method to locate these transactions is to double-click the total income amount on your Profit & Loss report. Doing so opens the Transaction Detail by Account report. At the top right of the report, select Sort By and choose Type. Within each income account group, QuickBooks will sort the transactions by transaction type. Review the report for non-sales form transaction types such as General Journal or Bill (to name a couple). If you find the bill form on this report, it can be due to improperly setting up your items. To determine how to fix this type of error, see the section titled "Correcting One-Sided Items," located in Chapter 3.

- **Income recorded as a result of vendor discounts**—If you have set up an income account for your vendor discounts in your bills preferences setting, you will need to deduct this amount from your total revenue when you compare the two totals. I always recommend that you create a separate income account for these discounts so that you can easily identify them.

Additionally, QuickBooks defaults the Sales Tax Liability report dates based on your preference setting, as detailed in the "Preferences That Affect Sales Tax" section.

Reconciling Sales Tax Liability to Balance Sheet Sales Tax Payable

Another equally important comparison to make is between the balance on your Balance Sheet Sales Tax Payable amount and the amount showing payable on your Sales Tax Liability report.

If you created your own Sales Tax Payable account, you might not be able to correctly compare the two reports. QuickBooks creates the Sales Tax Payable account automatically. You can learn more information about automatically created accounts in Chapter 2, "Reviewing the QuickBooks Chart of Accounts."

To compare the Balance Sheet Sales Tax Payable with the Sales Tax Liability report, follow these steps:

1. Click **Reports, Company & Financial** and choose **Balance Sheet Standard** (see Figure 12.16).

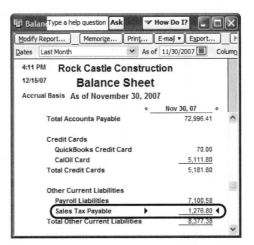

FIGURE 12.16

Balance Sheet Sales Tax payable should agree with your Sales Tax Liability report.

2. On the report, select the **As of Date** you are comparing to; this date must be the same ending date you will use when you prepare your Sales Tax Liability report in the next step.

3. Click **Reports, Vendors & Payables** and choose the **Sales Tax Liability** report. QuickBooks defaults the date range depending on your sales tax preference setting (see Figure 12.17).

Each month before preparing your sales tax return, compare the total of these two reports. If they do not agree, read the sections in this chapter titled "Reports to Review When Troubleshooting Sales Tax Errors" and "Correcting Sales Tax Errors."

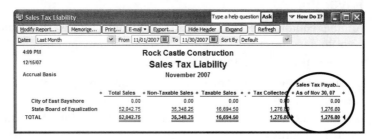

FIGURE 12.17

The total sales tax liability payable should agree with your Balance Sheet Sales Tax payable.

When a Check or Bill Form Is Used to Pay Sales Tax

A common mistake is to use a write check or vendor bill form to pay your sales tax payable. If these types of forms are used and the Sales Tax Payable account is assigned on the form, QuickBooks reduces the Sales Tax Payable amount on the Balance Sheet, but does not make the same adjustment in the Pay Sales Tax dialog, as discussed in the section titled, "Properly Paying Sales Tax."

Use this method to find the transaction(s) that might be the cause of not being able to compare your Balance Sheet Sales Tax Payable amount to your Sales Tax Liability report amount to be paid:

1. Open the Vendor Center by clicking the **Vendors** button on the Home page.

2. Select your sales tax vendor from the **Vendor List** dialog.

3. From the **Show** drop-down menu, select **Checks (or Bills)**, making sure that you are looking in the appropriate date range.

If you have found checks or bills, this could be one of the reasons your two reports do not agree with each other. The correct sales tax payment form is a type named TAXPMT when viewing transactions in your bank register.

Refer to the section titled, "Correcting Sales Tax Errors," to learn how to associate these check or bill payment forms to the lines in the Sales Tax Payable dialog.

Properly Paying Sales Tax

Now that you have your sales tax correctly set up, you need to know how to properly pay your sales tax.

As mentioned earlier, when you collect sales tax, you are acting as an agent for the state. Most often, you will simply pay the state or city taxing authority the same amount that you collected from your customers. Sometimes the state might allow you to discount the sales tax due for prompt payment or charge a penalty for paying late. Each of these situations is discussed in detail in this section.

Paying Sales Tax Without an Adjustment

After you have properly compared your Profit & Loss income total with your Sales Tax Liability report total sales and they agree, or if they don't agree and you have identified the differences, as discussed in the "Reports to Review When Troubleshooting Sales Tax Errors" section, you are ready to create the check to pay your sales tax.

1. Click **Vendors**, **Sales Tax** and select **Pay Sales Tax**. The Pay Sales Tax dialog box displays (see Figure 12.18).

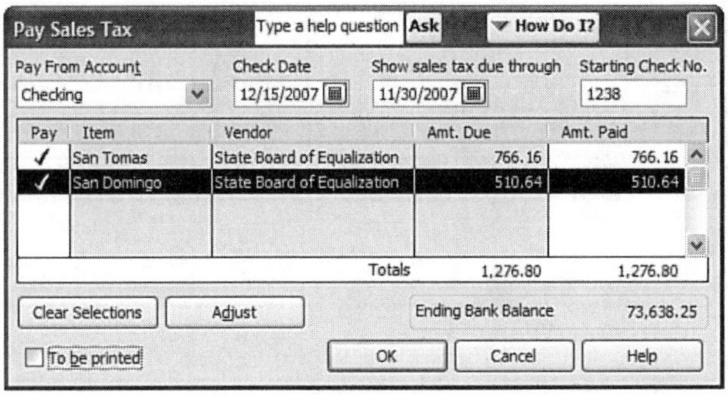

FIGURE 12.18

The Pay Sales Tax dialog.

2. From the **Pay From Account** drop-down, choose the correct bank account.

Digging Deeper

You can set a user-specific default account for this drop-down by Selecting Edit, Preferences, and then choosing the Checking preference and the My Preferences tab.

3. Select the date for the check.
4. Select the appropriate **Show sales tax due through** date. This date should default to your preference setting, as discussed earlier in this chapter. If the date is not the date you want to pay through, you can override it here.
5. If the check was manually created, put the check number in the **Starting Check No.** box. If you are going to print the check, place a check mark in the lower-left **To be printed** box. If you are not paying the amount in full, skip to the next section titled "Paying Sales Tax with an Adjustment."
6. Place a check mark in the **Pay** column on the left for the individual items you want to pay. QuickBooks creates or prints a separate check transaction for each line item with a different vendor.
7. Verify that the **Amt. Paid** column is in agreement with your Sales Tax Liability report for the same period.
8. Click **OK**; QuickBooks creates a transaction with the TAXPMT type viewable from your checkbook register, as shown in Figure 12.19.

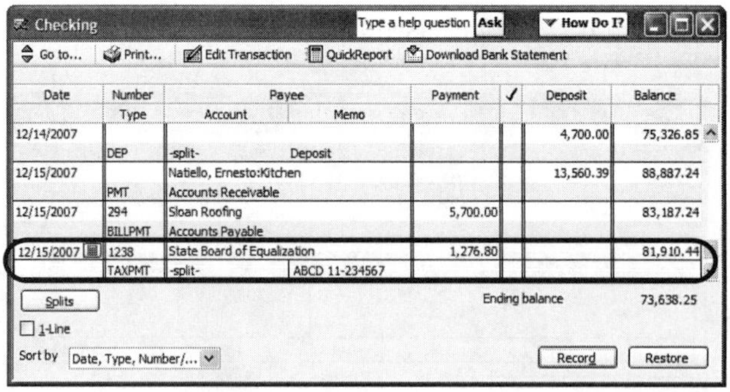

Checking
Type a help question Ask
How Do I?
Go to... Print... Edit Transaction QuickReport Download Bank Statement
Date Number Type Payee Account Memo Payment ✓ Deposit Balance
12/14/2007 DEP -split- Deposit 4,700.00 75,326.85
12/15/2007 PMT Natiello, Ernesto:Kitchen Accounts Receivable 13,560.39 88,887.24
12/15/2007 294 BILLPMT Sloan Roofing Accounts Payable 5,700.00 83,187.24
12/15/2007 1238 TAXPMT State Board of Equalization -split- ABCD 11-234567 1,276.80 81,910.44
Splits
1-Line
Sort by Date, Type, Number/...
Ending balance 73,638.25
Record Restore

FIGURE 12.19

View your checkbook register for the Sales Tax Payment type transaction.

Paying Sales Tax with an Adjustment

There are many reasons why your Sales Tax Payable doesn't agree with the amount the agency is expecting you to pay, including the following:

- Discount offered for early payment
- Penalty or fee assessed for late payment
- Credit received for overpayment on a prior period's sales tax return
- State sales tax holiday or rate reduction
- Rounding errors

If any of these apply to your business, follow these steps:

1. Perform steps 1 through 5 listed in the preceding section ("Paying Sales Tax Without an Adjustment").

2. In the **Pay Sales Tax** dialog, click **Adjust** to open the **Sales Tax Adjustment** dialog, as shown in Figure 12.20. Note: If you select the items to be paid **first**, and then select the Adjust button recording the discount or increase, QuickBooks will provide a warning (see Figure 12.21) that your previously selected check marks will be removed and you will need to select the line items again, including the new adjustment to be included with the payment.

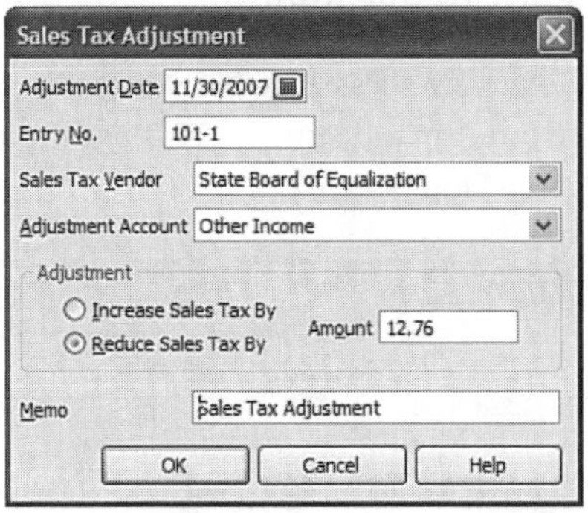

FIGURE 12.20

Use the Sales Tax Adjustment dialog to increase or decrease your sales tax payment.

3. Select the appropriate **Adjustment Date**. This date should be on or before the Show sales tax through date.

4. Enter an **Entry No.**, or QuickBooks will default a number if that preference is set.

5. Select the **Sales Tax Vendor** for which you are decreasing or increasing your payment.

6. Select from your chart of accounts the **Adjustment Account**. Ask your accountant what he prefers, but typically the account can be either of the following:

   ▪ Other Income, if you are recording a discount for early payment.

   ▪ Expense, if you are recording a penalty or fine.

7. Select the option to **Increase Sales Tax By** or **Reduce Sales Tax By** and enter the appropriate dollar amount.

8. In the **Memo** section, enter a description for your reports or accept the default description.

9. Click **OK** to record the sales tax adjustment. QuickBooks provides the warning message shown in Figure 12.21 when recording an adjustment to the sales tax.

FIGURE 12.21

QuickBooks warns when you are recording an adjustment to sales tax.

10. Click **OK** to close the warning.

   QuickBooks now shows the Pay Sales Tax dialog with an additional line showing the adjustment. This example shows a reduction in sales tax due (see Figure 12.22).

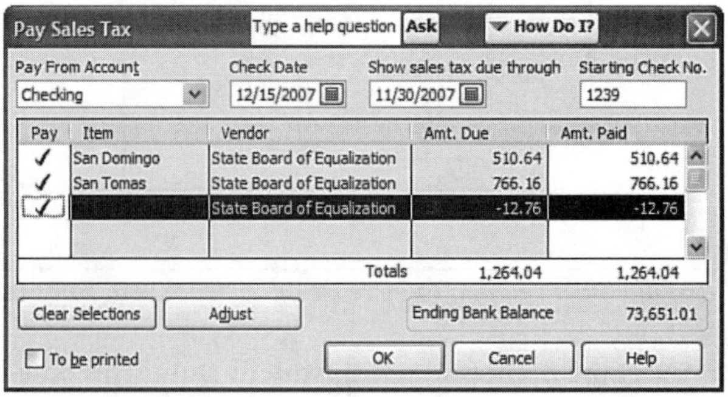

FIGURE 12.22

The Pay Sales Tax dialog includes the recorded sales tax adjustment.

QuickBooks automatically creates a General Journal Entries form when the sales tax adjustment is recorded, as shown in Figure 12.23.

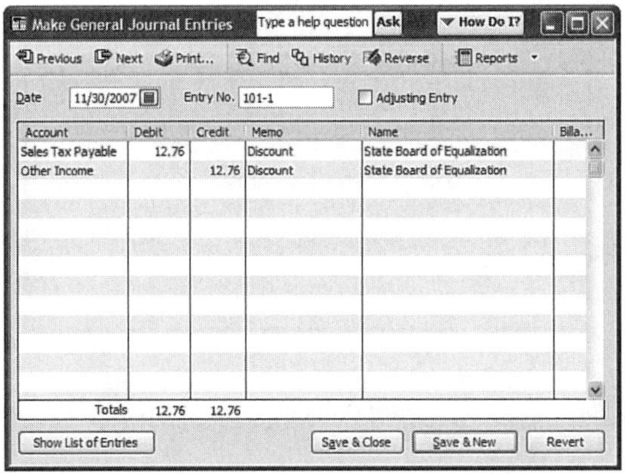

FIGURE 12.23

A General Journal Entries form is automatically created as a result of the sales tax adjustment.

Correcting Sales Tax Errors

Sales tax errors can be a bit tricky to fix, so make sure you have asked yourself the following questions:

- Have you made a backup of your data?
- Have taxes or financials been prepared using the data in its current state? If yes, then you need to be concerned about the dates and types of the corrections you make.
- If the QuickBooks sales tax due is incorrect, have you determined outside QuickBooks how much was or is due?

Print your sales tax reports before you begin to make corrections to your data file. Then, when your corrections are complete, print the same reports to be sure you achieved the desired end result. Of course, keep good paper documentation of why you did what you did in case you are subject to a sales tax audit.

When a Check or Bill Form Was Used to Pay the Sales Tax

In newer versions of QuickBooks, the error of using a check or bill form to pay sales tax should happen less often. QuickBooks provides messages to users attempting to pay their sales tax vendors incorrectly.

If you pay a vendor and assign the Sales Tax Payable account (created automatically by QuickBooks) on a check or bill form, QuickBooks provides the warnings shown in Figures 12.24 and 12.25.

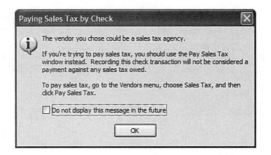

FIGURE 12.24

QuickBooks warns you when you create a check or bill to a vendor that is associated with a sales tax item.

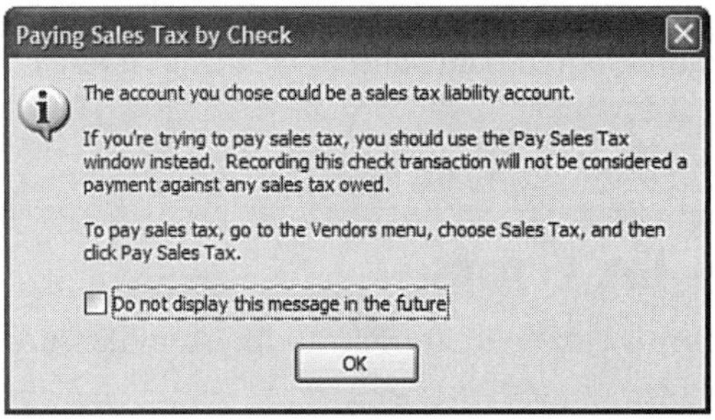

FIGURE 12.25

QuickBooks warns you when you create a check or bill form and use the Sales Tax Payable account.

If you find your payment was made by check (or bill form), first determine whether the check has been included in a bank reconciliation; if it hasn't, simply void the check and re-create the check per the instructions in the section titled "Properly Paying Sales Tax."

If the check has already been included in the bank reconciliation, use the following method to properly assign the check or bill form to the line items in the Pay Sales Tax dialog:

1. Select the check or bill form from the steps listed in the previous section titled "When a Check or Bill Form Was Used to Pay Sales Tax." Double-click the check or bill form to open the **Write Checks - Account or Enter Bills** dialog.

2. If not already assigned, assign the **Sales Tax Payable** liability account from in the **Account** column of the **Expenses** tab.

3. In the **Customer:Job** column, select the **Sales Tax Vendor** from the list of vendors (make sure it is a vendor and not an "other name" list item).

4. Click **Save & Close** to close the check (or bill) form.

5. Select **Vendors, Sales Tax**, and choose the **Pay Sales Tax** option.

6. Place a check mark next to each sales tax line item, including the line item with the correction to associate the check or bill payment form with the sales tax due (see Figure 12.26). If the net total amount is zero, you do not need to concern yourself with the other fields in the window.

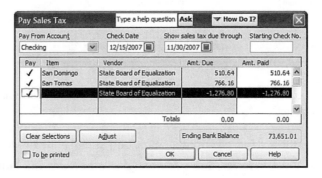

FIGURE 12.26

QuickBooks now enables you to assign the corrected check (or bill) form to the sales tax payable without issuing a new check.

The net entry is zero, so no check will be issued. However, QuickBooks will now associate your check or bill payment with the related sales tax due and when you return to the Pay Sales Tax dialog, the amount previously showing as unpaid will no longer be there. If the net entry was not zero, you might need to record a sales tax adjustment as discussed in the section titled "Properly Paying Sales Tax."

New for QuickBooks Premier Accountant 2009 as well as the QuickBooks Enterprise Solutions Accountant 9.0 is the Client Data Review feature. Available in the Client Data Review feature is a report that identifies these check forms that were used to pay sales tax liability. To learn more about these features, see Chapter 17, "New for 2009! Detecting and Correcting with the Client Data Review Feature."

When the Sales Tax Liability Report Shows Past Sales Tax Due

If your collected sales tax amount and the amount showing payable on the Sales Tax Liability report do not match, as shown in Figure 12.27, it is because there are sales taxes collected previous to the current report's Show sales tax through date that remain unpaid. Perhaps the payments were incorrectly paid using a check or bill form, in which case you should correct these errors following the instructions provided in the previous section.

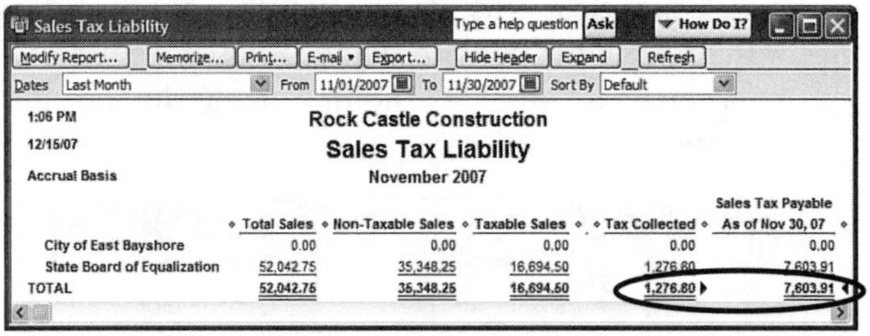

FIGURE 12.27

When the total collected and the sales tax payable do not match, prior sales taxes have not been recorded as paid.

Follow these steps to verify the totals and to make the needed corrections:

1. Click **Vendors, Sales Tax** and select the **Sales Tax Liability** report.

2. From the Dates drop-down list, select **This Month-to-Date**.

3. If the Tax Collected and Sales Tax Payable totals agree with each other for today's date, your sales tax payment made previously was probably given the wrong Show sales tax through date. To fix this error, you can void and reissue the payment or simply expect that the correction will catch up with you in the current month.

4. If the two totals do not match, verify that the tax collected for the current period is correct. You can verify this amount by reviewing the invoices you have issued for the month.

5. Verify that the tax collected for the prior period was correct.

6. Determine to what account(s) your sales tax payments were incorrectly recorded. The previously made payments would cause these accounts to be overstated.

   In the example in Figure 12.28, it was determined that a Sales Tax Expense type account was created, and the check and bill payments had been recorded to this expense account in error.

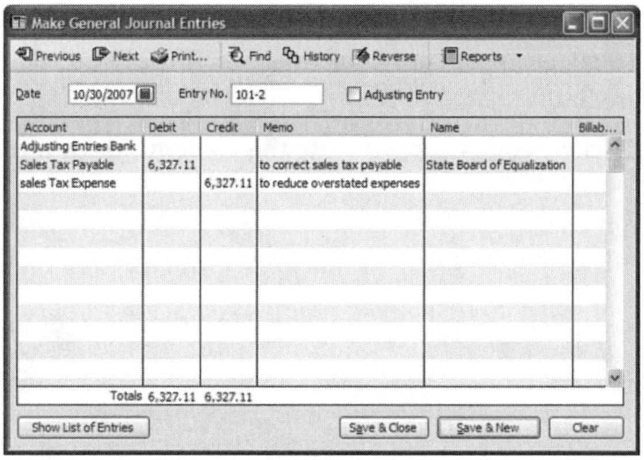

Make General Journal Entries

Account	Debit	Credit	Memo	Name	Billab...
Adjusting Entries Bank					
Sales Tax Payable	6,327.11		to correct sales tax payable	State Board of Equalization	
sales Tax Expense		6,327.11	to reduce overstated expenses		

Totals 6,327.11 6,327.11

FIGURE 12.28

You can create a General Journal entry to fix certain sales tax payable errors.

7. Select **Company, Make General Journal Entries** to create a correcting entry.

8. Date the entry in the period you are correcting.

9. Give the entry a number, or let QuickBooks automatically number it if that is a preference you have set.

10. Leave the first line of the General Journal Entries form blank.

Rescue Me!

Leave the first line of any Make General Journal Entries form blank because QuickBooks uses this line as the source line. Any list item in the Name column on the first line (source line) of a General Journal Entries form will also be associated in reports with the other lines of the same General Journal Entries form. See the sidebar titled "Caution When Using General Journal Entries" in Chapter 11.

11. On the second line in the Account column, select the Sales Tax Payable liability account.

12. Enter a debit amount if you are decreasing your sales tax payable amount; enter a credit amount if you are increasing your sales tax payable amount.

13. On the third line, select the account that was discovered to be over-stated or understated in your review (see step 6).

14. Enter the same amount from line 2 in the opposite column (debit or credit) from the previous line. Verify that your debits are equal to your credits.

15. Click **Save & Close** to close the General Journal form.

You will now be able to select this line item with other sales tax lines for future tax payments, as shown in Figure 12.29.

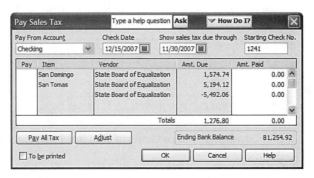

FIGURE 12.29

After you make the General Journal correcting entry, QuickBooks should show the correct amount due for the current period in the Pay Sales Tax dialog.

You might opt for this method to fix many months' errors with one journal entry and then have in place better controls for future sales tax management.

When Total Sales Does Not Equal Total Income

One of the important comparisons to make is the Sales Tax Liability total sales with the Profit & Loss Standard total income. Both of these reports are discussed in the section titled, "Reports to Review When Troubleshooting Sales Tax Errors." Before comparing the reports, make sure both are created using the same accounting basis: accrual or cash. The default basis for the sales tax report is defaulted from the Sales Tax Preference discussed earlier in this chapter. With the Report dialog open, you can click on the Modify button to change the basis being used for that report.

After you have reviewed your Profit & Loss statement and determined which transactions are causing the imbalance, you can create a General Journal Entries form to correct the records. To do this, follow these steps:

1. Verify that Total Sales on the Sales Tax Liability report does not agree with total income on the Profit & Loss Standard report. (See the section in this chapter titled, "Reports to Review When Troubleshooting Sales Tax Errors.")

2. Determine which items were used on invoices and were not mapped to an income account. (For a detailed discussion of this topic, see Chapter 3.)

3. Decide whether you will be correcting the items, as discussed in Chapter 3, and letting QuickBooks go back to fix previous transactions automatically. This method will affect prior period financials.

4. If you choose to *not* affect prior financials, select **Company**, **Make General Journal Entries**.

5. Enter a date for the transaction, typically in the current accounting period if you are not going to correct prior periods.

6. Enter a number for the transaction or let QuickBooks automatically assign the number.

7. Leave the first line of the General Journal blank, as discussed in the Rescue Me on page 339.

Unique Sales Tax Transactions

Over the years, I have come across some unique sales tax transaction tracking needs. This section addresses several that you might find useful if your state has similar guidelines.

As always, because you are acting as the "agent" for the state in collecting sales tax from your customers, you should take the time to research the sales tax guidelines for each state where you do business.

Tracking and Collecting Multiple Sales Tax Rates

The state you sell in might require you to collect and track multiple sales tax rates depending on where the customer is located. If you have a customer with different tax rate locations, you need to create a customer for each tax location if you want QuickBooks to automatically collect the correct tax amount because QuickBooks tracks the sales tax rate to the customer and not to the job.

See the section, "Sales Tax Items, Groups, and Codes" in this chapter for a complete discussion of how to handle this unique transaction type.

When Your State Imposes a Maximum Sales Tax

I have encountered having to track a state-imposed maximum sales tax a few times. If your state imposes a maximum sales tax for a certain type of sale, I recommend the following method:

1. Click **Lists, Item List**. From the **Item** drop-down menu, select **New** to create a new list item. The **New Item** dialog displays.

2. If you do not have a subtotal item on your list, choose **Subtotal** from the **Type** drop-down list.

3. To create the new sales tax item, follow steps 1 and 2 and select **Sales Tax Item** from the **Type** drop-down list.

4. For the **Sales Tax Name**, use **See Above**. This name is what is viewable by the QuickBooks user when selecting this sales tax item (see Figure 12.30).

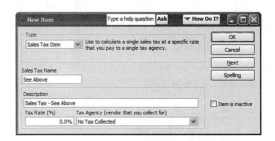

FIGURE 12.30

Create a sales tax item to be used on an invoice that has multiple sales tax rates charged.

5. For the description, I simply add at the end of the default description **See Above**. This is the description that prints on the customer's invoice.

6. Leave the **Tax Rate** at the default of **0.0%**.

7. For the **Tax Agency**, I create a vendor named **No Tax Collected** and do not assign it an address or any details. Because no tax will be collected with this item (because it has a rate of 0%), a check will never be prepared. Click **OK**.

8. To create the invoice to your customer, click **Customers, Create Invoices** and complete the invoice as detailed in steps 9 and 10.

9. Enter a subtotal line after the appropriate amount that is to have sales tax collected on it. In Figure 12.31, the example is of a customer that has sales tax collected only on the first $5,000.00 of sales on the same invoice. Sales in excess of $5,000.00 in this example are not taxable.

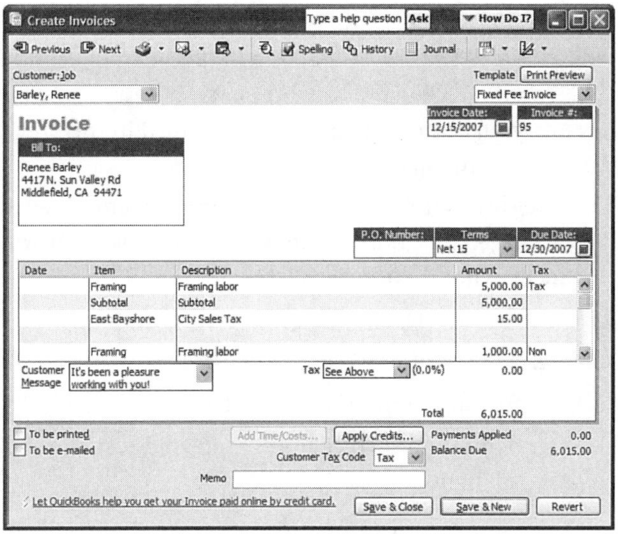

FIGURE 12.31

Example of a customer invoice that only has the first $5,000.00 of charges marked as taxable.

10. Enter the remaining items on the invoice, making sure to select the Non-taxable sales code for the lines not taxable or select the non-taxable items.

QuickBooks will now properly record the total sales of $6,000.00, but it shows only $5,000 in the Taxable Sales column of the Sales Tax Liability report, as shown in Figure 12.32.

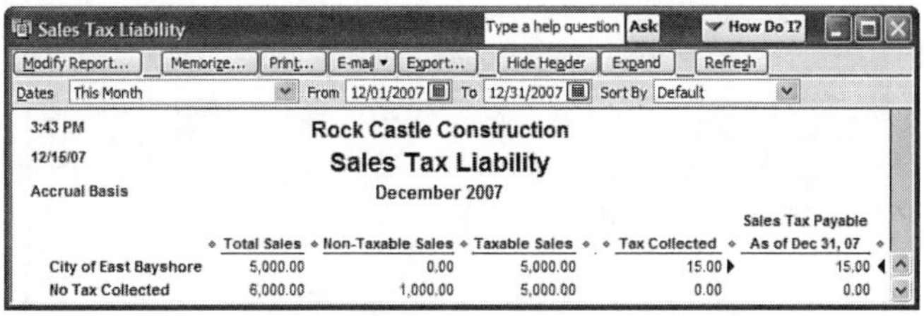

FIGURE 12.32

QuickBooks properly records the taxable revenue amount from the non-taxable sale amount.

Multiple Sales Tax Rates on One Invoice

In particular, if your business sells retail items, liquor, and food all on one sales form, chances are that each item type is subject to a unique sales tax rate. Follow the same steps listed in the preceding section for creating the subtotal item and 0% sales tax item. Assign this 0% "See Above" sales tax item to your customer.

Next, create your customer's invoice as detailed in the previous section, following these additional steps:

1. Make sure you have created a sales tax item for each sales tax rate to be charged and name them so that the customer will be able to tell exactly what the rate was for.

2. Enter the line item(s) subject to one tax rate.

3. Enter a subtotal line.

4. Enter the appropriate sales tax item.

5. Enter additional invoice lines, each with a subtotal and appropriate sales tax items.

QuickBooks will accurately collect and report on the correct amount of sales tax charged for the different item types being sold.

To further clarify this point, the example shown in Figure 12.33 does not track sales by customer, but just a retail summary for the day's sales. The example also shows how to charge multiple sales tax rates on a single invoice by placing a subtotal after each group of sales and then placing the correct sales tax rate after the subtotal.

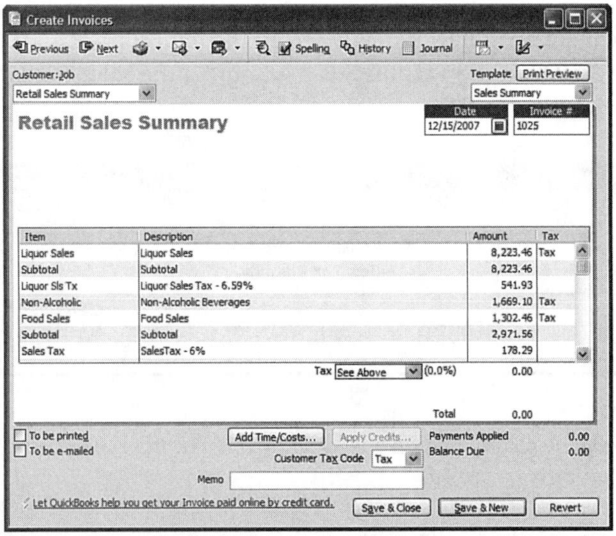

FIGURE 12.33

Creating an invoice with multiple sales tax rates charged.

If you would like more information on this, you can press the F1 key on your keyboard to open QuickBooks Help. Click on the Search tab and on the top search bar, type "sales summaries" and follow the link for more information on this topic.

Issuing Credit Memos When Sales Tax Should Not Have Been Charged

Although issuing customer credit memos is necessary for correct reporting when you file your sales tax on accrual basis (sales tax payment liability accrued as of the date of the customer invoice) and not required when you report sales tax liability on cash basis (sales tax payment liability not accrued until the date of customer's payment), I still recommend having controls in place that limit the ability to modify an invoice from a prior month.

After you have filed your sales tax return with your state, you should not adjust any invoices or sales tax payments recorded on or before your file-through date. If you do, QuickBooks recalculates the taxable sales, non-taxable sales, and amount owed, and your return as filed with the state will no longer agree with your QuickBooks data.

 Digging Deeper

> In Chapter 15, "Sharing Data with Your Accountant or Your Client," I discuss setting a closing date for your data. I recommend that this same control be placed in your file after preparing your monthly or quarterly sales tax returns for your state.

Instead of adjusting a customer's invoice, consider using the QuickBooks customer Credit Memos/Refund form. For example, suppose you charged sales tax to a non-taxable customer by mistake. Let's also assume that you have filed your accrual basis sales tax return for the month of that invoice, effectively overstating taxable sales.

Creating a credit memo reduces taxable sales, increases non-taxable sales, and credits the customer's invoice for the sales tax amount, all within the current sales tax month.

1. Click **Customers**, **Create Credit Memos/Refunds**.

2. From the **Customer:Job** drop-down menu, select the appropriate Customer or Customer:Job for which you need to issue the credit memo. Choose a date, often in the current sales tax month. For the detail beginning with line 1 of the credit memo, enter the line or lines of sales items exactly as they were recorded on the original invoice with positive amounts (see Figure 12.34).

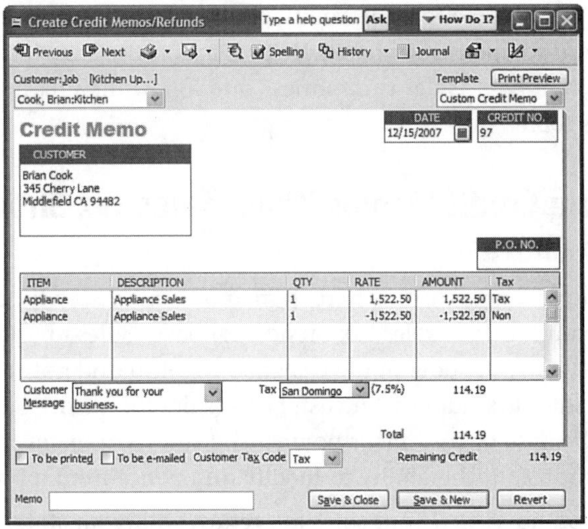

FIGURE 12.34

Issuing a credit memo to a customer who was charged an incorrect sales tax amount.

3. On the remaining lines, enter the same items, each with a negative rate, making sure that Non-taxable is the sales tax code assigned to these lines. The net effect of the credit memo will be to show a credit equal to the sales tax amount charged on the customer's original invoice.

4. Click **Save & Close**. QuickBooks opens the **Available Credit** dialog where you can choose how to handle the resulting credit (see Figure 12.35).

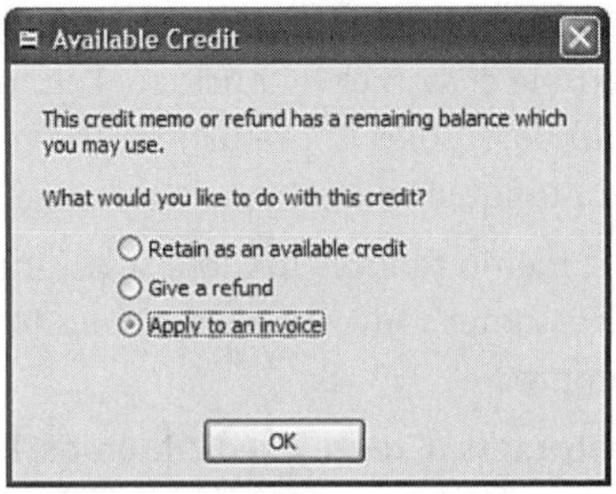

FIGURE 12.35

When saving the credit memo, QuickBooks asks what you want to do with the resulting credit.

Chapter **13**

Reviewing and Correcting the Opening Balance Equity Account

- Purpose of the Opening Bal Equity Account

- Transactions in the Opening Bal Equity Account

- Reports to Review and Troubleshoot the Opening Bal Equity Account

- Closing Opening Bal Equity into Retained Earnings

- Setting a Closing Date and Password

Purpose of the Opening Bal Equity Account

QuickBooks automatically creates the Opening Bal Equity account when you create a new data file. The Opening Bal Equity account serves the following purposes for a new data file:

- To keep your books in balance during the opening entries.

- To provide a common register so you can easily view your opening entries before "closing" to the Retained Earnings account.

- For QuickBooks versions 2005 or older, this account was used for bank reconciliation adjustments. (Note: Newer versions of QuickBooks use a new expense type account created by QuickBooks called Reconciliation Discrepancies to record any adjustments created in the bank reconciliation process.)

This chapter discusses all these purposes in detail.

Whether or not you choose to create the file using the QuickBooks EasyStep Interview (see Chapter 1, "Creating a New QuickBooks Data File," for more details), QuickBooks creates this chart of account list item in the Equity section of your Balance Sheet report.

If you are creating a QuickBooks file for an existing business (one that has had transactions prior to your QuickBooks start date, see the section titled "Select a Start Date" in Chapter 1), you will most likely use this Opening Bal Equity account when recording your beginning balances.

If you are creating a QuickBooks file for a new business without any historical transactions, you should not use this account for any of your opening balances. Instead, you will create your accounting transactions using the proper QuickBooks forms as presented throughout this book.

You know that a QuickBooks file is properly set up when the Opening Bal Equity account balance on the Balance Sheet report is zero after you have entered all your opening balances and properly closed any remaining balance to the Retained Earnings equity account.

Transactions in the Opening Bal Equity Account

QuickBooks automatically records the following transactions to the Opening Bal Equity account:

- Your ending bank statement balance transaction when you created a new bank account in the EasyStep Interview

- Opening balances for other Balance Sheet report accounts created in the Add New Account dialog

- Inventory total value balances entered in the New Item dialog
- Bank reconciliation adjustments for QuickBooks versions 2005 or earlier

Other common transactions that a user might assign to this account include

- Accrual basis opening accounts payable transactions as of the start date
- Accrual basis opening accounts receivable transactions as of the start date
- Uncleared bank checks or deposits (accrual or cash basis) as of the start date

Cash Basis Reporting and the Opening Bal Equity Account

If your business wants to review your QuickBooks financials on a cash basis (see the section titled "Choosing a Reporting Basis" in Chapter 4, "Easily Review Your QuickBooks Data"), you do not want to use items that are mapped to the Opening Bal Equity account for your opening entries. This is because QuickBooks will report cash basis revenue as of the date of the customer payment and cash basis expense as of the date of the bill payment or check using the income or expense account assigned to the item.

For example, suppose your QuickBooks start date is 01/01/2009. As of 12/31/08, you have an unpaid customer invoice for $1,000.00. For cash basis reporting, you should create the open invoice using the same product or service items that were originally sold.

When you receive the customer's payment sometime in year 2009, QuickBooks will record the revenue to the account associated with the item on the invoice as of the customer's payment transaction date.

If you have not used QuickBooks before, you will want to review Chapter 3, "Reviewing and Correcting Item List Errors," for more detailed information on the proper use of items on a customer invoice or expense form.

If you had used an item that was assigned to the Opening Bal Equity account, QuickBooks would not have any revenue account to record the income to when the customer made the payment.

Properly entering your startup invoices and bills enables you to prepare financials in either cash or accrual basis.

Bank Statement Ending Balance Entered in the EasyStep Interview

One of the automatically generated transactions by QuickBooks that is recorded to the Opening Bal Equity account is the ending balance information you entered during the EasyStep Interview, discussed at length in Chapter 1 (see Figure 13.1).

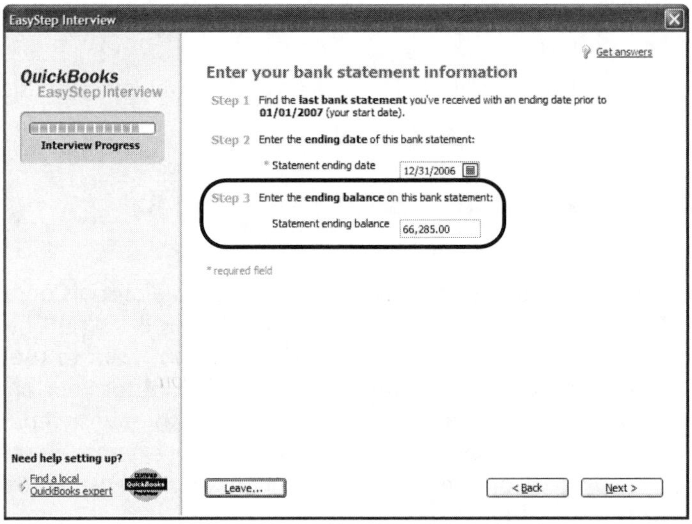

FIGURE 13.1

The bank statement ending balance recorded in the EasyStep Interview offsets the Opening Balance Equity account.

When you enter your ending statement balance, QuickBooks increases (in this example) your bank statement balance. In accounting terms, the increase is a debit to your Cash account. To complete the transaction, QuickBooks needs an "offsetting" account to put the credit side of the transaction to, and rather than require the user to select an account, QuickBooks defaults the other side of the transaction to the Opening Bal Equity account, as shown in Figure 13.2.

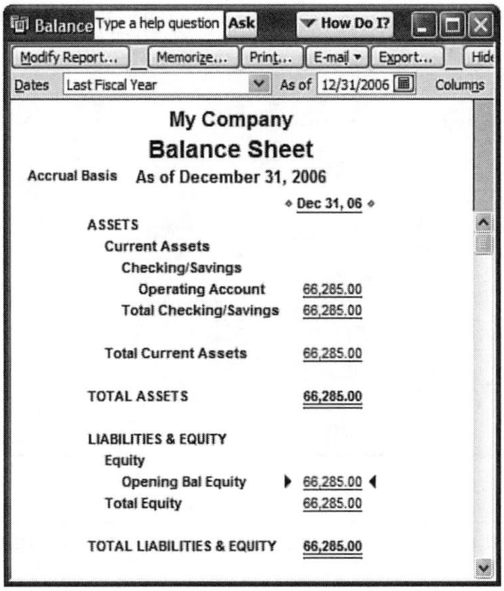

FIGURE 13.2

QuickBooks increases Cash and Opening Bal Equity when you enter a bank statement ending balance in the EasyStep Interview.

One of the more useful features of QuickBooks is that you do not need to know debit and credit accounting; that is, that every transaction must have an equal amount in debits and credits. However, because the concept of debits and credits is a standard accounting principle, QuickBooks does the work behind the scenes.

Opening Balance in the Add New Account Dialog

Another transaction QuickBooks automatically enters into the Opening Bal Equity account happens when you enter an opening balance via the Add New Account dialog, as shown in Figure 13.3.

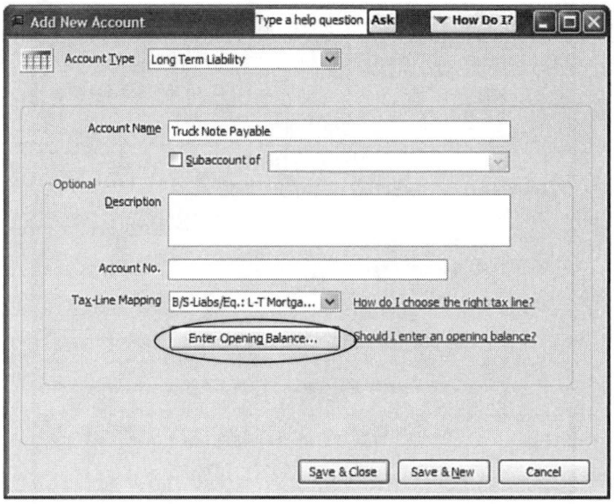

FIGURE 13.3

The Add New Account dialog permits you to add an opening account balance.

Digging Deeper

> If you have an existing business with prior accounting balances, you should consult your accounting professional before entering opening balances in QuickBooks. Your accounting professional can help guide you through this process.

If you are just starting with QuickBooks but you have transactions and account balances from before your QuickBooks start date, you can enter these beginning balances directly into the Add New Account dialog. You will not, however, be able to add the beginning balances with this method later when you edit the account.

To add a new account, follow these steps:

1. Click **Lists**, **Chart of Accounts** to open the chart of accounts dialog. Click the **Account** drop-down menu and select **New**.

2. The Add New Account: Choose Account Type dialog displays. Select the correct **Account Type** and click **Continue**. Note that only Balance Sheet account types will allow you to enter an opening balance into the Add New Account dialog. Income, Expense, Cost of Goods Sold,

Other Income, and Other Expense types do not offer you the option to enter an opening balance due to those accounts not having forward balances.

3. The Add New Account dialog opens with the selected account type at the top, as shown in Figure 13.3. Enter the **Account Name**.

4. Optionally, place a check mark in the **Subaccount of** check box and enter the appropriate account.

5. Enter an optional **Description** and **Account No.**, and choose a **Tax-Line Mapping**.

6. Click the **Enter Opening Balance** button to open the Enter Opening Balance dialog, as shown in Figure 13.4.

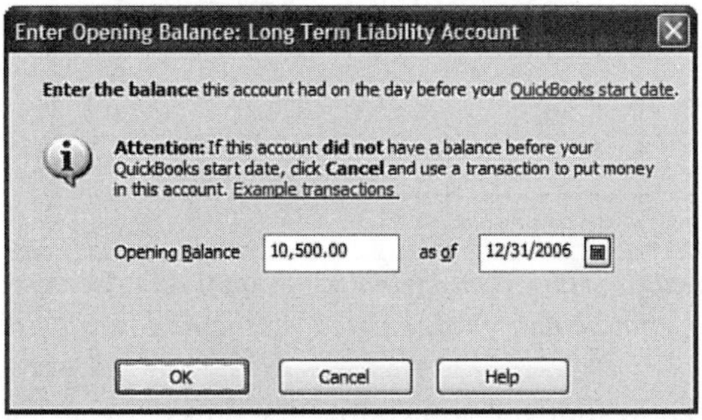

FIGURE 13.4

Click the Enter Opening Balance button in the Add New Account dialog to open the dialog for entering the opening balance.

7. Enter the **Opening Balance** amount and the **as of** date. This date should be one day before your start date. If you are entering a transaction dated after the start date, you should use one of the many common QuickBooks forms to record these "after start date" transactions. Refer to the chapter index in this book for specific chapters discussing the proper workflow and forms to use.

8. Click **OK**; the Add New Account dialog redisplays.

9. Click **Save & Close**.

The example shown in Figure 13.4 results in an increase (credit) to the Long Term Liabilities account and a decrease (debit) to the Opening Bal Equity account. See Figure 13.5.

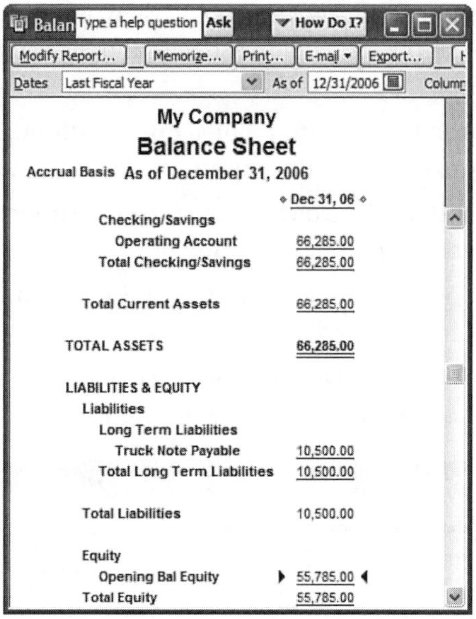

FIGURE 13.5

QuickBooks increased the Long Term Liabilities account and decreased the Opening Bal Equity account when an opening balance was entered via the Add New account dialog.

Did you know that you can control the dates in your file by setting the following date warning preference?

1. Click **Edit**, **Preferences** to open the Preferences dialog.

2. Select the **Accounting** preference.

3. Click the **Company Preferences** tab (you must be logged in as the Admin or External Accountant user and in single-user mode).

4. Specify the number of days in the past and into the future you want to be warned if the transaction exceeds this range of dates.

This preference helps prevent errors in the dates assigned to transactions, including these open balance transactions.

Entering a Total Value for a New Inventory Item

QuickBooks automatically creates an inventory adjustment transaction that records to the Opening Bal Equity account if you add a Total Value to your New Item dialog for inventory item types.

Figure 13.6 shows a new inventory item being created and a Total Value of $600.00 for the new item. In this example, QuickBooks increases (debit) your Inventory Asset account and increases (credit) your Opening Bal Equity account.

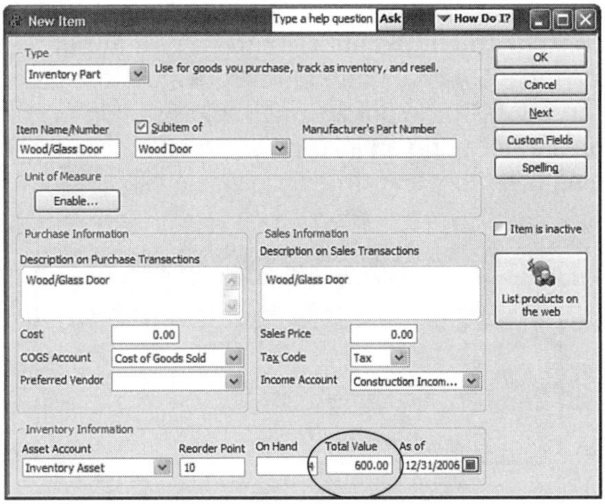

FIGURE 13.6

Entering a Total Value for a new inventory item increases the inventory asset account and increases the Opening Bal Equity account.

These transaction types are named INV ADJ, and the memo line of the transaction includes the inventory part name with the term Opening Balance so that these entries are easy to locate on a report or in the Opening Bal Equity register.

Entering Beginning Inventory Balances

Because you will often create your inventory items days or weeks before you begin actually using your QuickBooks data file, rather than entering an opening balance for the inventory item when you create the inventory list item you should instead create an inventory adjustment to record the beginning balance quantities when your set up work is complete. Then, create an inventory adjustment to record the on-hand quantity and value adjustment following these steps:

1. Click **Vendors, Inventory Activities** and select the **Adjust Quantity/Value on Hand** menu.

2. On the Adjust Quantity/Value on Hand dialog that opens, enter an **Adjustment Date**; if this entry is to put the original inventory quantity count into QuickBooks, the date selected should be one day before your QuickBooks start date.

3. Enter a **Ref. No.**

Continues...

4. Enter an **Adjustment Account**; if this entry is to put the original inventory quantity count into QuickBooks, use the Opening Bal Equity account. QuickBooks warns you, as shown in Figure 13.7, that you are not using an income or expense account. For this beginning inventory adjustment only, you can ignore this warning.

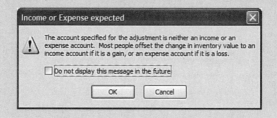

FIGURE 13.7

The warning provided when you enter an inventory adjustment to a non-income or expense account.

You can learn more about inventory adjustments in Chapter 10, "Reviewing and Correcting Inventory Errors." Look for the section titled, "Creating an Inventory Quantity Adjustment."

Bank Reconciliation Adjustments (QuickBooks 2005 or Older)

If your data file was created with QuickBooks version 2005 or older, and if you let QuickBooks automatically make adjustments to reconcile your bank account, then you might find these adjustments in your Opening Bal Equity account, the default account set by QuickBooks. If you updated your 2005 or older QuickBooks file to a more recent year, reconciliation adjustments will appear in an expense account QuickBooks creates called Reconciliation Adjustments.

QuickBooks provides a message similar to the one shown in Figure 13.8 when reconciling with an adjustment.

If you click Enter Adjustment in the Warning dialog shown in Figure 13.8, QuickBooks makes the requested adjustment to the bank account (either an increase or decrease to your bank balance) and the offsetting entry to the Opening Bal Equity account.

QuickBooks then creates a General Journal Entries transaction; the memo will say "Balance Adjustment," making the adjustment easy to identify in the Opening Bal Equity register.

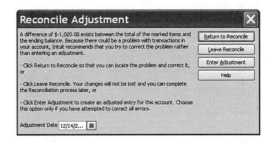

FIGURE 13.8

When reconciling with an adjustment in QuickBooks version 2005 or older, QuickBooks provides this warning.

 Digging Deeper

Beginning with QuickBooks 2006, all bank account reconciliation adjustments are no longer recorded to the Opening Bal Equity account. Instead, QuickBooks automatically creates an expense account called Reconciliation Discrepancies. This account is an Expense type as compared to Opening Bal Equity, which is an Equity type account.

Because most companies review the Profit & Loss report more frequently than the Balance Sheet report for the business, it is more likely now that users will see the bank reconciliation adjustments.

If you see a balance in the Profit & Loss report called Reconciliation Discrepancy, make sure you take the time to research the problem and reclassify the balance to another more appropriate account.

Accrual Basis Startup Records

Another type of transaction that might be recorded to the Opening Bal Equity account is one used strictly for accrual basis startup balances.

One method to enter individual customer invoices or vendor bills is to create an item that has the Opening Bal Equity account assigned to it, as shown in Figure 13.9.

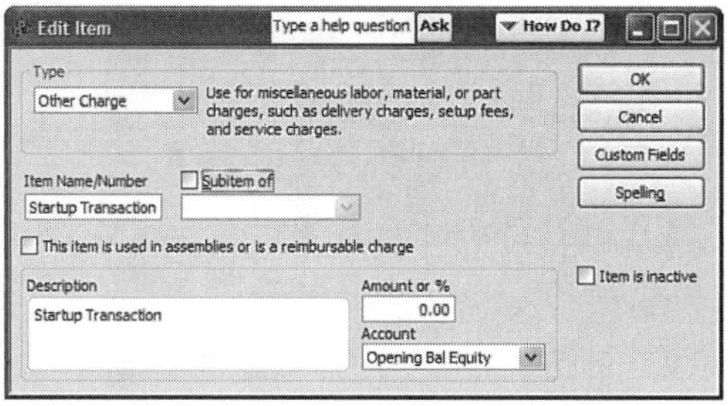

FIGURE 13.9

Using the Opening Bal Equity account for entering accrual basis startup records.

If your business reviews its financials only in accrual basis, this method is perfectly fine. It will, of course, cause transactions to also post to the Opening Bal Equity account.

Although this method for entering accrual basis startup transactions is easy and efficient, it can cause problems if it is used on transactions after the start date. So a good process would be to edit the item and make it inactive after all the startup transactions have been entered.

You can find a review of creating startup transactions in Chapter 1, in the section titled, "Setting Up a QuickBooks Data File for Accrual or Cash Basis Reporting." The method discussed in that chapter provides details on how to set up your transactions for accrual or cash basis financial reporting.

Reports to Review and Troubleshoot the Opening Bal Equity Account

Before you begin reviewing your data for transactions in the Opening Bal Equity account, verify that you do have a balance in this account.

To create a Balance Sheet Standard report, follow these steps:

1. Click **Reports**, **Company & Financial** and select the **Balance Sheet Standard** report.

2. Without adjusting the date, view the Equity section of the report to see whether a balance exists in the account, as shown in Figure 13.10.

Technically, the Opening Bal Equity account value should be equal to your prior year's Retained Earnings. So, if you have a balance in your Opening Bal Equity account, and if the balance is equal to your prior year's Retained Earnings amount, you might simply be able to "close" Opening Bal Equity into Retained Earnings—a topic that is discussed in the next section.

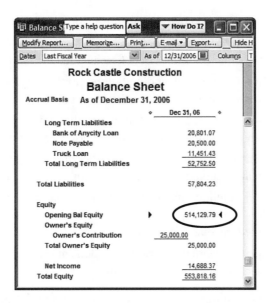

FIGURE 13.10

The Balance Sheet Standard report shows a balance in the Opening Bal Equity account.

If, however, a balance displays on the Balance Sheet report, and you have completed your opening balances—including closing Opening Bal Equity into Retained Earnings—you can review the individual transactions by creating the following report:

1. Click **Reports, Custom Transaction Detail Report**. The Modify Report dialog displays with the Display tab selected.

2. Select the **Report Date Range** you want to view. I recommend that you choose **All** from the Dates drop-down menu.

3. In the **Columns** section of the **Display** tab, click to place a check mark next to those data fields you want to see on the report, or click to remove the check mark from those you don't want to see on the report. Be sure to include **Type** near the top of the list.

4. Optionally, from the **Sort By** drop-down list, select **Type**. This option groups the report by type of transaction, which makes reviewing the source of the transactions easier.

5. Click the **Filters** tab.

6. In the Choose Filter pane, select **Account**; from the Account drop-down menu select the **Opening Bal Equity** account.

7. Click **OK** to create the report.

With the report sorted by type of transaction, you can begin to determine whether errors in entries were made.

Some of the more common errors I see include the following:

- Users enter a bank ending balance in the EasyStep Interview and also created a deposit form for the same value.

- Users enter an opening balance in the Add New Account dialog and then later enter the opening balance on another transaction.

- Users in QuickBooks 2005 or earlier allowed QuickBooks to make a reconciliation adjustment to agree with the bank statement.

- Users entering inventory for the first time enter a Total Value in the New Item dialog and then later enter an inventory adjustment to record the opening balance.

- Users inadvertently post transactions directly or indirectly (using items) after the QuickBooks start date.

One of the most important things to know about the Opening Bal Equity account is that when a file is completely and successfully set up, no balance should remain in the Opening Bal Equity account.

Closing Opening Bal Equity into Retained Earnings

I have mentioned a few times in this chapter that the Opening Bal Equity account should have a zero balance when a file is set up correctly.

When I refer to a correctly set up QuickBooks file, I assume the following:

- You *are not* converting your data from Quicken, Peachtree, Microsoft Small Business Accounting, or Office Accounting. Each of these products has an automated conversion tool available free from Intuit that eliminates the need to do startup transactions if you convert the data and not just lists.

- Your company had transactions prior to the QuickBooks start date. If it did not, you simply enter typical QuickBooks transactions using common forms with no need for unusual startup entries. If you did have prior transactions to the QuickBooks start date, you are *not* going to recreate these prior transactions in your QuickBooks data file.

- You have entered each of your unpaid customer invoices, unpaid vendor bills, and uncleared bank transactions and dated them prior to your QuickBooks start date.

- You have entered and dated your trial balance one day before your QuickBooks start date. (You might need to request the trial balance numbers from your accountant if you are not converting from some other financial software that provides you with a trial balance.)

- When you create a Trial Balance report in QuickBooks dated one day before your QuickBooks start date, it agrees with your accountant's trial balance or with the trial balance from your prior financial software with the exception that you have a balance in the Opening Bal Equity account.

If you answered yes to each of these assumptions, I would expect that your Opening Bal Equity account is equal to the Retained Earnings balance from your accountant's financials or from your prior software. If it doesn't agree, you need to continue to review the data to determine what the errors are. If it does agree, you are prepared to make the final entry in your start up process.

To create this closing entry, use a General Journal Entries form:

1. Click **Company, Make General Journal Entries** to open the Make General Journal Entries dialog.

2. Enter a **Date** (it should be one day before your QuickBooks start date).

3. Type an **Entry No.**

Rescue Me!

Leave the first line of any Make General Journal Entries form blank because QuickBooks uses this line as the source line. Any list item in the name column on the first line (source line) of a general journal entries form will also be associated in reports with the other lines of the same general journal entries form.

4. Leaving line 1 of the form blank, on line 2 of the Make General Journal Entries form (using the example as shown in Figure 13.11), decrease (debit) Opening Bal Equity by $514,129.79 and increase (credit) Retained Earnings by the same amount. This action "closes" Opening Bal Equity to Retained Earnings. Click **Save & Close**.

5. Click **OK** to the QuickBooks warning dialog that displays; QuickBooks saves the transaction. The warning advises that you are posting to a Retained Earnings account and that QuickBooks has a special purpose for this account. It is appropriate to post this entry to Retained Earnings. This warning is a result of a preference setting that you can access by clicking **Edit, Preferences** and selecting **Accounting** from the list on the left. Click the **Company Preferences** tab and choose the option to enable the warning. (You must be logged in as Admin or External Accountant user and in single-user mode to access this preference.)

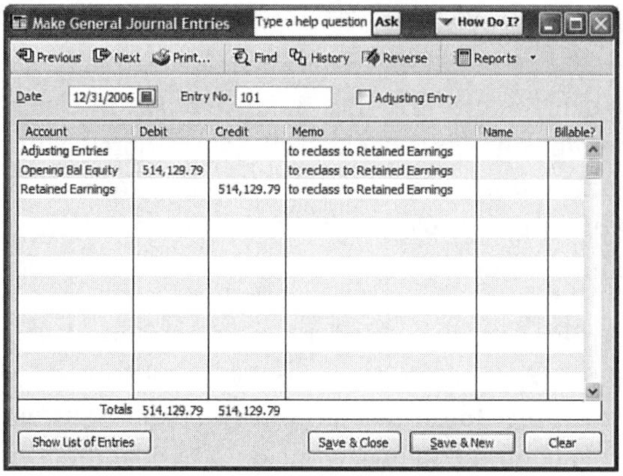

FIGURE 13.11

Use a Make General Journal Entries form to close Opening Bal Equity to Retained Earnings.

When the transaction is saved, create the Balance Sheet Standard report as explained earlier in this chapter and verify that your ending numbers are accurate; that is, that they match your accountant's or your prior software trial balance for the same period. Figure 13.12 now shows the proper Retained Earnings balance, and you no longer have a balance in Opening Bal Equity.

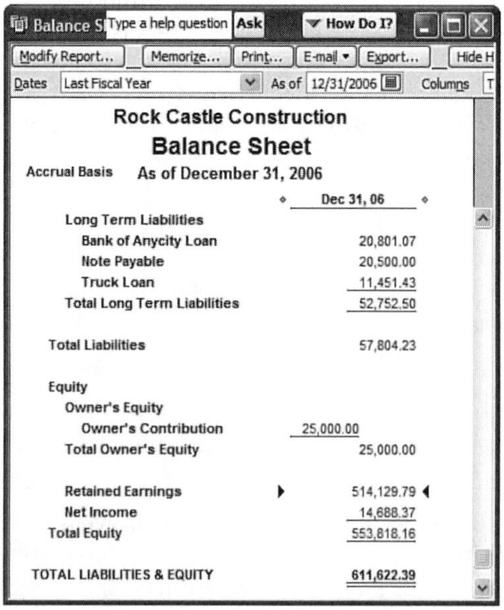

FIGURE 13.12

The Balance Sheet for the prior year after "closing" Opening Bal Equity to Retained Earnings.

Setting a Closing Date and Password

Congratulations—after all this work, you now have a properly set up a data file that matches the balances from your accountant or prior financial software. The next and final step is to protect your work from users making changes to the transactions by setting a closing date password. Although modifying and adding transactions to prior dates can provide great flexibility in getting the file ready for tax time, this flexibility can be disastrous, potentially wasting all the effort that has been put into ensuring the numbers are correct.

To set a closing date password, you must first be logged in as the Admin User (default user for a new QuickBooks data file) or new External Accountant user and in single-user mode then, follow these steps:

1. Click **Company**, **Set Closing Date** and the Accounting, Company Preferences dialog opens.

2. Click the **Set Date/Password** button to open the Set Closing Date and Password dialog.

3. In the Date pane, enter a closing date. Usually for a new data file, it is the day before your QuickBooks start date, or ask your accountant for the date that should be selected. Enter an optional **Closing Date Password** confirming the password.

4. Click **OK** to save the closing date and password. The User List dialog opens again. Click **OK** to close the Preferences dialog.

   Now that you have set a closing date and optional password, you need to make sure that users are given permissions to change or not change closed transactions. (Transactions dated on or before the closing date.)

5. Log into the file as the Admin user and click **Company**, **Set Up Users and Passwords** and select the **Set Up Users** menu option.

6. If your file has an Admin User password, a dialog opens where you will need to type the Admin password before continuing. Click **OK** to close the QuickBooks Login dialog and open the User List dialog.

7. To view the details of users' security, select a user from the list and click the **View User** button. The View user access dialog opens, as shown in Figure 13.13.

If you need to edit the setting for a user, see step 5 in the preceding list.

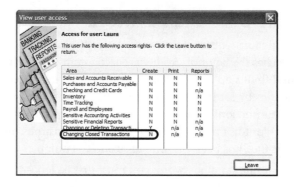

FIGURE 13.13

View user access rights to see whether a user is or is not allowed to change closed period transactions.

Here is how the closing date feature works depending on the Y or N in the Create column of the Changing Closed Transactions setting:

- **"N"**—The user will not be able to add or modify transactions dated on or before the closing date.

- **"Y"**—If only a closing date is set, the user will be warned when adding or modifying transactions dated on or before the closing date.

- **"Y"**—If both a closing date and closing date password were set, the user will be warned and required to enter the closing date password.

These are great controls to have in place, but remember that if a user has access to the Admin password, he can reset the closing date and closing date password.

Additionally, in Chapter 5, "Power Reports for Troubleshooting Beginning Balance Differences," you can learn more about reports that show when a closing date was changed and when transactions were posted to closed periods.

Chapter 14

Reviewing and Correcting Payroll Errors

- Payroll Service Options
- Payroll and Employees Preference
- Payroll Forms and Workflow in QuickBooks
- Using the Payroll Setup
- Using the Run Payroll Checkup Diagnostic Tool
- Reports to Review When Troubleshooting Payroll
- Adjusting Payroll Liabilities
- Unique Payroll Transactions and Processes

Properly setting up your payroll is one of the most important tasks you have when creating a new QuickBooks data file or reviewing an existing data file. This chapter shows you how to set up your payroll properly, efficiently review your data, and handle some of those unique payroll transactions.

If your company defines an employee as "a person in the service of another under any contract of hire, express or implied, oral or written, where the employer has the power or right to control and direct the employee in the material details of how the work is to be performed," your company is responsible for paying wages, collecting certain federal and state payroll taxes, and filing quarterly and annual forms.

Your company becomes an agent of the state and federal government because it must collect certain payroll-related taxes on predetermined payment schedules. The first step is to select a payroll service option. Intuit offers several choices, and one will fit your company's needs.

Payroll Service Options

To have QuickBooks automatically calculate your payroll, you need to purchase a payroll subscription from Intuit in addition to your QuickBooks software.

The QuickBooks Financial Software partnered with an Intuit-provided payroll service makes setting up payroll, collecting taxes, remitting timely payments of the collected taxes, and filing the required payroll reports easy.

When you create a new data file, or if you have not previously purchased a payroll subscription, you can click the New Payroll Options icon on the QuickBooks Home page to see your options or you can visit www.payroll.com.

As of the writing of this book, Intuit has the following payroll service options, one of which is sure to meet the needs of your company (see Table 14.1).

Table 14.1 Intuit 2009 Payroll Services and Feature Comparison

Key Payroll Features	Basic	Enhanced	Enhanced Payroll For Accountants	Assisted
Prepare your own payroll checks; optionally offer employees direct deposit	✓	✓	✓	✓
Keep your QuickBooks payroll taxes current with downloadable tax updates from the Internet	✓	✓	✓	✓
Let QuickBooks automatically calculate all taxes for your payroll records	✓	✓	✓	✓
Prepare and print completed federal and state payroll forms		✓	✓	✓
Conveniently use IRS e-file for payroll payments and reporting		✓	✓	
Have Intuit pay your payroll taxes and file your quarterly and annual returns, penalty-free guarantee				✓
Track worker's comp expenses		✓	✓	✓
Payroll technical callback support: assisted, live phone support	✓	✓	✓	✓
Process payroll for multiple client data files			✓	

Digging Deeper

Each of these payroll options requires a paid subscription. Visit the www.payroll.com website for current pricing.

Two other payroll services are offered: Intuit Online Payroll, which does not require QuickBooks financial software (but optionally can be downloaded into QuickBooks), and Intuit Payroll for QuickBooks Online, which works specifically with the QuickBooks Online Edition. Both of these payroll services are not discussed in this book.

You can select the Basic option if you are going to partner your payroll reporting with your accountant, or choose other options, such as Assisted if you want Intuit to make your payroll payments and file your forms.

Payroll and Employees Preference

After you sign up for one of the Intuit payroll subscription offerings, you need to enable payroll and set some payroll-specific and employee-specific preferences as follows:

1. Log in as the Admin or External Accountant user for your data file and in single-user mode.

2. Click **Edit**, **Preferences** and select the **Payroll & Employees** preference from the left side.

3. Click on the **Company Preferences** tab, as shown in Figure 14.1.

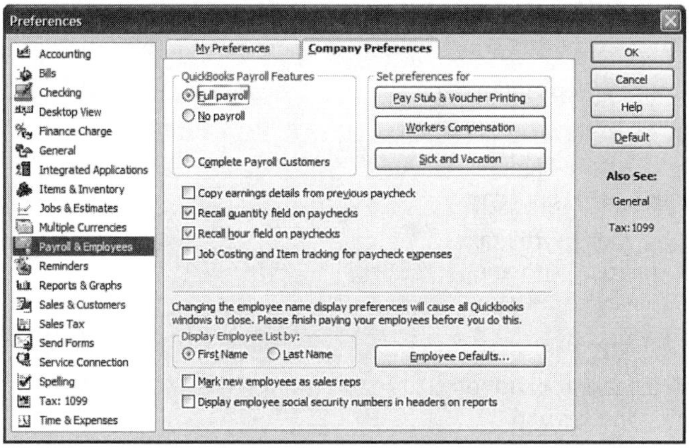

FIGURE 14.1

Payroll & Employee Company Preferences tab.

4. Click the **Full payroll** button in the QuickBooks Payroll Features pane. This button enables the remaining features in the Preferences dialog.

5. Click the check box next to the features that are appropriate to your business:

   ■ Copy earnings details from previous check (copies hours, rates, and Customer:Jobs from prior paycheck).

   ■ Recall quantity field on paychecks (recalls line 1 of a previous paycheck, payroll item, and rate only; no Customer:Job recalled).

   ■ Recall hour field on paycheck (recalls total hours only and places total number of hours on a single line even if prior paycheck had several lines).

■ Job Costing and Item tracking for paycheck expenses (enables QuickBooks to add the cost of company-paid taxes to the burdened costs for time that is assigned to a Customer:Job). QuickBooks also offers the Class Tracking by Paycheck or Earnings Item option if you have the class tracking preference enabled.

6. Display **Employee List** by selecting the button to display your employee lists by first name or last name.

7. Click the check box next to **Mark new employees as sales reps** if you want new employees automatically added to the sales rep list. An employee who is also a sales rep can be listed on a customer invoice form so that you can report on sales by rep.

8. Click the check box next to **Display employee social security numbers in headers on reports** if you want to display this sensitive information on reports.

9. Click the **Employee Defaults** button to set the following defaults for new employees:

   ■ Default earnings items

   ■ Default to use time sheets to create paychecks from

   ■ Default additions or deductions payroll items

   ■ Checkbox if employee is covered by qualified pension plan

   ■ Default payroll schedule

   ■ Default pay frequency

   ■ Default class

   ■ Default federal and state tax settings

   ■ Default sick and vacation settings

10. Click the **Set preferences for Paystub and Voucher Printing** button to open the Payroll Printing Preferences dialog shown in Figure 14.2. In the Printing Preferences dialog, you can customize what detail will print on employees' paycheck stubs.

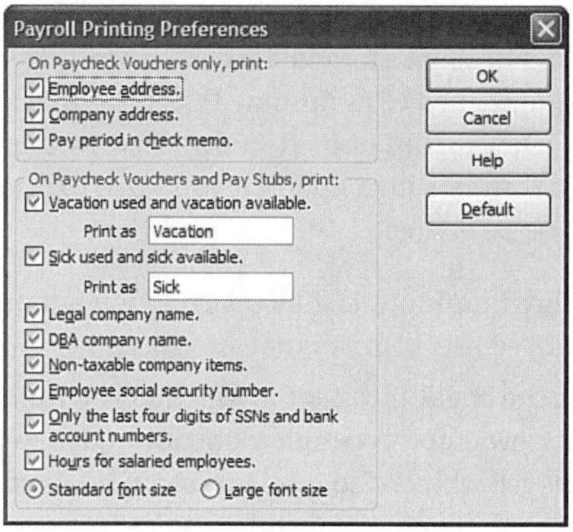

FIGURE 14.2

Printing preferences are customizable in QuickBooks.

11. Click the **Workers Comp** button in the Set Preferences for pane to set the preference to track worker's comp, to be warned when worker's comp is not assigned, and to exclude overtime hours from worker's compensation calculations.

12. Click the **Sick and Vacation** button to set default employee rates, tax preferences, pay schedule, and many other options. Using this setting can save data entry time when you are creating new employees because your common employee defaults will pre-fill when setting up new employees.

Payroll Forms and Workflow in QuickBooks

Payroll is like other areas of QuickBooks—it works best when the forms designed for use in this module are used to manage payroll expenses and liabilities. By following the proper payroll workflow, you can ensure that payroll is done correctly.

Payroll Forms

The following forms are unique to payroll processing:

■ **Paycheck**—The only form used by QuickBooks to pay an employee and automatically calculate all additions and deductions. You can identify these in your bank register as the transactions with a PAY CHK transaction type, as shown in Figure 14.3.

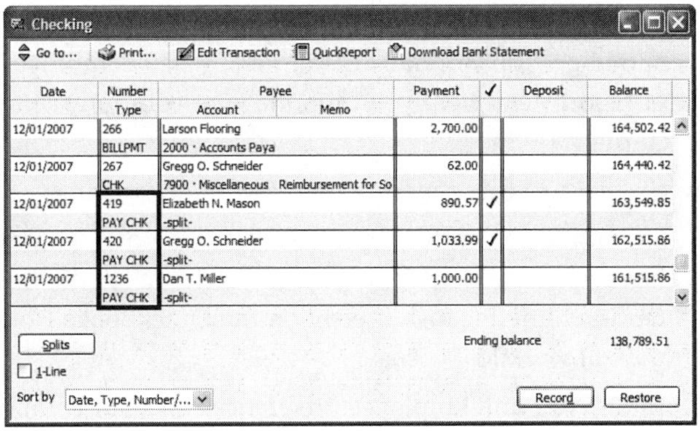

FIGURE 14.3
Properly created employee paychecks look like these transactions in your checkbook register.

- **Payroll Liability Adjustment**—The only form used by QuickBooks to modify the balances computed from actual paychecks. Click the **Employee radial** button if the adjustment needs to affect an employee's year-end W-2 form (see Figure 14.11 later in this chapter). This form also can affect your account balances, depending on what type of correction is to be made. For example, if the balance sheet report is correct but the payroll liabilities balances is incorrect, you can create a payroll liability adjustment and click **Accounts Affected** and choose to **Not Affect Account Balances**. You can identify these transactions in your bank register as transactions with a LIAB CHK transaction type.

- **Deposit Refund for Liabilities**—You use this special deposit form to record any refund received from overpaying your payroll liabilities. (See Figure 14.25 later in this chapter.)

You can conveniently create these forms from the Payroll Center, accessible from the QuickBooks Home page, Employees section.

These forms are the only ones recognized by the payroll module when you are preparing payments of payroll liabilities due or when preparing state and federal payroll reports in QuickBooks. (Your ability to prepare the state and federal forms is dependent on the type of payroll service subscription you have.)

Payroll Workflow

QuickBooks 2009 makes setting up and managing payroll tasks easier than before. Payroll tasks are defined and easily completed using the Employee Center, Payroll Center. Setting your Scheduled Payrolls and Scheduled Payroll

Liabilities practically eliminates the chance of making errors.

The preferred payroll workflow detail here, when combined with the proper review of reports, can help you manage your company's payroll efficiently and accurately.

Follow the steps in this general payroll workflow order:

1. Sign up for an Intuit Payroll Subscription at www.payroll.com or, if you have not signed up for a payroll service, click the **Learn about Payroll Options** link located directly on the QuickBooks Home page in the payroll workflow area.

2. Set Payroll and Employee preferences for your company. (See the section earlier in this chapter titled "Payroll and Employees Preference.")

3. Complete (if your data is new) the Payroll Setup or perform a payroll data review (for existing payroll) with the Run Payroll Checkup diagnostic tool. (See the sections "Using the Payroll Setup" and "Using the Run Payroll Checkup Diagnostic Tool" in this chapter.)

4. Set up scheduled payrolls and conveniently pay your employees directly from the QuickBooks Home page.

5. Pay your scheduled payroll liabilities, also accessible from Payroll Center. For more details on this newer feature, see the section in this chapter called "Scheduled Payroll and Liabilities."

6. Reconcile your bank account each month to identify any uncleared payroll checks that you do not expect to clear your bank.

7. Review and compare your financials and payroll reports frequently. (See the section "Comparing Payroll Liabilities Balances to the Balance Sheet" later in this chapter.)

8. Prepare your quarterly and annual state and federal payroll forms directly in QuickBooks (depending on which payroll subscription you have purchased).

The purpose of this book is to provide methods for reviewing and correcting existing data. With the enhancements made in QuickBooks, new users and advanced users will find payroll setup much easier to do. In addition, with the enhanced Run Payroll Checkup diagnostic tool, troubleshooting payroll just got a lot easier.

Using the Payroll Setup

Using the Payroll Setup tool is helpful to both new and existing QuickBooks payroll users.

- New Users to QuickBooks Payroll—The Payroll Setup helps you with your payroll setup.
- Existing Users QuickBooks Payroll—The Payroll Setup prefills the dialogs in the setup tool with your information, notifying you of any missing information.

For new QuickBooks payroll users, have the following information available before you begin the Payroll Setup tool:

- Compensation payment items: hourly, salary, and vacation to name just a few.
- Other additions or deductions to payroll.
- Employee name, address, and Social Security number, in addition to other relevant information you want to track.
- Payroll tax payment schedules and rates; that is, what frequency your business is required to pay payroll taxes, including the rate you pay for your state unemployment payroll tax, also known as SUTA.
- If starting payroll during the year, have available your employees' year-to-date amounts paid. It can be useful to have these amounts totaled by the payroll calendar quarter. (For more detailed information on this, see the section "Setting Up Payroll Mid-Year" later in this chapter.)
- Year-to-date payroll liability payments and other payroll payments made before using QuickBooks to produce your payroll liabilities.

To begin setting up payroll, after purchasing a payroll subscription, click Employees and choose the Payroll Setup menu option. QuickBooks takes a few minutes to load the Payroll Setup dialog. The first page of the payroll setup is shown in Figure 14.4.

Digging Deeper

When you click Employees, if you do not have a Payroll Setup menu choice, it is probably because you have not yet signed up for one of Intuit's payroll subscriptions. See the earlier section titled "Payroll Service Options" for more information.

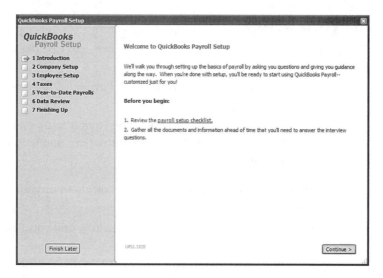

FIGURE 14.4

Use the Quickbooks Payroll Setup dialog to start a new payroll in QuickBooks or to check an existing payroll setup.

The Payroll Setup tool prompts with the following dialogs, which, if this is your first payroll setup, need to be completed in the order of the menus. If you have already set up your payroll, new for QuickBooks 2009, you can review the menus in *any* order:

1. **Introduction**—Explains some of the basics of this tool.

2. **Company Setup**—Define your compensation items and any employee benefits you offer.

3. **Employee Setup**—Enter personal information, pay rates, and form W-4 information, in addition to any direct deposit information.

4. **Taxes**—Identify your state tax identification number and tax agencies you pay, in addition to any applicable local payroll taxes.

5. **Year-to-Date Payrolls**—Provides the option to indicate whether you have had payroll earnings prior to starting payroll in QuickBooks. If you choose No to your company issuing prior paychecks, QuickBooks skips the remaining submenus of this step. If you choose Yes, QuickBooks provides new for 2009 summary screens to enter employee year-to-date earnings and record your prior payroll liability payments.

6. **Data Review**—QuickBooks reviews your wage and tax data and helps you find errors so that you can fix them.

7. **Finishing Up**—Overview information is provided about where you can find the information you have set up as well as instructions on how to use the Payroll Center. This menu is useful for any company new to using QuickBooks payroll.

Any time the Payroll Setup identifies an error, you can either correct the error at the time or select Finish Later to exit the Payroll Setup. You will be able to return to where you left off. Something new to QuickBooks 2009 is that after one payroll compensation item and an employee are set up, you can work on the remaining menus in any order. In versions prior to QuickBooks 2009, you could advance to the next menu in the payroll setup only when you had fixed any identified errors in the prior menu.

The next section discusses the Run Payroll Checkup menu option in QuickBooks.

Using the Run Payroll Checkup Diagnostic Tool

After you have subscribed to one of Intuit's payroll services, modified the payroll preferences to meet your company's specific needs, completed the payroll setup, and created payroll checks in QuickBooks, you are ready to complete the Run Payroll Checkup.

This menu option is similar to the previously listed Payroll Setup feature. In fact, when you open the Run Payroll Checkup diagnostic tool, it also opens the Payroll Setup feature, but some of the menus are modified.

What makes the Run Payroll Checkup tool different than the Payroll Setup tool? After you have set up your payroll, you will most likely use the Run Payroll Checkup tool to diagnose errors with both setup and transactions.

The QuickBooks Run Payroll Checkup enables you to "Finish Later" and return where you left off. Before you begin the Run Payroll Checkup dialog, make sure you have the following information available:

- Employees' names, addresses, Social Security numbers, and state for W-2s
- Compensation, benefits, other additions, or deductions your company offers
- Prior payroll wage and tax totals if starting a payroll mid-year

 Rescue Me!

When performing a diagnostic review of the previous quarter or current quarter payroll, you can select the Print button on the error screen to print the details, and then close the Run Payroll Checkup diagnostic tool to make the needed corrections.

The QuickBooks Run Payroll Checkup diagnostic tool (also known as Payroll Setup) assists in setting up or reviewing your existing payroll data for the following:

- Missing or incomplete information for employees, as shown in Figure 14.5.

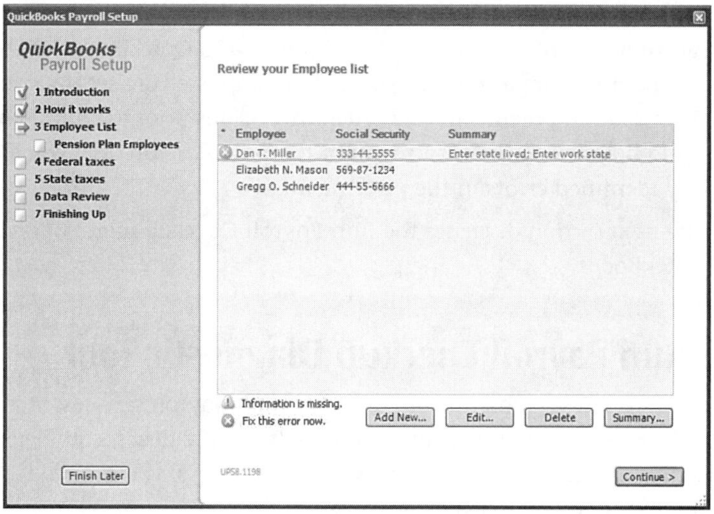

FIGURE 14.5

Employee information reviewed in the Payroll Setup diagnostic tool in QuickBooks.

- Compensation items, other additions, and deductions for missing or incomplete information (see Figure 14.6).
- For existing data, review of actual wage and tax amounts provides an alert if any discrepancy is found, as shown in Figure 14.7.

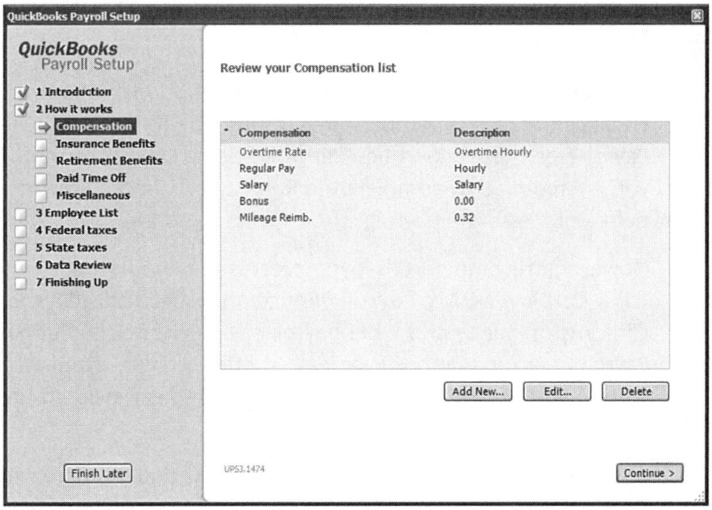

FIGURE 14.6

Compensation items reviewed in the Payroll Setup diagnostic tool in QuickBooks.

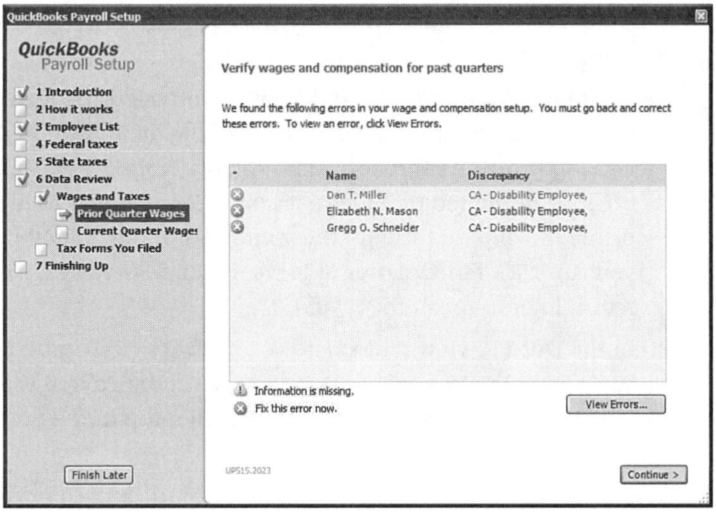

FIGURE 14.7

Alert provided if the QuickBooks Payroll Setup diagnostic tool detects wage or tax errors.

Digging Deeper

The Run Payroll Checkup diagnostic tool is optional for Intuit's Basic or Enhanced Payroll subscribers. If you subscribe to Intuit's Assisted Payroll (see the section titled "Payroll Service Options" in this chapter) you are required to complete the Run Payroll Checkup diagnostic tool before processing a payroll.

However, I recommend that you process the Run Payroll Checkup (click Employees, My Payroll Service and select Run Payroll Checkup) regardless of what payroll option you select. Running the Payroll Checkup diagnostic at least as often as once a quarter before your quarterly payroll tax returns are prepared can help ensure that your data is correct.

Be prepared to take the time to fix the errors that are detected. The QuickBooks Run Payroll Checkup diagnostic tool does not enable you to go to the next review dialog until the errors are corrected. You can, however, leave the tool and later return to where you left off.

To have the payroll diagnostic tool within QuickBooks review your payroll setup for missing information and paycheck data for discrepancies, do the following:

1. Click **Employees, My Payroll Service** and select the **Run Payroll Checkup** menu option. Follow each of the dialogs through step 5, clicking **Continue** through each window. Note: If QuickBooks detects an error in the setup, it identifies the error, and you need to correct it before moving on through the remainder of the payroll checkup, or you can click **Finish Later** to leave the Run Payroll Checkup and return later to finish the review.

2. In the **Data Review** dialog (step 6), click **Yes** (see Figure 14.8). Note: Be sure to say **Yes** to menu 6, Data Review, in the Payroll Checkup (Setup) tool. QuickBooks then checks the payroll setup and data you have recorded for accuracy.

3. If errors are detected (refer to Figure 14.7), click the **View Errors** button, and QuickBooks opens the error detail, as shown in Figure 14.9.

4. Click the **Print** button in the Payroll Item Discrepancies dialog, as shown in Figure 14.9. You must close this dialog before creating any adjusting entries.

5. Click the **Finish Later** button to close the Run Payroll Checkup diagnostic tool so that you can create correcting entries.

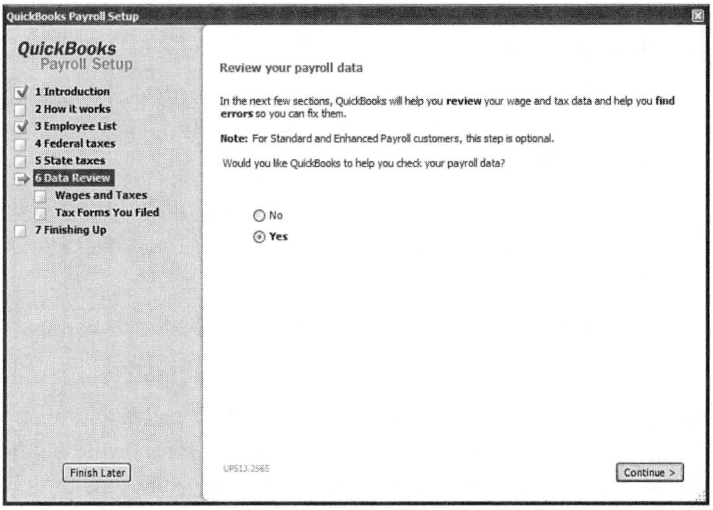

FIGURE 14.8
Click Yes when you want the Run Payroll Checkup diagnostic tool to verify wages and taxes for prior quarters and/or the current quarter.

FIGURE 14.9
You can print the report of errors in wages or accrued taxes for later review.

Rescue Me!

Carefully consider the adjustments that need to be made if they affect a prior calendar quarter that has already had the necessary payroll returns filed.

Be prepared to promptly file a correcting return with the federal government or state agency when you adjust your QuickBooks payroll data from what was previously reported.

Correcting prior quarters can often be the best choice, especially if your data is ever audited.

Using the errors displayed earlier in Figure 14.7 as an example, the following are the typical steps for correcting them. (Your errors will be different and might require adjustments to other types of payroll items than are displayed in this example.)

1. Click **Reports, Employees & Payroll** and select **Payroll Summary**. Review this report for either prior or current payroll quarters (depending on where the error was detected). In Figure 14.10, you can easily compare your Payroll Summary report to the Payroll Item Discrepancies report in Figure 14.9. The QB Amount should equal what your Payroll Summary report shows when printed today.

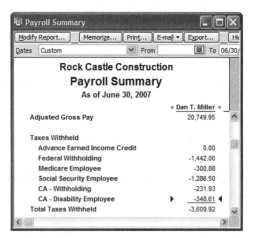

FIGURE 14.10

Compare your Payroll Summary report to your Payroll Item Discrepancies QB Amount column.

2. Click **Employees, Payroll Taxes and Liabilities**, and select **Adjust Payroll Liabilities** to open the Liability Adjustment dialog shown in Figure 14.11.

3. Enter the **Date** and **Effective Date**. Both should be dated in the quarter you want to effect the change.

4. Select either **Company** or **Employee** for the adjustment. **Company** indicates it is a company-paid adjustment. **Employee** indicates an employee-paid adjustment and will affect W-2 reported amounts.

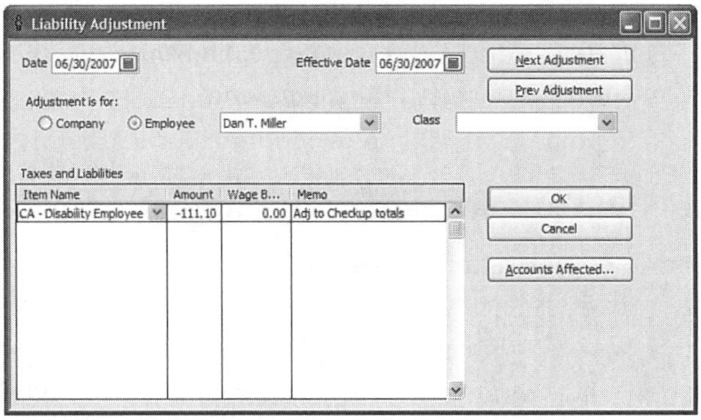

FIGURE 14.11

Create a payroll liability adjustment when correcting payroll from previously filed payroll quarters.

5. Optionally, assign a class if your business tracks different profit centers.

6. Click **Accounts Affected** only if you do not want to affect balances. This would be necessary if your Balance Sheet is correct but your Payroll Liabilities balances are incorrect.

7. Click **OK**.

8. QuickBooks might open another dialog (see Figure 14.12) with the default account that is going to be affected. QuickBooks shows you this dialog to suggest the recommended account for the adjustment based on how the payroll item is set up. If you need to change the account assignment, choose the appropriate account from the drop-down menu.

FIGURE 14.12

QuickBooks shows the default account that will be affected by the change.

9. Click **OK** to save the transaction.

10. Return to the Run Payroll Checkup menu to review your payroll data again after the correction. If your adjustments were successful, QuickBooks displays a Congratulations message showing all adjustments have corrected the discrepancies.

Need to Run Payroll Checkup for a Prior Year?

If you need to complete a Run Payroll Checkup diagnostic for a prior year, and if you are working in a multi-user environment, ask everyone to log out of the QuickBooks file and close the data file.

Next, change your computer system date to a date in the prior year. When selecting the date, keep in mind how QuickBooks will review and report on "prior quarters" dependent on this new system date.

Run the Payroll Checkup diagnostic, which QuickBooks now checks the payroll data that corresponds to the year of your computer's system date.

Don't forget to close the file and then reset your computer date to the current date before opening the file again and allowing other users into the system.

You might want to contact your computer professionals before changing the system date in a networked environment, because it might impact other running programs.

Reports to Review When Troubleshooting Payroll

Using the QuickBooks Run Payroll Checkup diagnostic tool can be one of the most useful ways to review and validate the accuracy of your payroll data. You can also review your data setup and accuracy manually by reviewing the reports detailed in this section.

Payroll Item Listing

One of the first reports I prepare when working with a client is the Payroll Item Listing.

Click Reports, Lists, and select Payroll Item Listing. You do not need to modify or filter this report (see Figure 14.13).

The Payroll Item Listing report provides several pieces of critical information (see Figure 14.13):

- **Type**—This is from a predefined list in QuickBooks. The type determines whether it is added to gross wages or deducted.
- **Amount**—This figure is determined by the QuickBooks-provided payroll tax tables, with the exception of State Unemployment, city, and local taxes, which are user defined.

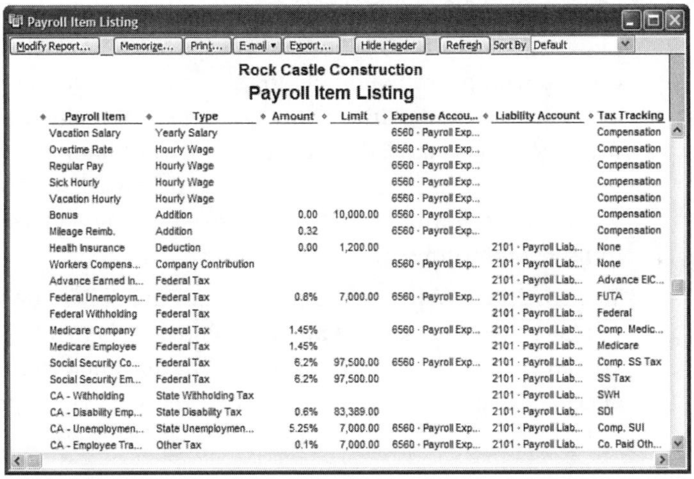

Rock Castle Construction

Payroll Item Listing

Payroll Item	Type	Amount	Limit	Expense Accou...	Liability Account	Tax Tracking
Vacation Salary	Yearly Salary			6560 · Payroll Exp...		Compensation
Overtime Rate	Hourly Wage			6560 · Payroll Exp...		Compensation
Regular Pay	Hourly Wage			6560 · Payroll Exp...		Compensation
Sick Hourly	Hourly Wage			6560 · Payroll Exp...		Compensation
Vacation Hourly	Hourly Wage			6560 · Payroll Exp...		Compensation
Bonus	Addition	0.00	10,000.00	6560 · Payroll Exp...		Compensation
Mileage Reimb.	Addition	0.32		6560 · Payroll Exp...		Compensation
Health Insurance	Deduction	0.00	1,200.00		2101 · Payroll Liab...	None
Workers Compens...	Company Contribution			6560 · Payroll Exp...	2101 · Payroll Liab...	None
Advance Earned In...	Federal Tax				2101 · Payroll Liab...	Advance EIC...
Federal Unemploym...	Federal Tax	0.8%	7,000.00	6560 · Payroll Exp...	2101 · Payroll Liab...	FUTA
Federal Withholding	Federal Tax				2101 · Payroll Liab...	Federal
Medicare Company	Federal Tax	1.45%		6560 · Payroll Exp...	2101 · Payroll Liab...	Comp. Medic...
Medicare Employee	Federal Tax	1.45%			2101 · Payroll Liab...	Medicare
Social Security Co...	Federal Tax	6.2%	97,500.00	6560 · Payroll Exp...	2101 · Payroll Liab...	Comp. SS Tax
Social Security Em...	Federal Tax	6.2%	97,500.00		2101 · Payroll Liab...	SS Tax
CA - Withholding	State Withholding Tax				2101 · Payroll Liab...	SWH
CA - Disability Emp...	State Disability Tax	0.6%	83,389.00		2101 · Payroll Liab...	SDI
CA - Unemploymen...	State Unemploymen...	5.25%	7,000.00	6560 · Payroll Exp...	2101 · Payroll Liab...	Comp. SUI
CA - Employee Tra...	Other Tax	0.1%	7,000.00	6560 · Payroll Exp...	2101 · Payroll Liab...	Co. Paid Oth...

FIGURE 14.13

Review the Payroll Item Listing report to manually verify that QuickBooks payroll is set up correctly.

- **Limit**—This figure is determined by the QuickBooks-provided tax tables and is not modifiable by the user. Incorrect limits could be due to a payroll tax table that is not current.

Digging Deeper

When you review your company's payroll item listing, do the tax limits listed not match up to what the IRS currently requires? You might need to update your QuickBooks payroll tax table. To update your payroll tax tables, your company's payroll subscription must be active.

Click Employees, Get Payroll Updates to see the current status of your payroll subscription. This information is also shown on the Payroll Center, which you can access from the Home page.

- **Expense Account**—If the payroll item type is considered an expense, users can define the default expense account from the chart of accounts list in the payroll setup. QuickBooks defaults this account to a generic Payroll Expense account that is created automatically by QuickBooks when payroll is enabled.

- **Liability Account**—This account is used for payroll items that are accrued with payroll and paid to the state or federal government. QuickBooks defaults these items to a generic liability account created when payroll is enabled. You can define what liability account is assigned, but you should use the one QuickBooks provides if you want to see certain warnings that are provided when you try to create a transaction incorrectly.

- **Tax Tracking**—When you create a new payroll item and select a payroll item type, QuickBooks provides a predetermined list of tax tracking types associated with that item type. Tax tracking determines how QuickBooks treats the item on the W-2 year-end employee tax form.

Comparing Payroll Liabilities Balances to the Balance Sheet

You should also compare your Balance Sheet payroll liabilities account balance to the amount on the Payroll Liabilities Balances report. To do so, follow these steps:

1. Click **Reports**, **Company & Financial** and select the **Balance Sheet Standard** report.

2. On the report dialog that opens, set the date to include the period you are reviewing.

3. Click **Reports, Employees & Payroll** and select the **Payroll Liability Balances** report.

4. Click the **Dates** drop-down menu and select **All** from the top of the list. Leave the **From** date box empty. In the **To** date box, enter the same date that was used on the Balance Sheet Standard report. Doing so ensures that you are picking up all transactions for this account, including any unpaid balances from prior years. Click **Print** if you want to have a copy of this report to compare to your Balance Sheet payroll liabilities balance.

These two reports should have matching totals. In the examples shown in Figures 14.14 and 14.15, the Balance Sheet and Payroll Liabilities reports do not match.

The totals might not match because of non-payroll transactions being used to record adjustments or payments to payroll liabilities using non-payroll forms, such as a General Journal Entry, Bill, or a Write Check form.

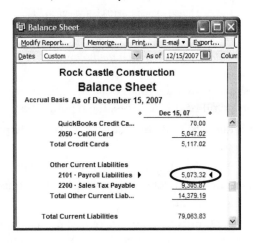

FIGURE 14.14

View your Balance Sheet payroll liabilities balance.

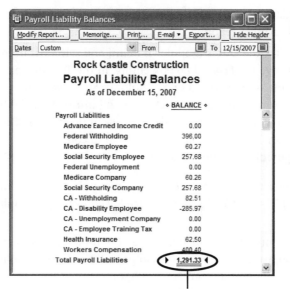

Should match Payroll Liabilities in Figure 14.14.

FIGURE 14.15

Total Payroll Liabilities balance should match the Balance Sheet for the same account.

To troubleshoot payroll liabilities differences, I prefer to work with the Custom Transaction Detail report. To access the report, follow these steps:

1. Click **Reports, Custom Transaction Detail Report**. The Modify Report dialog opens.

2. Click the **Dates** drop-down list and select **All**. Leave the **From** date box empty; in the **To** date box, enter the date you used on the Balance Sheet Standard report.

3. In the **Columns** box, remove or add a check mark for the information you want to display on the report. Be sure to include **Type**.

4. On the **Sort By** drop-down menu, select **Type**.

5. Click the **Filters** tab; in the **Choose Filters** pane, the Accounts filter is already selected. From the **Accounts** drop-down menu to the right, select the **Payroll Liabilities** account.

6. Click **OK** to create the report.

QuickBooks creates a useful and telling report, as shown in Figure 14.16. When this report is sorted by type of transaction, you can easily see what non-payroll related transactions are affecting your Balance Sheet Standard report Payroll Liability balance and are *not* affecting your Payroll Liability Balances report.

If you are an accounting professional working with the Client Data Review feature, new for QuickBooks 2009, you can also select the "Find Incorrectly Paid Payroll Liabilities" custom report from the Payroll Cleanup Task pane. More information about the usefulness of this tool is documented in Chapter 17, "New for 2009! Detecting and Correcting with the Client Data Review Feature."

Custom Transaction Detail Report						
Modify Report...	Memorize...	Print...	E-mail ▼	Export...	Hide Header	Refresh
Dates	Custom	▼	From		To	12/15/2007	Total By	Total only	▼	Sort By

Rock Castle Construction
Custom Transaction Detail Report
Accrual Basis
As of December 15, 2007

Type	◇	Date	◇ Num ◇	Name	◇	Memo	◇	Amount	◇
▶ General Journal		09/30/2007				Opening balance as of start date		3,781.99	◀
Liability Adjust		06/30/2007		Dan T. Miller		Adj to Checkup totals		-111.10	
Liability Adjust		06/30/2007		Elizabeth N. Mason		Adj to checkup		-90.26	
Liability Adjust		06/30/2007		Gregg O. Schneider		Adj to checkup		-105.56	
Liability Adjust		06/30/2007		Dan T. Miller				-2.01	
Liability Check		02/07/2007	302	Employment Devel...		987-6543-2		-99.19	
Liability Check		02/07/2007	302	Employment Devel...		987-6543-2		-4.16	
Liability Check		02/07/2007	302	Employment Devel...		987-6543-2		-218.20	
Liability Check		02/07/2007	302	Employment Devel...		987-6543-2		-191.81	
Liability Check		02/07/2007	303	Great Statewide B...		00-7904153		0.00	

FIGURE 14.16

Use the Custom Transaction Detail Report to easily identify non-payroll transactions that are recorded to the Payroll Liabilities account.

 Digging Deeper

QuickBooks makes viewing details of transactions easy. Hover your mouse pointer over a transaction and click to select (highlight) the transaction.

With the transaction selected, simultaneously press the Ctrl+Y keys on your keyboard.

QuickBooks provides the transaction detail in the traditional debit and credit format, as shown in Figure 14.17.

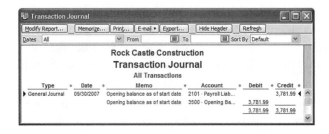

FIGURE 14.17

Optionally, view your transactions in debit and credit format.

You can double-click on any of the listed transactions to see more detail about the transaction. If you want to view the transaction in the form it was originally created in, double-click the transaction to open up the original form.

 Digging Deeper

Because the General Journal Entries form is not a recommended form for managing payroll liabilities balances, it is better to use the Payroll Liabilities Adjustment Transaction form as discussed in the section titled "Adjusting Payroll Liabilities."

Compare Payroll Summary to Filed Payroll Returns

Has your company ever received a notice from the IRS indicating that your year-end payroll documents do not agree with your quarterly payroll return totals, or have you received a similar notice from your state payroll tax agency?

Listed in this section are some basic comparisons that you should do both before filing a payroll return and after, in the event that you allow users to make changes to transactions from previous payroll quarters. You can avoid these period changes by following the advice listed in Chapter 15, "Sharing Data with Your Accountant or Your Client," in the section titled "Instructing Your Client to Set a Closing Date.."

Compare the following items routinely while doing payroll in QuickBooks:

- When reviewing the Payroll Summary, verify that each calendar quarter in QuickBooks agrees with your filed payroll return totals. Look at these specific areas:
  - Total Adjusted Gross Pay in QuickBooks agrees with the Federal 941 Form, Wages, Tips, and Other Compensation.
  - Federal Withholding in QuickBooks agrees with the Federal 941 Form, Total income tax withheld from wages, and so on.

- Employee and Company Social Security and Medicare in QuickBooks agree with the computed Total Taxable Social Security and Medicare on the Federal 941 Form.
- Ensure total payroll tax deposits for the quarter in QuickBooks agrees with your paper trail. Whether you file online or use a coupon that you take to the bank, check to make sure that you recorded the correct calendar quarter with the IRS for your payments.
- Total Adjusted Gross Pay for the calendar year in QuickBooks agrees with the reported Gross Wage total on the annual Federal Form W-3, Transmittal of Wage, and Tax Statements.
- Total Adjusted Gross Pay for the calendar quarter in QuickBooks agrees with the Total Gross Wage reported to your state payroll agency.
- Total Payroll expense from the Profit & Loss report agrees with total Adjusted Gross Pay on the Payroll Summary report.

Reviewing these critical reports with your federal and state tax filings will ensure that your data agrees with the payroll tax agency records.

Adjusting Payroll Liabilities

With recent versions of QuickBooks, it is less likely that you will make any errors setting up or managing payroll from pay period to pay period. This is due in great part to the Payroll Setup feature. If you do not have this menu choice, you first need to subscribe to one of Intuit's payroll offerings. There is a service that is just right for your company's payroll needs.

QuickBooks payroll works best when you perform all activity from within the payroll menus. This includes paying your accrued payroll taxes to the respective taxing authorities. If your company has written checks or vendor bills paying for these liabilities, and the QuickBooks-created Payroll Liabilities account was assigned, a warning message displays, as shown in Figure 14.18.

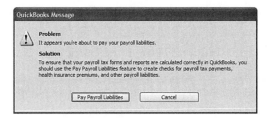

FIGURE 14.18

The warning message that displays if you try to create a liability payment using a check (or bill) and assign the QuickBooks-created Payroll Liabilities account.

This warning prevents users from using the wrong type of payment form when attempting to make payroll liability payments. When the user clicks the Pay Payroll Liabilities button in the warning message, the user is directed to the Select Date Range for Liabilities dialog (see Figure 14.19). The message directs the user to create the proper form for a payroll liability check.

Select Date Range For Liabilities

Select the date range for the payroll liabilities you want to pay.
Tip: Base your dates on the dates of the paychecks you issued, not on your pay period dates.

Show Payroll Liabilities

Dates Custom   From 01/01/2007   Through 07/31/2007

OK   Cancel   Help

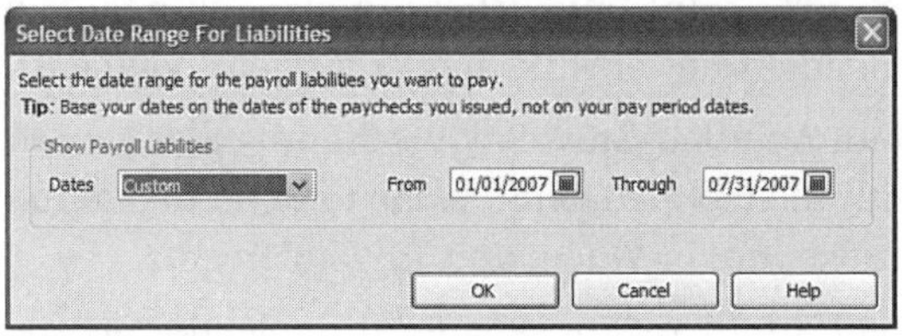

FIGURE 14.19

QuickBooks redirects you to create a proper payroll liability check if you attempt to use a check or bill form.

Rescue Me!

The warning in Figure 14.18 displays only if you are assigning your payroll liabilities to the QuickBooks automatically created Payroll Liabilities account, not an account you manually created and called Payroll Liabilities.

For more information on the importance of using these automatically created accounts see Chapter 2, "Reviewing the QuickBooks Chart of Accounts," in the section titled "Accounts That QuickBooks Creates Automatically."

New for QuickBooks Premier Accountant 2009 as well as the QuickBooks Enterprise Solutions Accountant 9.0 is the Client Data Review feature. From this feature, you can prepare a report that provides details of non-payroll transactions paying payroll liabilities. To learn more about these features, see Chapter 17.

You can also use this process to identify when non-payroll forms were used to complete payroll tax payments to vendors with a check or bill:

1. Click the **Vendors** tab from the QuickBooks Home page to open the Vendor Center.

2. Select the vendor to which you pay your payroll liabilities.

3. On the right, click the **Show** drop-down menu and select **Checks** or **Bill Payments**, and then review whether a check or bill payment form was used to pay payroll liabilities.

4. Make a note of what chart of account list item the check or bill form was assigned to.

You have two methods for correcting these. First, if you have identified non-payroll forms paying for your payroll liabilities, you can properly fix them after determining that the check or bill payment check has not cleared the bank and has not been included in the current monthly bank reconciliation.

Void the existing check or bill that is paying the payroll liabilities and recreate it correctly by clicking Employees, Payroll Taxes & Liabilities and selecting Pay Scheduled Liabilities.

If you need to add a new or edit your existing liability payment schedules, click Employees, Payroll Taxes & Liabilities and select Edit Payment Due Dates/Methods (see Figure 14.20). QuickBooks opens the Payroll Setup tool specifically on the Schedule Payments (for a new schedule) or Edit Payment Schedule (existing schedule) dialog. After setting this schedule, QuickBooks reminds you on the Payroll Center dialog when the payment is due.

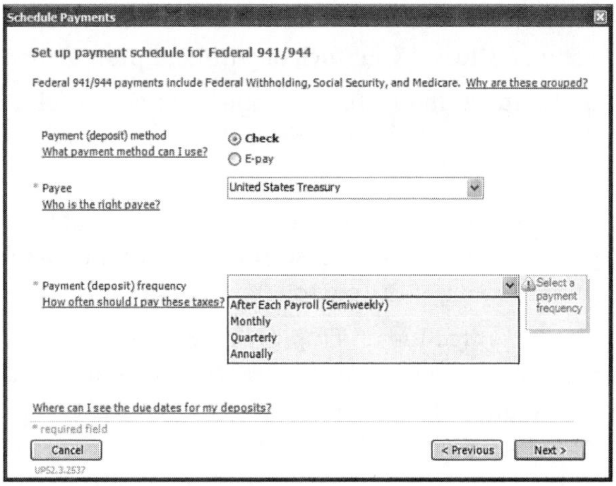

FIGURE 14.20

Set a schedule for properly paying your payroll taxes.

You can use a second method if you have marked the check (or bill payment check form) that improperly paid your payroll liabilities as cleared in the bank reconciliation. You do not want to void the check or bill payment check because it would negatively affect your recorded bank reconciliation.

Digging Deeper

In recent versions of QuickBooks, you rarely make the mistake of not properly paying your payroll liabilities. However, to have QuickBooks automatically warn you when improperly paying these payroll liabilities, the payroll liabilities account must be the chart of accounts list item that QuickBooks created automatically (see the section titled "Accounts That QuickBooks Creates Automatically" in Chapter 2). Using any other user-created payroll liabilities chart of account does not provide the valuable user warning.

Beginning with QuickBooks version 2008, the warning directs you to the proper menu for paying payroll liabilities.

Rather than using a General Journal Entries form to correct payroll liability errors, use the Payroll Liability Adjustment form following these steps:

1. Click **Employees, Payroll Taxes & Liabilities** and select **Adjust Payroll Liabilities** to open the Liability Adjustment dialog. (Refer to Figure 14.11.)

2. Choose **Employee** if you want to effect the change on the employee's W-2, or **Company** if you want to effect the change only for the Federal Form 940 or 941.

3. Assign a **Class** if you track department profitability.

4. In the Taxes and Liabilities pane, Item Name column from the drop-down menu, select the **Payroll Item** your review indicated that needed to be adjusted.

5. In the Amount column, enter the amount of the adjustment. Enter a positive number to increase or a negative number to decrease the selected totals of the payroll item on that line.

6. If you are creating an Employee adjustment, an additional column displays for Wage Base. Typically, you should not adjust what defaults in this column. (If your adjustment was for the Company selection, you do not see the wage base column.)

7. Optionally, enter a memo that displays in detailed reports.

8. Click **Accounts Affected** to open the Accounts Affected dialog, as shown in Figure 14.21. Here, you have these two important options:

   ■ **Do not affect accounts**—Selecting this option adjusts only your Pay Scheduled Liabilities dialog totals and not Balance Sheet or Profit & Loss report totals.

- **Affect liability and expense accounts**—Selecting this option adjusts your Pay Scheduled Liabilities dialog and your Balance Sheet and/or Profit & Loss accounts.

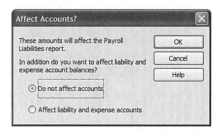

FIGURE 14.21

Choose to not affect accounts with a liability adjustment when only the Pay Scheduled Liabilities amounts are incorrect.

9. Click **OK** to save your Affect Accounts selection.

10. Click **OK** to save the payroll liability adjustment.

11. Click **Employees, Payroll Center** and verify that the correct amounts to be paid are listed in the Pay Scheduled Liabilities dialog. (See Figure 14.22.)

✓	Send By	Status	Payment	Period	Amount Due
	01/15/08	Upcoming	Federal 941/944	Dec 2007	1,038.90
	01/31/08	Upcoming	CA Withholding and Disabilit...	Q4 2007	417.71

Total Selected Items: 0.00

Related Payment Activities ▾   Check E-payment Status   View/Pay

FIGURE 14.22

The Pay Scheduled Liabilities total should now agree with what you currently owe.

Unique Payroll Transactions and Processes

This section discusses a few of the more unusual payroll transactions or processes.

 Digging Deeper

Although several acceptable methods exist for accomplishing these tasks, the ones discussed in this section are those that I recommend to my clients.

Scheduled Payroll and Liabilities

One of the most useful features in recent versions of QuickBooks payroll is the capability to define a scheduled payroll and scheduled payroll liabilities.

A scheduled payroll enables you to set multiple payroll frequencies to organize your payroll; for example, you can pay your clerical staff weekly and the management staff biweekly.

To create a scheduled payroll, follow these steps:

1. Click **Employees, Add or Edit Payroll Schedules**. The Payroll Schedule List dialog displays.

2. Click the **Payroll Schedule** drop-down menu and select **New** as shown in Figure 14.23. Or, if you selected an existing payroll schedule in step 1, you can choose **Edit Payroll Schedule**.

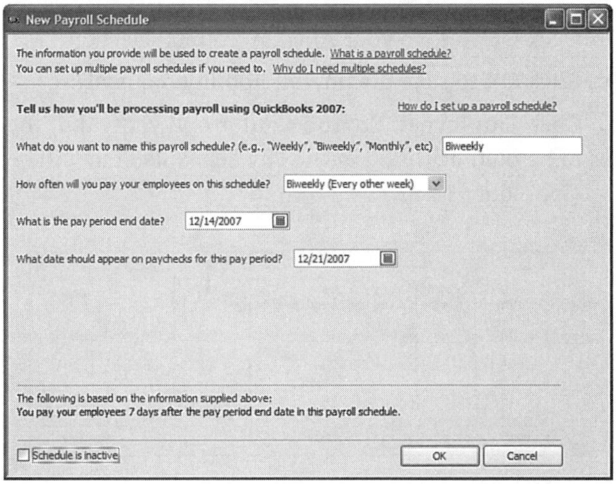

FIGURE 14.23

Adding a scheduled payroll to QuickBooks helps keep payroll processing timely and organized.

3. For a new schedule, give the schedule a name, select from a predetermined list of frequencies, enter the pay period ending date, and select the date the paychecks will be given out. Click **OK**.

    QuickBooks displays the payroll schedules you have created, making an easy task of processing payrolls that have different pay periods. Click the red **X** in the upper right to close this list.

4. To schedule or edit your payroll liabilities (if you have not already done so with the Run Payroll Checkup), click **Employees, Payroll**

Taxes and Liabilities and select the option to **Edit Payment Due Dates/Methods**. QuickBooks opens the Payroll Setup tool, but shows only the specific menu for scheduling your tax payments. (See Figure 14.24.)

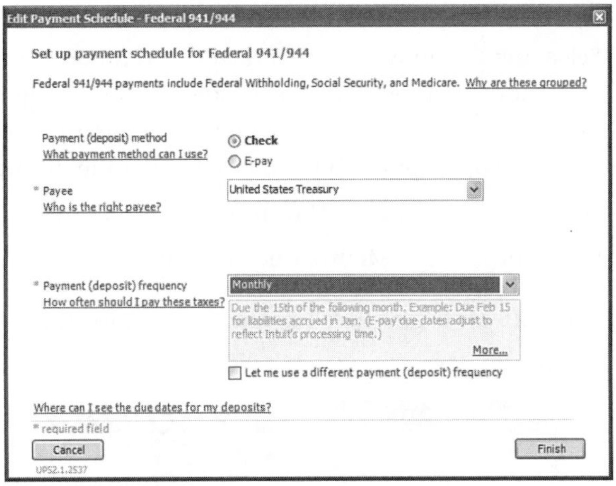

FIGURE 14.24

Set a schedule for paying payroll liabilities.

With a payroll schedule defined and payroll liabilities scheduled, QuickBooks can make your payroll processing more efficient and accurate.

Deposit a Refund of Payroll Liabilities

If you received a refund from an overpayment of payroll taxes, you would not want to add it to a Make Deposits form (like other deposit documents you create). If you did, the refunded amount would not correct your overpayment amount showing in the payroll liability reports and in certain payroll forms.

This type of payroll error should rarely, if at all, occur in current versions of QuickBooks thanks to improved messaging and ease in working from the QuickBooks Home page. However, if you were paying your payroll liabilities outside the QuickBooks payroll menus and you had an overpayment that you requested and received a refund for, the following is the proper method to use to record the deposit if you want your payroll reports to reflect receipt of the overpayment:

1. Click **Employees, Payroll Taxes and Liabilities** and select **Deposit Refund of Liabilities**. The Refund Deposit for Taxes and Liabilities dialog displays.

2. Select the name of the vendor.

3. Enter the **Refund Date** (the date of your deposit).

4. Enter the **For Period Beginning** date (this should be the payroll quarter the overpayment was in).

5. Enter the **Deposit Total** of the refund.

6. Select the Group with other undeposited funds radial button if this item is included on a bank deposit ticket with other deposit amounts. Or select the Deposit To radial button to create a single deposit entry and select the appropriate bank account from the drop-down list.

7. Select the **Payroll Item** that needs to be adjusted.

8. Optionally, add a **Memo**, and click **OK**.

See Figure 14.25 for a completed Refund Deposit for Taxes and Liabilities form.

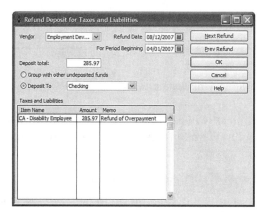

FIGURE 14.25

Deposit refunded payroll liabilities with a form from the Employees menu.

Reprint a Lost Payroll Check

When any other check in QuickBooks is lost, you typically void the check in QuickBooks and report it to your bank so that it cannot be cashed.

With payroll, you need to be a bit more cautious about voiding the transaction because when you void a payroll transaction and then reissue it, certain payroll taxes could be recalculated on the replacement check different from the originally issued payroll check.

Certain payroll taxes are based on limits; for example, Social Security, federal unemployment, and state unemployment taxes are examples of taxes that are charged to employees or to the company up to a certain wage limit. When you void a previously issued check, QuickBooks recalculates these taxes for the current replacement check, and these amounts might differ from the original check, potentially affecting the net amount of the check.

Proper control would be to report the missing check to your bank so that it cannot be cashed. In QuickBooks, instead of voiding the payroll check and then recreating it, print a new payroll check (from the same original payroll check details) and record the new check number, and then separately create a voided Write Check form for the lost check. Follow these steps to record these transactions:

1. Locate the lost check in your checking register by clicking **Banking, Use Check Register**.

2. From the **Select Account** drop-down menu, select the bank account that has the missing check and click **OK** to open the bank register.

3. Find the check in the register that was reported missing. With your cursor, double-click the list item to open the paycheck form and make a note of the check number, date, and payee.

4. On the open Paycheck dialog, place a check mark in the **To Be Printed** check box.

5. Print the paycheck form singly or with others by clicking the **Print** button at the top of the check form.

6. QuickBooks asks for the check number. After printing the check, QuickBooks assigns the new check number and uses the check date and totals assigned to the original check.

7. To keep track of the lost check in your accounting, click **Banking, Write Checks**. Using the original check number, date and payee, record the check with a zero amount to an account of your choosing. You might get a message warning not to pay employees with a check, but because you are recording a zero transaction, you can ignore this warning.

8. With the lost check created in step 7 still open, click **Edit, Void Check**. QuickBooks prefills with a "0" amount and the Memo line of the check with "Void." This now shows this check as voided in your register just in case the employee was able to cash the check. You would notice when reconciling that you have marked it as voided.

Using this method for printing a lost payroll check ensures that you do not inadvertently change any prior period payroll amounts and reported payroll totals; at the same time, recording the lost check helps keep a record of each check issued from your bank account.

Setting Up Payroll Mid-Year

In the accounting community, the term "mid-year" refers to setting up payroll at any other time than at the beginning of the year. Interestingly, when accountants use the term mid-year, they are technically saying that you are starting your first payroll in QuickBooks sometime during the calendar year (not at the beginning of the calendar year) for a business that has already paid out payroll to employees in the same calendar year (perhaps using other software, or using an outside payroll agency).

This method is needed only for companies converting to QuickBooks payroll in a calendar year that had prior payroll in the same year produced from some other source.

When you make the decision to begin using QuickBooks payroll in a year that you have already had payroll transactions, you can:

- Manually recreate in detail all your previous payroll transactions, and then you do not need to follow the steps in this section.

- Record year-to-date totals for previously issued payroll checks and liability payments, following the steps given in this section.

You need to record year-to-date (YTD) payroll amounts in QuickBooks for the payroll process to calculate state and some federal taxes correctly. In addition, this will enable you to print accurate quarterly or annual state and federal forms.

Before beginning this process, make sure you have accurate records of the prior period payrolls, preferably subtotaled by calendar quarter.

To set up mid-year payroll YTD amounts using the Payroll Setup, complete the following steps:

1. Click **Employees, Payroll Setup** and complete the setup process through step 4 (Taxes).

2. On step 5 (Year-to-Date Payrolls), QuickBooks first determines whether you have had payroll in the current year or the last year. If you answer Yes, QuickBooks opens the Payroll Summary dialog, new for QuickBooks 2009 (see Figure 14.27).

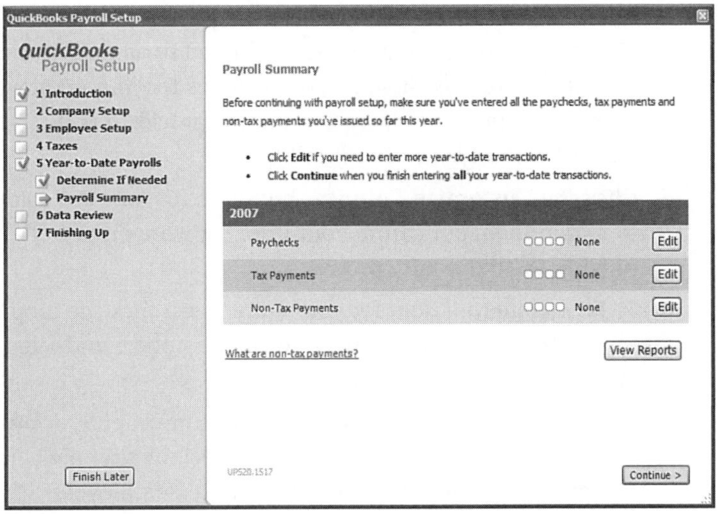

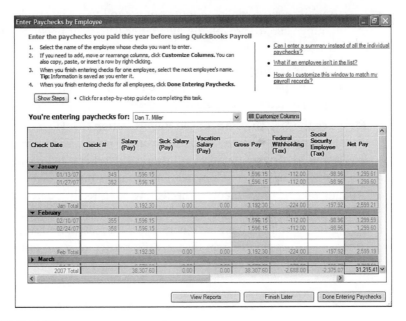

FIGURE 14.26

Answering Yes to the previous payroll question enables you to record year-to-date payroll information for employees.

> **3.** Click the **Edit** button on the Payroll Summary dialog to begin entering your employee's prior year payroll totals as shown in Figure 14.27.

FIGURE 14.27

New interface in QuickBooks 2009 makes entering year-to-date payroll easier and improves accuracy.

4. The Enter Paycheck by Employee dialog opens as shown in Figure 14.28. This new dialog, similar to Microsoft Excel functionality, streamlines the task of entering year-to-date payroll totals for your employees. Click the **Show Steps** button to have QuickBooks provide a pop-up dialog of what information is typed in each cell.

5. Click the **Customize Columns** button to arrange the columns of data to match the reports from your prior software or payroll provider, simplifying the data entry process.

6. To begin entering data for your employees, click the drop-down menu for **You're entering paycheck for** menu option and select the employee you are starting with.

7. Right-click with your mouse pointer to conveniently copy, paste, insert, or delete rows. This functionality is especially useful when entering repeating information such as for salaried employees.

8. Conveniently check your monthly and annual totals as you type directly from the Enter Paychecks by Employee dialog to make sure your data entered agrees with your prior payroll records.

9. QuickBooks 2009 includes two new reports to help report on the accuracy of the setup details. Click **View Reports** and the Historical Paycheck-Basic dialog opens as shown in Figure 14.28.

   Use this report to validate that your payroll totals by employee and by earnings item or payroll tax item agree with your previous payroll records.

10. Click the **Compress** button to squeeze more columns of data into the report by placing the column headers on a slant and click **Print** or **Export to Excel** to document your work.

11. Click the **Switch to Advanced Report** button (see Figure 14.29) to open the Historical Paycheck Report-Advanced report. The Advanced report compares the combination of historical paycheck detail with any employee or company payroll liability adjustments. If your historical payroll and adjustments (if needed) were correctly entered, the QuickBooks-Calculated amount column should equal your totals for those payroll tax items as reported to your federal and state governments. Click the red **X** in the top right corner to return to the Enter Paychecks by Employee dialog.

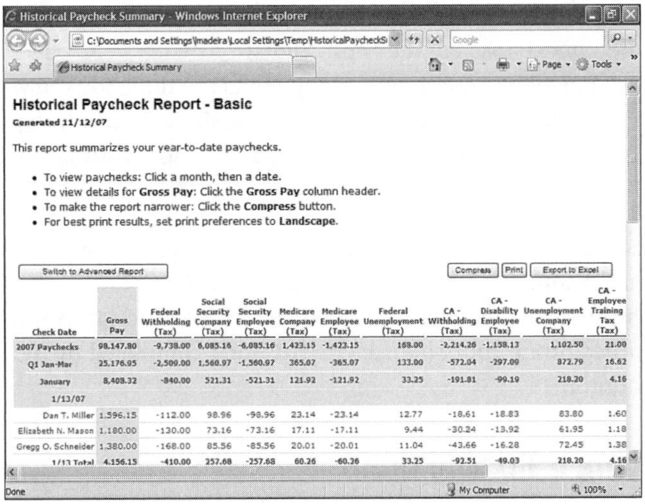

FIGURE 14.28

Use the Historical Paycheck-Basic report to review the data you have entered for accuracy.

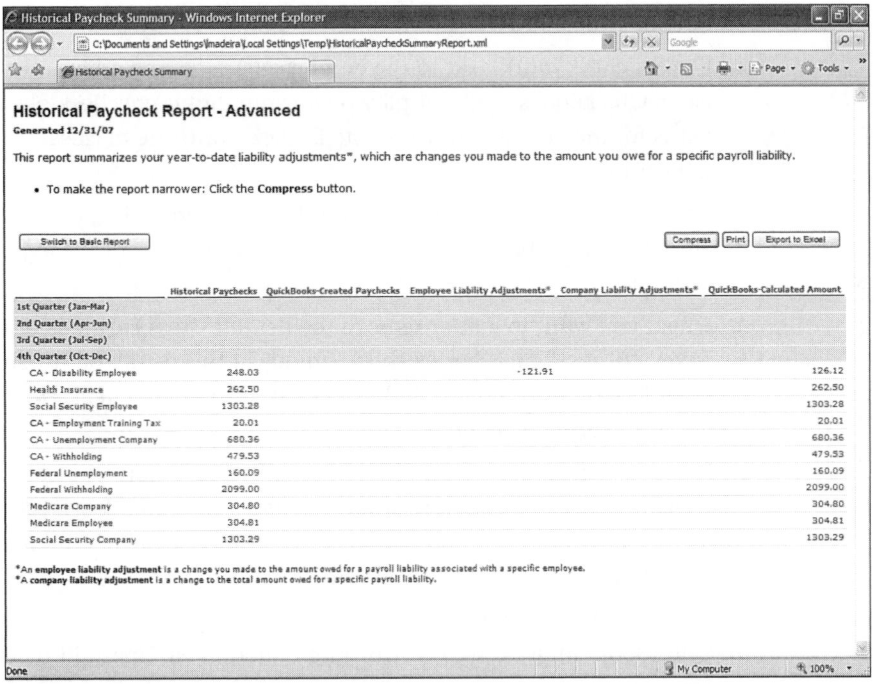

FIGURE 14.29

Use the Historical Paycheck-Advanced review accuracy of your reporting.

12. Click the **Done Entering Paychecks** button to return to the QuickBooks Payroll Setup Dialog. As each task, paychecks, tax payments, and non-tax payments are done (as shown previously in Figure 14.26), the boxes will be shaded green progressively until each task is complete, making it easy to return and pick up where you left off.

These balances entered in these Year-to-Date payroll windows affect the Payroll Summary and all payroll forms but do not affect the Balance Sheet or Profit & Loss reports. Your balances for these accounts will be included in your beginning trial balance entry usually completed by the company's accountant.

Paying a Taxable Bonus

When you pay employees a bonus, you create an unscheduled payroll. This payroll is included in their total taxable wages. To do so, complete the following steps:

1. Click **Employees**, **Pay Employees** and select the **Unscheduled Payroll** option. The Enter Payroll Information dialog displays.

2. Place a check mark next to the employee(s) receiving a bonus check. Note: QuickBooks might display a warning that a paycheck already exists for the date you have selected. Click **Continue** to close the warning.

3. You are returned to the Enter Payroll Information dialog, and if the employee is paid hourly, you can adjust the hours from the regular pay column.

4. Often, you want to edit or remove the default Gross Earnings or Federal Taxes Withheld on a bonus check. To adjust this detail, on the same Enter Payroll Information dialog, click the **Open Paycheck Detail** button to modify the default amounts.

5. If you are using Intuit's Enhanced Payroll subscription, you can also select the check box to **Enter Net/Calculate Gross** on the paycheck detail. Selecting this option enables you to specify the net amount and QuickBooks then calculates what the gross amount should be to cover taxes and withholdings.

6. QuickBooks might display a warning dialog titled "Special Calculation Situation" to inform you that certain payroll items have reached their limits.

7. In the example shown in Figure 14.30, the Federal Withholding amount that was automatically calculated was removed. QuickBooks now shows that this paycheck was adjusted.

Adjust paychecks cautiously, making sure that you do not adjust those items that have a predefined tax table amount, such as Social Security and Medicare. If you do, and the adjustment causes the calculated totals to be incorrect for the year, QuickBooks "self adjusts" the taxes on the next payroll check you create for this employee. You should also obtain the advice of your tax accountant before adjusting taxes withheld on bonus payroll checks.

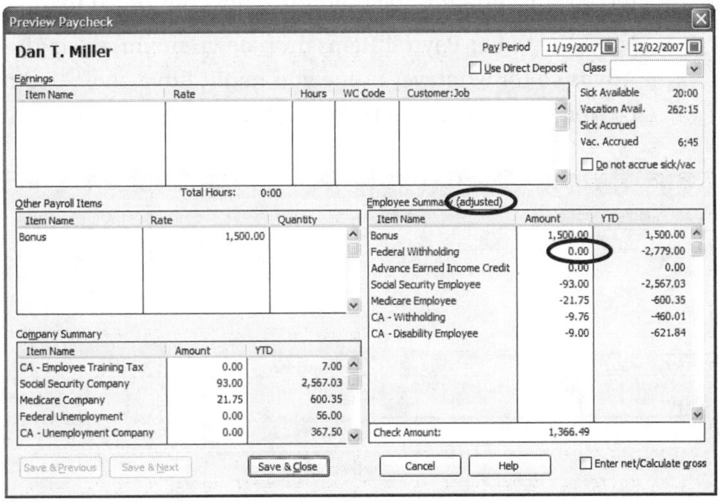

FIGURE 14.30
QuickBooks identifies when a paycheck has been adjusted.

Employee Loan Payment and Repayment

Your business might offer a loan to an employee in advance of payroll earnings. This amount should not be taxed at the time of payment if you expect the loan to be paid back to the company.

Creating the Employee Loan Payment Check

When you offer to pay employees an advance on their earnings, you are creating a loan payment check. If this is a loan to be paid back to the company, follow these steps:

1. Click **Employees**, **Pay Employees** and select **Unscheduled Payroll** to open the Enter Payroll Information dialog.

2. Place a check mark next to the employee you are creating the loan check for.

3. QuickBooks might warn that a paycheck for that period already exists. Click **Continue** if you want to create the loan payment check. You are returned to the Enter Payroll Information dialog.

4. To modify the check to be an employee loan check, click the **Open Paycheck Detail** button from the same Enter Payroll Information dialog.

5. Remove any amounts from the Earnings box (if you expect to be repaid this amount, the amount is not considered taxable earnings).

6. From the Other Payroll Items drop-down menu, select the **Employee Advance** (or whatever name you might have given it) Addition type payroll item, as shown in Figure 14.31, and skip to step 15.

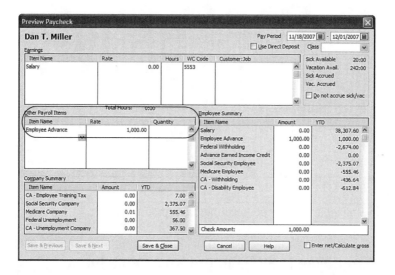

FIGURE 14.31

Use an Addition type payroll item in the Other Items pane to record a nontaxable loan (advance).

If you do not have an employee advance Addition type payroll item, you can easily create one right from this Preview Paycheck dialog. Click **Add New** from the **Other Payroll Items** pane drop-down menu, as shown in Figure 14.32, and continue with step 7.

7. From the Add new payroll item dialog, select the button for the **Addition** type and click **Next**.

8. The Add new payroll item (Addition) dialog opens. Name the item
   Employee Advance (do not select the Track Expenses by Job box).
   Click **Next**.

9. The Expense account dialog opens. From the drop-down menu, select
   your **Employee Loans, Other Current Asset** account. You can also
   scroll to the top of this menu and click **Add New** in this dialog to create the Other Current Asset account. (See Chapter 2 for more details on
   creating accounts.) Click **Next**.

10. For the **Tax Tracking** type from the drop-down menu, select **None**
    (at the top of the list) and click **Next**.

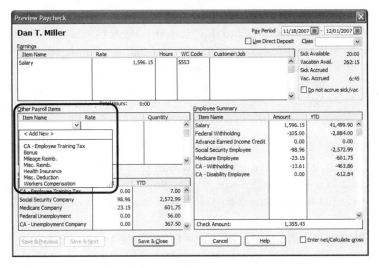

FIGURE 14.32
Easily create your employee loan addition item from the Preview Paycheck dialog.

Rescue Me!

Carefully consider what option you choose when selecting the Tax
Tracking type for a new payroll item or editing an existing payroll
item. The selection you choose here affects how QuickBooks taxes or
doesn't tax the payroll item on paychecks and how QuickBooks handles reporting the payroll item on forms, such as the W-2 form given
to employees at the end of a calendar year.

When you select each Tax Tracking type, QuickBooks provides detailed
information about how it will be treated for tax calculations and form
preparation. Be sure to take the time to read these. If you are unsure
of the proper tax tracking type, consult your accounting professional.

11. The Taxes dialog opens. On this dialog, do not select any of the options, but leave the defaults. Then, click **Next**.

12. The Calculate Based on Quantity dialog opens. Leave the default of **Neither** selected and click **Next**.

13. In the Gross vs. Net dialog, leave the default of **Gross**. This setting has no impact because you are setting it up with a tax tracking type of None. Click **Next**.

14. The Default Rate and Limit dialog opens. Leave it blank because you define the limit amounts individually for each employee. Click **Finish** to close the Add new payroll item setup or Edit payroll item setup dialog.

15. You are returned to the Preview Paycheck dialog. From the **Other Payroll Items** pane, in the **Item Name** column, select the **Employee Advance** payroll addition item from the drop-down menu. Enter the dollar amount of the loan you are providing the employee in the **Rate** column. QuickBooks creates a payroll advance check without deducting any payroll taxes (see Figure 14.31 shown previously). (Note: You do not need to enter anything in the Quantity column.)

Now, QuickBooks has on record a loan paid to the employee. If you have defined payment terms with the employee, you need to edit the employees' record so that on future payroll checks the agreed to amount will be deducted.

Automatically Deducting the Employee Loan Repayments

When a company provides an advance to an employee that is to be paid back over time in installments, you can have QuickBooks automatically calculate this amount and even stop when the total of the loan has been completely paid back to the company.

Follow these steps to record a payroll deduction on the employee's setup so that QuickBooks automatically deducts loan repayments from future payroll checks.

1. From the icon bar in QuickBooks, click the Employee Center to open the list of employees.

2. Select the employee who was given a payroll advance or loan.

3. Click the **Edit Employee** button from the **Employee Center**. The Edit Employee dialog opens.

4. From the **Change tabs** drop-down menu, select the **Payroll and Compensation Info** menu. The Payroll tab dialog opens.

5. In the Additions, Deductions, and Company Contributions pane, in the Item column, select your **Employee Loan Repay** deduction item (and skip to step 15) or click **Add New** to open the Add new payroll item dialog.

6. If creating a new item, select type **Deduction**.

7. Name the item **Employee Loan Repay** and click **Next**.

8. The Add new payroll item (Deduction) dialog opens. Leave the Agency Name and Number field blank. For the Liability account, select the drop-down menu and choose your Employee Loans, Other Current Asset account created previously when you created the employee advance check. Click **Next**.

9. The Tax Tracking type dialog opens. Leave the default for **Tax Tracking** type of **None** and click **Next**.

10. The Taxes dialog opens. Accept the default of none of them selected and click **Next**.

11. The Calculate Based on Quantity dialog opens. Leave the default of **Neither** selected and click **Next**.

12. The Gross vs. Net dialog opens. Leave the default of **Gross**. This setting has no impact because you are setting it up with a tax tracking type of None. Click **Next**.

13. The Default Rate and Limit dialog opens. Leave it blank, because you define the limit amounts individually for each employee. Click **Finish** to return to the New Employee or Edit Employee payroll info pane.

14. From the Additions, Deductions, and Company Contributions pane in the Item Name column, select a line. From the drop-down menu, choose the **Employee Loan Repay** deduction item that was just created.

15. In the **Amount** column, enter the per pay period amount you want to deduct.

16. In the **Limit** column, enter the amount of the total loan. QuickBooks stops deducting the loan when the limit is reached. Click **OK** to record your changes to the employee setup.

QuickBooks is now properly set up to deduct the stated amount on each paycheck until the employee loan has been fully paid back. If you provide additional employee loans, do not forget to go back to step 16 and add the new amount to the previous loan total.

Reporting Employee Loan Details

It is equally important to track the actual details of the employee loan. Use a modified version of my favorite report, Custom Transaction Detail report (as shown in Figure 14.33), following these steps:

1. Click **Reports, Custom Transaction Detail Report**. The Modify Report dialog displays.

2. From the **Report Date Range** drop-down menu, choose the date range you are reviewing.

3. In the **Columns** pane, select or deselect the detail you want to see displayed on the report.

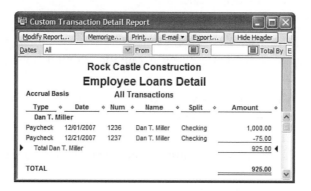

FIGURE 14.33

Create a report to track your employee loan details.

4. From the **Total by** drop-down menu, select **Employee**.

5. Click the **Filters** tab; Account is already selected in the Choose Filters pane. From the **Account** drop-down menu to the right, select the **Employee Loans**, Other Current Asset account.

6. In the Choose Filters pane, select the **Amount** filter and optionally select an amount greater than or equal to .01. Doing so provides a report of only those employees with non-zero balances.

7. Optionally, click the **Header/Footer** tab and customize the report title.

8. Click **OK** to view the modified report.

9. Optionally, click **Memorize** to save the report for use later.

You are now prepared to advance money to an employee and track the employee's payments against the loan accurately. Don't forget to review the balances and to increase the limit when new loans are paid out.

Adjusting an Employee Paycheck

Few reasons exist why you should adjust a paycheck record in QuickBooks. However, one reason might be if you hand-prepared the check, and then later noticed that the net amount that QuickBooks calculated was different than your hand-prepared check net total.

In this example, the check amount cashed by the employee differs from what QuickBooks computed, so adjusting the QuickBooks paycheck is acceptable.

To adjust a prepared employee check before it is printed, or to adjust a paycheck that had the wrong amount in QuickBooks from what was recorded on the actual check, follow these steps:

1. Locate the paycheck in your checking register by clicking on **Check Register** from the **Banking** section on the QuickBooks Home page.

2. If you have multiple checking accounts, select the one that the paycheck was recorded to and click **OK** to open the bank register.

3. Find the check with the incorrect amount; open the paycheck form by double-clicking with your cursor on the check.

4. Click the **Paycheck Detail** button to display the detail of the check to be modified.

5. Click **Unlock Net Pay** and review the message that QuickBooks provides about cautiously changing net pay on existing checks. Click **OK** to close the message, as shown in Figure 14.34.

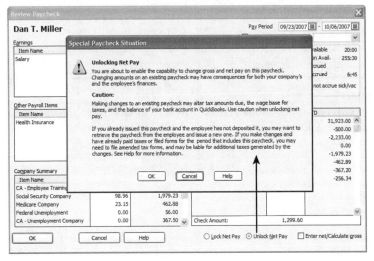

FIGURE 14.34

QuickBooks protects inadvertent changes by requiring you to unlock net pay before modifying a paycheck record.

6. Modify the check as needed, being careful not to modify the Social Security or Medicare taxes. In Figure 14.35, the Federal Withholding was modified, and the net check changed to reflect the actual check amount that cleared. (Your paycheck detail might vary depending on what payroll subscription you have purchased. The Enter Net/Calculate Gross option is available only with the Enhanced for Accountants payroll subscription.)

7. Click **OK** to close the paycheck detail dialog.

8. Click **Save & Close** to save the changes to the paycheck.

Cautiously consider the effect of changes you make to existing paychecks. To prevent these types of changes, consider setting a closing date password, discussed in Chapter 15.

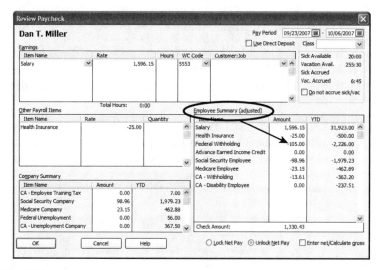

FIGURE 14.35

QuickBooks also identifies on the Preview Paycheck window when the automatically computed information was adjusted.

Sharing Data with Your Accountant or Your Client

- Sharing QuickBooks Data

- QuickBooks File Types

- Data Sharing for the Business Owner

- Data Sharing for the Accountant

Sharing QuickBooks Data

One feature that truly sets QuickBooks apart from other business accounting software is the ease and flexibility of sharing a copy of the data between the business owner and the accounting professional. With QuickBooks 2009, you will find sharing your or your client's data easier and more efficient than ever before with the Accountant's Copy file feature, greatly enhanced over the last couple of years.

Partner the Accountant's Copy functionality with the new Client Data Review feature, allowing the accountant to work smarter not harder! This Client Data Review feature is available in Intuit QuickBooks Premier Accountant 2009 and QuickBooks Enterprise Solutions Accountant 9.0. Additionally, accounting professionals that log into a client's file as the new External Accountant user have access to the Client Data Review tool in Intuit QuickBooks Pro 2009 and non-accountant Premier 2009 and Enterprise 9.0 editions.

To learn more about how this new feature adds power to an accountant's review of a client's data file, see Chapter 17, "New for 2009! Detecting and Correcting with the Client Data Review Feature."

Benefits for the Business Owner

As a business owner, you will want to have your accounting professional review your data; after all, you are using this data to make important management decisions. Additionally, you need to provide the results of your data to your accounting professional when preparing your federal and state tax returns.

So what might be some of the benefits of sharing your QuickBooks business data with your accountant?

- Your accountant can review your current financials and provide timely feedback without interrupting your day-to-day workflow. (Accountant's Copy File sharing method.)

- You have less stress because you do not need to prepare multiple reports for your accountant to review.

- You can share critical tasks with your accountant, such as reconciling a bank account. (Accountant's Copy File sharing method.)

- Your accountant can use your data to compile the information needed for your tax returns.

■ You can choose from multiple sharing methods, and select one that is just right for your business.

■ Periodic review of your data by your accountant can save precious time at year end and provide more accurate financials during the year.

Benefits for the Accountant

Periodically reviewing your client's data has become more important in recent years, as strict accounting guidelines are established. Often your clients are even unaware of these changes.

As an accountant, you can benefit from sharing your client's data by doing the following:

■ Working more efficiently by reviewing your client's data at your office at a time convenient for you or your staff.

■ Completing key reviewing tasks, while enabling your client to continue their day-to-day transactions. (Accountant's Copy File sharing method.)

■ Using the many accountant-specific tools to facilitate this review offered in your QuickBooks Premier Accountant or Enterprise Solutions Accountant including new for QuickBooks 2009 the Client Data Review feature.

■ Completing critical tasks for your client, such as reconciling a bank account making your services more valued by the client. (Accountant's Copy File sharing method.)

■ Providing your client with more frequent and timely analysis of their data.

This chapter is a guide for how both the business owner and the accountant can share QuickBooks data. Of particular interest are the improvements to the Accountant's Copy file sharing method in QuickBooks 2009, detailed in this chapter.

QuickBooks File Types

There is much flexibility in how a business owner or accountant can share a common QuickBooks data file. Some of the benefits of sharing data using the Accountant's Copy file were previously listed. This chapter discusses details of all the choices offered in facilitating this sharing.

Table 15.1 lists the common QuickBooks file types used for sharing data. Knowing these file types is important as you make decisions on the best method for your business or your clients' data sharing needs.

Table 15.1	QuickBooks File Types		
Extension	**File Type**	**Description**	**QuickBooks Editions***
.QBW	QuickBooks for Windows regular working file	This is the working data file type created when a user creates a new QuickBooks file. To open a .QBW file from within QuickBooks click File, Open or Restore Company and choose the Open a Company File option.	Simple Start Pro Premier (all editions) Enterprise (all editions)
.QBB	QuickBooks for Windows backup file	The most secure and complete method for protecting your data with a backup. Click File, Save Copy or Backup and choose the Backup Copy option.	Simple Start Pro Premier (all editions) Enterprise (all editions)
.QBM	QuickBooks for Windows portable company file	This is a compressed version of your QuickBooks .QBW data file. Used primarily to email or move the file to another location. Click File, Save Copy or Backup and choose the Portable Company File option.	Simple Start Pro Premier (all editions) Enterprise (all editions)
.QBX	Accountant's Copy (export file)	This file type is created by the business owner to save or send data to the accountant. Click File, Save Copy or Backup and choose the Accountant's Copy option.	Pro Premier (all editions) Enterprise (all editions)
.QBA	Accountant's Copy (converted .QBX file)	QuickBooks creates this file when open/convert a .QBX file is performed (usually by the accountant). Click File, Accountant's Copy and choose the Open and Convert Accountant's Copy Transfer File.	Pro Premier (all editions) Enterprise (all editions)

Extension	File Type	Description	QuickBooks Editions*
.QBY	Accountant's Copy (import file)	This is the file the accountant sends to the business owner after making changes. To import the accountant's changes click File, Accountant's Copy and choose Client Activities. Select Import Accountant's Changes.	Pro Premier (all editions) Enterprise (all editions)

*Not shown in Table 15.1 are QuickBooks Online and QuickBooks for Mac. Both of these versions have a different file structure, and neither of them supports the Accountant's Copy feature discussed at length in this chapter.

How the QuickBooks Year and Version Affect Your Data Sharing Choices

The choices of how you can share your or your clients' data depend on the version and release year of QuickBooks that you and your client use.

The QuickBooks product line includes Simple Start, Pro, Premier (general and industry-specific versions), Enterprise (general and industry-specific versions), QuickBooks for Mac, and QuickBooks Online.

Additionally, Intuit releases a new QuickBooks version each year, often represented by the year included in the name. For example, QuickBooks Premier 2009 is the Premier version usually released in the fall prior to the stated year. This version is separate from the updates that QuickBooks provides throughout a year to add functionality and fix issues discovered with a version.

To determine your current version and release, with QuickBooks open, press Ctrl+1. At the top of the Product Information dialog that displays is the product name (and industry edition if Premier or Enterprise), year, and release number.

So that you can see how the version year can affect your choices for sharing data, in this chapter I discuss the Accountant's Copy features, which are not available for Simple Start, QuickBooks Online, or the QuickBooks for Mac edition or for any QuickBooks product prior to the 2007 version.

Choosing a Method to Share Data

QuickBooks offers flexibility in how data is shared between a business owner and an accountant. Different methods can be used at different times during the year, depending on the nature of the changes to be made.

Options available might also be determined by the edition of QuickBooks you use and whether your data is in an older version of QuickBooks. The enhancements made in recent years for sharing your data with your accountant make it a perfect time to upgrade to the newest release.

To compare different QuickBooks products, go to www.intuit.com.

You might even choose to use multiple data sharing methods during the course of a year, after you know the advantages and limitations associated with each type.

Before choosing an option, review the pros and cons of each file type (shown earlier in Table 15.1) in the sections that follow.

.QBW: Regular Working Copy of the Data

This is the file type in which each client file is originally created. Here is a list of some of the advantages and limitations of sharing this type of data file:

- The accountant *cannot* take the file to his office and work in the file and later merge changes into the business owner's file.

- The accountant has access to all transaction activities.

- The accountant can access this file at the business owner's office or with a remote Internet-assisted program (QuickBooks partners with Remote Access by WebEx).

- The file often can be too large to send as an attachment in an email.

.QBB: QuickBooks Backup File

This file type remains as it has for years—it's the best choice for securing a data backup of your work. If needed, this file can be restored to a .QBW file. Here is a list of some of the advantages and limitations of sharing this type of data file:

- The file cannot be opened first without being restored. To restore a backup file, click File, Open or Restore Company and select the Restore a Backup Copy option.

- When restored, the file extension becomes a .QBW (see the pros and cons listed earlier).

- Changes made to a restored version of this file type *cannot* be merged later into the original data file.

.QBM: QuickBooks Portable Company File

This file type has been offered only for a couple of years; however, it does not replace the usefulness of the QuickBooks .QBB file type. Here is a list of some of the advantages and limitations of sharing this type of data file:

- The compressed file size makes a .QBM a perfect choice for attaching to an email or moving from one computer location to another.
- The file type does not replace a .QBB backup because it lacks some of the needed transaction logs.
- The file cannot be opened until it is restored. To restore a portable company file, click File, Open or Restore Company and select the Restore a Portable File option.
- When restored, the file extension becomes a .QBW (see the pros and cons listed earlier).
- Changes made to a restored version of this file type *cannot* be merged later into the original data file.

.QBX: Accountant's Copy (Export File)

As a business owner, if you choose to share your data with your accountant using the Accountant's Copy functionality, this is the file type that will be sent to your accounting professional. Here is a list of some of the advantages and limitations of sharing this type of data file:

- This file type is created by the business owner and enables your accountant to review and make needed changes to your data while you continue recording your day-to-day transactions in the file at your office.
- Any changes or additions your accountant makes *can* be imported (merged) into your company's data file. (There are some limitations on what changes can be shared, as noted in the section "What the Accountant Cannot Do.")
- The compressed file size makes it a perfect choice for attaching to an email or moving from one computer location to another.
- The file type does not replace a .QBB backup because it lacks some of the needed transaction logs.
- The file cannot be opened; it must be converted to a .QBA file type. The accountant will convert this file to a .QBA file type from within the QuickBooks Premier Accountant or QuickBooks Enterprise Accountant software.

.QBA: Accountant's Copy (Working File)

Only the accountant will work with this type of file, converted in the accounting professionals Premier Accountant or Enterprise Solutions Accountant. Here is a list of some of the advantages and limitations of sharing this type of data file:

- This file type is a converted .QBX file and is created by the accountant from within the QuickBooks Premier Accountant or QuickBooks Enterprise Solutions Accountant.

- The .QBA file type is the file that the accountant will open and make changes to. It will be converted to a .QBY file for the client to import.

- The file can be saved to your computer and opened and closed as needed while you (the accountant) do your review work.

.QBY: Accountant's Copy (Import File)

The business owner receives this file from the accountant, and it includes any accounting changes made to the original .QBX file. Here is a list of some of the advantages and limitations of sharing this type of data file:

- This file type is created by the accountant in the Export Changes function found in the QuickBooks Premier Accountant and QuickBooks Enterprise Solutions Accountant software.

- The file includes the changes made by the accountant to the original .QBX file the business owner provided the accountant.

- The file cannot be opened; it must be imported into the data file that *originally created* the Accountant's Copy data file. For details on how to use this file type, see the section titled "Importing Your Accountant's Changes" later in this chapter.

QuickBooks offers your business many options in how you want to share your data with your accountant. Select a solution that works for both you and your accountant.

Data Sharing for the Business Owner

Few business owners with whom I have worked over the years have a college degree in accounting. That situation is exactly what makes QuickBooks so appealing to a growing business: You don't need to be an accountant to use it. However, you will need an accountant to review your financials, perhaps at tax time or when you need a statement of your business's financial condition to give to a bank when requesting a business loan.

QuickBooks provides several different methods of sharing data with your accountant. See the previous Table 15.1 for details on the QuickBooks file types the business owner can choose.

When Your Accountant Is Using QuickBooks 2009

If you are using a version of QuickBooks 2008 or newer or Enterprise Solutions version 8.0 or newer and you choose to share your data using the Accountant's Copy feature, your accountant can use the QuickBooks 2009 Premier Accountant or Enterprise Solutions Accountant 9.0 version to open your 2008, or 2009 company file and make changes. When the file is returned with the accountant's changes, you will be able to import the changes back into your QuickBooks file, even though the accountant used a newer version of QuickBooks. The QuickBooks Premier Accountant 2009 and Enterprise Solutions Accountant 9.0 offer a level of what is considered backward compatibility.

If you are sharing any other file type (other than the Accountant's Copy) with your accountant, there is no backward compatibility. When your accountant restores a .QBB (backup) or .QBM (portable) company file in her 2009 version, the file will be updated to 2009; if the file is returned to you, you need to update your QuickBooks version to the same release year as your accountant.

For example, suppose you are currently using a QuickBooks 2008 version. Your accountant is using QuickBooks 2009 Premier Accountant. When your accountant restores your QuickBooks file backup, she will have to update the file to the QuickBooks 2009 release. If your accountant returns the data to you, you will only be able to open it with QuickBooks 2009 software.

So, as you decide which method to use, consider discussing with your accountant the QuickBooks version you are using. QuickBooks accountants who have serviced companies for many years often have several versions of QuickBooks installed.

However, only QuickBooks Enterprise Solutions software can open another Enterprise data file. If you open a Simple Start, Pro, or Premier data file with the Enterprise Solutions software you will no longer be able to open the same data file in its original QuickBooks edition.

Reviewing Your QuickBooks Data

No matter what method you choose to share your data file with your accountant, one of the most important things you can do is review your data for accuracy, especially in the areas of Accounts Payable and Accounts Receivable—areas that you will know better than your accountant.

To begin, pick a chapter of this book that covers the area of QuickBooks that you need to review. You might want to start with Chapter 4, "Easily Review Your QuickBooks Data." This chapter shows you quick and easy data checks that you can do before your accountant formally reviews your data. Performing this quick review can also help you identify any potential errors for which you will need your accountant's consulting advice when correcting.

Using the Accountant's Copy Feature

The Accountant's Copy method of sharing your data can be the most efficient because it enables your accountant to work in the data file from her office without interrupting your day-to-day work pattern.

 Rescue Me!

Only the Admin or new External Accountant user can create an Accountant's Copy or import the .QBY Accountant's Copy import file that contains the changes the accountant made to your data.

You must consider the following before making the choice to use the Accountant's Copy file sharing type:

- If you choose to create an Accountant's Copy, you want to determine how you will get the Accountant's Copy data file to your accountant. QuickBooks version 2008 and 2009 offer you these options:

  - Send an encrypted copy of your data to your accountant via Intuit's free secure Accountant's Copy File transfer service.

  - Attach the saved file to an email.

  - Copy it to a storage device such as a USB drive or CD.

- You also will be required to set a dividing date, as shown in Figure 15.1. The dividing date is a specific date in the past that determines the restrictions you and your accountant will have when adding or editing transactions.

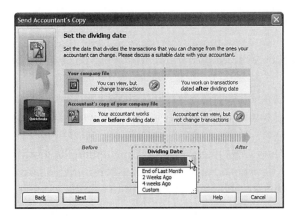

FIGURE 15.1

Setting a dividing date is required when creating an Accountant's Copy.

The following list briefly identifies the date restrictions with a dividing date in place when you share an Accountant's Copy of your data with your accountant. For example, if you choose a sample dividing date of 12/31/08, the following restrictions exist:

- **On or before the dividing date**—You cannot add, delete, or modify transactions. The accountant can add, delete, or modify transactions.

- **After the dividing date**—You can add, delete, or modify transactions. The accountant can add transactions but cannot delete or modify them.

Rescue Me!

When a dividing date or closing date is set, you cannot add, modify, delete, or void any transaction dated prior to the dividing date or closing date, including nonposting documents such as estimates, sales orders, and purchase orders. This limitation can be terribly inconvenient for the business owner, so discuss it ahead of time with your accountant. If appropriate, you should change the date of these open "nonposting" documents to a date after the expected dividing date or closing date.

See the section titled, "What the Business Owner Can and Cannot Do" for any restrictions that affect you, the business owner.

Preparing an Accountant's Copy of Your Data

To create an Accountant's Copy of your data that your accountant can review and modify while you continue to do your daily transactions, follow these steps:

1. Close all your active QuickBooks windows, and then click **File**, **Accountant's Copy** and choose **Client Activities**. Click the **Save File** menu option to open the Save As Accountant's Copy dialog.

2. Choose the **Accountant's Copy** option, as shown in Figure 15.2. (The other option includes the Portable Company or Backup file; both will not allow the accountant to export any changes made or you to import the changes.)

3. Click **Next**. The Set the Dividing Date dialog opens.

4. From the **Dividing Date** drop-down menu, choose one of the date options as previously shown in Figure 15.1, or choose **Custom** to select your own specific dividing date. (See the section titled "Using the Accountant's Copy Feature" for how the date affects your data entry options.)

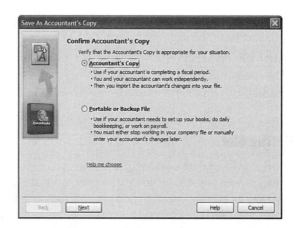

FIGURE 15.2

Saving a file as an Accountant's Copy creates a file that your accountant can work in and later merge the changes with your file.

5. Click **Next**. QuickBooks opens the Save Accountant's Copy dialog, where you can browse your computer for the location where you want to save the Accountant's Copy export file (.QBX file).

6. Click the **Save** button. QuickBooks provides the message shown in Figure 15.3, indicating that you successfully created an Accountant's Copy and telling you where the file was stored, as well as other useful information.

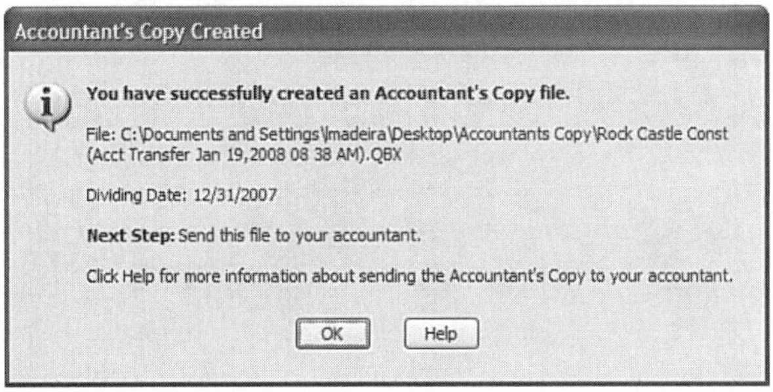

FIGURE 15.3
After you click Save, QuickBooks provides information about where the file was saved.

> **7.** Click **OK**. As shown in Figure 15.4, the QuickBooks title bar now identifies your file as having Accountant's Changes Pending.

FIGURE 15.4
Your QuickBooks title bar will indicate whether you have accountant's changes pending.

> **8.** Now send this file to your accountant (it will have a .QBX extension) as an email attachment, or copy it to a removable data storage device. Or for QuickBooks 2008 or newer, you can use the method of encrypting your data through the new Intuit Secure Accountant's Copy file transfer service (see the next section).

Sending the File via Intuit's Secure Accountant's Copy File Transfer Service

Offered with the 2008 and newer versions of QuickBooks Pro, Premier, and Enterprise is the option to use a secure, Intuit-hosted site to encrypt and transfer data to your accountant without needing to create a file and attach it to an email.

Follow these steps to send data to your accountant with the new encrypted file service:

> **1.** Click **File, Accountant's Copy** and choose **Client Activities**. Click **Send to Accountant**. The Confirm sending an Accountant's Copy dialog, shown in Figure 15.5, appears, further detailing the service and what types of shared work are recommended with this type of file and what types are not.

FIGURE 15.5

Confirming dialog that the Accountant's Copy is the appropriate choice for the shared work you and your accountant will be doing.

2. Click **Next**. The Set the Dividing Date dialog appears.

3. From the **Dividing Date** drop-down menu, choose one of the date options shown in Figure 15.1, or choose **Custom** to select your own specific dividing date. (See the previous section titled "Preparing an Accountant's Copy of Your Data" for how the date affects your data entry options.)

4. Click **Next**. The Information for sending the file (1 of 2) dialog appears, as shown in Figure 15.6. In it, you indicate the email address to notify your accountant and your name and return email. Your accountant will receive an email notification that your data file is ready to download. The download is only available for 14 days.

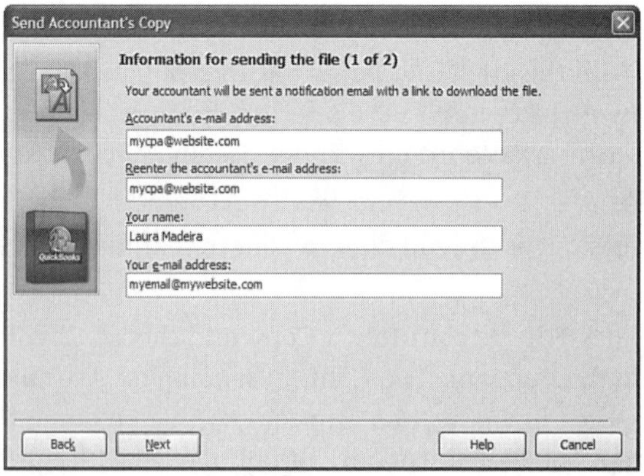

FIGURE 15.6

Identify the email address you want your accountant notified at, as well as your own name and email address.

5. Click **Next**. The Information for sending the file (2 of 2) dialog appears, as shown in Figure 15.7.

6. Enter a strong password that is seven characters long and contains at least one capital letter and one digit. Optionally, type a note to your accountant but do not include the password in the communication.

7. Click **Send**. QuickBooks gives you a message that the .QBX transfer file is being sent.

8. Click **OK** to the message that QuickBooks has to close all windows to create the Accountant's Copy. Note: QuickBooks also provides an information message only (no action to be taken) that the transfer might take a few minutes, even though it might seem as if it's not being responsive.

9. Click **OK** on the QuickBooks Information dialog that appears, indicating the file was sent successfully.

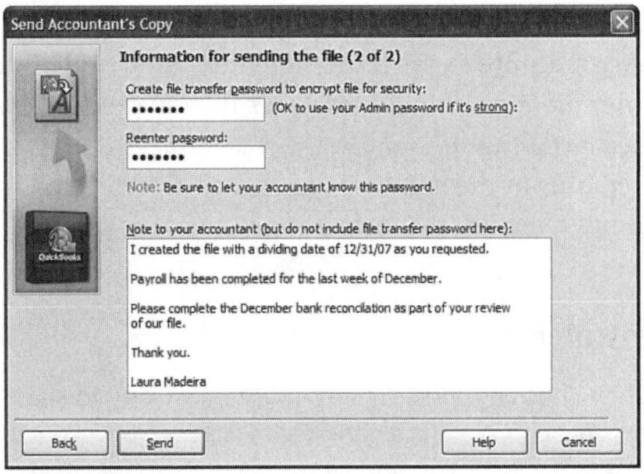

FIGURE 15.7

Set a strong password and add an optional note for your accountant.

The QuickBooks title bar identifies your file as having Accountant's Changes Pending, as shown earlier in Figure 15.4. This title bar change indicates you have successfully created a file for your accountant to review, edit, modify, and later return the changes to you without interrupting your work.

What the Business Owner Can and Cannot Do

The QuickBooks release in 2009 further improves the Accountant's Copy features for both the accountant and business owner. With this newly enhanced Accountant's Copy, your accountant can be assured that the information in the file she is working in will not change for dates prior to the dividing date.

The following list details what you can and cannot do with your data file while an Accountant's Changes are pending:

- **Transactions**—You can add, edit, and modify transactions with a date after the dividing date.

- **Accounts**—You can add a new chart of accounts list item.

- **Subaccounts**—You cannot add a subaccount to an existing account.

- **Editing, merging, or inactivating accounts**—You cannot edit, merge, or inactivate a chart of accounts item (your accountant can).

- **Editing lists (other than the chart of accounts)**—You can add, edit, and inactivate your list items. If you and your accountant make changes to the same item, the accountant's changes will override your changes.

- **Deleting lists**—You cannot delete or merge list items (your accountant can).

- **Reconciling the bank account**—In the .QBW file with pending Accountant's Copy, if the statement date and all transactions involved into the reconciliation are *after* the dividing date and accountant didn't reconcile this account in the Accountant's Copy, reconciliation work remains in the .QBW file after the import. Bank reconciliations for dates *on or before* the dividing date are rolled back at the import time.

Rescue Me!

When choosing to use the Accountant's Copy to share your data, you can only complete the bank reconciliation for reconciliations where the bank statement date and all transactions to be cleared are dated after the selected dividing date.

This is a new option and is only available in QuickBooks 2009 data files. (See the section in this chapter titled "Preparing an Accountant's Copy of Your Data.")

Click Banking, Reconcile and choose your bank account. The bank reconciliation dialog opens. On this dialog you must enter the following dates to begin reconciling the bank account (see Figure 6.1 in Chapter 6, "Bank Account Balance or Reconciliation Errors"):

■ **Statement Date**—Must be a date *after* the specified dividing date (see the section in this chapter titled, "Preparing an Accountant's Copy of Your Data")

■ **Service Charge Date**—Must be a date *after* the specified dividing date

■ **Interest Earned Date**—Must be a date *after* the specified dividing date

Your bank reconciliation work will remain after the import of your accountant's changes if:

■ None of the transactions that you mark as cleared are dated on or before the Accountant's Copy dividing date.

■ Your accountant did *not* also complete a bank reconciliation for the same bank account.

■ Your accountant doesn't undo any reconciliations for this account in the Accountant's Copy.

You might still want to proceed with the reconciliation now, even if it might be rolled back later, to verify that your books are correct.

Importing Your Accountant's Changes

When you make an Accountant's Copy from your data file, QuickBooks creates a file for you to give to your accountant. Your accountant then works in this file, adding and editing transactions, and even reconciling your bank account. When the accountant finishes with the review, she exports the changes for you, and QuickBooks creates a file with the extension of .QBY, also referred to as the Accountant's Copy (import file).

To successfully import your accountant's changes, follow these steps:

1. Make sure your accountant has given you the QuickBooks file with the .QBY extension.

2. With your QuickBooks data file open, verify that the title bar indicates that the accountant's changes are pending (refer to Figure 15.4). You might also see the message shown in Figure 15.8 when you open your data file. To begin the import, go to step 3.

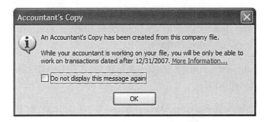

FIGURE 15.8

The message you get when QuickBooks opens the data file indicating that your accountant's changes are pending.

   3. Click **File**, **Accountant's Copy** and select **Client Activities**. Click the **Import Accountant's Changes** menu option.

   4. Browse to the location where you stored the .QBY Accountant's Copy (import file) your accountant sent to you.

   5. Select the file and click **Open**. The Incorporate Accountant's Changes dialog opens, enabling you to view the details of the changes to be imported (see Figure 15.9).

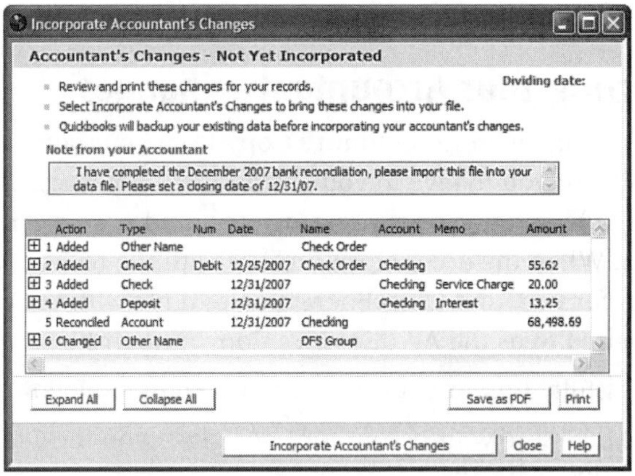

FIGURE 15.9

View the accountant's changes and notes before they are imported into your data.

   6. Click the + in front of a transaction to see more details about that specific transaction, or click **Expand All** to see the details of all the transactions.

   7. Click **Print** or **Save As PDF** to save the details for your future reference.

   8. Click the **Incorporate Accountant's Changes** button when you have finished reviewing the changes.

9. The Accountant Import dialog opens, instructing you to close any open QuickBooks windows. Click **OK**.

10. The *Save Backup Copy* dialog opens, indicating that you must first make a backup of your data before the import. In the **Save In** drop-down choose a location to save the backup file and in the **File Name** field, type a name if you don't want to accept the default name provided. Click **Save**.

11. Click **OK** to close the message that informs you where the backup was stored. QuickBooks displays a progressive message that it is incorporating the changes. When it is finished, the Accountant's Changes Incorporated dialog appears.

12. Click **Close** after viewing the accountant's changes that were incorporated. Click **Print** or **Save As PDF** if you did not do so earlier. This is your last opportunity to do so.

13. Click **OK** to complete the process or **Cancel** if you want to return and print the details.

14. Click **Yes** in the Closing Date dialog if your accountant has asked you to set a closing date. I recommend that you set a closing date the same as the dividing date to protect the accountant's work. Beginning with QuickBooks 2009, your accountant might have already included a closing date for you in the imported file. If a closing date was set, you will see the details on the Incorporate Accountant's Changes report you view prior to importing the changes.

 Digging Deeper

When the accountant's changes are imported, the dividing date and all the restrictions associated with it are removed. The accountant can include with his changes a closing date that transfers to your file so that you do not inadvertently add, delete, or modify transactions prior to the closing date. The Incorporate Accountant's Changes report that you preview prior to importing your accountant's changes will show if a closing date was already set by your accountant.

15. If you selected **Yes** to setting a closing date, the Company Preference window appears. Click the **Set Closing Date** button. The Set Closing Date and Password dialog appears.

16. Enter an optional password and a closing date—typically the same date that was used for the dividing date.

17. Click **OK** to accept the closing date and optional closing date password.

18. To be certain that the Closing Date control is managed properly, review all users for their specific rights for changing transactions prior to a closing date. Click **Company**, **Set Up Users and Passwords** and select the **Setup Users** menu to open the User List dialog. (This is the menu path for QuickBooks Pro or Premier Edition menu; QuickBooks Enterprise Solutions Edition has more robust security setting options not discussed in detail in this book.)

19. To view existing security by user, from the User List dialog opened in the previous step, select the user with your cursor and click the **View User** button, as shown in Figure 15.10.

FIGURE 15.10

To see the user's specific security rights in summary, click the View User button.

20. The View user access dialog opens, as shown in Figure 15.11. Any user who should not have rights to change closed period transactions should have an "N" appearing in the last menu option in the Create column.

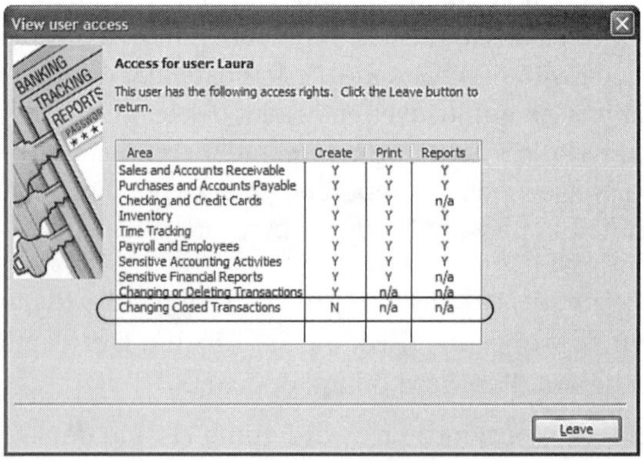

FIGURE 15.11

You can easily view the user's access rights from one summary window.

21. If after reviewing the access for each employee you need to edit this setting for an employee, click **Leave** to close the View User Access dialog.

22. You are returned to the User List dialog. With your cursor, select the employee and click **Edit User**.

23. The Access for User dialog opens. Choose the **Selected Areas** option and click **Continue** through the screens until you reach page 9 of 10, as shown in Figure 15.12. Click **Next** (page 10 of 10) to see a summary of the employee's security settings or **Finish** to return to the User List dialog.

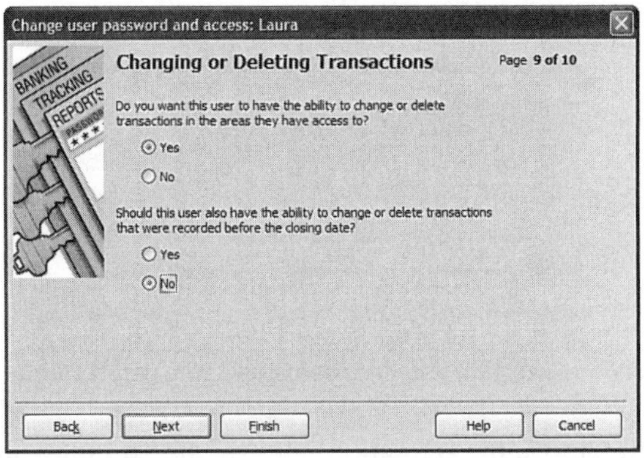

FIGURE 15.12
On the second option, place a mark in the No button to prevent the user from changing transactions in closed periods.

24. Click **Close**.

Canceling an Accountant's Copy

It's possible for you to cancel an accountant's copy of your data if necessary. The following are some of the reasons to cancel the accountant's changes:

- Your accountant has delayed the review of your file.

- You have found corrections you would like to make prior to the dividing date.

- You cannot modify nonposting documents (purchase orders, sales orders, and estimates) dated prior to the dividing date.

- Your accountant needs to work in your file without any transaction restrictions, making an appointment to come to your office to work or perform the work remotely via the Internet.

Before canceling or removing restrictions on your data file, discuss this option with your accountant. After the Accountant's Copy is canceled, your accountant's changes file cannot be imported into your data file.

To remove the restrictions placed on your file by an Accountant's Copy, click File, Accountant's Copy and choose the Remove Restrictions menu option. The Remove Restrictions dialog appears, warning you that your accountant will no longer be able to import her changes back into your file, as shown in Figure 15.13.

FIGURE 15.13

The Remove Restrictions warning you get when canceling an Accountant's Copy file.

After you remove the restriction from the file, no more data restrictions are imposed by the dividing date, and the top bar of your data file no longer displays the Accountant's Changes Pending message.

Data Sharing for the Accountant

Earlier, Table 15.1 listed the types of QuickBooks files with which business owners and accountants have the options of working. This section discusses the options from the perspective of the accountant.

As the accountant, you will want to review the variety of file types and the pros and cons of using each file type for sharing data with your client as discussed in the section titled "QuickBooks File Types" earlier in this chapter.

Digging Deeper

If you're not sure in which year's release your client's .QBW or .QBA data file type was last opened, use Windows Explorer to locate the file, and place the cursor over the file supplied by your client (as shown in Figure 15.14). QuickBooks gives you important information about the file, including the following:

- Type of file (QuickBooks Company or QuickBooks Accountant's Copy file)

- Date modified

- Size of the file

- Last opened with QuickBooks 200x

However, this tool will give you this information only for the .QBW windows working file or the .QBA, the Accountant's Copy working file. Other file types do not display the same information.

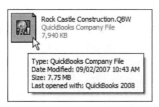

FIGURE 15.14

Use Windows Explorer to determine in what year's version your client's .QBW file type was created.

Creating an External Accountant User Type

New for QuickBooks 2009 is the option to create a new user "type." If you log into the client's data file as an External Accountant you will:

- Separate the changes you make in the data file from the changes your client makes.

- Use the Client Data Review feature more efficiently (see Chapter 17 for more information).

- Access all areas of QuickBooks except creating new users or viewing sensitive customer credit card numbers.

To create this unique type of user, you must be logged into the data file as the Admin user and you or the client must create the new user *before* the client creates the Accountant's Copy file for your use.

You will then use this new login when you begin working with the client's data file.

Another important feature of the new External Accountant type user designation is the ability to "unlock" the Client Data Review feature in the QuickBooks Pro 2009 or QuickBooks Premier 2009 (non-Accountant Edition versions). Certain limitations exist when using the Client Data Review feature in a client's Accountant Copy file. See Chapter 17 for more details.

Preparing Your Client for the Data Exchange

As an accounting professional, you probably will be able to choose the method you and your client use to share the data. However, you might not be able to control the condition in which you receive the file. I am speaking specifically of the accounting accuracy. Some accounting professionals don't worry much about this until they receive the data file; others might want their client to take certain steps to ensure the accuracy of the data before beginning the review. Encourage your clients to review specific chapters in this book to help better prepare their file for your review, making your review time more profitable!

Ask clients to review the following in their file before sharing the data with you:

- Accuracy of their book bank balances (QuickBooks 2008 and newer, Accountant's Copy feature will allow you to reconcile bank accounts for your client while they continue working)
- The open customer invoices in Accounts Receivable
- The unpaid vendor bills in Accounts Payable

Other critical numbers to review are usually easier to reconcile by asking for documents from sales tax authorities or from banks, such as bank loan documents, or comparing with filed payroll returns.

After your client has reviewed the information and provided the documents you requested, you are ready to choose a method for sharing the data with your client. Choose from one of the options discussed in the earlier section, "QuickBooks File Types."

Working with an Accountant's Copy File

After reviewing the advantages or limitations of each file type in the section titled "QuickBooks File Types," you can see that one of the most functional methods is the QuickBooks Accountant's Copy file feature. With it, your clients can continue their day-to-day accounting tasks, and from the convenience of your office you can review and make needed changes to their data, later importing these changes into the file they have been using.

 Digging Deeper

> If you are using QuickBooks Premier Accountant 2009 or QuickBooks Enterprise Solutions Accountant 9.0, you can convert your client's QuickBooks 2008 or newer Accountant's Copy file (.QBX file extension), work with it in your Premier Accountant 2009 or Enterprise Solutions Accountant 9.0, and return it to your client to import back into their QuickBooks 2008 or 2009 version! This feature is available only with the Accountant's Copy file-sharing feature and does not apply to other file types. (See the Rescue Me on page 442.)
>
> QuickBooks Premier can open a Simple Start, Pro, QuickBooks for Mac, or any of the Premier industry-specific editions, and when the file is returned to the client, they will be able to work again with the file in their product edition.
>
> When you open a Simple Start, Pro, or any of the Premier industry specific editions with QuickBooks Enterprise Solutions the file is converted to an Enterprise edition and cannot be opened again as Simple Start, Pro, Mac, or Premier product.

The functionality associated with changes allowed while working with an Accountant's Copy file has been improved with the release of QuickBooks 2009. More information will be provided later in this chapter on the specific transactions allowed or restricted.

Before your clients prepare an Accountant's Copy of their QuickBooks data for you (see the steps in the previous section titled "Preparing an Accountant's Copy of Your Data"), be sure to discuss the following with them:

- The dividing date selection. You should communicate what this should be.
- How current are the bank reconciliations in the data file? In the Accountant's Copy, your bank reconciliation work is returned to the client only for statement dates on or before the dividing date. Additionally, the client can only mark as cleared items dated after the Dividing Date. (See the Rescue Me! on Page 442.)

- Verify that the data file has users set up with restrictions for editing or modifying transactions prior to the closing date. (This step is optional, but when you are working in the Accountant's Copy file, you can send back with your changes the closing date. More details were provided previously in "Importing Your Accountant's Changes.")

- Instruct them *not* to cancel or remove restrictions on the Accountant's Changes Pending without first consulting you.

- Discuss with your clients the options for sending this file to you. New for QuickBooks 2009 and 2008, users have these options:

  - Send you an encrypted copy of their data via Intuit's secure Accountant's Copy File transfer service, a free service to you and your client. Be sure your client knows the email address where you would like to be notified.

  - Attach the saved file to an email.

  - Copy it to a storage device, such as a USB drive or CD.

If your client chooses the Intuit's Accountant's Copy File transfer service to get the data to you, you are notified at the email address the client provides in the transfer process, and you are directed to a secure site to download your client's file. This service offers your client simplicity in getting the data to you while aiding in the encrypted security of the transfer of sensitive data over the Internet. Downloads are only available for 14 days, so don't delay!

Have your client follow the steps to create and send to you the Accountant's Copy file of the data as outlined in the section, "Preparing an Accountant's Copy of Your Data."

Follow these steps to work with your client's Accountant's Copy (.QBX) file type your client sent to you or that you downloaded:

1. Click **File, Accountant's Copy** and choose **Open & Convert Accountant's Copy Transfer File**. The Open & Convert Accountant's Copy Transfer File dialog appears, as shown in Figure 15.15. This summary provides you with an overview of the workflow when using an Accountant's Copy.

2. Click **Next**. The What the Accountant's Copy Can and Cannot Do dialog appears, giving you another option to make sure this file type will work with the transaction types you will be adding or modifying.

3. Click **Next**. The Save As Accountant's Copy dialog opens.

4. You are directed to browse to the location where you stored the Accountant's Copy file (.QBX file extension). With your mouse pointer on the file, Click **Open**.

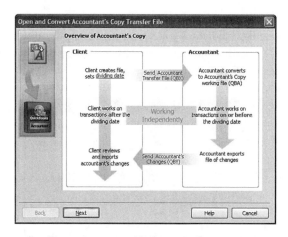

FIGURE 15.15

Overview of the Accountant's Copy workflow.

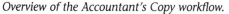

If you have not previously disabled this message, a QuickBooks Save As Accountant's Copy dialog appears, notifying you that the file will be converted and that prior to converting you need to name the new file and save it. Click **OK**.

5. In the Save As Accountant's Copy dialog choose a location and name for the new file. I usually put the accounting period being reviewed in the name, such as <Company Name_YE_12_31_07.QBA>, as in the example shown in Figure 15.16. Click **Save**, and QuickBooks will prompt with a message that the conversion is taking place.

FIGURE 15.16

When you save the file, give it a name that will help you identify it later.

If you have not previously disabled this warning, you will see the message that indicates you are opening an Accountant's Copy and shows you the dividing date that was chosen by your client, as shown in Figure 15.17.

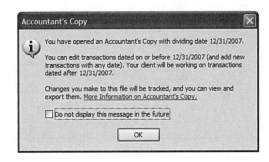

FIGURE 15.17

This is the QuickBooks notification that you are opening an Accountant's Copy file and the selected dividing date.

6. If you received the message in Step 5, click **OK** to close the message. (See the following sidebar, "Reinstate Warnings," for information about reenabling these one-time messages if they have been disabled.)

   Your QuickBooks 2009 Premier Accountant title bar will show that you are working with an Accountant's Copy and what the dividing date for that file is (see Figure 15.18).

> Rock Castle Construction (Acct Copy, Div Date 12/31/2007)

FIGURE 15.18

You can be certain you are working in the correct file by looking at the title bar of your Accountant's Copy .QBA file.

As the company's accounting professional, you can now review, add, and edit the data file, secure that your client cannot modify the balances prior to the dividing date that was set, all while the client continues her day-to-day accounting tasks.

Reinstate Warnings

If you do not see some of the dialogs mentioned in this section, a user might have selected the Do Not Display This Message (or Page, and so on, depending on which dialog is open) option, causing future users not to see these messages.

To turn these one-time messages back on:

1. Click **Edit**, **Preferences**. In the dialog that appears, choose **General** on the left side.

2. Click the **My Preferences** tab.

3. Place a check mark in the **Bring Back All One-Time Messages** box.

I often do this task in my client's file (prior to making an Accountant's Copy), especially if I have found errors that might have been prevented if the user had heeded the warning of a message.

What the Accountant Can Do

The release of QuickBooks 2009 greatly improves those tasks that you can do with an Accountant's Copy of your client's data.

The restrictions invoked by the dividing date set by your client affect your ability to add or edit transactions. If these restrictions prevent you from completing your tasks, you can convert the Accountant's Copy to a working QuickBooks data file (.QBW file extension). However, your changes cannot be imported into your client's file. See the section, "Converting the Accountant's Copy to a Regular Company File," later in this chapter, for more information.

The Accountant's Copy in QuickBooks 2008 and 2009 now provides a unique way to determine whether your changes will be sent back to the client. Any field that is colored beige will transfer back to your client. If the field is white, you might be able to modify it for your own purposes but the change will not be sent back to your client.

For example, if part of your correction to your client's file was to modify an existing list item, only the fields identified in Figure 15.19 would be sent back to your client's data file. All other fields can be modified for your purposes but would not transfer back to your client's file. If you and your client make changes to details on the same item, your changes will override the client's when the changes are imported.

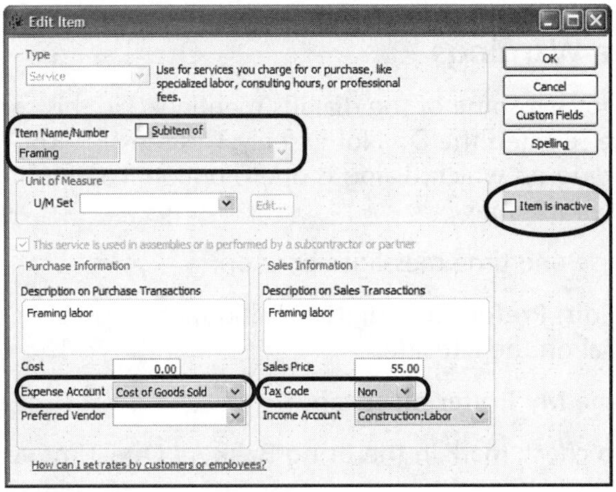

FIGURE 15.19

When adding or modifying your client's list items, note that any fields shaded beige (non-white) will be sent back to your client's file.

The following sections describe more specifically what you, the accountant, can do (with noted limitations) while working in the Accountant's Copy of your client's file.

Accounting Activities

With the release of QuickBooks 2008 and 2009 enhancements were made to the accounting activities that you can do with the client's data when sharing an Accountant's Copy file type.

- **Reconcile the bank statements for dates prior to the dividing date—** You can create and edit transactions necessary to perform the bank reconciliation. Additionally, your changes to a reconciled item will also be sent back to the client.

   New for QuickBooks 2009, your client can reconcile the bank account when the statement date and all cleared transactions are dated after the selected dividing date. However, if you *also* reconcile this account, her bank reconciliation work will be rolled back to the transactions cleared status as of the time the Accountant's Copy was created.

- **Set 1099 account mappings—**New for QuickBooks 2009, you can assign the proper chart of account to the Federal Form 1099 category.

- **Reconcile the bank statements for dates after the dividing date—** You can do this if it helps your review. However, these reconciliations will not be sent back to the client's data. Any transactions added will be sent back to the client.

- **Set tax-line mappings—**Used to assign the tax form line to a chart of accounts. Use this feature if you are integrating the QuickBooks data with Intuit's tax preparation software ProSeries or Lacerte.

QuickBooks Lists

Also enhanced with the release of QuickBooks 2008 and 2009 is your ability to manage your client's list items when performing data corrections.

- **Chart of Accounts—**No restrictions, including the ability to merge charts of account list items. (See Chapter 2, "Reviewing the QuickBooks Chart of Accounts," for more information about merging accounts.)

- **List Items—**In general you can add, edit, delete, and inactivate list items you create in the Accountant's Copy.

- **Items List—**For lists with items dated before the dividing date, you can edit the Item Name/Number, Subitem, Expense Account, Tax Code, and Income Account and also make the item inactive. So you know what changes will and won't be sent back to the client, beige fields represent fields that can be modified; your changes to these fields will be sent back to the client. Note: If you and your client both make changes to the same item, the accountant's changes will override that of the client when the changes are imported.

- **Customer, Other Names List—**Add to or edit the Name field only.

- **Vendor—**Add to or edit the Name and Social Security fields only. Your changes will override the same information in the client's file when imported.

- **Employee List—**Add to or edit the Name and Social Security fields only.

- **Class List, Fixed Asset Item—**New for 2009 is the ability to merge class list items. Additionally, you can add to or edit the Name field only.

- **Sales Tax Code—**Add to or edit the Name field only. No sales tax rates will be sent back to your client.

Transactions

Generally, you can add any transaction type before or after the dividing date with the following limitations on editing, voiding, or deleting:

- **Bills and checks**—Edit, void, or delete only those dated before the dividing date.

- **Vendor credits**—Add or delete, but don't edit or void before and after the dividing date.

- **Item receipts**—Add or delete, but don't edit or void before and after the dividing date.

- **Bill payments by credit card**—Add or delete, but don't edit or void before and after the dividing date.

- **Inventory quantity/value adjustments**—Add or delete, but don't edit or void before and after the dividing date.

- **Customer payments**—Add or delete, but don't edit or void before and after the dividing date.

 Rescue Me!

If you are working with a client's Accountant's Copy file created from a QuickBooks 2008 version, you will not have the same editing privileges listed earlier because the enhanced editing options were made available beginning with the QuickBooks 2008 and enhanced with the 2009 Accountant's Copy. Several of these options are recognized only when they're returned to a QuickBooks 2008 or newer data file.

With QuickBooks 2009, you have more features to help you work productively in your client's file while doing review work. Now is an excellent time to encourage your clients who share data with you to upgrade to QuickBooks 2009.

What the Accountant Cannot Do

Here is what you, the accountant, cannot do while working in the Accountant's Copy of your client's file:

- Payroll transactions.

- Nonposting transactions, such as estimates, sales orders, or purchase orders.

- Transfers of funds between accounts. Although you cannot use the transfer form, you can create the same effect on the accounts with a journal entry or deposit form.

- Build assemblies.

- Sales tax payments.

Although you cannot make changes to these types of transactions in your client's file with an Accountant's Copy file type, you can conveniently make these changes using Remote Access discussed in the section titled "QuickBooks Remote Access for Accountants" later in this chapter.

Returning the Accountant's Copy Change File to the Client

One of the most important features of using the Accountant's Copy to share your client's data is that when your changes are complete, you can send back an updated file for your client to import into her file.

For QuickBooks 2009, you can use the Accountant's Copy feature in your QuickBooks Premier Accountant (as well as QuickBooks Enterprise Solutions Accountant) to open and work with your client's 2008 or newer data file. After you complete the review and changes to the client's Accountant's Copy file, you can return the file to the client, so that she can open it in her 2008 or newer version.

Creating an Import File for Your Client

To return the corrected file to your client after you make all your changes, follow these steps:

1. Click **File**, **Accountant's Copy** and choose the **View/Export Changes for Client** to open the View/Export Changes for Client dialog, as shown in Figure 15.20.

2. Review your changes and add a note for your client. New for QuickBooks 2009, you can set the Closing Date in the Accountant's Copy of your client's file. The Closing Date setting is noted in the Incorporate Changes details for your client.

3. If you need to make additional changes or edit the changes you have made, click **Save Note & Close**.

4. If your changes are complete, click **Create Change File for Client**. The Save Accountant Change File To dialog appears.

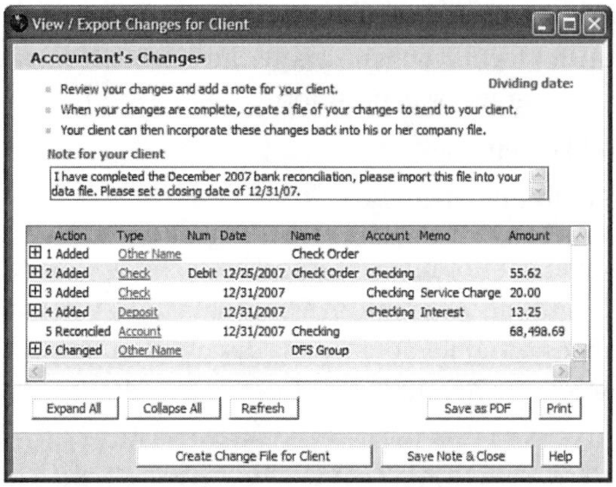

FIGURE 15.20

The View/Export Changes for Client dialog, where you can review your changes and include a note for your client.

> **5.** Browse to the location where you want to save the file and optionally edit the filename to be saved. QuickBooks creates a file with an extension of .QBY.
>
> **6.** If you have already exported these changes for the client, you will see the message in Figure 15.21 informing you that if your client has already imported the previously exported changes file, she will not be able to import these changes. Click **OK** if you still want to export the changes.

FIGURE 15.21

If you have previously exported the changes, QuickBooks provides this warning message.

> **7.** Click **Save**. A QuickBooks information dialog appears, letting you know the file was successfully created.
>
> **8.** Click **OK** to close the information message. QuickBooks returns you to the .QBA file.

To complete the process, simply give this newly created .QBY (Accountant's Copy import file) back to the client. You can copy it to a removable storage device or attach it to an email.

Instruct your client to follow the steps listed in the section, "Importing Your Accountant's Changes," to import your changes. Your client will be able to review your changes in detail before accepting or incorporating the changes into her file.

Instructing Your Client to Set a Closing Date

When your client imports the changes you have made to the Accountant's Copy of her file, the dividing date restrictions are removed. If you do not want the client to add or edit transactions prior to the dividing date, make sure that you also set a closing date prior to exporting the data for the client.

New for QuickBooks 2009 data files, when the accountant sets a closing date in the client's converted .QBA file (Accountant's Copy) the closing date will transfer back to the client's file and the client will *not* be asked to set the closing date. Information that a closing date was set is included in the information the client previews before incorporating the accountant's changes.

If you are working with a client's QuickBooks 2008 data Accountant's Copy, the import changes process takes the client to the Closing Date menu automatically, so if you communicated in your Accountant's Copy Changes note what the desired closing date should be, the changes you made to balances cannot be changed.

If your changes are not "fixed" and can be modified, you might not need your client to set a closing date, and she will be able to select No when asked to update the closing date and password.

Review the details of setting a closing date and reviewing each employee's access rights to changing transactions prior to the closing date in the section titled "Importing Your Accountant's Changes."

QuickBooks Remote Access for Accountants

If as the accountant you would like to take more control over the import of your changes into your client's file as well as setting the closing date, you might want to consider using a remote access program to log in to your client's file through the Internet.

QuickBooks partners with WebEx to bring you a solution that makes it easy to work remotely in your file or your clients' files. You can use this option if you need to make data changes that are not allowed in an Accountant's Copy, for example, changes to payroll transactions. You can also use this tool to perform the import of your changes into your client's data file.

I find working in the remote environment a perfect choice for simplifying the entire process for clients. For more information, select Accountant, Remote Access to learn about this useful service that QuickBooks has partnered with.

What to Request from the Client When the Import Is Complete

The process for the client of importing your changes is structured with simple, easy-to-follow menus, as described in the section titled "Importing Your Accountant's Changes." However, you might want to request a few items from the client after the import to be sure the process was completed successfully:

- **Trial Balance**—You should review the trial balance as of the dividing date to compare with the same information from your copy of the client's file. Click Reports, Accountant, Trial Balance. Identify for the client cash or accrual basis if the client's company report default is not what you need to compare with. (You can find more information on these report modifications in Chapter 4.)

- **Closing Date**—If you are working with a client's 2009 data file and you set a closing date, your client did not have to say "yes" to setting a closing date and you can rest assured that your closing date was part of the import changes process.

  If you are working with a clients 2008 data file, verify with your client that she did set the closing date you requested. Instruct your client to click Company, Set Closing Date. Doing so opens the Company Preference tab for Accounting Preferences. Have your client verify the closing date (or any date at all), as shown in Figure 15.22. (See the section, "Importing Your Accountant's Changes.")

- **User security rights**—Verify with your client the access rights each employee has for changing transactions dated prior to the closing date. Instruct your client to click Company, Set Up Users and select the Set Up Users menu option. In the User List dialog that opens, select the employee and the View User tab on the right. A "Y" in the Changing Closed Transactions permission allows that user to add or edit transactions dated prior to the closing date. If a closing date password was set, the user will have to type that password first. A creative password that I have used is "call laura," prompting the client to call me first before making the change!

FIGURE 15.22

A good practice is to verify with the client that a closing date was set after importing the Accountant's Copy changes.

You can save yourself some time by offering to use the WebEx Remote Access tool spoken of previously and import the client's changes for him or her. Take note, however, of the Rescue Me! on page 421 when setting a closing date.

Converting the Accountant's Copy to a Regular Company File

What can you do if after beginning to work in the Accountant's Copy you determine some of the changes that need to be made cannot be accommodated with this file type? You can now convert the client's Accountant's Copy (.QBX) file type to a regular QuickBooks (.QBW) file type following these steps.

Click File, Utilities, and choose the Convert Accountant's Copy to Company File (.QBW) menu option. A QuickBooks information dialog appears, recommending that you contact your client to discuss this change (see Figure 15.23).

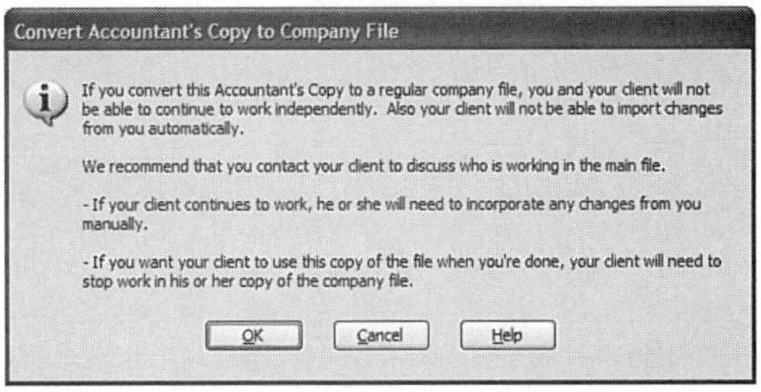

FIGURE 15.23

You can optionally create a regular company file (.QBW) from an Accountant's Copy file type.

You have to make the following decisions:

- Have the client manually repeat your changes in her file.
- If the client is going to use your file, the client must stop working in the file she has.

QuickBooks 2009 offers accountants more flexibility than in prior versions in how you choose to share and work in your client's data. These improvements help make the workflow for you and your client more efficient, making your accounting business more profitable.

Chapter **16**

Reporting Tips and Tricks

- Intuit Statement Writer—*New for 2009!*

- Company Snapshot—*New for 2009!*

- Using the Report Center

- Reporting Preferences

- Modifying Reports

- Report Groups

- Memorized Reports

- Exporting and Importing Report Templates

- Exporting Reports to a .CSV File or to Excel

- Emailing Reports

- About Financial Statement Designer

Intuit Statement Writer—*New for 2009!*

Intuit Statement Writer (ISW) is a new, extremely powerful and flexible reporting tool available in the QuickBooks Premier Accountant 2009 (fee applies) and all editions of QuickBooks Enterprise Solutions 9.0 (included in all editions with no additional fee). With the Intuit Statement Writer, you can create Generally Accepted Accounting Principles (GAAP) compliant financials from your client's QuickBooks data.

Intuit Statement Writer uses Microsoft Excel as the platform for creating customized financial reports from your client's QuickBooks data. Additionally, ISW keeps the statements synchronized with changes in the QuickBooks data.

The Intuit Statement Writer works with Excel 2003 or newer. (Note: ISW will *not* work with Microsoft Excel 2003 Standard Edition, 2003 Student Edition, or 2003 Small Business Edition.)

Rescue Me!

For the Intuit Statement Writer 2009 to work properly, Microsoft Excel must be installed *before* the QuickBooks software. If it is not working properly, try uninstalling the QuickBooks software and reinstalling QuickBooks including any patches that you have previously installed.

For additional information about working with Microsoft Excel 2007, click on the link "About Opening Statements with Microsoft Excel 2007" from the Welcome to Intuit Statement Writer 2009 dialog.

Digging Deeper

The ISW feature replaces the Financial Statement Designer (FSD) reporting tool used in prior versions of QuickBooks. However, your previously created Financial Statement Designer documents can be converted and used with the new Intuit Statement Writer.

To convert your previously stored Financial Statement Documents to ISW format, download this free conversion tool:

`http://accountant.intuit.com/isw_convert`

Benefits of Using the Intuit Statement Writer

The ISW tool is used primarily by accounting professionals who produce financials directly from their client's QuickBooks data. Benefits of using the new Intuit Statement Writer include:

- Creating customized, professional financial statements from your client's QuickBooks data.
- Using one of the many templates to create your own statements. Templates come in a variety of formats for Balance Sheets, Income Statements, Cash Flow Statements, and Budget to Actual Statements.
- Using Microsoft Excel (Excel 2003 or newer) as the platform for customizing, adding all the additional features, and reporting flexibility available in Excel.
- Refreshing customized financials with current QuickBooks data without leaving the ISW tool.
- Combining multiple QuickBooks account lines into one line on financial statements without changing your client's QuickBooks data.
- Adding your own rows or columns of detail.
- Drilling down to QuickBooks data and making changes to transactions within the ISW tool.
- Easily viewing and adding any missing accounts not included in the current statement.
- *NEW* preparing customized Budget versus Actual reports from QuickBooks data (*not* available with the Financial Statement Designer).
- Create supporting documents using your Client's QuickBooks data.

Functions of the Intuit Statement Writer

Customizing your client's financials with QuickBooks Premier Accountant 2009 or QuickBooks Enterprise Solutions 9.0 is easy with all the built-in flexible features of the Intuit Statement Writer.

 Digging Deeper

When you first launch the Intuit Statement Writer 2009 from your QuickBooks data, you have the options to use it free for 30 days, go online to purchase, or to enter you license and product code from your purchase.

The ISW tool is available without an additional charge for QuickBooks Enterprise Solutions 9.0 clients.

ISW Icon Functionality

The Intuit Statement Writer tool functionality is simplified by the use of ISW specific icons. These icons are only available when you have launched an ISW statement from QuickBooks. Hover your mouse over these icons for quick one-click access to common features in the ISW tool (see Table 16.1).

Table 16.1	**Intuit Statement Writer Icon Functionality**	
Icon	**Icon Description**	**Function**
	Create a new statement	Select to begin generating a new statement from one of the many templates. Opens a new Excel window.
	Open an existing statement	Opens an existing statement (.qsm file extension).
	Save the statement	Saves the current statement to a default path.
	Save As	Option to save as a .qsm with a different name or to a different location.
	Roll up selected rows	Customize financials by "grouping" multiple rows together into one row.
	Refresh from QuickBooks	Use to refresh statement data when QuickBooks data has changed.
	Zoom into QuickBooks	Available from a QuickBooks data cell, switches the active window to QuickBooks, displays detail for that account or group of accounts.
	Statement Writer Help	Opens ISW tool help.

Statement Properties

When you need to modify properties that will affect the entire statement, not just a specific row or cell, you will probably find the feature in the Statement Properties pane of the ISW Document Actions.

The Statement Properties pane (as shown in Figure 16.1) controls changes made to the entire financial statement:

- **Statement Date**—Custom dates or a variety of preset dates.
- **Basis**—Accrual or Cash financial reporting.
- **Refresh from QuickBooks**—Updates the current statement when changes have been made to the QuickBooks data.

■ **Change Appearance**—Opens a separate dialog that enables you to customize font, size, colors, and other settings affecting the appearance of the financials.

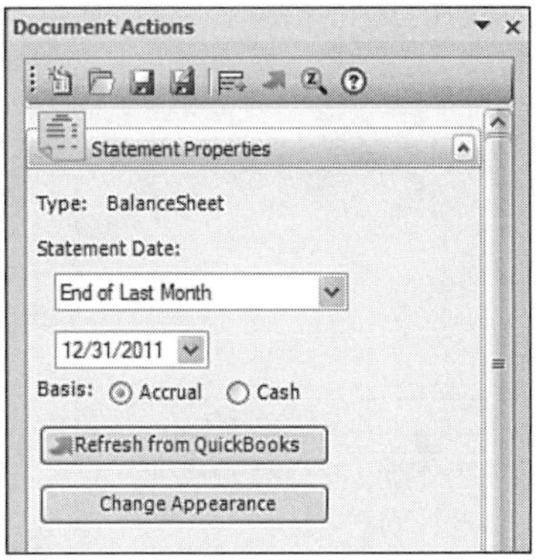

FIGURE 16.1

Statement Properties control options for the entire statement.

Row Properties

To make a change to a specific row, and not affect other rows, you will want to review the features of the Row Properties pane of the ISW Document Actions.

The Row Properties shown in Figure 16.2 affect formatting for the selected row and offer the following functionality:

■ Changing the label of the cell (with the cell selected); the default is the account name.

■ Rolling up accounts (combining multiple lines into one row).

■ Splitting out rows that were previously combined.

■ Removing accounts from a statement.

■ Reversing all the positive and negative numbers in the row by using the Reverse sign.

 Digging Deeper

Did you know that to change the text in a row label, you can make the change directly in the Row Properties pane with the row selected, or simply type the new text directly into the appropriate cell of the spreadsheet? Entering new text using either of these options updates the Row Properties pane and the row label viewed for the statement.

FIGURE 16.2

Use the Row Properties options to control the data you view in a particular row.

Column Properties

Use the Column Properties pane (see Figure 16.3) to affect the properties of an Excel column. The options available in the Column Properties pane change, depending on the type of column that is current when the pane is selected.

- **Type**—Choose the type of data in the column; Accounts (the column or statement header), Normal (blank), % of Budget (budget templates), % of the whole (column total), QuickBooks Data, and Variance are all choices. Each type has its own unique column property options.

- **Heading**—Use to modify the column header; the benefit is that changing it in ISW will not change the column header for that same report in QuickBooks.

- **Delete Column**—Click to select the column you want to delete and then select the Delete Column button on the Column Properties pane. You have to use the ISW Delete Column function because the Excel worksheet is protected from using the Excel delete command.

- **Date Type**—Just as in QuickBooks, we can prepare reports for "Current Month," "Current Fiscal Year," and "Current Month to Date" as well as "Custom" to name just a few of the choices. The ISW tool also offers these "dynamic" date options. Create a statement with a "dynamic" date and each time you prepare the statement, QuickBooks will look to refresh with current data for that requested accounting period.

- **Show me data as of**—Use to create multi-period statements, for example, this period and this year-to-date. Use when you have more than one column of data in your statement.

- **Class**—If your client uses "classes" in QuickBooks, you also create an Income Statement by Class. Only income, other income, cost of goods sold, expenses, and other expense type accounts can be reported by "class."

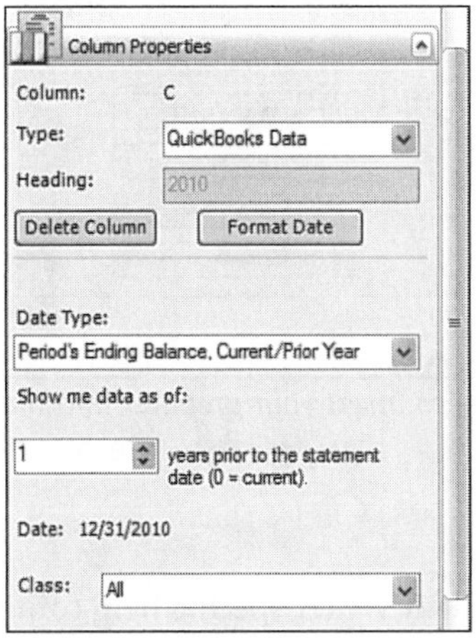

FIGURE 16.3

Column Properties control the contents of the currently selected column.

Rescue Me!

Although column properties include the option to prepare financials by "class," the list that QuickBooks uses to departmentalize financials, the ISW tool, offers only an Income Statement by Class, *not* a Balance Sheet by Class.

General

These General ISW actions shown in Figure 16.4 include:

- **Accountant Information**—Firm name, address, and other similar information. Once this information is stored, it will be available for all client data files opened with your registered copy of QuickBooks Premier Accountant 2009 or QuickBooks Enterprise Solutions 9.0.

- **Edit Appearance**—Same options as the "Change Appearance" under the Statement Properties pane.

- **Insert**—Option to insert specific information into a specific cell of the Statement. Information that can be inserted includes accountant information, client information, reporting basis, and statement date.

- **Format Statement Date**—Options to tell the ISW tool how to present dates, in alpha numeric, numeric only on the statement. You can also indicate how you want to customize the heading text for the date range.

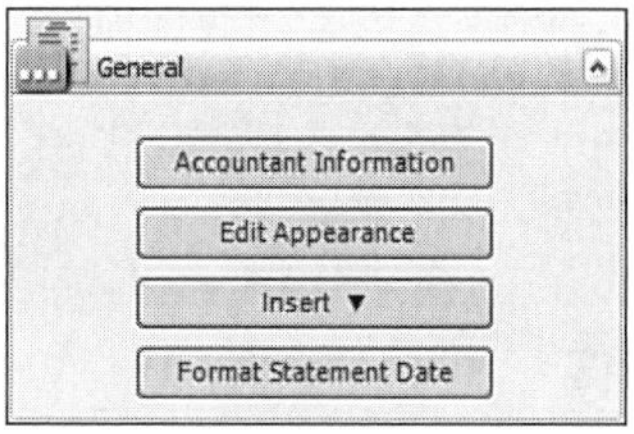

FIGURE 16.4

Use the General menu option to insert your preparer information as well as other items.

Help?

With Intuit Statement Writer specific help content, you can search for a specific topic or show a table of contents.

How to Use the Intuit Statement Writer

You have been introduced to the menu options available in the new ISW. The following section provides more detailed instructions for you to try the many features available.

Follow along with these instructions using your data or your client's data. Remember, this tool is only available with QuickBooks Premier Accountant 2009 (fee applies) or QuickBooks Enterprise Solutions 9.0 (all editions, no additional fee).

1. Click the Accountant menu (or, alternately, the Reports menu) and select Intuit Statement Writer. The Welcome to Intuit Statement Writer 2009 dialog opens as shown in Figure 16.5.

Opens the New
Statement dialog with
predefined templates

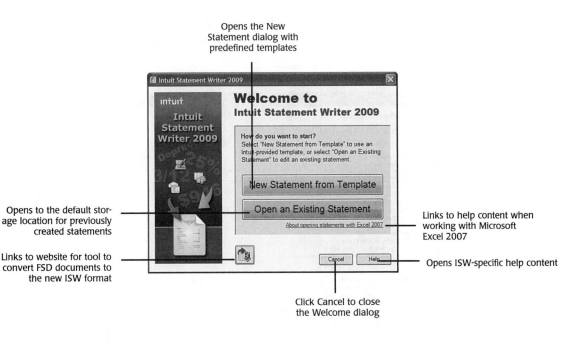

Opens to the default storage location for previously
created statements

Links to website for tool to
convert FSD documents to
the new ISW format

Links to help content when
working with Microsoft
Excel 2007

Opens ISW-specific help content

Click Cancel to close
the Welcome dialog

FIGURE 16.5

Welcome screen after launching the Intuit Statement Writer 2009 from within QuickBooks.

2. Select the option to create a **New Statement from Template** (as shown in Figure 16.6). Choose from the listed templates or Open an Existing Statement that was previously created and saved; these file types will have a file extension of .qsm.

3. To try these features for the first time using the following detailed instructions, from the New Statement dialog select the **Balance Sheet**, choosing the **Selected and Prior Year** template.

 Digging Deeper

You can also convert your previously saved Financial Statement Designer documents to the Statement Writer format by selecting the icon on the lower left as shown in Figure 16.5. When this icon is selected you are directed to the http://accountant.intuit.com/isw_convert website to download a conversion tool you will need to launch when converting your FSD documents to an ISW statement.

If you are opening a previously stored ISW statement, the default path for these is "My Documents\Intuit\Intuit Statement Writer\[Company Name – e.g. Rock Castle]\statement name. qsm."

Don't forget to include this folder in your backup process. Backing up a QuickBooks data file does not include backing up your ISW statements.

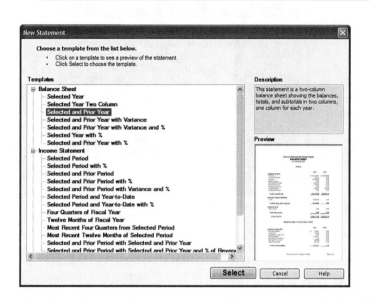

FIGURE 16.6

QuickBooks provides templates to make creating your own customized financials easy.

4. If this is the first time you have launched the ISW tool, you will be asked to grant permission (see Figure 16.7) for this application to access the QuickBooks data file. Simply select the appropriate radial button to enable this application to read and modify the QuickBooks data. Click **Continue**.

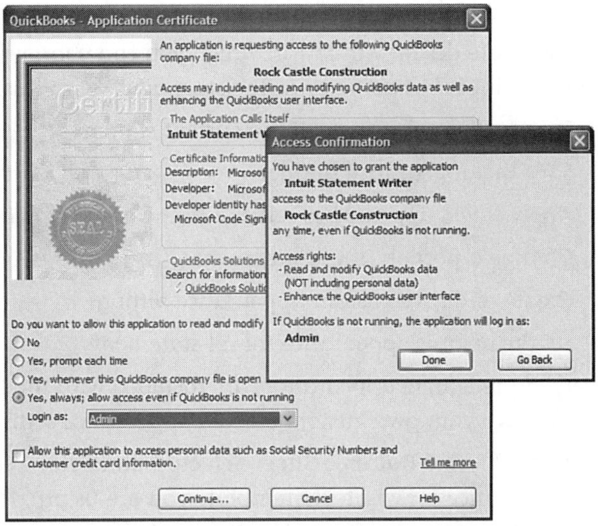

FIGURE 16.7
Initially, you will be asked to grant permission to this application to access the QuickBooks data file.

5. The Access Confirmation dialog opens notifying you that you have granted access for this application to the QuickBooks data. Click **Done**.

6. Select the **Statement Date** from the available drop-down options, or choose to put in a custom date. Click **Create**.

7. Click **Close** after reviewing the tips on the Getting Started with Intuit Statement Writer dialog. Optionally, select the box in the lower left to **Don't show this** dialog again.

8. Microsoft Excel opens with the selected Template using data from the currently opened QuickBooks file.

You are now prepared to try each of the following exercises.

Modifying the Statement Appearance

When you want to change the font, bold a column header, or even apply italicized formatting, you will use the features of the Change Appearance button.

Clicking the Change Appearance button in the Statement Properties pane opens a separate design window in which you can change the fonts, size, and other text settings that are used in the statement. With this tool you can:

- Specify the appearance of the current statement
- Save the appearance settings
- Apply saved appearance settings to the entire statement
- Change a portion of the statement
- Create and save custom appearance settings
- Set the default appearance for all statements

A variety of predefined appearances are included with the ISW. You can also create and save your own custom created appearance settings.

1. To modify the **Balance Sheet-Selected and Prior Year** statement's appearance (or whatever template you are using), follow steps 1–7 in the section titled "How to Use the Intuit Statement Writer."

2. With the ISW statement opened, select the **Statement Properties** from the ISW Document Actions pane. Expand the view by clicking on the arrow.

3. Click on the **Change Appearance** tab.

4. An Edit Appearance dialog opens showing a "Preview using Sample Data" as shown in Figure 16.8.

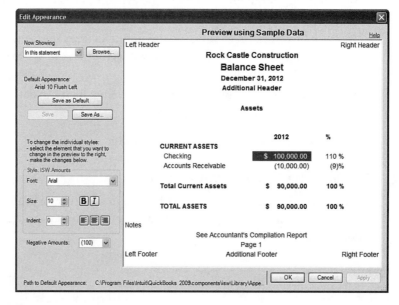

FIGURE 16.8

Conveniently use the Edit Appearance dialog to create default styles for your statements.

5. Click with your mouse on any of the sample data fields or heading fields shown in the sample preview dialog and to the left will be options to change the font, font size, and how to present negative amounts on your financials.

6. Optionally, select your changes to **Save as Default** or click **Save As** to store your changes to the current statement.

Saving these format changes for future use can save time when creating statements for other client's customized financials. The statement appearance is saved with a .qss file extension and can only be opened and used when in the Intuit Statement Writer tool. In a multi-user QuickBooks environment, save these statement appearance files to a shared network location for all users to access.

Modifying the Column and Statement Data Reported

When customizing your client's financials, you can add more years to the statement or change the number of years displayed.

Select the Statement Date drop-down menu to modify the specific accounting period being reported in a single column of your statement.

1. To modify column data (and affect the entire statement's data) in the **Balance Sheet-Selected and Prior Year** statement (or whatever template you are using), follow steps 1–7 in the section titled "How to Use the Intuit Statement Writer."

2. With the ISW statement opened (in this example, the **Balance Sheet-Selected and Prior Year**), click with your mouse cursor Column C to select that specific column of data.

3. On the right is a pane specific to the ISW tool called Document Actions. Select the **Column Properties** section and expand the view by clicking on the arrow.

4. From the options available, select **Show me data as of** and change the **1** to **2** to represent two years.

5. Click on the **Refresh from QuickBooks** icon as shown in Figure 16.9 to refresh the current statement with the new dates.

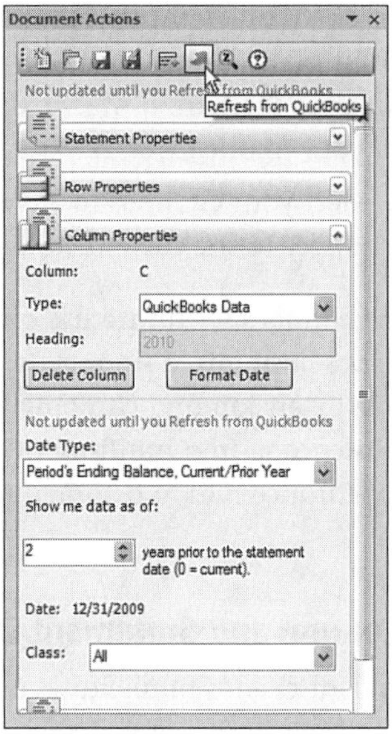

FIGURE 16.9

Intuit Statement Writer provides a warning that the statement has changed and the data needs to be refreshed.

      6. ISW changes the data and date for the column selected.

Remember, when you want to modify data in a column, make sure that you click with your mouse pointer in the column you want to change, selecting the appropriate column.

Adding a Column

Intuit Statement Writer offers improved functionality and ease when you want to add columns of data.

      1. To add a column in the **Balance Sheet-Selected and Prior Year** statement (or whatever template you are using), follow steps 1–7 in the section titled "How to Use the Intuit Statement Writer."

      2. With the ISW statement opened (in this example, the **Balance Sheet-Selected and Prior Year**), click with your mouse cursor in Column D.

      3. With Column D selected, as shown in Figure 16.10, select the **Type** drop-down menu and choose the type of column you will add. In this example, we are adding a Variance column type. ISW creates a new variance column displaying the difference between Column B and C as shown in Figure 16.11.

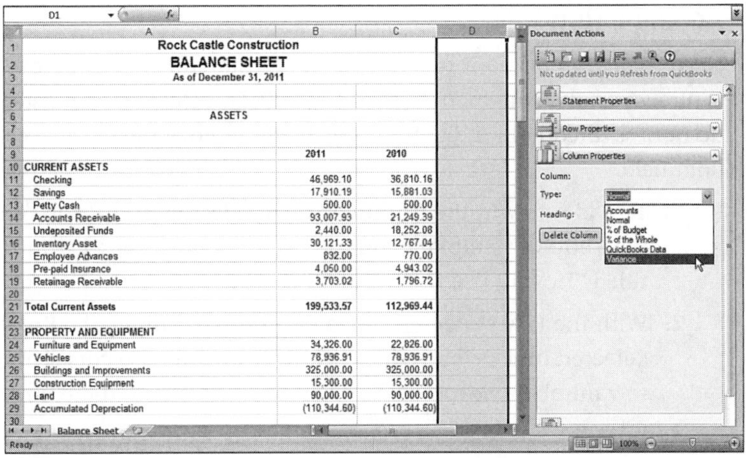

FIGURE 16.10

Adding columns and customizing the type of column offers even more flexibility when creating financials that meet your client's specific needs.

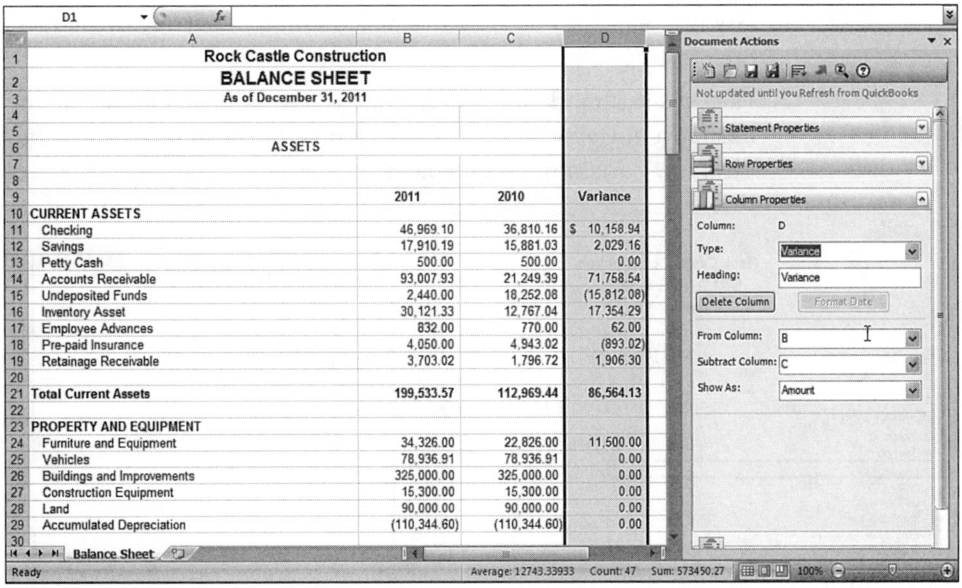

FIGURE 16.11

This statement now includes a variance column easily added from the Column Properties actions.

Adding a Row

Need to add an account row to your stored statement? Not sure if the account is already in the statement? Rest assured that if the ISW tool detects the account is already in a different row, it will remove the extra occurrence of the data field.

1. To add a row in the **Balance Sheet-Selected and Prior Year** statement (or whatever template you are using), follow steps 1–7 in the section titled "How to Use the Intuit Statement Writer."

2. With the ISW statement opened (in this example, the **Balance Sheet-Selected and Prior Year**), click with your mouse cursor on the Excel row number *one row below* where you want to add the new row.

3. With the entire row selected, right-click with your mouse pointer, and select the Excel option to Insert. Excel will insert a blank row.

4. Place your mouse pointer in the newly created blank row.

5. With the newly created row selected, open the **Row Properties** and select the **Add Accounts** button.

6. ISW will open an Add Accounts dialog listing in red any accounts that are missing.

7. Place a check mark in the account(s) you want to add to the statement as shown in Figure 16.12. In this example, we are adding the Petty Cash row back into the statement.

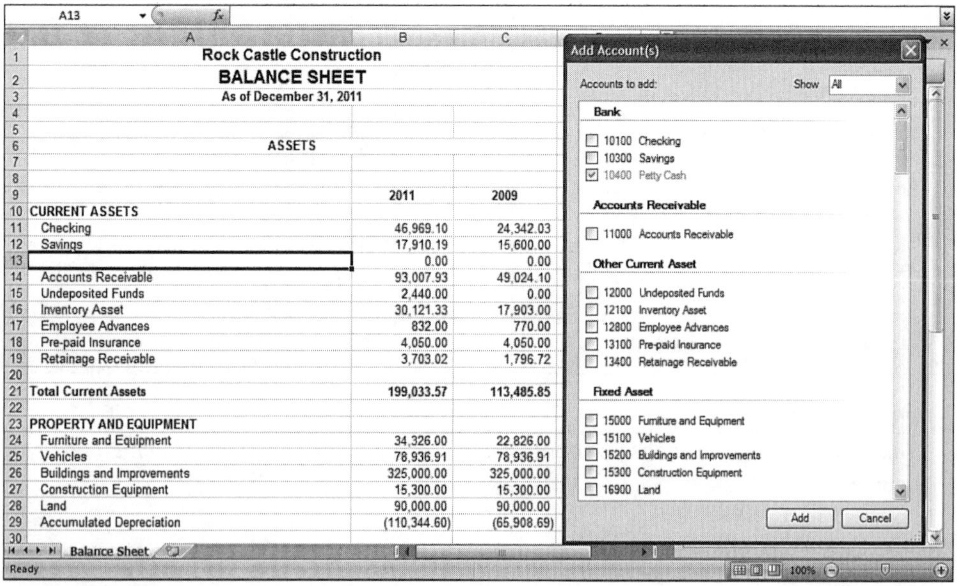

FIGURE 16.12

Selecting the Add Accounts from Row Properties, ISW displays in red any missing accounts.

8. If you need to add a missing account to an existing row, click your mouse pointer in the row you want to add the account to. Open the **Row Properties**, and from the **Accounts in this Row** pane select the specific QuickBooks account (if more than one is shown) and select the **Add** button.

9. ISW will add the total of the newly added account to the existing row data. A red diamond will appear in the top right of the cell for the displayed statement. Hover your mouse over the diamond and ISW provides details of what accounts are included in that cell.

Combining Account Rows

QuickBooks offers users a lot of flexibility when working with a chart of accounts. Often, too many chart of account list items have been created since your last review of the data. The ISW tool enables you to create customized financials grouping accounts together without affecting the client's original chart of accounts.

1. To combine accounts in the **Balance Sheet-Selected and Prior Year** statement (or whatever template you are using), follow steps 1–7 in the section titled "How to Use the Intuit Statement Writer."

2. With the ISW statement opened (in this example, the **Balance Sheet-Selected and Prior Year**), click with your mouse cursor, highlighting any two or more cells that you want to combine into a single row. In the example shown in Figure 16.13, we have selected the cells for the amount in Checking, Savings, and Petty Cash.

3. With the cells or rows selected that you want to "roll up," simply click on the **Roll up selected rows** icon from the ISW toolbar. The rows automatically roll up into one, as shown in Figure 16.14.

4. Optionally, rename the label either in the Row Properties pane or directly in the cell. Figure 16.14 shows the row was renamed to *Cash and Cash Equivalents*.

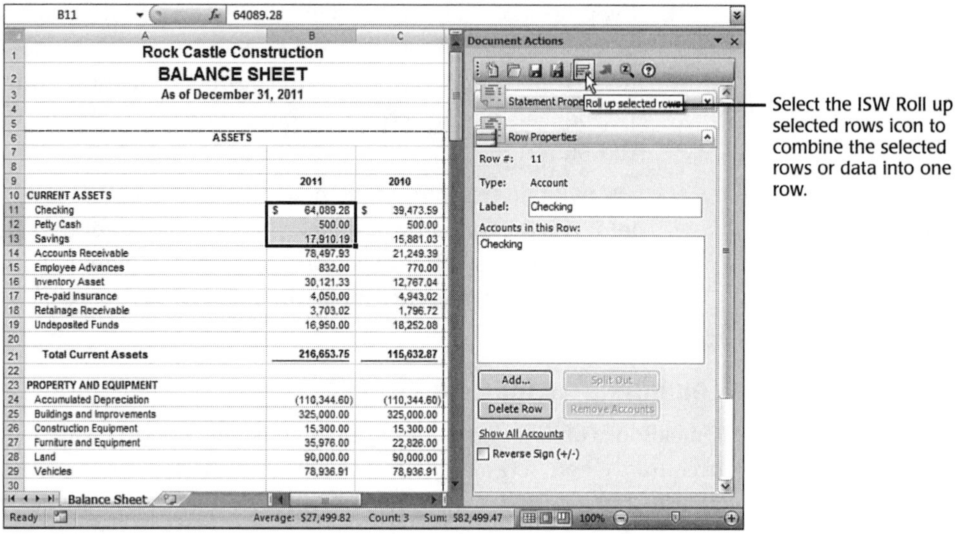

Select the ISW Roll up selected rows icon to combine the selected rows or data into one row.

FIGURE 16.13

Select multiple rows of data to roll up into one row.

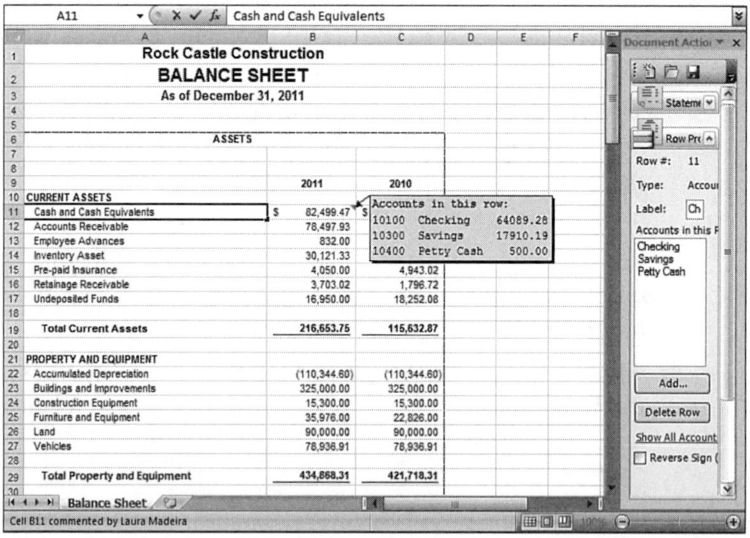

FIGURE 16.14

Multiple cash rows have rolled up into one single row of data.

  5. Hover you mouse over the red triangle that appears in the upper right corner of the cell to see a note of what accounts are included in the new cell total.

One of the most efficient uses in customizing your client's financials is the capability to combine "like" rows of data into a single row. Your financials will be more professional in appearance, while not affecting the client's chart of accounts.

Splitting Out Previously Combined Account Rows

Use the Split Out button if after reviewing your ISW prepared financials, you determine that you need to "split out" rows that were previously grouped into one row.

1. To split out previously combined accounts in the **Balance Sheet-Selected and Prior Year** statement (or whatever template you are using), follow steps 1–7 in the section titled "How to Use the Intuit Statement Writer."

2. With your mouse, select the Excel cell with multiple accounts assigned that you want to "split out."

3. Open **Row Properties** from the Document Actions pane. Click on the arrow to expand the details.

4. The multiple accounts assigned will appear in the pane titled Accounts in this Row. Highlight in the box the account (or use the shift key on your keyboard to select multiple accounts).

5. With the account(s) selected in the **Accounts in this Row**, click on the **Split Out** button. In the example shown in Figure 16.15, selected is the cell for the amount in Cash and Cash Equivalents.

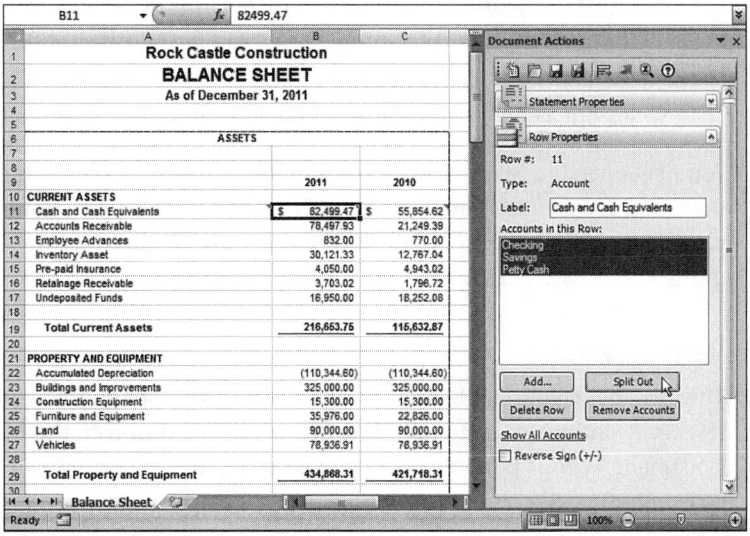

FIGURE 16.15

Split out previously combined rows of data.

6. The ISW tool removes the previously combined rows and places them as individual rows on the statement, updating the total balances. Don't forget to rename the first account row label with its original default account name.

When a New Account Is Added to QuickBooks

The ISW tool will provide you with a list of new accounts that have been added to the QuickBooks data since last preparing the statement. You no longer have to use a "work-around" to determine exactly what new accounts your customer created since your last data review.

1. To test this functionality, use the **Balance Sheet-Selected and Prior Year** statement (or whatever template you are using) and follow steps 1–7 in the section titled "How to Use the Intuit Statement Writer."

2. With the ISW statement opened (in this example, the **Balance Sheet-Selected and Prior Year**), return to QuickBooks by clicking on the QuickBooks menu option on your computer task bar.

3. In QuickBooks, create a new account. Select **Lists**, **Chart of Accounts** and on the **Account** drop-down menu, select **New**.

4. Select the radial button for **Bank Account** (or whatever type of account you want to create).

5. Click **Continue** after selecting the appropriate type of account.

6. Give the account a name. Click **Save & Close**.

7. Return to the Intuit Statement Writer. Click on the **Refresh from QuickBooks** button from the Document Actions icon pane.

8. Your ISW Statement data is updated to include this new account and a message is provided indicating the new account was added.

You never need to worry about your statement being "out of balance" from the QuickBooks data. The ISW Show all Accounts link in the Row Properties pane displays in red any accounts found in QuickBooks that are not included in the current statement.

Deleting Rows

The ISW tool creates a "locked" worksheet that will not enable you to delete rows in a statement using the Excel delete option. However, the ISW Document Actions pane provides you with the tool to delete rows.

1. To remove rows in the **Balance Sheet-Selected and Prior Year** statement (or whatever template you are using), follow steps 1–7 in the section titled "How to Use the Intuit Statement Writer."

2. With the ISW statement opened (in this example, the **Balance Sheet-Selected and Prior Year**), click with your mouse cursor in any row that you want to delete.

3. From the Document Actions, select **Row Properties**. From the Row Properties in the **Accounts in this Row** option, select the account you want to delete.

4. Click the **Delete Row** button.

5. ISW removes the row and adjusts the statement total. A Delete Row(s) dialog appears as in Figure 16.16, detailing the account that was deleted and letting you know that the account is now missing from the statement.

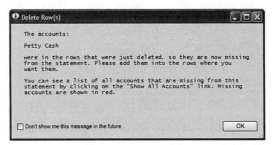

FIGURE 16.16

The ISW tool provides details whenever an account is removed from statement.

See the following section for details on how to view accounts that have been removed from a statement.

Viewing Missing Accounts

This section details how to easily view all the accounts included in the current statement as well as identifying in red any accounts missing in the statement but appear in the currently open QuickBooks data file.

The Accounts dialog is in an easy-to-view Trial Balance format, so you can see not only which accounts are not included but the value of the data assigned to that account.

Additionally, after removing an account from the statement using the instructions in the previous section, you can see a list of missing accounts in the statement.

1. To view missing accounts in the **Balance Sheet-Selected and Prior Year** statement (or whatever template you are using), follow steps 1–7 in the section titled "How to Use the Intuit Statement Writer."

2. Click the **Show All Accounts** link in the **Row Properties** pane.

3. ISW provides a list of all accounts in Trial Balance format with missing accounts listed in red, as shown in Figure 16.17.

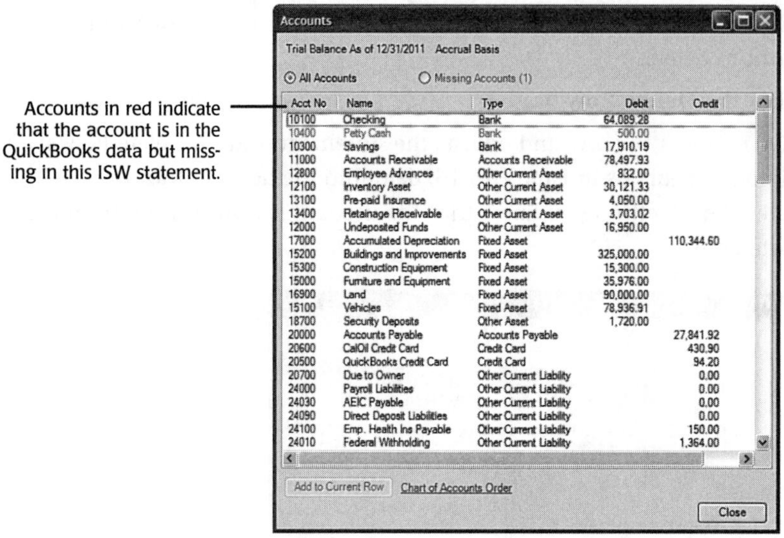

Accounts in red indicate that the account is in the QuickBooks data but missing in this ISW statement.

FIGURE 16.17

The Accounts dialog will list all the accounts in the statement; those in red are not currently included in the statement.

4. To add the missing row, select the row in the Accounts dialog and select the button to **Add to Current Row**. If you are not adding to a current Excel row, create a new row to add the data to. Detailed instructions are included in the section titled "Adding a Row" earlier in this chapter.

With this trial balance view of all accounts, changes your clients made to accounts between reviews will be easily detected.

Deleting Columns

The ISW tool creates a "locked" worksheet that will not enable you to delete a column in a statement using the normal Excel delete option. However, the ISW Document Actions pane provides you with the tool to delete columns.

1. To delete a column in the **Balance Sheet-Selected and Prior Year** statement (or whatever template you are using), follow steps 1–7 earlier in the section titled "How to Use the Intuit Statement Writer."

2. With the ISW statement opened, click with your mouse cursor in any column that you want to delete.

3. From the Document Actions pane, select **Column Properties**. Click the **Delete Column** button to remove the column.

Adding Preparer Information

The ISW tool is designed primarily for accounting professionals to assist in the preparation of customized GAAP compliant financials as stated in the beginning of this chapter.

The ISW tool provides a menu option to add your specific preparer information to your statements. Once this information is added, it will be available for all ISW statements for different clients.

1. To add preparer information in the **Balance Sheet-Selected and Prior Year** statement (or whatever template you are using), follow steps 1–7 in the section titled "How to Use the Intuit Statement Writer."

2. If this is your first time using the ISW tool and you have not previously stored your preparer information, select the arrow on the **General** menu option from the Document Actions pane to open up the general menu options.

3. Click on the **Accountant Information** button and enter the information you want to appear on your customized financials (see Figure 16.18).

   The information entered here will appear for all client files you open with this registered copy of QuickBooks.

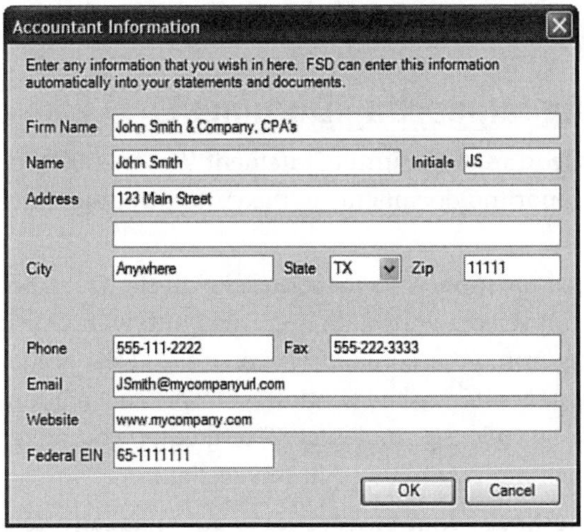

FIGURE 16.18

Enter your preparer information used for all statements from the General properties.

4. Click **OK** to close the Accountant Information pane.

5. Click on the **Edit Appearance** button. These options are the same as was detailed in the section titled "Modifying the Statement Appearance" earlier in this chapter.

6. Click on the **Insert** button to add your accountant information (and other details) to a statement template. Place your mouse pointer in the cell where you want the information included. You can choose to add Accountant Information, Client Information, Basis, and Statement Date.

7. Click on the **Format Statement Date** to open the Format Date dialog with several options for how to present the text of a date on the financials. Options include To-date, From-date and To-date, and Number of Months to name just a few.

Now that you know the features available with the new Intuit Statement Writer as well as how to use it, create financials for your client's business needs easily and conveniently directly from your client's QuickBooks data. Print these financials or store them as PDF documents for future review.

Don't forget to include additional value for your clients by creating customized bar graphs or charts from your QuickBooks data. It is beyond the scope of this book to detail these and the many other options you have available using Microsoft Excel tools.

The following sections detail more specifics on reporting for both the accountant and business owner. The information provided in the remaining sections of this chapter is about features available in QuickBooks Pro, Premier (all editions), and Enterprise (all editions).

Creating Supporting Documents

Another feature of the Intuit Statement Writer 2009 tool is the capability to create supporting documents to the customized statements created in the ISW tool.

This added functionality was released with the QuickBooks R2 update patch. To see what release your data is currently at, with QuickBooks open, select the F2 key from your computer keyboard and the Product Dialog window displays. At the top of the window, your product edition, year, and release are listed. If your release number is R2 or greater, you have the supporting statement functionality discussed in this section.

Most QuickBooks data files are set to automatically detect when an update patch is released. You can also manually download updates by going to www.quickbooks.com/support and clicking on the Product Updates link at the top of the window. Follow the instructions on the window for manually down-loading the update to your QuickBooks file.

The following sections detail how to use the existing templates, edit the templates, or create your own templates for supporting documents.

Using the Default Set of Supporting Document Templates

Included with the Intuit Statement Writer is a set of default supporting document templates including Accrual Basis Compilation Report With or Without Disclosures, Cash Basis Compilation Report With or Without Disclosures, and a Title Page. You can use these templates to create your supporting documents by following these steps:

1. Launch the ISW tool from within QuickBooks, using the instructions provided in Steps 1–7 in the section titled "How to Use the Intuit Statement Writer."

2. Open any ISW statement (for the supporting document functionality you have to be in the ISW tool).

3. Carefully select the appropriate Statement Date; the content of the supporting document might include this date.

4. In Microsoft Excel 2007, from the **Add-Ins** tab on the Ribbon (see Figure 16.19), select the **Statement Writer** menu.

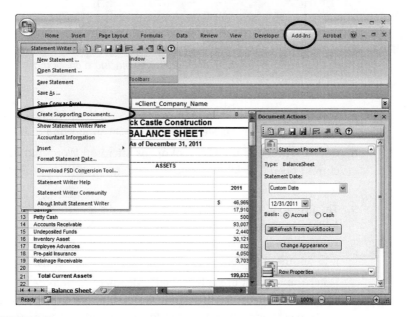

FIGURE 16.19

To access Supporting Documents, click the Add-Ins Tab from Excel 2007.

5. From the drop-down menu, select the **Create Supporting Documents**. The Create Supporting dialog opens with the built-in templates listed.

6. In Step 1 of the Create Supporting dialog, click to place a check mark in one of documents. For this example, I selected the Accrual Basis Compilation Report without Disclosures (see Figure 16.20).

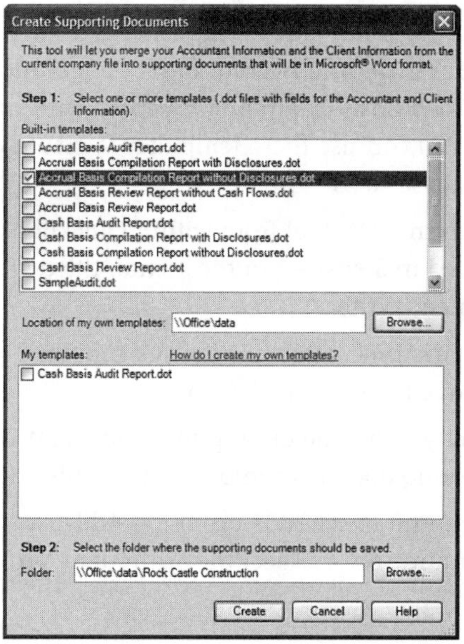

FIGURE 16.20

Select a supporting document (or multiple documents) by placing a check mark in the box in front of the document name.

7. Browse to the client folder you want to save these created supporting statements to. (This is Step 2 of the Create Supporting dialog).

8. Click **Create**, and the ISW tool opens Microsoft Word and merges your current open QuickBooks data with the merge fields in the stored template.

9. The ISW tool saves a copy of the prepared supporting document in the folder you selected in step 7. Because a copy is already stored for you, you can close the Word document or select File, Save or Save As to save it to another location.

Note: You will not use this "saved" document to prepare future supporting documents for this client. Instead, return to step 6 when creating a new supporting document for a new statement date.

Conveniently create supporting documents from predefined templates helping you to more productively prepare customized financials with the Intuit Statement Writer tool.

Editing a Predefined Template or Existing Word Document

You might want to modify the content or the merge fields included with the ISW predefined templates or maybe you have already created your own supporting documents in Word.

For ISW to be able to merge select fields from the ISW financial statement dates or client data from the currently open QuickBooks data file, you need to make sure you save your changes as a Word template file.

Follow these steps to modify an existing predefined supporting document or to modify your own Word document:

1. Create a folder (on your network server if multiple users will use the modified template) to copy the predefined template or your Word documents to.

2. Browse to the default storage path for the predefined ISW Supporting Document templates: <drive where data file is located>:/Program Files/Intuit/QuickBooks Premier 2009/Components/ISW/ Library/Templates.

   If you are using QuickBooks Enterprise, they are stored in the <drive where data file is located>:/Program Files/Intuit/QuickBooks Enterprise Solutions 9.0/Components/ISW/Library/Templates.

3. Using windows copy function, select the document template (.dot file extension), and then copy and paste to the newly created folder from step 1.

4. Alternately, open your own Word supporting document (.doc or .docx extension) and select **File, Save As**, choosing the Word Template option, and save to the newly created folder. Your original Word supporting document will now have the file extension of .dot.

FIGURE 16.21
Use the Word Save as Template option, so that ISW can link QuickBooks data to the newly created document.

5. To modify the static text (text that does not change with each created supporting document), using Word, open the template (.dot file) and make changes as needed to the text (see Figure 16.22).

6. To modify the dynamic data, or merge fields, add a specific named field that ISW recognizes (see Figure 16.22). In your template Word file, place your mouse where you want the merged data inserted.

7. In Word 2007, from the Insert tab, select Quick Parts and select the Field menu option.

8. The Field dialog displays. In the Please choose a field pane, with your mouse pointer, select **MergeField**. The right side of the dialog now opens a text box for Field Properties.

9. Type exactly the field name you want to merge into your modified supporting document. See Figure 16.23, which indicates that the Client Phone Number is added to the template. These fields are detailed in Table 16.2.

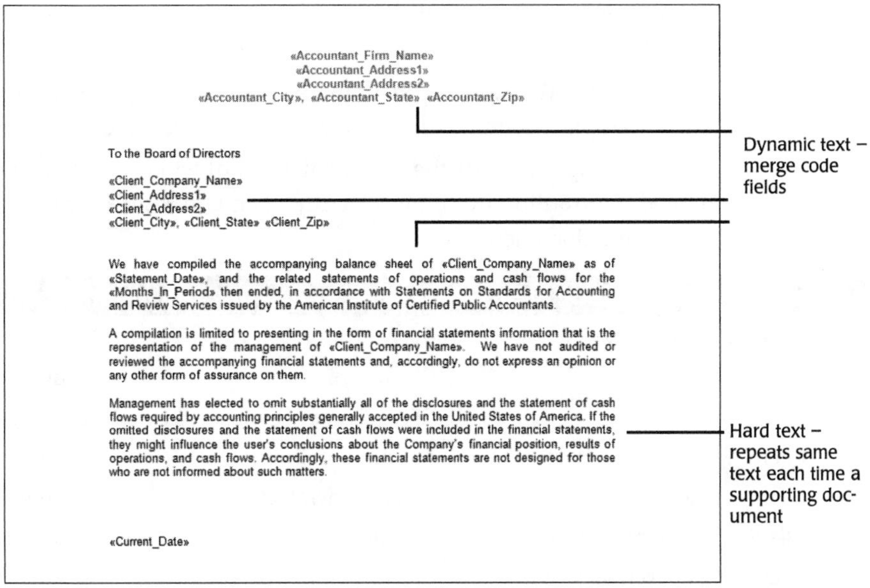

«Accountant_Firm_Name»
«Accountant_Address1»
«Accountant_Address2»
«Accountant_City», «Accountant_State» «Accountant_Zip»

To the Board of Directors

«Client_Company_Name»
«Client_Address1»
«Client_Address2»
«Client_City», «Client_State» «Client_Zip»

We have compiled the accompanying balance sheet of «Client_Company_Name» as of «Statement_Date», and the related statements of operations and cash flows for the «Months_In_Period» then ended, in accordance with Statements on Standards for Accounting and Review Services issued by the American Institute of Certified Public Accountants.

A compilation is limited to presenting in the form of financial statements information that is the representation of the management of «Client_Company_Name». We have not audited or reviewed the accompanying financial statements and, accordingly, do not express an opinion or any other form of assurance on them.

Management has elected to omit substantially all of the disclosures and the statement of cash flows required by accounting principles generally accepted in the United States of America. If the omitted disclosures and the statement of cash flows were included in the financial statements, they might influence the user's conclusions about the Company's financial position, results of operations, and cash flows. Accordingly, these financial statements are not designed for those who are not informed about such matters.

«Current_Date»

Dynamic text – merge code fields

Hard text – repeats same text each time a supporting document

FIGURE 16.22
Supporting statements created in ISW can include both "static" text and "dynamic" text.

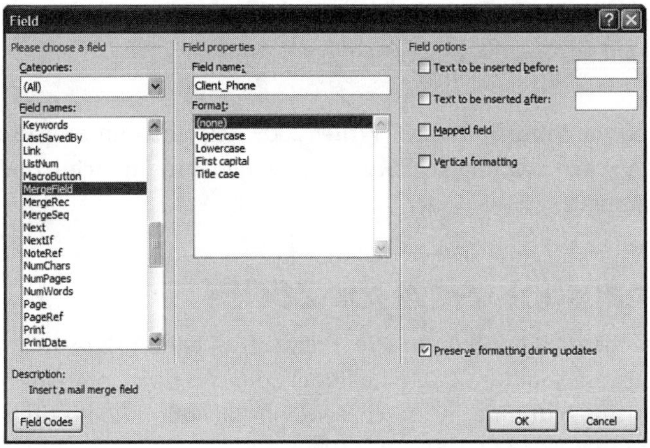

FIGURE 16.23
To add merge fields, you must type the field name exactly as included in the Help menu for ISW.

10. Select **OK** to place the merge code field name into the template document.

11. Select **File, Save As** and choose the Word Template option, giving the template a name and storing it in the selected folder.

The following table lists the merged fields that will accurately place the related information from the currently open QuickBooks data file into an ISW supporting document.

Table 16.2 Merge Code Fields Used With Supporting Document		
Client_Company_Name	Client_Phone	Accountant_Zip
Client_Address1	Client_Fax	Accountant_Phone
Client_Address2	Client_Email	Accountant_Fax
Client_City Client_Website	Accountant_Email	Accountant_Website
Client_State	Client_Federal_EIN	Accountant_Name
Client_Zip Client_SSN	Accountant_Federal_EIN	Accountant_Initials
Client_Legal_Company_Name	Client_Company_Type	Statement_Date
Client_Legal_Address1	Accountant_Firm_Name	Months_In_Period
Client_Legal_Address2	Accountant_Address1	Current_Date
Client_Legal_City	Accountant_Address2	
Client_Legal_State	Accountant_City	
Client_Legal_Zip	Accountant_State	

Using the Intuit Statement Writer 2009 helps accountants work more productively when creating customized management, financial, and supporting documents.

Company Snapshot—*New for 2009!*

New for 2009 QuickBooks Pro, Premier (all editions), as well as QuickBooks Enterprise Solutions 9.0 (all editions) offers a new Company Snapshot for reporting real-time critical company information and a single location to perform specific QuickBooks tasks.

These reporting tools are commonly referred to as digital dashboards and offer real-time visual views of a company's critical information. The new QuickBooks Company Snapshot is shown in Figure 16.24.

The Admin or External
Account user can select
this link to change the
Select the drop-down to   company preferences
change reporting dates.   for reminders.

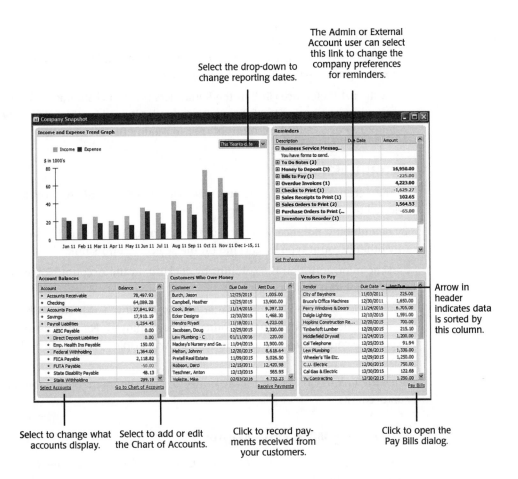

Select to change what   Select to add or edit   Click to record pay-   Click to open the
accounts display.   the Chart of Accounts.   ments received from   Pay Bills dialog.
your customers.

FIGURE 16.24

Company Snapshot, new reporting tool in QuickBooks 2009.

Income and Expense Trend Graph

This section of the Company Snapshot shows graphically your income
compared to your expenses of your business. Click on the drop-down arrow
in the Income and Expense Trend Graph pane to select a different date range
to view.

Place your mouse on a bar in the graph to see a total for that bar. Double-
click with your mouse pointer on any bar to see the QuickInsight: Income and
Expense Graph for that period. Continue to double-click on the report detail to
get to the original transactions.

Reminders

The Reminders pane is a selection of predefined lists and tasks that the Admin user decided to view on the dashboard.

Click the Set Preferences link in the Reminders pane to customize what information you are reminded of. You will need to be logged into the file as the Admin user or External Accountant user to modify the preferences.

Account Balances

In the Account Balances pane, users can view the financial balances for selected accounts.

By default only Balance Sheet accounts are shown. You can add to this view any other account type by clicking on the Select Accounts link.

Sort the information in the columns by clicking on the Account Name or Balance column headers.

Double-click with your mouse pointer on any account. For Balance Sheet accounts, the register for that account will be displayed. For Income and Expense accounts, an Account QuickReport will display for the selected account.

Click the link to Go to Chart of Accounts to open the menu option to add or edit accounts.

Customers Who Owe Money

To sort the data displayed, click on the Customer Name, Due Date, or Amt Due column headers.

The Due Date shown is the earliest due date for all invoices or statement charges for that customer. Overdue items are shown in red.

The Amt Due column is the total ending balance for that customer.

Double-click with your mouse pointer on any line item to open the Customer Open Balance report, listing the individual open transactions.

Click the Receive Payment link to open the Receive Payments form in QuickBooks. You might also be directed to information on taking credit card payments from your customers.

Users must have security rights to Sales and Accounts Receivable functions to complete the Receive Payment function. If not, they will be able to view the balances, prepare a report of the balances, but not actually receive payment from the customer.

Vendors to Pay

Stay on top of what you owe your vendors with this quick snapshot in the Vendors to Pay pane.

To sort the data displayed, click on the Vendor Name, Due Date, or Amt Due column headers.

The Due Date shown is the earliest due date that the vendor bills are due.

The Amt Due column is the total ending balance for that vendor.

Double-click with your mouse pointer on any line item to open the Vendor Open Balance report, listing the individual transactions that make up the balance shown.

If you click on an open balance for your sales tax vendor, a vendor QuickReport will open for that vendor for all dates.

Click the Pay Bills link to open the Pay Bills dialog in QuickBooks.

Users must have access to the Purchases and Accounts Payable security functions to be able to access the Pay Bills dialog from the link on the Vendors to Pay pane.

Defaulting the Company Snapshot as Home Page

If you wish to have the Company Snapshot default when you open a company file, follow these instructions:

1. Open the Company Snapshot by clicking the **Company Snapshot** icon or from selecting Company Snapshot from the Company menu.

2. From the **Edit** menu, select **Preferences** and choose the **Desktop View** preference from the left margin.

3. On the **My Preferences** tab, select the **Save Current Desktop** radial button.

4. Uncheck the option to Show Home page when opening company file. When you open your data file, the Company Snapshot will default as the new Home page.

A word of caution about this setting is that not only will QuickBooks open with the Company Snapshot, but it will also open and rebuild any transactions or reports you had open at the time you closed QuickBooks, which can slow down the speed at which the file will open.

Rescue Me!

If your company has created user restrictions in QuickBooks, the user will have access only to activities of the Company Snapshot that he has been provided permission to access. If you do not want the user to see the Income and Expense of the company, you will have to set restrictions for both the Sensitive Accounting Activities and Sensitive Financial Reporting. To modify a user's security rights, you must be logged into the data file as the Admin user.

After you have set up the security, log in as that user and verify whether the behavior is what you were expecting.

For more complex user security settings, consider using QuickBooks Enterprise Solutions 9.0.

Using the Report Center

Up to this point in the book, I have discussed ways to review your data. Throughout each chapter, I often included step-by-step instructions for creating specific reports to assist you with your data review. This chapter instead discusses ways you can make reporting work for you using many of the reporting tools found in QuickBooks.

If you are new to QuickBooks or if you have never reviewed the QuickBooks Report Center, in this section you can find out about the many features available for simplifying your reporting needs in QuickBooks.

The Report Center is available in the following editions of QuickBooks: Pro, Premier (all editions), and Enterprise (all editions).

To access the Report Center, follow these steps:

1. Click the **Report Center** icon from the QuickBooks icon bar or click **Reports, Report Center**. The Report Center appears, as shown in Figure 16.25. (The image shown in Figure 16.25 might differ from your selection of reports depending on the QuickBooks version you are using.)

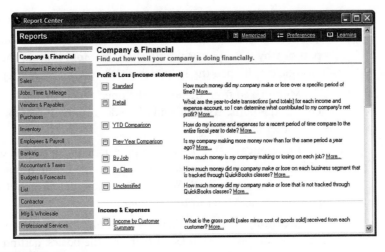

FIGURE 16.25

The QuickBooks Report Center.

2. On the left of the Report Center are buttons for the different report groups in QuickBooks. Click on the desired group to see all the prepared reports for that group.

3. Hover the mouse pointer over the small icon image in front of the report name and QuickBooks will display a preview of the report (see Figure 16.26).

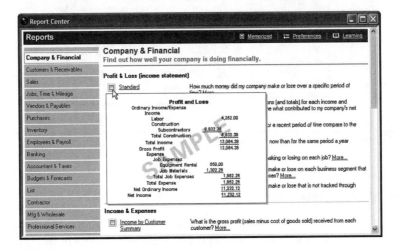

FIGURE 16.26

Preview the report with sample data right from the Report Center.

4. Click the **Report Name** link to run the report using your data.

5. If you need additional information about the expected content of the report or why the report is useful, click the **More** links in the text. QuickBooks will open the help menu text specific to that report.

6. Click **Memorized** from the top of the open report dialog to access memorized reports. You can find more details about memorizing reports later in this chapter.

7. Click **Preferences** to set personal report preferences as well as company preferences (if you are logged into the data file as the Admin or External Accountant user). You can find more details about setting report preferences later in this chapter.

8. Click **Learning** to open the Reports Learning Center, shown in Figure 16.22. On this page are links for learning the basics, getting the most out of a report, and managing reports (not shown in Figure 16.27).

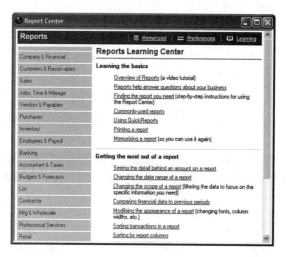

FIGURE 16.27

For additional help with creating reports, click Learning in the Report Center.

Reporting Preferences

QuickBooks makes customizing reports globally through the use of the Reporting Preferences easy. Reporting Preferences come in two types: My Preferences, or those that are unique to a logged-in user, and Company Preferences, which can be set only by the Admin or External Accountant user and represent global settings for all users.

My Preferences

The My Preference setting for reports is user specific. These preferences are set only for the currently logged-in user. To access user-specific preferences for reports:

1. Choose **Edit, Preferences** and select the **Reports and Graphs** from the preferences dialog that opens.

2. Click the **My Preference** tab.

You can specify the following settings that will be unique for the currently logged-in user (if using QuickBooks in a multi-user mode):

- **Prompt to modify report**—When selected, this option causes QuickBooks to open the Modify Report window when each report is opened.

- **Reports and Graphs refresh**—You have a choice, when report details have changed, to request QuickBooks to prompt you to Refresh (this is the default option for a new data file), Refresh Automatically, or Don't Refresh. I usually select the Refresh Automatically option. However, if the report is lengthy and you have multiple users entering data, you might want to review a report, make changes, and not have QuickBooks refresh at the time the change is made.

- **Graphs Only**—This option offers settings for drawing in 2D (which is faster) or using patterns.

Company Preferences

Different from the My Preference setting for Reports and Graphs, the Company Preferences can only be set by the Admin or External Accountant user and are global settings for all users.

To access Company Preferences for reports, log in as the Admin or External Accountant user in single-user mode:

1. Choose **Edit, Preferences** and select the **Reports and Graphs** from the preferences dialog that opens.

2. Click the **Company Preference** tab and set global defaults (for all users) for each of the following items.

You can set defaults for the following options for all users:

- **Summary Report Basis**—You can choose Accrual (default) or Cash Basis. For business owners, I suggest that you discuss this option with your accountant.

- **Aging Reports**—You can choose to age from the due date (default) or age from the transaction date. This setting determines the aged status of your accounts receivable or accounts payable reports.

- **Format**—Click the Format button to set the following options globally for all reports.

Click the **Header Footer** tab to set:

- **Header Information**—I recommend leaving each of these choices selected and not modifying them in this window.

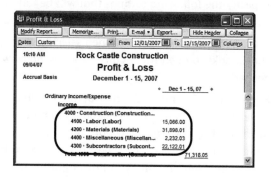

FIGURE 16.28

When the Name and Description report preference is selected and if account numbering is enabled.

- **Show Footer Information**—Here you can enter an additional footer line, such as "Confidential Information" or the like.

- **Page Layout**—Standard (the default), left, right, or center justified.

- **Fonts**—You can set this on the **Fonts & Numbers** tab. Use this to set fonts for all text or specific text lines. As you select the text line on the left, QuickBooks will display the current font choice and size for that text.

- **Show Negative Numbers**—Format choices include normal –300.00; in parentheses (300.00) or with a trailing minus 300.00–. Optionally, you can select to have these numbers print in red.

- **Show All Numbers**—Use this setting to divide all numbers by 1,000, to not show zeros, or to show numbers without the cents. These options are most often used by accounting professionals when providing a statement to a bank and so on.

You can display accounts by Name Only (the default), Description Only, or Name and Description. These are fields you completed in the Add New

Account or Edit Account dialogs, as shown in Figure 16.29. More detail on creating or editing your chart of accounts can be found in Chapter 2, "Reviewing the QuickBooks Chart of Accounts." The options are as follows:

- **Name Only**—Shows account name and account number, as shown in Figure 16.30 (if the use account numbers preference is enabled, see Chapter 2 for more details).

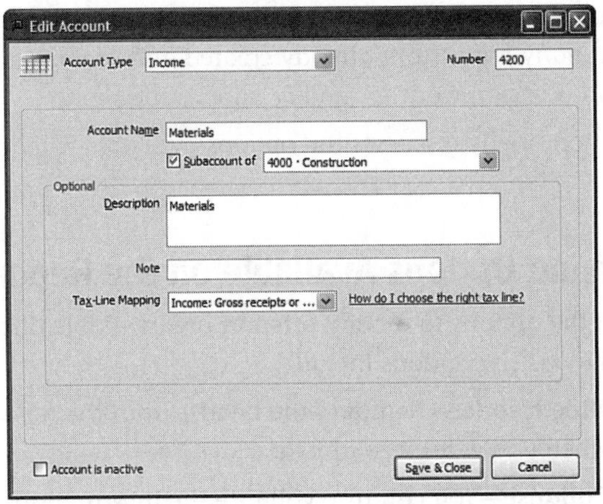

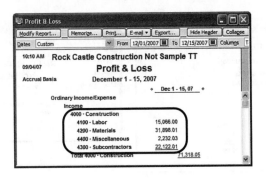

FIGURE 16.29
Optionally, include a description in addition to the account name.

FIGURE 16.30
Resulting report when the Name Only report preference is selected in addition to having the account numbering preference enabled.

- **Description Only**—Shows only the information typed in the Description field (shown in Figure 16.29).
- **Name and Description**—Shows account number, account name, and description, as shown in Figure 16.28.

- **Statement of Cash Flows**—Click the **Classify Cash** button to open the Classify Cash dialog. In it, you define your Balance Sheet accounts as Operating, Investing, or Financing cash flow types.

Modifying Reports

QuickBooks makes gathering information from your data quick and easy. Though many reports are already created and organized for your use, you might on occasion want to modify an existing report.

This section briefly discusses the options available when you want to modify a report.

Modifying Options Available on the Report Window

A few of the options to modify a report are available directly on any active report dialog. The options include

- **Hide Header**—Removes the header from the report. Click Show Header when you want it to appear.

- **Collapse**—You can also collapse the information, as shown in Figure 16.31. When you click the Collapse button, QuickBooks removes the subaccount detail from view only. The report details are not changed, just viewed with fewer line details.

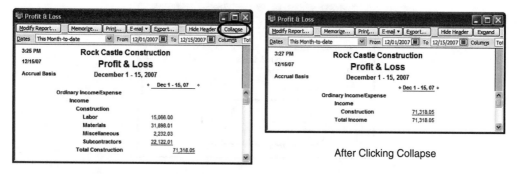

Before Clicking the Collapse Button

After Clicking Collapse

FIGURE 16.31

Click the Collapse button on a report to roll up the subaccounts into the main account.

- **Columns**—For certain reports, you can easily control how the data is subtotaled or grouped and add additional columns or subcolumns.

- **Sort By**—Use this to group the detail into useful ways for your review. I use this frequently, especially when looking at reports with many lines of detail.

Other options on the active report window simply enable you to email, print, or export the report to an Excel format. The additional option to memorize a report is discussed in a following section.

Modify Report Button

You can modify the report further by clicking the Modify Report button at the top left of the open report dialog. The options for modifying reports vary by report type. Some reports offer the following choices; others might not offer the same report modification choices.

- **Display tab**—This tab opens automatically when you choose to modify an existing report. From this window you can modify the following:

    - **Report Date Range**—Choose from the QuickBooks predefined date ranges, or set a custom date range for your report.

    - **Report Basis**—You can choose Accrual or Cash. This option is not available on all reports.

    - **Columns**—This setting is useful for selecting what information you want to see and whether you want it sorted or totaled by a specific field on the resulting report.

    - **Advanced tab**—This tab is often overlooked, but its settings enable users to display active, all, or non-zero rows as well as the desired reporting calendar.

- **Filters tab**—Use these options to filter for specific accounts, names, or transaction types as well as many other fields that can be filtered on.

 Digging Deeper

Filtering a report is easy and convenient to do when you want only specific information from a longer report.

If you do filter, you might want to modify your report title so that it identifies what has been filtered. For example, if you are filtering a report to show employee advances detail, you might want to modify the report title to *Employee Advances Detail* so that those who read the report will know it is pulling out specific information.

- **Header/Footer tab**—Use this tab to modify the report title and the appearance of the information that appears on the report. You can set this information globally for all users; see the section, "Company Preferences" earlier in this chapter.

- **Fonts & Numbers tab**—Use this tab to specify fonts for specific line text as well as how numbers appear in your reports. You can set this information globally for all users; see the section, "Company Preferences" earlier in this chapter.

Report Groups

If you have not set up your own customized report groups, you might not know how easy they are to work with and how efficient they can make reporting on your QuickBooks data. This section highlights how to create, use, and manage report groups.

Creating Report Groups

For accountants, this feature can save you precious time each period that you work with your client's data. You can create a group of reports that you will want to review each time you work with the client's file.

 Digging Deeper

If my clients were prone to making mistakes when entering data, I would teach them how the data should look, give them their own report group, and request that they review these reports before my appointment.

To create a report group, follow these steps:

1. Choose **Reports, Memorized Reports** and select the **Memorized Report List** menu. The Memorized Report List dialog appears (showing predefined groups and associated reports).

2. Click the **Memorized Report** drop-down menu at the bottom of the list and select **New Group** menu.

3. In the New Memorized Report Group dialog, provide a name for the group. Click **OK** to return to the Memorized Report List dialog. QuickBooks places your new group alphabetically in the existing list of report groups.

4. Click on the red X in the upper right to close the Memorized Report List dialog.

Digging Deeper

If you are going to be creating several reports that will be included as part of this report group, you will want to move this newly created report group to the top of the list. While you memorize reports for this group, QuickBooks defaults the report group in the Memorize Report dialog to the first one on the list.

When you are done memorizing the reports to this report group (see the next section), then you can move the group list item back alphabetically within the rest of the memorized reports or groups.

To move a report group up or down the list, place your cursor over the diamond shape in front of the report group name. Drag the item up or down. Figure 16.32 shows the new Monthly Reports group being moved to the top of the list.

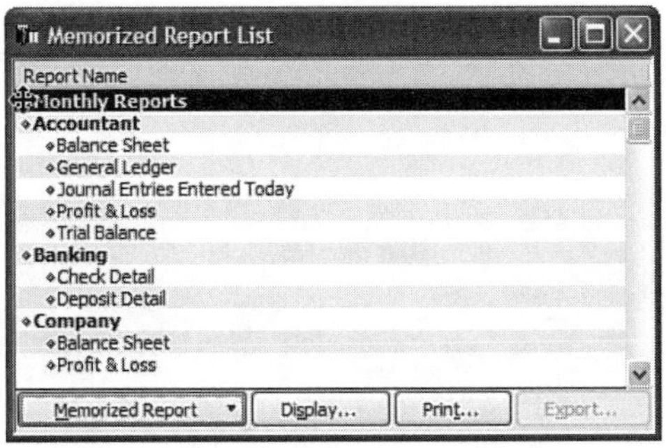

FIGURE 16.32

Create a report group so you can easily display or print multiple reports at one time.

Using Report Groups

The primary purpose of report groups is to simplify displaying or printing multiple reports at one time.

To display a group of reports, follow these steps:

1. Click **Reports, Process Multiple Reports**. The Process Multiple Reports dialog appears.

2. From the **Select Memorized Reports From** drop-down menu, select the specific group of reports you want to create, as shown in Figure 16.33. Figure 16.34 shows the Banking report group selected.

3. Remove the check mark for any report you do not want to process in the group.

4. In the **From** and **To** columns, change the date as needed. Be aware
    that these changes are not permanent. The next time you create the
    report group, the original date range stored with the report will appear.
    If you want the new dates to appear next time, you need to memorize
    the report again and select the Replace button to replace the previously
    stored report with the report with the new date range.

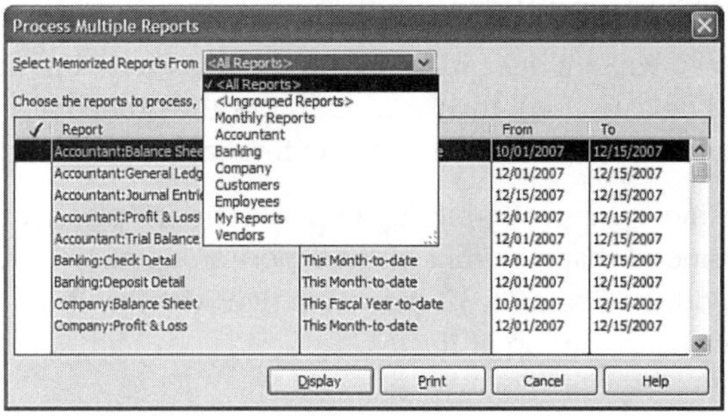

FIGURE 16.33

*The Process Multiple Reports dialog enables you to choose what group you want to conve-
niently display or print.*

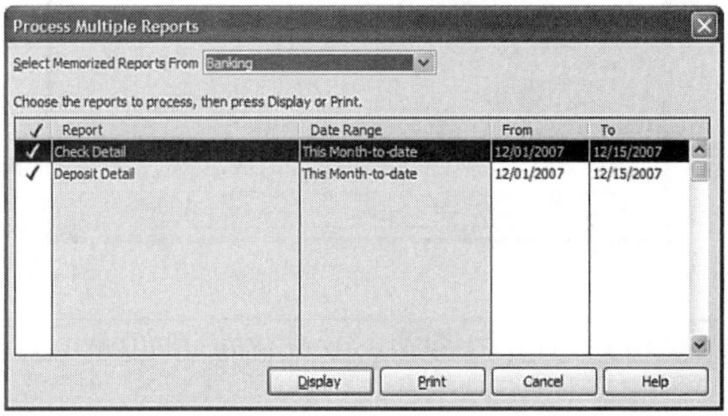

FIGURE 16.34

*The Banking report group has been selected, and those reports memorized with this group are
shown.*

Digging Deeper

When memorizing a report that you will add to a report group, be
aware of the date range selected. If you want to see the dates for the
current month-to-date, you would select This Month-to-Date for the
date range for the report so that the report, whenever it is generated,
will use data from the current month-to-date.

If you select a specific range of dates on a memorized report, QuickBooks considers those dates custom and will always generate the report with those specific dates.

5. Click **Display** to view the reports on your computer screen or click **Print** to send the selected reports to your printer.

Your report group will now generate the multiple reports for you to view or print. I often create a report group, for my clients called either Monthly or Quarterly Reports. In this group, I put certain reports I want them to review before my appointment. This method helps them help me in keeping their QuickBooks data reporting organized.

Managing Report Groups

To manage a report group, follow these steps:

1. Click **Reports, Memorized Reports** and select **Memorized Report List**. The Memorized Report List dialog appears (showing predefined groups and associated reports).

2. Click the **Memorized Report** button at the bottom of the list to choose the following memorized report list options:

   - **Edit Memorized Report**—Edit the name of an existing report list item or which group it is associated with (you do not edit the date ranges or filters from this dialog).

   - **New Group**—Used to create an association of multiple reports, discussed in the previous section.

   - **Delete a Memorized Report**—Helpful in managing the list and changes over the years.

   - **Print the List**—Do this if needed to manage what reports are useful.

   - **Re-sort the List**—Not often needed with this list, but if used, your list will return to its original order before any custom changes to the organization of the list items.

   - **Import or Export a Template**—Create and then use reports for multiple client data files. See the section titled "Exporting and Importing Report Templates."

3. To rearrange your reports, simply place your cursor on the diamond in front of the report name, and click and drag down and to the right, as demonstrated in Figure 16.35. Release the mouse button when the report is in the proper position.

From the memorized report list, you can also export your reports to Excel without first displaying them in QuickBooks. Use these report groups to streamline your data reviews. You can use the Memorize feature for many of the special reports discussed in this book and place them in a report group for easy and frequent access.

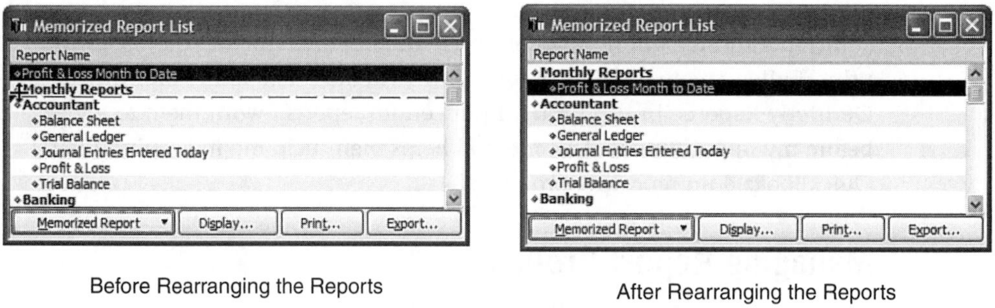

Before Rearranging the Reports

After Rearranging the Reports

FIGURE 16.35

Click and drag the diamond in front of any report or group to rearrange the list manually.

Memorized Reports

After you have created a report group, you will want to use the memorize feature for the reports that you want in that group. Placing your memorized reports in a group is optional, but using groups will help keep your memorized reports organized.

To memorize a report, simply click the Memorize button at the top of an open report, as shown in Figure 16.36. QuickBooks asks you to give the report a Name and lets you assign it to a report group (optional). (You must first create the report group so it appears in the drop-down list in the Memorize Report window.)

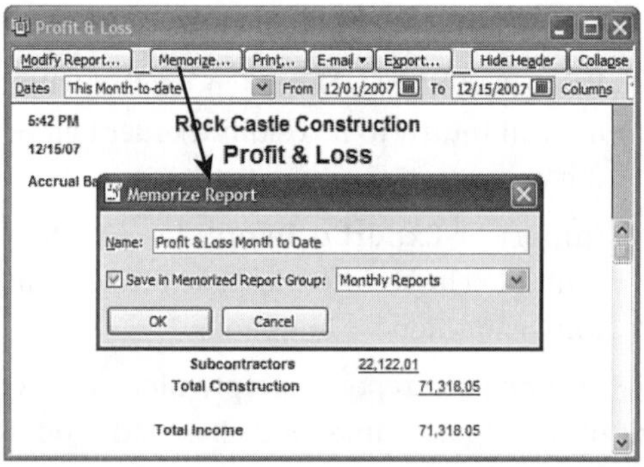

FIGURE 16.36

Click Memorize in any report, give the report a name, and (optionally) assign it to a report group.

If you choose not to assign a report group, your memorized reports are listed individually at the top of the Memorized Report List, as shown in Figure 16.37.

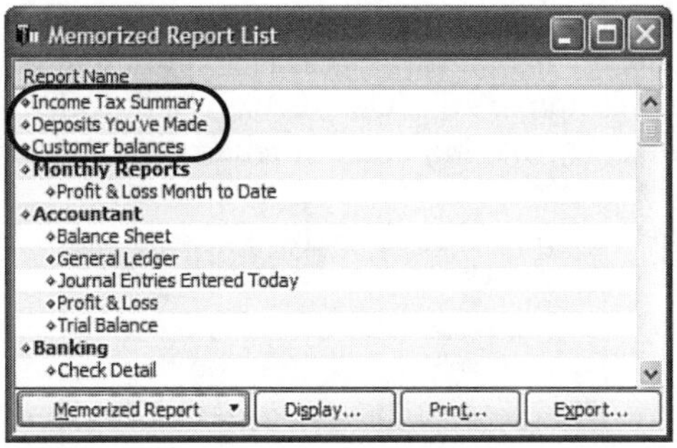

FIGURE 16.37

You do not need to assign memorized reports to a report group. If they are not assigned, they will appear at the top of the Memorized Report List.

Exporting and Importing Report Templates

QuickBooks offers the option to export and import report templates. This feature is useful for accountants who want to save time by having several clients use the same report template.

Only the format and filter settings are stored with report templates. If you create a report template and then have several clients use it, when the client imports it, the desired report is generated with the current client's data, not the data that it was created with.

You can export and import a single report or a group of reports only from the Memorized Report List. So before you attempt to export a report, be sure QuickBooks memorizes it first.

Exporting a Report or Report Group Template

To export a report or report group template, follow these steps:

1. Click **Reports, Memorized Reports**. The Memorized Reports List dialog appears.

2. On the Memorized Reports List dialog, select **Export Template** from the **Memorized Reports List** drop-down menu.

3. The Specify File Name dialog appears in Windows Explorer, enabling you to select a location to store the template (.QBR extension).

4. Simply attach the stored report template or report group to an email, or copy it to a removable storage device such as a USB drive to share with other QuickBooks data files.

Rescue Me!

Certain restrictions exist when creating a template for export. For example, if you filter for a specific account that might not be present in every customer's file, QuickBooks will provide the message shown in Figure 16.38, warning that this report cannot be exported.

FIGURE 16.38

If your report has too many specific filters, you might not be able to export and share it with multiple data files.

Importing a Report or Report Group Template

To import a report or report group template, follow these steps:

1. Click **Reports, Memorized Reports**. The Memorized Reports List dialog appears.

2. On the Memorized Reports List dialog, select **Import Template** from the **Memorized Reports List** drop-down menu.

3. The Specify File Name dialog appears in Windows Explorer, enabling you to select the stored location of the .QBR template.

4. Select the appropriate .QBR report or report group template.

5. Click **Open**. The Memorize Report dialog appears for you to assign a name for the report and optionally assign it to a group.

6. Click **OK** to add the report to your memorized report list.

Digging Deeper

Did you know that an abundance of reports are already created for you to import into your or your client's data file?

Both business owners and accountants will find these reports useful and unique to what you already have in QuickBooks.

Go to www.quickbooksgroup.com. On the left, select QB Library and from the QB Library menu dialog, select Reports. QuickBooks provides a long list of reports available for you to download and import into your or your client's own QuickBooks data file.

Exporting Reports to a .CSV File or to Excel

You might have occasions where you want to export your reports to Excel to manipulate them in some more extensive method than is available while working in QuickBooks.

Rescue Me!

I generally try to discourage exporting to Excel and do my best with a client to find the appropriate report in QuickBooks, simply because any changes you make to your report in Excel do not "flow" back into your QuickBooks data file. Also, any changes you make to your QuickBooks data file do not change the information in an existing exported Excel copy of your QuickBooks report.

To export a report to either .CSV or Excel format, follow these steps:

1. From the open report, click the **Export** button at the top of the report. The Export Report dialog appears.

2. Choose between the .CSV or Excel format.

3. On the **Basic** tab of the Export Report dialog, you can select to export to a new Excel file or an existing Excel file. In Figure 16.39, I selected a new Excel workbook.

FIGURE 16.39
The Export Report dialog enables you to choose the format for the export as well as to create a new file or import into an existing file.

4. On the **Advanced** tab of the Export Report dialog are options for preserving QuickBooks formatting, enabling certain Excel features, and printing options. Test these options a few times and alternate what features or print options are selected. You might be surprised at the outcome.

5. Click **Export** to create the exported report, as shown in Figure 16.40.

Remember, however, that exported reports are "static"—their information is fixed in time. Changes made to the Excel report do not go back into QuickBooks and changes in QuickBooks do not update the Excel report until it is exported again. So, use the export tool with caution so that you do not create more work for yourself.

If you are customizing a Balance Sheet, Profit & Loss, or Budget vs. Actual report, review the first section in this chapter that discusses the new Intuit Statement Writer tool offered with the release of QuickBooks 2009.

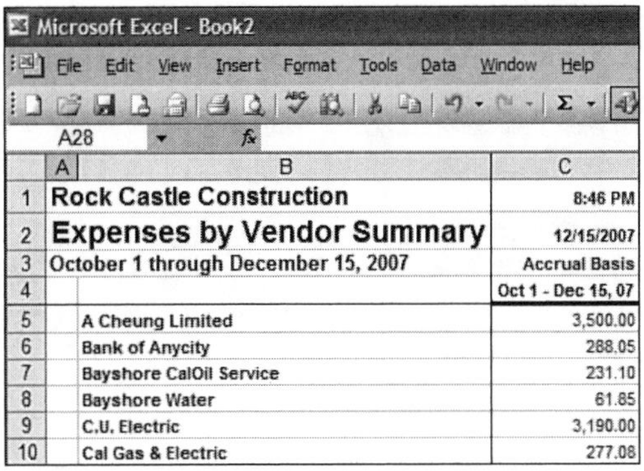

FIGURE 16.40

Easily convert any QuickBooks list or report to a .CSV or Excel format.

Emailing Reports

Did you know that you can email reports from your QuickBooks data? This can be a convenient way to get paper data to your customers, vendors, and even accountant. The release of QuickBooks 2008 greatly enhanced the functionality of email, offering Outlook users the option of sending reports and forms through their own Outlook account, the benefit of having a record kept in the "sent" folder.

When you email the report, QuickBooks offers two options: You can create a separate Adobe PDF for each report, or you can choose to create an Excel file that is attached to the email. You must have an Internet connection on the computer that is used to send the report.

If you want to set Outlook as your default e-mail, select Edit, Preferences, Send Forms. Select the My Preferences tab where you can set the default e-mail application to be Outlook or QuickBooks.

To email a report, follow these steps:

1. From the open report, click **Email** and choose whether to send the **Send Report as Excel** or to send the **Send Report as PDF**.

2. If a security message appears indicating that sending information over Internet email is not secure, click **OK** to continue or click **Cancel**.

   Beginning with the release of QuickBooks 2008, if you clicked OK, QuickBooks launches Outlook (if it's not already open) within QuickBooks and creates a new message with the report attached, as shown in Figure 16.41. This feature enables you to use your Outlook database for email addresses as well as track your sent items.

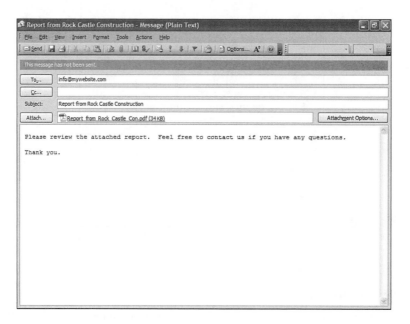

FIGURE 16.41

Reports sent as PDF or Excel attachments can use your own Outlook account to send.

If you do not use Outlook for your email, QuickBooks continues to send the email through QuickBooks Business Solutions, which has been available for years. Figure 16.42 shows how the email is created within QuickBooks when Outlook is not your email program.

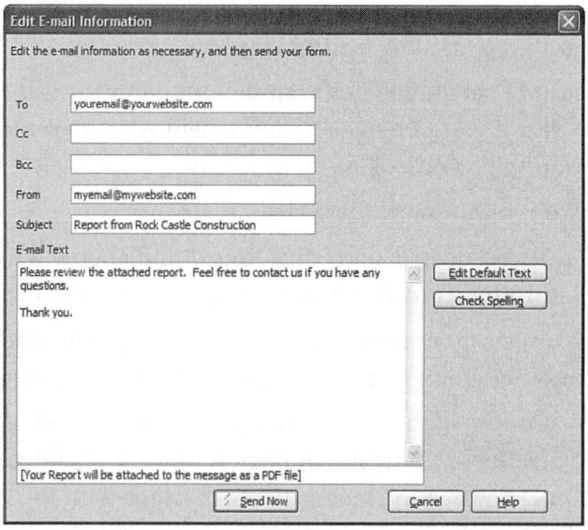

FIGURE 16.42

Send a report as an attachment through QuickBooks (when you don't use Outlook).

3. If you are sending the report through Outlook, simply add your email address and any additional comments to the email. Click **Send** when done. You are returned to your QuickBooks data file, and the email is stored in your Outlook sent folder.

If you are not using Outlook for email, simply click **Send Now** and QuickBooks transmits the email for you.

 Digging Deeper

QuickBooks offers an automated sync of contacts with Microsoft's Outlook. To obtain this tool, simply download it from http://support.quickbooks.intuit.com/support/tools/contact_sync/.

This free tool will create a menu option in your Outlook program where you can sync your QuickBooks contacts to Outlook or Outlook to QuickBooks.

The tool has been improved greatly during the last few years, and any business using both QuickBooks and Outlook can be more efficient when syncing shared data between the two programs.

We have discussed methods to enhance your use of QuickBooks reports; the next sections will offer even more flexibility in creating reports that meet your or your client's specific business needs.

About Financial Statement Designer

The Financial Statement Designer, commonly referred to as FSD, has been replaced with a much more robust reporting tool called Intuit Statement Writer, which is discussed at the beginning of this section. The Intuit Statement Writer is an add-one (a fee applies) for Premier Accountant 2009 and is included free with editions of QuickBooks Enterprise Solutions 9.0.

How does Financial Statement Designer differ from the new Intuit Statement Writer? Most importantly, ISW uses the Microsoft Excel platform for creating and modifying your customized financials. The FSD tool has limited Excel-like functions. So, if you use Microsoft Excel for reporting, you will find the Intuit Statement Writer offers far more flexibility with its integrated Excel functionality.

For users who desire to continue using Financial Statement Designer, download the FSD tool for use in QuickBooks Premier Accountant 2009 and QuickBooks Enterprise (all editions) 9.0.

Digging Deeper

Do you want to continue using Financial Statement Designer with your QuickBooks Premier Accountant 2009? Intuit does not deliver the FSD tool on the product CD, but you can download the add-on free at:

http://accountant.intuit.com/isw_fsd

The Financial Statement Designer will launch from a menu icon outside of your QuickBooks Premier Accountant 2009 data.

The Financial Statement Designer, commonly referred to as FSD, offers accounting professionals the ability to create a standard set of financial statements that comply with Generally Accepted Accounting Principles (GAAP) without changing the way that the client works or reports in QuickBooks.

For example, with FSD you can combine all the cash accounts within QuickBooks into one "Cash & Cash Equivalents" line on your GAAP-compliant financials, all without changing the client's QuickBooks data.

A few of the other benefits of using FSD include the following:

- Excel spreadsheet-like tools enable you to customize data fields and format your report in any way that meets your specific reporting needs.
- FSD is linked in "real time" to the QuickBooks data, which means that you can click on a number in the FSD report and it will take you into the QuickBooks data where you can edit the transaction. Unlike exporting to Excel, changes made in FSD do affect your QuickBooks data.
- FSD comes with many different templates for the Balance Sheet, Income Statement, and Statement of Cash Flows, as well as Compilation and Review letters. Or you can start from scratch and create your own.
- FSD is only available with QuickBooks Premier Accountant 2009 and QuickBooks Enterprise Solutions 9.0 all editions as a free download. FSD has been replaced with Intuit Statement Writer 2009.
- FSD limits the need to use outside programs to produce a complete set of financials. FSD offers you the ability to design your title page as well as review letters in addition to customizing the financials.
- FSD lets you assign the order in which you want to print the documents making it simple to produce a complete set of professional-looking financials right from within QuickBooks.

Discussing in detail how to work with the Financial Statement Designer tool is beyond the scope of this book.

Chapter 17

New for 2009! Detecting and Correcting with the Client Data Review Feature

- Introduction: Features and Benefits

- Starting a Client Data Review

- Customizing the Client Data Review Center

- Account Balances

- Review List Changes

- Accounts Receivable

- Accounts Payable

- Sales Tax

- Inventory

- Payroll

- Bank Reconciliation

- Miscellaneous

- Finishing a Client Data Review

- Reopening a Client Data Review

- Reporting on Review Activity

- Creating an External Accountant User

Introduction: Features and Benefits

New for QuickBooks 2009 is the Client Data Review (CDR) feature, shown in Figure 17.1. CDR is a new feature used primarily by accounting professionals to streamline the many tasks involved in reviewing, troubleshooting, and correcting a client's QuickBooks data.

The Client Data Review feature is available with QuickBooks Premier Accountant 2009 and QuickBooks Enterprise Solutions Accountant 9.0.

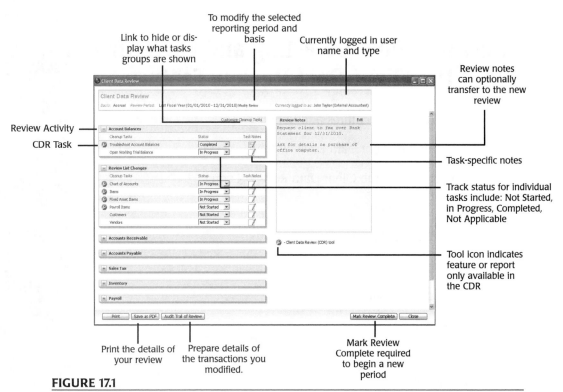

FIGURE 17.1

New for QuickBooks 2009—the CDR feature.

However, as an accounting professional you can also gain access to the Client Data Review features from any client's QuickBooks 2009 Pro, Premier (all editions), or Enterprise Solutions 9.0 (all editions) when you log into the client's file using a new type of user called External Accountant. (See the "Creating an External Accountant User" section for more details.) The CDR feature is not available for use with QuickBooks Simple Start files.

Additionally, CDR can be used when working with a client's Accountant's Copy file type (.QBX file extension). Some feature limitations apply when working in an Accountant's Copy file sharing type. Refer to Chapter 15, "Sharing Data with Your Accountant or Your Client," for more details on the

benefits of working with this file type and for improvements made to the
Accountant's Copy for QuickBooks 2009.

Typically, the workflow for using the new CDR is as follows:

1. Review with the client Accounts Receivable, Accounts Payable, and
   other balances for which the client has current information.

2. Begin your review of the client's data file using the CDR specific tasks
   and reports.

3. Make data corrections and set QuickBooks defaults.

4. Mark the Review Completed, letting CDR "store" your reviewed
   balances (client cannot change these!).

5. Print a report of the Review Details.

6. Print a report of your modified transactions.

7. Begin your next review and let QuickBooks detail for you any and all
   changes to transactions and lists since your last completed review!

Your steps might differ slightly if you are working in a client's Accountants
Copy file type.

 Digging Deeper

> The CDR feature is a QuickBooks single user activity; while you are
> working on tasks in the CDR, other users cannot open and work in the
> same data file.
>
> This limitation makes it more functional to choose to work with a
> client's Accountant's Copy file. You can complete the review from your
> office, and then merge your changes with the client's file while he or
> she continues day-to-day transactions.

There are specific tasks and reports that can be accessed only from within the
CDR. These tasks are indicated with the CDR icon; for example, see the icon
next to the Troubleshoot Account Balances task, as shown in Figure 17.1.
Other tasks listed without the icon indicate a feature or report that is available both in and outside of the CDR.

With the new CDR comes more robust tracking of the changes your client
makes to the data between your reviews. If your client is using QuickBooks
2009 Pro, Premier (all editions), and Enterprise Solutions 9.0 (all editions),
and the client has created an External Accountant user login for you, you will
have access to these key benefits and features:

  ■ New troubleshooting tools and reports are available only in the CDR.
    These are identified in this chapter with the "tool" icon ![tool icon], such as

the Troubleshooting Account Balances task, which is a CDR-dependent feature.

■ A trial balance window that "saves" the previously reviewed balances, compares them to the same prior dated balances in QuickBooks as of today. Your previously reviewed and stored QuickBooks reviewed balances cannot be modified by the client!

■ Identifies what chart of accounts balances differ and the amount of the difference when compared to your prior period of reviewed financials.

■ QuickBooks suggests an adjusting journal entry to make so that your prior period reviewed balances agree with the current QuickBooks data for that period. You remain in control, deciding if you want to modify the detail in the journal entry.

■ Tracking changes to the items lists, such as additions, name changes, and even tracking accounts or list items that were merged.

■ Tracking changes list items, accounts assigned, or for payroll items when a change to a rate is made.

■ Working with the Open Windows dialog? CDR displays in the Open Windows dialog enabling you to move efficiently between activities in QuickBooks and the Client Data Review activities.

■ Conveniently work on CDR in QuickBooks and modify or add transactions as normal with an immediate refresh of the data in your review.

■ Access the CDR while working in a client's Accountant's Copy file sharing format. Some feature limitations apply when working in an Accountant's Copy file sharing type. (Some limitations specific to Accountant's Copy apply.) See Chapter 15 for more details.

There is not a better time to encourage your client's to update to the newest version of QuickBooks. Only QuickBooks 2009 client files will offer this new innovative Client Data Review functionality!

Starting a Client Data Review

You are ready to begin a review of your client's file using the CDR when one of the following conditions exists:

■ You are at the client's place of business working in a QuickBooks 2009 Pro, Premier (all editions), or Enterprise 9.0 (all editions) data file.

■ You are working remotely (via Remote Access or other Web-enabled tools) in a client's QuickBooks 2009 Pro, Premier (all editions), or Enterprise 9.0 (all editions) data file.

■ You are working from the convenience of your office with a client's QuickBooks 2009 Accountant's Copy file. (The file extension is .QBA converted from the .QBX file the client sent to you. See for more details).

■ You have an External Accountant type user login with an optional password assigned. See the "Creating an External Accountant User" section at the end of this chapter.

 Digging Deeper

Beginning with QuickBooks 2009 Pro, Premier, and Enterprise 9.0, if a user logs in with the External Accountant user, he will have access to the CDR in QuickBooks Pro as well as all non-accountant industry editions of Premier and Enterprise 9.0.

It is easy in CDR to see the type and name of the user currently logged into the file. See Figure 17.1. In the top, right of the figure, notice the logged in user name and identification as an External Accountant user type displays.

If you do not log into a data file as the External Accountant user type, you will have access only to the CDR from the QuickBooks 2009 Premier Accountant Edition and all editions of QuickBooks Enterprise 9.0.

You will most likely not want to perform the tasks in the CDR if you are not working in the live, working data file or an Accountant's Copy file. If your client sends to you a QuickBooks 2009 backup file (.QBB extension) or portable company file (.QBM file extension), both of these files when restored will enable you to use the CDR, but your changes will not be able to be merged into the client's data file.

Chapter 15 discusses the benefits of using the Accountant's Copy file, a preferred data-sharing method if you need to use the CDR while your client continues day-to-day work in the file. Chapter 15 also details the improvements that were made to the Accountant's Copy for QuickBooks 2009.

Customizing the Client Data Review Center

You can customize the view you have in the CDR center to make it unique for each client's QuickBooks 2009 file. To gain access to these features, you need to launch the CDR:

1. From the **Accountant** menu, select **Client Data Review**. (The feature is also accessible from the Company menu of QuickBooks Pro 2009, Premier 2009, and QuickBooks Enterprise 9.0 if you are logging in as an External Accountant type user, refer to the last section in this chapter.) You can also launch CDR from the QuickBooks icon bar if you are using QuickBooks Premier Accountant 2009 or Enterprise Solutions Accountant 9.0, as shown in Figure 17.2.

Conveniently open Client Data Review from the icon bar.

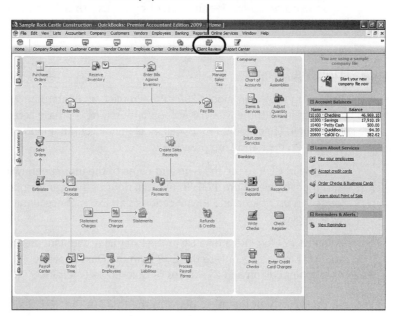

FIGURE 17.2

Launch the Client Data Review feature from the icon bar.

> **2.** If this is your first review for this client, the Client Data Review—Start
> Review dialog displays, as shown in Figure 17.3. From this dialog,
> select the default **Review Date Range** shown, or select a date range
> from the following options in the drop-down menu:
>
> ▪ Last Fiscal Year (your default fiscal year is defined in the
> QuickBooks Company, Company Information menu)
>
> ▪ Last Fiscal Quarter
>
> ▪ Last Month
>
> ▪ Custom (you will select the from and to dates)
>
> **3.** Select the **Review Basis—Accrual or Cash**. This basis defaults from the
> preference setting in the QuickBooks file for reports. To set your report-
> ing preferences, select Edit, Preferences. From the preferences on the
> left, select **Reports and Graphs**. You will need to be logged in as the
> Admin or External Accountant user in single-user mode to change the
> global preference for reporting basis.

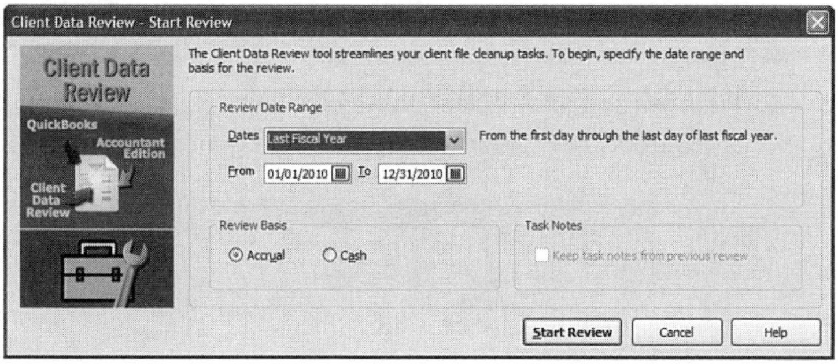

FIGURE 17.3

After launching the CDR for the first time, you will select your review period and reporting basis.

> **4.** Click **Start Review** and the Client Data Review dialog displays as was shown in Figure 17.1.

With the CDR open, you can now customize the view uniquely for each client.

Modifying the Review Date and Basis

The Basis and Review Period shown in the CDR defaulted from the QuickBooks data file preferences when the CDR was launched, or the date range was manually selected on the Client Data Review—Start Review dialog.

If after beginning a review, you need to change either of these settings, simply click on the Modify Review link in the CDR, top center, to be returned to the Start Review dialog, as shown in Figure 17.3.

Changing the Task Display

You might have some clients who do not need a review of some of the task groups in their QuickBooks data. For example, you are working in a client's file that does not have to track or pay sales tax. To remove the sales tax task group (or any of the other tasks) from the CDR, follow these steps:

> **1.** Complete steps 1 through 4 in the "Customizing the Client Data Review Center" section of this chapter. The CDR feature is launched.
>
> **2.** Click the **Customize Cleanup Tasks** link on the CDR dialog (see Figure 17.1).

3. The **Client Data Review—Customize** dialog displays as shown in Figure 17.4.

4. Place your mouse pointer on any list item and click once to unselect that specific task or group of tasks. Clicking again will reselect the list item.

FIGURE 17.4

Customer Client Data Review to show or hide specific cleanup tasks uniquely for each client's file.

 Digging Deeper

If you are attempting to perform a data review and you don't see a task group listed (for example, the Sales Tax task group doesn't display), you can select the Customize Cleanup tasks link on the CDR to enable this task group, as previously shown in Figure 17.1.

If the client's data file does not have the sales tax preference enabled in the QuickBooks file, that task group will not display in the CDR.

A link to setting the Sales Tax and other preferences is included in the Miscellaneous task group of the CDR.

5. Click the **Restore Defaults** button to return to the original settings.

6. Click **Help** to open the help topic specific for CDR.

7. Click **Save Changes** or **Cancel** if you do not want to make the changes.

You have successfully changed the lists of tasks that displays for this client's data file only.

Hiding and Showing Task Groups

You might not want to remove the task completely, but instead, you might want to minimize the task. In the CDR, follow these steps:

1. Complete steps 1 through 4 in the "Customizing the CDR Center" section of this chapter. The CDR is launched.

2. Click the (-) before a task group name to minimize the task group details.

3. Click the (+) before a task group name to maximize the task group details.

In the example shown in Figure 17.5, you will select the (-) before the Sales Tax task group header. The result, as shown in Figure 17.6, is to minimize the task for Sales Tax. The Hide and Show Task state for each task group on the CDR is company-file dependent. The changes you make in one company file will not be made in other QuickBooks client files.

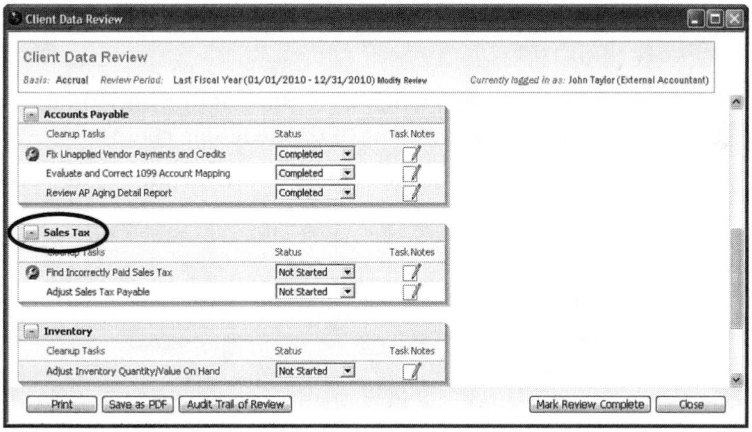

FIGURE 17.5

View before minimizing tasks.

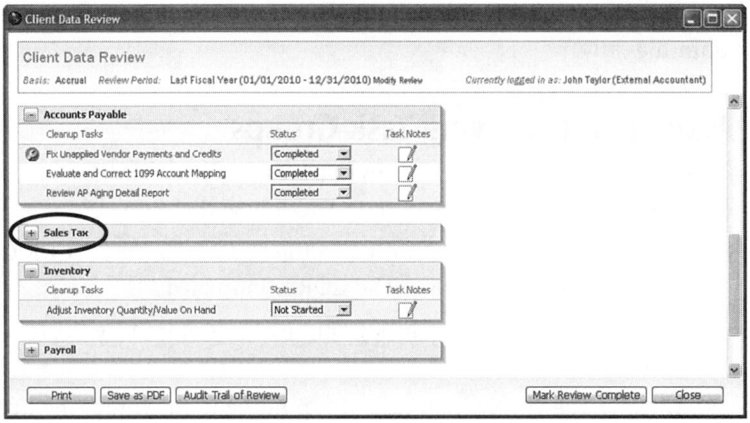

FIGURE 17.6

Selecting the (-) in front of a task group minimizes those tasks.

Assigning Status and Notes to Review Tasks

To help in managing the review of a client's file, you have an associated status you can optionally assign to each task. This feature is useful if you are unable to finish a review or if several accounting professionals are reviewing the same file.

To assign a new status or change an existing status, click on the status drop-down menu and choose from one of the available choices:

- Not Started (which is the default status assigned to all tasks when a review is started)
- In Progress
- Completed
- Not Applicable

Optionally, you can record a note about a particular task. Click on the task note icon to the right of a task as was shown in Figure 17.1. The task notes pad will display where you can document specific review notes for that task. After saving the task note, the Task Notes icon image changes to include "lines," which indicate that there are notes included. These notes are included in the CDR notes when printed.

When you return to a CDR in progress, or if you share the review with another accounting professional at your firm, each individual can see the progress of a particular task in review.

After customizing the CDR to show or hide specific task groups, you should take one more precaution.

Before beginning the review and making changes to a client's file, make sure you are logged in with the new External Accountant type user. This will ensure that your changes can be tracked separately from those made by the client and will also give you complete access to the Admin activities available in the CDR. For more information, read the "Creating an External Accountant User" section later in this chapter.

To see the currently logged in user, look to the top, right of the CDR. In Figure 17.1 the user name and External Accountant user type are identified. You are now ready to begin the review process. The following sections provide more details about the unique features and results that you can expect when reviewing and correcting your client's data file using this new innovative feature. You'll never want to do a review the "old fashioned" way again!

Account Balances

Although you do not have to do the review task groups in any particular order, I do recommend that you begin with the Account Balances task group. A reliable client date file review depends on accurate balance sheet reporting, which includes financial numbers from prior periods.

If a closing date was not set previously, or if the user was granted access to adding, modifying, or deleting prior year transactions, your ending balances that QuickBooks reports now might be different from those you used to prepare financials or tax return documents. Setting a closing date and password can help to control changes to prior period transactions.

The Account Balances review tasks display in trial balance, debit, and credit formats including the following columns of information, as shown in Figure 17.7.

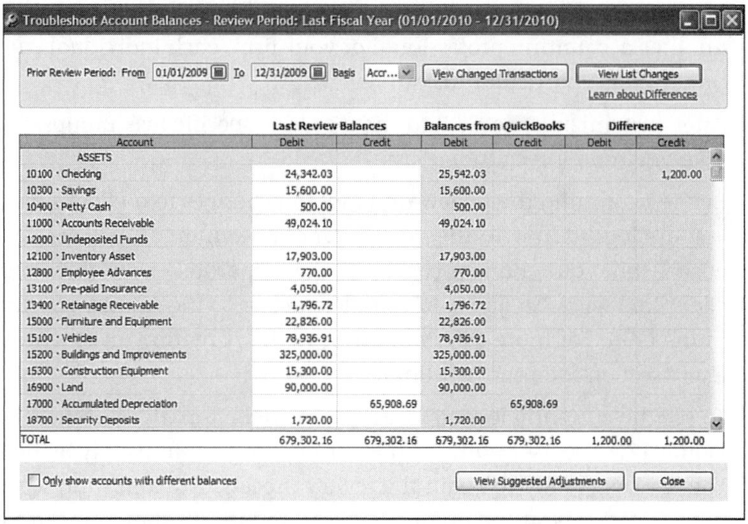

	Last Review Balances		Balances from QuickBooks		Difference	
Account	Debit	Credit	Debit	Credit	Debit	Credit
ASSETS						
10100 · Checking	24,342.03		25,542.03			1,200.00
10300 · Savings	15,600.00		15,600.00			
10400 · Petty Cash	500.00		500.00			
11000 · Accounts Receivable	49,024.10		49,024.10			
12000 · Undeposited Funds						
12100 · Inventory Asset	17,903.00		17,903.00			
12800 · Employee Advances	770.00		770.00			
13100 · Pre-paid Insurance	4,050.00		4,050.00			
13400 · Retainage Receivable	1,796.72		1,796.72			
15000 · Furniture and Equipment	22,826.00		22,826.00			
15100 · Vehicles	78,936.91		78,936.91			
15200 · Buildings and Improvements	325,000.00		325,000.00			
15300 · Construction Equipment	15,300.00		15,300.00			
16900 · Land	90,000.00		90,000.00			
17000 · Accumulated Depreciation		65,908.69		65,908.69		
18700 · Security Deposits	1,720.00		1,720.00			
TOTAL	679,302.16	679,302.16	679,302.16	679,302.16	1,200.00	1,200.00

FIGURE 17.7

New for QuickBooks 2009, compare current QuickBooks data to your prior period reviewed balances.

The Troubleshoot Account Balances dialog includes:

- Accounts, grouped by account type:
  - Assets
  - Liabilities
  - Equity
  - Income
  - Cost of Goods Sold
  - Expenses
- Last Review Balances, debit and credit columns
- Balances from QuickBooks, debit and credit columns
- Difference Column, debit and credit columns

Troubleshooting Account Balances

The primary purpose of this task is to provide a window where QuickBooks can compare the prior year's ending balances (as you used to prepare financials, tax returns, or monthly and quarterly reviews) with what QuickBooks currently shows for that same prior date range.

The workflow for this activity is:

1. First time you use the Troubleshooting Account Balances, manually enter the amounts in the Last Review Balances columns to agree with your last reported financials or filed tax return.

2. For each remaining review, QuickBooks will transfer your saved CDR balances to the Last Review Balances columns after selecting Mark Review Complete.

3. Differences in balances are identified in the Debit and Credit Difference columns of the Troubleshoot Account Balances dialog. If this is not your first review for this client's data file, you can click on any difference amount to see what transactions made up that difference.

4. Optionally, click the View Changed Transactions to see all changes. (This report is generated after your first review is completed.)

5. View list changes.

6. View suggested adjustments; QuickBooks prepares an adjusting journal entry for your review.

7. Let QuickBooks create the journal entry or modify the suggested amounts and accounts assigned.

8. Optionally, create a reversing journal entry in the current period or on any date you choose.

Your work is complete in this window when there are no amounts in the difference columns indicating that the Last Review Balances agree with the QuickBooks data for that same prior period date.

Entering Last Review Balances

If this is your first time using CDR with your client's data, you will need to manually enter the Last Review Balances columns in debit and credit spreadsheet format. This is the only time you will be required to manually enter the balances. For future reviews, QuickBooks will populate the Last Reviewed Balances columns with the reviewed balances as recorded when you selected the Mark Review as Complete at the bottom, right of the CDR.

The Troubleshoot Account Balances dialog compares these prior balances to the current balances QuickBooks has for each account for the same prior date range. QuickBooks is determining for you which accounts have a discrepancy from the last review! Imagine the time saved! A very time-consuming task is automatically done for us with the CDR!

These balances would have been less likely to change if a closing date and password had been entered in your client's data file.

Rescue Me!

When preparing an Account Balances review, which involves a chart of account listing that was marked as inactive in QuickBooks, but has a balance in the account as of the date range in the review, the Client Data Review dialog for Account Balances will include that account listing.

In Figure 17.7, there is a difference for accounts 10100-Checking and 63900-Rent (not shown). The next section will detail how these CDR-dependant tasks will help you locate these "differences."

Viewing Changed Transactions

If this is your first time using the Client Data Review for a client's data file, QuickBooks will not be able to detail the specific changed transactions in the Differences columns. However, after the first CDR is Mark Review as Complete, QuickBooks will begin tracking from that time-specific changed transactions.

To determine what transactions dated on or before your last completed review date have been modified, click the button in the top right of the CDR titled, "View Changed Transactions" or double-click any amount displayed in the Differences column. The Transaction Change Report is displayed as shown in Figure 17.8. The report identifies for you the specific transactions that have been added, modified, or deleted since you selected Mark Review as Complete.

![Audit Trail window showing Transaction Change Report for Rock Castle Construction]

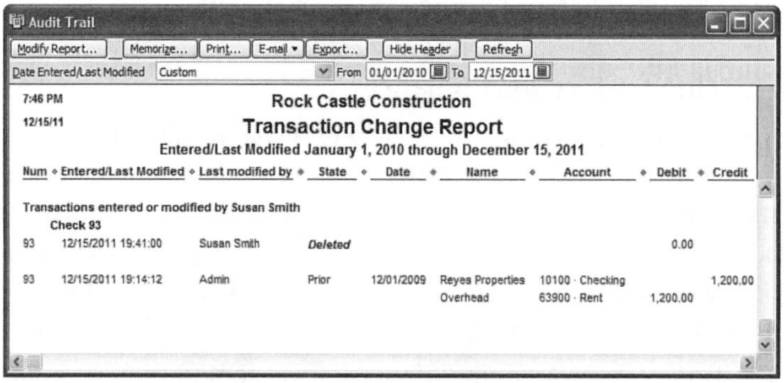

FIGURE 17.8

The Transaction Change Report easily identifies those transactions that are in the Difference column.

The Transaction Change Report is filtered for transactions modified since the completed date given to your last review to today's current date. You can limit what you see on the report by choosing the Filter button on the displayed report. You can filter for Days Entered/Last Modified to see only those transactions that were changed after you finished your review.

This one feature alone is why we want our client's using QuickBooks 2009. Think of all the time you will save on future reviews of your client's data! Indeed, who will want to do a review the "old fashioned" way!

Viewing List Changes

You can also select the Review List Changes; this feature is discussed in more detail in the "Review List Changes" section.

View Suggested Adjustments

When QuickBooks detects any difference between your reviewed prior period balances and the current balances for that same prior period review date, a suggested adjusting journal entry is prepared for you to review.

To have QuickBooks assist in the preparation of this adjusting journal entry:

1. Click the **View Suggested Adjustments** button and QuickBooks opens a Make General Journal Entries form marked as adjusting and dated as of the last date in your review (see Figure 17.9). If your debits and credits are equal in the Review Last Balances columns, this journal entry should also have debits equal to credits for any differences that were detected. Note, you will not be able to save the journal entry unless debits and credits are equal.

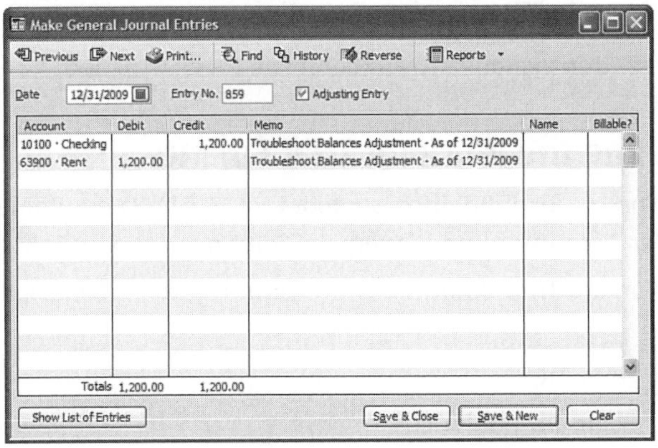

FIGURE 17.9

QuickBooks prepares an adjusting journal entry to agree with your reviewed balances for the prior period.

Rescue Me!

If you selected View Suggested Adjustments, and you had adjustments to both an Accounts Receivable and Accounts Payable account, you will receive a warning message that you cannot adjust accounts receivable and accounts payable in the same journal entry. Instructions are given to remove one of the lines and the corresponding balancing line and enter it in a separate journal entry form.

2. If you are working in an Accountant's Copy file, you might also get a notice that any changes made to shaded fields in the journal entry will transfer back to the client. Select **OK** to close this message.

3. Click **OK** to close the message about automatically numbering your journal entries.

4. Click **Save & Close** to close the **Make Journal Entries** dialog.

5. Click **View Suggested Reversing Entries** if after these adjustments are made you need to reverse them; it is useful if the client corrected the error in a future accounting period. Or, select the **Don't Reverse** button to close the **Reversing Entries** dialog.

The Troubleshooting Account Balances task is complete when there are no amounts in the Differences column. Optionally, enter a task note for the Troubleshooting Account Balances task. Select the Mark as Complete button on the bottom of the Troubleshooting Account Balances CDR feature.

When the Mark Review Complete button is selected on the CDR dialog, CDR will take the Balances from the QuickBooks column and transfer them to the Last Review Balances column in the Troubleshooting Account Balances dialog. The Last Review Balances amounts *will not* change when clients add, modify, or delete transactions in your completed review period.

Opening the Working Trial Balance

The Working Trial Balance is a tool that has been available for years in the Premier Accountant and Enterprise Solutions Accountant.

The Working Trial Balance, as shown in Figure 17.10, displays the following details:

- Account
- Beginning Balance
- Transactions (for the selected date range)
- Adjustments (total of adjusting journal entries)

- Ending Balance

- Workpaper Reference notes

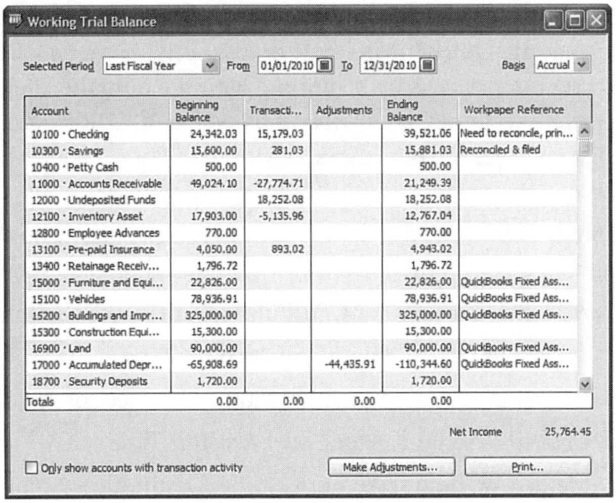

FIGURE 17.10

The Working Trial Balance window enables you to easily view the current period balance and make adjusting journal entries.

The Working Trial Balance provides a working window to manage changes to a client's ending balances. You normally use this tool after you have matched the prior year balances in the Troubleshoot Account Balances task with your records and you need to review and correct the next accounting period.

Click on the Make Adjustments button to create an adjusting journal entry and watch the net impact to your client's Net Income with each change. When you are finished, click the Print button to prepare a report of your work.

Review List Changes

New for QuickBooks 2009 Pro, Premier (all editions), and Enterprise 9.0 (all editions), QuickBooks will now track changes made to list items as of the date your client updates the file to QuickBooks 2009. The Review List Changes feature is available only in the CDR. The type of changes tracked are specific to each task as detailed in the next several sections. Remember, if a task has the Client Data Review icon in front of it, it indicates that the task can only be done with the Client Data Review. If any other tasks are listed, they simply link to the respective menu in QuickBooks for that activity.

This feature is only available for QuickBooks 2009 users. So perhaps now, more than ever before is the best time to upgrade to the newest version!

Chart of Accounts

Reviewing the Chart of Accounts, correcting setup errors, making an account inactive, and merging like accounts was covered in detail in Chapter 2, "Reviewing the QuickBooks Chart of Accounts." This new CDR feature now tracks list changes activity beginning with the date the client installs and upgrades his data to QuickBooks 2009. When a CDR is marked as Completed, these list changes are also marked with an "R" for reviewed so that in future reviews, you can conveniently "hide" those changes.

Click on the Chart of Accounts task in the Review List Changes task group. QuickBooks displays the Review List Changes dialog as shown in Figure 17.11.

The Review List Changes for Chart of Accounts track the following accounts:

- Added—Account Name and Account Type
- Changed—Marked Inactive, Name changed, or Account Type changed
- Deleted—Account Name and Account Type
- Merged—Original Account Name, Destination Account, Name and Account Type

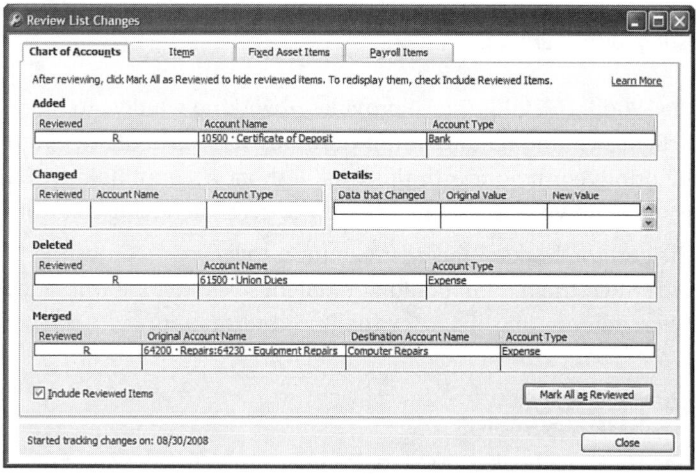

FIGURE 17.11

QuickBooks 2009 tracks changes made to list items.

For changes your client has made that you want to indicate as "Reviewed," click the Mark All as Reviewed button. For changes you make to the lists while logged in as the new External Accountant user, they are automatically marked as reviewed.

The tabs at the top enable easy access to the remaining tracked list changes. Click Close when you have completed this task.

⚙️ Items

Chapter 3, "Reviewing and Correcting Item List Errors," details methods to find and troubleshoot item setup errors. This new feature now tracks this activity beginning with the date the client installs or upgrades his data to QuickBooks 2009. When the review is marked as Completed, an "R" is placed next to each line item change to indicate that it has been reviewed. In future client data reviews, you can conveniently hide these previously reviewed changes.

Click the Items task in the Review List Changes task group. QuickBooks displays the Review List Changes dialog, as shown in Figure 7.12.

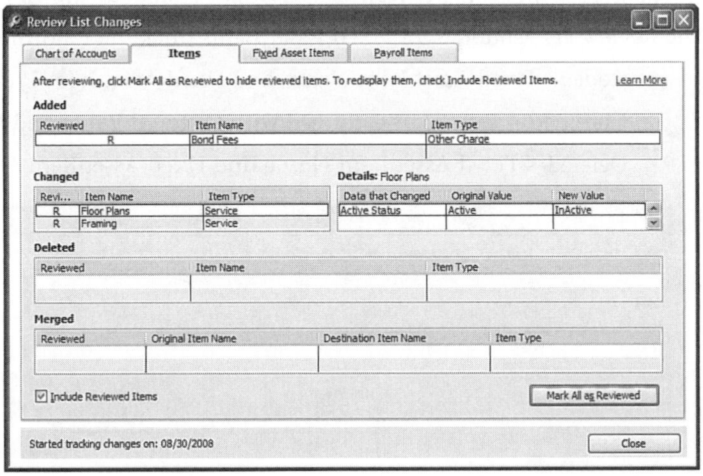

FIGURE 17.12

New for QuickBooks 2009, list changes are tracked.

The Review List Changes for Items track the following items:

- Added—Item Name and Item Type
- Changed—Data that Changed with Original Value and New Value
- Deleted—Item Name and Item Type
- Merged—Original Item Name, Destination Item Name, and Item Type

When the Mark All as Reviewed button is selected, CDR feature will place an "R" in the Reviewed column for each item list change your client made. If you are logged into the file as an External Accountant user type, as you make list changes, they are automatically marked as Reviewed.

Tabs at the top enable easy access to the remaining tracked list changes. Click Close when you have completed this task.

🕐 Fixed Asset Items

Reviewing the purpose of Fixed Asset Items was covered in detail in Chapter 3. Details were also provided in that chapter about how to create a Fixed Asset item type. This new feature now tracks this activity beginning with the date of when a client installs or upgrades his data to QuickBooks 2009. When the Mark Review as Completed option is selected, an "R" is placed next to each fixed asset item change to indicate that it has been reviewed. In future client data reviews, you can conveniently hide these previously reviewed changes.

Click on the Fixed Asset Items task in the Review List Changes task group. QuickBooks displays the Review List Changes dialog, as shown in Figure 7.13.

The Review List Changes for Fixed Asset Items track the following fixed assets:

- Added—Fixed Asset Item Name and Fixed Asset Item Type
- Changed— Data that Changed with Original Value and New Value
- Deleted— Fixed Asset Item Name and Fixed Asset Item Type

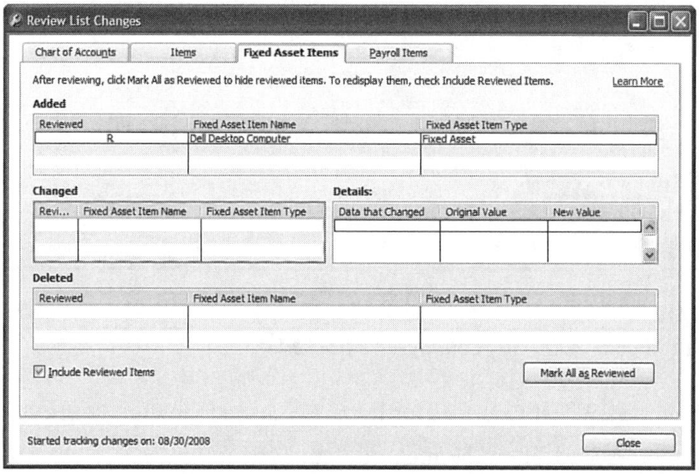

FIGURE 17.13

QuickBooks 2009 tracks changes to the Fixed Asset Item list.

When the Mark All as Reviewed button is selected, the Client Data Review will place an "R" in the Reviewed column for each fixed asset item list change your client made. If you are logged into the file as an External Accountant user type, as you make list changes, they are automatically marked as Reviewed.

Tabs along the top of the Review List Changes dialog enable easy access to the remaining tracked list changes. Click Close when you are completed with this task.

⊚ Payroll Items

Reviewing the purpose of Payroll Items was covered in detail in Chapter 14, "Reviewing and Correcting Payroll Errors." Details were also provided in that chapter to correct payroll setup errors. This new feature now tracks changes made to payroll items beginning with the date the client installs or upgrades his data to QuickBooks 2009. When the review is marked as Completed, an "R" is placed next to each payroll item change to indicate that it has been reviewed. In future client data reviews, you can conveniently hide these.

Click on the Payroll Items task in the Review List Changes task group. QuickBooks displays the Review List Changes dialog, as shown in Figure 17.14.

The Review List Changes for Payroll Items track the following payroll items:

- Added—Payroll Item Name and Payroll Item Type
- Changed—Data that Changed with Original Value and New Value
- Deleted—Payroll Item Name and Payroll Item Type
- Merged—Original Payroll Item Name, Destination Payroll Item Name, and Payroll Item Type

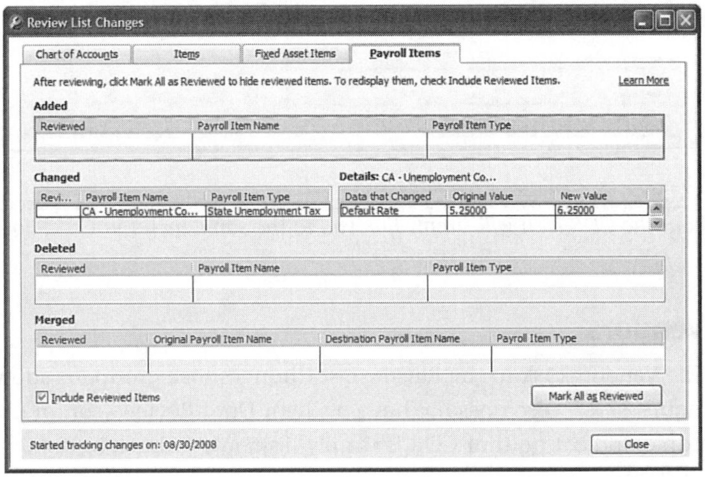

FIGURE 17.14

QuickBooks 2009 also tracks changes to payroll list items.

When the Mark All as Reviewed button is selected, the CDR will place an "R" in the Reviewed column for each item list change your client made. If you are logged into the file as an External Accountant user type, as you make list changes, they are automatically marked as Reviewed.

Tabs at the top enables easy access to the remaining tracked list changes. Click Close when you have completed this task.

Customers

Notice how in Figure 17.15, the Customers task in the Review List Changes pane does *not* have a Client Data Review icon in front of the name, indicating that CDR is simply linking you back to the original Customer Center.

Refer to Chapter 7, "Reviewing and Correcting Accounts Receivable Errors," for more details on how to use the Customer Center to gather information and easily find specific transactions.

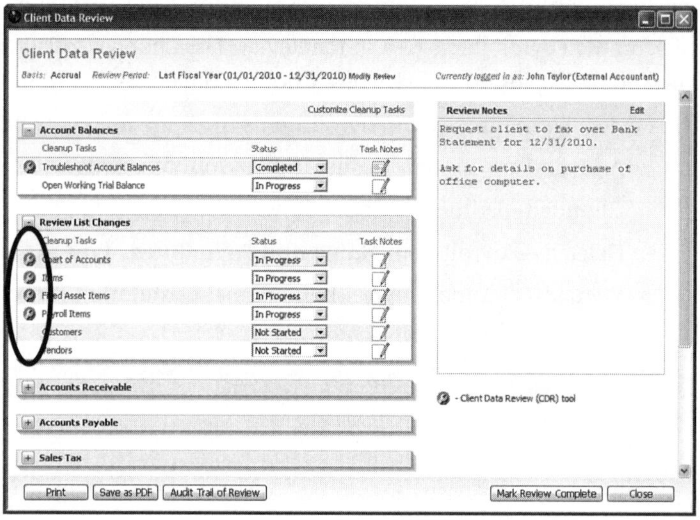

FIGURE 17.15
Tasks without the CDR icon will simply link you to the same menu in QuickBooks.

Vendors

The Vendors task in the Review List Changes task group, as shown in Figure 17.15, also does *not* have a Client Data Review icon in front of the name, indicating that CDR is simply linking you back to the original Customer Center.

Refer to Chapter 11, "Reviewing and Correcting Accounts Payable Errors," for more details on how to use the Vendor Center to gather information and easily find specific transactions.

Accounts Receivable

A complete review of Accounts Receivable, including the proper process to use in QuickBooks for potentially avoiding the corrections detailed in this section can be found in Chapter 7 and Chapter 8, "Reviewing and Correcting Errors with the Undeposited Funds Account."

The tasks listed in the Accounts Receivable task group of the CDR will help you easily correct client mistakes made when the client recorded a customer payment or made a deposit form, but *did not* assign the transaction to an open customer payment.

More recent versions of QuickBooks will help discourage this with messaging that warns the user not to use a Make Deposit form to record a customer payment. If recording a customer payment without assigning to an open invoice, QuickBooks provides a message that the credit will be left in the customer's account.

The AR Aging Detail Report is listed last in the Accounts Receivable task group. I recommend reviewing the AR Aging Detail Report and other reports prior to making corrections with the CDR. Properly reviewing your client's data will help you make the most informed decisions about the corrections that might be needed.

Fixing Unapplied Customer Payments and Credits

If your client entered a customer payment, but did not apply the payment to an invoice, this tool will help simplify the task of assigning the unapplied payment to the proper invoice, saving you time over the processes detailed in Chapter 8.

To begin fixing unapplied customer payments and credits, follow these steps:

1. Complete steps 1 through 4 of the "Customizing the Client Data Review Center" section of this chapter. The CDR feature is launched.

2. Click the **Fix Unapplied Customer Payments and Credit** link from the Accounts Receivable task group.

3. On the left, the tab for **Customers** will default, and on the right, the tab for **Invoices and Charges** will default.

4. With your mouse pointer, select any of the customers on the list, as shown in Figure 17.16. With a customer selected on the left, the **Invoices and Charges** pane will display unapplied payments and credits (left side) and open invoices (right side) for that specific customer.

5. On the **Invoices and Charges** pane, place a check mark next to the payment or credit on the left pane and a check mark next to the associated open invoice on the right you want to apply the payment to.

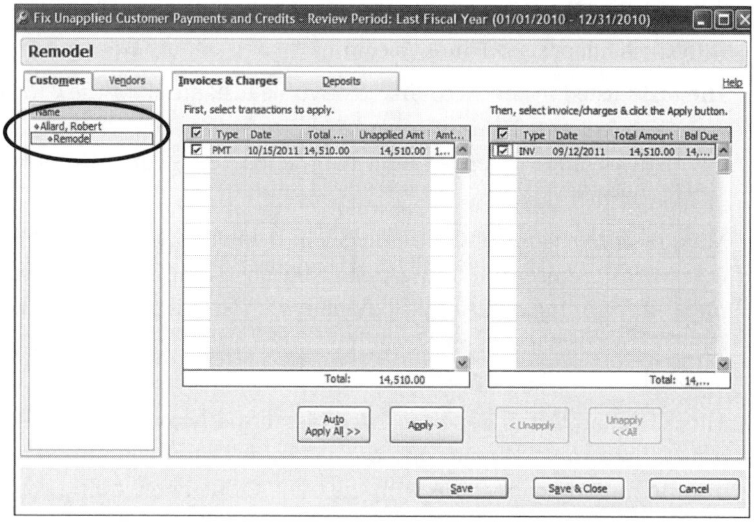

FIGURE 17.16

Assign unapplied customer payments or credits to an open invoice.

6. Enter in the **Amt to Apply** column an amount if different than the payment amount you want to apply.

7. Optionally, click the **Auto Apply All** button to apply all of the unapplied payments to the invoices on the right.

8. Or, click the **Apply** button to assign the payments or credits selected on the left to the selected open invoices on the right. The items are then grayed out to indicate that you have already assigned them.

9. Click **Save** to begin working on another customer record or **Save & Close** to complete the task.

Rescue Me!

Cash basis reporting taxpayers should take caution when using this tool. In cash basis reporting, the date of the customer payment form is the date that revenue is recorded. If an unapplied customer payment received in a prior year is assigned to a customer invoice, QuickBooks will assign the unapplied payment to the invoice. The transaction will increase (debit) accounts receivable and increase (credit) income as of the date of the customer payment form.

If correcting entries were made previously for those years, this correction will change those prior period financials. The CDR *does not* recognize the controls associated with setting a closing date. Additionally, QuickBooks does not provide any warnings that you are modifying a transaction dated on or before the closing date.

Recent editions of QuickBooks make this error less likely to occur with the many warnings that are provided.

Clearing Up Undeposited Funds Account

Have you ever worked with a client's data file that had an incorrect undeposited funds balance? Did your client create a separate deposit form without assigning the receive payment to the deposit?

The undeposited funds account is a current asset type on the Balance Sheet. Like using a safe, payments received are recorded in QuickBooks and then later gathered and totaled on one deposit ticket. This is similar to the purpose of the undeposited funds account type; more details are provided in Chapter 8.

The Clear-up Undeposited Funds Account task can help you assign those undeposited funds to the deposit form that was created incorrectly. Recent editions of QuickBooks make this error less likely to occur with the many warnings that are provided.

It is important to know that this feature will work when both of the following conditions apply:

- Receive Payment form was recorded and assigned to the Undeposited Funds account without assigning the payment to an open customer invoice.

- Make Deposits form was recorded, the Received From column included the Customer or Customer:Job name and the Account From column has an account assigned, which is (typically an income account). See Figure 17.17. Without the Received From column including the Customer or Customer:Job name, CDR *will not* display the deposit.

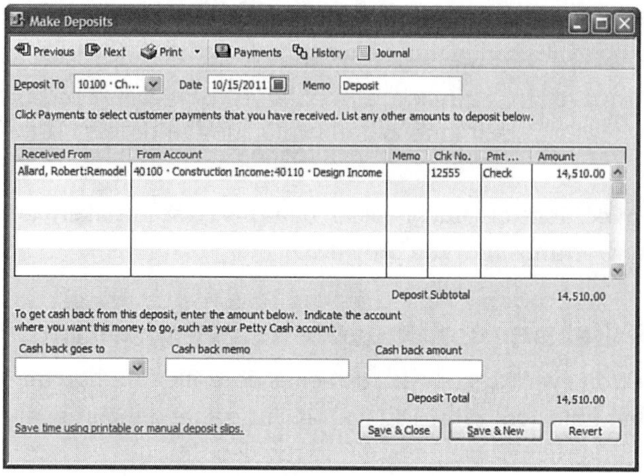

FIGURE 17.17

Example of a customer payment recorded improperly.

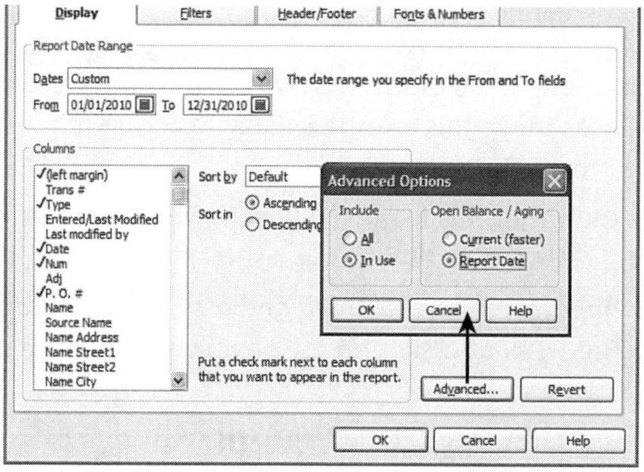

FIGURE 17.18

Associate the customer payment in Clear up Undeposited Funds to the incorrectly recorded Make Deposit form.

To begin correcting the Undeposited Funds Account balance, as shown in Figure 17.18 follow these steps:

1. Complete steps 1 through 4 of the "Customizing the CDR" section of this chapter. The Client Data Review is launched.

2. Click the **Clear-up Undeposited Funds Account** link from the Accounts Receivable pane.

3. The **Customers** tab on the top left and the **Deposits** tab on the right are selected by default.

4. With your mouse pointer, select any of the customers on the list to the left. The **Deposits** pane will display undeposited payments on the left for that specific customer. On the right, will be displayed Make Deposit forms also assigned to that customer.

5. Place a check mark next to the payment on the left and the make deposit form on the right you want to associate the payment with.

6. Click the **Apply** button to assign. The list items are grayed out, indicating they have been applied to each other.

7. Click **Save** to begin correcting records for the next customer or **Save & Close** to complete the task.

Digging Deeper

Need to return to the original transaction in QuickBooks during your review? Simply double-click with your mouse pointer on any transaction to open the original transaction form.

You are now ready to move on with your review. While the AR Aging Detail Report tasks is listed last on the Accounts Receivable task group, I recommend looking at it first to get a general idea of the types of corrections you may need to make with the remaining accounts receivable tasks.

Reviewing the AR Aging Detail Report

Check the AR Aging Detail Report before fixing transactions, an individual transaction can be deceiving if you don't see its relationship with other related transactions.

When you select the Review AR Aging Detail Report link, QuickBooks opens the same titled report. From this report, you can view open credits and invoices comparing this total with your balance sheet balance for the selected report date.

What exactly are you looking for on the aging report? You might be looking for customer credits that are aged and have not been applied to current open customer invoices. Or, perhaps as Chapter 7, "Reviewing and Correcting Accounts Receivable Errors," documented, you may want to remove an open balance from a customer's invoice.

I prefer to use the Open Invoices report because it groups the data by Customer or Customer:Job. If you are reviewing for a previous date, you will need to modify the report to show your balances as of that prior date. To do this, follow these steps:

1. Click **Reports, Customers & Receivables, Open Invoices**. This report includes all payments made by your customer as of today's computer system date.

2. Review the report with today's date first. This will help you identify what corrections you may want to make using the tasks defined in this section. Reviewing it with today's date will also show if the correction you may have needed on a previous date has already been corrected.

3. If you are reviewing for some date in the past, it is important that you click **Modify Report**, select the **Display** tab, and click **Advanced**. In the **Open Balance/Aging** pane of the Advanced Options dialog, select the **Report Date** option (see Figure 17.19). This modification to the report enables you to see each invoice balance detail as of the report date (see Figure 17.20). If you do not modify this report, QuickBooks will display the date on the report, but will also reduce the balances owed for payments made after the report date.

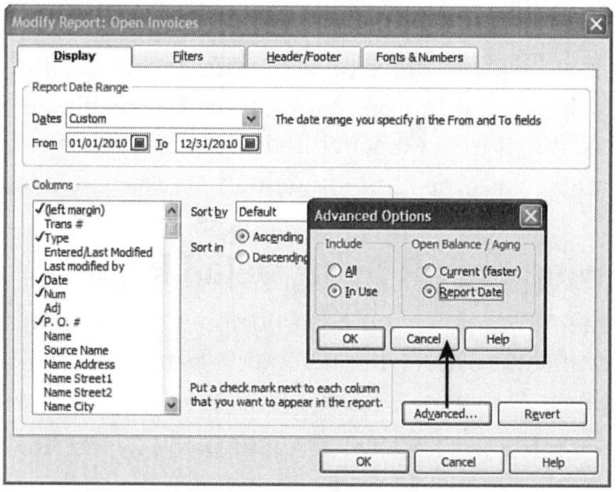

FIGURE 17.19

Open Invoices report, when modified, can be compared to the totals on your Balance Sheet report for some time in the past.

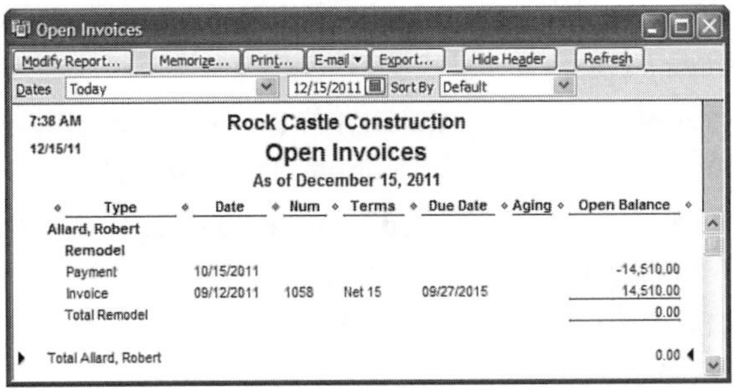

FIGURE 17.20

I prefer this report because it easily shows unpaid balances and any unapplied customer credits.

You are now complete with the Accounts Receivable tasks. Don't forget to review Chapters 7 and 8 for more details on the many QuickBooks preferences that will enable better control while your client's record undeposited funds and accounts receivable transactions and other Accounts Receivable troubleshooting suggestions.

Accounts Payable

A complete review of Accounts Payable, including the proper process to use in QuickBooks that potentially avoids the corrections detailed in this section can be found in Chapter 11, "Reviewing and Correcting Accounts Payable Errors."

The tasks listed in the Accounts Payable section of the CDR feature can help you easily correct client mistakes made when the client has created a vendor credit and did not assign it to the open vendor bill.

The AP Aging Detail Report is listed last in the Accounts Payable task group. I recommend reviewing the AP Aging Detail Report as well as other reports prior to making corrections with the Client Data Review. Properly reviewing your data will help you make the most informed decision on the corrections that might be needed.

Fixing Unapplied Vendors Payments and Credits

Chapter 11 detailed the proper accounts payable process that when a vendor bill is created, the Pay Bills dialog should be used to pay the bills. Some QuickBooks users might have entered the Bill form and later recorded a Write Check form as payment for that vendor bill instead of properly using the Pay Bills dialog.

To assign an unapplied vendor credit forms to an open vendor bill using CDR, follow these steps:

1. Complete steps 1 through 4 of the "Customizing the Client Data Review" section of this chapter to launch CDR.

2. Click the **Fix Unapplied Vendor Payments and Credits** link from the Accounts Payable task group.

2. The **Vendors** tab on the top left and the **Bills** tab on the right will be selected by default.

3. With your mouse pointer, select any of the vendors on the list to the left. The **Bills** pane will display all unapplied vendor credits for the vendor selected on the left. On the right of the Bills pane will display any open vendor invoices for that specifically selected vendor.

4. Place a check mark next to the credit on the left and the open vendor bill form on the right you want to apply the payment to (see Figure 17.21).

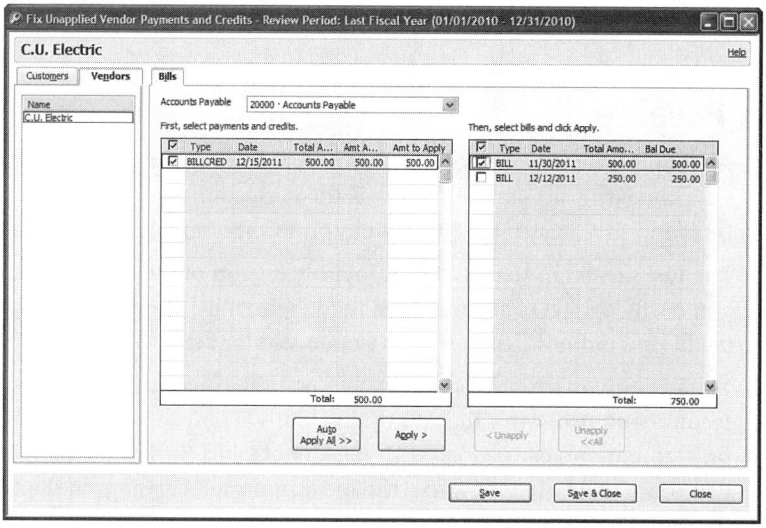

FIGURE 17.21

Assigning a Vendor Credit to an open Vendor Bill.

5. Optionally, click the **Auto Apply All** button to apply all of the unapplied payments to the invoices on the right.

6. Or, click the **Apply** button to assign that specific vendor credit form with that specific vendor bill. The items selected will be grayed out, indicating that you have assigned them.

7. Click **Save** to begin correcting transactions for another vendor or **Save and Close** to complete the task.

Evaluating and Correcting the 1099 Account Mapping

Setting up your vendors for proper 1099 status is important. However, be assured that if after reviewing this information you determine the original setup was incorrect, any changes made here will correct prior- and future-dated reports and forms.

When you select the link in the Accounts Payable task group for Evaluate and Correct 1099 Mapping, the preference dialog for 1099's is displayed.

In the preference setting for Tax:1099, you can click the Yes button to select the Do You File option to let QuickBooks know that you will be providing 1099 forms to your vendors at the end of the year.

The dialog shown in Figure 17.22 lists several 1099 categories such as rents, royalties, and so on. However, QuickBooks will track the information but only prints the 1099—Misc. Income form (or the Box 7 data).

To finish setting this option, you must assign a QuickBooks account on the specific 1099 category and box detail line. Highlight the appropriate 1099 category you want to assign, and from the drop-down menu in the account column, select an account. You can also assign multiple accounts from the account drop-down menu, select Multiple accounts at the top of the list, and place a check mark next to the appropriate accounts.

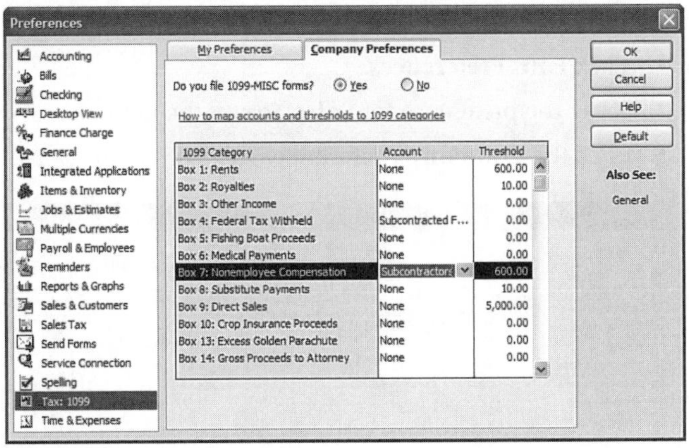

FIGURE 17.22

Setting the Tax:1099 preference to map to specific or multiple accounts.

See the section titled, "Reviewing and Printing Year-end Vendor Tax Forms" in Chapter 11, "Reviewing and Correcting Accounts Payable Errors," for more information on how to properly set up vendors and prepare 1099 documents at the end of the year.

Reviewing the AP Aging Detail Report

One of the first tasks you should do with your client is review the AP Aging Detail Report, primarily because the client will know best if the bills that are open are still due and payable to the vendor.

What exactly are you looking for on the aging report? You might be looking for vendor credits that are aged and have not been applied to current open vendor bills. Or, as Chapter 11 documented, you may see several aged item receipts for vendors you know the client has paid.

Use the information collected from this report to help determine the corrections that should be made with the tasks listed in the Accounts Payable task group of the CDR.

Sales Tax

The CDR feature offers the basic in the reviewing of sales tax errors. Before beginning the tasks listed in this section, you should review the client's settings (preferences) for sales tax.

Additionally, the Sales Tax task group will not display in the Client Data Review if the Sales Tax feature has not been enabled. To locate that preference setting for enabling sales tax, you must log in as the Admin or new External Accountant type user in single-user mode:

1. Click **Edit**, **Preferences**.

2. Select the preference for **Sales Tax** in the left pane.

3. Click the **Company Preferences** tab (see Figure 17.23).

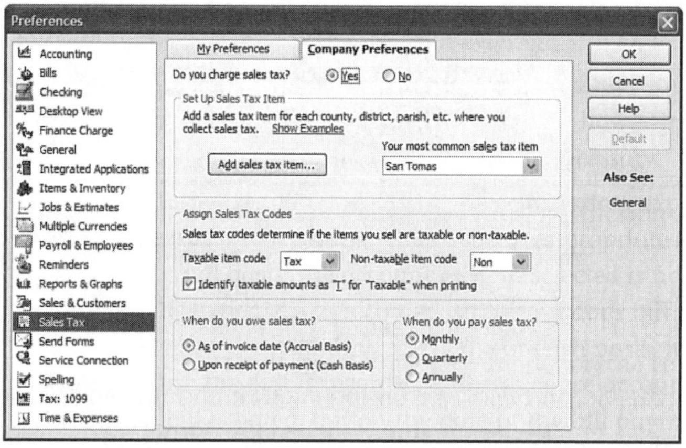

FIGURE 17.23

Review Sales Tax preferences before making any corrections.

Alternatively, you can access the Sales Tax preferences from the Home page by selecting Manage Sales Tax.

After reviewing and correcting your client's sales tax preference settings, you are prepared to begin the following CDR tasks.

🕘 Finding Incorrectly Paid Sales Tax

The Client Data Review icon in front of this name indicates that this task is only available from within the CDR center.

QuickBooks uses a special Pay Sales Tax dialog (as shown in Figure 17.24) to properly record the sales tax liability payments. When payments are made using other form types, such as a write check, bill, or make journal entries forms, the Pay Sales Tax dialog may not accurately reflect the payments.

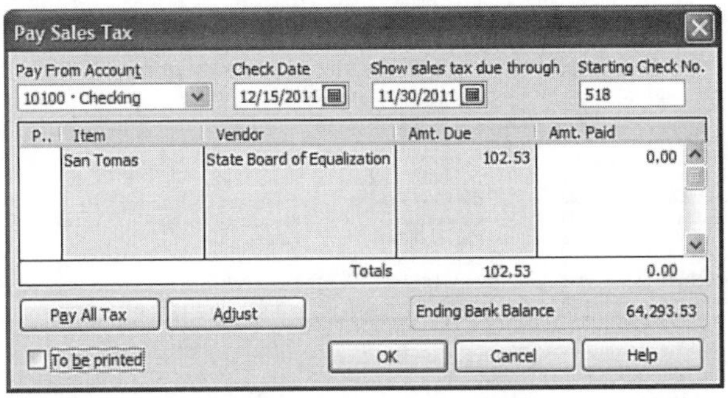

FIGURE 17.24
Properly paid sales tax will be recorded from this dialog.

The Find Incorrectly Paid Sales Tax task will help you identify when a client paid his sales tax liability outside of the Pay Sales Tax dialog, as shown in Figure 17.25. Properly recorded sales tax payments will have a transaction type of TAXPMT in the checkbook register.

To begin the review, click the task link to display the report titled "Incorrectly Recorded 'Sales Tax Payable' Payments," as shown in Figure 17.26.

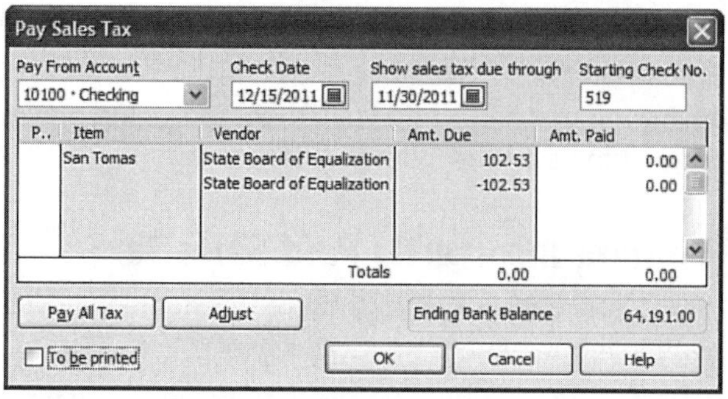

FIGURE 17.25

Pay Sales Tax dialog when an imporperly recorded sales tax payment was made.

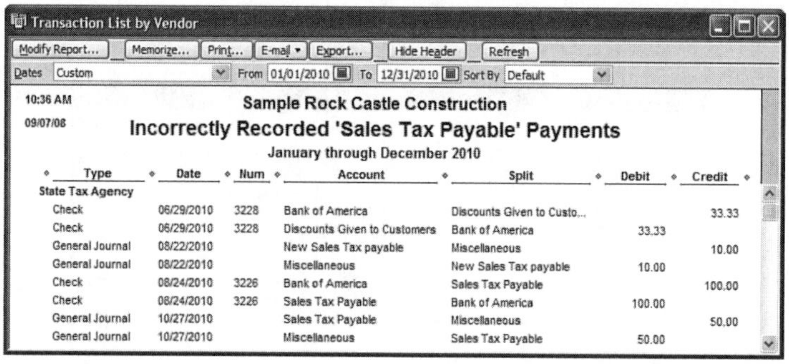

FIGURE 17.26

Report helps to identify incorrectly paid sales tax payments.

What exactly is this report finding? The report will identify non sales-tax payable type transactions used to pay sales tax liability.

The report will list the following:

- Write Checks—payable to a vendor and assigned to the default QuickBooks created Sales Tax Payable account.

- Write Checks—payable to a vendor assigned to a sales tax item and assigned to any type of account.

- Make Journal Entries—when both a debit or credit amount is assigned to any account type and a sales tax vendor is included on that line.

You will review these transactions to determine what expense or liability account your client assigned the payments too; this review will help you know the correct account to make the sales tax adjustment to.

Rescue Me!

The default date range for this report will match your selected CDR dates.

If this is your first review, you may want to change the report date range to "All" from the Dates drop-down menu. This ensures that you are seeing all sales tax payable transactions that were improperly recorded.

Adjusting Sales Tax Payable

Your review of the Incorrectly Recorded 'Sales Tax Payable' Payments report provided you with a list of transactions that were paying sales tax payable without using the proper QuickBooks sales tax payment form.

In addition to reviewing this report, I recommend that you review the following before and after adjusting sales tax payable. When comparing these reports and the Pay Sales Tax dialog, make sure that each report is using the same Accrual- or Cash- Basis and is prepared with the same reporting date.

Compare the following reports to each other for sales tax payable balances:

- Balance Sheet—Sales Tax Payable balance. Select Reports, Company & Financial and choose the Balance Sheet Standard report option. Optionally, click the modify button to change the report basis and date.

- Sales Tax Liability Report—Sales Tax Payable as of <date> column total. Select Vendors, Sales Tax and choose the Sales Tax Liability report option.

- Pay Sales Tax—Amt. Due column total. Select Vendors, Sales Tax and choose the Pay Sales Tax menu option.

The end result of a properly made sales tax adjustment is that each of these totals mentioned will agree with each other after making the sales tax adjustment.

To begin the Adjust Sales Tax Payable task, follow these steps:

1. Complete steps 1 through 4 of the "Customizing the Client Data Review" section of this chapter to launch the Client Data Review.

2. Click the **Adjust Sales Tax Payable** link in the Sales Tax task group of the CDR.

3. The Sales Tax Adjustment dialog shown in Figure 17.27 displays.

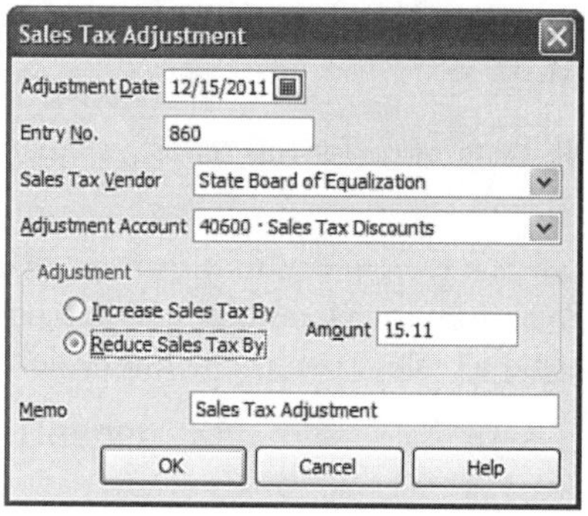

FIGURE 17.27

Properly discounting sales tax payable.

4. Select the **Adjustment Date**.

5. Type in **an Entry No.**

6. Select your **Sales Tax Vendor** from the drop-down menu.

7. Select the **Adjustment Account** from the drop-down menu.

8. In the Adjustment pane, select the **Increase Sales Tax By** or **Decrease the Sales Tax By** radial button. Enter an amount for the adjustment.

9. Enter a **Memo** or select the default memo.

10. Click **OK** to save the transaction.

QuickBooks will create a Make Journal Entries form with a decrease (debit) or increase (credit) to Sales Tax Payable account with the resulting debit or credit in the account that was selected in step number seven listed previously.

After the adjustment, go back to the reports listed in this section and review that they agree with each other. More details on the proper setup of Sales Tax can be found in Chapter 12 "Reviewing and Correcting Sales Tax Errors."

Inventory

For the accounting professional, this is commonly one area of QuickBooks that is the least understood. Often when working with a client's file with inventory tracking, I will see a journal entry used to adjust inventory. Although this does make the adjustment to the inventory account balance on the Balance Sheet report, it does not reflect the adjustment in the Inventory Valuation Summary or Detail report.

Why is it that a journal entry shouldn't be used to adjust inventory? Consider that inventory value on a balance sheet is the quantity of an item multiplied by a cost. When you create a journal entry, you can enter an amount for the adjustment, but you cannot associate it with an actual inventory item.

Before completing the Adjust Inventory Quantity/Value on Hand task, you should review the Inventory Valuation Summary report and compare the information in that report with a physical inventory count.

To assist your client in performing a physical inventory:

1. Prepare a **Physical Inventory Worksheet** and request that your client compare the reported totals with a physical count from their inventory location noting any discrepancies on the worksheet, as shown in Figure 17.29.

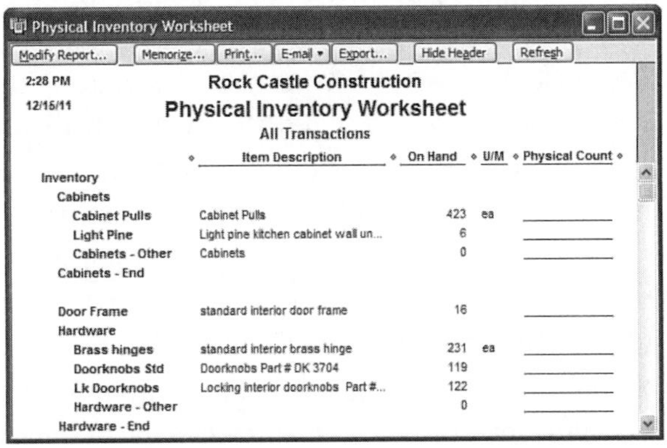

FIGURE 17.28

Physical Inventory Worksheet is used to record differences when doing a physical inventory count.

2. The client provides you, the accounting professional with the results of the physical count, noting which items in inventory need to be adjusted for quantity or value.

Performing a physical inventory count is a vital activity to the success of a correctly made inventory adjustment.

Adjusting Inventory Quantity/Value on Hand

Before you perform this task, you need to know what the actual ending quantity and value for each inventory item is currently. This is determined by completing a physical inventory count. Without this important step, you might make an adjustment that might not be supported by the actual count.

Quantity Inventory Adjustment

The following instructions detail the steps to making an inventory quantity adjustment. With this type of adjustment, QuickBooks will use the average cost associated with the item (or if none exists, will use the default cost on the New or Edit Item dialog) to determine the actual value of the quantity adjustments. If there was no recorded average cost and your items do not have a default cost in the New or Edit Item dialog, no financial change will be created for this inventory adjustment. More detailed information is provided in Chapter 10, "Reviewing and Correcting Inventory Errors."

To properly adjust the quantity on hand to agree with a physical inventory count, follow these steps:

1. Complete steps 1 through 4 of the "Customizing the Client Data Review" section of this chapter to launch the CDR.

2. Click the **Adjust Inventory Quantity/Value on Hand** link in the Inventory pane of the Client Data Review center.

3. Enter an **Adjustment Date** and optional **Ref. No.** Optionally, assign a **Customer:Job** and select your **Adjustment Account** chart of accounts (this can be either a Cost of Goods Sold or Expense type account).

4. In the **New Qty** column, enter your count from the completed physical inventory, or, optionally enter the change in the **Qty Difference** column.

5. QuickBooks will provide the **Total Value of the Adjustment** at the bottom of the dialog for your review as you make the needed changes. Select **Save & Close** when you are done.

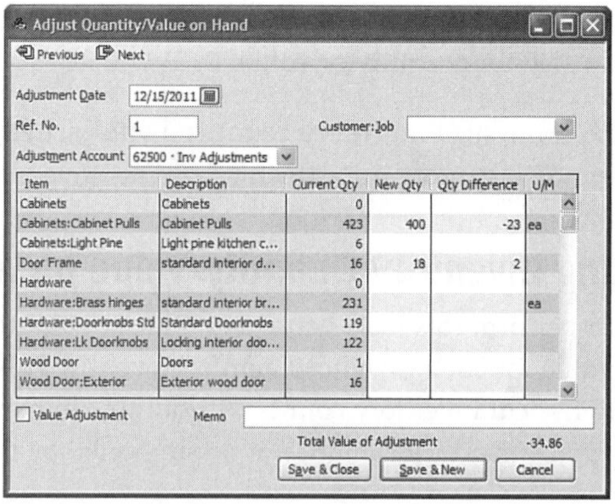

FIGURE 17.29

Record an adjustment for inventory quantity differences after performing a physical inventory count.

The accounting effect of the transaction in Figure 17.29 is to reduce the quantity on hand for one inventory item and increase the quantity for another. The net effect on the financials is to reduce (credit) the Inventory asset balance by $34.86, and increase (debit) the Inventory Adjustments account (either a Cost of Goods Sold type or Expense type).

This section has discussed using the CDR feature to access the Inventory Adjustment menu in QuickBooks. Inventory adjustments are normally done to adjust for quantity decreases perhaps due to damage or theft, or even increases when perhaps a prior inventory count left out some items not yet on the shelf.

The next section discusses a different type of inventory adjustment called a Value Adjustment.

Value Inventory Adjustment

When deciding whether to use a Quantity on Hand or Value Adjustment only, be sure of the net result you wish to obtain. A value adjustment will not change the quantity on hand, but it will assign a new average cost by dividing the units in inventory by the new value.

Timing is important when doing a valuation adjustment. Value adjustments, if appropriate, should be carefully considered for their impact on the company's resulting financials.

The following instructions detail the steps to making an inventory value adjustment:

1. Complete steps 1 through 4 of the "Customizing the Client Data Review Center" section of this chapter to launch the CDR tool.

2. Place a checkmark in the **Value Adjustment** box in the lower-left of the Adjust Quantity/Value on hand dialog.

3. In the **New Value** column, enter your current total dollar value for the inventory, as shown in Figure 17.30.

4. QuickBooks will provide the Total **Value of the Adjustment** at the bottom of the dialog for your review as you make the needed changes. Select **Save & Close** when you are done.

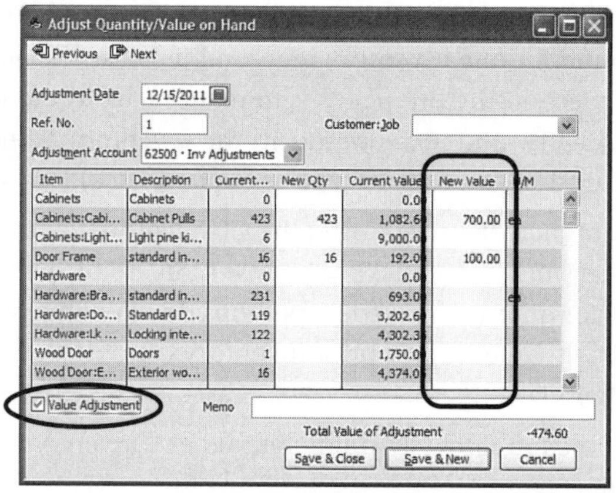

FIGURE 17.30

Record an inventory value adjustment.

The accounting result of this inventory value adjustment, as shown in Figure 17.30, is no net change to inventory quantities, a decrease (credit) to your Inventory Asset account, and an increase (debit) to your Inventory Adjustments account (either a Cost of Goods Sold type or Expense type). A new average cost will be computed based on the (Original Asset Value + or - the Value Difference) / Quantity on Hand as recorded on the inventory value adjustment.

Payroll

To have QuickBooks automatically calculate payroll, you or your client needs to purchase a payroll subscription from Intuit. When payroll is not prepared properly, many of the QuickBooks payroll forms and calculations will not work correctly or at all. For more detail information on the payroll subscriptions offered as well as details of the proper payroll process, see Chapter 14.

The CDR tasks for payroll will help you find payroll errors and set defaults in your client's file that will help to avoid future mistakes.

Digging Deeper

Your ability as the accountant to make changes in a client's payroll setup as well as adjust payroll transactions is possible when:

- You are working in a client's working data file (.QBW file extension). You cannot make changes to payroll transactions when working in an Accountant's Review file copy.

- If you are working on-site or remotely logged into the client's file (via the Internet) and your client has a current paid payroll subscription. The payroll features available will be limited by the payroll subscription they own.

- If you are working with the client's file at your place of business, and you have a paid payroll subscription from Intuit. Accounting professionals providing payroll services for their clients will benefit from using the QuickBooks Enhanced Payroll for Accountants subscription. See Chapter 14 for more specific details.

Finding Incorrectly Paid Payroll Liabilities

Details about the proper methods to prepare payroll and how to pay the accrued liabilities were provided in Chapter 14. . Some QuickBooks users may choose to use the write check form when preparing their payroll liability payments. Incorrectly prepared payments will adjust the balance sheet balances, but will not be reflected accurately in the Payroll Center. However, over the last several years, payroll liability payment errors are less likely to occur due to improved error messaging that encourages the QuickBooks user to properly prepare these liability payments.

QuickBooks 2009 CDR delivers another time-saving tool, helping you the accounting professional easily and quickly find payroll liability payments that were not recorded using the correct form.

When you select the link to Find Incorrectly Paid Payroll Liabilities from the Payroll task group, QuickBooks prepares a report titled "Payroll Liabilities Paid by Regular Check." See Figure 17.31. This report will find a Write Check form that was payable to a payroll item vendor.

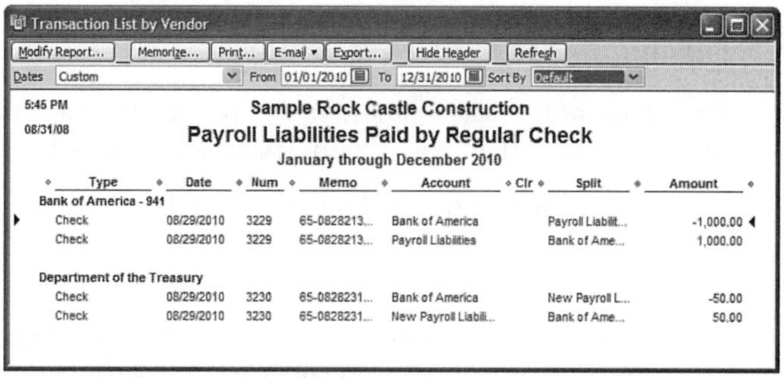

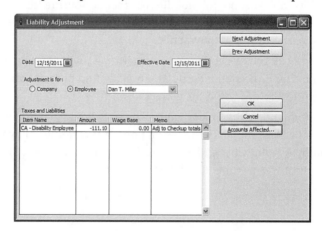

FIGURE 17.31

This report will find incorrectly paid payroll liability payment transaction types.

Use the details from this report to determine where your client has recorded these payroll liability payments to. Did they record them to the payroll liabilities account or did they select an expense account by mistake?

After you determine what account the entries are posted to, you can complete a Payroll Liability Adjustment as follows:

1. Click **Employees, Payroll Taxes and Liabilities**, and select **Adjust Payroll Liabilities** to open the Liability Adjustment dialog shown in Figure 17.32.

2. Enter the **Date** and **Effective Date**. Both should be dated in the quarter you want to effect the change.

3. Select either **Company** or **Employee** for the adjustment. Company indicates it is a company-paid adjustment. Employee indicates an employee-paid adjustment and will affect W-2 reported amounts.

FIGURE 17.32

Create payroll liability adjustment when correcting payroll from previously filed payroll quarters.

4. Optionally, assign a Class if your business tracks different profit centers.

5. You click **Accounts Affected** only if you do not want to affect balances. This would be necessary if your Balance Sheet is correct, but your Payroll Liabilities balances are incorrect.

6. Click **OK**.

7. QuickBooks might open another dialog with the default account that is going to be affected. QuickBooks shows you this dialog to suggest the recommended account for the adjustment based on how the payroll item is set up. If you need to change the account assignment, choose the appropriate account from the drop-down menu.

8. Click **OK** to save the transaction.

You can check this and other details of your client's payroll setup by completing the Run Payroll Checkup discussed in the next section.

Run Payroll Checkup

The Run Payroll Checkup tool is used after a payroll has been set up, and its primary purpose is to test the setup and optionally test the accuracy of the transactions reported in payroll.

A well hidden feature, until now! The CDR includes this in the payroll activities.

What makes the Run Payroll Checkup tool different than the Payroll Setup tool? After you have set up your payroll, you will likely use the Run Payroll Checkup tool to diagnose errors with both setup and transactions.

The QuickBooks Run Payroll Checkup enable you to "Finish Later" and return where you left off. Before you begin the Run Payroll Checkup dialog, make sure you have the following information available:

- Employees' names, addresses, social security numbers, and states for W-2's.

- Compensation, benefits, other additions, or deductions your company offers.

- Prior payroll wage and tax totals if starting a payroll in the middle of the year.

Rescue Me!

When performing a diagnostic review of the previous quarter or current quarter payroll, you will not be able to continue to the next screen without successfully correcting any discrepancies found.

Print the details of the error screen, and then close the Run Payroll Checkup diagnostic tool to make the needed corrections.

The QuickBooks Run Payroll Checkup diagnostic tool (also known as Payroll Setup) assists in setting up or reviewing your existing payroll data including:

- Compensation items, other additions, and deductions for missing or incomplete information, as shown in Figure 17.33.

- For existing data, review of actual wage and tax amounts provides an alert if any discrepancy is found, as shown in Figure 17.34.

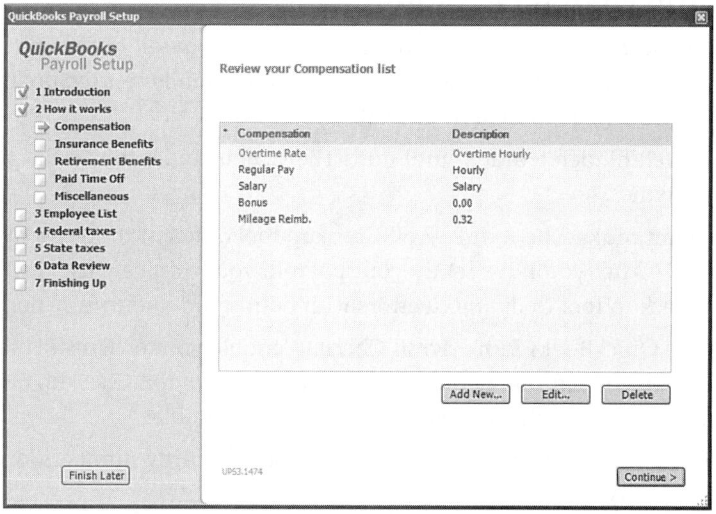

FIGURE 17.33

Compensation items reviewed in the Payroll Setup diagnostic tool in QuickBooks.

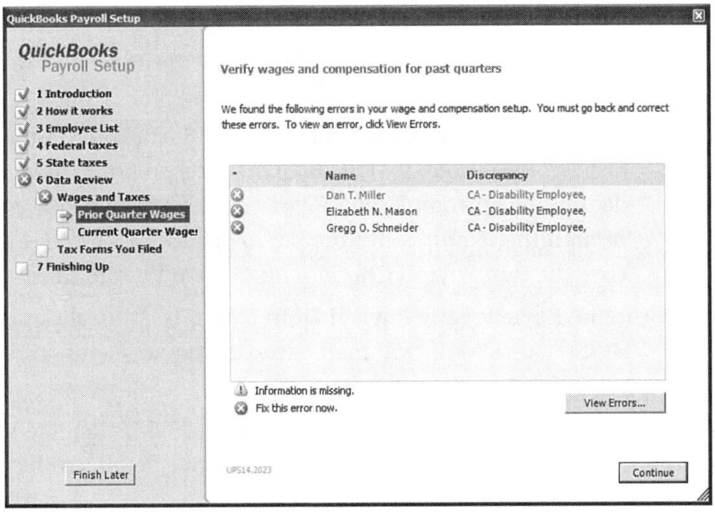

FIGURE 17.34

Alert provided if the QuickBooks Payroll Setup diagnostic tool detects wage or tax errors.

Digging Deeper

The Run Payroll Checkup diagnostic tool is optional for Intuit's Standard or Enhanced Payroll subscribers. If you subscribe to Intuit's Assisted Payroll (see the "Payroll Service Options" section in this chapter), you are required to complete the Run Payroll Checkup diagnostic tool before processing a payroll.

However, I recommend that you teach your clients to run this process directly from the QuickBooks menus. Click Employees, My Payroll Service and select Run Payroll Checkup regardless of what payroll option your client has selected. Running the Payroll Checkup diagnostic at least as often as once a quarter before quarterly payroll tax returns are prepared will help ensure that the client's data is correct.

To have the payroll diagnostic tool within the CDR feature review your client's payroll setup for missing information and paycheck data for discrepancies, do the following:

1. Complete steps 1 through 4 of the "Customizing the Client Data Review Center" section of this chapter to launch the CDR.

2. Click the **Run Payroll Checkup** link in the Client Data Review payroll pane.

3. Select **Yes** to updating your payroll subscription if provided that dialog.

4. The QuickBooks Payroll Setup dialog opens (also known as the Payroll Checkup).

5. Follow each of the dialogs through step 5, clicking Continue through each window. Note: If QuickBooks detects an error in the setup, it will identify the error and you may need to correct it before moving on through the remainder of the payroll checkup, or click **Finish Later** to leave the Run Payroll Checkup and return later to finish the review.

6. In the **Review Your Payroll Data** dialog (step 6), click **Yes** (see Figure 17.35). QuickBooks will then check the payroll setup and data you have recorded for accuracy.

7. If errors are detected as shown in Figure 17.34, click the View Errors button and QuickBooks will open the error detail, as shown in Figure 17.36.

8. Click the **Print** button in the **Payroll Item Discrepancies** dialog, as shown in Figure 17.36. You must close this dialog before creating any adjusting entries.

9. Click the **Finish Later** button to close the Run Payroll Checkup diagnostic tool so that you can create correcting entries.

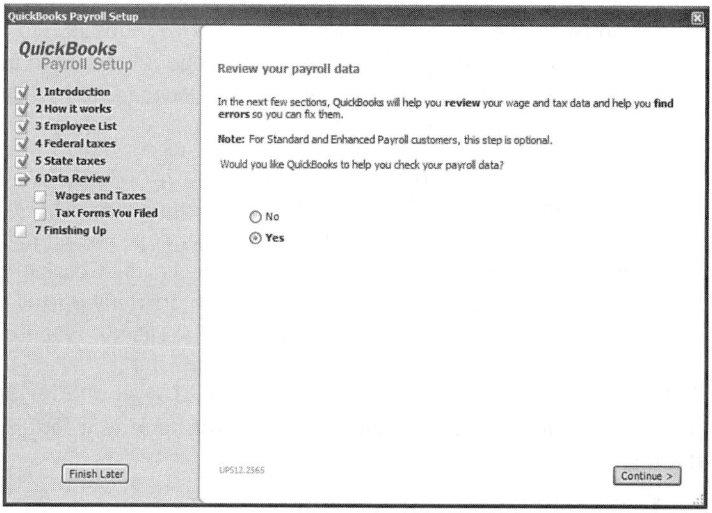

FIGURE 17.35
Click Yes when you want the Run Payroll Checkup diagnostic tool to verify wages and taxes for prior quarters and/or the current quarter.

FIGURE 17.36

You can print the report of errors in wages or accrued taxes for later review.

Chapter 14 offers more detailed instruction on how best to correct errors the Run Payroll Checkup may find.

Need To Run Payroll Checkup for a Prior Year?

If you need to complete a Run Payroll Checkup diagnostic for a prior calendar year, you will need to adjust your computer system date to a date in the prior year. When selecting the date, keep in mind how QuickBooks will review and report on "prior quarters" dependent on this new system date.

Run the Payroll Checkup diagnostic, which QuickBooks will now perform on the payroll data that corresponds to the year of your computer's system date.

Don't forget to close the file and then reset your computer date to the current date before opening the file again and allowing other users into the system.

You might want to contact your computer professionals before changing the system date in a networked environment because it might impact other running programs.

Reviewing Employee Default Settings

QuickBooks 2009 Client Data Review feature provides easy access to another feature that has been well hidden! Reviewing employee defaults will help your client process new payroll with fewer mistakes, making future payroll reviews less time-consuming.

To set the employee preferences, you will need to be logged in as the Admin or new External Accountant user.

1. Complete steps 1 through 4 of the "Customizing the CDR" section of this chapter to launch CDR.

2. Click the **Review Employee Default Settings** link in the Payroll task group of CDR.

3. The Preferences for Payroll & Employees, Company Preferences dialog opens, as shown in Figure 17.37.

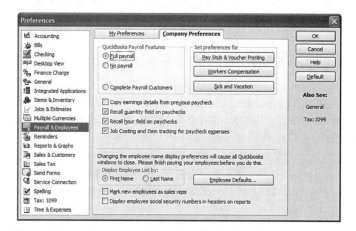

FIGURE 17.37

Payroll & Employee Company Preferences tab.

4. Click the **Full Payroll** button in the QuickBooks Payroll Features pane. This button enables the remaining features in the Preferences dialog.

5. Click the check box next to the features that are appropriate to the client's business:

    ■ Copy earnings details from previous check (copies hours, rates, and Customer:Jobs from prior paycheck).

    ■ Recall quantity field on paychecks (recalls line 1 of a previous paycheck, payroll item, and rate only; no Customer:Job recalled).

- Recall hour field on paycheck (recalls total hours only and places total number of hours on a single line even if prior paycheck had several lines).
- Job Costing for paycheck expenses (enables QuickBooks to add the cost of company-paid taxes to the burdened costs for time that is assigned to a Customer:Job). QuickBooks also offers the Class Tracking by Paycheck or Earnings Item option if you have the class tracking preference enabled.

6. Display Employee list by selecting the button to display your employee lists by first name or last name.

7. Click the check box next to Mark new employees as sales reps if you want new employees automatically added to the sales rep list and available to be added to a customer invoice form.

8. Click the check box next to Display employee social security numbers in headers on reports if you want to display this sensitive information on reports.

9. Click the **Pay Stub and Voucher Printing** button to open printing preferences. In this dialog, you can customize what detail will print on employees' paycheck stubs or vouchers (if direct depositing the check).

10. Click the **Workers Compensation** button to set the preference to track worker's comp, to be warned when a worker's comp code is not assigned, and to exclude overtime hours from workers compensation calculations. This feature is available with the Enhanced Payroll subscription service.

11. Click the Employee Defaults button to set default employee rates, tax preferences, pay schedule, and many other options. Setting these preferences can save data entry time when your client is creating new employees because the common employee defaults will pre-fill when setting up new employees.

Setting preferences for your client can save precious data entry time and help to avoid future mistakes. The client will appreciate the time you take to make his job easier.

Entering After-The-Fact Payroll

No longer is entering after-the-fact payroll time consuming!'. Now, 'with the new CDR, the accounting professional has access to this important feature. You or your client must have an active payroll subscription. If you or your client do not have an active payroll subscription; the After-The-Fact Payroll task will not be displayed in the Payroll task group. Keep this in mind if you are working at the client site or remotely logged into the client's data file. To begin entering payroll in this manner, follow these steps:

1. Complete steps 1 through 4 of the "Customizing the Client Data Review Center" section of this chapter to launch the CDR.

2. Click on the **Enter After-The-Fact Payroll** link in the Payroll task group of the CDR.

3. The After-The-Fact Payroll dialog opens as displayed in Figure 17.38.

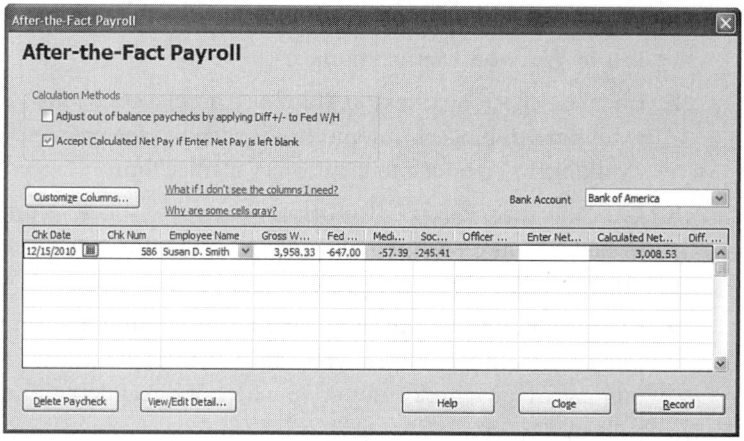

FIGURE 17.38

Conveniently enter After-The-Fact payroll.

4. In the **Calculations Method** pane, you can choose to let QuickBooks adjust any out-of-balance amount to Federal Withholding. Or, choose the option to accept the net pay as calculated.

5. Optionally, click the **Customize Columns** button to open a dialog that will let you place the columns of detail in your preferred order. This is especially useful if you are working from some other manual book-keeping form or computer-generated details when entering into QuickBooks.

6. Select the **Bank Account** drop-down menu from the right of the dialog, the appropriate bank account that this payroll record is going to be paid from.

7. Complete the fields in the familiar spreadsheet format, including check date, check number, employee, gross wages, federal withholding, and depending on your selection in step 4, let QuickBooks calculate the net or choose to enter the net paycheck.

8. Optionally click on the **View/Edit Detail** button at the bottom of the dialog. This Preview Paycheck dialog will open, allowing you to assign a job, service item, and workmen's compensation code. Select **Save & Close** to close the Preview Paycheck dialog.

9. Click **Record** when you have completed a single row of detail or simply enter through to the next line. Click **Close** when you want to close the After-The-Fact Payroll dialog.

10. Optionally select from the status drop-down, the current status of the task and record a task note.

Payroll entered through the After-The-Fact Payroll processing will also be included in all of the federal and state forms that QuickBooks payroll subscriptions offer.

Bank Reconciliation

When I am reviewing a client's file, I look closely at the bank reconciliation results. I look to see if the bank reconciliation has been completed recently and how old outstanding, uncleared bank transactions are.

There are many ways to troubleshoot bank reconciliation issues with your client's data. The CDR feature provides a quick link to three important tasks. For more information on other options you have and reports you can customize for your clients, see the "Troubleshooting an Incorrectly Reconciled Bank Account" section in chapter 6, "Bank Account Balance or Reconciliation Errors."

Reconciling Accounts

You can use the Reconcile Accounts link in the Bank Reconciliation task group of the CDR feature to troubleshoot or complete your client's monthly bank reconciliation. If you working with a client's Accountant Copy, you will be able to reconcile any and all months, but only the reconciliations for dates prior to the "Dividing Date" set in the client's file will be returned with your changes. More details about this topic can be found in Chapter 15, "Sharing Data with Your Accountant or Your Client."

1. Access steps 1 through 4 of the "Customizing the Client Data Review Center" section of this chapter to launch CDR.

2. Click on the **Reconcile Accounts** link in the Bank Reconciliation task group of the Client Data Review. If your client has more than one bank account, select from the Account drop-down menu the bank account you are reviewing.

3. Access the following tasks from the Begin Reconciliation dialog shown in Figure 17:39:

- Review the date listed as last reconciled.

- Compare the beginning balance with the ending balance of the last completed bank statement from the financial institution.

- Begin a new bank reconciliation by entering the statement ending balance from the printed bank statement and optionally entering service charges or interest earned on this statement. Then click Continue.

- Locate discrepancies, as discussed in more detail in the following section.

- Undo the last reconciliation used when you need to restart the last bank reconciliation. When selected, you are returned to the prior months bank reconciliation dialog. All of your previously marked transactions are now no longer marked cleared. Any added service charges or interest income transactions were not removed. Note: You can "roll back" as many months as you need to, one month at a time.

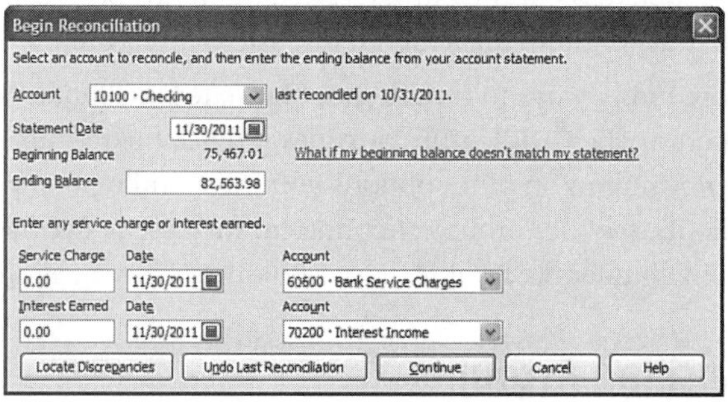

FIGURE 17.39

The Begin Reconciliation dialog has other useful task links.

In my years of working with clients QuickBooks files, the bank reconciliation is the task I most frequently see not completed at all, or not completed correctly, yet it is one of the most important tasks to complete when wanting to look at trusted financials. The CDR feature helps you, the accountant, work with your client's data file when reviewing or completing the bank reconciliation.

Locating Discrepancies in Bank Reconciliation

After reviewing the client's previous bank reconciliations, you determine the beginning balance that was once correct is no longer correct. Perhaps your client modified, voided, or deleted a previously cleared transaction.

The Locate Discrepancies in Bank Reconciliation report will help you to easily find these.

1. Complete steps 1 through 4 of the "Customizing the Client Data Review Center" section of this chapter to launch CDR.

2. Click **Locate Discrepancies** in Bank Reconciliation in the Bank Reconciliation task group.

3. From the **Specify Account** drop-down menu, select the bank account.

4. The "Previous Reconciliation Discrepancy Report" displays. 'For each transaction on this report, you will see the modified date, reconciled amount, type of change (amount added or deleted), and the financial effect of the change (see Figure 17.40) grouped by bank statement date.

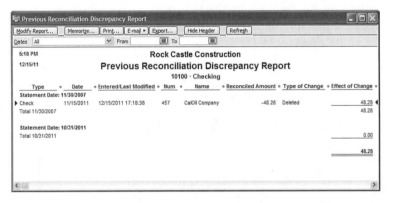

FIGURE 17.40

View details of previously cleared transactions that have been modified or deleted.

You can click Modify Report and add the user name that modified the transaction to help in identifying who made the change to the transaction.

After you have found the reconciliation discrepancy, you can view the Voided/Deleted Report to help determine how to correct the transaction(s). To prepare this report, select Reports, Accountant & Taxes, and choose the Voided/Deleted Transactions Summary or Detail report.

Rescue Me!

Troubleshoot your beginning balance differences with the Previous Reconciliation Discrepancy Report *before* completing the next month's reconciliation. Doing so is important because QuickBooks removes all details from the discrepancy report when you complete a new reconciliation. This is due to QuickBooks determining that you have solved the issue or you would not have completed the next month's bank reconciliation.

This report will not track discrepancies caused by changing the bank account associated with a transaction. However, now with the Client Data Review, Review List Changes task will track changes made from adding, deleting, or even merging charts of accounts and other list items in QuickBooks.

Reviewing Missing Checks

This is a useful report when reviewing the accuracy of your client's bank account data. This report can help you determine whether any check transactions are missing or duplicated.

Complete steps 1 through 4 of the "Customizing the Client Data Review Center" section of this chapter. The CDR will be launched.

Select the Review Missing Checks task in the Banking task group. When the Specify Account dialog displays, select the appropriate bank account from the drop-down menu.

The resulting Missing Checks report shows all check or bill payment check type transactions sorted by number (see Figure 17.41). You will look for any breaks in the detail with a `*** Missing` or `*** Duplicate` warning.

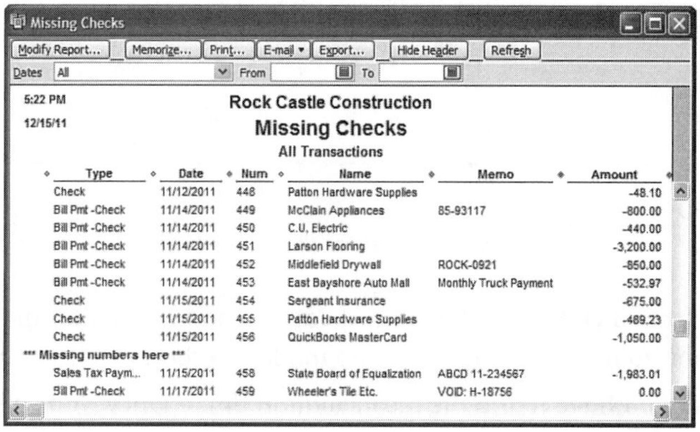

Type	Date	Num	Name	Memo	Amount
Check	11/12/2011	448	Patton Hardware Supplies		-48.10
Bill Pmt -Check	11/14/2011	449	McClain Appliances	85-93117	-800.00
Bill Pmt -Check	11/14/2011	450	C.U. Electric		-440.00
Bill Pmt -Check	11/14/2011	451	Larson Flooring		-3,200.00
Bill Pmt -Check	11/14/2011	452	Middlefield Drywall	ROCK-0921	-850.00
Bill Pmt -Check	11/14/2011	453	East Bayshore Auto Mall	Monthly Truck Payment	-532.97
Check	11/15/2011	454	Sergeant Insurance		-675.00
Check	11/15/2011	455	Patton Hardware Supplies		-489.23
Check	11/15/2011	456	QuickBooks MasterCard		-1,050.00
*** Missing numbers here ***					
Sales Tax Paym...	11/15/2011	458	State Board of Equalization	ABCD 11-234567	-1,983.01
Bill Pmt -Check	11/17/2011	459	Wheeler's Tile Etc.	VOID: H-18756	0.00

FIGURE 17.41

The Missing Checks report can help you determine whether you need to enter any missing transactions before you reconcile.

Miscellaneous

This section of the CDR can be one of the most useful to you because it shows you how to set preferences to make your client's work more accurate and how to set a closing date that will prevent or discourage a user from making changes to your reviewed data. If you are working with a client's Accountants Copy, you will be able to set the Closing Date and optional Closing Date Password, but other preferences set will *not* transfer over to the client's file.

Setting the Closing Date and Password

QuickBooks offers flexibility for accounting professionals who want to protect prior period data and those that need or want to make changes to prior period accounting records.

What exactly is a "closed" accounting period? Well, a business can decide to close a month when tasks such as a bank reconciliation is done or a sales tax return is filed, or a business can simply close once a year when the data is finalized for tax preparation. Because QuickBooks does not require you to close the books, it is a decision of the accounting professional and business owner (see Chapter 15, "Sharing Data with Your Accountant or Your Client").

The option of setting a closing date and password makes it easy to protect prior period transactions from unwanted modifications. With additional user-specific security settings, the business owner and accountant can also manage who has the privilege to make changes to transactions dated on or before a specific closing date.

Step One—Setting the Date and Assigning the Password

The first step in controlling changes to closed accounting periods is to set a closing date and optionally a closing date password that the user must provide when adding or modifying a transaction dated on or before the closing date.

Another important reason for setting a closing date is to track additions, modifications, or deletions to transactions dated on or before a closing date. The Closing Date Exceptions report will not track these changes when a closing date is not set.

To set the closing date and optionally a password (different from the Admin or External Accountant password), follow these steps:

1. Complete steps 1 through 4 of the "Customizing the Client Data Review Center" section of this chapter to launch the Client Data Review.

2. Click the **Set Closing Date and Password** link in the Miscellaneous task group of the CDR center.

3. Click the **Set Date/Password** button. The Set Closing Date and Password dialog displays.

4. Enter a closing date and optional password. Consider using your phone number as the password or "Call Accountant" to encourage your client to call you before making changes to closed period transactions.

5. Click **OK**.

Setting a closing date is only step one. Next, you must set user-specific privileges for users you want to allow access to adding or modifying a transaction dated on or before the closing date.

Step Two—Setting User-Specific Security

To be certain that the closing date control is managed properly, review all users for their specific rights to change transactions prior to a closing date. To view the following menu, you need to log into the file as the Admin user, (External Accountant User type does not have the capability to create new users):

1. Click **Company**, **Set Up Users and Passwords** and select the option to **Set Up Users**. The User List dialog opens.

2. To view a user's existing security privileges from the User List dialog, select the user with your cursor and click the **View User** button. You will be able to view in summary form the security settings for that user, as shown in Figure 17.42.

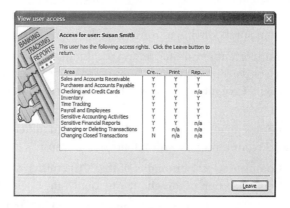

FIGURE 17.42

Review in summary form the user's security privileges.

3. Any user who should not have rights to changing closed period transactions should have an "N" placed in the last setting, Changing Closed Transactions.

4. If after reviewing a user's existing security privileges, you need to edit the setting referenced earlier, click **Leave** to close the View User Access dialog.

5. QuickBooks returns you to the User List dialog. Select the username and click the **Edit User** button.

6. On the Change User Password and Access dialog optionally modify the user name or password. Click **Next** to continue.

7. The User Access dialog for the specific user displays. Select Selected Areas and click **Next** to continue through each of the security selections until you reach the selection on Page 9 as shown in Figure 17.43.

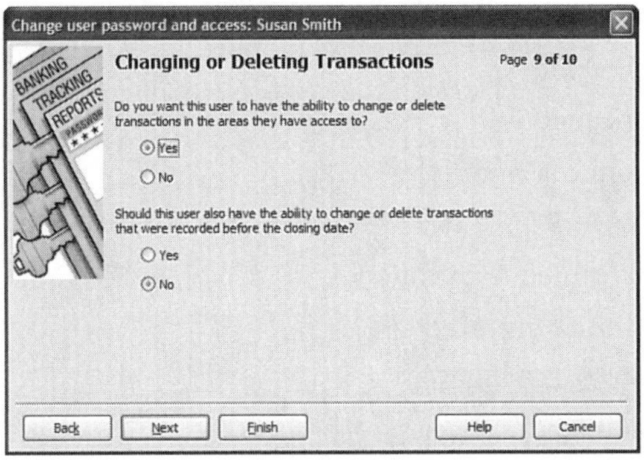

FIGURE 17.43
Be sure that each user is also set to No for changing closed period transactions.

With the ease of doing client reviews, and now the security of knowing your hard work is documented and protected with a closing date, your future reviews should take even less time to complete, giving you more time to help your client with important management decisions!

Reviewing Quickbooks Preferences

Don't forget during your review to properly manage the many useful preferences that will help you and your client work more efficiently and accurately in the QuickBooks data file.

QuickBooks offers two types of preferences:

- My Preferences—Choices selected on this tab are being defined only for the currently logged in user. If you are setting preferences for your client, you should log in with his user name, and then set the My Preferences. These settings can be set in a multiuser environment (when others are in the date file).

- Company Preferences—Preferences set on these tabs are global for all users in the QuickBooks data file. Often, these preferences can be set only when you are in single-user mode, meaning other users cannot be working in the file when you set Company preferences. Both the Admin and the new External Accountant type user can modify Company Preferences.

There are preferences specific for accounting you will want to review. As the trusted accounting professional for your client, you will benefit by reviewing each of the available preferences, including:

- Accounting
- Bills
- Checking
- Desktop View
- Finance Charge
- General
- Integrated Applications
- Items & Inventory
- Jobs & Estimates
- Multiple Currencies – *New for 2009!*
- Payroll & Employees
- Reminders
- Reports & Graphs
- Sales & Customers
- Sales Tax
- Send Forms
- Service Connection
- Spelling
- Tax: 1099
- Time and Expenses

Of the preferences, those that can enhance the accounting accuracy of a QuickBooks file are discussed in more depth in the related chapter. For example, the Sales & Customer preferences that improve the client's accuracy in QuickBooks are detailed in Chapter 7, "Reviewing and Correcting Accounts Receivable Errors."

With a password set and preferences reviewed, your next review of your client's data should take even less time using the Client Data Review.

Finishing a Client Data Review

You can leave a CDR open for as long as it takes you to finish. When you close out of task, your work is saved. Additionally, as you are working, you can conveniently select a QuickBooks menu outside of the Client Data Review and CDR will refresh automatically, including transactions created and modified.

Optionally, as you work through the many tasks, you can record an overall note for the review or individual notes assigned to specific tasks.

Saving the Review as a PDF

You can print the details of your Client Data Review to paper or save as a PDF file. The information included with this document as shown in Figure 17.44:

- Company File Name
- Review Period (Last Fiscal Year, Quarter, Month, or Custom)
- Date Printed
- Dates included in this review
- Basis: Accrual or Cash
- Client Data Review Note
- Cleanup Tasks and subtasks
- Status
- Task note
- File name and path where the report is stored if prepared in PDF format.

Marking Review Complete

When you have completed all tasks in the CDR and you select the Mark Review Complete button, QuickBooks will:

- Provide the option to set a closing date and password.
- Change the Prior Review Period Dates in the Troubleshoot Account Balances Task.
- In the Troubleshoot Account Balances tasks, transfer your final reviewed balances to the Last Review Balances column. (These amounts will not change even if a customer makes a change to a transaction dated in that review period!)
- Provide the option to carry over task notes to the next review.

Specific to the Troubleshoot Account Balances task, you do not have to Mark the Review as Complete for each review. However, your ending balances will be recorded only in the Last Review Balances column when you mark the review as completed. Marking a review as completed still gives you the option to reopen a previously closed review.

Rock Castle Construction

Review Period: **Last Fiscal Year**	Date Printed: **12/15/2011**
Dates: **01/01/2010 - 12/31/2010**	Basis: **Accrual**

Review Notes:

Request client to fax over Bank Statement for 12/31/2010

Ask for details on purchase of new office computer

Cleanup Tasks	Status	Task Notes
Account Balances		
Troubleshoot Account Balances	Completed	
Open Working Trial Balance	Completed	
Review List Changes		
Chart of Accounts	Completed	
Items	Completed	
Fixed Asset Items	Completed	
Payroll Items	Completed	
Customers	Completed	
Vendors	Completed	
Accounts Receivable		
Fix Unapplied Customer Payments and Credits	Completed	
Clear-up Undeposited Funds Account	Completed	
Review AR Aging Detail Report	Completed	Review Aged Receivables report with client.
Accounts Payable		
Fix Unapplied Vendor Payments and Credits	Completed	
Evaluate and Correct 1099 Account Mapping	Completed	
Review AP Aging Detail Report	Completed	
Sales Tax		
Find Incorrectly Paid Sales Tax	Completed	
Adjust Sales Tax Payable	Completed	
Inventory		
Adjust Inventory Quantity/Value On Hand	Completed	
Payroll		
Find Incorrectly Paid Payroll Liabilities	Completed	
Run Payroll Checkup	Completed	
Review Employee Default Settings	Completed	
Enter After-The-Fact Payroll	Completed	
Bank Reconciliation		
Reconcile Accounts	Completed	
Locate Discrepancies in Bank Reconciliation	Completed	
Review Missing Checks	Completed	
Miscellaneous		
Set Closing Date and Password	Completed	
Review QB Preferences	Completed	

FIGURE 17.44

Print or Save to PDF the details of the review for your paper files.

Reopening a Client Data Reviw

After marking a review as complete and before you start the next review, you will have the option to reopen the previously marked completed review. After you start a new review, you will no longer have the option to reopen the previously completed review, see Figure 17.45.

FIGURE 17.45

Before starting a new review, you will have the option to open a previously closed review.

Reporting on Review Activity

Also available on the CDR center is a link to the Audit Trail of Review report. You can use this report to detail the transactions you have added, modified, or deleted during your review. The Audit Trail report will not report on changes made to list items.

Additionally, if you used the new External Accountant type of login access, you were given all the rights of the Admin user (except adding or modifying users and viewing sensitive customer credit card information) and you can see your changes separate from the Admin or other users on this report.

The Audit Trail report provides details of additions and changes made to transactions, grouping the changes by username. The detail on this report shows the prior version of the transaction and the latest version of the transaction, if it was edited. The Audit Trail of Review report defaults to changes made as of today's date. This filter date can me modified for your needs.

To create the Audit Trail report shown in Figure 17.46, click Reports, Accountant & Taxes, and then select the Audit Trail report.

The audit trail report can be lengthy to review; however, if as an accountant you try to track down specific user activity with transactions, this can be a useful report to review because the changes are grouped by username.

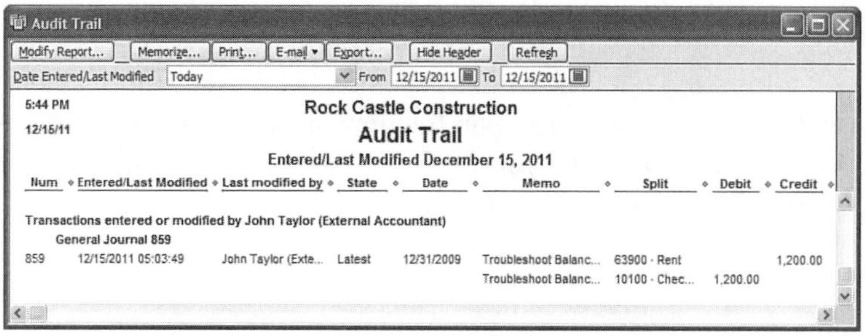

FIGURE 17.46

The QuickBooks Audit Trail report helps to identify what changes were made to transactions and by which user.

Optionally, you can export the current audit trail report to Excel for added filtering functionality as instructed in the following steps (this requires Excel 2003 or newer). This functionality would be useful if there are several individuals at a firm reviewing, adding or modifying transactions in a client's data file. These steps will allow you to filter transactions for a specific user.

1. Select **Reports, Accountant & Taxes** and choose the **Audit Trail**.

2. Modify the report dates as needed for your review.

3. Select the **Export** button on the open Audit Trail dialog.

4. The Export Report dialog displays on the Basic tab.

5. Select the appropriate radial button for the desired output into a new Excel workbook or existing Excel workbook.

6. If you selected the existing radial button, you will need to browse to find the Excel workbook and identify what worksheet to import the details into.

7. Select the **Advanced** tab.

8. Select the **Auto Filtering** option by placing a checkmark in the box, as shown in Figure 17.47.

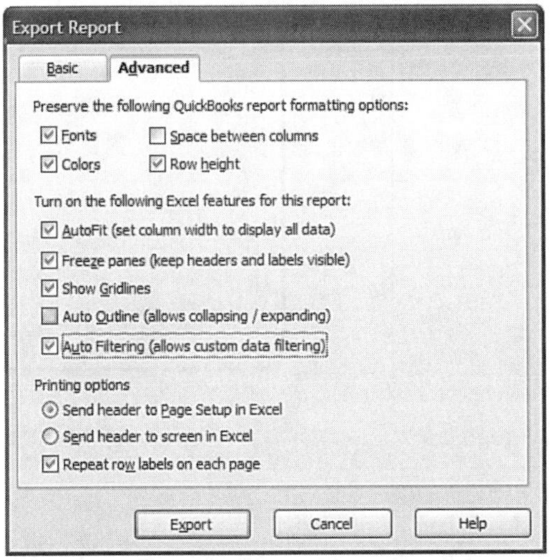

FIGURE 17.47

Exporting the Audit Trail report with Auto Filtering enabled.

9. Click **Export** to prepare the workbook from the QuickBooks Audit Trail report.

10. The Audit Trail report displays in Excel with auto-filtering enabled.

11. In the Excel document, select the **Last modified by** drop-down menu. Each user name will have a check mark next to its user name; deselect those users you want to "filter out" of the results of the auto-filtering. In Figure 17.48, John Taylor is selected, the user assigned the External Accountant user type in this chapter. The resulting data now shows only those transactions in the Audit Trail that this specific user added or modified.

12. The Excel workbook will display only those transactions in the Audit Trail report added or modified by the selected user.

13. Print the newly filtered Audit Trail report for you or your client's records.

14. Optionally save your Excel workbook.

If you are using the CDR feature with your client's Accountant's Copy data file sharing method, you will also have access to a detailed report of all changes made to a file available only in the Accountant's Copy.

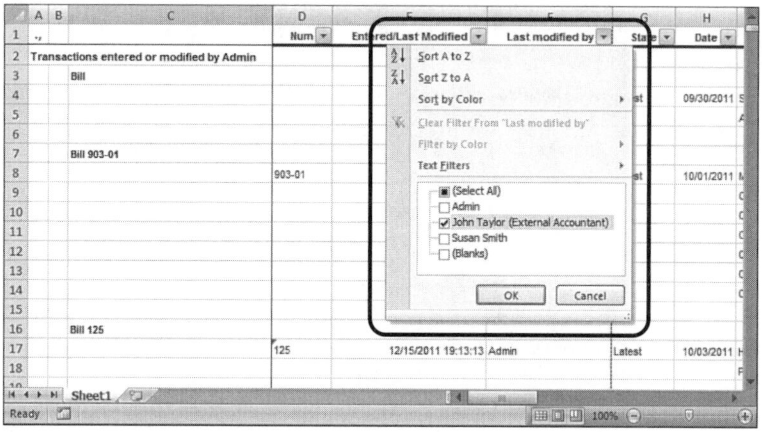

FIGURE 17.48

Using auto-filtering to limit the data that is displayed in the Audit Trail report.

If you find undesired transaction changes, consider setting a closing date password and setting specific user security privileges as detailed earlier in this chapter.

Creating an External Accountant User

Setting up a QuickBooks user for each person that enters data provides a level of control over the sensitive data to be viewed by this user and gives access to specific areas in QuickBooks. For additional control, a user-specific password can also be assigned.

New for QuickBooks 2009 is a new type of user called the External Accountant. When you create a new user (or edit an existing user) in QuickBooks, you can assign that user as an External Accountant.

As an accounting professional using the CDR, you will want to request that your client create a user name for you and assign the new External Accountant Type. If you then log into the client file with this new user type, you will benefit from:

- Complete Admin access, except you cannot create users or view sensitive customer credit card numbers.

- Reports like the Audit Trail can be filtered in Excel for a specific user name, enabling you to see your transactions separate from the client's transactions.

- Access to the CDR in a client's QuickBooks Pro, Premier (all editions), and Enterprise (all editions).
- Client Data Review distinguishes in the dialog if your login is the new External Accountant type (see Figure 17.1).

If you are reviewing your client's data using the Accountant's Copy file type or if you are not given the Admin login, this new External Accountant will have to be created before your client creates the Accountant's Copy or has you review his data file.

To create an External Accountant, follow these steps:

1. Open the QuickBooks data file using the Admin user (the default user that QuickBooks creates with a new QuickBooks file) and enter the appropriate password if one was created.

2. From the **Company** menu, **Set Up Users and Passwords**, select the **Set Up Users** menu option.

3. Enter the Admin user password if one was originally assigned. Click **OK**.

4. The **User List** dialog opens; it lists the current users set up for this file.

5. Click the **Add User** button to create a new user, or with your mouse pointer, select an existing user name and click the **Edit User** button.

6. The Set up or Change user password and access dialog is opened.

7. In the **User Name** field, type the name you want the user to be identified by in the file.

8. In the **Password** field, enter an *optional* password, and in the **Confirm Password** field, retype the password for accuracy.

9. Optionally, click the box to **Add** this user to my QuickBooks license. (See the explain link for more details.)

10. Click **Next**. You may receive a No Password Entered message, click **Yes** or **No** to creating a password. If you select Yes, you will be taken back to step number 8. Optionally, select the **Do not display** this message in the future.

11. The Access for User:<user name> dialog opens.

12. Select the radial button for **External Accountant**, as shown in Figure 17.49.

13. Click **Next**.

14. QuickBooks provides a warning message, confirming that you want to give this new user access to all areas of QuickBooks except customer credit card numbers. Select **Yes** to assign the new External Accountant type privileges to this new or existing user.

15. The Access for User:<user name> dialog opens. The message restates that the new External Accountant user will have access to all areas of QuickBooks except sensitive customer credit card data. Click **Finish** to complete the process.

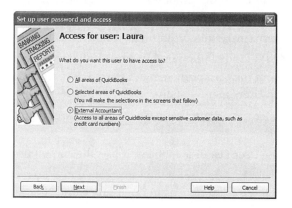

FIGURE 17.49

Ask your client to create an External Accountant type user for your login.

You can now log in with the privileges assigned to the External Accountant as detailed in the "Introduction: Features and Benefits" section in the beginning of this chapter.

Index